JUST CAUSE
THE SEVEN TESTS

JUST CAUSE
THE SEVEN TESTS

Adolph M. Koven
Susan L. Smith

Second Edition
Revised by Donald F. Farwell

BNA
BOOKS

The Bureau of National Affairs, Inc., Washington, D.C.

Copyright © 1992
The Bureau of National Affairs, Inc.

Fourth Printing, August 1997

Library of Congress Cataloging-in-Publication Data

Koven, Adolph M.
   Just cause : the seven tests / Adolph M. Koven, Susan L. Smith. --
2nd ed. / rev. by Donald F. Farwell.
      p.   cm.
   Includes index.
   ISBN 0-87179-708-9
   1. Labor discipline--Law and legislation--United States.
   2. Employees--Dismissal of--Law and legislation--United States.
   I. Smith, Susan L. II. Farwell, Donald F.   III. Title.
   KF3540.K68   1992
   344.73 ' 012598--dc20
   [347.30412598]   92-4399
                                                                          CIP

Published by BNA Books, 1250 23rd St., N.W., Washington, D.C. 20037

Printed in the United States of America
International Standard Book Number: 0-87179-708-9

Dedicated to the Memory of
Adolph M. Koven
(1917–1990)

Preface

This second edition of a book devoted to the seven tests of just cause formulated by Arbitrator Carroll R. Daugherty, like the first edition, reflects the conviction of Arbitrator Adolph M. Koven that the tests represent a practical and effective way to determine whether just cause is present for discharge or other disciplinary action—or, applied prospectively, whether proposed disciplinary action is firmly and fairly grounded.

In his nearly 40 years of experience as arbitrator and mediator, Kove was called upon to decide countless discipline and discharge cases in every conceivable occupational setting, both private and public. That experience informs every page of this book. The many representatives of management and labor who came to know Kove over the years will recognize in these pages the intelligence, humanity, and (not least) wit which he brought to the arbitration process. We are fortunate that when he died in March 1990, he left this book, his two films on arbitration, and his many published cases as a continuing legacy.

At the time of his death, Kove had begun work on the second edition of this book. He had drafted the notice chapter, had done much of the preliminary research needed to update and revise the other chapters, and had made notes regarding changes he believed were desirable in various places throughout the book. That work is reflected in the pages that follow, and an effort has been made to carry out what could be inferred to have been Kove's wishes.

Dr. Susan L. Smith, co-author with Kove of the first edition, and now a professor at the University of California at San Diego, worked closely with the undersigned in preparing the second edition. She reviewed the manuscript and made many valuable suggestions. Kove's close collaborator for more than a decade, she was uniquely qualified to provide guidance as to both the organization and the treatment of the subject matter. In effect, she served as both a penetrating critic and an expert editor.

The undersigned brought to the project many years' expe-

rience with the arbitration field as an editor and publisher with
The Bureau of National Affairs, Inc. He was associated with
Kove and Dr. Smith during the preparation of the first edition
of this book as well as *Arbitration: The Seven Tests of Just Cause*, a
film devoted to Arbitrator Daugherty's tests, and a second book,
ALCOHOL-RELATED MISCONDUCT. He also is an attorney and a
member of the Labor Panel of the American Arbitration Association.

Much of the first edition has been carried over to this second
edition. Coverage has been expanded in a number of areas; in
particular, there is much new material dealing with a topic of
great current interest, drug and alcohol abuse in and outside the
workplace. The book continues to focus primarily on relatively
recent arbitration cases, although "lead cases" from prior years
also are extensively cited.

The book has three purposes, as follows:

to provide a general treatment, for managers, union
representatives, and practitioners and students of labor relations, of the concept of just cause and the seven tests;

to offer guidance for determining what (if any) disciplinary action is warranted in particular cases of employee
misconduct;

to provide a reference for those who want to know
what the authorities in the field have had to say.

DONALD F. FARWELL

July 1991

Contents

Introduction

The Concept of Just Cause

"No employee shall be disciplined or discharged except for just cause"[1] is one of the shortest, simplest clauses in any contract.[2] But it is also one of the most frustrating to manage-

---

[1]The less frequently seen terms "cause" and "proper cause" are customarily interpreted by arbitrators in the same manner as "just cause"; see, e.g., *Higgins, Inc.*, 24 LA 453, 456 (Morvant, 1955) (violation of safety rule): "[T]he company's argument that the term 'discharge for cause' cannot be interpreted to mean discharge for 'just' or 'good' cause . . . abjures the basic principles of all labor-management agreements. . . . To agree with the company that 'cause' in this instant case means 'any reason' would make meaningless all of the rights of the individual worker." In agreement, see, e.g., *Eagle-Picher Indus., Inc.*, 70-2 ARB ¶8469 (Merrill, 1970) (sleeping), with many additional citations; *Atlantic Richfield Co.*, 69 LA 484 (Sisk, 1977) (absenteeism); *Wilderness Foods*, 84-1 ARB ¶8242 (Daniel, 1984) (absenteeism); *Weyerhaeuser Co.*, 88 LA 270 (Kapsch, 1987) (absenteeism).

[2]Arbitrator Wallen, in *Atwater Mfg. Co.*, 13 LA 747 (1949) (punching another employee's time card), expressed the widely accepted view that the just cause standard is implied by the very existence of the collective bargaining agreement, since one of the fundamental purposes of the agreement is to assure the security of the employee in his or her job. See also *Anderson Hickey Co.*, 50 LA 1217, 1219 (Volz, 1968) (strike participation) ("implied covenant of fair dealing and good faith" on which agreement is based "imposes upon management a standard of reasonableness where a 'just cause' provision has not been included in the contract"); *Maclin Co.*, 52 LA 805 (Koven, 1969) (arbitrability of discharges); *Shell Oil Co.*, 90 LA 112 (Massey, 1988) (dishonesty); *Binswanger Glass Co.*, 92 LA 1153 (Nicholas, 1989) (performance deficiencies); *Sterling Chems., Inc.*, 93 LA 953 (Taylor, 1989) (failure to complete employee assistance program); *Press Democrat Publishing Co.*, 93 LA 969 (McKay, 1989) (misuse of computer), and cases cited in F. ELKOURI & E. A. ELKOURI, HOW ARBITRATION WORKS 652 (4th ed. 1985). Said the arbitrator in *Binswanger*, 92 LA 1153, 1155: "In the absence of a specific grant to Company to terminate employees in a 'just because' fashion, the Arbitrator concludes that some indicia of cause for discharge must be seen. To hold otherwise would mean that the discretion Company purports to possess would render its employees, in effect, employees at will." But in *Westvaco*, 92 LA 1289 (Nolan, 1989) (absenteeism), the arbitrator refused to imply a just cause standard because the parties had failed to add one after another arbitrator found that the implication of such a standard was beyond his authority. The only restrictions on the company's authority, he stated, were that it was not free to use its discharge power to undermine another provision of the contract and its actions must not be arbitrary, capricious, or discriminatory.

1

ment, especially first-line supervisors. Why? Because, as arbitrators long have recognized, the just cause standard cannot be defined absolutely.

> *Arbitrator Platt:* To be sure, no standards exist to aid an arbitrator in finding a conclusive answer to such a question . . . .[3]

> *Arbitrator Nicholas:* [T]he concept of "good" or "sufficient" cause cannot be seen in an absolute sense.[4]

The law is no stranger to inexact standards but relies in many instances on doctrines that cannot be reduced to a simple rule or formula. The example that is perhaps most comparable to just cause is the so-called "reasonable person" standard, which is used in the law to determine whether an individual is guilty of negligence. That standard requires that a particular individual act as a person of ordinary sense, exercising ordinary caution and judgment, would act under the circumstances.

But what does "ordinary sense" mean? And how can one define "ordinary caution and judgment" with certainty? Why the "reasonable person" standard is vague, and why more specific rules of conduct cannot be defined, has been explained by Prosser, the great authority on civil wrongs (or torts):

> The whole theory of negligence presupposes some uniform standard of behavior. Yet the infinite variety of situations which may arise makes it impossible to fix definite rules in advance for all conceivable human conduct. The utmost that can be done is to devise something in the nature of a formula [i.e., the "reasonable person" standard], the application of which in each particular case must be left to the jury, or to the court.[5]

The same reasoning applies to the just cause standard. To paraphrase Prosser in just cause terms:

- The theory of "just cause" presupposes some uniform standard of behavior in the area of discipline and discharge.
- Yet the possible variety of industrial misconduct, and the circumstances that might surround any act of misconduct, are so diverse that a single standard would not cover them all.

---

[3]*Riley Stoker Corp.*, 7 LA 764, 767 (1947) (use of company time for personal business, loafing).

[4]*Indal Aluminum Gulfport*, 84 LA 124, 127 (1985) (use of profanity).

[5]Prosser & Keaton on the Law of Torts 173 (5th ed. 1984).

- The utmost that can be done is to devise something in the nature of a formula, the application of which in a particular case (if the parties cannot resolve it themselves) must be left to the arbitrator.

"Something in the nature of a formula" has in effect been proposed by a number of arbitrators.

Arbitrator Platt: It is ordinarily the function of the Arbitrator in interpreting a contract provision which requires "sufficient cause" as a condition precedent to discharge not only to determine whether the employee involved is guilty of wrong doing . . . but also to safeguard the interests of the discharged employee by making reasonably sure that the causes for discharge were just and equitable and such as would appeal to reasonable and fair-minded persons as warranting discharge.[6]

Arbitrator Harris: Without attempting precisely to define "cause," it is the arbitrator's view that the true test under a contract of the type involved here is whether a reasonable man, taking into account all relevant circumstances, would find sufficient justification in the conduct of the employee to warrant discharge.[7]

Arbitrator Doyle: Just cause is a standard which should be applied in a manner that will distinguish the unduly harsh, unfair, biased, prejudiced, or arbitrary action from the fair and reasonable judgment in which reasonable minds would concur.[8]

Arbitrator Volz: [E]mployees with seniority are not to be terminated by action which is deemed by the reasonable man to be arbitrary, unduly harsh, or disproportionate to the offense.[9]

A fundamental question still needs to be answered, however. Who decides what it means to be "reasonable"?

The "Intrinsic" Approach

Not surprisingly, many employers take the position that the "reasonable person" is management, as long as it has established

---

[6]*Riley Stoker Corp., supra* note 3, at 767. In *Atlas Press Co.*, 9 LA 810, 812 (1948) (drinking in plant), Platt expanded his definition to include the following: "[I]t is an Arbitrator's function and duty . . . to decide, according to the habits and customs of industrial life and the standards of justice and fair dealing prevalent in the community, whether the penalty imposed is equitable and just and not seriously disproportioned to the offense."

[7]*RCA Communications, Inc.*, 29 LA 567, 571 (1957) (refusal to testify before congressional committee).

[8]*Iowa Beef Packers, Inc.*, 66-2 ARB ¶8527, 4808 (1966) (absenteeism).

[9]*Philip Morris, Inc.*, 68-2 ARB ¶8773, 5689 (1968) (possession of alcohol).

some standard that defines misconduct and what the appropriate penalties are, and sticks to that standard in actual cases.
This approach to just cause:

- is intrinsic or unilateral in the sense that management's
  conduct may be successfully challenged only if it has acted
  unreasonably—that is, been arbitrary, capricious, or discriminatory—according to whatever standards it has set
  for itself;[10]
- subjects the employer's claim of reasonableness in a particular case only to such factors as its own past practice
  with respect to enforcing plant rules and imposing like
  penalties for like misconduct;
- implies that an arbitrator has no right to substitute his or
  her own judgment for that of the employer as to what is
  "reasonable." The arbitrator's task is to judge whether the
  employer has produced reasons for its action within its
  own value structure;
- concludes that the arbitrator who goes further than this—
  whether in assessing the cause for discipline or the penalty
  imposed by the employer—is exceeding his or her authority.

Do arbitrators agree? Many arbitrators follow the intrinsic
approach in at least one crucial area—management's right to
detemine the penalty for misconduct, once the misconduct has
been admitted or proved.

> *Arbitrator McCoy:* Where an employee has violated a rule or en-
> gaged in conduct meriting disciplinary action, it is primarily the
> function of management to decide upon the proper penalty. If
> management acts in good faith upon a fair investigation and fixes
> a penalty not inconsistent with that imposed in other like cases,
> an arbitrator should not disturb it.
>   The mere fact that management has imposed a somewhat

---

[10]This approach is reflected in the following statement by the arbitrator in *Ohio
State Highway Patrol*, 94 LA 58, 61 (Bittel, 1990):
  Only if the [employer's] view of the seriousness of [the] offense lacks rationality
  and fairness can the Arbitrator overturn the discharge for just cause. . . . [D]eter-
  mination of the issue of just cause does not call for the Arbitrator's independent
  decision as to what the appropriate discipline should be, or whether the Grievant,
  due to personal worth, deserves to have his job back.
  See also *Pepsi-Cola Bottlers of Akron, Inc.*, 87 LA 83, 88 (Morgan, 1986) (absenteeism)
("only question the Arbitrator has the right to resolve is whether or not the facts gave
the employer the right to act as it did").

different penalty or a somewhat more severe penalty than the arbitrator would have, if he had had the decision to make originally, is no justification for changing it. The minds of equally reasonable men differ. A consideration which would weigh heavily with one man will seem of less importance to another. A circumstance which highly aggravates an offense in one man's eyes may be only slight aggravation to another.

If an arbitrator could substitute his judgment and discretion for the judgment and discretion honestly exercised by management, then the functions of management would have been abdicated, and unions would take every case to arbitration. The result would be as intolerable to employees as to management.

The only circumstances under which a penalty imposed by management can be rightfully set aside by an arbitrator are those where discrimination, unfairness, or capricious and arbitrary action are proved—in other words, where there has been abuse of discretion.[11]

The "Extrinsic" Approach

Just cause involves more than the question of the proper penalty, however. The arbitrator usually must also determine whether the company had adequate proof that the employee was guilty as charged. In such matters of fact, arbitrators consistently evaluate employers' decisions according to criteria derived from court proceedings, though these criteria are applied more informally in arbitration proceedings.[12]

Many arbitrators also adopt an "extrinsic" approach to other questions which are raised by just cause, including the controversial question of whether the penalty was reasonable.

---

[11]*Stockham Pipe Fittings Co.*, 1 LA 160, 162 (1945) (fighting). See also *Owl Drug Co.*, 10 LA 498 (Pollard, 1948); *Bauer Bros. Co.*, 23 LA 696 (Dworkin, 1954); *Kellogg Co.*, 28 LA 303 (Meltzer, 1957) (attack on fellow employee); *Trans World Airlines, Inc.*, 41 LA 142 (Beatty, 1963) (damage to equipment, negligence); *Iowa Beef Packers, supra* note 8. In a variation on this theme, Arbitrator Teple held in *Packaging Corp. of America*, 37 LA 338 (1961) (failure to attend meeting), that an arbitrator should not disturb penalties short of discharge. Other cases have held that arbitrators should be more reluctant to substitute their judgment for that of management where the cause of discipline is directly work-related, *e.g.*, inefficiency, negligence, etc. See FAIRWEATHER'S PRACTICE AND PROCEDURE IN LABOR ARBITRATION 444-47 (R. J. Schoonhoven, ch. ed., 3rd ed. 1991) (with many other citations on the arbitrator's authority to alter penalties).

[12]See, e.g., *Retail Clerks Int'l Ass'n*, 69-2 ARB ¶8552 (Bothwell, 1969) (poor attitude) (arbitrator must resolve conflicts in evidence and may not accept employer's version of facts at face value); *Inland Steel Container Co.*, 60 LA 536 (Marcus, 1973) (marijuana) (just cause standard requires employer to prove misconduct by at least preponderance of evidence).

But by whose standards is the employer's decision to be evaluated? Not the arbitrator's personal standards—what he or she would have done as the employer—but the standards of the industrial community as a whole, which have been set forth over many years of management-labor practice and arbitral review.

> *Arbitrator Hon:* There is no absolute answer to the question of what constitutes just or sustainable discharge, but the test most commonly used is whether experienced and impartial persons familiar with the habits and customs of industrial life would find the penalty just.[13]

> *Arbitrator Platt:* The inquiry must be not only whether the disciplined employee was guilty of the acts charged but also whether they were committed in the course of his employment and whether they constitute industrial misconduct. And, too, the inquiry must be into whether the penalty imposed is such a one as would appeal to fair minded persons, mindful of the habits and customs of industrial life and of the standards of justice prevalent in the community as just, under all the circumstances of the case.[14]

The extrinsic approach to just cause therefore:

- is extrinsic in the sense that the company's conduct is subject to challenge if the company has acted unreasonably, not just according to its own standards but according to "outside" standards;
- gives the arbitrator greater flexibility than the intrinsic standard, especially with respect to deciding on the appropriate penalty;[15]
- still, however, requires that the arbitrator not merely substitute his or her personal judgment for the employer's,

---

[13]*Waste King Corp.*, 66-1 ARB ¶8007, 3028 (1965) (incompetence, inefficiency).

[14]*Republic Steel Corp.*, 23 LA 808, 810 (1955) (arrest on charge of burglary). In *Trans World Airlines*, 93 LA 167 (Eisler, 1989) (damaging company image), the arbitrator rejected an employer contention that he could not consider the appropriateness of the penalty imposed where the union's submission only questioned whether just cause existed. He quoted a statement by a U.S. district court in *Physicians and Surgeons Community Hosp. v. Service Employees Local 597*, 114 LRRM 2876 (N.D. Ga. 1983), that "'just cause' encompasses not only whether the grievant in fact committed the alleged disciplinary rule violation, but also what range of penalties can fairly be meted out . . . ."

[15]Among the many cases holding that arbitrators have the authority under a just cause provision to determine whether a penalty was reasonable are *Davis Fire Brick Co.*, 36 LA 124 (Dworkin, 1960) (negligence); *Phillips Petroleum Co.*, 64-3 ARB ¶8907 (Mittenthal, 1964); *Kaiser Sand & Gravel*, 49 LA 190 (Koven, 1967) (drinking); *Eagle-Picher Indus., Inc., supra* note 1; *Abex Corp.*, 70-2 ARB ¶8867 (Volz, 1970); *Pacific Tel. & Tel. Co.*, 56 LA 581 (Hughes, 1971) (alcohol, marijuana violations); *Trans World Airlines, supra* note 14.

but rather evaluate its disciplinary actions according to standards generally accepted in industrial relations practice.

Why an extrinsic standard? To return to the law of negligence, the "reasonable man" standard means that no individual is free to act solely according to some personal idea of what constitutes reasonably prudent behavior.[16] Because we live in society with other people who may be affected adversely by our actions, we are at least to some degree subject to society's idea of what kind of behavior is prudent and responsible, as defined and enforced by courts and juries.

> *Arbitrator Volz:* Reasonableness is a fact question and ordinarily must be determined on the basis of a comparison with an accepted general standard. The question as to what is reasonable in a particular instance normally is judged by what similarly situated people in the locality do under the same or similar circumstances.[17]

The individual employer is not strictly bound by the prevailing standards of industrial justice in the same way that the individual citizen is accountable to principles of law. But, the proponents of the extrinsic approach would argue, if every employer could be the sole judge of what kind of conduct is reasonable, the just cause standard would provide employees little protection since almost any decision could be backed up with reasoning of some kind. The result would be that the employer could successfully claim that discharge for the most trivial offense was for just cause—a result the extrinsic approach is designed to guard against.[18]

---

[16]Arbitrator Lessley, in *Allied Employers, Inc.*, 70-2 ARB ¶8782, 5626 (1970) (poor attitude): "The term 'just cause' must be objective, not subjective; it must be in relation to a job to be done, not to the supervisor's sense of outrage . . . ." Arbitrator Smith, in *The Maccabees*, 27 LA 99, 102 (1956): "[T]he employer may no more determine, finally and beyond challenge through the grievance procedure, what does in fact constitute chronic tardiness than it can finally and beyond challenge determine what constitutes 'incompetence' or 'insubordination,' or any of the other categories of fault specified in general language as grounds for discharge . . . ." See also *Perini, M-K, Leavell*, 46 LA 1044 (Merrill, 1966) (assault on supervisor).

[17]*Bowater Carolina Corp.*, 64 LA 1206, 1210 (1975) (medical benefits). See also *Shepard Ambulance, Inc.*, 85-2 ARB ¶8336 (Krebs, 1985) (alcoholism).

[18]As Arbitrator Cantor put it, in *Memphis Publishing Co.*, 67-1 ARB ¶8233, 3821 (1967) (outside employment operating a "go-go" establishment):

> The concept of what [employee conduct] is detrimental must be subject to review of an arbitrator as to whether it is reasonably within the meaning of the word and the circumstances of the contract. A contract is intended to be the protection of both parties by being specific as to what terms or circumstances may lead to given

"Intrinsic" and "Extrinsic" Combined

In practice, neither the intrinsic nor the extrinsic approach is carried to an extreme. Arbitrators normally take into account both the particular company's ways of doing things and external criteria in reaching their decisions; where the balance is struck depends partly on the individual arbitrator's views and partly on the circumstances of the particular case.

A combination of intrinsic and extrinsic factors appears in a discussion of just cause by Arbitrator McGoldrick. Misconduct for which an employee may be discharged with just cause, according to McGoldrick, (1) involves duties, such as honesty, sobriety, and punctuality, owed by the employee to the employer; and (2) has been recognized by one or more of the following authorities as industrial misconduct warranting discipline:

- day-to-day practices of the particular employer and union (the intrinsic approach);
- traditional industry practices (here, extrinsic standards begin to creep in);
- decisions of arbitrators and the courts (with this, a wider choice of extrinsic standards becomes available).[19]

Just Cause Versus Employer Rules

What happens when a contract contains *both* a general provision requiring just cause for discipline or discharge *and* a specific set of rules and penalties? If the arbitrator's own notions of just cause requirements happen to clash with the negotiated rules and penalties, in the view of Arbitrator Jonathan Dworkin,

---

results. Therefore, the concept of what is detrimental is not the sole or singular choice of Management, but is subject to an appeal to reason and the review of an arbitrator . . . .

See also *Higgins, Inc.*, 24 LA 453 (Morvant, 1955) (violation of safety rule); *Binswanger Glass Co.*, 92 LA 1153 (Nicholas, 1989) (performance deficiencies).

[19]*Worthington Corp.*, 24 LA 1 (1955) (refusal to testify about Communist Party affiliation). Among many other variations on the definition of just cause, see *Sooner Rock and Sand Co.*, 48 LA 336 (Bentley, 1967) (insubordination); *Ditrich Indus., Inc.*, 70-1 ARB ¶8265 (Waldron, 1969); *Conner Mfg. Co.*, 63 LA 1102 (Mulhall, 1974) (intoxication); *Lear Siegler, Inc.*, 63 LA 1157 (McBrearty, 1974) (garnishment); *MGM Grand Hotel*, 77-2 ARB ¶8324 (Weiss, 1977) (insubordination); *Washington Metal Trades, Inc.*, 80 LA 1 (Keltner, 1982) (sleeping); *Koch Refining Co.*, 86 LA 1211 (Miller, 1986) (tardiness).

the negotiated standards prevail and the arbitrator's views must be put aside.

> It is broadly recognized that contractual disciplinary rules, coupled with stated penalties, usually override broader just-cause requirements. This is an entirely proper way for arbitrators to interpret contracts. Just cause is an amorphous term which lacks a concrete definition. When its principles control the outcome of a dispute, an arbitrator is invested with broad authority—much broader than in any other kind of "rights" grievance. Rulings on just-cause cases routinely call for application of an arbitrator's concepts of fairness, justice, and equity. By negotiating rules and penalties, parties express their intent to circumscribe arbitral authority. In effect, their agreement defines what is just cause for disciplining an identified breach of employment responsibilities, and narrows the issue. It does away with the more speculative decision-making implicitly licensed by a just-cause standard.[20]

Dworkin went on to say that the same is not true of rules and penalties adopted unilaterally by the employer. These simply tell employees what the employer expects of them, give notice of the relative importance the employer attaches to particular violations, and show how the employer intends to achieve evenhandedness in discipline; and their enforcement is subject to just cause requirements.[21]

Influence of the Courts

In the landmark *Steelworkers Trilogy*, the U.S. Supreme Court gave arbitrators broad license to interpret collective bargaining agreements without interference by the courts. The Court ruled that a lower court must enforce an arbitration award whether or not it agrees with the arbitrator's interpretation of the contract. Said the Court:

> The function of the court is very limited when the parties have agreed to submit all questions of contract interpretation to the arbitrator. It is confined to ascertaining whether the party seeking arbitration is making a claim which on its face is governed by the contract. Whether the moving party is right or wrong is a question of contract interpretation for the arbitrator. In these

---

[20]*Northern Ohio Red Cross Blood Serv.*, 90 LA 393, 397 (1988) (poor performance).

[21]Arbitrator Barrett made the same points with respect to both negotiated rules and unilateral rules in *Bemis Co.*, 89-2 ARB ¶8324 (1989) (threatening supervisor).

circumstances the moving party should not be deprived of the arbitrator's judgment, when it was his judgment and all that it connotes that was bargained for.

The courts, therefore, have no business weighing the merits of the grievance, considering whether there is equity in a particular claim, or determining whether there is particular language in the written instrument which will support the claim.[22]

The critical question for a court, said the Supreme Court in another case decided at the same time, is whether the arbitrator's award "draws its essence from the collective bargaining agreement" and does not merely represent "his own brand of industrial justice."[23]

Nearly a quarter of a century later the Court spelled out an exception to the hands-off policy it had established for the courts. It held that a court should refuse to enforce a collective bargaining agreement that is "contrary to public policy," adding that "the question of public policy is ultimately one for resolution by the courts." The Court further stated, however, that an arbitration award interpreting a contract could be denied enforcement only where the contract as interpreted would violate an explicit, well-defined public policy; "general considerations of supposed public interests" are not a sufficient basis for refusing to enforce an award.[24]

This public-policy exception was seized upon by several courts to overturn arbitrators' decisions holding that discharges were not for just cause, especially in cases involving alcohol and drug use. One of these involved an employee who was fired for possessing drugs on company premises. Although the police found marijuana in the employee's car while it was parked on the employer's lot, this fact did not become known to the employer until six months after the discharge. The arbitrator ruled that the company had insufficient evidence to prove the charges against the employee when it fired him, and the discharge therefore was not for just cause.[25]

The arbitrator's order reinstating the employee with back pay and full seniority was appealed by the employer, and the

---

[22]*Steelworkers v. American Mfg. Co.*, 363 U.S. 564, 567–68, 46 LRRM 2414 (1960) (footnote omitted).

[23]*Steelworkers v. Enterprise Wheel & Car Corp.*, 363 U.S. 593, 596, 46 LRRM 2423 (1960).

[24]*W. R. Grace & Co. v. Rubber Workers*, 461 U.S. 757, 766, 113 LRRM 2641 (1983).

[25]*Misco, Inc.*, 89 LA 137, 88-2 ARB ¶8503 (Fox, 1983).

district court vacated the award on the ground that it violated public policy. This decision was affirmed by the Fifth Circuit Court of Appeals, which held that reinstatement would violate the public policy "against the operation of dangerous machinery by persons under the influence of drugs or alcohol."[26]

The Supreme Court ruled that the appeals court was wrong on all counts. It was wrong to delve into the facts of the case, it was wrong to question the arbitrator's refusal to consider the postdischarge evidence, and it was wrong to apply the public-policy exception. On the last point, the Court had this to say:

> The Court of Appeals made no attempt to review existing laws and legal precedents in order to demonstrate that they establish a "well defined and dominant" policy against the operation of dangerous machinery while under the influence of drugs. Although certainly such a judgment is firmly rooted in common sense, we explicitly held in *W. R. Grace* that a formulation of public policy based only on "general considerations of supposed public interests" is not the sort that permits a court to set aside an arbitration award that was entered in accordance with a valid collective-bargaining agreement.[27]

This narrow reading of the public-policy exception, taken together with the Supreme Court's ringing reassertion of the relative immunity of arbitrators' decisions to court review, might seem to foreshadow diminished resort to the courts by losing parties seeking to overturn arbitration awards. But in fact, as the 1980s came to an end, this did not seem to be the case. Some courts were showing a willingness to review the merits of arbitrators' decisions overturning discharges on just cause grounds,[28] and this can be expected to have an impact on the further development of the just cause doctrine. In particular, some arbitrators may be less willing to infer just cause requirements in the absence of contractual references to just cause.

---

[26]*Paperworkers v. Misco*, 768 F.2d 739, 120 LRRM 2119 (5th Cir. 1985).

[27]*Paperworkers v. Misco, Inc.*, 484 U.S. 29, 44, 126 LRRM 3113 (1987). For discussion of the decision and its implications for arbitration, see J. E. Dunsford, *The Judicial Doctrine of Public Policy:* Misco *Reviewed*, 4 LAB. LAW. 669–82 (1988); J. Parker, *Judicial Review of Labor Arbitration Awards:* Misco *and Its Impact on the Public Policy Exception*, 4 LAB. LAW. 683–714 (1988); J. Vetter, *Public Policy Post-*Misco, ARBITRATION 1988 75–88 (Proceedings of the 41st Annual Meeting, National Academy of Arbitrators 1989).

[28]See, e.g., *Iowa Elec. Light & Power Co. v. IBEW Local 204*, 834 F.2d 1424, 127 LRRM 2049 (8th Cir. 1988); *Delta Air Lines v. Air Line Pilots*, 686 F. Supp. 1573, 127 LRRM 2530 (N.D. Ga. 1987); *Stead Motors v. Machinists Lodge 1173*, 843 F.2d 357, 127 LRRM 3213 (9th Cir. 1988); *S. D. Warren Co. v. Local 1069*, 846 F.2d 827, 128 LRRM 2432 (1st Cir.), *cert. denied*, 129 LRRM 3082 (1988).

Arbitrator Estes has made this assessment of the prospects for increased judicial scrutiny of arbitration awards:

> More intensive judicial examination of arbitrators' findings of "ambiguity" in contract language and increased attention to the "plain meaning" of contract clauses could result in judicial expansion of the [*Steelworkers*] *Trilogy* "essence" test. Such inquiries could bring about judicial review that is closer to an examination of disputes than apparently was intended under the *Steelworkers* and *Misco* decisions.
>
> A wide and distinct division among the circuits may be required before the Supreme Court agrees to hear another case relative to the application of the *Trilogy* standards of judicial review of labor arbitration awards. In the meantime, more attorneys for losing parties in arbitration may advise their clients to test the waters of their circuits in attempts to use an expanded "essence" test as a basis for vacating awards. Even if unsuccessful, such litigation could have the effects of undermining labor arbitration finality and adding burdens to an already crowded court system.[29]

The Milieu of Just Cause

Just cause is not a free-floating notion without a set of referents, but is part of the larger milieu of forces and factors within which the basic institution of labor-management relations operates. Conflict in our industrial society is a fact of life, and to seek (or hope) to eliminate conflict from the collective bargaining relationship is unrealistic (though one might argue that it has materially changed in its scope and goals over the years to suit adjustments in the power relationship between the parties and their goals).

That said, every collective bargaining relationship has its own personality, a personality reflected in the discharge and disciplinary system which the parties have evolved. That system may be permissive or rigid; it may emphasize rehabilitation more than punishment. But whatever the system's personality, it does not exist in a vacuum. It would be impossible, for example, for the parties to approach their differences in a relatively flexible and cooperative spirit if they did not have a disciplinary system that reflected a close working relationship.

---

[29]R. W. Estes, *Life After* Misco, ARBITRATION 1989 174–75 (Proceedings of the 42d Annual Meeting, National Academy of Arbitrators 1990).

Arbitration, too, is not only an *extension* of the collective bargaining process (as it is commonly put) but also a *reflection* of the particular collective bargaining relationship. How the parties deal with each other in arbitration will mirror how they deal with their problems generally.

Labor and management are "organic" institutions, linked together in a living, ever-changing relationship, albeit one that is always potentially impermanent. Thus, if a highly cooperative relationship is for the time being to the parties' mutual advantage, their arbitration system and their dealings with each other will reflect that fact. Conversely, if they are for the time being at odds, their arbitration system will mirror that condition. If the parties have a distant, formal collective bargaining life, their arbitration system will tend to be legalistic; if they deal with each other more informally, their arbitrations will tend to be more freewheeling.

It is also true that how the arbitrator plies his trade in a case where just cause is in dispute (or, indeed, any other type of case) is inseparable from his view of the nature and goals of arbitration. Arbitrators differ among themselves on a variety of issues that arise in connection with just cause tests (e.g., whether constitutional privileges apply at the work place), and more often than not such varying points of view mirror differences in their theories of arbitration. The same differences are found among employers and unions.

A Continuing Collective Bargaining Relationship

The continuing character of the collective bargaining relationship cannot be overemphasized since, from a practical point of view, it has no parallel elsewhere in the judicial world (except for domestic relations).

In the legal world, the confrontation is between two individual parties. But once the litigation is over, the two typically go their separate ways and probably never meet again. In the labor-management world it is very different—no matter that a specific bit of litigation is over and done with, the parties are nonetheless destined to continue dealing with each other, not only in other grievances, arbitrations, and NLRB proceedings but in a variety of other involvements—negotiations, safety meetings, government inquiries of one kind or another, pension and retirement matters, and the like.

> *Arbitrator McDermott:* [The parties] not only will continue to see each other every day in the plant, as most parties to judicial proceedings will not, but much more—they must continue to cooperate with each other every day in the future in the efficient operation of their enterprise. Whatever they do, or make, or sell, their long- and short-range interest is in continuing to do it efficiently, and they cannot do that if their various spokesmen and representatives are treated in arbitration as if all were liars, cheats and scoundrels, or as if what one party or the other sees as a serious problem were time and time again shut off from rational treatment on the merits by overly formal objections borrowed from the public system of the law . . . .[30]

The continuing character of the relationship is probably the single most important fact about the relationship, and this large and basic fact colors all that goes on between the parties.[31]

The Two "Parents" of Arbitration

The arbitration process can be said to owe its origin to two "parents," the collective bargaining process and the judicial system. As such, it is a "quasi-judicial" system, and its hybrid personality can be expected to express itself repeatedly in both direct and subtle ways throughout the arbitration process.

Perhaps this split personality is best exemplified by the place the rules of evidence occupy in the process. On the one hand, the rules of evidence are rules the parties are supposed to take into account in pursuing or defending their cause; on the other, either by statute or custom or both, the rules do not have to be observed. Thus, there are regular outcries from the judicial side of the aisle of "objection—that's hearsay" or "objection—that's irrelevant," to which comes the response of the arbitrator (or reminders from the collective bargaining side of the aisle): "Hearsay? That's admissible," or "Irrelevant? Oh, well, let it in for what it's worth."

---

[30]DECISIONAL THINKING OF ARBITRATORS AND JUDGES 11 (Proceedings of the 33d Annual Meeting, National Academy of Arbitrators 1980).

[31]Illustrating this is *Todd-Pacific Shipyards*, 86 LA 171 (Draznin, 1985) (insubordination), where the arbitrator disapproved the suspension of the grievant, even though he had been insubordinate, because the labor relations manager had decided at a grievance meeting not to impose discipline. Higher management overruled him and suspended the grievant for 10 days. The arbitrator reasoned that the union must be able to rely upon statements made at grievance meetings. However, to put the grievant on notice that such conduct would not be tolerated in the future, he directed that a copy of his decision be placed in the grievant's personnel file.

Voluntary Selection of Arbitrators

Major effects flow from the fact that the "judge" in arbitration is voluntarily selected. Many arbitrators themselves develop a continuing relationship with the parties, which in turn becomes part of the parties' own continuing relationship. Harry Shulman, for example, spent many years as the permanent umpire for Ford Motor Co. and had a far-ranging impact upon the relationship between the company and the United Auto Workers (as well as upon the field of arbitration itself). Since the parties have had a hand in choosing whom they want to serve as their "judge" and often know the arbitrator well, the atmosphere in the hearing room is likely to be much less aggressive and challenging than in the courtroom, particularly in reference to the attitude of the adversaries toward their "judge." And since the adversaries ordinarily are not involved in a "one-shot" affair and can expect to have further and continuing dealings with each other (and perhaps also with the arbitrator), a concern for credibility and good reputation is likely to be a top priority.

It is not the arbitrator but the parties themselves who are the "authors" of the arbitral law under which they try cases. That is so because the viewpoints of the particular arbitrator ultimately are subject to veto or adoption by the parties. An arbitrator whose approaches are unacceptable to practitioners will eventually fade away. The opposite is also true—the arbitrator whose thinking is compatible with the views of the parties will be listened to and will continue to hear their cases.

Balancing Two Benefits of the Doubt

Most arbitrators would agree that in matters of discipline and discharge, other things being equal, the benefit of the doubt goes to the grievant (and the union), whereas in matters of management rights the benefit of the doubt goes to the employer. Part of the reason for this approach is that the employer has the burden of proof in discipline and discharge situations, whereas in other matters the burden of proof falls upon the union.

Beyond that, some would say that the outcome of a discharge and discipline case is generally more important to the union than to the employer. A discharge threatens the employee's livelihood, and many unions hold to the notion that discharge is "industrial capital punishment." Moreover, the grievant not only is an employee who has been discharged but may also be or become a union member. Sooner or later, he or she is likely to be a voter in a union election.

"Political" Versus "Politics"

Both management and labor can be said to have political considerations on their minds. But clearly they are not involved in politics in the same way. "Politics" in a company means that jockeying and infighting may be going on with respect to such matters as recognition and advancement.

But a company can not be called a "political institution." No one is running for office, and no one needs to compete for the loyalty of a group of employees for the purpose of getting elected. Union officials, on the other hand, like members of Congress, know that sooner or later they are going to have to stand for reelection. We can see the union in its role as a "political institution" when it brings cases to arbitration which it knows are without merit and sure losers.

It might be said that there is no difference between a union's "sure loser" and management's knowingly backing a supervisor who is clearly in the wrong. But there is a basic difference between the two events—a union's purpose is politically or institutionally motivated, whereas management's purpose is business or personally oriented, namely, to let the supervisor know that management has a policy of "my supervisor, right or wrong."

Past Practice

Because of its vitality and influence, past practice (or "custom of the shop," as the Supreme Court has called it) is a benchmark for much that goes on between the parties. Indeed, it is indispensable to a proper focusing of the principles that compose the content of just cause.

In discharge and discipline cases, past practice is inseparable from all seven tests of just cause. It is most likely to arise, however, with respect to equal treatment, where the treatment of a particular employee is often compared with how the company has dealt with other employees in the past; and penalty, as a basis for reducing or eliminating the punishment or justifying what the employee has done.

Two Theories of Arbitration

There are four ways to look at arbitration. Two of these—arbitration as a search for truth and as a fact-finding procedure[32] and arbitration as a therapy session[33]—are not much in vogue these days. Two others—arbitration as a judicial process and arbitration as a continuation of the collective bargaining relationship—both have many adherents. What follows is a review of the two major ways of looking at arbitration and some observations about the collective bargaining environment which are intended to place just cause within the larger perspective.

A Judicial Process

> *Arbitrator Platt:* Arbitration is essentially a judicial process. Unlike a mediator or conciliator in a labor dispute, the function of an arbitrator is not to reach a settlement, or for himself to strive for a compromise solution, but to determine the rights and duties of the disputants upon the issue before him.[34]

Those who support this view urge that arbitration is a substitute for litigation in two senses. First, arbitration is literally a substitute for litigation because many aspects of the employer-employee relationship are regulated by federal and state statutes

---

[32]This view is discussed in PROBLEMS OF PROOF IN ARBITRATION 285, 315 (Proceedings of the 19th Annual Meeting, National Academy of Arbitrators 1967). For criticism of this approach, see DECISIONAL THINKING OF ARBITRATORS AND JUDGES, *supra* note 30, at 198; P. Seitz, *Some Observations on the Role of an Arbitrator,* ARB. J. 65 (1979); and S. Vladek, Comment on L. A. Crane, *The Use and Abuse of Arbitral Power,* LABOR ARBITRATION AT THE QUARTER-CENTURY MARK 83 (Proceedings of the 25th Annual Meeting, National Academy of Arbitrators 1972).

[33]The major statement of this position is that of Arbitrator William E. Simkin:
    One of the fundamental purposes of an arbitration hearing is to let people get things off their chest, regardless of the decision. The arbitration proceeding is the opportunity for a third party to come in and act as a sort of father confessor to the parties to let them get rid of their troubles, get them out in the open . . . .
(Conference on Training of Law Students in Labor Relations, Vol. III, Transcript of Proceedings 636–37 (1947), cited in F. ELKOURI & E. A. ELKOURI, HOW ARBITRATION WORKS 298 (4th ed. 1985). For criticism, SEE PROBLEMS OF PROOF IN ARBITRATION, *supra* note 32, at 265ff.

[34]*The Arbitration Process in the Settlement of Labor Disputes,* 31 J. AM. JUDICATURE SOC. 54 (1947).

as well as by the collective bargaining agreement, so that the parties have recourse to the courts to settle many conflicts if they so choose.[35] The parties opt for arbitration not because they could not go to another forum, but because they see arbitration as a viable substitute for litigation.[36]

Moreover, one who calls arbitration a substitute for litigation is urging that the arbitrator should function much like a judge and that an arbitration is a one-shot "Jones v. Smith" type of confrontation. The parties' "relationship" is irrelevant to what arbitration is all about.[37] The arbitration hearing, in this view, should take on something like the full trappings of a trial before a judge and jury, with "full and vigorous resort by counsel to the so-called rules of evidence, a demand for meticulous adherence to strictures of trial practice relating to the examination (on direct and cross-examination) of witnesses, and an aura of adversarial hostility and aggressiveness."[38] Arbitration is thus a "system of adjudication that industry has elected in lieu of resorting to the courts."[39]

Some strong words are used by critics of this view.[40] (Critics

---

[35]Familiar examples include the Equal Pay Act of 1963, Title VII of the Civil Rights Act, and the Occupational Safety and Health Act. On the inroads which the availability of legal proceedings has made (or threatened to make) upon arbitration's traditional orbit, see D. Feller, *Arbitration: The Days of Its Glory Are Numbered*, 2 INDUS. REL. L. REV. 97–130 (1977); S. R. Reinhardt, *Arbitration and the Courts: Is the Honeymoon Over?*, ARBITRATION 1987 25–39 (Proceedings of the 40th Annual Meeting, National Academy of Arbitrators 1988); Dunsford, *supra* note 27; Parker, *supra* note 27.

[36]*E.g.*, because the parties have the opportunity voluntarily to select their own "judge," they can expect the arbitrator (unlike a court judge) to be an expert in the labor business and to have a direct and continuing commitment to them and to the profession; the time and cost of arbitration are much less than those of a court proceeding; the parties get a "once and for all" resolution of their dispute, without a potentially lengthy appeal process; and arbitrators, unlike judges, are not strictly bound by precedent—they can call individual cases "as they see them."

[37]L. L. Fuller, *Collective Bargaining and the Arbitrator*, COLLECTIVE BARGAINING AND THE ARBITRATOR'S ROLE 8 (Proceedings of the 15th Annual Meeting, National Academy of Arbitrators 1962). The classic statement of the arbitrator-as-judge position is that of American Arbitration Association vice president J. Noble Braden in his article *Problems in Labor Arbitration*, 13 Mo. L. Rev. 149 (1948).

[38]R. A. Smith, *The Search for Truth*, TRUTH, LIE DETECTORS, AND OTHER PROBLEMS IN LABOR ARBITRATION 48 (Proceedings of the 31st Annual Meeting, National Academy of Arbitrators 1979).

[39]A. Rubin, *Arbitration: Toward a Rebirth*, TRUTH, LIE DETECTORS, AND OTHER PROBLEMS IN LABOR ARBITRATION 31, *supra* note 38.

[40]Arbitrator Emanuel Stein: "[A] frustrating kind of legalism has crept into labor relations because the arbitrator has come to function like a judge and the parties have come to treat arbitration like litigation, with all the canons of construction familiar to the law of contracts." *Creeping Legalism in Labor Arbitration: An Editorial*, 13 ARB. J. 129

of this view tend, of course, to be proponents of the second view and vice versa.[41]) They argue as follows: (1) The formalities and technicalities of the courtroom do not belong in arbitration and ultimately can destroy it.[42] (2) The arbitrator cannot really act like a judge, even if he or she wants to, since his or her penalty and remedy powers are very different from those of a judge.[43] (3) The strict "judicial" approach in arbitration overlooks the key fact that the parties have a continuing relationship with each other.

An Extension of the Collective Agreement

> *Arbitrator Shulman:* To consider . . . arbitration as a substitute for court litigation or as the consideration for the no-strike pledge is to take a foreshortened view of it. . . . The arbitration is an integral part of the system of self-government. And the system is designed to aid management in its quest for efficiency, to assist union leadership in its participation in the enterprise, and to secure justice for the employees. It is a means of making collective bargaining work . . . .[44]

Grievance arbitration, in this view, must go beyond a narrow determination of contract rights and interests, since the contract often reflects only a partial meeting of minds and does not anticipate every problem that might arise during its term. "The role of the arbitrator as the final voice in the grievance procedure is to fill in these gaps of understanding. Arbitration

---

(1959). See also L. L. Fuller, *Collective Bargaining and the Arbitrator, supra* note 37, at 9: "The critics of this conception have a less flattering view of it. To them it is unrealistic, prudish, purist, legalistic, an abandonment of common sense, a chasing after false models motivated perhaps by a secret hankering for the glamour and security of judicial office."

[41]For a lively, thoughtful, and informed discussion of the merits of the "judicial" and "collective bargaining relationship" approaches, see the Socratic dialogue between Arbitrators McDermott and Roberts in *The Presidential Address—An Exercise in Dialectic: Should Arbitration Behave as Does Litigation?*, DECISIONAL THINKING OF ARBITRATORS AND JUDGES, *supra* note 30, at 1–18.

[42]McDermott & Roberts, *supra* note 41, at 12: "[M]any attitudes and devices found satisfactory in court are entirely unsatisfactory when transferred to arbitration—so much so that they distort what arbitration is meant to do and, if not fought with tooth and nail, will destroy it."

[43]H. Shulman, *Reason, Contract and Law in Labor Relations*, 68 HARV. L. REV. 1017 (1955).

[44]*Id.* at 1024.

awards and grievance settlements involve, therefore, not only administering the agreement, but completing the agreement."[45] The arbitrator who takes this approach is not so much a judge as a problem-solver who tries to do justice to the parties' continuing relationship.

Critics of the second view argue as follows: (1) The parties' continuing relationship is their lookout, not the arbitrator's.[46] (2) The arbitrator who thinks of himself as a "problem solver" may easily overstep the authority the parties have given him,[47] and may even think he can "play God."[48]

Types of Arbitrators

In practice, few arbitrators are "judicial" types or "relationship" types to the exclusion of the other. An arbitrator who is inclined toward the relationship view, for example, may shift to a more judicial posture if he or she believes a particular case calls for it. Such an arbitrator might also make adjustments if the parties are accustomed to functioning in a relatively legalistic, arm's length manner, or if for some reason they want to go strictly "by the book" in a particular case.

The only arbitrators who would tend not to adapt to the parties' expectations are those who have a very definite conception of the arbitrator's role in the collective bargaining process and believe that the arbitration process is best served if they play that role, whatever the expectations of the parties. Most arbitrators would agree that the arbitrator cannot be completely the creature of the parties and should bring to the process a detached and independent perspective. But in so doing, the arbitrator is not precluded from deciding whether a "judicial" stance or a "relationship" stance is more appropriate to the particular situation.

A "relationship" arbitrator is more likely to:

- try to mediate the dispute if he or she believes this is possible, to get the parties to achieve their own "meeting of minds";[49]

---

[45]Chicago Panel Report, DECISIONAL THINKING OF ARBITRATORS AND JUDGES, *supra* note 30, at 63-64.

[46]*Id.* at 167.

[47]Vladek, *supra* note 32, at 70.

[48]Fuller, *supra* note 37, at 122.

[49]The use of mediation as the arbitrator's primary tool in resolving disputes was urged by George W. Taylor, who has historically represented the arbitration-as-

- tailor his or her part in the proceeding to meet the parties' needs;
- run a more informal hearing than the "judicial" arbitrator;
- take a broader view of contract construction than the judicial type, placing more reliance on past practice and other principles outside the literal language of the agreement to "fill in the blanks";
- take into account questions of equity and how a decision may affect the parties' long-term relationship.

The Search for a Just Cause Standard

A Range of Approaches

By now, one should have a fair idea of how tricky it is to pin down the concept of just cause. The just cause standard presents a cluster of issues (such as the scope of the arbitrator's authority versus that of the employer) and consists of a number of different elements, and some arbitrators emphasize one whereas some give more weight to others. Proof of misconduct is the key for some; others tend to stress due process considerations, such as the employer's obligation to investigate all the circumstances before making any decision about discipline. Finally, some arbitrators emphasize "equity over law," stressing the spirit rather than the letter of the just cause standard.

By becoming familiar with these different elements and how they have been applied in specific cases, one can get a feel for what just cause means by reflected light, so to speak. It is in the service of that purpose to take a look at some further approaches to the concept of just cause.

> *Arbitrator Tyree* (common sense, knowledge, and understanding): About all that an impartial arbitrator can do . . . is to decide the justice or injustice of the discharge . . . in the light of (a) common sense, (b) common knowledge of generally prevailing industry

---

extension-of-the-contract view; see his article, *Effectuating the Labor Contract Through Arbitration*, THE PROFESSION OF LABOR ARBITRATION 20 (1957) (reprint of his 1949 speech before the National Academy of Arbitrators). While few arbitrators today would agree with Taylor that mediation is the goal of arbitration, probably only the very extreme "judicially inclined" would not step in and attempt mediation if it became clear during the hearing that agreement was just within reach and the parties agreed to accept the arbitrator's temporary shift to a mediation role.

standards for employee deportment and (c) common understanding of when—*absent specific criteria mutually agreed on* an employer may fairly and justly discharge an employee with seniority
rights.[50]

Arbitrator Turkus (proof of misconduct, fairness of penalty): In
applying the test of "just cause," the arbitgrator is generally required to determine two factors: (a) has the commission of the
misconduct . . . been adequately established by proof; and (b) if
proven or admitted, the reasonableness of the disciplinary penalty imposed in the light of the nature, character and gravity
thereof . . . .[51]

Arbitrator Karlins (consider all the facts): The words "just cause"
necessarily imply some investigation, fact finding, and weighing
of the circumstances.[52]

Arbitrator Belshaw (a "fair shake"): [Just cause] seems to be that
cause which, to a presumably reasonable determiner (Is there one
here?) appears to be (not necessarily is) fair and reasonable when
all the applicable facts and circumstances are considered, and are
viewed in the light of the ethic of time and place. That's a mouth-
ful of words but it really is only, bottom-line, another expression
of the now-common expression "fair shake."[53]

Arbitrator Platt (safeguard both parties' interests): It is the Arbitrator's function . . . not only to safeguard the employer's right to
discipline for cause where its exercise is necessary to the efficient
operation of his business, but also safeguard the interests of the
disciplined employee by making sure that the cause asserted for
disciplining him is just and the penalty is also fair and not disproportionate to the offense.[54]

Arbitrator Dworkin (three essential obligations): To comply with
just-cause requirements, the company had to perform three essential obligations. It needed to determine that disciplinary misconduct had indeed taken place; it had to issue discipline even-

---

[50]*Campbell Soup Co.*, 10 LA 207, 208 (1948) (absenteeism) (arbitrator's emphasis).
[51]*The Great Atl. & Pac. Tea Co.*, 63-1 ARB ¶8027, 3090 (1962) (improper handling
of receipts). To the same effect, *Indal Aluminum Gulfport*, 84 LA 124 (Nicholas, 1985)
(use of profanity); *Federal Paper Bd. Co.*, 88-1 ARB ¶8002 (Mathews, 1987) (fighting).
[52]*Farmbest, Inc.*, 44 LA 609, 613 (1965) (fighting).
[53]*Hiram Walker & Sons, Inc.*, 75 LA 899, 900 (intoxication).
[54]*Gardner-Richardson Co.*, 11 LA 957, 960 (1948) (misuse of confidential information). To the same effect, see *National Screw & Mfg. Co.*, 33 LA 735 (Dworkin, 1959)
(unauthorized absence due to arrest); *National Carbide Co.*, 49 LA 692 (Kesselman, 1967)
(absence from work station).

handedly without singling out any employee for disparate treatment; it was required to assess individual circumstances.[55]

Arbitrators Abrams and Nolan (employees' duties stressed): Just cause . . . embodies the idea that the employee is entitled to continued employment, provided he attends work regularly, obeys work rules, performs at some reasonable level of quality and quantity, and refrains from interfering with his employer's business by his activities on or off the job.[56]

A Practical Approach: Seven Key Tests

The basic elements of just cause which different arbitrators have emphasized have been reduced by Arbitrator Carroll R. Daugherty to seven tests. These tests, in the form of questions, represent the most specifically articulated analysis of the just cause standard as well as an extremely practical approach.[57] The comprehensiveness of these tests, their utility, and the widespread acceptance they have received in the 25 years following their first publication in 1966 have led us to structure this book around them.

A "no" answer to one or more of the questions means that just cause either was not satisfied or at least was seriously weakened in that some arbitrary, capricious, or discriminatory element was present.

1. NOTICE: Did the Employer give to the employee forewarning or foreknowledge of the possible or probable consequences of the employee's disciplinary conduct?
2. REASONABLE RULE OR ORDER: Was the Employer's rule or managerial order reasonably related to (a) the orderly, efficient, and safe operation of the Employer's business, and

---

[55]*Orrville Prods.*, 88 LA 204, 207 (1987) (failure to meet production quotas). A three-step just cause ladder is set up fairly frequently in arbitration, although the nature of the steps may differ somewhat from case to case. E.g., *Continental Grain Co.*, 85-2 ARB ¶8599 (Yarowsky, 1985) (fighting) (known infraction, proper notice, equal treatment); *Indianapolis Power & Light Co.*, 87 LA 826 (Volz, 1986) (proof of misconduct, disciplinary procedures followed, appropriate penalty); *Consolidation Coal Co.*, 87 LA 729 (Hoh, 1986) (drug use) (dischargeable offense, adequate proof, consideration of mitigating or extenuating circumstances).

[56]R. Abrams & D. R. Nolan, *Toward a Theory of "Just Cause" in Employee Discipline Cases*, DUKE L.J. 601 (1985).

[57]The seven tests were described on p. 2 of the newspaper of the American Arbitration Association, *Arbitration Times* (Spring 1988), as "the most practical and incisive criteria for employee discipline and discharge."

(b) the performance that the Employer might properly expect of the employee?

3. INVESTIGATION: Did the Employer, before administering the discipline to an employee, make an effort to discover whether the employee did in fact violate or disobey a rule or order of management?

4. FAIR INVESTIGATION: Was the Employer's investigation conducted fairly and objectively?

5. PROOF: At the investigation, did the "judge" obtain substantial evidence or proof that the employee was guilty as charged?

6. EQUAL TREATMENT: Has the Employer applied its rules, orders and penalties even-handedly and without discrimination to all employees?

7. PENALTY: Was the degree of discipline administered by the Employer in a particular case reasonably related to (a) the seriousness of the employee's *proven* offense, and (b) the record of the employee in his service with the Employer?[58]

The Seven Tests Applied

During the years since they were formulated by Arbitrator Daugherty, and especially during the past decade, the seven tests have been cited and applied by arbitrators in a wide variety of discipline and discharge cases.[59] They also have been incorporated in training materials for management and union represen-

---

[58]*Enterprise Wire Co.*, 46 LA 359 (1966) (absenteeism). Arbitrator Daugherty's decision, including his notes to the seven tests, is reprinted in the Appendix.

[59]Some of the cases in which most or all of the seven tests were applied are the following: *Thompson Culvert Co.*, 84-1 ARB ¶8077 (Newmark, 1984) (insubordination); *Holiday Inns, Inc.*, 84-1 ARB ¶8184 (Concepcion, 1984) (safety violation); *Aeroquip Corp.*, 85-1 ARB ¶8031 (Roumell, 1984) (fighting); *Signal Delivery Serv., Inc.*, 86 LA 75 (Wies, 1985) (intoxication); *Kidde, Inc., Weber Aircraft Div.*, 86 LA 681, 86-1 ARB ¶8200 (Dunn, 1985) (sexual harassment); *Olin Corp.*, 86 LA 1096 (Seidman, 1986) (sleeping on job); *County of Meeker*, 87 LA 51 (Kapsch, 1986) (insubordination); *Western Auto Supply*, 87 LA 678 (O'Grady, 1986) (poor performance); *Southern Cal. Edison*, 89 LA 1129 (Collins, 1987) (falsification of records); *Burlington N. Motor Carriers*, 90 LA 585 (Goldstein, 1987) (threatening company president); *Timken Co.*, 88-1 ARB ¶8056 (Duda, 1987) (falsification of clock-in time); *Hillhaven Corp.*, 91 LA 451 (McCurdy, 1988) (patient abuse by nursing aide); *Anderson-Tully Co.*, 88-1 ARB ¶8151 (Rice, 1988) (insubordination); *Fleming Foods of Tex., Inc.*, 89-1 ARB ¶8259 (Fox, 1988) (leaving job without permission); *General Tel. of the Midwest*, 89-2 ARB ¶8370 (Canestraight, 1988) (accessing unpublished number to pursue personal dispute); *Tucson Unified School Dist.*, 92 LA 544 (White, 1989) (theft); *Phillips 66 Co.*, 93 LA 607 (Goodstein, 1989) (refusal to work overtime; nonunion situation); *Carrier Corp.*, 89-1 ARB ¶8188 (Wilmoth, 1989) ("banking" of production); *H. J. Heinz Co.*, 95 LA 82 (Ellmann, 1990) (absenteeism).

tatives in both the private and public sectors.[60] Thus it may be said that the tests, apart from their impact on the arbitration process, have helped to improve the fairness of disciplinary processes in business, industry, and government.

Some have raised objections to Daugherty's tests of just cause on the ground that their use may degrade the decision-making process. "[T]he difficulty is that a process whose strength and uniqueness lies in the personal responsiveness of the decision maker to the daily problems of flesh and blood human beings in the shop may be transformed into an academic exercise, as tests and rules imported from extraneous sources begin to dominate the discretion and judgment of the arbitrator."[61] It was never Daugherty's intention, however, that the just cause tests be applied mechanically without regard to the setting in which they were applied. As he explained:

> The above-mentioned Questions and Notes [setting forth the seven tests] do not represent an effort to compress all the facts in a discharge case into a "formula." Labor and human relations circumstances vary widely from case to case, and no formula can be developed whereunder the facts can be fed into a "computer" that spews out the inevitably correct answer on a sheet of paper. There is no substitute for sound human judgment. The Questions and Notes do represent an effort to minimize an arbitrator's consideration of irrelevant facts and his possible human tendency to let himself be blown by the variable winds of sentiment on to an uncharted and unchartable sea of "equity."[62]

The seven tests have been described as embodying the common law of arbitration, and indeed Arbitrator Daugherty stated that his tests were grounded on the "innumerable discipline cases [that] have developed a sort of 'common law' definition of

---

[60]For a review of the development of the seven tests by Arbitrator Daugherty and the impact they have had on labor-management relations, see D. S. McPherson, *The Evolving Concept of Just Cause: Carroll R. Daugherty and the Requirement of Disciplinary Due Process*, 38 LAB. L.J. 387–403 (1987). For a critical view of the seven tests, see J. E. Dunsford, *Arbitral Discretion: The Tests of Just Cause*, ARBITRATION 1989 23–50 (Proceedings of the 42d Annual Meeting, National Academy of Arbitrators 23–50 (1990). The seven tests are the subject a film, *Arbitration: The Seven Tests of Just Cause*, featuring Adolph M. Koven, distributed by BNA Communications. They also are the basis for another book by A. M. KOVEN & S. L. SMITH, ALCOHOL-RELATED MISCONDUCT (1984).

[61]Dunsford, *supra* note 60, at 37.

[62]*Whirlpool Corp.*, 58 LA 421, 427 (1972) (horseplay). Recognition of this caution is reflected in *Holiday Inns, Inc.*, *supra* note 59, at 3847: "The standards for determining just cause do include the elements cited by the Union; however, all the elements are not always applicable in all situations and common sense must be applied."

just cause."[63] As such, an arbitrator may find their application to be inappropriate where the contract itself sets forth the standards of just cause. "In matters where clear contract language exists concerning the characteristics of the process and the standards to be used in determining whether just cause exists, it is the parties' contract that must prevail . . . ."[64] Thus, in a case involving the discharge of a long-service employee who had admitted taking $1.78 worth of overripe tomatoes without paying for them, the arbitrator was constrained from applying the just cause tests because under established company policy termination was automatic even if removal of the tomatoes was inadvertent, as the employee claimed. Though he said he regarded the employer's action as "draconian," the arbitrator found no alternative to upholding the discharge.[65]

Another caveat regarding the seven tests is that one or more negative answers to the questions do not necessarily mean that discharge or other discipline is not justified. This is most often the case where the arbitrator finds that the employer's investigation was deficient in some respect. If the deficiency was such that the grievant was not prejudiced, the arbitrator may well see no reason to disturb the discipline imposed by the employer.[66] Similarly, a failure to meet the literal requirements of notice, reasonable rule, equal treatment, and penalty may be excused by the arbitrator, either because there was no demonstrable injury to the grievant or because the employer acted within the bounds of its reasonable discretion. The most nearly inviolable test is that of adequate proof, since "if no infraction has been proved, then no penalty is just."[67] To repeat Daugherty's admonition, "[t]here is no substitute for sound human judgment."

---

[63]*Enterprise Wire Co.*, *supra* note 58, at 362.

[64]*Philips Indus., Inc.*, 93 LA 1133 (Dilts, 1989) (refusal to submit to drug screen).

[65]*Kroger Co.*, 89-2 ARB ¶8504 (Seidman, 1989).

[66]See, e.g., *Hillhaven Corp.*, *supra* note 59.

[67]*Arizona Aluminum Co.*, 82-1 ARB ¶8212, 3975 (Sass, 1982) (damage to company property).

Chapter 1

Notice

"Did the employer give to the employee forewarning or foreknowledge of the possible or probable consequences of the employee's disciplinary conduct?"

"Forewarning" and "foreknowledge" in Daugherty's first test mean notice. "'[N]otice' means information, an advice, or written warning, in more or less formal shape, intended to apprise a person of some proceeding in which his interests are involved, or informing him of some fact which it is his right to know and the duty of the notifying party to communicate."[1] To put notice in the context of industrial relations:

> *Arbitrator Koven:* [I]t is well recognized that before an employee can be justifiably disciplined for a breach of an employer's rules or regulations, he must have knowledge of the rule or regulation which he is charged with violating. In most cases, such employee knowledge is not to be inferred, but is required to be evident by the publication of such rules so that employees can be presumed to be aware of them.
>
> Only certain egregious conduct, such as stealing, intoxication while at work, or fighting with supervisors or co-workers, is so evidently a violation of commonly accepted notions of work conduct that it will be presumed that the employee is on notice that such conduct is unacceptable and that he can be penalized for violating such rules.[2]

Or, as Arbitrator Marlatt has put it:

---

[1]Black's Law Dictionary 957 (5th ed. 1979).

[2]*Bay Area Rapid Transit Dist.*, 80-2 ARB ¶8612, 5734 (1980) (unauthorized phone calls, false overtime claim). To the same effect, *Federal Mogul Corp.*, 86 LA 225, 231 (Blinn, 1985) (delay in obtaining leave extension): "Basic due process and fairness require that the employee be given fair warning" of the use of automatic termination on the presumption of voluntary quit.

No Company has to post a Shop Rule saying, "Employees are forbidden to steal Company property, to beat up the Foreman, or to break the windows on purpose." Any employee knows that he does such things at the risk of his job.[3]

But there are less obvious rules, governing such matters as how long employees may wear their hair, where and when they may smoke, how many absences are acceptable before discharge will follow, and the like. So

> when just cause for discipline is involved, and particularly when that discipline takes the form of discharge, there is a clear burden on the Company to see to it that the employees fully understand the rules and procedures which they must follow and more importantly, that they also understand what will happen to them if they do not follow the rules and procedures.[4]

The subject of notice can be approached from a number of different angles, which overlap to some degree. For management, notice normally comes up through one of three questions: First, of what, exactly, does the employer have to give notice? Second, what form does notice have to take? Third, what are the common pitfalls where notice is in issue?

I. Two Requirements: Misconduct and Its Consequences

Notice of Misconduct—What Actions Can Lead to Discipline?

A fundamental component of the just cause standard is that employees must be told what kind of conduct will lead to discipline—especially if the penalty is to be discharge. An employee can hardly be expected to abide by rules the employer

---

[3]*Texas Mills Supply & Mfg., Inc.*, 74-2 ARB ¶8703, 5671 (1975) (failure immediately to report missing merchandise). See also Arbitrator Marlatt's distinction in *Baker Marine Corp.*, 84 LA 627, 629 (1985) (failure to pass certification test), between theft-type cases and work standards and qualifications cases in which "the employer needs to spell it out"; *Hyatt Hotels Palo Alto*, 85 LA 11 (Oestreich, 1985) (sexual harassment held wrong per se, thus notice not required); *Hospital Employees' Div.*, 87-2 ARB ¶8524 (Frost, 1987) (no rule or notice required for dishonesty); *Furr's, Inc.*, 87-2 ARB ¶8365 (Blum, 1986) (same for lying); *Ohio Edison Co.*, 86-1 ARB ¶8299 (Kates, 1986) (same for marijuana use).

[4]*Texas Mills Supply & Mfg. Co., Inc., supra* note 3, at 5671. See also *Beverly Enterprises d.b.a. Leisure Lodge*, 86-1 ARB ¶8102 (Nelson, 1985) (use of toxic cleaning substance); *Southland Corp.*, 84-1 ARB ¶8134 (Marcus, 1984) (theft).

has not communicated, and no arbitrator is likely to uphold a penalty for conduct that an employee did not know was forbidden.[5]

It would be next to impossible to catalog all the different kinds of behavior for which employees may not be disciplined if not put on notice that their actions will be considered misconduct. As a rule of thumb, notice is required for any action that is misconduct by definition of the employer and does not fall under any of the well-known exceptions to formal notice requirements set forth below.

Arbitrators have revoked or reduced penalties where employees were not clearly told they had to have a supervisor's permission before leaving their work stations;[6] that they could not distribute political campaign leaflets on company premises;[7] that break-time card playing was prohibited;[8] that, as postal employees, they could not backdate postmarks on personal mail;[9] that they could not leave the plant during breaks;[10] that they must report for overtime;[11] that they could not attend college classes while on sick leave;[12] that punching another employee's time card, even without an intent to defraud the

---

[5]In *Trizec Props., Inc.*, 87-2 ARB ¶8324, 5104 (Keefe, 1987) (insubordination), where the employer was found not to have given its security guards written information on what was expected of them with regard to such matters as their lunch breaks and check-in times, the arbitrator advised the employer that "stability in its dealing with the workers will emerge from written promulgation of reasonable, businesslike rules and procedures so that individual employees will be able to know the expectations the Employer requires to have fulfilled." In *McKeown Trans. Co.*, 84 LA 600 (1985) (dishonesty), Arbitrator Armstrong pointed out that one consequence of failure to give proper notice is that the union is deprived of an opportunity to prepare a defense, which in turn may set in motion a number of other consequences, such as waiver by the employer of the right to object to potential step variations in the grievance procedure that may have occurred. See also *Goldberg & Solovy Foods, Inc.*, 85-2 ARB ¶8440 (Rothschild, 1985) (unexcused absence); *County of Meeker*, 87 LA 51 (Kapsch, 1986) (insubordination); *Central Tel. Co.*, 93 LA 185 (Hardbeck, 1989) (negligence).

[6]*Schenley Indus., Inc.*, 67-2 ARB ¶8514, 4802 (Koven, 1967):
    Obviously, no violation of any rule can occur unless employees are on clear and unequivocal notice of such rules. . . . The requirement of clear and emphatic notice of the existence of the rule was particularly required in the case of irrigators because of their work situation which admittedly did not demand their full attention in the afternoon. Unless such notice was given, it is reasonable to conclude that, so long as work requirements were satisfactorily met, no penalty would follow from not being physically present at all times . . . .

[7]*Four Wheel Drive Auto Co.*, 4 LA 170 (Rauch, 1946).

[8]*Inland Underground Facilities*, 70-1 ARB ¶8042 (Talent, 1969).

[9]*U.S. Postal Serv.*, 62 LA 293 (Killion, 1974).

[10]*Owens-Illinois, Inc.*, 76 LA 994 (Koven, 1981).

[11]*Canteen Corp.*, 86 LA 378 (Hilgert, 1986).

[12]*Niemand Indus., Inc.*, 88-1 ARB ¶8070 (Sargent, 1987).

company, was wrong;[13] that they were forbidden to enter non-job-related or copyrighted programs into the computer;[14] and that they must submit to a blood-alcohol test or be discharged.[15]

Lack of notice concerning proper work procedures has led to the disallowance of discipline for negligence or for damaging company property,[16] while the company's failure to make clear its policies, for example, as to what constitutes an "excused" absence[17] or when a doctor's slip is required for return to work,[18] has brought reversal of many a penalty for absenteeism. An employee recovering from alcohol and cocaine addiction was improperly discharged for not following the prescribed after-care treatment program, where the company had not adequately told him what it expected of him.[19] Even discharge for urinating in a company parking lot was set aside (and full back pay awarded) where the practice was common and the company had no published rule against it.[20]

Where Working Life and Private Life Overlap

Misconduct that is more directly connected with an employee's personal life than with his work life is a fairly common source of notice problems. Arbitrator Healy explains why: "Unlike the more blatant offenses which have a direct bearing on the employer-employee relationship (e.g., poor quality work, absenteeism, tardiness, insubordination, etc.), this type of offense [wage garnishment] might not occur to one as affecting one's acceptability as an employee."[21] Wage garnishment, for example, affects the employer-employee relationship only indirectly, either by imposing a bookkeeping burden or by casting doubt on the employee's character. Thus, garnishment should not be an occasion for discipline unless the employer has expressly said it would be.

---

[13]*Cranston Print Works Co.*, 36 LA 179 (Maggs, 1960).

[14]*U.S. Army Tank-Automotive Command*, 93 LA 767 (Smith, 1989).

[15]*Fitzsimmons Mfg. Co.*, 92 LA 609 (Roumell, 1989). See also *Englehard Corp.*, 89-1 ARB ¶8033 (Mathews, 1988) (improper to discharge employees testing positive for drugs, where adequate notice of disciplinary consequences not given to employees or union).

[16]*Tennessee Forging Steel Corp.*, 69-1 ARB ¶8282 (Owen, 1968).

[17]*John A. Volpe Construction Co.*, 45 LA 532 (Dunlop,1965); *American Standard*, 30 LA 231 (Thompson, 1958).

[18]*Abex Corp.*, 47 LA 441 (Kates, 1966).

[19]*Peoples' Gas Light & Coke Co.*, 89 LA 786 (Smith, 1987).

[20]*Kentucky Textile Indus.*, 70-1 ARB ¶8127 (Williams, 1969).

[21]*D. M. Watkins Co.*, 14 LA 787 (Healy, 1950).

Discipline cannot as a rule be imposed for other reasons falling in the "twilight zone" between personal and working life, such as residency outside the company's geographical area, marriage to a fellow employee, conflict of interest, and the like, unless company policy on these matters has been clearly made known.[22] Certain types of off-premises criminal acts, such as drunk driving, have also been held to be subject to notice requirements where the misconduct in question has no direct impact on the individual's employment.[23]

Exceptions to Formal Notice Requirements

Conduct Wrong in Itself. There are some kinds of activities that every employee should know will not be tolerated on the job. For misconduct of this kind, "forewarning or foreknowledge" is given by common sense rather than by any specific written rule or explicit oral direction. To put it another way, notice that actions in this category are wrong is "implied."

> *Arbitrator Keeler*: [A] Company does not have to establish that it had, or that it had communicated specific rules for certain well-recognized proven offenses such as drunkenness, theft, or insubordination . . . .[24]

> *Arbitrator Cohen*: Certainly, the Union does not seriously contend that violent conduct need be tolerated or that employees are unaware that violence may result in disciplinary action simply because a "do not injure your coworker" rule has not been mailed to the Union or posted on the bulletin board. Employees are assumed to have a modicum of common sense and employers have a right to expect that even such a minimal degree of common sense is exercised by the employees.[25]

---

[22]*Quaker State Corp.*, 92 LA 898 (Talarico, 1989) (residency requirement); *Northwest Airlines, Inc.*, 72-1 ARB ¶8290 (Koven, 1972) (conflict of interest).

[23]*Lamb Glass Co.*, 32 LA 420, 423 (Dworkin, 1959) (drunk driving conviction): "Since as a matter of 'common law' applicable to industrial relations, what an employee does on his own time is not a subject of regulation by the employer, any qualifying restriction must be expressly set out in clear and unequivocal language." Similarly, in *Gamble Bros.*, 68 LA 72, 74 (Krislov,1977) (marijuana use on lunch break away from plant): "[W]hen the company discharges an individual for an offense (despite its illegality) which has become quite common, . . . employees have not been given proper notice."

[24]*Philco Corp.*, 45 LA 437, 441 (1965) (obscene language). To the same effect, *Signal Delivery Serv., Inc.*, 86 LA 75 (Wies, 1985) (intoxication).

[25]*Davey Co.*, 60 LA 917, 919 (1973) (fighting).

As a rule, discipline may be imposed without specific advance notice for two classes of misconduct:

Socially disapproved—actions that society as a whole prohibits or disapproves, including:

- misconduct involving property, such as theft, willful destruction of property, or arson;[26]
- misconduct directed against persons, such as threats of bodily harm, unprovoked assaults,[27] police brutality,[28] carrying of firearms on company premises,[29] rape, or sexual harassment;[30]
- other illegal or socially unacceptable misconduct such as selling drugs, many forms of gambling, and the like.[31]

---

[26]*Norwich Pharmacal Co.*, 5 LA 536, 539 (Shipman, 1946): "It is one thing where the act upon which a discharge is premised is wrong per se. Typical, even though extreme, would be the case of an employee stealing company property. Here notice is unnecessary. It is presumed." See also *Capital Area Transp. Auth.*, 77-1 ARB ¶8170, 3744 (Brown, 1976): "There was no rule . . . which specifically covered the defacing or destroying of company property. . . . Employers do not have to publish rules that prohibit conduct that is so clearly wrong that common sense would dictate that the employer would regard such acts as misconduct."

[27]*New York Central R.R. Co.*, 44 LA 552, 553 (Wyckoff, 1965): There "are certain types of conduct such as murdering passengers or wrecking trains that could hardly be condoned for the want of a rule." See also *Omar, Inc.*, 26 LA 641, 642 (Beatty, 1956): "[E]very mature person must know that engaging in a violent fist fight on Company property . . . is detrimental to the business and can be injurious to property and persons and that it cannot be condoned."

[28]*County of Santa Clara*, 88-1 ARB ¶8157 (Barrett, 1987). In this case a police officer was discharged for using excessive force on an intoxicated, handcuffed prisoner, to the point where the prisoner required hospital treatment. Citing *City of Hartford*, 62 LA 1281 (Blum, 1974), in which discharge for excessive force was reduced to an eight-month suspension, the *Santa Clara* arbitrator upheld the discharge, since he regarded the conduct of the officer as much more serious than that of the grievant in *City of Hartford*. To similar effect, see *City of Redwood*, 83 LA 1254 (Concepcion, 1984), and *City of Pomona*, 84 LA 1118 (Collins, 1985).

[29]*Brown & Williamson Tobacco Corp.*, 50 LA 403, 412 (Willingham, 1968): "Common sense alone would dictate that a weapon such as a loaded firearm would not be permitted on the premises of any employer except in the possession of a duly authorized plant protection man." *Jeffrey Mining Mach. Div., Dresser Indus., Inc.*, 79-1 ARB ¶8002, 3014 (Leach, 1978): "[C]onduct involving the creation of fear through brandishing what Grievant had to know would be believed to be a real gun, is conduct that is inherently wrong and known by every reasonable person to be wrong. That kind of conduct needs no specific prohibiting rule of the Company."

[30]*Dover Corp.*, 78-2 ARB ¶8465, 5164 (Haemmel, 1978) (forcing sexual advances on another employee): "[T]he grievant cannot complain of receiving no express warnings; such male versus female aggressions on the job predate the very first collective bargaining agreement and such a prohibition remains part of the unwritten law of the shop."

[31]*News Syndicate Co.*, 43 LA 511, 513–14 (Berkowitz, 1964): "The Company need not post notices forbidding employees to gamble any more than it need post notices forbidding employees to break other aspects of the laws of the land." See also *Safeway*

In practice, most companies have rules or even contract provisions covering socially disapproved misconduct. But there are some situations, however serious, that an employer might not anticipate.

> **EXAMPLE:** One afternoon and evening, various company personnel received anonymous telephone calls at the plant and at their homes warning that a time bomb had been set to go off on company premises and the plant should be evacuated. An employee who was on disciplinary suspension at the time subsequently was fingered as the culprit and was fired. The union argued that making threatening telephone calls was not prohibited by the plant rules set forth in the contract, and hence that the employee's termination was not for just cause.

Nonsense, the arbitrator said in effect. Rule or no rule,"in the general exercise of its management, the company is specifically given the power . . . to discharge for just and proper cause in the event that some specific conduct of an employee is of such a serious nature as to justify discharge even on a first offense of such a conduct." Making telephoned bomb threats is certainly "of such a serious nature" because such conduct could cripple operations, by forcing evacuations and causing shutdowns, and cannot be tolerated. Discharge was sustained.[32]

Discharge without specific notice for even less obviously damaging misconduct has been upheld when such misconduct is widely accepted to be wrong. Such was the case where an employee was terminated for spreading rumors about illicit relationships between the store manager and store owner and female employees. The arbitrator pointed out that society has always condemned slander and made such activity actionable in court. Rumor mongering is a particular problem in a business environment, he noted, where poor morale can threaten the very existence of the organization.[33]

Stores, Inc., 82-1 ARB ¶8207 (Phelan, 1982) (selling illegal drugs); *Cooper Airmotive, Inc.*, 63 LA 896 (Sartain, 1974) (loan sharking).

[32] *Vulcan Materials Co.*, 64 LA 773 (Ipavec, 1975). In *Columbia Broadcasting Sys., Inc.*, 57 LA 77 (Sembower, 1971),the arbitrator held that a broadcasting company could not reasonably have foreseen that an employee would secretly "bug" a union meeting in a company conference room; therefore, it could not be faulted for not having a rule covering such "bizarre"conduct. Nevertheless, discharge was set aside on the ground that the bugging incident was "no great act of espionage" and that tape recording was so common a practice in the industry that discharge without notice was improper.

[33] *Food Wagon Tom Boy Store*, 71-1 ARB ¶8021 (Sembower, 1970).

Industrially disapproved—activities that violate fundamental principles of the employer-employee relationship, including:

- refusing to follow legitimate work orders (insubordination);[34]
- neglecting one's duties (e.g., by sleeping,[35] leaving one's work station in order to avoid work,[36] being absent too frequently,[37] getting drunk during working hours, leaving work early without permission);[38]
- poor work performance;[39]
- dishonesty in any form (e.g., falsifying a time card, fraudulently collecting incentive pay);[40]
- sabotage.

As Arbitrator Schmidt has explained:

Published rules and regulations are not necessary to inform an employee that conduct of the nature described may subject him to discharge from the company's employ. Every employee, working in an industrial plant, is presumed to know that the plant cannot operate without a reasonable measure of discipline and

---

[34]*Ross Gear & Tool Co.*, 35 LA 293, 295–96 (Schmidt, 1960):
It is implicit in the employer-employee relationship that an employee must conform to certain well known, commonly accepted standards of reasonable discipline and proper conduct while engaged in his work at the plant. Among these obligations are the duty to perform his work as directed . . . . An industrial plant is a place for the production of goods and the performance of work. While it is not a military barracks, neither is it a place for barroom conduct, indifference to a supervisor's instructions, or childish outbursts of defiant insubordination accompanied by abusive and profane language.
[35]*Ashland Oil Co.*, 28 LA 874 (Bradley, 1957); *Whittaker Corp.*, 70-1 ARB ¶8302 (Geissinger, 1970).
[36]*Friden, Inc.*, 52 LA 448, 449 (Koven, 1969) (loafing, lack of cooperation, negligence): "[I]rrespective of formalization into rules, misconduct of the type with which the grievant is charged is subject to disciplinary action."
[37]*Sterling Drug, Inc.*, 70-1 ARB ¶8033, 3128 (Berkowitz, 1969): "No formal rule is needed to set forth the notion [that] an employee is expected to be at work on time and not to be excessively absent."
[38]*American Auto-Felt Corp.*, 41 LA 770, 772 (Howlett, 1963):"[T]he lack of a rule regulating departure from work or the plant does not give employees license to leave the plant at any time during working hours. The absence of rules does not signify shop anarchy. That an employee, once having reported, work all of a scheduled work day unless excused is a normal standard of employee conduct."
[39]*Anchor Hocking Glass Corp.*, 67-1 ARB ¶8209 (Stouffer, 1967).
[40]*Southern Cal. Edison Co.*, 70-1 ARB ¶8066 (Sinclitico, 1969) (dishonesty in using company-assisted purchase plan). The grievant, who held a position of fiduciary responsibility as a senior accounting clerk, should have known that a breach of trust would destroy the company's confidence in him. Actual notice of the consequences of his action was unnecesssary.

without a reasonable attitude of respect from the employees for the authority of their supervisors.[41]

But even in the case of conduct that is so clearly improper in the industrial setting that no rule prohibiting it is necessary, notice problems can arise in particular situations.

EXAMPLE: One Friday an employee spoke to her foreman about her husband's desire to go fishing the following Monday and was led to believe that he gave her permission to take Monday afternoon off. She was subsequently fired for leaving the plant early in violation of a company rule requiring employees to get permission for early departures from either the company president or the general manager. The union contended that there was no such rule.

There was no general notice problem. "[L]ack of a rule regulating departure from work or the plant does not give employees license to leave the plant at any time during working hours," the arbitrator commented. But "in the specific" it was another matter; employees had not been adequately notified that permission to leave early could be granted only by the president or the general manager and by no other supervisor. For that reason, the discharge was set aside.[42]

"And Similar Offenses." Specific notice that a particular action is prohibited may not be needed if that action is so similar in character to misconduct that *has* been prohibited that notice is implied. When management sits down to draft plant rules, obviously it cannot anticipate every conceivable act by an employee that might—at some time in the future—warrant discipline. Indeed, management may deliberately choose not to make its plant rules too specific, to avoid having the union turn the tables and claim that if the employer had intended to prohibit a particular kind of conduct, it would have said so.

Employers often try to cover all bases by finishing off their

---

[41]*Ross Gear & Tool Co.*, *supra* note 34, at 296.

[42]*American Auto-Felt Corp.*, *supra* note 38. See also *Everett Piano Co.*, 79-1 ARB ¶8158, 3667–68 (Casselman, 1979): "While it is not entirely clear by what method the rules were announced, it is obvious that any employee possessed of average intelligence would know that shutting down the line for no reason . . . is a very serious offense, punishable by a major penalty, including discharge." The arbitrator went on to observe, however, that shutdowns of the line at this company had been a fairly frequent occurrence, and management had "failed to establish specific and *clear cut* rules defining the limitations on the right to shut down the line and the circumstances when shut downs are prohibited." The grievant's discharge was therefore set aside.

lists of prohibited conduct with phrases like "and similar offenses" or "among other reasons," which are designed to put
employees on notice that they may be held liable for misconduct
which is not spelled out but which common sense dictates is
"similar" to actions that are subject to penalty.

> *Arbitrator Kupsinel*: There is no need for a Company to post a rule
> concerning every specific type of activity which merits discipline.
> Section 1 of Article 20 lists a number of specific reasons giving
> the Company the right to discipline or discharge and adds "or
> any just and sufficient cause," which is a catch-all of obvious, but
> unlisted *serious* offenses. There is no doubt that the Grievant
> knew, or should have known, that possession of marijuana is a
> criminal offense and that possession on the Company premises
> would warrant severe discipline.[43]

Even in the absence of such "catch-all" language, management may make the judgment that a particular kind of action
not explicitly mentioned in its rules is comparable to conduct
that is proscribed, and impose discipline on that basis. The test
of "similarity" or "comparability" must be applied on a case-by-
case basis and comes down to a decision as to whether the
misconduct in question is so similar to specifically proscribed
misconduct that the employee should reasonably have known
that discipline would result.

> **EXAMPLE NO. 1:** An employee was discharged for placing a
> "fire bomb" in a dump area adjacent to the company's parking
> lot. The bomb was timed to go off immediately after work as
> employees were going to their cars to kick off an after-hours
> party. The employer compared the device to a "deadly weapon,"
> possession of which was ground for immediate discharge under
> the employer's posted rules and regulations. The union asserted
> that the "fire bomb" was in reality no more than a firecracker
> or noisemaker and likened the employee's action to a harmless
> prank.

Who was right? Both, said the arbitrator. After hearing
testimony from law enforcement and fire-fighting authorities,
he concluded that the device set by the employee did not

---

[43]*KLM Royal Dutch Airlines*, 66 LA 547 (1975). See also *Flxible Co.*, 48 LA 1227,
1230 (Teple, 1967), where a rule prohibiting destruction of company property was
found to apply to the grievant's abuse of a vendor-owned soft drink machine: "The
preface to the plant rules clearly indicates that the violations are typical and that other
similar violations may also call for proper discipline based on the nature of the offense."

have the lethal potential that the employer claimed it had, nor was it a fighting instrument as implied by the word "weapon." The employee was therefore not on notice that he could be fired for planting his explosive device, and his discharge was set aside.

However, the arbitrator made a "comparability" or "similarity" judgment of a different kind in imposing a lesser penalty. The device was potentially more dangerous than a simple firecracker, and the employee certainly was guilty of irresponsibility in setting it to go off where someone might have been injured if it had exploded accidentally. Since the rules stated that the employer "endeavors to employ only persons of good character and judgment" and provided that the employer could discipline employees for "other reasons" as well as listed offenses, the appropriate punishment was a 60-day suspension.[44]

> **EXAMPLE NO. 2:** When two employees got married, one of them resigned her job in accordance with a rule requiring one spouse or the other to resign within 30 days of their marriage. Two years later they divorced, and the woman sucessfully reapplied for a job. The following year the two began living together again, though they did not remarry. When the employer found out, it informed the couple that one of them would have to go. Both refused, and both were terminated.

Reinstating them, the arbitrator did not interpret cohabitation as equivalent to marriage. The employees did not hold themselves out publicly as being married; the state in which they lived did not recognize common law marriages; and the Internal Revenue Service considered them single individuals. Cohabitation was not a common practice at the time the employer's rule was instituted, and it was not clear that the employer foresaw

---

[44]*Coleman Co.*, 54 LA 281 (Springfield, 1970). "Comparability" was also found in *Safeway Stores, Inc.*, 82-1 ARB ¶8207, 3954 (Phelan, 1982):

> Both Section 1 and Section 8 of Article VII indicate that the use of illegal drugs is a continuing concern of the Company and the Union and this concern is reinforced in the Employee Handbook's working rules which forbid the possession of any drug which affects work performance. It stands to reason that the concern of the parties would be just as great, if not more so, with an employee dealing with the distribution of illegal drugs.

See also *Ethyl Corp.*, 74 LA 953 (Hart, 1980) (prohibiting possession of marijuana would seem to follow logically from prohibiting its use); *Alden's Inc.*, 73 LA 396 (Martin, 1979) (rule allowing company to search employees' purses did not impliedly exclude other types of searches; discipline affirmed for grievant who refused security guard's order to raise her conspicuously bulging pants leg).

the change in mores and intended that cohabitation and marriage be treated alike. Thus the couple had no reason to know that the employer would consider cohabitation to be the same as marriage.[45]

Other Exceptions. In a number of cases arbitrators have relaxed or disregarded the requirement of notice, not because of the nature of the misconduct but because the circumstances persuaded them that strict adherence to the usual notice rules was not warranted. Such circumstances include the following: where the failure to give proper notice did not result in harm to the employee;[46] where the employee knew of the rule and the consequences of violating it;[47] where the problem was not misconduct as such but rather failure to meet known job responsibilities;[48] where the employer met the spirit though not the letter of the rule in regard to notice;[49] and where violation of the notice requirement was merely technical.[50]

Notice of Penalty

The requirement of notice, as arbitrators have generally understood it, means that the employer must let employees know not only what kinds of conduct will lead to discipline, but what discipline is likely to result. Notice of penalty is particularly important if the penalty is discharge; employees guilty of conduct they knew or should have known was unacceptable have sometimes been put back to work because they were not warned that they could be fired.[51]

---

[45]*Public Serv. Co. of New Mexico*, 78-1 ARB ¶8247(Springfield, 1978). See also *Port Auth. of Allegheny County*, 71-2 ARB ¶8694 (Duff, 1971) (rule prohibiting bus drivers from wearing political campaign buttons did not cover button expressing black nationalist sentiments); *Trane Co.*, 12 LA 559 (Graff, 1949) (smearing greasy handprints on screen in men's room not comparable to "defacing company property").

[46]*Stroh Brewery Co.*, 85 LA 89 (Boyer, 1985) (insubordination); *Pan Am Support Servs.*, 89-1 ARB ¶8306 (Odom, 1988) (use of offensive language).

[47]*Shell Oil Co.*, 85-2 ARB ¶8556 (Bennett, 1985) (absenteeism).

[48]*Apex Paving Co.*, 87 LA 1136 (Yarowsky, 1986) (unacceptable performance).

[49]*Calho Chems., Inc.*, 84-1 ARB ¶8023 (High, 1983) (insubordination); *Dominick's Finer Foods*, 88 LA 847 (Traynor, 1987) (improper cash refunds).

[50]*American Inks & Coatings Corp.*, 87 LA 691 (Di Lauro, 1986) (absenteeism).

[51]*E.g., Bumper Works*, 87 LA 586 (Schwartz, 1986) (absenteeism); *Packaging Materials, Inc.*, 84-1 ARB ¶8137 (Maniscalco, 1984) (absences); *Star Markets, Ltd.*, 84-1 ARB ¶8207 (Tsukiyama, 1983) (pilfering). In *Tuohy Furniture Co.*, 88-2 ARB ¶8517 (Jacobowski, 1988), two factors combined to persuade the arbitrator that no penalty was justified where an employee failed to show up for voluntary Saturday overtime work: (1) the employee had not been warned that his work record and performance were so bad that he would be subject to termination if he did not improve or if another serious infraction

Arbitrator Ipavec: An occasion for discipline is not necessarily an appropriate occasion for discharge. The Employee should be aware of the significance which the Company attaches to a prohibited act and, in a case of disobedience, that sanction will be immediate discharge.[52]

EXAMPLE: During his lunch break an employee noticed two-pieces of copper cable in a scrap heap. Thinking his 12-year-old son could make use of the cable in a home smelter he had constructed, he put it in his dinner bucket with the intention of taking it home at the end of the day. When a supervisor by chance discovered the cable in the dinner bucket, the employee was discharged under a company rule providing discipline or discharge for "stealing, misappropriating, or wrongfully converting to his own use the property of the Company or another employee." The employee claimed he thought the cable had been abandoned and was of no value to the employer, although he admitted he knew he was supposed to seek permission before taking it. He did not do so, he said, because he believed permission would routinely have been granted.

Noting a lack of evidence that any employee had ever been discharged for taking material from the scrap pile, the arbitrator concluded that the employee reasonably could have believed the cable was up for grabs. If the employer had clearly and unequivocally warned him and others that the penalty for taking material from the scrap pile without permission was summary discharge, the arbitrator would have sustained the discharge. But under the circumstances, especially in view of the employee's exemplary work record over a period of 12 years, termination was not justified. Because the employee failed to seek permission, however, the arbitrator concluded that a 60-day suspension would have been proper.[53]

Lack of clear notice that discharge would be the penalty has played a crucial role in cases involving sleeping,[54] cash short-

---

occurred; (2) the employee already had been disciplined for the offense by a warning notice from his foreman.

[52]*Gray Drug Stores, Inc.*, 70-1 ARB ¶8115, 3403 (1969) (failure to record sales). To the same effect, *U.S. Postal Serv.*, 62 LA 293, 299 (Killion, 1974) (backdating postmark on personal mail): "It is . . . an established tenet of Industrial Jurisprudence that an employee must not only be apprised of the content of an Employer's work rule but in addition thereto must also be warned of the consequences of its violation."

[53]*Consolidation Coal Co.*, 92 LA 813 (Seidman, 1989).

[54]*Whittaker Corp.*, 70-1 ARB ¶8302 (Geissinger, 1970).

ages,[55] fighting,[56] possession of alcohol,[57] excessive sick leave,[58] and a variety of other offenses.[59]

Notice that discharge is in the offing is particularly important in the common situation where discharge is to be imposed for an accumulation of minor infractions, none of which in itself would justify a severe penalty but which together add up to an unacceptable unemployment record.[60] An employee is entitled to know, for example, at exactly what point another absence,[61] garnishment,[62] production lapse,[63] or other act of minor misconduct[64] will prove to be the "last straw."

---

[55]*Gray Drug Stores, Inc.*, *supra* note 52.

[56]*Farmbest, Inc.*, 44 LA 609 (Karlins, 1965), in which the arbitrator found that lack of notice would not prevent the discharge of someone for provoking a fight. But where the company made no attempt to determine whether the grievant had been the aggressor or the unwilling victim, and where no notice had been given that discharge would result merely from taking part in a fight, discharge was too harsh. See also *City of Massillon*, 92 LA 1303 (Elkin, 1989), where the arbitrator reduced a discharge for starting a fight to a lengthy suspension since neither the contract nor a written rule required discharge for fighting, the company was partially to blame for not defusing the situation, and the grievant had no prior disciplinary record.

[57]*Red Arrow Freight Lines, Inc.*, 78 LA 141 (Baroni, 1982).

[58]*Mare Island Naval Shipyard*, 89 LA 861 (Wilcox, 1987). In *Oglebay Norton Co.*, 84-1 ARB ¶8294 (Duda, 1984), the arbitrator reinstated with back pay an employee who was discharged because he had been absent 60% of the time over an eight-year period. The great bulk of the employee's absences were due to two major injuries which together incapacitated him for 852 days, and the company had not warned him that even excused absences would be counted in determining what was excessive absenteeism.

[59]*Western Contracting Corp.*, 77-1 ARB ¶8004 (Laughlin, 1976) (stopping truck by roadside); *Metal Powder Prods., Inc.*, 35 LA 409 (Dworkin, 1960) (walking off job before end of shift); *Artco-Bell Corp.*, 61 LA 773 (Springfield, 1973) (refusal of work assignment); *Jeffrey Mining Mach. Div.*, 79-1 ARB ¶8002 (Leach, 1973) (flourishing gun at company-sponsored sports event); *Milgram Food Stores, Inc.*, 68-2 ARB ¶8655 (Madden, 1968) (gambling); *Gamble Bros.*, 68 LA 72 (Krislov, 1977) (marijuana use on lunch break away from plant); *Los Angeles Soap Co.*, 69 LA 62 (Kaufman, 1977) (leaving plant by scaling fence).

[60]*Ampex Corp.*, 44 LA 412, 415 (Koven, 1965), is a classic case of this type:
> [W]hat emerges from this record is a compendium of minor fracases, temper, emotionality, lack of self-discipline, refusal to follow the rules, and in short, a kind of niggling circumvention of the businesslike behavior expected of employees. . . . The grievant's total conduct was in the nature of Peck's Bad Boy, a behavior which in the context of a business relationship obviously becomes a problem.

[61]In *Caterpillar Tractor Co.*, 67 LA 203, 209 (Wolff, 1976), the arbitrator refused to subscribe to the company's view that it need not have warned the grievant that her next absence might result in her discharge, pointing out that "if, as the Company believes, grievant was prone to accidents, a warning that her next accident-caused absence might result in the loss of her job might cause her to be more careful." See also *General Elec. Co.*, 69 LA 707 (Jedel, 1977), and other cases cited under "The Problem of Degree," p. 40.

[62]*Trailmobile, Inc.*, 27 LA 160 (McCoy, 1956).

[63]*Stuck Mould Works, Inc.*, 78-1 ARB ¶8255 (Dyke, 1978); *O'Brien Corp.*, 77-2 ARB ¶8405 (Wright, 1977).

[64]*Ohio Crankshaft Co.*, 48 LA 558 (Teple, 1967) (painting designs on machine and tool box); *Ryan Aeronautical Co.*, 39 LA 58 (Spaulding, 1962) (flouting supervisor's authority, falling behind in production).

Without clear notice, an employee may have no incentive to correct his or her behavior.[65] In some instances, an employer's failure to give warning that an employee is flirting with discharge can lead to the conclusion that the employee's past behavior could not have been so horrendous as the employer later tries to make out.[66] In others, the employer's failure to mention any penalty has been interpreted as implied condonation of the grievant's actions.

> *Arbitrator Pinkus:* Actions do speak louder than words, and the Company's inaction on so many incidents which it now finds blameworthy can only have lulled [the grievant] into a false sense of security. . . . It is open to management to tighten its standards of conduct and discipline but it must give fair and adequate notice to employees who have grown accustomed to a more lenient regime.[67]

Exceptions to Formal Notice of Penalty

Just as common sense should tell employees that some types of "socially disapproved" and "industrially disapproved" misconduct can lead to discipline, common sense should tell them that some misconduct is so serious that discharge is likely to result.

> *Arbitrator Teple:* There is no doubt that with any infraction which is sufficiently serious, by itself, to warrant immediate discharge no particular warning system is necessary. It is well known that

---

[65]*U.S. Postal Serv.*, 62 LA 293, 299–300 (Killion, 1974) (backdating of personal mail):

> That Grievant should have here had foreknowledge of the consequences of his action is a fair and reasonable condition precedent to the right to discharge. The reason is simple. Under a system of corrective discipline the test in determining "just cause" for discharge is not what the Grievant did in the case at issue but whether he has now proven himself beyond rehabilitation. And it cannot be reasoned that he is now incorrigible if he did not know the seriousness and consequences of the rule violation and would not have violated it if he had known that the consequences would be discharge.

[66]As in *Weyerhaeuser Timber Co.*, 25 LA 634, 637 (Wyckoff, 1955), where the company failed to make an issue of the grievant's supposed careless workmanship over a period of 13 years: "In the absence of any prior reprimand or warning about his competence, an employee with this man's length of service is entitled to conclude that the Company considered the general quality of his performance to be satisfactory . . . ."

[67]*Woodward's Spring Shop, Inc.*, 63 LA 367, 372 (1974) (unauthorized absences, insubordination, abusive language, rudeness to customers). See also *Shell Chem. Co.*, 81-2 ARB ¶8570 (Nutt, 1981) (absenteeism).

major misconduct is likely to result in a penalty as severe as discharge.[68]

Theft, striking a supervisor, gross insubordination, and intoxication in a hazardous work environment are some examples of misconduct for which no express notice need be given that discharge can be the consequence.[69] Even where the contract or rules list particular offenses for which summary discharge may be imposed, and require that a prior warning be given for other offenses, arbitrators have found that the employer may impose discharge without warning for an unlisted offense if it is so serious that the employee should have anticipated the consequences. The contract and the rules, in other words, are not the only sources of "notice," according to this view.

Take a case where the union argued that the employer was precluded from discharging an employee for a first offense of using or selling drugs on company property. The contract required the employer to give at least one warning before firing an employee for any offense other than dishonesty, drunkenness, or recklessness resulting in an accident. That language was "strong and clear," the arbitrator conceded. Nevertheless, "[c]arried to its logical conclusion, this could mean that in a situation where an employee unmercifully assaulted a Supervisor without just reason the Company could not discharge such an employee failing the showing of a written warning in advance. Such a situation is unthinkable . . . ."[70]

---

[68]*Ohio Crankshaft Co.*, 48 LA 558, 562 (1967). See also *Kennecott Copper Corp.*, 52 LA 822 (Roberts, 1969) (insubordination, fighting); *Capital Area Transp. Auth.*, 77-1 ARB ¶8170 (Brown, 1976) (defacing or destroying company property).

[69]In *Bayou Steel Corp.*, 92 LA 726, 731 (1989), Arbitrator Chumley saw no need to inform employees of or post a rule providing discharge as the penalty for reporting to work intoxicated. "A person coming to work in that condition is not only a danger to himself, but also to his fellow workers and to anyone driving on the same highway. It especially cannot be tolerated at an industrial plant, and is the reason why such conduct is always subject to discharge."

[70]*S. F. Kennedy-New Prods., Inc.*, 64 LA 880, 883 (Traynor, 1975). A more severe penalty than the contract or rules expressly called for was also upheld in *Safeway Stores, Inc.*, 82-1 ARB ¶8207 (Phelan, 1982) (selling illegal drugs); *Mississippi River Grain Elevator, Inc.*, 73-2 ARB ¶8598 (Marcus, 1973) (marijuana smoking); *R. E. Phelon Co.*, 75 LA 1051 (Irvings, 1980) (leaving work area without authorization); *Covington Furniture Mfg. Co.*, 75 LA 455 (Holley, 1980) (insubordination). An exception is *J. Weingarten, Inc.*, 77-1 ARB ¶8050 (Helburn, 1977), in which the arbitrator found that contract language requiring prior written warning except for a few specified offenses was "clear and unambiguous" and could not be interpreted "as providing illustrations rather than a complete list of discharge without warning infractions." The grievant's discharge for calling a company customer a whore was not sustained.

May, Might, Must

A rule that states that a particular type of misconduct *may* result in discharge or may make a violator *subject* to discharge, or that discharge is "possible,"[71] generally cannot be interpreted as requiring or permitting discharge under any and all circumstances. Arbitrator Dworkin explains why, in a case where an employee was discharged under a rule stating that on-the-job intoxication "may be cause for immediate discharge":

> In the judgment of the arbitrator the rule is not *per se* improper. However, the rule itself recognizes that an offense "may" be the cause for immediate dismissal, which suggests that immediate dismissal would not automatically follow for every violation of the rule where it is the first offense. The language of the rule contemplates that the determination of the penalty shall result from the exercise of sound judgment on the part of management. . . . The appropriate penalty in a given case is therefore subject to the requirements of reasonableness and just cause.[72]

When he refers to "reasonableness," Dworkin has in mind such things as an employee's length and quality of service; the circumstances surrounding the misconduct (e.g., in an intoxication case, whether drinking led to additional misconduct such as sleeping or insubordination); and other factors that are customarily taken into account in determining whether a penalty is proper.

What this means is that conditional language—such as "may," or "could be," or "subject to"—cannot be interpreted as putting employees on notice that discharge can be imposed for *any* violation of the rule in question.

Mandatory Penalties: The Pros and Cons

Management strengthens its position with respect to notice when it informs employees in advance that discharge (or some

---

[71]*Volunteer Elec. Coop.*, 84-1 ARB ¶8079 (Rayson, 1983) (residency requirement).

[72] *Continental Can Co.*, 68-2 ARB ¶8785, 5726–27 (1968). Cases to the same effect include *Standard Oil Co.*, 11 LA 689 (Updegraff, 1948) (leaving post); *Lone Star Brewing Co.*, 45 LA 817 (Merrill, 1965) (violence against coworker); *Southern Cal. Edison Co.*, 51 LA 869 (McNaughton, 1963) (misuse of employee purchase plan); *Louisville Cooperage Co.*, 70-2 ARB ¶8652 (Volz, 1970) (draining untaxed whiskey out of used barrels); *Altamil Corp.*, 71-1 ARB ¶8198 (Volz, 1971) (drinking on the job); *Food World, Inc.*, 77-1 ARB ¶8203 (Leach, 1977) (failure to follow check-cashing policies); *Prismo-William Armstrong Smith Co.*, 73 LA 581 (Jedel, 1979) (insubordination); *National Hose Co.*, 73 LA 1048 (Robins, 1979) (failure or refusal to work scheduled overtime); *R. E. Phelon Co.*, *supra* note 70 (leaving work area without pemission); *Red Arrow Freight Lines, Inc.*, 78 LA 141 (Baroni, 1982) (possession of alcohol).

other specified penalty) not only *may* attach to but *will* attach to certain misconduct,[73] especially if it shows that it means business by discharging violators without exception.[74] Few arbitrators will venture to disturb a penalty, including discharge, when the "rules of the game" are well known and well established.

Even for relatively minor infractions, discharge for a first offense has been sustained in some instances where company rules warn employees in no uncertain terms that infractions will result in summary discharge, or where the company has announced its intention to crack down on the conduct in question.[75] The union of notice and practice has the effect of letting employees know that even if most employers have other ideas, their own employer will penalize violations with a firm hand.

Most employers, however, do not follow rigid rules of disciplinary cause and effect, and for good reason. One consideration is that arbitrators have sometimes found mandatory penalties, especially discharge, to be arbitrary and unreasonable and therefore in conflict with the just cause standard.[76]

But even if the inherent reasonableness of mandatory penalties were not in question, there are good arguments for a

---

[73] As in *City of Richland Center*, 76-1 ARB ¶8258 (Yeager, 1976), where a rule stating that any change of an employee's residence outside city limits "shall be grounds for termination of employment" gave ample notice of the consequences of a prohibited move; and *Atlantic Steel Co.*, 50 LA 173 (Hebert, 1968), where the rules stated explicitly that a first offense of possession of alcohol would lead to discharge.

[74] In *Day and Zimmermann, Inc.*, 75 LA 699, 701 (Sisk, 1980), where the company had given clear notice of its policy and fired every person over many years who had been found to be under the influence of alcohol, in every case using the level of 0.10% blood alcohol as its definition of intoxication, the arbitrator commented: "It is difficult to conceive how a company could be more consistent in its application of a rule."

[75] In *AMF Lawn & Garden Div.*, 64 LA 988, 992 (Wyman, 1975), the arbitrator found that "[s]tanding alone as an isolated case, discharge for the first offense of the sole act of possessing alcoholic beverages on company premises . . . might be adjudged too severe." But since the company had undertaken a well-publicized and intensive campaign to eliminate all alcohol-related misconduct from its premises, a discharge for such a first offense was allowed to stand.

[76] In *Nineteen Hundred Corp.*, 6 LA 709, 712 (Zeigler, 1946), the arbitrator found that a new rule advising employees that any act of carelessness resulting in property damage "will be cause for discharge" did not make adequate provision for consideration of the degree of carelessness and mitigating factors that might be present in individual cases. "Mass discipline or automatic discharge as proposed by the company is not the proper course." In *Safeway Stores, Inc.*, 70-1 ARB ¶8393 (Coffey, 1970), the grievant had been put on notice that his next absence would mean a five-day suspension. The arbitrator found, however, that the reason for that "next" absence, when it occurred, should have been taken into account by the company, and suspension should not have been automatic. In *Alcan Co.*, 67-2 ARB ¶8475 (Daugherty, 1967), a policy making discharge the automatic penalty for a second wage garnishment was held too inflexible to protect employees from mistaken or illegal wage demands.

flexible approach. Thus, a company may find itself in a situation where it wishes to ignore a notice of mandatory discharge or deviate from a previously established schedule of penalties but be unable to come up with an objective reason for doing so.[77] Suppose, for example, that a long-term, highly skilled employee reports back after lunch one day high as a kite. Assume that the company has had problems with lunchtime drinking in the past and for several years has, without exception, fired people who have come to work intoxicated. What are its options?

It may be able to work out an agreement with the union that the employee can go back to work on a non-precedent-setting basis. If not, it must either bite the bullet and let a valued employee go or run the risk that other employees will think it is getting soft on drinking, or that the next man discharged will prevail on an equal-treatment defense.

The combination of notice and practice has advantages to a company, in that whatever penalties have been announced in advance as mandatory and given the "muscle" of consistent past practice stand a better-than-average chance of being upheld if they should be challenged in arbitration. But such rigidity also may bind the company to certain disciplinary actions when it would rather have leeway to take factors like length of service and quality of work into account.

II. Forms of Notice

Some Definitions

As a quasijudicial system (or, as some have called it, a "queasy" judicial system), arbitration can be said to have two parents. One parent is the judicial system and the other is the collective bargaining process. With respect to notice, arbitration owes its fundamental concepts to the judicial system; on the other hand, such concepts as past practice, lax enforcement, and just cause are traceable in their origins and content primarily to the needs of the collective bargaining relationship.

---

[77]E.g., in *Baumfolder Corp.*, 78 LA 1060 (Modjeska, 1982), where an employee reported under the influence, the arbitrator required the company to stick to its written schedule of disciplinary penalties, which specified a two-day suspension as the penalty for a first infraction. A separate rule that made discharge the penalty for intoxication and drinking on the premises was found to have been improperly applied.

In the world of courts, judges, pleadings, demurrers, inter-pleaders, and legal papers of all sorts and descriptions, notice can take several different forms. One basic classification, *statutory notice*, that is, notice required by legislative enactment, essentially plays no role in the world of arbitration and industrial relations. But other forms of notice come up in one way or another.

> *Actual notice* has been defined as notice expressly and actually given, and brought home to the party directly. . . . The term "actual notice," however, is generally given a wider meaning as embracing two classes, *express* and *implied*. *Express notice* includes all knowledge of a degree above that which depends upon collateral inference, or which imposes upon the party the further duty of inquiry. *Implied notice* imputes knowledge to the party because he is shown to be conscious of having the means of knowledge.
>
> *Constructive notice* is information or knowledge of a fact imputed by law to a person (although he may not actually have it), because he could have discovered the fact by proper diligence, and his situation was such as to cast upon him the duty of inquiring into it.[78]

Some have drawn distinctions between the terms "notice" and "warning."[79] The point is made that customarily a "notice" is both more general and broader in scope and is ordinarily given *before* any specific incident has taken place. Thus, "notice" is viewed as being directed at a class or group of employees with respect to prohibited conduct; a posting on the bulletin board "There shall be no smoking in the boiler room" is obviously directed at everyone.

In contrast, a warning has a particular person or persons in mind and is said to be concerned with a specific incident *after* that incident has taken place with a view to putting the recipient(s) "on notice" as to future behavior. For example, a foreman says to one of his crew: "Harry, if you are caught one more time smoking in the boiler room, you will be fired!" (There are some who use the term "advance warning." As with "notice," "advance warning" is a more general term calling the recipient's attention to his conduct *before* any incident has occurred; but, like "warning," it is at the same time directed to a particular individual or individuals.)

---

[78]Black's Law Dictionary 957–58 (5th ed. 1979).
[79]See, e,g., *Pacific Bell*, 84 LA 710 (Oestreich, 1985) (negligence).

What has all this to do with notice at the workplace and in arbitration?

A Range of Options

In the typical employment setting, employees receive information in many different ways. So it is with notice. Management ordinarily is not required to use any particular form of communication to inform employees of the rules of the shop.

> *Arbitrator Murphy*: So long as the rules exist, and are known to the employees, the sufficiency of the rule is established. There is no one way of either establishing or publicizing a rule. The key point is whether or not the employees are aware of it.[80]

Murphy's point is that what counts is the substance, not the form, of notice. How employees come to know about a rule or policy is less important than that they do in fact know what is expected of them. Thus, something less than directly communicated knowledge—as where one becomes aware of what is expected through chance or inadvertence—may be as binding as notice in the form of a posted bulletin.[81] Some arbitrators, however, would say that proposition is subject to modification if the company's practice has been to give notice by one particular method to the exclusion of others. Arbitrator McCoy stated in one case, for example: "But even if he had had a verbal warning in lieu of the [required] second written warning, the Company's case would be none too strong. Policy and practice required that such warnings be in writing."[82]

McCoy was suggesting that once the company commits itself to a particular notice policy, a notice, to be effective, must be given in the prescribed form. Most arbitrators, though, take a

---

[80]*Eastern Air Lines, Inc.*, 44 LA 459, 461 (1965) (noncompliance with safety rule). In *Ross Gear & Tool Co.*, 35 LA 293 (Schmidt, 1960) (absence from work station; threatening supervisor), the arbitrator found that contract language giving the company the right to establish formal rules did not make the publication of rules mandatory. In agreement, see, among others, *Watt Car & Wheel Co.*, 4 LA 676 (Blair, 1946) (possession of alcohol); *Davey Co.*, 60 LA 917 (Cohen, 1973) (fighting).

[81]See *Cessna Aircraft Co.*, 86 LA 1064 (Krislow, 1986) (poor attendance).

[82]*Trailmobile, Inc.*, 27 LA 160, 162 (McCoy, 1956) (wage garnishment). See also *PPG Indus., Inc.*, 67 LA 835 (Van Wart, 1976) (failure to post new corrective discipline policy); *Ball Corp.*, 74-1 ARB ¶8050, 3192–93 (Shanker, 1974): "[A]rbitrators generally agree that where termination, the supreme penalty in industrial relations, is involved, then all doubts and technicalities set out in the Labor Agreement must be resolved in favor of the employee."

more pragmatic approach to notice, even where the contract or practice calls for notice in the form of posted rules or some other particular method.

> *Arbitrator Merrill:* The purpose of provisions for the posting of rules is to insure that the employees know what standards of conduct they should observe. If they get this knowledge from other sources, the failure to post the rules has not harmed them. It is a general rule of law that where the subject of requiring notification is to give information or to expedite its receipt, knowledge of the matter is an effective substitute for the formal notification.[83]

To the "pragmatists" it is only where actual notice cannot be clearly proved—or, though proved, is defective in some way—that an employer's failure to give notice in its customary way has fatal consequences.[84] Take a case where the supervisor testified that he had "spoken to" and "talked to" an employee about using the proper door to enter the warehouse, but the employee maintained he was only doing what other employees did. The fact that the employer had consistently used written notices to advise employees about prohibited conduct, but issued

---

[83]*Patterson Steel Co.*, 37 LA 862, 864 (1961) (leaving work to attend union meeting). In the same vein, an employee's claim that he must be given an order in writing or a "direct order," and that he could choose whether or not to follow any other kind of management direction, was rejected in *Lee Dodge*, 84 LA 1073, 1076 (Chandler, 1985) (insubordination). Observed the arbitrator: "This must be considered an intolerable situation . . . ." See also *Illinois Dep't of Corrections*, 84 LA 925 (Meyers, 1985), holding that information received in a training program put an employee on notice; *Gulf South Beverages, Inc.*, 87 LA 688 (Caraway, 1986), where a job description put employees on notice that they must be clean shaven.

[84]*Lucky Stores, Inc.*, 42 LA 837, 839 (Koven, 1964):

As to the Union's main argument that the grievant could not have been insubordinate by refusing to obey a house rule which was not posted, if it had been shown that the grievant was unaware of the rule against picture taking, management's failure to post the rule would be decisive, and the Arbitrator would absolve the grievant from blame. But the record is clear that . . . the Company not only informed the grievant of the rule, but even vigorously, if not angrily, put him on notice not to violate the rule.

In *McKissick Prods.*, 83-1 ARB ¶8168, 3756 (Gowan, 1983), the arbitrator for the same reason rejected the union's argument that oral notice to an employee about excessive absenteeism was not an adequate substitute for written notice called for by company policy and practice:

Again, the key is communication and employee understanding of that communication. . . . This case could have taken an entirely different turn if Grievant had alleged and shown that he had somehow been misled or caused to take comfort in a false sense of security by the failure to give his last warning in writing, but such is not the case.

See also *Continental Oil Co.*, 69-2 ARB ¶8856 (Howlett, 1969) (negligence).

no such notice in this case, led the arbitrator to question not only whether adequate notice had actually been given, but also whether the employee's offense was really all that serious.[85]

Changes in Existing Rules: Sometimes Special Requirements

It may be even more important for an employer to follow its customary procedures for giving notice when an existing rule is being modified than when an entirely new rule is being promulgated.[86] The reason: When employees have come to expect notice to be in a particular form, notice otherwise clothed may not be recognized as having equal status, and employees may be confused as to whether the old or the new rule applies.[87]

Say that an old rule makes a written reprimand the penalty for a first offense of participating in a work stoppage, and the employer decides to change the penalty to a three-day suspension. However, the employer fails to consult the union before making the change, though it consulted the union about the original work-stoppage rule and all other plant rules. Notice of the change in such a situation was defective, Arbitrator Kotin ruled, and several employees who were suspended under the new rule should only have been reprimanded. "Absent such consultation, the employees could logically assume that the orig-

---

[85]*Michel Warehousing Corp.*, 67 LA 565 (Mallet-Prevost, 1976). The facts and reasoning are similar in *Fontaine Converting Works*, 24 LA 555 (Marshall, 1955) (inefficiency, loafing).

[86]*Atlantic Richfield Co.*, 86 LA 393 (Dunn, 1986) (absenteeism), sets forth an approved way of giving proper notification of a changed rule even though the program it was replacing had never been posted or distributed. The company distributed the revised program to all employees, sent letters to all employees who had been disciplined and were being brought into the revised program, and granted an amnesty period for absences between the date of the last discipline and the effective date of the revised program. In contrast, in *Menasha Corp.*, 90 LA 427 (Clark, 1987), application of a seven-absences-per-year standard to the grievant was improper since the published rule was vague, practice had been to discipline after 10 absences, and the new standard was not communicated to employees.

[87]*Ball Corp.*, *supra* note 82, at 3192:
What is more, the failure of the Company to post a written shop rule regarding its new policy for dealing with chronic, albeit excused, absences was bound to cause confusion among the employees. As matters now stand, Shop Rule 26 . . . is the *only* posted rule touching on the subject of absenteeism. As such, it could well be interpreted (and apparently was interpreted by many employees and the Union) as the *exclusive* rule dealing with absenteeism. . . . If the employees' reliance on the exclusivity of posted Shop Rule 26 and the Company's own past practice was to be changed, then, clearly, it is desirable that it be made by announcement comparable to that originally given to Shop Rule 26; namely, by posting on the department bulletin boards . . . .

inal rule [was] still in effect."[88] The same is true of an existing practice. Although the employer has a right to change a practice, it must give notice of the change because employees otherwise have reason to believe the prior practice is still in effect.[89]

Posted Rules and Constructive Knowledge

Written, posted rules, even if they are not a strictly necessary form of notice, have one major advantage over other forms of notice: there can be no question of inadequate communication.

> **EXAMPLE:** An employee was apprehended by a security guard drinking beer in the company parking lot and was discharged for violating a rule against possessing or drinking any intoxicating beverage on company premises. The employee testified that he did not recall mention of such a rule during his orientation; however, an orientation form acknowledging receipt of a copy of the company's rules bore his signature.

Does the employee's argument fly? The arbitrator commented:

> [The employee] may not have read the book of rules, but his failure to do so was not the Company's responsibility. It had discharged its responsibility by making the rules available to the employee. The Arbitrator must conclude that the Company's rule communication program was adequate and [the employee] was aware of the rule.[90]

The arbitrator thus presents us with a sample of "constructive knowledge."

Management gets a leg up on potential notice problems by distributing written rules to employees individually or posting them prominently on bulletin boards. When this is done, an employee, except in a few special cases,[91] will be charged with "constructive knowledge" of those rules, and any claim that he "didn't know the score" will fall flat.[92]

---

[88]*Armstrong Rubber Co.*, 52 LA 501, 506 (1969). See also *Iowa-Illinois Gas & Electric Co.*, 84 LA 868 (Keefe, 1985) (tampering with equipment); *Kansas Power & Light Co.*, 87 LA 867 (Belcher, 1986) (change in no-fault policy).

[89]*Clinchfield Coal Co.*, 85 LA 382 (Rybolt, 1985) (absence without leave).

[90] *AMF Lawn & Garden Div.*, 64 LA 988, 990 (Wyman, 1975). But see *Texstar Corp.*, 84 LA 900 (Thornell, 1985) (reporting of absences), where posting had taken place more than four years earlier and there was dispute as to when it was last seen by anyone.

[91]See *infra*, p. 57.

[92]*Friden, Inc.*, 52 LA 448, 449 (Koven, 1969) (unsatisfactory work record): "Even if the grievant's testimony is credited to the effect that he had not seen the rules since the time when he was first hired, we know that these rules were posted in a conspicuous place and that, at the least, he is charged with constructive knowledge." See also *Village of Herkimer*, 84 LA 1298 (Klein, 1985) (discharge for economic reasons); *Goodyear Aerospace Corp.*, 86 LA 403 (Fullmer, 1985) (possession of pistol and marijuana).

Arbitrator Marlatt: [T]here is at least a rebuttable presumption that an employee understands the Company's procedures if he is personally handed a copy, written in language appropriate to a workman's level of education, and told that he must familiarize himself with it or find himself in big trouble.[93]

Other Accepted Forms of Notice

Distributing written rules and posting them may be the best ways of making sure employees know the rules of the game, but they are by no means the only acceptable methods. Other ways include individual oral or written notice,[94] past practice,[95] and oral notice to employees as a group.[96]

---

[93]*Texas Mills Supply & Mfg. Co.*, 74-2 ARB ¶8703, 5671 (1975) (failure to report missing merchandise).

[94]*E.g., Chris Craft Corp.*, 45 LA 117 (Autrey, 1965), where the fact that the grievant had been told personally by his foreman that he was not to use the rest room in another department overcame the union's claim that notice had not been given because no general notice about which rest rooms were off limits had been posted. In *Capitol Area Transp. Auth.*, 77-1 ARB ¶8170 (Brown, 1976), the grievant was found to be on notice that writing graffiti on company walls could lead to discharge because he and several other employees were present when a supervisor informed the union president that anyone caught defacing company property would be fired. See also *Continental Oil Co.*, 69-2 ARB ¶8856 (Howlett, 1969) (production errors); *Sterling Drug, Inc.*, 70-1 ARB ¶8033 (Berkowitz, 1969) (that grievant may not have been handed copy of rules was irrelevant; he had received numerous oral warnings that his level of tardiness and absenteeism was unacceptable); *Ohio Power Co.*, 64 LA 934 (High, 1975) (grievant told on four occasions his expense claims were too high and he had to reduce his expenditures); *White Mfg. Co.*, 74 LA 1005 (LeBaron, 1980) (running check-cashing business on company premises); *Union Carbide Corp.*, 74 LA 681 (Bowers, 1980) (absenteeism).

[95]See, e.g., *Eastern Air Lines, Inc.*, 44 LA 459, 461 (Murphy, 1965) (noncompliance with safety rule): "[A] rule can become a rule through the accumulation of experience and practice and need not be announced at a given time and place that 'this is the rule.'" Although no formal rule requiring safety helmets be worn was ever promulgated, the fact that employees in the grievant's department were wearing helmets demonstrated they were aware of the helmet requirement. In *Stoppenbach, Inc.*, 68 LA 553 (Lee, 1977), the fact that a certain production standard had long been followed without protest from the union indicated to the arbitrator that the standard was generally known to employees, and the grievant had no basis for claiming he had not been told what was expected of him. And in *Stella D'Oro Biscuit Co.*, 48 LA 349 (Cahn, 1967), the arbitrator rejected the grievant's claim that he was unaware that carrying unauthorized passengers in his truck was prohibited, since in the past he had always made a point of asking pemission to carry riders. Note, however, that where a policy is not enforced with regularity, that factor can contribute to "uncertainty as to [its] existence." *Van Nuys Communication Co.*, 84 LA 881, 886 (Gentile, 1985) (ban on employment of relatives).

[96]See *Ohio Power Co.*, 50 LA 501 (Teple, 1967), where the arbitrator rejected the union's argument that employees had not been officially notified that coffee-making by individuals was to be discontinued, since discontinuance of the practice was announced at a general employee meeting, followed up by communications from individual supervisors; and *Capital Area Transp. Auth., supra* note 94 (notice that graffiti would not be tolerated communicated by supervisor to employees in a group).

Oral Notice to the Union. If notice has been given to the union, the inference can be drawn in many circumstances that notice has reached union members as well. Arbitrator Dykstra reasoned as follows in imputing to employees awareness of information conveyed to the union:

> [T]he Union placed considerable stress on the fact that the men were not personally instructed nor reprimanded during the days in question. Although this may be true, the record does disclose that Union leaders were frequently consulted as to difficulties. It further reveals that these representatives realized the Company believed a slowdown was in progress. There is every reason to assume that this information was conveyed to the employees and that they shared the consciousness that greater cooperation was desired.[97]

Word of Mouth or Grapevine. The "grapevine" may not be the most reliable method of giving notice. Nevertheless, if the evidence in a particular case clearly establishes that the grievant was in fact tuned in, the effect may well be the same as if information had been imparted in a more formal manner. In one case even friendly urgings to modify his aggressive behavior were viewed as enough to establish that an employee was sufficiently aware that his belligerent manner, if not corrected, would surely get him in trouble.[98]

The grapevine proved to be effective in a case where the union asserted that the grievant, a telephone repairman, was unaware that pocketing overflow coins from a pay phone constituted a dishonest act under the company's "honesty in the business" policy. But the arbitrator found that the grievant was not the first employee to be disciplined for taking coins; that he knew of at least one other repairman who had been disciplined for the same offense; and that he had heard rumors that the company was maintaining surveillance on certain coin tele-

---

[97]*Kennecott Copper Corp.*, 41 LA 1339, 1344 (1963). In another such case, *Patterson Steel Co.*, 37 LA 862 (Merrill, 1961), the company discussed its new absentee policy with union representatives, and as a result the policy was publicized at union meetings. See also *Oil Center Tool Div.*, 73-2 ARB ¶8335, 4240 (Emery, 1973): "Union Committee's spreading the word that the Company was determined to clear the plant of the drug [marijuana] went far toward giving the same notice that a posted rule would have."

[98]*Continental Grain Co.*, 85-2 ARB ¶8599 (Yarowsky, 1985). But see *Grand Trunk W. R.R. Co.*, 86 LA 475 (Bendixsen, 1985) (derailment of locomotive), where it was held that the inadvertent overhearing of an instruction was not the same as having been warned.

NOTICE   53

phones and using marked money. Moreover, his shop steward had advised him to be careful.

> It would, of course, have been infinitely better for the Company to have issued some direct communication when it changed the rules of the game. However, we do not think that it was unreasonable for the Company to conclude that X was aware that his act could result in serious consequences . . . .[99]

Implied Notice. This final form of notice is really a restatement, from a slightly different perspective, of the principle that some kinds of misconduct are so serious that no specific, formal notice is required before discipline can be imposed. The consequences of an employee's carelessly putting himself in danger, stealing company property, striking a supervisor, and the like are so patently unacceptable that employees should know that discipline can be expected. Notice is "implied" by the very nature of the misconduct.[100]

Implied notice of another kind is given when an action, not specified in the rules (e.g., reporting to work under the influence of marijuana), is so similar or comparable to misconduct that the rules prohibit (e.g., reporting to work under the influence of alcohol) that notice of the one amounts to notice of the other.[101] But "comparability" must be genuine—not a matter of wishful thinking on the company's part.

> **EXAMPLE:** After his truck accidentally slid off the road and became stuck in mud and snow, the driver spent two hours trying to dig the truck out before a supervisor found him. He was subsequently suspended under two rules—one prohibiting negligence, the other prohibiting the wasting of time (since the driver did not call in to report the accident and get assistance as soon as he realized he was in trouble).

---

[99]*Pacific Northwest Bell Tel. Co.*, 48 LA 498, 502 (Lovell, 1967).

[100]*Capital Area Transp. Auth.*, *supra* note 94, at 3744: "Employers do not have to publish rules that prohibit conduct that is so clearly wrong that common sense would dictate that the employer would regard such acts as misconduct." See also *Southern Cal. Edison Co.*, 70-1 ARB ¶8066 (Sinclitico, 1969) (dishonesty); *Memphis Light, Gas & Water Div.*, 77-1 ARB ¶8202 (Flannagan, 1977) (unauthorized reconnection of electric service); *Bruce Hardwood Floors*, 84-1 ARB ¶8103 (Marcus, 1984) (leaving work without permission); *Palmer Terrace Nursing Center*, 84-1 ARB ¶8221 (Kossoff, 1984) (patient abuse); *Freeman United Coal Co.*, 84-1 ARB ¶8266 (Roberts, 1984) (possession of intoxicants; use of dangerous equipment); *Boise-Cascade Paper Group*, 86 LA 177 (Marlatt, 1985) (sleeping on the job); *Ohio Edison Co.*, 86-1 ARB ¶8299 (Kates, 1986) (sale and use of drugs).

[101]*Porcelain Metals Corp.*, 73 LA 1133 (Roberts, 1979) (reporting under the influence of prescription drug).

The arbitrator found that neither rule applied to this case. The accident was not the driver's fault, so he was not guilty of negligence, and his strenuous efforts to free the truck hardly constituted wasting time. He might have used better judgment by looking for a phone to call in right away; but "nothing in the rules indicates that an individual . . . who is involved in an accident should immediately notify the company. The rules are not indicative of any act to be made in that situation and it can hardly be said that the grievant was violative of any known rule of the facility."[102]

The moral of this story: If there is no genuine "similarity" or "comparability" between the grievant's actions and misconduct covered by the rules, the employer cannot get around a failure to give notice by twisting an existing rule to fit a situation it does not really cover.

Notice Received: There's Many a Slip

Oral Notice

Although arbitrators may say that written and oral notice are equals, the fact is that oral notice is a second-class citizen and often turns out to be "less equal" in practice.

> **EXAMPLE:** A route salesman for a soft drink manufacturer was discharged for taking orange juice on one occasion and milk on another from a customer's refrigerator and leaving some of the company's product in exchange. The policy the salesman violated, according to the company, permitted sales people only to exchange a warm company product from his truck for a cold company product in the customer's refrigerator. The salesman asserted, however, that he understood the policy to require the exchange of customer goods for company product on an equivalent-value basis. He did not realize that he was allowed to take only his employer's brand of soft drink.

The company's problem in this case was that every route salesperson who testified at the hearing understood the exchange policy differently, one stating that company soft drinks could be exchanged for other soft drinks, another that taking a competitor's product was forbidden, and so on. There also was no consensus as to whether the customer had to be notified of

---

[102]*Stocker & Sitler Operating Co.*, 74 LA 752 (Feldman, 1980).

each exchange. Said the arbitrator: "Had the Employer been able to establish that its exchange policy was clearly communicated to the Grievant, there would be no question of the propriety of discharge. However, where the parameters of the policy are fuzzy and the Grievant's act not clearly outside them, discharge is unwarranted."

Why the "fuzzy parameters"? Largely because the company had no written exchange policy but left it up to individual supervisors to communicate policy to new employees as they came on the job. As a result, many different "policies" were in existence, not just one unambiguous company rule.[103]

The case of the misinformed soda salesman underscores one of the major difficulties with unwritten rules. They are more susceptible to being misunderstood[104] and misremembered[105] (or at least to claims that they have been misunderstood or misremembered) than rules set down in writing. Oral warnings may also not be taken as seriously as written warnings, especially if given in an informal manner.[106]

> *Arbitrator Kates:* A shop rule to be enforceable must, in my view, be specific enough to be clearly understood by the shop employees. An unwritten shop rule ought not to be held binding if reasonable doubt exists in the minds of the work force or of an alleged violator as to what the rule states, means or requires. . . .

---

[103]*Coca-Cola Bottling Co. of Los Angeles*, 79-1 ARB ¶8101 (Randall, 1979). See also *Empire Tractor & Equip. Co.*, 85 LA 345 (Koven, 1985) (tardiness); *Ludlow Flexible Packaging* , 86-2 ARB ¶8598 (Curry, 1986) (tardiness).

[104]In *Texas Mills Supply & Mfg. Co.*, 74-2 ARB ¶8703, 5672 (Marlatt, 1974), the arbitrator found that notice given at occasional employee meetings was not specific enough to let delivery employees know they had to inform the company by telephone immediately of any discrepancies between the number of cartons a customer had ordered and the number of cartons actually sent. "There is no indication that these employees were even told to take notes at the meeting, or that [the company official] had followed any written agenda." Employees were told to report problems with deliveries, but there was no evidence that discrepancies were among the problems the company had in mind.

[105]*Reserve Mining Co.*, 38 LA 443, 449–50 (Sembower, 1962):

[T]he affirmative statement of the rule is left to a rather nebulous conjecture, at best, based upon conflicting testimony as to what happened at the Jan. 5th safety meeting. . . . The weaknesses of human recollection are so great that it is doubtful if at this date it would ever be possible to reconstruct sufficiently what was said . . . .

[106]As in *Times Publishing Co.*, 40 LA 1054 (Dworkin, 1963), where supervisors had voiced oral criticism of the grievant's work but never made those criticisms a matter of record or told her explicitly that she was subject to disciplinary action. See also *Bowman Transp., Inc.*, 88 LA 711 (Cocalis, 1987), in which oral notice was held unacceptable where formal notice (though not written notice) was specified.

An employer takes an unnecessary risk of enforcement in failing to put all its shop rules in written form.[107]

Then, too, "the word" may not reach every employee if the company relies on informal types of notice,[108] or different employees may be told different things by different supervisors.[109] Unwritten rules also have a greater tendency to invite inconsistent application than do rules whose meaning is set down in writing. Where an employer relied on word of mouth to disseminate its policy concerning the employment and retention of close relatives, confusion about what the policy really meant resulted in some close relatives being allowed to continue on the job only if they lived in separate households, while others living under the same roof were kept on.[110]

Last but not least, oral notice is also, by its very nature, more "deniable" than written notice. Typical is a case in which a supervisor testified that he recalled "to the point of certainty"

---

[107]*Abex Corp.*, 47 LA 441, 442–43 (1966) (absenteeism and tardiness). To the same effect, *Cajun Elec. Power Coop., Inc.*, 73-2 ARB ¶8365, 4345 (Williams, 1973):

> By not reducing their understanding to writing and signing it, the parties run the risk of having it misconstrued or misunderstood. An Arbitrator should be reticent to sustain disciplinary action (and particularly discharge) against an employee, in the face of what was at best a verbal understanding . . . .

See also *Trizec Props., Inc.*, 87-2 ARB ¶8324, 5104 (Keefe, 1987): "Without . . . written guidelines on which each side can rely, chaos can, and almost assuredly will, creep in." In *Coca-Cola Bottling Co. of New York, Inc.*, 2 LA 130 (Cole, 1946), the arbitrator went so far as to direct the parties in his award to draft and post the previously unwritten rule that truck drivers who deviated from their assigned delivery routes would be subject to discharge.

[108]In *Kentucky Textile Indus., Inc.*, 70-1 ARB ¶8127, 3453 (Williams, 1969), some employees, but not others, had been told that urinating in the company parking lot was prohibited. Thus, "[t]he Company's attempt to promulgate such a rule was incomplete, and therefore insufficient to bind the employees who are entitled to reasonable notice of new rules." In *Allstates Air Cargo, Inc.*, 61 LA 640 (Sands, 1973), the arbitrator rejected the company's contention that all its truck drivers must have received the word that stopping at a diner during working hours was prohibited because three employees had been reprimanded for making unauthorized stops, since there was no evidence that the reprimands had been shown to other employees or posted where all could see them. In *Swift & Co.*, 72 LA 513 (Rentfro, 1979) (marijuana), company policy was announced at a union meeting, but there was no evidence that the grievant was present at that meeting. The arbitrator found that this "indirect method," unaccompanied by a posted statement or other formal notice, fell short of giving the required notice.

[109]*Hayes Indus., Inc.*, 65-1 ARB ¶8425, 4565 (Teple, undated):

> Although everyone who testified seemed to be aware of some policy on the subject, this knowledge was dependent entirely upon word of mouth. No precise description of the policy has ever been issued. . . . To add to the confusion, the subject was outlined in various ways to the employees at the time of hiring, one Union witness testifying that the matter was not brought to her attention at all.

[110]*Food Basket Stores*, 71 LA 959 (Ross, 1978).

that the grievant had been expressly informed that a conviction for drunk driving would mean discharge—testimony that was flatly contradicted by the grievant. The arbitrator decided that oral notice was not proved and fell back on the key facts not in conflict: "that the rule had not been the subject of negotiation with the union, that it was not in written form and was not posted on the bulletin board." The grievant's discharge was rescinded.[111]

In another case, the employer claimed that "in actual shop practice a set of procedures was followed so routinely that they had acquired the force of formal work rules." The grievant, however, asserted that he had always applied his own methods without interference from management. Since no concrete evidence supported either side, the arbitrator decided that "the Company's assertion that the grievant violated established procedures . . . remains open to question."[112]

Written Notice

Although written notice is reliable as a general rule, it is by no means foolproof.

The "Desk Drawer" Problem. A written rule is not an effective form of notice if management keeps the rule to itself. That may seem obvious—but the problem arises more frequently than one might imagine.

In the "close relatives" case mentioned above, the employer in fact had a written rule. The problem was that the written document was kept in the front office and not made available to employees; only members of management had access to it, and not even all supervisors knew what it said, judging by their varying interpretations of the rule. Similarly, a policy requiring drug screening for employees returning from disability leave of more than one year was held to be improper and unenforceable, where the employer communicated the policy in writing only to a few members of management.[113] Equally ineffective was a

---

[111]*Lamb Glass Co.*, 32 LA 420, 423 (Dworkin, 1959).

[112]*Solano Contract Warehouse Corp.*, 80-1 ARB ¶8065, 3304 (Koven, 1979).

[113]*Donaldson Mining Co.*, 89-1 ARB ¶8089 (Zobrak, 1988). In *Fort Wayne Hotel*, 66-1 ARB ¶8218 (Keefe, 1966), a policy relating to personal phone calls was held not to have been properly communicated even though it was posted, since there was no evidence that it remained posted long enough for employees to have seen it.

prohibition against firearms that a company added to its list of written rules, where the addition was not disseminated.[114]

Rules? What Rules? Even where the employer has a policy of distributing written rules to employees, problems have arisen where it did not follow through properly.

> **EXAMPLE:** When an employee set up a small business selling marine equipment and supplies, he bought gasoline for resale to his customers from a competitor of his employer. The employee subsequently was discharged for violating a conflict-of-interest rule set forth in a company rule booklet. Booklet or no booklet, the employee protested that he never had been made aware of any such rule.

The discharge was overturned. Why? The principal employer witness testified that, as a general practice, new employees received rule booklets and that revised editions were either handed out or placed on a table for employees to pick up. The problem was that he did not know whether this particular employee had ever been given a booklet. He testified that he had once told the employee he could not sell a competitor's gasoline, but the employee denied this. Nor was there evidence that the union had ever received a copy of the rules. Thus, the employer failed to prove that the employee had knowledge of the policy he was discharged for violating.[115]

Another example is provided by an employer's laxity in distributing or posting copies of its employee handbook. The handbook, which set forth the employer's policy on absenteeism, was held ineffective as a form of notice.[116]

In at least one case, the arbitrator found that even where employees had the written rules in hand, the mere distribution of those rules had not been sufficient to impress upon employees what their responsibilities were; an extra step was required.

> If these rules were discussed with the employee at the orientation and the booklet used for later reference, knowledge of rules could not be denied. However, it is a risky assumption for a firm to give rules to workers in a written form and then expect them to read

---

[114]*Bright-O, Inc.*, 54 LA 498 (Mullin, 1970) (possession of firearms).

[115]*Phillips Petroleum Co.*, 47 LA 372 (Caraway, 1966).

[116]*Rockwell Int'l Flow Control Div.*, 1975 ARB ¶8036 (Knee, 1975) (absenteeism). In *Lester Eng'g Co.*, 43 LA 1268 (Klein, 1965), a policy on garnishment had been negotiated, but the new contract had not been printed and made available to employees prior to the grievant's discharge.

and understand them without some type of follow-up to confirm reading and clarity of understanding.[117]

An employee may also be able to make out a credible case that he never received a written warning—as in the case where the grievant claimed he did not receive a warning notice despite management's assertion that it had been mailed to him. He had been on vacation when the notice was mailed, and the employer was not able to produce a receipt, even though it had sent the notice by certified mail. The grievant's discharge for absenteeism was set aside.[118]

Signed Acknowledgment. The problem of claimed nonreceipt can be avoided if management has a signed statement from the employee acknowledging receipt and understanding of the company rules or a written warning about particular misconduct. In most cases such a statement is adequate proof of notice. But suppose an employee claims the employer has no right to require such a signed receipt. Does the employee have a case? Not according to Arbitrator Dworkin, who relied on the management rights clause of the contract in upholding the employer's position.

> The right of the employer to make and enforce rules and regulations governing its operations and the conduct of its personnel includes the right to exercise this authority in an effective and practical manner, thereby according some latitude and discretion as regards the manner and form to be employed. The requirement that each employee receiving a copy acknowledge same by signing and returning a copy, does not involve any act which is inconsistent with any of the express provisions of the labor agreement, nor does it subject the employee to any hazard or act in violation of any state or federal law.[119]

Arbitrators generally have agreed with Dworkin's position. However, in cases where the contract required that rules be promulgated in a particular form, it has been held that the

---

[117]*Ethyl Corp.*, 74 LA 953 (Hart, 1980) (marijuana). The company's failure to conduct any follow-up to determine whether employees had in fact familiarized themselves with a rule book that was passed out to them also was cited by the arbitrator in *U. S. Spring & Bumper Co.*, 5 LA 109 (Prasow, 1946) (gambling).

[118]*Jessop Steel Co.*, 68-1 ARB ¶8004 (Wood, 1967).

[119]*Metromedia, Inc.*, 46 LA 161, 166 (Dworkin, 1966) (insubordination).

employer needed the union's consent to add a signature requirement on top of what the contract called for.[120]

The Employee's Obligation. Just as management has an obligation
to notify employees of the consequences of their misbehavior,
so employees have an obligation not to impede the employer's
efforts to communicate with them. On this basis an arbitrator
found irrelevant the lack of warning of the consequences of
walking off the job where the employee made such warning
impossible by hanging up on his supervisor, leaving his phone
off the hook, and then leaving his job.[121]

Progressive Discipline as Form of Notice

"Inherent in the concept of 'cause' or 'just cause' or 'proper
cause' is the concept of 'progressive discipline,'"[122] which is not
something for which the union must bargain.[123] Moreover, "inherent in the concept of progressive discipline is the idea that
employees enjoy certain rights of due process and one of those
rights is notice of problems on the job."[124] For all but the most
serious types of misconduct (e.g., theft), progressive discipline
functions as a graduated system of penalties for repeated rule
infractions.

> *Arbitrator Duff:* The principle of progressive discipline requires
> that for the first minor infractions, verbal warnings be given to
> an employee. If the verbal warnings do not lead an errant em-
> ployee to reform, and a repetition of the offense, or a similar
> infraction occurs, then more severe punishment should be im-
> posed. Written reprimands place an employee on notice that
> heavier penalties will be imposed for future acts of misconduct.
> . . .
>
> Management's continued reliance upon a repetition of gen-
> tle verbal rebukes that were not effective did not adequately warn
> the Grievant that the Company would not continue to tolerate
> such conduct. . . . Prompt and adequate penalties should have
> been imposed . . . .[125]

---

[120]See *Springfield Sugar Co.*, 61 LA 639 (Blum, 1973), where the contract required
only that rules be posted.

[121]*S. B. Thomas*, 92 LA 1055 (Chandler, 1989).

[122]*Southwest Elec. Co.*, 54 LA 195 (Bothwell, 1969).

[123]*Western Contracting Corp.*, 77-1 ARB ¶8004 (Laughlin, 1976) (negligence).

[124]*City of Thief River Falls*, 88-1 ARB ¶8111, 3541 (Ver Ploeg, 1987).

[125]*Armco Steel Corp.*, 52 LA 101, 104 (1960) (poor employment record).

A system of progressive discipline has two primary objectives. First, progressive discipline is a system of penalties for misconduct. Second, and equally important, progressive discipline serves to put an employee on notice that he must correct his behavior or eventually face discharge.

The second objective of progressive discipline was highlighted in a case where an employee was given an oral warning and a written warning and then was discharged, all on the same day, for three unexcused absences. The arbitrator held that the requirement of proper notice had not been met because such compression of the steps of progressive discipline gave the employee no chance to improve.[126] As Arbitrator Dawson has explained further:

> The concept of a warning implies an opportunity for correction. This in turn implies opportunity for sober reflection and in many cases resolves itself into a question of how much time has elapsed between the warning and the final discharge.[127]

Query: Does a progressive discipline policy always require a warning at the first step? "The answer is clearly NO," according to Arbitrator Oestreich, reflecting the general arbitral view.[128] If, however, the contract sets forth a rigid schedule of progressive discipline steps, management departs from the schedule at its peril. A case in point involved a school district that sent a letter to a teacher stating that "[f]ailure to observe any of these guidelines will result in discipline up to and including discharge." Progressive discipline was stated in the contract to consist of four steps—oral reprimand, written reprimand, suspension, discharge. Since no oral reprimand preceded the letter, the arbitrator reasoned that the letter was not part of progressive discipline but instead was an improper attempt to bargain individually with the teacher as to the matters in question.[129]

---

[126]*Rockford School Dist.*, 88-2 ARB ¶8367 (Traynor, 1987) (improper behavior by teacher toward student). See also, among many other cases, *Times Publishing Co.*, 40 LA 1054 (Dworkin, 1963); *Armstrong Cork Co.*, 71-1 ARB ¶8242 (Wolf, 1971); *Ohio Power Co.*, 64 LA 934 (High, 1975).

[127]*Standard Shade Roller Div.*, 73 LA 86, 90 (1979).

[128]*Pacific Bell*, 84 LA 710 (Oestreich, 1985) (negligence), citing FAIRWEATHER, PRACTICE AND PROCEDURE IN LABOR ARBITRATION 243 (2d ed. 1983).

[129]*Rockford School Dist.*, supra note 126. See also *Simplex Prods. Div.*, 91 LA 356 (Byars, 1988) (failure to send warning letters under progressive discipline policy showed company did not intend to apply notification rule).

Disciplinary Suspensions Versus Warnings Only

Progressive discipline typically begins with verbal and/or written reprimands and then, upon repetition of the same or a similar offense, follows up with a suspension or suspensions of increasing duration, culminating in discharge. Some systems of progressive discipline, however, consist of warnings only. Warnings-only systems have been used mostly in connection with absenteeism caused by illness, the theory being that such absenteeism cannot be treated the same as other violations of plant rules because illness is an involuntary condition on which suspension could not be expected to have a corrective effect.

Warnings-only policies, as well as the more familiar forms of progressive discipline, have been upheld in a number of cases.[130] However, from the particular standpoint of notice, many arbitrators have held that a system of progressive discipline that follows up oral or written warnings, or both, with at least one disciplinary suspension has several advantages over a system that relies exclusively on warnings and counseling.

Shows that the company means business. Time off without pay has the effect of unmistakably impressing upon the employee that the company is serious about enforcing its work rules. A suspension goes beyond an oral or written warning in that it not only serves notice but serves notice punitively, by depriving the employee of income.[131] Sometimes, as Arbitrator Teple put it, "talk and meetings simply are not enough and as the disciplinary procedures which include suspension in many industries indicate, an actual layoff may be necessary to bring the point home."[132]

---

[130]*Atlantic Richfield Co.*, 69 LA 484 (Sisk, 1977); *Union Carbide Corp.*, 46 LA 195 (Cahn, 1966); *Logan Metal Stampings, Inc.*, 53 LA 185 (Kates, 1969), in which the contract provided for a progressive discipline system, including a three-day suspension, for excessive absenteeism, but made an exception for absenteeism due to chronic illness. Other cases in which absentee control programs based on warnings only have been accepted include *Pacific Tel. & Tel. Corp.*, 32 LA 178 (Galenson, 1959); *Cannon Elec. Co.*, 46 LA 481 (Kotin, 1965); *American Brakeblok Div., Abex Corp.*, 52 LA 484 (Wagner, 1969); *Koenig Iron Works, Inc.*, 53 LA 594 (Ray, 1969); *Sterling Drug, Inc.*, 70-1 ARB ¶8033 (Berkowitz, 1969); *Jaeger Mach. Co.*, 55 LA 850 (High, 1970); *Globe-Union, Inc.*, 57 LA 701 (High, 1971); *Doxsee Food Corp.*, 57 LA 1107 (Farinholt, 1971); *Beaunit Fibers*, 71-2 ARB ¶8455 (Amis, 1971); *Avco Corp.*, 64 LA 672 (Marcus, 1975); *Husky Oil Co.*, 65 LA 47 (Richardson, 1975); *Hoover Ball & Bearing Co.*, 66 LA 764 (Herman, 1976); *Pacific Southwest Airlines*, 70 LA 833 (Jones, 1978).

[131]*General Tel. of Cal.*, 44 LA 669 (Prasow, 1965).

[132]*White Motor Corp.*, 50 LA 541, 544 (1968) (fighting). See also *Ryder Truck Rental, Inc.*, 82-1 ARB 8186, 3862 (Allen, 1982) ("sometimes a suspension will 'shock' an impish and sarcastic worker into the full realization of the dangerous direction in which his

Leaves an employee in no doubt as to where he stands. This point is closely related to the first. Warnings-only policies, especially when warnings begin to pile up for the same infraction, may foster a false sense of security.

> *Arbitrator Laughlin:* In the face of mere oral warnings, ignored and repeated and ignored again, an employee is likely to become convinced that he is immune from meaningful corrective action. The absence of penalties of increasing severity is tantamount to ignoring the numerous violations.[133]

Lays the foundation for "the straw that broke the camel's back." Even though an individual act of misconduct is not of such severity as to warrant summary discharge, it may be "the straw that broke the camel's back." It can only be the last straw, however, if the employee has been put on notice of a continuing problem and the prospect of more severe disciplinary action, including dismissal. A suspension achieves this, since it puts the employee on clear notice that he or she must shape up. Typically three conditions must be met in such cases: (1) there must have been a genuine "last straw" (i.e., a present offense must have been committed); (2) the grievant's overall record must be as bad as the employer contends; and (3) the requirements of progressive discipline must have been satisfied.[134]

More difficult to deny. When warnings are followed by suspension, an employee ordinarily cannot claim lack of notice about his pattern of misconduct or plead ignorance of the employer's intention to penalize continued misconduct with discharge.[135]

Warnings-Only System. A warnings-only system of progressive discipline can work if the employer takes special care to make sure that notice obligations are fulfilled. Within the context of progressive discipline in an absenteeism control program, for example, those obligations would be satisfied by telling the employee clearly and unequivocally at each step that he or she has failed to meet the company's attendance standard; what

---

attitude is taking him"); *Rochester Tel. Corp.*, 45 LA 538 (Duff, 1965) (use of obscene language); *Ohio Crankshaft Corp.*, 48 LA 558 (Teple, 1967) (insubordination, disruptive conduct); *Armco Steel Corp.*, 52 LA 101 (Duff, 1969) (overall misconduct); *Eastex, Inc.*, 69-2 ARB ¶8459 (Marshall, 1969) (absenteeism); *Wolf Mach. Co.*, 72 LA 510 (High, 1979) (absenteeism, other misconduct).

[133]*Western Contracting Corp.*, 77-1 ARB ¶8004, 3026 (Laughlin, 1976).

[134]*Mobil Oil Corp.*, 87 LA 837 (Koven, 1986) (insubordination).

[135]*Union Carbide Corp.*, 74 LA 681 (Bowers, 1980) (absenteeism).

standard must be met in order to avoid further sanctions; and, most critically, at what point further absences will result in termination.[136]

In cases where the employer's attendance rules do not provide for suspension as the step prior to discharge, one of the most common factors that have led arbitrators to reinstate grievants' has been uncertainty as to whether they were in fact on notice that their jobs were in jeopardy.[137] Such uncertainty can be avoided or at least minimized if a warnings-only system is defined in specific terms (for example, how many days of absence will bring an employee to each successive step) and clearly communicated to employees and the union (for example, by written notice, meetings, or whatever means are appropriate at the particular work site to bring home to employees that discharge will follow a final warning even if suspension is not imposed).

Many conflicts about whether notice was given can be avoided if the employer has a record showing that the employee received and understood the warning at each step (for example, a written memorandum of an oral counseling session, or the employee's signature on a written warning acknowledging its receipt). The union might also be sent copies of written notices, especially the final warning of termination.

The "Last Chance" Agreement

A special addition to progressive discipline is the "last-chance" agreement, an understanding among the three parties (employer, union, and employee) that no further misconduct will be tolerated. In a sense, such an agreement exists whenever the employee has been warned that further misconduct will result in discharge; but the last-chance agreement comes into being when the employee already has engaged in misconduct meriting termination and is being given one final opportunity to keep his or her job. In such cases, Arbitrator Dworkin has held, the usual just cause standards do not apply; the employee may be fired for even a trivial rule violation.[138] The employee

---

[136]E.g., *Phillips Petroleum*, 64-3 ARB ¶8907 (Mittenthal, 1964); *General Elec. Co.*, 69 LA 707 (Jedel, 1977); *Union Carbide Corp.*, *supra* note 135.

[137]E.g., *Kaiser Aluminum & Chem. Corp.*, 68-2 ARB ¶8606 (Hebert, 1968).

[138]*Butler Mfg. Co.*, 93 LA 441 (1989) (absenteeism; insubordination); see also *Linde Gases of the Midwest, Inc.*, 94 LA 225 (Nielsen, 1989) (refusal to take alcohol test). In *Ohio Dept. of Highway Safety*, 96 LA 71 (1990), however, Arbitrator Dworkin ruled that a last-chance agreement was unreasonable on its face in holding the grievant's discharge "in

need not be given explicit notice when he or she commits the further infraction,[139] and no further progressive discipline is required.[140]

But even last-chance agreements have their limits. It may still be appropriate to take account of strongly mitigating circumstances. Take a case where the employee's unexcused absence was caused by a serious family emergency. The employee's pregnant wife had become violent, and the employee feared for the safety of his two children; he was unable to advise the company of his situation because his wife had ripped the telephone out of the wall. In this extreme case the arbitrator held that discharge was not justified, though he denied back pay on the theory that the company was not financially responsible for the employee's absence.[141]

A different kind of mitigation is illustrated by the case of an employee who was terminated for filing a spurious claim for overtime pay after he had received a "final warning" that any further violation of written or unwritten shop rules would result in his suspension or discharge. The arbitrator reversed the discharge because the employee had filed the claim in the belief that it was valid and without intent to defraud or steal. Absent a clear expression of the parties' intent as to the scope of the warning, he held, it was unreasonable to conclude that discharge was contemplated for the filing of an unacceptable overtime claim.[142]

III. Typical Notice Pitfalls

Written Notice or Oral—Two Common Failings

By its very nature, since it is designed to let employees know what they can and cannot do, a notice needs to be drawn with

---

abeyance" on condition that she complete a rehabilitation program and refrain from further drug or alcohol abuse, since it failed to specify an expiration date.

[139]*Allied Maintenance Corp.*, 87 LA 121 (Duda, 1986) (work rules).

[140]*Champion Int'l Corp.*, 86 LA 1077 (Chalfie, 1986) (absenteeism).

[141]*Chicago Transit Auth.*, 89-1 ARB ¶8129 (Goldstein, 1988); see also *Food Marketing Corp.*, 88 LA 98 (Doering, 1986) (not clear employee fully understood implications of last-chance agreement).

[142]*San Francisco Newspaper Agency*, 93 LA 322 (Koven, 1989).

sufficient clarity to leave them in no doubt as to the company's expectations.[143] Notices may fall short in one of two ways.

The Problem of Specificity—Who, What, Where, When

Even though the employer has a rule intended to cover the general category of misconduct in which the employee has engaged, the rule may not be worded specifically enough to cover all situations. The "where," "when," and other such details must be spelled out if discipline is to be sustained.

Take a case involving "when." An employee was caught napping on "fatigue time" and discharged for violating a no-sleeping-on-the-job rule. Did the parties intend sleeping on fatigue time to be covered by that rule? This was not clear from the rule itself, the arbitrator found; and there was evidence that on one occasion a company representative had told some employees they could do whatever they wanted during fatigue time. So the discharge was invalidated.[144] "When" was the critical factor also in a case where an employee was told to "go take care of himself" by having a medical examination and no specific date was set for his return. Then he was fired for overstaying his leave. This discharge, too, was overturned.[145]

Or take a "where." When an employee lit a cigarette on the loading platform, was it proper to give him a two-day suspension for violating a rule against carrying matches "in the working area"? The employee argued that the rule did not apply because it was not clear that the loading dock was part of the working area. Right, said the arbitrator; if employees are subject to punishment, they are entitled to know in detail the activities that warrant punishment.[146]

And finally, a "what." Take the case of the garage mechanic

---

[143]See, e.g., *Piggly-Wiggly* T-212, 81 LA 808, 815 (Nelson, 1983), in which the arbitrator reversed the discharge of an employee because he had not received clear instructions concerning the cleanliness of his department and the labeling of meat: Employees must "be put on clear notice as to exactly what they are doing that is inappropriate or unacceptable, and warned that if inappropriate or unacceptable behavior continues, discipline and/or discharge will result. This requirement . . . is an implied but thoroughly understood part of 'just cause.'" See also *Stella D'Oro Biscuit Co.*, 48 LA 349 (Cahn, 1967) (unauthorized carrying of rider); *Owens-Illinois, Inc.*, 76 LA 994 (Koven, 1981) (leaving plant without permission, overstaying break).

[144]*Wade Mfg. Co.*, 21 LA 676 (Maggs, 1953).

[145]*General Tel. Co.*, 85-2 ARB ¶8579 (Cloke, 1985).

[146]*Duke Laboratories*, 70-1 ARB ¶8382 (Silverstone, 1970). See also *North American Aviation, Inc.*, 19 LA 183 (Komaroff, 1952) (not clear whether rest room was "place of work" under rule requiring employees to remain at place of work until close of shift).

who was discharged for recklessness when he "rocked" a stalled pickup truck to free it from its restraining rails and lost control so that the truck rolled down a ramp, seriously damaging several parked vehicles and almost injuring several employees. The discharge was overturned because the company had never issued instructions as to the exact procedure to be followed in getting stalled trucks down the ramp.[147] Or consider the dilemma of a grocery clerk who was suspended for failing to comply with a rule barring "flamboyant, extreme hair styles or colors." He wore his hair short on the sides, long on top, and it appeared to be dyed on top so as to be two-toned. The arbitrator, while sympathizing with the employer's need to protect its image in a highly competitive industry, found that the rule gave employees little guidance as to what was required. Whether the clerk's hair style was flamboyant or extreme was a subjective judgment; as for the color, the two-tone effect could have been the result of bleaching by the sun, as claimed by the clerk. The clerk cut his hair two or three times in an effort to meet the employer's objections. In the absence of evidence that the employer's customers objected to his hair style, the arbitrator found that the suspension was not for just cause.[148]

However, even though a rule is vague on its face, if the evidence shows that the particular employee knew how the rule was being applied in practice, the vagueness may not save him.

EXAMPLE: A meter reader for a utility company had the utilities at his home disconnected for nonpayment of the bill. About a month later, the company found that his meter was back up and running and again disconnected it. Again the meter reader turned on the juice. He was subsequently discharged for violating a written memorandum issued less than a month earlier stating that employees would face severe disciplinary action, including discharge, if they "illegally reconnect services for themselves or

---

[147]*Solano Contract Warehouse Corp.*, 80-1 ARB ¶8065, 3304 (Koven, 1979): "To establsh that the grievant was guilty of 'willful negligence,' the Company would have to demonstrate that established safety procedures had been violated. But the existence of such practices is itself in question. The Company admits that such practices were never formally defined for employees." See also *General Tel. Co. of Cal.*, 86 LA 138 (Maxwell, 1985) (failure to define misuse of telephone).

[148]*Lucky Stores, Inc.*, 91 LA 624 (Ross, 1988). See also *Van Nuys Communication Co.*, 84 LA 881 (Gentile, 1985) (no-relative policy); *U.S. Army Corps of Eng'rs*, 86 LA 939 (O'Grady, 1986) (seat belt rule); *Rainbo Baking Co.*, 86-1 ARB ¶8181 (Taylor, 1986) (dishonored check); *Warner Jewelry Case Co.*, 87 LA 160 (Atleson, 1986) (double insurance coverage); *Lake Terminal R.R. Co.*, 89 LA 728 (Duda, 1987) ("excessive" speed); *RMS Technologies, Inc.*, 94 LA 297 (Nicholas, 1990) (definition of "outrageous behavior").

others . . . or otherwise obtain utility service without proper authorization." The meter reader claimed he thought the memorandum referred only to wiring "straight through" so that the electricity would bypass the meter or the meter would run backward. He pointed out that he had previously been allowed to reconnect his own service after paying a delinquent bill.

This story did not impress the arbitrator. The meter reader must have known that "proper authorization" was required, since on the prior occasion he had asked for and received permission to reconnect his service. Moreover, since the company had disconnected his service not once but twice, he should have known he would have to pay his bill before service could be restored.[149]

One little caveat: "For a past practice to be as enforceable as a written rule, it must consist of a constant, clearly defined pattern of conduct."[150] In a case where the employer contended that its written rule prohibiting the wearing or displaying of "campaign buttons" had been interpreted to prohibit buttons or pins of any kind, credible testimony established that employees had worn St. Patrick's Day shamrocks, Knights of Columbus and American Legion badges, and buttons of many other kinds. Under these circumstances, the arbitrator found that, contrary to the employer's claim, the rule had been applied literally, and the grievant had not been given adequate notice that wearing a button with the inscription "Free Angela Davis" (a black activist) was improper.[151]

Specificity Regarding Notice of Penalty. A disciplinary notice may also be deficient if it fails to tell employees how future misconduct will be punished. A phrase such as "appropriate disciplinary action," for example, is too vague.[152] A supervisor's "mild

---

[149]*Memphis Light, Gas & Water Div.*, 77-1 ARB ¶8202 (Flannagan, 1977).

[150]*Port Auth. of Allegheny County*, 71-2 ARB ¶8694, 5646 (Duff, 1971).

[151]*Id.*

[152]*Potter Electric Signal Co.*, 75 LA 50 (Madden, 1980) (grievant had no reason to think "appropriate disciplinary action" would be two-day suspension, especially since others guilty of same offense were only reprimanded). In *Oil Transp. Co.*, 89-2 ARB ¶8484 (Goodstein, 1989), the arbitrator reversed the discharge of an employee who had delivered merchandise to the wrong company, improperly begun work early, and loaded the wrong product. The employee had been warned that in the event of future infractions, "disciplinary action will be taken," but this was viewed as insufficient to warn of discharge. Other drivers had received lesser penalties after getting similar warnings, and the infractions in this case were not of the type for which immediate discharge was provided.

complaints" or hopes that an employee will improve are likewise
not sufficient to let the employee know his job is in jeopardy.[153]
And if the penalty for an offense has been increased, employees
have a right to be warned through proper notice that a sterner
standard is being adopted.[154]

As in the cases discussed in the preceding section, ambiguity
often is a problem when employees are told what punishment
they can expect for misconduct.

> **EXAMPLE:** An employer had an established policy that a first
> wage garnishment would result in a reprimand; a second garnish-
> ment, in a reprimand and a three-day suspension; and a third
> garnishment, in discharge. When an employee's wages were gar-
> nished for the second time, his foreman persuaded the Personnel
> Department to forego the written reprimand and three-day sus-
> pension because the employee had convinced him that he would
> pay his debts promptly and because Christmas was close at hand.
> The foreman warned him, however, that if his wages were again
> garnished, "there would be nothing more I could do for you."
> When another garnishment came through, the employee was
> fired.

The employer argued that the foreman's words should have
put the employee on notice that, despite the employer's leniency
on the occasion of his second garnishment, he could expect
discharge the next time. The arbitrator disagreed. The foreman's words were equivocal. "They might mean either that he
would be discharged, as the Company contends, or that [the
foreman] would not be able to relieve him of a three-day suspension the second time." Given this ambiguity, and the fact that
a written notice of reprimand was not issued for the second
garnishment, the arbitrator ruled that the employee had not
had the required two warnings prior to discharge.[155]

A language problem of a different sort was presented in
the case of a Spanish-speaking employee who was discharged
for failing to report as ordered on the day he wanted to observe
as his birthday holiday. The employee knew his supervisor
wanted him to work, but he did not understand the consequences of not showing up. Bilingual employees were available
to translate, but the supervisor, who spoke no Spanish, failed to

---

[153]*Fontaine Converting Works*, 24 LA 555 (Marshall, 1955) (inefficiency, loafing).
[154]*Iowa-Illinois Gas & Elec. Co.*, 84 LA 868 (Keefe, 1985) (tampering with utility
meters).
[155]*Trailmobile, Inc.*, 27 LA 160 (McCoy, 1956).

call upon one of them to assure effective communications. The arbitrator therefore reduced the penalty to a two-week suspension.[156]

Notice of penalty may also be defective if the company fails to state clearly what type of future misconduct will trigger discharge (or other penalty). That problem is highlighted in a case where an employee had received three written warnings advising him that failure to reduce his tardiness level to 5 percent would lead to discharge. When he was cited again for leaving his work area without permission and failing to attend a safety meeting, the employer fired him in accordance with its policy that a fourth warning meant discharge.

Notice was deficient in this case because the employee's first three warnings all were directed to his tardiness problem; he was never given notice that a fourth warning for some other infraction would lead to discharge.[157] A parallel situation arose where an employee was informed that if he again showed up on company premises drunk or with whiskey on his breath, he would be fired. That warning was not sufficient, the arbitrator decided, to put him on notice that drinking a beer during his lunch break would lead to the same penalty.[158]

The Problem of Degree—How Much Is Too Much?

Notice may also be deficient if the employer fails to tell an employee in no uncertain terms how much misconduct will land him in the soup. The two most obvious areas where the question of degree may become important are absenteeism and tardiness—how many absences or how many late reports before discipline will be imposed? If discipline is to stick in these and other areas where the number of infractions is pivotal, the rules of the game must be communicated in advance.[159]

---

[156]*Sterling Beef Co.*, 91 LA 1049 (Watkins, 1988).

[157]*General Elec. Co.*, 69 LA 707 (Jedel, 1977). See also *General Bag Co.*, 86 LA 739 (Klein, 1985) (negligence).

[158]*Altamil Corp.*, 71-1 ARB ¶8198 (Volz, 1971). See also *James River Corp.*, 89-1 ARB ¶8164 (Gershenfeld, 1988), where a three-day suspension for failure to give notice of lateness was set aside because a prior warning had specified only that notice of absence had to be given, even though posted notices required notice of both absence and lateness.

[159]*E.g.*, *W. R. Grace Co.*, 62 LA 779 (Boals, 1974) (employee told to improve attendance with no criteria as to extent of improvement required). Cases to the same effect include *Ball Corp.*, 74-1 ARB ¶8050 (Shanker, 1974); *Rockwell Int'l Flow Control Div.*, 1975 ARB ¶8036 (Knee, 1975); *Shepard Niles Crane & Hoist Corp.*, 71 LA 828 (Alutto, 1978).

Arbitrator Kabaker: It becomes incumbent upon the Company to establish a clear figure or benchmark as to what or how many reprimands will constitute an "accumulation." If the Company decides to use the reason as a regular procedure, it must promulgate a clear rule on this subject and make reasonably certain that all employees are aware of the rule and fully forewarned.[160]

The question of degree can come up in many less obvious ways as well.

EXAMPLE NO. 1: Trying to figure out why her production was below average, an employee's foreman concluded that one factor slowing down her output was her long fingernails. He directed her to cut them. She refused—not once, but twice—and was given a three-day and then a 10-day suspension. Upon returning from her 10-day suspension, she declared that she had finally complied with the foreman's order and displayed the nail clippings in a plastic bag. Still too long, the foreman decided—and fired her.

The problem? The foreman never told the employee how short to cut her nails; he just said to make them short enough so she could work at a proper pace. For that reason, the employee was reinstated with back pay—and the company was directed to prescribe a reasonable fingernail length for all employees in the department and to communicate that standard properly.[161]

EXAMPLE NO. 2: When an employee reported for work with the smell of alcohol on his breath, he was given a breathalyzer test which showed he had a 0.14 percent blood alcohol level—well above the standard of 0.10 percent which would have made him subject to arrest for driving under the influence. As a result, he was fired.

Since the company had not told employees in advance what blood alcohol level it would regard as proof of intoxication (or even announced that a sobriety test might be required), the employee's discharge was overturned, and he was reinstated with back pay.[162]

---

[160]*Canton Drop Forging & Mfg. Co.*, 80-2 ARB ¶8450, 5013 (1980) (absenteeism and tardiness).

[161]*Honeywell, Inc.*, 74 LA 918 (Belshaw, 1980).

[162]*Northrop Worldwide Aviation Servs., Inc.*, 64 LA 742 (Goodstein, 1975). See also *Anaconda Aluminum Co.*, 62 LA 1049 (Warns, 1974) (excessive use of telephone). Other "degree" cases include *Inland Underground Facilities*, 70-1 ARB ¶8042 (Talent, 1969) (number and length of coffee breaks); *Automotive Pattern Co.*, 77-2 ARB ¶8435 (Daniel, 1977) (definition of lateness).

Inconsistent Enforcement of Company Rules: The Problem of
"Negative Notice"[163]

Past practice—that is, how the parties have lived together on a day-to-day basis—has already been discussed as one of the unwritten forms in which notice of a rule or policy may be given. Past practice and notice are connected in other ways as well.

"Everybody's Doing It"

If the employer has permitted a certain kind of conduct to go on among employees without doing anything about it, a later claim that employees are "on notice" that such conduct is unacceptable becomes difficult to sustain. The suspension of an employee for spending a minute or two reading a magazine article when she had no work was overturned, for example, where the arbitrator found that her behavior was not out of line. The employer had no rule prohibiting employees from reading when they had no work, and the employee had seen other employees talk, show one another family photographs, sell raffle tickets, and engage in other personal activities on company time without interference from supervisors.[164]

Indeed, even a written rule covering certain misconduct may not be enforceable if management has knowingly let violations go unpunished, thereby giving employees a kind of "negative notice" that such misconduct is acceptable. Two employees with terrible attendance records were the beneficiaries of this negative notice even though they had been warned that their next violations would result in discharge and the contract provided for discharge in such cases. The arbitrator rescinded their discharges upon finding that the policy had been unevenly applied with poor

---

[163]The problem of inconsistent enforcement from the point of view of equal treatment is covered in Ch. 6.

[164]*Litton Indus., Inc.*, 62 LA 1195 (Karasick, 1974). See also *Stevens Shipping & Terminal Co.*, 70 LA 1066, 1072 (Hall, 1978), where the employer was found guilty of "some misleading permissiveness" for not having adopted formal work rules and for having allowed horseplay and other misconduct for which the grievant was discharged to go unchecked. "Leniency and stern-fairmindedness are noble traits; but they backfire when they become condonation." In *Georgia-Pacific Corp.*, 94 LA 667 (Shearer, 1990), the arbitrator reduced to a four-week suspension the discharge of an employee who admittedly took a light fixture from a company salvage trailer, even though he knew he needed permission to do this, where the company had not clearly informed the employee that it had discontinued the practice of giving away some salvage items. The employee had no intent to steal, the arbitrator found, and he could reasonably have believed the fixture had no further value to the company.

maintenance of records and some supervisors showing favoritism. Moreover, the intent of progressive discipline had not been realized—the employees had been given insufficient opportunity to improve after being warned of discharge.[165]

The point is that a party to a collective bargaining agreement must live with the consequences of its past conduct. A companion proposition is that employees are entitled to be told the rules of the game from the beginning.

> **EXAMPLE:** A Hispanic employee was terminated after he painted the words "paz" (peace), "amor" (love), and "hermanos" (brothers) on a door frame in his work area. No one thought he was motivated by anything but noble sentiments; but the employer still insisted that he violated a rule against "misusing, destroying, damaging, or defacing company property." The union argued that the discharge should be overturned because a wide variety of words, slogans, and drawings scrawled or painted by other employees had been on the walls for a long time—certainly during this employee's entire term of employment.

The effect of those graffiti, the arbitrator found, was to neutralize the effect of the notice given in the written rule. If management truly objected to such scribblings, and wanted to impress upon employees that expressing themselves with a paint brush could lead to discipline, "why did it allow the sporadic scrawls and drawings on its walls . . . to remain visible and undisturbed for so long? Certainly such a long-term omission on the part of management was hardly calculated to bring home to its employees that it regarded such prior markings as actual 'defacements' of its property."[166]

---

[165]*Worcester Quality Foods, Inc.*, 88-2 ARB 8432 (Rocha, 1988). In *Macmillan Bloedel Containers*, 92 LA 592 (Nicholas, 1989), the arbitrator held that progressive discipline was required for employees charged with violating a rule prohibiting the use, possession, or being under the influence of alcohol or drugs. The employer had been lax in enforcing the rule, and the arbitrator reasoned that employees could reasonably conclude that the employer did not intend to impose discharge for a single violation. In *Fedders Air Conditioning, U.S.A.*, 95 LA 449 (Cooper, 1990), the arbitrator disapproved the suspension of employees who failed to report for mandatory Saturday overtime work that had been posted on the bulletin board, even though the contract permitted suspension in such cases. A six-year practice of imposing suspension only in cases of failure to report for personally assigned and accepted overtime work, the arbitrator found, misled employees into believing they would not be suspended for failing to report for posted overtime work.

[166]*Russell Stanley Corp.*, 66 LA 953 (Kornblum, 1976). In *Lockheed Corp.*, 75 LA 1081, 1085 (Kaufman, 1980), where the company had allowed drinking and marijuana smoking to go on in its parking lot for a considerable time, the arbitrator refused to excuse management's delay in taking disciplinary action even though the delay was caused by the company's desire not to jeopardize a police investigation into drug traf-

"Negative notice" may be individual as well as general, as where just one employee has previously engaged in misconduct without being disciplined. Where management had taken a long-suffering attitude toward an employee's many offenses (which included leaving his work area, distracting other employees from their work, and arguing with and insulting supervisors), his eventual discharge, though long overdue in the arbitrator's opinion, was set aside because the employer had failed ever to tell him clearly that his conduct was intolerable and had to stop.[167]

As the arbitrator explained in another case, "the rationale of weighing past condonation as a mitigating factor is the inherent unfairness of punishing an employee for a present violation after he may have been led to believe that such conduct was condoned by management."[168] Another kind of implied condonation occurs when the employer gives an employee a "final warning" or "last chance" but then fails to follow through, as in the case of a maintenance man who worked without wearing a safety hat, with his supervisor's knowledge, at least 10 times after he had been given a "final warning" to wear the helmet or be discharged.[169]

Tightening Up On Enforcement

The fact that an employer has been haphazard about enforcing its rules, or about letting certain kinds of conduct go on without issuing a rule on the subject, does not mean it cannot decide at some point that enough is enough.

Arbitrator Allman: The company has the right to take steps to tighten discipline, but its agreement with the Union, and general

---

ficking among its employees. "[W]hat counts when it comes to enforcing Company rules, rather than criminal statutes, is the impact of the Company's inaction upon the employees, not the Company's motivation. As the Union points out, the practical effect, despite the posted rules, was that the employees 'looked upon the lots as sanctuaries for this relaxation . . . .'"

[167]*Armco Steel Corp.*, 52 LA 101 (Duff, 1969). See also *New York Central R.R. Co.*, 44 LA 552 (Wyckoff, 1965) (attorney could not be discharged without warning for representing plaintiff in suit against employer, since he had done same thing before with company's knowledge and without punishment); *M. Pascale Trucking, Inc.*, 59 LA 47 (Rodio, 1972) (employee improperly discharged for working second job because management had known of his moonlighting for some time and effectively condoned practice); *Northwest Eng'g Co.*, 72 LA 486 (Grubb, 1979) (condonation of failure to wear safety glasses).

[168]*Hilo Coast Processing Co.*, 74 LA 236, 240 (Tanaka, 1980).

[169]*Tumwater Valley Dev. Co.*, 64 LA 981 (Peck, 1975). See also *Mazza Cheese Co.*, 84 LA 947 (La Cugna, 1985); *Worcester Quality Foods, Inc.*, *supra* note 165.

labor relations principles, require that when the Company has tolerated a condition and decides to end its toleration, there must be some indication of the change in policy.[170]

In other words, the employer must live with whatever has been going on until it gives employees clear notice that things will be different in the future. Where an old rule exists, but has been allowed to wither on the vine by nonenforcement, such notice should go beyond merely reposting or restating the old rule to make it unmistakably clear that the employer means business.

The following notice informed employees in no uncertain terms of a crackdown on a persistent problem involving holiday drinking:

NOTICE
As we approach the Holiday Season, we would like to remind you that drinking and work do not mix. Last year we had some bad experiences here at the plant with people reporting for work under the influence of alcohol.

You are reminded that this is a violation of the Shop Rules and cannot be tolerated. Therefore, you are asked not to report for work under the influence of alcohol. Also, there will be no alcoholic beverages admitted into the plant at all. Violations will result in severe disciplinary action.[171]

Such a notice of a change in policy may take any of the customary forms of notice: posting on bulletin boards, memo to the union, distribution to employees individually—whatever method or combination of methods will get the message across.

Another example of the employer's doing it right involved the discharge of an employee for poor performance. She had received no formal complaints in her first 13 years of employment, but then the employer began an effort to increase efficiency. Thereafter, despite persistent efforts by management personnel to help her overcome her problems, the employee repeatedly failed both written and practical qualifying tests, and she was disciplined four times in four years for job neglect. Ultimately, after concluding that she was incapable of meeting the job requirements and giving her a final opportunity to pass the qualifying tests, the employer terminated her. Sustaining

---

[170]*Genest-Midwest, Inc.*, 67-2 ARB ¶8569, 4994 (1967) (reporting to work under the influence).

[171]*Burnham Corp.*, 73-1 ARB ¶8036, 3244 (Pollock, 1973).

the discharge, the arbitrator found that the employee was held to no higher standard than other employees and that there was no classification for her to be demoted to.[172]

Change in how a rule is to be enforced. Notice is just as crucial when the employer intends to change the way in which it enforces an existing rule. The name of the game is (again) *advance* notice, not notice of the change *after the fact.*

> **EXAMPLE:** For a number of years an employer had had a policy—posted conspicuously on a bulletin board—that employees must open their lunch boxes and other personal packages upon request when leaving company premises. The policy had been consistently enforced for night-shift employees but neglected on the day shift until the oversight came to management's attention. The first day a supervisor was assigned to check day-shift lunch boxes, one of the first employees to leave the warehouse refused to open his lunch box when requested. He walked away and reappeared two minutes later with an empty lunch box. He was subsequently suspended for five days for refusing to comply with a reasonable inspection procedure.

The union's complaint: Even though the rule undeniably existed, the company's decision to start enforcing the rule on the day shift amounted to a change in policy that was made too abruptly. The arbitrator agreed. Notice of the change should have been given, even by way of some explanation by the supervisor as employees approached her at the exit, thus minimizing the element of surprise. "Foreknowledge removes any chance of misunderstanding or suggestion that something has occurred which has created a suspicion of dishonesty among the workers or that a trap is being laid to identify a miscreant."[173]

---

[172]*Marathon Petroleum Co.*, 91 LA 824 (Grimes, 1988).

[173]*Nipak, Inc.*, 76-2 ARB ¶8434 (Ruiz, 1976). Similar reasoning prompted the arbitrator in *City of North Las Vegas*, 88-1 ARB ¶8242 (Richman, 1988), to disapprove the transfer of an employee to a position where he would have closer supervision. The employee had received above-average to excellent evaluations for six years, but a new supervisor determined that his work was substandard. If the company's standards were changing, the arbitrator commented, the employee was entitled to notice and the opportunity to conform before action was taken against him. See also *Lawrence Bros., Inc.*, 28 LA 83 (Davis, 1957), where the employer was required to give advance notice before enforcing a pants-only rule for women for reasons of "good taste and decorum," since the rule previously had been applied only when safety considerations dictated that pants be worn.

Questions of Timing

When the employer decides only after the fact that a particular kind of misconduct is out of bounds, the reasons for its decision may be suspect. Especially where the employer has allowed the conduct in question to go on without interference in the past, a sudden crackdown without advance warning may raise the suspicion that the rule was resurrected for arbitrary reasons, perhaps to "get" an employee.

> **EXAMPLE:** An employee put up a poster in his office displaying a picture of Emiliano Zapata, whom he described as a Mexican folk hero, and the slogan "Viva la Revolución." When his supervisor ordered him to remove the poster, the employee complied. But then he took the matter up with the front office, where he was told that he could not rehang the poster because of a company policy permitting the posting only of signs having to do with the employer's business. He protested that other employees had put up signs and posters of various kinds and replaced the Zapata poster. The company thereupon directed that all personal items be removed from its walls and issued a bulletin stating that nothing might be posted that did not relate to company business. The offending employee was suspended indefinitely for refusing to comply with the rule.

The fact that employees had freely posted a wide variety of pictures and notices before this employee tacked up his poster belied the employer's claim that putting up non-business-related posters had been forbidden all along. By getting tough only after the Zapata poster made its appearance, the employer opened itself to the charge that its action was discriminatory. The employer's real objection, the union argued, was not to posters and pictures as such but to the Zapata poster because of its political content.

The arbitrator's analysis: "The new bulletin or 'clarification,' was issued in such great haste that one is entitled to conclude that the bulletin (which was intended to show a detached, objective, long-standing and implemented Company policy) instead comes into the record as having been thought up solely for the purpose of resisting this particular Zapata poster."[174]

---

[174]*California Processors, Inc.*, 56 LA 1275, 1281 (Koven, 1971).

IV. Notice: Some Final Issues

Notice and Management Rights

Where no rule has been promulgated either by the employer or by the parties jointly to cover behavior that is suddenly and without notice treated as misconduct, an arbitrator normally will refuse to fill the vacuum for the parties—even if there is a crying need for a guideline to cover the behavior in question. One reason is that arbitrators are reluctant to add to, change, or otherwise modify the collective bargaining agreement—indeed, they are often expressly barred from doing so. Moreover, a fundamental principle is that it is management's right to make its own rules.

> **EXAMPLE:** Needing a vehicle in a hurry to transport cut lumber to the production line and not finding one handy, an employee solved his problem by dumping the contents of an unused hand truck onto the mill floor. The employer took the position that the "promiscuous" dumping of lumber interfered with the orderly and disciplined running of the shop and amounted to "unruly behavior," "resisting authority," and insubordination. Two days' suspension was the penalty.

The arbitrator agreed—up to a point. Dumping lumber was not particularly "orderly." But the employer had never forbidden dumping by written rule, or even by oral instructions, and the employee could not be fairly disciplined for disobeying a nonexistent order. The employer was free to issue a new rule prohibiting dumping if it chose. "What the Arbitrator refuses to do, however, . . . is to write a rule or order which the Company has not put into force in the past."[175]

Though it is management's right and indeed duty to make

---

[175]*McCray Corp.*, 48 LA 395 (Witney, 1967). To the same effect, see *Reserve Mining Co.*, 38 LA 443, 449 (Sembower, 1962) (refusal to unload explosives):

> It is not the main purpose of the arbitrator . . . to write safety standards for the parties. He can make certain 'findings of fact' in the light of expert testimony at the hearing, but the development of full standards is a technical matter which may already have been fulfilled in fuller measure by the management with the advice of its scientists and engineers or perhaps by the parties working jointly through their safety committees.

Similarly, in *Canton Drop Forging & Mfg. Co.*, 80-2 ARB ¶8450, 5013 (Kabaker, 1980) (tardiness and absenteeism): "The Arbitrator is exceedingly aware that he has no authority to establish a 'yardstick' for the Parties and he is equally conscious that if any such yardstick is desired by the Parties they have the means to implement it."

its own rules, the employer may act in such a way as to lose the right to do so in a particular area. An example is an employer that sought to impose certain conditions to exemptions from its absenteeism-control program. When the union brought a grievance, the arbitrator agreed that the employer had acted improperly. The reason? To induce employees to ratify the union contract the employer had advertised the exemptions without mentioning the conditions, and the conditions applied only to union-negotiated exemptions. Imposing the conditions, therefore, was tantamount to changing a negotiated condition of employment.[176]

Notice and Insubordination

Insubordination is universally recognized as misconduct for which employees can be penalized even in the absence of formal notice. No employee needs to be told straight out: "Refusing to obey a legitimate work order of a member of management can lead to discipline, including discharge."

Nevertheless, notice is at the heart of many insubordination cases. If an employee is to be disciplined (and especially discharged) for disobeying a supervisor's order, the order itself must meet two fundamental criteria with respect to notice: First, the order must be clear and specific enough to let the employee know exactly what is expected. Second, the employee must be told exactly what the penalty will be if he or she refuses to comply.

> *Arbitrator Young:* Arbitrators and Arbitration Boards have consistently held that essential to making discharges stand up are: (1) very clear instructions; and (2) even more explicit statements about the penalty for failure to comply.[177]

> **EXAMPLE NO. 1:** A bus driver who had returned late to his station because of a heavy snowstorm was asked by his dispatcher to turn around and take the next run. When he gave the dispatcher the "thumbs downs" sign and said, "It's an extra man's job, not mine," the dispatcher stared at him and then arranged for someone else to take the run. A few days later the driver was discharged for failing to complete his assignment and not following a supervisor's instructions.

---

[176]*Tyson Foods, Inc.*, 92 LA 1121 (Goodstein, 1989).
[177]*Micro Precision Gear & Machine Corp.*, 31 LA 575, 579–80 (1958).

The driver was put back to work by the arbitrator because the dispatcher's "order" was fatally flawed—one of the most common reasons charges of insubordination fall apart. An employee is entitled to know before his fate is sealed what will happen if he persists in his course of conduct. "In fact," the arbitrator pointed out, "not to do this is *a form of entrapment*, involuntary though it may be, on the part of the employer." He continued:

> The basic and fundamental reason for requiring the alleged wrongdoer to be put on notice directly and informed that he is comporting himself in a manner inconsistent with his obligations to the Company, is that, if he is properly apprised of the fact, he might conceivably change his erring ways and comply with orders or instructions given him, which up to now he has not done.[178]

EXAMPLE NO. 2: A contract rule requiring employees to get a supervisor's permission before leaving work in the middle of a shift was altered by means of a posted notice stating that an employee need only inform a supervisor that he was taking off. One evening an employee told his foreman that he had to leave work to get gas because his car's tank was so nearly empty that he wouldn't be able to make it home and the stations all close at midnight—before the end of his shift. The foreman said to him, "There's a station on 55th Street that's open. You have work to do." The employee went anyway and was discharged the next day for leaving work without permission.

The employee was reinstated by the arbitrator. Why? Because he was not given adequate notice that if he left work he would be discharged. The contract had been modified, and the foreman had given him no indication that he intended to "override" the posted notice.[179]

What should the foreman have done. He should have told the employee unambiguously, "I'm directing you not to leave before your shift is up. If you do, you can be discharged." Going through all the steps of giving a proper work order may sometimes seem unnatural to a supervisor; he knows what he means, and he may think the employee knows what he means, too. He may even be right. But if a dispute arises later, an arbitrator will not assume the employee was a mindreader. "Or-

---

[178]*Safeway Trails, Inc.*, 38 LA 218, 224 (Seidenberg, 1962).
[179]*Fawn Eng'g Corp.*, 63 LA 1307 (Fitch, 1974).

ders" in the form of "Do what you feel you should do,"[180] or "You do what you want to do and I will do what I have to do,"[181] are just too vague to serve as adequate notice of what the employer expects.

Notice, Drugs, and Drug Testing

Issues relating to drugs and drug testing have assumed vastly greater importance in the employment setting in recent years. Employers, reflecting the attitudes of society generally, have become increasingly concerned about substance abuse by employees, and the goal of a drug-free workplace has become commonplace. Concern over drug abuse is heightened by the fact that the effects of drugs used off employer property can show up in the workplace in the form of erratic performance and increased absenteeism. More and more employers have thus become engaged "in a delicate process of balancing employee rights and interests, struggling to avoid potential liability under such emerging legal doctrines as wrongful discharge, invasion of privacy and emotional distress."[182]

Under the Drug-Free Workplace Act of 1988,[183] each employer holding federal contracts for $25,000 or more is required to publish a statement notifying employees that the unlawful manufacture, distribution, dispensation, possession, or use of a

---

[180]*Ethyl Corp.*, 78-1 ARB ¶8151, 3719 (Taylor, 1978). Those were the words used when an employee stood up during a safety meeting and protested that he did not have to attend and did not intend to remain. He and three fellow employees were suspended for insubordination for walking out of the meeting. The arbitrator decided that the supervisor's words could have been taken as permission to leave and that he "failed to give the employees explicit warning of the consequences if they failed to comply."

[181]*Central Foundry Co.*, 72 LA 531, 533 (Rutherford, 1979). The grievant had announced to his supervisor that he intended to take his vacation during the ensuing three weeks, although he had not gone through the proper vacation-scheduling procedures. The arbitrator found that, although it was reasonably clear that the grievant knew he had not been given permission to take off as he wished, it was also plain that the supervisor did not make clear what would happen to him if he did. "The Grievant should not be required to 'guess' what might happen." See also *City of Anaheim, Cal.*, 71-1 ARB ¶8159 (Gentile, 1971) (statement that employees could not watch World Series game on TV after break in training session not clear order to turn off radio one man was listening to in class); *Silva Harvesting, Inc.*, 81-2 ARB ¶8575 (McKay, 1981) (order not to leave "early" not clear); *FMC Corp.*, 92 LA 483 (Dworkin, 1989) (supervisor's saying he would "pass the information on" justified employee's leaving after requesting relief from mandatory overtime; supervisor had duty to respond clearly and immediately to request).

[182]*Oil, Chem. & Atomic Workers*, 88-1 ARB ¶8084, 3406 (Miller, 1988).

[183]Pub. L. No. 100-690.

controlled substance in the workplace is prohibited and specifying the penalties for violating the prohibition. Each such employer also must establish a drug-awareness program to inform
employees about (1) the dangers of drug abuse in the workplace;
(2) the policy of maintaining a drug-free workplace; (3) any
available drug counseling, rehabilitation, or employee assistance
program; and (4) the penalties for drug abuse violations. Employees working on federal contracts must be required, as a
condition of employment, to notify the employer within five
days of a conviction for violation in the workplace of any criminal drug statute, and the employer must either penalize them
or require their participation in a drug-abuse assistance or rehabilitation program.

The customary rules of notice, as set forth earlier in this
chapter, apply to drug-related misconduct on company property or company time with the same force as to other kinds of
misconduct. For example, despite his denial, it was reasonable
to believe that an employee had seen a posted notice that unannounced searches for drugs would be made.[184] Similarly, informing employees that unannounced searches might take place
was held to be an effective notice, so that employees could not
complain simply because a particular search was not announced
in advance.[185] And in the case of the sale and use of drugs on
company premises, an employee could be held to a "should have
known" standard even in the absence of a written policy.[186]

As part of their efforts to ensure that their operations are
not adversely affected by drug abuse among employees, many
employers have introduced testing for drugs on a routine basis
or in particular situations—for example, upon return from layoff or leave of absence or when an employee experiences an
industrial accident. Many of the objections to drug-testing programs raised by employees and unions are concerned with the
proper place of notice and other due process considerations.[187]
Related questions, some of which are broader in scope, such as
to what extent employees' traditional right of privacy should be
reexamined, have also begun to make their presence known.

---

[184]*Shell Oil Co.*, 84-1 ARB ¶3021 (Hanes, 1983) (search for guns, drugs).

[185]*Consumer Plastics Corp.*, 88 LA 208 (Garnholtz, 1987); *Concrete Pipe Prods. Co.*,
87 LA 601 (Caraway, 1986).

[186]*Ohio Edison Co.*, 86-1 ARB ¶8299 (Kates, 1986).

[187]Other aspects of the drug problem raise issues relating to some of the other
tests, especially investigation, proof, and reasonable rules. Those considerations will be
dealt with in the chapters devoted to those other tests.

Arbitrators agree that an employer has a right to establish rules designed to prevent drug and alcohol use from affecting its operations adversely, and this right may extend to drug testing or "screening" of employees. If a drug-testing program is to pass muster in arbitration, however, a rock-bottom requirement is that adequate notice be given to employees and the union. Where a program of drug testing has been disapproved, the reason frequently has been that notice was deficient. The failure to give adequate notice of testing, and of the disciplinary consequences of refusing to submit to testing, has been viewed as depriving employees of due process.

> **EXAMPLE:** Because employees were exposed to toxic materials in the course of their employment, a chemical company agreed in negotiations to pay for periodic physical examinations to determine whether employees were suffering any harmful effects. After the examination program had been in effect for some time, the employer unilaterally added a drug screen to the other tests being given. An employee who refused to submit to the drug screen was fired for insubordination. The employer argued that it had the right to add the drug screen to other tests given in the physical examinations. Alternatively, it claimed it could institute drug testing under its management prerogatives.

Neither argument impressed the arbitrator. Since the company had bargained over the physical examination program to begin with, he reasoned, it could not unilaterally add a drug screen to the other tests. Nor could it require an employee to submit to drug testing under its management prerogatives without some evidence of impairment; to do so was an invasion of privacy and an unwarranted requirement to furnish confidential medical information. And in any case, prior notification of both the union and employees, as well as sound reasons, would have been necessary to justify the requirement of a drug screen. The employee's refusal to submit to testing was found to have been justified, and he was reinstated with back pay.[188]

This is not to say that employees must always be notified in advance of particular drug tests. It is notification of the policy concerning drug tests, not of the intention to apply the policy

---

[188]*Gem City Chems., Inc.*, 86 LA 1023 (Warns, 1986). See also *Donaldson Mining Co.*, 89-1 ARB ¶8089 (Zobrak, 1988) (policy requiring drug screening of employees returning from disability leave of more than one year was improper, where policy communicated only to certain members of management).

on specific occasions, that is required. Thus, where an employee was known to have a substance abuse problem and was aware that he was subject to testing, the arbitrator upheld his discharge for failing to provide a urine sample for an unannounced drug test. The employee claimed he was unable to urinate in the doctor's office because of anxiety; if this was so, the arbitrator commented, his anxiety was reasonably attributable to a fear of testing positive.[189]

Given adequate notice of testing, and of the consequences of noncooperation, discharge for refusal to take a drug test has been upheld. Where an employee became agitated when the plant manager refused to accept a signed prescription form in lieu of a physician's note and then balked at submitting to a drug test, for example, the arbitrator ruled that the company properly could fire him. The test order, he noted, was based on the manager's personal observation of the employee, the company never had accepted a prescription form as an excuse for absence, the manager told the employee three times to take the test or be discharged, and the company's drug policy was properly adopted, reasonably announced, and fairly applied.[190]

Similarly, an employee who tests positive in a properly conducted drug screen is subject to discipline, and perhaps can even be shown the door, if notice and other just cause requirements have been satisfied. Thus, summary discharge was held to be

---

[189]*Philadelphia Gas Works*, 89-2 ARB ¶8481 (Simpkins, 1989). But in *Union Oil Co. of Cal.*, 88 LA 91 (Weiss, 1986), the arbitrator found no just cause for the suspension of four employees who tested positive for cocaine or marijuana, in part because the company had no published policy declaring that employees could be tested without advance notice and could be suspended if they tested positive.

[190]*Crescent Metal Prods.*, 91 LA 1129 (Coyne, 1989). *Warehouse Distribution Centers*, 90 LA 979, 982 (Weiss, 1987): "Arbitrators have generally accepted the view that if an employer has reasonable grounds to believe that an employee has consumed an illegal drug, it may require him to submit to a test and the employee's refusal to take the test, may, in itself, constitute just cause for discharge." See also *Bowater Carolina Co.*, 92 LA 162 (Clarke, 1989) (employee properly discharged for failure to provide urine sample over period of seven hours, where return to work after conviction of cocaine possession conditioned on agreeing to random drug testing); *Philadelphia Gas Works*, 89-2 ARB ¶8481 (Simpkins, 1989) (employee known to have substance abuse problem properly discharged for failure to provide urine sample for unannounced drug test, where employee had previously provided urine specimens under similar conditions). In *Oklahoma Transportation & Park Auth.*, 88 LA 492 (Harr, 1986), discharge for refusal to provide a urine sample for a drug test was overturned because the employee was not warned of the disciplinary consequences; and in *Morton Thiokol, Inc.*, 89 LA 572 (Nicholas, 1987), a discharge for refusal to take a breathalyzer test was held not justified because of doubt that the employee understood the consequences of his refusal.

warranted for an employee whose urine revealed a high concentration of marijuana in two tests conducted during work time 12 days apart. The arbitrator pointed out that the testing procedure was scientifically sound, employees had notice that drug testing would be included in annual physical examinations, an expert witness testified that the employee was "impaired" when he gave the urine specimens, and work rules permitted discharge for reporting to work under the influence of illegal drugs.[191]

---

[191]*Amoco Oil Co.*, 88 LA 1010 (Weisenberger, 1987). See also *Thomas Steel Strip Co.*, 87 LA 994 (Feldman, 1986) (employee properly discharged for testing positive for marijuana while on six-month probation imposed after earlier positive test, since he was on notice that further positive result would subject him to discharge). Cases in which discharges have been overturned because of the failure to warn of the disciplinary consequences include *CFS Continental, Inc.*, 86-1 ARB ¶8070 (Lumbley, 1985) (failure to warn deprived employees of due process); and *Engelhard Corp.*, 89-1 ARB ¶8033 (Mathews, 1988) (improper to discharge employee testing positive in drug screen, since adequate notice of disciplinary consequences not given to union or employees).

Chapter 2

Reasonable Rules and Orders

"Was the Employer's rule or managerial order reasonably related to (a) the orderly, efficient, and safe operation of the Employer's business, and (b) the performance that the Employer might properly expect of the employee?"

I. What Does It Mean to Be Reasonable —or Unreasonable?

Few propositions in labor relations are more firmly established than the proposition that the employer has the right to make reasonable rules and give reasonable orders in the conduct of its business.

> *Arbitrator McIntosh:* The basic rule of labor management relations is that management has all rights except those which it has bargained away in the Contract. Among the prerogatives of management there has always been the right to make reasonable rules for the governing of the conduct of the plant and its employees.[1]

The employer and the union may, of course, agree that basic rules of conduct will be jointly negotiated, even incorpo-

---

[1]*Dover Corp*, 33 LA 860, 861 (1956) (rest breaks). To the same effect, Arbitrator Dworkin:

> An employer retains the inherent right to exercise reasonable control over the conduct of its employees during their scheduled hours of work. Although this authority is frequently acknowledged in the form of a management rights clause, thereby according contractual recognition to the principle, the absence of such language in the labor agreement does not serve to diminish the employer's right in these matters."

Cited in *Brown-Graves Co.*, 43 LA 465 (Stouffer, 1964) (unauthorized breaks). In *U.S. Pipe & Foundry Co.*, 84 LA 770 (Singer, 1985) (insubordination), the arbitrator rejected a union argument that plant rules were unreasonable because they had never been recognized by the union and had been challenged in arbitration. Many additional cases on the employer's right to adopt reasonable work rules are cited in F. ELKOURI AND E. A. ELKOURI, HOW ARBITRATION WORKS 553–56 (4th ed. 1985).

rated into the contract. But unless the employer has explicitly agreed to surrender its rule-making prerogatives in whole or in part,[2] the employer's right unilaterally to tell employees what to do and what not to do has been overwhelmingly upheld in arbitration—subject, however, to two limitations:

- that management's rules and orders must be reasonable, both in themselves and in their administration,[3] and
- that the question of reasonableness is subject to the grievance procedure.[4]

That management has reasons—any reasons—for issuing a particular rule or giving a particular directive does not necessarily satisfy criteria that arbitrators use for assessing "reasonableness."[5] As stated in the discussion about the "reasonable man" in the Introduction, reasonableness must be determined not by management's standards alone but by standards acceptable to the labor relations community. Each of the following three arbitrators gives a slightly different twist to the meaning of reasonableness as applied to company rules:

> *Arbitrator Volz:* In order to prevail, the Union must show that [the rule] was invalid. It may do this by establishing (1) that it violates an express provision in the Contract, (2) that it materially changes a past practice or working condition which through mutual acceptance has acquired the status of a contractually-protected right,

---

[2]Such as in a case where the employer was barred from adopting a new rule making criminal conduct, on or off company premises, a disciplinary offense by a contract clause providing that "[t]he Company's rules for employees are mutually adopted by the Company and the Union." The company's argument that the clause covered only rules in effect when the contract was negotiated was rejected by the arbitrator since the agreement also stated that if additional rules were established "employees will be notified of such mutually adopted 'rules' by posting on bulletin boards." That provision clearly showed that new rules, too, would be subject to negotiation. *Consolidated Papers, Inc.*, 66 LA 1256 (Gunderman, 1976).

[3]"There should be no question that the company has the right to promulgate rules to govern the unsatisfactory behaviour of its employees. However, it is also important that the implementation and administration of such rules be consistent, fair and reasonable." *Armstrong Tire Co.*, 88 LA 323, 327 (Kindig, 1986) (negligence).

[4]"Plant rules designed to govern the operation of a company's business must be obeyed, subject, however, to the right of the union to challenge the reasonableness of a particular rule, and its application in individual cases, through the grievance procedure." *H. K. Porter Co.*, 46 LA 1098, 1103 (Dworkin, 1966) (productivity).

[5]In the discussion that follows, standards for evaluating the reasonableness of general rules apply in most cases to individual work orders and to individual causes for discipline (which may or may not come under the umbrella of a general rule), even if the term "work order" or "cause" is not mentioned.

or (3) that the [rule] is unreasonable either on its face or in its administration.[6]

Arbitrator Daugherty: It is a settled rule of arbitration that a company has the right unilaterally to issue and enforce rules that (1) do not conflict with any provisions of the parties' agreement or of law and (2) are reasonably related to the safe, orderly, and efficient operation of the company's business.[7]

Arbitrator Sisk: If a rule is related to the attainment of the goals and objectives of a company, and if that rule is not arbitrary, capricious or discriminatory, it is generally considered to be reasonable.[8]

To some extent, "reasonableness" is a shifting concept in the labor relations world. The labor-management relationship is inevitably influenced by what is happening in the society as a whole. When it became fashionable among young people a generation ago to wear longer hair and more abundant facial hair, many employers responded by rewriting rules governing workplace grooming and dress. Some of these rules were held to be reasonable, while others were not. Changing views on smoking provide another example. Company rules today take into account what are thought to be nonsmokers' rights to a much greater degree than was the case, say, 30 years ago.

Now society is experiencing a serious drug problem, and as a consequence drugs in the employment setting have increasingly become the focus of rule making. Society as a whole has broad concerns over the impact of drug use on crime, violence, and public health; in the business environment, concern about drug use focuses more specifically on its impact on production and productivity, workplace safety, the employer's reputation, and other work-related problems. Managements and unions are developing new plant rules, especially on drug testing and the use of drugs away from the workplace. In both areas notions of privacy are clashing with business needs, and prevailing standards of reasonableness are called into question.

Tomorrow the concern over drugs may recede somewhat and be replaced by a new societal problem that cannot now be foreseen. The result will be further refinement of what is meant by the reasonableness of the rules of the workplace.

---

[6]*Metal Specialty Co.*, 39 LA 1265 (1962) (unauthorized rest breaks).
[7]*Industrial Finishing Co.*, 40 LA 670 (1963) (reporting of absences).
[8]*Pullman Trailmobile Corp.*, 238 AAA 12 (1978).

II. Five Categories of "Unreasonable" Rules

1. Rules or Orders That Are Inconsistent With the Contract

The management rights principle typically allows the employer broad residual and discretionary power over matters not specifically covered in the contract. Thus, an employer could properly discharge an employee who was involved in 14 industrial accidents over a seven-year period, despite the absence of any contract provision or rule covering a situation of that kind. The employee had proved himself unable to carry out his work assignments without hazard to himself and others, the arbitrator reasoned, so the company had just cause to discharge him.[9]

Management may not, however, exercise its rule-making power in a manner that is inconsistent with the contract. Obvious? Perhaps. But many disputes that come before arbitrators involve rules claimed to be in conflict with the agreement. There are two particular problem areas:

- Where the employer adopts special policies or procedures to implement contract provisions.

EXAMPLE: The parties' agreement provided that if an employee became ill on the job, he was either to report his illness to his foreman, who would excuse him or send him to the plant hospital, or, if the foreman was not available, to report directly to the hospital after leaving word for the foreman with a fellow employee. The company changed that procedure to require a sick employee to obtain a special pass from the foreman before leaving work. Even though the new procedure improved the company's record-keeping, it was inconsistent with the intent of the contract, the arbitrator found, making the change unreasonable.[10]

- Where business needs that arise or become more acute after the contract has been negotiated call for (in the employer's view) revised rules or procedures.

EXAMPLE: Concerned over increasing drug and alcohol abuse and reports linking mine accidents to drug and alcohol use, a mining company adopted new rules which added drug and alco-

---

[9]*Dinner Bell Meats, Inc.*, 84-1 ARB ¶8080 (Heinsz, 1984). See also *Holiday Inns, Inc.*, 84-1 ARB ¶8184 (Concepcion, 1984) (no need to show violation of specific rule to justify discharge of employee whose disregard of safety procedures had potentially serious consequences).
[10]*Bucyrus-Erie Co.*, 69 LA 970 (Fleischli, 1977).

hol screening tests to preemployment physical exams and work-related physicals, including return-to-work physicals. The new rules also provided for testing after work-related accidents in certain cases. Confirmed positive test results were stated to be ground for disciplinary action, including discharge. The union protested the new rules because the employer had not bargained over them and because they were, in the union's view, unreasonable.

The arbitrator noted that the employer already had a policy on drugs and alcohol that permitted screening tests in some situations, and he did not buy the union's claim that it could not unilaterally change that policy. In principle he recognized the employer's right to make and change work rules; nevertheless, he found the new policy to be in conflict with the parties' contract. The agreement, he pointed out, gave employees the right to challenge determinations that they were unfit to work for medical reasons. The new policy would deny them that right by making positive test results ground for disciplinary action, including termination. For this and other reasons, the arbitrator ruled that the new policy could not be enforced as written.[11]

Rules have sometimes been judged improper not because they clashed with the contract directly but because they gave general contract language too restrictive a meaning. Thus, a rule requiring union officials to give the employer 48 hours' notice before leaving work on official union business was in conflict with a contract provision allowing union officers to take leaves of absence upon "reasonable" notice, since "[t]he term

---

[11]*Maple Meadow Mining*, 90 LA 873, 878 (Phelan, 1988). In *Luria Bros.*, 70-2 ARB ¶8601 (Walsh, 1970), a newly adopted absenteeism policy under which any failure to report was counted as an absence was found to violate a contract making overtime work voluntary. In *Sweco, Inc.*, 73 LA 684 (Hardbeck, 1979), a new no-fault policy in which absences for any reason could count against an employee was found to be inconsistent with a contract provision guaranteeing that an employee would not lose seniority because of illness. A similar conflict was identified by the arbitrator in *Central Tel. Co. of Va.*, 68 LA 957 (Whyte, 1977), between a new no-fault attendance program and contract language recognizing "excused" absences for purposes of holiday pay and vacation eligibility. See also *Sylvania Elec. Prods., Inc.*, 32 LA 1025 (Wallen, 1958) (progressive discipline providing for immediate discharge upon reaching last step conflicted with contract provision requiring one week's notice of discharge); *Chromalloy Am. Corp.*, 64 LA 853 (Emery, 1975) (placing employees with unacceptable absence records on medical leave of absence violated contract language whereby nondisciplinary leaves could be initiated only by employees).

'reasonable' is not one which either side, or in fact both sides, excepting by express understanding, can limit to an exact number of hours."[12]

Not only may the employer find itself in trouble if it adopts a rule that violates the letter of the contract; it may have difficulty defending rules that violate the contract's spirit as well—rules that impinge on the fundamental rights of individual employees or of the union as an institution.

A rule prohibiting employees from conducting any union business on company time without advance permission, for example, was held by an arbitrator to be too broad. Had it merely defined the circumstances under which an employee or union representative could interrupt work, the rule might have passed muster. But "[a]s written, it is an invasion of basic rights of the employees subsisting under a Collective Bargaining Agreement" and would allow union business to be conducted only "at the permissive indulgence of the employer"—not as required to protect employees' legitimate contractual rights.[13]

2. Rules That Conflict With an Established Past Practice

Past Practice as a Bar to New Rules

Management's right to make reasonable rules is limited not only by written contract terms. Whether it is a question of a new rule or a change or clarification of an existing rule, the company's action may be successfully challenged by the union if it conflicts with a past practice that meets certain criteria. As set forth by Arbitrator Mittenthal, these are (1) clarity and

---

[12]*Ampco Metal, Inc.*, 3 LA 374, 379 (Updegraff, 1946). Similarly, in *Electrical Repair Serv. Co.*, 67 LA 173 (Towers, 1976), the employer was barred from establishing a rule subjecting to discipline employees who failed to report an intended absence or tardiness at least 12 hours before starting time when the contract required only that employees notify their immediate supervisor "prior to scheduled work time."

[13]*United-Carr Tenn.*, 59 LA 883, 888 (Cantor, 1972). See also *Solar Turbines, Inc.*, 85 LA 525 (Kaufman, 1985) (rule on standards of employee conduct may not be applied as if it superseded contractual just cause provision); *Ohio Adjutant General's Dep't*, 91 LA 727, 733 (Dworkin, 1988) (unilateral regulations can be adopted only as general guidelines and may not supplant negotiated rights and protections).

consistency, (2) longevity and repetition, and (3) acceptability to both parties.[14]

> *Arbitrator Updegraff:* [I]t is unlikely an entirely new rule made by an employer would be sustained if inconsistent with long established past practice of such sort as would justify employees in reasonably relying upon its indefinite continuance.[15]

> *Arbitrator Volz:* Day to day practice mutually accepted by the parties may attain the status of contractual rights and duties, particularly where they are not at variance with any written provision negotiated into the contract by the parties and where they are of long standing and were not changed during contract negotiations.[16]

The employer's unilateral right to make or change rules that are inconsistent with existing practices has been held to be restricted by:

- a contract provision that expressly calls for negotiation before the employer may change a past practice;[17]
- general contract language that provides for maintenance of benefits and working conditions not specifically dealt with elsewhere in the agreement;[18] or

---

[14]*Past Practice and the Administration of Collective Bargaining Agreements*, ARBITRATION AND PUBLIC POLICY 32–33 (Proceedings of the 14th Annual Meeting, National Academy of Arbitrators 1961). Or as stated by Arbitrator Justin: "[P]ast practice, to be binding on both parties, must be (1) unequivocal; (2) clearly enunciated and acted upon; (3) readily ascertainable over a reasonable period of time as a fixed, established practice accepted by both parties" (cited in *Roadway Express*, 87 LA 465 (Chapman, 1986) (absenteeism)).

[15]*Standard Oil Co.*, 11 LA 689, 690 (1948) (leaving work post).

[16]*Metal Specialty Co.*, 39 LA 1265, 1269 (1962) (unauthorized rest breaks).

[17]The problem for an arbitrator in this situation is often simply whether the asserted practice did or did not exist. See, e.g., *Utah Army Nat'l Guard*, 74 LA 770 (Wiggins, 1980), where disagreement focused on whether the employer had, in fact, permitted beards to be worn during hunting season.

[18]The distinction between rules that affect "working conditions" and "benefits" (areas that have been held to be subject to bargaining by the NLRB and are often protected by contract language) and other rules (which generally are not subject to negotiation) is not always clear cut. In *United Baking Co.*, 43 LA 337 (Kreimer, 1964), the arbitrator found that the employer had to bargain over rules affecting wages, hours, or conditions of employment but could unilaterally set standards for employee conduct; where the line was to be drawn, however, he did not specify. Another arbitrator has suggested that nonnegotiable company rules cover "standards for personal performance and behavior. . . . Personal *conduct* as opposed to work-related objectives is the differentiating feature between a company rule and a work assignment." *Tappan Appliance Group*, 64 LA 1269, 1272 (Knee, 1975) (insubordination). Yet another arbitrator held in *Maple Meadow Mining*, *supra* note 11, that unilateral work rules do not become past practices or customs and may be changed without agreement or bargaining with the union.

- NLRB rulings making rules affecting working conditions mandatory subjects for bargaining (unless the union has expressly waived its right to bargain over rules).[19]

Even where none of the three foregoing factors has been present, past practice has been widely held by arbitrators and the courts to limit management's freedom of action with respect to new work rules.

EXAMPLE: For more than 10 years the employer had had a succession of tardiness-control policies. All provided for some form of progressive discipline, and recent programs had allowed as many as 24 incidents of lateness in a 12-month period. Under a new plan, however, an employee could be late no more than 12 times during a calendar year. Warning notices were no longer sent; employees were expected to keep track of their own tardiness records. When someone was fired for lateness, the union protested that the new tardiness rule had been adopted unilaterally; that it was arbitrary and discriminatory; and that it violated the contract, which said only that employees might be discharged for "chronic tardiness" without specifying the number of occurrences.

The arbitrator's analysis illustrates how what has gone on in the past can become a standard of reasonableness. For the employer to define "chronic tardiness" as a fixed number of instances in a given time period was not unreasonable in itself. What was unreasonable was the drastic reduction from what the employer had tolerated in the past. Unreasonable, too, was the elimination of the long-established practice of sending warnings to employees when discharge was imminent.[20]

---

[19]Arbitrators differ as to whether their decisions should conform to rulings of the NLRB, some holding that arbitration decisions should be consistent with NRLB policy, others taking the view that the arbitrator's job is to interpret the contract without reference to external law, and still others taking an "in between" approach as particular cases seem to warrant. For the arguments pro and con, see R. G. Howlett, *Why Arbitrators Apply External Law*, and R. Mittenthal, *Why Arbitrators Do Not Apply External Law*, LABOR ARBITRATION: A PRACTICAL GUIDE FOR ADVOCATES 257–86, 287–94 (1990). For a case in which the NLRB position with respect to changes in work rules is followed (and many citations are set forth), see *Portec, Inc., Paragon Div.*, 72 LA 804 (Ellmann, 1979). See also *Keebler Co.*, 75 LA 975 (Morris, 1980) (attendance rules).

[20]*The Maccabees*, 27 LA 99 (Smith, 1956). In *General Tel. Co. of Ky.*, 71-2 ARB ¶8430 (Seinsheimer, 1971), a 20-year practice of permitting employees to go outside for a stroll, smoke, or cup of coffee during their breaks barred the company from adopting a rule prohibiting them from leaving the building during the work day. See also *Kentile Floors, Inc.*, 52 LA 771, 772 (Kornblum, 1969) (longstanding practice whereby employees had access to plant at any time before work "had assumed the dignity of an established working condition," which company could not unilaterally change by new rule prohibiting employees from entering plant more than 30 minutes before start of

Past practice that gives meaning to ambiguous contract language can also determine reasonableness of a new rule. Where a contract stated that a nurse on "restricted call" could either sleep at the hospital or remain at home if she could reach the hospital "promptly," the hospital could not enforce a new policy that required such nurses to respond to calls immediately—that is, to remain at the hospital. The reason: A prior written policy and the parties' past practice had established that "promptly" meant within 15 minutes. "[H]aving published its reasonable clarification of an ambiguity, it cannot unilaterally publish another rule which goes beyond clarification and actually amends the contract word from 'promptly' to 'immediately.'"[21]

Six Situations in Which Past Practice Is Not Binding

Past practice does not always stop the clock as far as management's rule-making powers are concerned. Some arbitrators have held flatly that if management can make rules in the first place, it also can change them or make new ones without restriction.[22] More often, however, where arbitrators have upheld the employer's right to make or change a rule in the face of a longstanding past practice, one or more of the following conditions has been present:

---

shift); *Formica Corp.*, 44 LA 467 (Schmidt, 1965) (rest periods); *S. S. White Dental Mfg. Co.*, 48 LA 1337 (Turkus, 1967) (requirement of doctor's certificate to verify illness). A past practice may also prevent an employer from stepping up penalties for certain offenses, as in *Wolverine Aluminum Corp.*, 74 LA 252 (Dobry, 1980), where a new rule imposing stiff penalties for late returns from lunch was found to be in conflict with a past practice of applying progressive discipline to such returns.

[21]*Youngstown Hosp. Ass'n*, 71 LA 1266 (Strasshofer, 1979).

[22]See, e.g., *Maple Meadow Mining, supra* note 11, at 878:

There is no requirement that the Union agree to the personnel policies before the Company puts them into effect, and there is no intent that they become binding agreements for the future. They are simply work rules which the Employer puts into effect under its reserved authority to manage, and the work rules may be changed by the Employer under that same authority when the circumstances warrant.

See also *Sylvania Elec. Prods., Inc.*, 32 LA 1025 (Wallen, 1958) (absenteeism and tardiness) (since management may make reasonable rules, it may change them, provided changes are reasonable); *Stroh Die Casting Co.*, 72 LA 1250, 1254–55 (Kerkman, 1979):

The Union argues that the Company is obligated to bargain over the changed work rules at issue here, pursuant to its responsibilities under the Labor Management Relations Act. . . . Under the facts in the instant matter, the undersigned concludes that the Company properly bargained with the Union with respect to work rules when the parties agreed in their Collective Bargaining Agreement that the right to establish reasonable work rules were [sic] invested exclusively in the Company.

1. Changed Conditions.

Arbitrator Cahn: It must be stated as a general proposition that once the conditions upon which a past practice has been based are changed or eliminated, the practice may no longer be given effect.[23]

EXAMPLE: Soon after the employer moved into a new facility, it began having housekeeping problems with disposable beverage containers that employees brought to their work areas from vending machines and with employees taking too many breaks. So it issued a new rule limiting vending machine visits to official break times and requiring that any beverages brought onto the shop floor be in vacuum bottles or other nondisposable containers. The union protested one employee's discharge on the ground that the new rule changed a longstanding practice permitting employees to bring disposable soft-drink containers to their work areas.

The past practice was left behind when the employer moved into the new facility. Said the arbitrator:

The previous permission to bring soft drink containers to the work area must be regarded not as a condition of employment but as a matter which management saw fit to tolerate under the conditions of the old plant but found impractical and had the right to change under conditions in the new plant.[24]

The installation of a sound system over which radio programs were broadcast was reason enough for banning personal radios, which had been permitted for many years, in another case. The arbitrator reasoned that the company did not so much withdraw a benefit as change the method of providing the benefit.[25] The same analysis might be applied to a situation where an employer put an end to a longstanding practice of letting employees make their own coffee when it moved into a new building and made coffee available to them for the first time.[26]

---

[23]*Gulf Oil Corp.*, 34 LA 99, 100 (1959) (changing work week).

[24]*Kast Metals Corp.*, 70 LA 278, 282 (Roberts, 1978). A "changed conditions" claim did not help the company in *General Tel. Co. of Ky.*, *supra* note 20. There the company adopted a new rule prohibiting employees from leaving company premises during breaks, in part because break-time facilities had finally been provided on the premises. But because the company had allowed the old practice of allowing employees to go where they pleased on their breaks to continue for many months after the new facilities were made available, the arbitrator was not persuaded that changed conditions justified nullifying a 20-year practice.

[25]*Qonaar Corp.*, 62 LA 258 (Woodward, 1974).

[26]*Mac Tools, Inc.*, 73-1 ARB ¶8139, (Geissinger, 1973).

2. Abuse of a Benefit. Similar to the changed-conditions scenario is the case where employees take advantage of a practice to an extent that the company finds disruptive.

> **EXAMPLE:** For many years management had allowed employees to take hourly breaks from their heavy work and to visit the vending machines for refreshment. Declining productivity finally caused management to take stock, however, and it found that employees' breaks had been getting longer and longer—some as long as 20 to 25 minutes. It decided to allow only two 10-minute break periods. Soon several employees were suspended for violating the new rule.

The arbitrator made a distinction between past practice and the abuse of a practice. The longstanding practice of hourly breaks was entitled to recognition, and could be changed only through negotiation. But, said the arbitrator,

> inherent in every practice is the principle that it is not to be abused and that, if it is, reasonable corrective action may be taken. It cannot be inferred that the other party has accepted or acquiesced in the excesses constituting the abuse so as to make them binding. From the evidence it seems apparent that the men themselves changed the practice by more of them taking breaks and for longer and longer times.

The appropriate remedy, he determined, was restoration of the practice as it had prevailed before employees began to abuse it.[27]

To the arbitrator in another case, putting an end to employees' freewheeling practice of taking breaks at times of their own choosing was "not a change in working conditions, but a mere establishment of order in the plant." The employer was thus within its rights to start requiring employees to take their refreshment breaks at specified times.[28]

---

[27]*Metal Specialty Co.*, 39 LA 1265, 1269-70 (Volz, 1962). See also *St. Regis Paper Co.*, 77-1 ARB ¶8069 (Draper, 1977) (abuse of break times).

[28]*Dover Corp.*, 33 LA 860, 862 (McIntosh, 1959). In *Dover Corp.*, 69 LA 779, 781 (Edes, 1977), the arbitrator found that a past practice of letting employees make emergency telephone calls on company time did not preclude the adoption of a reasonable rule to discourage unnecessary, nonemergency calls.

The fact that the phones may have been used by employees for almost any reason they wished and for seemingly limitless periods does not establish such practice as a privilege. A privilege is the grant of *permission* to do something or enjoy a benefit which a person is then entitled to enjoy or exercise with immunity. The company never granted any such *right* to its employees.

3. Past Practice Not Proved. To be binding, a practice must meet three criteria—that it be clear and consistent, that it have continued for a long time, and that it be known to management. If any of these elements is missing, there simply is no past practice.

> **EXAMPLE:** The union challenged a new rule prohibiting employees from listening to radios during working hours, claiming it amounted to withdrawal of an established benefit. The contract required that all privileges previously enjoyed by employees be maintained, and the union asserted that radio playing had gone on for a long time. It turned out, however, that only six employees out of about 600 at the facility had actually played radios, and the union's witness was vague as to how often he saw radios in use. Supervisors were aware of radio playing only on special occasions—during the World Series, for example—when they were asked for, and gave, permission.

In reaching the conclusion that a binding past practice had not been established, the arbitrator gave particular weight to the fact that employees had not openly listened to radios without supervisors' consent. "[T]he evidence that the practice was subject to permission is significant to an evaluation of its strength as a 'privilege' and the reserved right of the Employer to say 'no' as well as 'yes.'"[29]

4. Prior Acceptance of New Rule by Union. If the union has acquiesced in the past when the employer issued new rules that changed longstanding practices, past practice may preclude the union from challenging a rule that is not to its liking on the ground that it was unilaterally adopted and therefore unreasonable. Thus, a union's claim that the employer could not unilaterally change rules that were in existence when the contract was signed was rejected by the arbitrator, who observed: "It is clear from the record that for some 16 years the Union did not question the right of the company to revise or amend plant rules." Stated another way, the union's prior acceptance of the employer's right to issue new rules during the contract term amounted to a past practice which the union was not entitled unilaterally to change.[30]

Similarly, if the union passes up an opportunity to bargain

---

[29]*Eastern Air Lines, Inc.*, 65-2 ARB ¶8545, 5038 (Yagoda, 1965). See also *Roadway Express*, 87 LA 465 (Chapman, 1986) (consideration of on-the-job injuries as basis for discipline).

[30]*Butler Mfg. Co.*, 50 LA 109 (Larkin, 1968).

over proposed changes in work rules, its inaction may be viewed as acceptance of the company's right to make the changes in question unilaterally. Such was the case where a union, over a period of years, declined to bargain over the substance of rules on absenteeism and tardiness but maintained its right to challenge the reasonableness of the rules through the grievance procedure. The arbitrator found that neither party intended to bargain over the substance of the absenteeism and tardiness program, and concluded that the union had waived its right to bargain by agreeing to the management clause, which reserved to the company the right to establish reasonable rules.[31]

5. Failure of Union to Lodge Timely Complaint. In the case where the employer discontinued a practice of individual coffee making (see Exception No. 1 above), the arbitrator noted that the employer had informed the union during the parties' most recent negotiations that it intended to change the coffee-making rule. The union, therefore, "had full and ample opportunity to question the matter had they so desired. The Company made its position clear prior to execution of the new Agreement. The ball was passed to the Union. There is no question here of a unilateral change following the execution of the Agreement."[32]

6. Extreme Necessity. The reasonableness of a rule change may be determined not only by what has gone on in the past but by what might happen in the future.

> **EXAMPLE:** Permitting employees to smoke at their work stations had been a practice for many years, and when the employer tried to enforce a new rule restricting smoking to break periods, the union's protest was loud and clear. Among its arguments: In past contract negotiations, the company had accepted the right to smoke as a subject for bargaining, and so it could not justifiably claim that it had an unrestricted right to make new no-smoking rules.

Though sympathetic to the union's past-practice argument, the arbitrator gave greater weight to compelling evidence that smoking was a serious fire hazard in the plant because of the presence of wood, plastic, masonite, sawdust, and other ex-

---

[31]*Litton Sys., Inc.*, 84 LA 688 (Bognanno, 1985). See also *Department of the Air Force*, 84 LA 617 (O'Grady, 1985), in which the arbitrator approved the employer's unilateral adoption of a rule requiring the wearing of seat belts, citing the union's failure to bargain over the rule when given an opportunity to do so.

[32]*Mac Tools, Inc., supra* note 26, at 3523–24.

tremely flammable materials. "Not only had there been several previous fires but the no-smoking rule was forcefully supported by the Fire Marshall and Company insurance carriers. Finally, the industry as a whole does not permit smoking in woodworking operations."[33]

3. Rules or Orders Affecting Employees' Life on the Job

"Business-Relatedness"—The Basic Test

> *Arbitrator Block:* The test of reasonableness . . . is whether or not the rule is reasonably related to a legitimate objective of management . . . .[34]

Many kinds of employee conduct are related to legitimate management objectives and therefore may be regulated by company rules. Whatever an employee may do—or not do—that affects any of the following elements is conduct in which the employer has a rightful interest:

- the employee's ability to perform his or her own job with reasonable efficiency and safety;
- the effective functioning of supervisory employees;
- the personal security of other employees;
- the security of the employer's product and other property.

Thus, such matters as absenteeism, tardiness, sleeping on the job, negligence, intoxication, insubordination, and theft all would clearly fall within the foregoing criteria. The problems that arise are typically found in the "gray area" that lies just outside the well-established boundaries of management's legitimate concern, namely, where the employee's *personal rights* (as he or she sees them) clash with the employer's *business needs* (as it sees them). Thus, the standard becomes whether the employer is pursuing a legitimate objective of management when it seeks

---

[33]*Lumber and Mill Employers Assn.*, 72-2 ARB ¶8612 (Koven, 1973).
[34]*Robertshaw Controls Co.*, 55 LA 283, 286, 70-2 ARB ¶8756 (1970) (falsifying employment application).

to control employee conduct or whether it has overstepped and invaded employees' legitimate private affairs.[35]

The following cases bring into focus the confrontation between the business needs of the employer and the personal rights of the employee and put in issue, as such cases always do, the criterion of whether the restrictions placed upon an employee's freedom of action serve a legitimate business need.

> **EXAMPLE NO. 1:** An employee had made a practice of bringing a small, battery-operated television set to work and watching TV at her desk during her lunch break. When her section chief discovered what she was doing, he ordered her not only to stop her lunchtime viewing but to stop bringing her TV onto company premises. Everyone in the employee's section had lunch at the same time, and no one had complained of being disturbed by her TV. The contract provided that employees might listen to music on radios or cassette players, as long as the productivity of the individual or the unit was not disturbed. The employer cited two "business needs" to justify the no-TV directive: first, the employee's television viewing might distract other employees; and second, it might make an unfavorable impression upon outsiders passing through her section.

Neither claim by the employer was persuasive to the arbitrator. He found that productivity could not be affected, since no one was working around the employee during the lunch break; and watching television was not likely to create a worse impression than card playing—a lunch-break activity to which the company had given its blessing. Since no clear business need was demonstrated, the arbitrator decided, the company had no good reason to interfere with the employee's right to use her free time as she wished. The order not to bring her TV set to work he found "particularly objectionable." "There is nothing inherently dangerous or distasteful or which automatically constitutes a nuisance in bringing a small TV on government prop-

---

[35] As summarized by Arbitrator Yagoda:

[T]he rule-maker, and in turn the arbitrator who judges the product of the rule-maker, must decide whether those rules are appropriate to the needs of the particular industrial community in which they are to operate. The obvious questions are: "Do they uphold the needed authority for getting things done? Do they preserve the orderly routine of the productive process? Do they articulate the accepted norms of interpersonal deportment and work application so as to minimize friction and encourage fruitful performance?"

The Discipline Issue in Arbitration—Employer Rules, 15 Lab. L.J. 562ff. (1964). Personal rights on and off the job are discussed in F. ELKOURI & E. A. ELKOURI, HOW ARBITRATION WORKS 725–802 (4th ed. 1985).

erty where the purpose for carrying the device might be completely unrelated to playing it on the job, such as taking it to a party or on a trip after working hours."[36]

EXAMPLE NO. 2: When the husband of a nursing home resident was assaulted and robbed at the home, the employer demanded that one of the orderlies, who was in the area where the crime took place and who had a criminal record involving both assault and robbery, take a lie-detector test. When the orderly refused to do so, he was discharged. The union argued that the orderly had a right to refuse to take the test under his right of privacy and that his criminal record was unfairly being held against him.

The arbitrator decided that the nursing home had a right to insist that the orderly take the lie-detector test. He observed: The employee's personal integrity and rights of privacy are and should be recognized and jealously protected in labor arbitration settings just as they are in criminal constitutional law. In either setting, however, the individual's right of privacy is not absolute, yielding instead at times to more compelling social interests.

Here, he reasoned, given the facts confronting it and its reasonable suspicion of the orderly, the nursing home had a right to expect the orderly to cooperate fully in its investigation.[37]

---

[36]*Social Sec. Admin.*, 71 LA 963, 968 (Ables, 1978). The same "overstepping" of management's prerogatives without adequate business justification has also been found in rules requiring employees to punch in and out at the foreman's desk when going to and returning from the rest room; see, e.g., *Gremar Mfg. Co.*, 46 LA 215 (Teele, 1965), and *Detroit Gasket & Mfg. Co.*, 27 LA 717 (Crane, 1956). For a different view, see *Penn Transformer Corp.*, 278 AAA 1 (Eischen, 1982). In *Ideal Cement Co.*, 13 LA 943 (Donaldson, 1950), a rule prohibiting employees from sitting down at any time during their shift was found to be unreasonable where operations were at least semi-automatic and therefore to an extent monotonous, temperatures at least at some spots were high, and floors were hard. ELKOURI AND ELKOURI, *supra* note 35, at 784–91, discuss the rest-room question and other rules that affect employees' privacy at the work place. See also R. W. Fisher, *Arbitration of Discharges for Marginal Reasons*, 19 MONTHLY LAB. REV. 1–5 (1968), and R. S. Wolters, *Moral Turpitude in the Industrial Environment*, 27 LAB. L.J. 245–54 (1976), for discussions of obscene language, "love triangles," and other issues involving the clash between an employee's personal and working lives.

[37]*Orthodox Jewish Home for the Aged*, 91 LA 810, 816 (Sergent, 1988). In *Eureka Co.*, 93 LA 513 (Wolff, 1989), the arbitrator held that a company could properly discipline an employee who inserted religious sermons under a rule requiring "quality of product acceptable to customers," although given the employee's good intentions he found that discharge was too stiff a penalty. See also *Grey Eagle Distribs.*, 93 LA 24 (Canestraight, 1989) (use of abusive language to members of public was cause for discharge, even though contract did not include this as a dischargeable offense); *Internal Revenue Serv.*, 92 LA 233 (Lang, 1989) (discourtesy to taxpayers and putting

Times change. Where the line is to be drawn between an employee's private rights and his employer's business needs is constantly being modified as a result not only of changing business circumstances but of changing conditions in society. No-smoking rules offer a good example. Until the past decade or so, the reasonableness of no-smoking rules was evaluated primarily according to whether smoking interfered with the needs of the business, for example, by causing a safety hazard or sanitation problem. Only recently has an individual's right to smoke at work been weighed against nonsmokers' right to clean air, as in a case where the employer tried to enforce a blanket no-smoking rule, relying on medical research suggesting that "second hand" smoke is a health hazard to nonsmokers.[38]

Drug Testing. Rules relating to drug testing of employees offer another striking example of society's changing attitudes toward the clash between business needs and employee rights. Not so long ago, a rule requiring that all employees undergo periodic blood or urine tests probably would have struck the average person—and almost certainly the average arbitrator—as unreasonable in the extreme. Now, because drug abuse has become a serious national problem, a growing number of public and private employers require that some or all employees undergo testing for drug or alcohol abuse.

The National Labor Relations Board has ruled that drug testing of current employees, but not applicants for employment, is a mandatory subject of bargaining under Section 8(d) of the National Labor Relations Act.[39] This means that an employer subject to Board jurisdiction[40] may not adopt a drug-testing

---

them on hold was cause for discipline, even though putting calls on hold was not specific violation of code of conduct).

[38]*Union Sanitary Dist.*, 79 LA 193 (Koven, 1982). The rule was reasonable in principle, the arbitrator found, but unreasonably applied where nonsmoking employees had no objection to their coworkers' cigarettes. See also *Akron Brass Co.*, 93 LA 1070 (Shanker, 1989), in which the arbitrator held that banning smoking altogether would be a "reasonable" managerial action only if there were proof that a total ban was needed to protect the health of nonsmokers. But see *Worthington Foods*, 89 LA 1069, 1079 (McIntosh, 1987), where the arbitrator approved a rule eliminating smoking within the work place on the basis of the "overwhelming and wide spread documentation of the probable adverse effects of smoking on particularly the non-user . . . ."

[39]*Johnson-Bateman Co.*, 295 NLRB No. 26, 131 LRRM 1393 (1989); *Cowles Media Co., Star Tribune Div.*, 295 NLRB No. 63, 131 LRRM 1404 (1989).

[40]NLRB jurisdiction is limited to private-sector employers. In *Regional Transp. Dist.*, 94 LA 117 (Hogler, 1989), the arbitrator found that a public employer's substance-abuse policy that included drug and alcohol testing was not invalid by reason of the

policy applicable to current employees without first bargaining with the union representing its employees, unless the union has waived its right to bargain over drug testing. After negotiating to impasse over the issue, an employer is free to put a drug-testing program into effect unilaterally—but not until the expiration of the current contract. The U.S. Supreme Court has held, meanwhile, that drug testing involves a "search" within the meaning of the Fourth Amendment to the Constitution but that regulations requiring blood, urine, and breath analyses might be "reasonable" even "in the absence of a warrant or reasonable suspicion that any particular employee may be impaired."[41] In other words, random testing of employees is not unconstitutional if required by an important governmental interest.

Within this framework, some arbitrators have held that an employer has the right to impose mandatory drug testing where there are compelling reasons for doing so. In a case involving a nuclear facility, the arbitrator approved a requirement that all employees having unescorted access to protected areas undergo random drug and alcohol testing. "Random testing without probable cause is abhorrent to any fair minded person," he stated. Nevertheless, "I specifically find that the paramount

---

employer's failure to bargain over it. Public-sector legal precedent, he said, was inconclusive with respect to the question of bargaining over testing programs, and the union failed to prove that the company had refused a valid demand that it bargain over the substance-abuse policy.

[41]*Skinner v. Railway Labor Executives Ass'n*, 489 U.S. 602, 633 130 LRRM 2857 (1989). Most arbitrators take the position that constitutional guarantees, including the Fourth Amendment protection against unreasonable search, have their origin in concerns about the abuse of governmental power and the need to protect individuals against the power of the state. (See Ch. 3, p. 186.) Thus the application of the *Skinner* decision is usually limited to public employers and to private employers that are subject to government regulations mandating drug testing in particular situations. How public employers are affected is illustrated by two rulings of the U.S. Court of Appeals for the Third Circuit. In *Transport Workers Local 234 v. Southeastern Pa. Transp. Auth.*, 863 F.2d 1110 (3rd Cir. 1988), the court upheld random drug testing of operating employees holding "safety sensitive" positions in a public mass transit system. But in *Bolden v. Southeastern Pa. Transp. Auth.*, 59 USLW 2614 (3rd Cir. 1991), the court ruled that subjecting a maintenance custodian to drug and alcohol tests of his bodily fluids before he was returned to work pursuant to an arbitrator's decision was an unreasonable search in violation of the Fourth Amendment. The custodian was not in a "safety sensitive" position, the court observed, and drug testing of employees in non-safety-sensitive positions may not be justified by the need to protect such employees from themselves. That the custodian had been told in advance that he would be tested for drugs, the court stated, did not lessen the invasion of his privacy.

public interest in maintaining a safe nuclear facility . . . out-
weighs the employee's right to privacy."[42] Another arbitrator
found a random drug testing program reasonable in view of the
existence of a widespread drug problem in the plant and the
fact that other control measures had proved ineffective. Safety
considerations in an extremely hazardous environment, he said,
justified the intrusion into employee privacy.[43]

In the absence of compelling reasons, such as the safety of
the public or extremely hazardous conditions, arbitrators for
the most part have found random testing of employees unreasonable.[44] What is normally required for a drug test is "probable

---

[42]*Arkansas Power & Light Co.*, 88 LA 1065, 1070-72 (Weisbrod, 1987). In *Boston Edison Co.*, 89-2 ARB ¶8406 (Fraser, 1988), the arbitrator ruled that the proposed addition of a drug screen to the annual physical examination of office and clerical workers at a nuclear power facility was improper. There was no evidence of a drug problem, the employees' work was not of a sensitive nature, and errors they might make would not have serious consequences.

[43]*Dow Chem. Co.*, 91 LA 1385 (Baroni, 1989). In *Day & Zimmermann, Inc.*, 94 LA 399 (Nicholas, 1990), an ammunition plant's random testing program was upheld in the face of a contention that it was more burdensome upon older employees. The arbitrator reasoned that employees under the influence of drugs could subject themselves and many coworkers and visitors to serious or fatal injuries. Implementation of several diverse programs based on workforce demographics, he said, would not promote safe and efficient operation of the plant.

[44]Arbitrator Jones, in *Southern Cal. Rapid Transit Dist.*, 89-1 ¶8117, 3588 (1988) (mandatory testing of driver involved in accident causing injury or property damage, regardless of fault):

> The vice of random drug testing is that it is deeply offensive to persons who are innocent of wrongdoing to be involuntarily subjected to a test the purpose of which is to require them to prove their innocence. It is perceived as an insulting affront to the personal dignity and sense of integrity of any innocent person, and particularly so when there are no implicating circumstances which raise any rational suspicion of guilt.

See also *Gem City Chem. Co.*, 86 LA 1023 (Warns, 1986) (unilateral addition of drug screen to physical examinations was invasion of privacy and unwarranted requirement to furnish confidential medical information); *Maple Meadow Mining*, 90 LA 873 (Phelan, 1988) (testing of active employees without cause held arbitrary and unenforceable); *Stone Container Corp.*, 91 LA 1186, 1191 (Ross, 1988) ("[r]andom testing of employees has been routinely declared an improper exercise of managerial control except in certain situations where the benefits derived from such invasive activity out-
weigh the legitimate right of privacy"); *Southern Champion Tray Co.*, 92 LA 677 (Williams, 1988) (mandatory blood testing as part of unilateral wellness program unreasonably invaded privacy of employees where no direct relationship between test and employees' jobs); *Phelps Dodge Copper Prods. Co.*, 94 LA 393 (Blum, 1990) (unilateral expansion of drug-control policy to include random testing constituted enormous invasion of privacy and went far beyond expression of residual managerial power); *Wheatland Farms*, 96 LA 596 (Nelson, 1991) (unilaterally modified program providing for random drug testing was unreasonable on its face). But see *Amoco Oil Co.*, 88 LA 1010, 1017 (Weisenberger, 1987):

> Until such time as a court of final jurisdiction rules on this matter, I find that drug testing of employees by employers is not prohibited so long as the program is

cause"—i.e., a reasonable belief that a person is impaired.[45] Thus, arbitrators have found it unreasonable to require employees to undergo a drug screen merely because they have been involved in an industrial accident.[46] They also have found it unreasonable to require all employees returning from layoff or leave of absence to undergo testing.[47]

Where it is established that a company may properly require testing, arbitrators have upheld discharge or other discipline of employees who refuse to submit to testing[48] or to provide urine specimens.[49] But just cause requirements apply in such cases— for example, the particular order to test must be reasonable, the employee must have been clearly warned of the consequences of refusal, any mitigating circumstances must be taken into account, and the employee must be treated the same as other employees similarly situated.[50] By the same token, a positive test result is cause for discharge or other discipline in accordance with the employer's substance abuse policy if the test was appropriately given, subject to the same just cause requirements. Note,

---

administered in a non-discriminatory and scientifically sound fashion; the employees have sufficient prior notice of the testing and the decision of the employer based upon a positive test result has a reasonable relation to the workplace.

[45]*Pepsi Cola Bottling Co. of San Diego*, 93 LA 520 (Randall, 1989). In *Fitzsimmons Mfg. Co.*, 92 LA 609 (Roumell, 1989), the arbitrator ruled that more than slight suspicion or conjecture was required to justify mandatory alcohol testing. Showing up for work with red, watery eyes and smelling of beer was not enough, where other classic signs were missing.

[46]*North County Transit Dist.*, 89 LA 768 (Collins, 1987); *Stone Container Corp.*, *supra* note 44.

[47]See, e.g., *ITT Barton Instruments Co.*, 89 LA 1196 (Draznin, 1987); *Harshaw/Filtrol Partnership*, 89-1 ARB ¶8204 (Rimmel, 1988); *Southern Cal. Rapid Transit Auth.*, 92 LA 995 (Concepcion, 1989); *Day & Zimmermann, Inc.*, *supra* note 43.

[48]*Albuquerque Publishing Co.*, 87-2 ARB ¶8427 (Fogelberg, 1987); *Crescent Metal Prods.*, 91 LA 1129 (Coyne, 1989); *Regional Transp. Dist.*, *supra* note 40; *Marigold Foods*, 94 LA 751 (Bognanno, 1990) (discharge approved, even though refusal to be tested was based on advice of lawyer). In *Faygo Beverages, Inc.*, 86 LA 1174 (Ellmann, 1986), however, the arbitrator made the point that a refusal to submit to testing cannot be taken as proof of intoxication. It is the refusal itself, not the presumed violation of a rule on alcohol or drug abuse, that provides cause for discipline.

[49]*Bowater Carolina Co.*, 92 LA 161 (Clarke, 1989) (failure to provide urine specimen over seven-hour period was cause for discharge, where employee's return to work after conviction of cocaine possession was conditioned on agreement to random testing); *Philadelphia Gas Works*, 89-2 ARB ¶8481 (Simpkins, 1989) (discharge justified for failure to provide urine specimen over three-hour period, where employee was known to have substance abuse problem and had previously provided specimens under similar conditions).

[50]See, e.g., *Gem City Chem. Co., Inc.*, *supra* note 44 (probable cause lacking, no notice); *Faygo Beverages, Inc.*, *supra* note 48 (test required on mere suspicion of misuse of alcohol); *Fruehauf Corp.*, 88 LA 366 (Nathan, 1986) (test order unreasonable).

however, that a positive test result is not proof of fault in an accident situation or of being under the influence of alcohol or drugs.[51]

Rules That Are Arbitrary, Capricious, or Discriminatory

Another way of saying that a rule or work order is unreasonable is to say that it is arbitrary, capricious, or discriminatory, three terms that mean much the same thing.[52] Broadly speaking, they mean simply that a rule or order has no legitimate business purpose.

"Arbitrary" sometimes has the additional connotation of being overly rigid, as, for example, in the case of the lunchtime television viewing discussed above (see p. 100). The arbitrator responded to the employer's objection that outsiders might get the wrong idea if they saw the employee absorbed in "the tube" by pointing out that she could be instructed to put her TV away if visitors were expected on a particular day. What was arbitrary was to impose a blanket prohibition when everyday business conditions did not necessitate it.

Excessive rigidity was also a problem with a rule stating that an employee who left his work station to make an emergency telephone call would be docked 15 minutes' pay and required to remain in the telephone area for the full 15 minutes. The rule was arbitrary because there was no connection between the 15-minute provision and the amount of time that might actually be needed to make a call. Moreover, the rule could have the

---

[51]See, e.g., *Southern Cal. Rapid Transit Dist.*, *supra* note 44, where the arbitrator held that the discharge of a bus driver who tested positive for marijuana after an accident was not justified. There was no evidence, he found, that the driver was impaired in any way on the day of the accident or at any other time during the preceding two years. But see *Roadway Express*, 87 LA 224 (Cooper, 1986), where discipline was upheld following a positive test result because the parties' contract equated "presence of drugs in grievant's system" with "under the influence."

[52]Arbitrator Roberts, in *Schien Body & Equip. Co.*, 77-2 ARB ¶8565, 5475 (1977) (smoking): "The differences in meaning when applied to a rule are so subtle as to render the substantive difference *de minimis*. The words are frequently used as synonyms." Arbitrator Teele, in *Brodie Indus. Trucks, Inc.*, 68-1 ARB ¶8356, 4223 (1968) (carrying concealed weapons), defined "arbitrary" as "something the Company did on a whim, or in a manner unrelated to its judgment of the circumstances"; while Arbitrator Benewitz stated, in *Penns Grove Upper Penns Neck Regional School Dist.*, 71-1 ARB ¶8234, 3780 (1971) (transfer): "A decision is arbitrary or capricious if a prudent man in the normal course of his affairs COULD NOT have arrived at the decision in question after consideration of the facts and circumstances of the situation." For further discussion of how these terms are related, see P. Prasow & E. Peters, Arbitration and Collective Bargaining 210–12 (1970).

result of keeping an employee away from work longer than necessary, frustrating the very purpose of the rule—to keep people on the job.[53]

Both "arbitrary" and "capricious" may also be used to characterize a rule or order that appears to reflect merely the whim or personal convenience of the employer, without regard to any legitimate business need. Arbitrariness and capriciousness are seen clearly in the following case:

> **EXAMPLE:** An employee arrived at work one day about 25 minutes before his shift was scheduled to begin. Parking was at a premium because many spaces were still occupied by employees on the shift before his and because construction in the area had temporarily reduced the size of the parking lot. Just as the employee pulled into a parking space, he was spotted by the supervisor, who at the same time noticed a foreman driving around looking for a space. The supervisor sent someone down to direct the employee to move his vehicle. The employer had no rule reserving certain parking spaces for supervisors, and the employee refused. About an hour into the shift, the supervisor sought the employee out and, even though the foreman had long since found a place to park, told the employee he would have to move his vehicle or go home. The employee again refused—and lost the rest of the day.

In the absence of a rule on parking, and given the fact that the foreman and everyone else had found spaces, the supervisor had no valid reason to tell the employee to move. The order amounted to "the sole determination of the supervisor that he wanted the employee to bend to his will and move his car. . . . While the arbitrator does not feel that this was a discriminatory matter, the capriciousness of it certainly borders close to being discriminatory." In trying to force the employee to yield to the supervisor, the employer went beyond what it could legitimately require of the employee.[54]

---

[53]*Dover Corp.*, 69 LA 779 (Edes, 1977). In *City of Richfield*, 89 LA 1040 (Bard, 1987), on the other hand, the arbitrator rejected a union contention that a rule requiring patrol officers to meet a monthly quota of at least one traffic citation per shift was arbitrary and thus unenforceable. He found that the police department was within its rights in establishing the quota, and the fact that all other officers were able to meet it led him to infer that an officer who failed to do so was guilty of nonfeasance.

[54]*General Refractories Co.*, 64 LA 1051 (McIntosh, 1975). The connection between "arbitrariness" and personal preference is also seen in *Big Star No. 35*, 73 LA 850, 857 (Murphy, 1979), involving the question of acceptable hair length for two grocery clerks. The arbitrator found that

> there was simply no evidence that the line drawn had any rational connection with the operation of the business enterprise. It was like saying that management

Safety Rules

What makes a safety rule reasonable? Here is the basic consideration:

> *Arbitrator Rutherford:* While it is true that the Employer may promulgate safety rules, these rules must be reasonably related to an alleged safety hazard. The mere fact that the Employer calls a new rule a safety regulation does not automatically give it legitimacy.[55]

Arbitrator Clare McDermott has set forth the following widely recognized standards:

> *Objective hazard.* "'Reasonableness' implies the existence of some objectively recognizable hazard of sufficient seriousness . . . ."

> *Geographic proximity.* "'Reasonable' also implies that the objectively recognizable hazard be in such geographic proximity to the employees that their compliance with the rule in question will contribute in some appreciable degree to reducing the risk involved."

> *Past experience.* "In deciding whether the hazard involved is real or only supposed, consideration must be given in significant measure to the number and severity of accidents, near accidents and hospitalizations resulting from the operation in question."

> *What measures have been taken.* "'Reasonable' carries with it consideration of what these parties have done about the particular hazards in these and other plants, and of what is being done by men and Management in . . . other industries faced with identical or similar hazards."

> *A balancing act.* "'Reasonable' implies that the ultimate question is one of judgment in balancing whether and to what extent compliance with the rule involves interference with employees' personal choices, comfort and convenience against the probability of injury and the severity of it if it does occur."[56]

"feels" that all male employees will now have crew cuts, or wear red wigs and those who disobey will lose their tenure, their seniority and their jobs.

[55]*Colt Industries,* 71 LA 22 (1978). The fact that the contract provides for consultation with the union on health and safety issues (e.g., through joint safety committees) normally does not dilute the employer's right to adopt or change safety rules unilaterally. See, e.g., *General Tel. Co. of Pa.,* 71 LA 488 (Ipavec, 1978). On the topic of safety rules and workplace safety generally, see F. ELKOURI & E. A. ELKOURI, HOW ARBITRATION WORKS 708–24 (4th ed. 1985). See also R. L. Britton, *Courts, Arbitrators and OSHA Problems: An Overview,* DECISIONAL THINKING OF ARBITRATORS AND JUDGES 260–84 (Proceedings of the 33rd Annual Meeting, National Academy of Arbitrators 1981).

[56]Cited in *Babcock & Wilcox,* 73 LA 443, 445 (Strasshofer, 1979).

Thus, when safety rules present a problem in the work place, a "balancing of interests" is required—the values or needs of the employee matched against those of the employer.

EXAMPLE: An employee was discharged for violating a company rule requiring that all employees wear pants for safety reasons after she persisted in wearing a skirt to work. Her reason: Her religious beliefs prevented her from wearing men's clothing at any time. The union contended that the supposed dangers of wearing a skirt or dress were greatly exaggerated and that the employee should have been permitted to wear a skirt with several pairs of long socks to protect her legs.

Was the rule reasonable? The arbitrator offered a model analysis.

First, a real hazard was demonstrated. The employee's legs were exposed regularly to sharp edges on machinery and pipes; metal bands, nails, and splinters on crates; and hot water and acid. The employer also introduced 15 injury investigation reports, all involving cuts and bruises to the lower part of the body sustained by employees moving and loading pipe—tasks that this employee performed.

Second, there was a reasonable connection between the hazard and the rule. While pants might not prevent injury completely, common sense and past accidents indicated that they offered more effective protection to employees' legs than the heavy socks the employee proposed to wear. As the company pointed out, socks would tend to hold hot water and acid close to the skin, rather than repel it as pants would; and they would still leave her thighs exposed.

Finally, the alternative was unsatisfactory. A dress or skirt would pose one of two problems. If a straight skirt, bending, squatting, and climbing would be restricted; and if flowing or flared, it would catch on protruding machinery and other sharp edges and perhaps cause a tripping problem.

Thus, the pants-only rule was reasonable, and safety considerations had to prevail over the employee's right to exercise her religious beliefs at the work place. The arbitrator sustained her discharge—though he directed the company to rehire her if she agreed to abide by its safety rules.[57]

---

[57]*Colt Industries, supra* note 55. For another instructive analysis of factors that make a safety rule reasonable, see *U.S. Steel Corp.*, 66-3 ARB ¶9039 (Dybeck, 1966), involving a requirement that employees wear side shields on their safety glasses. Analyzing more than 23 separate hazards the employer claimed the shields were designed to protect

Dress and Grooming Rules

> *Arbitrator Fleischli:* While it is true that an Employer may establish rules regarding dress and grooming that are reasonably related to a legitimate Employer interest, an Employer does not have an unlimited right to regulate the dress and grooming of employees for reasons related to personal preference or taste.[58]

Arbitrators are generally agreed that an employer may adopt dress and grooming rules that restrict employees' choices as to personal appearance, provided that (like other plant regulations) these rules serve a reasonable business purpose. For both dress and grooming rules, "business purpose" typically involves one or more of three considerations—*company image*, *safety*, and *sanitation*. The major difference between dress rules and grooming rules is that the employer is often held to a stricter standard of proof in the case of grooming rules, since these commonly place greater restrictions on employees' personal freedom (a beard, unlike a pair of jeans, cannot be left in the locker room until after work).[59]

How an arbitrator strikes the balance between a proper business purpose and employees' personal rights is illustrated by the case of an employee who objected to wearing a prescribed

---

than 23 separate hazards the employer claimed the shields were designed to protect against, the arbitrator agreed with the union that the rule was unreasonable with respect to some of those hazards; e.g., although he found that falling two-by-fours, slipping plate hooks, and protruding piles of plate and other items posed a real danger,

> [e]ye protection devices, and particularly side shields, can be expected reasonably to prevent injury to the eye only from material that is not so large and heavy that it would, on impact, demolish the entire, or substantial portions of, the protective device itself.

But flying wood and metal slivers, wires that break and flip when used in tying down loads, and blowing bits of slag constituted so great a hazard (much more hazardous to the eye than small bits of dust or other foreign material, as the union claimed) that neither the lack of previous accidents nor the 10% reduction in peripheral vision caused by the side shields could tip the scales in the union's favor.

[58]*Checker Cab Co.*, 62 LA 1107 (1974). Arbitrator Marlatt, in *Computer Science Corp.*, 87-2 ARB ¶8357, 5285 (1986):

> There is, of course, a limit on an employee's freedom to wear whatever he or she chooses in any work environment. Dress which is patently offensive to other employees may properly be banned (e.g., T-shirts printed with obscenities or racial slurs, or clothing soiled to the point of being noticeably unhygienic).

For a general discussion, see R. Valtin, *Changing Life Styles and Problems of Authority in the Plant—I. Hair and Beard in Arbitration*, and other articles in LABOR ARBITRATION AT THE QUARTER-CENTURY MARK 235–81 (Proceedings of the 25th Annual Meeting, National Academy of Arbitrators 1973).

[59]*Allied Chem. Corp.*, 74 LA 412 (Eischen, 1980).

arbitrator found that the employer could require him to wear the uniform because it had substantial business reasons for doing so—ease of identification, maintenance of public image, cost considerations—even though the employee's doctor said he experienced stress from wearing the uniform. But the employee had a right to wear a hat, not part of the uniform, to conceal a scar on the top and back of his head, since there was no business purpose in preventing him from doing this.[60]

Some employers, especially retailers, have a special kind of dress-code rule prohibiting the wearing of buttons or pins while on duty. Often such rules are used to prevent the display of union insignia. If sufficiently general in coverage—that is, if they apply to all buttons and pins, or all that do not have a specific business purpose—such rules may be found reasonable. But where a company forbade employees to wear buttons identifying them as shop stewards while they were on the selling floor, the arbitrator, after applying 27 "balancing" tests, found that the ban was unreasonable and ordered the company to stop enforcing it. The tests included such factors as the presence of anti-union animus, origin of the rule, consistency of its enforcement, interference with work or discipline, and public reaction; on balance, their application was found to favor permitting employees to wear their identifying insignia.[61]

Company Image Justification. Where employees are in contact with the public (customers or passengers, for example) and the employer wishes to maintain a professional, conservative, youthful, or other image, the company may reasonably require employees to present an appropriate appearance. Arbitrators have applied several criteria, however, in testing the reasonableness of rules that primarily concern image.

- Is the same or a similar style customarily worn in similar work settings?
- Are the restrictions consistent with contemporary community standards of appearance for the work in question?
- Do affected employees have regular contact with the public?

---

[60]*Veterans Admin.*, 89-1 ARB ¶8053 (Tilbury, 1988), with many citations to cases upholding the right of management to control dress or appearance of employees, as well as about as many disapproving dress or appearance requirements.

[61]*Pay Less Drug Stores, Northwest, Inc.*, 87-2 ARB ¶8311 (Tilbury, 1987).

The following three cases illustrate how these criteria have been applied:

EXAMPLE NO. 1: Although an individual with a neat and clean beard might well be considered well groomed by contemporary community standards, the company might still require employees to conform to a more conservative corporate image, with which beards might reasonably be considered out of step. In a case in the airline industry, the arbitrator found a no-beard rule reasonable on the ground that all airlines provide essentially the same service, and the employer could adopt a particular image in seeking a competitive edge.[62]

EXAMPLE NO. 2: Not every business depends upon public image to the same degree as an airline. No business justification was found for a rule requiring haulers of concrete to remain clean shaven, for example, since the business was not highly sensitive to public reaction, truck drivers had little contact with the public, and no adverse effect on the company's business was demonstrated. The grievant's dealings were with employees of the company's customers—some of whom wore some form of facial hair themselves.[63]

EXAMPLE NO. 3: Where the grievant, a radio room telephone operator, was only "indirectly visible" to persons visiting the company's general business office, and where customers entered his room only rarely to claim lost property, a rule prohibiting his wearing blue jeans was arbitrary and unreasonable. But since

---

[62]*Northwest Airlines*, 68 LA 31, 77-1 ARB ¶8075 (Bloch, 1977). But what makes for a conservative image must be considered in the light of community standards, according to the arbitrator in *Pacific Gas & Elec. Co.*, 55 LA 459 (Eaton, 1970). He decided that to most people in the employer's service area (the San Francisco Bay region), neat moustaches and goatees (but not full beards) would qualify as "conservative." See also *Bismarck Food Serv.*, 84 LA 870 (Ellmann, 1985) (management's right to require reasonable standards of neatness took precedence over vendor's claim that his garb had been tolerated for three decades); *Fisher Foods*, 88 LA 1084 (Richard, 1987) (company properly may forbid grocery-store baggers to wear "punk" or "new wave" haircuts under right to have reasonable standards of dress). On the question of whether dress and grooming rules that apply to only one sex amount to sex discrimination under Title VII of the 1964 Civil Rights Act, see Ch. 6, p. 346.

[63]*Arrow Redi-Mix Concrete, Inc.*, 71-1 ARB ¶8252 (Fleischli, 1971). In *City of Pana*, 86-2 ARB ¶8335 (Talent, 1986) the arbitrator held that the police chief could not properly refuse to allow an officer to grow a beard. There was no mention of beards in the city's restrictions on personal appearance, the arbitrator noted; the chief's action was based on personal prejudice and not on legitimate concern for the department's public image. But see *Fraternal Order of Police*, 89-1 ARB ¶8110 (Bittel, 1988) (okay to suspend police officer who persistently refused to have hair cut in accordance with regulations).

he had some public contact, the operator reasonably could be required not to wear clothes that were frayed, torn, or soiled.[64]

One caveat: An arbitrator probably will not rubber stamp a restrictive dress and grooming rule merely because the employer asserts that it needs to present a certain image to its customers. In questionable cases he or she is likely to require that the employer show that it has actually received customer complaints about the forbidden styles of dress or grooming or provide other concrete evidence that its rule is necessary.[65]

Safety Justification. One's personal preferences in dress and grooming must give way in the face of a threat to life or limb. Thus, a rule requiring a maintenance mechanic to shave his full beard was reasonable where his duties required him to make frequent use of an acetylene torch in awkward positions that made it difficult for him to protect his beard from flying sparks, and where the danger was increased by the presence of grease and oil.[66]

There are limits, however, even where safety is in issue. In order to qualify as reasonable on safety grounds, dress and grooming rules must serve a bona fide safety purpose, as measured by the criteria which have already been discussed in connection with safety rules in general. A rule prohibiting employees from wearing beads or finger rings (even wedding rings) would be reasonable if limited to occasions on which employees were around moving machinery. Sentimental value that can be "preserved only by continuous wearing" must give way to reasonable safety restrictions. However, a blanket prohibition upon the wearing of jewelry might be unacceptable if not all

---

[64]*Checker Cab Co.*, *supra* note 58.

[65]In deciding whether a rule prohibiting cemetery workers from wearing tank tops was necessary to preserve decorum in the cemetery, the arbitrator in *City of Racine*, 68 LA 473, 77-1 ARB ¶8143 (Schoenfeld, 1977), noted that no member of the public had ever complained about seeing employees wearing tank tops. He concluded that the rule was unreasonable because the ban on tank tops merely reflected the employer's view that T-shirts looked better. In *Grocers Supply Co.*, 72 LA 1055 (Williams, 1979), on the other hand, customers' complaints about an employee's wearing short pants while making deliveries were a factor in the arbitrator's deciding that the company could require him to be clad "from shoulder to ankle" while on duty. Actual evidence, not mere surmise, that airline passengers wished male flight attendants to be clean shaven was required in *Hughes Air Corp.*, 72 LA 588 (Bloch, 1979).

[66]*United Parcel Serv. of Pa., Inc.*, 58 LA 201 (Duff, 1971). See also *American Smelting & Ref. Co.*, 69 LA 824 (Hutchison, 1971).

job classifications worked where jewelry might pose a safety hazard.[67]

Sanitation Justification. This consideration is important mainly in companies whose business is the processing, delivery, and serving of food and in hospitals and other health care facilities. In a food processing plant, for example, rules that require employees to wear hair nets or hats, or limit the length of facial hair, would obviously be reasonable if designed to protect the product from contamination.[68]

Rules Covering Break Time

Rules that directly affect what employees may do on meal or rest breaks—whether on or off company property—generally have been regarded as unreasonable if no effect on production needs or the orderly running of the plant can be shown.[69] Where an employer required employees to take their coffee breaks standing up, for example, the arbitrator judged its rule unreasonable. There was no evidence, he pointed out, that their sitting would interfere with production. Management's assumption that employees would be more likely to loaf or to overstay their breaks if they sat down was not sufficient basis for the no-sitting rule.[70]

Where a real business need can be demonstrated, however, employees' break-time activity may justifiably be regulated. Two examples: (1) A rule against employees' sleeping during their breaks was held to be reasonable because of potentially hazardous conditions, where employees might have to respond quickly in an emergency, and stages in the production process might be missed if employees overslept.[71] (2) To prevent the public from getting the idea that its employees were "shirkers," which could

---

[67]*Babcock & Wilcox*, 73 LA 443 (Strasshofer, 1979). See also *Union Carbide Corp.*, 84-1 ARB ¶8231 (Goldman, 1984) (unreasonable to require employees to be clean shaven because of possibility they might have to use respirators requiring close fit to face).

[68]*E.g.*, in *Kellogg Co.*, 70-2 ARB ¶8876 (Shearer, 1970), where a rule prohibiting beards and setting limits on the length of mustaches, hair, and sideburns was found to be reasonable in order to protect the company's products, such as prepared breakfast cereals.

[69]Problems involving the application during break periods of rules primarily intended to govern work times (no fighting, no profanity, and the like) are discussed below, p. 134.

[70]*Ross Clay Prods. Co.*, 64-3 ARB ¶8933 (Kabaker, 1964).

[71]*Ashland Chem. Co.*, 62 LA 371, 73-2 ARB ¶8624 (Robins, 1974).

adversely affect its rate structure, it was reasonable for a public utility company to establish a rule that more than three of its trucks parked outside a coffee shop would be considered "congregating," for which drivers could be disciplined.[72]

4. Rules or Orders Affecting Employees' Private Lives off the Job

The Right of Privacy Versus Business Needs

In society generally the right of privacy or the right to be left alone is one of our most cherished freedoms. Something in the nature of a right of privacy frequently is an issue in the employment setting by reason of rules and regulations that restrict employees' personal freedoms on the job. The right of privacy becomes a far more pressing issue when the employer makes rules that tell employees how to lead their personal lives off the job—rules that affect something as consequential as where they may live or something as minor as where they may park their cars. Rules concerning where employees may reside,[73] whom they may marry,[74] how they conduct their financial af-

---

[72]*Peoples Gas Light and Coke Co.*, 73 LA 357 (Gundermann, 1979).

[73]Reasons typically cited are the need to report to work promptly in emergencies (see, e.g., *City of Appleton Water Comm'n*, 62 LA 1116 (Knudson, 1974), with citations to prior cases, and *Morrow Elec. Coop., Inc.*, 77-1 ARB ¶8022 (Draper, 1976)); and the need for first-hand knowledge of the employer's community, applied chiefly to government workers such as police and firemen (see, e.g., *City of Richland Center*, 66 LA 613, 76-1 ARB ¶8258 (Yaeger, 1976). In *Quaker State Corp.*, 92 LA 898, 89-2 ARB ¶8386 (Talarico, 1989), a requirement that new hires live within 10 miles of the plant was held not enforceable since it was not reasonably related to the efficient operation of the plant and the employer did not show a need for rapid response in emergencies.

[74]Among the reasons often cited in support of rules prohibiting the employment of spouses or other close relatives are the possibility of work scheduling problems and simultaneous sick and personal leaves (*American Mach. & Foundry Co.*, 68 LA 1309 (Novak, undated)); the possibility that an employee might have divided loyalties as between the company and a relative (*Robertshaw Controls Co.*, 55 LA 283, 70-2 ARB ¶8756 (Bloch, 1970); *Studebaker Corp.*, 49 LA 105 (Davey, 1967)); and possible carryover of marital disharmony to the work place (*National Tea Co.*, 69 LA 509 (Kelliher, 1977)). For cases in which these considerations were found not to apply (e.g., because the close relatives worked in different departments of a large organization), see *Sierra Pac. Power Co.*, 1975 ARB ¶8343 (Eaton, 1975), and *Hayes Indus., Inc.*, 65-1 ARB ¶8425 (Teple, undated). Accepted business justifications for close-relatives rules are discussed in I. Kovarsky & V. Hauck, *The No-Spouse Rule, Title VII, and Arbitration*, 32 LAB. L.J. 366–74 (1981).

fairs,[75] and other personal matters all have been considered reasonable because of special circumstances.

What is involved in discipline for off-the-job conduct is a balancing of the employee's right to lead his or her own life and the employer's right to run its business as profitably as it can. As a general proposition, arbitrators agree that, to the extent that employees' off-the-job conduct has a bearing either on their ability to do their jobs or on the employer's ability to run the business, the employer may properly be concerned with that conduct. As Arbitrator Shulman put it, "the jurisdictional line which limits the Company's power to discipline is functional, not physical."[76] In other words, the employer's right to discipline does not stop at the workplace door. But a strict standard of reasonableness must be met.

> *Arbitrator Kates:* As I see the matter, a rule, in order to be reasonable, such as a residency rule which applies not only during an employee's working hours but also during his more numerous hours away from work, must not unreasonably interfere with the employee's outside freedom, must bear a fair relationship to the employer's needs and legitimate business interests, and must not be more restrictive than those needs and interests reasonably require.[77]

Granting, then, that the employer may have a legitimate interest in employees' off-the-job behavior, the question becomes how far the employer may go before the employee may justifiably claim, "The line is drawn here." Arbitrators Hill and Kahn have identified the following five criteria applied by arbitrators in determining whether off-duty conduct is a legitimate concern of the employer:

---

[75]Rules subjecting employees to disciplinary penalties for wage garnishments are normally justified on the ground that garnishments may cause substantial clerical work and financial loss to the employee. See, e.g., *Alcan Co.*, 67-2 ARB ¶8475 (Daugherty, 1967); *Lear Siegler, Inc.*, 63 LA 1157 (McBrearty, 1974); and *Simon Stores, Inc.*, 49 LA 569 (Koven, 1967), for a review of circumstances in which penalties for garnishments have been upheld. An employer's right to penalize employees for garnishments is restricted by both Title III of the Consumer Credit Protection Act and the 1971 Federal Truth in Lending Act, which provide that an employee may not be discharged by reason of the fact that his wages have been attached for any one indebtedness. See also *Owens-Illinois*, 71-1 ARB ¶8066 (Brown, 1970), and *Delta Concrete Prods. Co.*, 71 LA 538, 78-2 ARB ¶8435 (Bailey, 1978).

[76]Quoted in *New York City Health & Hosps. Corp.*, 76 LA 387, 388 (Simons, 1981).

[77]*Wilkinsburg-Penn Joint Water Auth.*, 73-1 ARB ¶8117, 3452 (1973) (residency rule).

- the characteristics of the employer—whether the employer has high public visibility so that adverse publicity might affect its reputation or sales;
- the location of the employer—e.g., a prominent employer in a small town may legitimately be more sensitive to scandal based on off-duty misconduct than an anonymous employer in a large metropolitan area;
- the nature of the misconduct—whether it is violent or destructive and whether, if criminal, it is a misdemeanor or a felony;
- the occupation of the offender—whether there is a link between his or her duties and responsibilities and the outside conduct;
- the extent and kind of publicity—whether the public's attention has been focused on the misconduct.[78]

"Moonlighting" Rules

The process of balancing an employee's right to lead his or her own life and the employer's business interests is well illustrated by cases in which employees are barred from working elsewhere, or "moonlighting," one of the most common types of off-the-job rules. Typically, rules of this type have been held to be reasonable on the basis of either adverse impact or a conflict of interest.

An outside job can have adverse impact on the primary employer, for example, by causing excessive absenteeism or tardiness or both, or by preventing the employee from giving his full attention and effort to his primary job.[79]

An excellent illustration is offered by a case in which the pressure of working two jobs caused a bus driver not only to miss time from his primary job but to falsify the reasons for his absences and accept sick leave benefits under false pretenses. This was truly a case where the employee could be said to have

---

[78]M. Hill, Jr., & M. L. Kahn, *Discipline and Discharge for Off-Duty Misconduct: What Are the Arbitral Standards?*, ARBITRATION 1986 121–54 (Proceedings of the 39th Annual Meeting, National Academy of Arbitrators 1987).

[79]Arbitrator Roberts, in *Amerace Corp.*, 68-1 ARB ¶8238, 3832 (1968):

In return for wages paid, employees are under an obligation to regularly report for work and, to the best of their abilities, meet the physical demands placed upon them by their duties. If they are engaged in other activities which in any way make it difficult or impossible to fulfill these responsibilities, management acts with full justification when enforcing prohibitions against such outside conduct.

"two-timed" his employer and his time card as well, and he could hardly expect to continue his double life when the primary employer found out what he was doing.[80]

But every "moonlighting" case has to be considered on its own facts. In a case that presented obvious parallels to the case of the two-timing bus driver, a pressman was discharged after he had been spotted pumping gas and performing other chores at a gas station of which he was part owner. He had taken the day off because of an ankle injury. What distinguished his case from that of the bus driver was that the chores he performed at his gas station were much less strenuous than his regular work. Furthermore, at the gas station he could sit down and rest for long periods of time. Thus, unlike the bus driver, he neither worked his outside job at his primary employer's expense nor falsified his reasons for being absent. Because it was not adversely affected, the primary employer had no right to restrict the pressman's outside work.[81]

A conflict of interest is created when an employee goes to work for a competitor of his primary employer and might divulge his employer's trade secrets to the competitor or put technical skills, developed at his employer's expense, at the competitor's disposal.[82] This reflects the well-known maxim that "a man cannot serve two masters."[83]

---

[80]*Alameda-Contra Costa Transit Dist.*, 76 LA 770 (Koven, 1981). See also *Interlake Steel Corp.*, 70-1 ARB ¶8444 (Helbling, 1970), and *Harvard Mfg. Co.*, 69-1 ARB ¶8314 (Kates, 1968). Even where no actual misconduct had taken place, an employee was required to choose between his primary job and his outside employment where he had had a serious attendance problem even before taking on his second full-time job. "[I]t is reasonable to assume that he 'couldn't cut it' if he were permitted to continue holding his second job . . . ." *Goodyear Tire & Rubber Co.*, 1975 ARB ¶8135, 3560 (Di Leone, 1975).

[81]*Amerace Corp.*, *supra* note 79. See also *Standard Brands, Inc.*, 69-2 ARB ¶8633 (Trotta, 1969), where discharge was held too severe for an employee who, while on sick leave, tended bar for a few hours at a friend's tavern without pay because he enjoyed the work, lived alone, and considered the tavern his "second home." In *Randle-Eastern Ambulance Serv., Inc.*, 65 LA 394 (Sherman, 1975), the employer improperly discharged a driver for riding a tiger in a race track exhibition while on injury leave in violation of a company rule requiring employees to seek advance permission before accepting outside work. The driver knew from prior experience that the tigers were lethargic, and, since there was no actual race, the danger of further injury was almost nil.

[82]In *Sperry Rand Corp.*, 57 LA 68 (Koven, 1971), the arbitrator set forth the following criteria (with additional case citations): (1) whether the quality or quantity of the employee's work suffered; (2) whether trade secrets or skills were involved; (3) whether direct evidence was present that the employee caused or intended to cause harm to his employer or that his actions were illegal; (4) whether the employee operated in direct competition with the employer or sold a competitor's products; (5) whether the employee indicated that he knew he was doing wrong by being secretive about his outside employment.

[83]Arbitrator Dworkin made the further point, in *Ravens-Metal Prods., Inc.*, 39 LA 404 (1962), that if the conflict of interest is direct, actual detriment does not have to be

EXAMPLE: Two heavy-duty-truck mechanics set up a repair business on their own time. The mechanics performed the same type of work as they did for their employer, and they pursued their enterprise in a regular and consistent manner. They even went so far as to solicit business from company customers, using their knowledge of the company's pricing policies to underbid the company.

The activities of these grievants convinced the arbitrator that discharge was justified. What they did amounted to more than an occasional moonlighting job or an unpaid favor for a friend. They took in substantial amounts of money, and on one occasion they used their employee discount privileges to purchase parts for some of their own repair work. In effect, they were competing with their employer, and application of the conflict-of-interest rule was proper.[84]

In sharp contrast was a case where the meat manager of a large supermarket was suspended for helping out his son, who had recently opened a small grocery store. The son's shop could not reasonably be characterized as a real competitor of the supermarket, since it was located 10 miles away and could not hope to undercut supermarket prices or offer the same variety of products or services. Moreover, the manager did not receive any compensation for instructing his son in meat cutting. His suspension was therefore set aside.[85]

The kinds of considerations discussed above lead to other questions about the balance to be struck between an employee's obligations to the employer and his right to lead his life as he chooses. For example, suppose a rule only prohibits outside work that interferes with an employee's primary job and does

---

demonstrated in order for a conflict-of-interest rule to be enforced. As Arbitrator Keller put it in *Mechanical Handling Sys., Inc.*, 26 LA 401, 403 (1956):

> Work for competing employers tends to breed suspicion and distrust and to destroy the confidence and sense of cooperation between employer and employee. . . . Granting that actual detriment to the principal employer may not exist, the possibility of its existence must be present in the minds of both employers, no matter how scrupulous the employee is to see that no harmful consequences result to his primary employer.

[84]*Alaska Sales and Serv. Co.*, 73 LA 164 (Axon, 1979). See also *Ravens-Metal Prods., Inc.*, *supra* note 83; *Heinrich Motors, Inc.*, 68 LA 1224 (Hildebrand, 1977); *Country Club Markets*, 85 LA 286 (Bognanno, 1985).

[85]*Great Atl. & Pac. Tea Co.*, 75 LA 640 (Calhoon, 1980). Absence of a meaningful competitive situation also led to discipline's being revoked in *Albertsons's, Inc.*, 65 LA 1042 (Christopher, 1975); while in *William Feather Co.*, 68 LA 13 (Shanker, 1977), a folding machine operator's knowledge of the company's operating methods was found to be too rudimentary to be of any benefit to a competitor, so that there could be no conflict of interest sufficient to justify discharge.

not specifically state that employees must report outside employment. Does an employee have a duty voluntarily to disclose that he has taken on a second job? It could be argued that unless his outside job causes him either to start missing work or reporting late, or not to "put out" on the job, what he does on his own time is none of the employer's business. On the other hand, one might argue that the employer is entitled to be told anything that might even potentially affect the quality of an employee's work performance, permitting the employer to decide whether the employee's "moonlighting" is acceptable.

Other "Private Life" Issues

The always touchy and sometimes controversial issues that are raised when an employer attempts to discipline an employee for off-the-job activities are illustrated by the following situations, which give a sense of the limits upon the employer's right to intrude into an employee's personal life.

Would it be reasonable for an auto dealership to prohibit employees from purchasing and driving cars made by a competitor? For a mechanic in the service department, no valid employer interest ordinarily would be present. Where a mechanic purchased the car of a competing auto maker, and there was no showing that he had ever "bad-mouthed" his employer's product to customers or to fellow employees, an arbitrator found that discharge for driving the car of his choice was not justified.[86]

For a car salesman, on the other hand, the result might be different. It could reasonably be argued that it is desirable that a salesman like and use the product he sells in order to persuade others to buy that product. If, for example, a Ford salesman drives a Chevy, a prospective buyer might well wonder whether to believe a sales pitch touting the merits of Fords.

Can a company validly preclude an employee from marrying a nonemployee? An arbitrator answered "yes" to that question when an airline ticket sales clerk married the owner of a travel agency. The clerk had access to privileged information (on forthcoming rate changes and similar matters) that could help her husband and potentially hurt the employer's business with other travel agents. Under these circumstances the airline could remove her from her job since her marriage created a conflict of interest.

---

[86]*Paul Swanson,* 61-2 ARB ¶8303 (Gochnauer, 1961).

The clerk's discharge was not sustained, but the company was permitted to transfer her to a different job where she would not be privy to sensitive information.[87]

This case also raises questions about the duty of disclosure. Most arbitrators would agree that an employee in the ticket sales clerk's position has an obligation to be frank with the employer when a potential conflict of interest arises. But what about a situation in which two employees took employment tests at another company on their own time and failed to tell their employer they were planning to do so? Did they have a duty to disclose their intentions? Clearly, an arbitrator ruled, their failure to disclose was not an act of disloyalty, and the employer did not have just cause to terminate them.[88]

Suppose the company adopts a rule stating that an employee will be discharged if his political activities pose a threat of violence. Would the rule be reasonable? This question raises the issue of community standards. The conflict between an employer's right to protect its business and its employees from harm, and an employee's right to exercise his or her constitutional right to free speech, was raised by the discharge of a bus driver who was also a local Ku Klux Klan leader.

The arbitrator gave full consideration to the driver's argument that his political beliefs and off-duty political activity were protected by the First Amendment and no business of the employer's. But the paramount consideration to him was not the driver's beliefs but the fact that he had made inflammatory public speeches in support of those beliefs. The speeches created a clear and present danger of violence involving persons and property on buses driven, or believed to be driven, by this driver; a strike by fellow drivers; and an economic boycott by company patrons, about half of whom were black. All of this justified the driver's termination.[89]

This case graphically illustrates, first, how every employer operates within the framework of pressures that can be applied

---

[87]*Northwest Airlines, Inc.*, 72-1 ARB ¶8290 (Koven, 1972). Many cases in which an employee was terminated or transferred following marriage to an outside party have involved the airline business, in which "singles only" policies for flight attendants at one time were common. However, in this industry, too, it has been the general rule for some years that a concrete business need must be demonstrated if no-marriage rules are to be upheld. See, e.g., *Southern Airways, Inc.*, 47 LA 1135 (Wallen, 1966); *Allegheny Airlines, Inc.*, 67-1 ARB ¶8244 (Kelliher, 1967).

[88]*Perkins Contracting Co.*, 92 LA 408 (Hilgert, 1988).

[89]*Baltimore Transit Co.*, 47 LA 62 (Duff, 1966).

by the community, whose standards may have a direct and negative impact on the company's ability to operate peacefully and profitably; and second, how community standards help determine how far an employer may go in intruding into an employee's private affairs. For some arbitrators, to whom constitutional guarantees of free speech are paramount, community standards might not play so decisive a role. If an arbitrator were to put the driver back to work in a case like this one, the question then would be what remedy the employer would have if, for example, a boycott did result.

Application of Job Rules to Employees off the Job

An employee may also become subject to disciplinary action if he or she engages in activities off the job that are defined as misconduct under the company's work rules. The test of reasonableness is again that of "business-relatedness."

> *Arbitrator Ferguson:* The general rule is that an employee upon being employed by a company places himself under the jurisdiction of the employer so far as their relationship is concerned.
>
> While it is true that the employer does not thereby become the guardian of the employee's personal life and does not exercise parental control, it is equally true that in those areas having to do with the employer's business and reputation, the employer has the right to terminate the relationship if the employee's wrongful actions injuriously affect the business.[90]

> **EXAMPLE:** When an employee went to work in the employer's Assembly Department, a coworker jumped to the conclusion that she was literally "throwing her weight around"—bumping other employees when passing through the narrow aisles. The employee in turn, felt insulted by uncomplimentary personal remarks the coworker made about her privately and in the presence of other employees. Finally deciding she had had enough, the employee attacked her tormenter one day during the lunch break. While the latter was walking toward a local restaurant, the employee leapt upon her from behind with a fingernail cleaner in hand, scratching her face and cutting her clothes. The ensuing struggle, in which two other employees became involved, was finally broken up by a bartender from a nearby tavern. Both women were discharged.

---

[90]*Inland Container Corp.*, 28 LA 312, 314 (1957). For a short general discussion of the off-premises-misconduct problem and some additional case citations, see F. ELKOURI & E. A. ELKOURI, HOW ARBITRATION WORKS 656–58 (4th ed. 1985).

This altercation is a classic case of off-premises misconduct that justifies discipline because of its connection to the employees' working lives. Said the arbitrator:

> Such relationship to employment resulted from the geographical nearness of the attack, the time of the attack, the origin of the difficulty, the fact that other employees should have expected to become and did become involved, and in the fact that plant operations, morale and efficiency were actually disrupted.[91]

Another example of off-premises misconduct that directly affects an employer's business is an attack upon a supervisor that grows out of the working relationship. The general rule is that a supervisor is entitled to do his job without fear of harm or reprisal whether on or off company premises.[92] However, arbitrators have sometimes found that discharge was too severe a penalty for behavior that did not result in physical injury to members of management.[93]

---

[91]*Victorian Instrument Co.*, 40 LA 435, 436 (Kates, 1963).
Generally speaking, personal misconduct of an employee if it occurs away from the plant, and if it is not connected with the employment, and if it is not of such nature as to reflect upon the employer's reputation or business or to impair plant operations, morale, safety or efficiency, ordinarily is not the proper subject of disciplinary action against the employee by the employer. These conditions, however, were not present in the instant case.
For counter examples, see *Modine Mfg. Co.*, 52 LA 128 (Sullivan, 1969) (insufficient evidence that employee's use of profanity and abusive language to coworkers away from work place would lead to disruptions on job); *Gamble Bros.*, 68 LA 72 (Krislov, 1977) (discharge too harsh for employee who smoked small quantity of marijuana away from plant on lunch break and was not under the influence); *Honeywell, Inc.*, 68 LA 346 (Goldstein, 1977) (no evidence that fight over off-premises card game involved "bad blood" that would affect participants' ability to work together).
[92]In *NCR, Appleton Papers Div.*, 70 LA 756, 759 (Gundermann, 1978), the grievant had vandalized his supervisor's home and automobile, and the arbitrator reasoned that his return to work would have a "negative impact on supervisory personnel thus affecting the Company's ability to direct the workforce." In *B. F. Goodrich*, 84 LA 240 (Nicholas, 1985), a company rule barring threats against or intimidation of management personnel was held applicable to threats made off company premises to a doctor who had testified for the company in a prior arbitration. And in *Lima Elec. Co.*, 84-1 ARB ¶8252 (Modjeska, 1984), suspension was held proper for an employee who made late night calls to supervisors' homes consisting of obscene utterances and belching. But in *Integrated Metal Technology, Inc.*, 89-1 ARB ¶8052 (Ellmann, 1988), a rule barring "threatening, intimidating, coercing or interfering with employees or supervision" was held not to apply to obscene phone calls allegedly made by an employee to a coworker and to a supervisor, or to an altercation between the employee and a coworker during off-duty hours. The arbitrator found no nexus between these actions and the employment relationship and no understanding that the rule would apply to off-duty conduct.
[93]In *Keebler Co.*, 92 LA 871, 89-2 ARB ¶8562 (Roumell, 1989), discharge was found to be too severe for an employee who assaulted a supervisor while off duty and threatened him and perhaps his family. The assault involved pushing not intended to inflict harm, the confrontation ended when the supervisor told the employee to stop,

Alcohol and Drug Use off the Job

Does the employer have a right to discipline an employee because he or she drinks or uses drugs while off duty? The answer to this question is clearly "yes" if—but only if—the off-duty behavior has some effect on the employee's work or on the company's business. Thus, if an employee develops an absentee-ism problem because of alcohol or drug abuse, discipline is appropriate—but only because of the absenteeism, not because of the off-duty behavior as such.[94] Also subject to discipline is the employee who shows up for work under the influence of alcohol or drugs, or whose ability to do his or her job is otherwise adversely affected by off-duty behavior.[95] Whether there is an adverse effect on the employer's business frequently depends upon whether the employee gets in trouble with the law or the misconduct becomes public knowledge (see below).

When there is no job connection, however, the company will be on shaky ground if it disciplines an employee for off-duty use of alcohol or drugs. "[A]n employer does not have the right to attempt to control an employee's conduct away from the work place. As pertinent to a drug abuse case, the ingestion

---

and the threats were not considered extreme. In *Buck Co.*, 89-2 ARB ¶8491 (Howard, 1989), discharge was held not justified where the assault was mostly verbal and any physical force was controlled, the employee apologized a few minutes later and civil conversation then ensued, and the supervisor did not even report the incident to the company.

[94]See, e.g., *American Airlines, Inc.*, 46 LA 737 (Sembower, 1966) (failure to work or call in because jailed for being drunk); *Cities Serv. Oil Co.*, 41 LA 1091 (Oppenheim, 1963) (inability to work because of involvement in automobile accident while driving drunk); *Lick Fish & Poultry*, 87 LA 1062 (Concepcion, 1986) (inability to work because of drug-induced psychosis); *Kimberly-Clark Corp.*, 88-2 ARB ¶8424 (Ross, 1988) (poor attendance caused by depression and alcohol abuse); *Boston Edison Co.*, 89-2 ARB ¶8310 (Bornstein, 1988) (refusal of leave of absence and subsequent discharge for absenteeism of employee serving alcohol-related jail sentence).

[95]In *New York Dep't of Correctional Servs.*, 87 LA 165 (Babiskin, 1986), the arbitrator ruled that two correctional officers were properly discharged after they were observed "snorting" cocaine in a night-club parking lot while off duty. He found that there was a direct and substantial relationship between their off-duty conduct and their fitness to perform their duties as correctional officers. See also *Wayne State Univ.*, 87 LA 953 (Lipson, 1986) (university facilities manager properly discharged after being arrested for possession of cocaine, since position required substantial contact with community and success depended upon leadership and trust attributes; *Angelica Corp.*, 62 LA 1227 (Bryan, 1974) (reason to believe truck driver guilty of drunk driving while off duty might do the same while on duty); *Motor Cargo*, 96 LA 181 (Jones, 1990) (use of cocaine at home while in possession of company truck was ground for discharge, since employee would have returned truck the following morning while still impaired had he not been arrested on drug charges and employer would have been liable for injury or damages resulting from employee's operation of truck).

of drugs must act to impair work performance."[96] Even where an employee gets into trouble with the law for drug use, an arbitrator may see no just cause for discharge if there is no adverse effect upon the employment relationship. Thus, discharge was held improper where an employee's arrest and conviction for marijuana and cocaine possession was not shown to have any effect on either his work or the company.[97]

A safe rule (applicable to other types of off-duty behavior as well): Discipline for the work-related consequences of off-duty alcohol- and drug-related misconduct, not the misconduct itself.

Criminal Arrests and/or Convictions[98]

It is not difficult to appreciate the emotional reaction that an employer may have when an employee gets into trouble with the law—even when the conduct involved is not a felony or other serious legal matter. The company may become uneasy about the employee's reliability; it may feel that an individual who breaks the law (any law) cannot be relied upon to perform

---

[96]*Pennwalt Corp.*, 89 LA 585 (Kanner, 1987). Since the employee in question was absent for three days because of off-duty cocaine use, the arbitrator found cause for discipline, though not discharge. In *Crucible Materials Corp.*, 94 LA 540 (Harkless, 1989), the arbitrator held improper the discharge of an employee for refusing to agree to conditions for continued employment, including completion of a drug-rehabilitation program, following the disclosure during an annual physical exam that he had smoked marijuana daily for 15 years. The employer, the arbitrator found, had reasonable safety concerns, but the plant rules contained no prohibition upon off-duty drug use, the employee had no notice that he would be required to enter the rehabilitation program, and there was no evidence of impairment on the job.

[97]*Virginia Elec. & Power Co.*, 87 LA 1261 (Jewett, 1986). In *U.S. Customs Service*, 88-1 ARB ¶8171 (Jedel, 1987), the purchase and use of marijuana by a customs inspector was found not to be cause for discharge. Though his off-duty activity was in conflict with his job duties, there was no public awareness and no adverse effect on job performance; hence the agency as a whole was not harmed. Moreover, a two-year delay between management's awareness of what the inspector was doing and the decision to fire him was "wholly inconsistent with the proper administration of discipline." A two-month suspension, however, was approved. See also *Lockheed Aeronautical Sys. Co.*, 92 LA 669 (Jewett, 1989) (discharge of employee indicted for off-duty sale of marijuana not for just cause because no nexus to employment relationship shown); *United States Penitentiary*, 96 LA 126 (Hendrix, 1990) (off-duty arrest for possession of cocaine and marijuana not just cause for discharge of corrections officer who voluntarily underwent counseling and rehabilitation, where there was no evidence public or inmate population were affected). But see *Union Oil Co.*, 87-2 ARB ¶8360 (Doering, 1987) (company may discharge employee dealing drugs without waiting to catch him doing so on company property); to the same effect, *Trane Co.*, 96 LA 435 (Reynolds, 1991).

[98]For distinctions among arrests, indictments, and convictions, see Ch. 5.

his job and conform to the standard of conduct the company requires at the workplace.

But even illegal activity cannot be a cause of discipline unless that activity has the same direct connection to the employer-employee relationship as the noncriminal kinds of off-premises misconduct already discussed.

> *Arbitrator Ables:* Most people would not argue with the proposition that an employer is justified in discharging an employee from his job if he has been convicted of a felony such as rape. Conversely, most people would argue with the proposition that an employer is justified in discharging an employee from his job for his first unaggravated offense of speeding. And yet both offenses are in violation of law.
>
> The difference between the two examples, of course, lies in the belief of the general public that a person who commits rape has such personality disorders as to make it unlikely he will do his job properly whatever the job—even if there is absolutely no chance that he will commit rape while on the job.[99]

The following three factors, as set forth by Arbitrator Kesselman,[100] have been widely accepted as criteria for determining when off-premises criminal activity justifies discharge or other form of discipline:

---

[99]*Eastern Air Lines*, 45 LA 932, 933 (1965). In *Muskegon Heights Police Dep't*, 88 LA 675 (Girolamo, 1987), the arbitrator held that even reprehensible conduct, if off duty, is not cause for discharge unless there is a link between the conduct and the employment relationship. At issue was the fate of a police officer who privately abused his girl friend because he found her in bed with another man. A not-guilty jury verdict was not binding upon him, the arbitrator commented, but it increased the department's burden of persuasion in defending its decision to fire the officer. See also *Indiana Bell Tel. Co.*, 93 LA 981 (Goldstein, 1089), where an employee's arrest on drug charges, subsequently dismissed, was found not to be cause for discharge under the employer's substance-abuse policy. The employee only accepted mail delivery of marijuana addressed to her husband, and the spousal relationship was not automatically detrimental to the employer. The arbitrator found suspension pending disposition of the criminal charges justified, however, despite the employee's 24-year unblemished record. But see *Alameda/Contra Costa Transit Dist.*, 87 LA 842 (Concepcion, 1986), where the arbitrator upheld the discharge of a bus driver convicted of off-duty, off-premises possession of cocaine with intent to sell, regardless of any impact of the misconduct on the employer's operations. The basis for his ruling was company rules providing that "conviction of a felony while employed by the district shall be sufficient cause for discharge."

[100]These criteria were set forth by Arbitrator Kesselman in *W. E. Caldwell Co.*, 28 LA 434 (1957). Well-reasoned analyses of criminal misconduct also appear in *Inspiration Consolidated Copper Co.*, 60 LA 173 (Gentile, 1973); *New York City Health & Hosps. Corp.*, 76 LA 387 (Simons, 1981); *Iowa State Penitentiary*, 89 LA 956 (Hill, 1987); and *City of Shawnee*, 91 LA 93 (Allen, 1988).

"Behavior harms company's reputation or product." *Barroom brawling:* A corrections officer who drank too much at a local bar and was arrested for making a false "officer in distress" call to local police was properly disciplined for violating a rule against employees bringing discredit on the employer. That incident, on top of the officer's prior history of "barroom brawling" and flourishing his revolver, "hardly reflected credit on the Department's or a Peace Officer's public image as an instrument and adjunct of law enforcement."[101]

Shoplifting: Two airline stewardesses were properly discharged after they were caught shoplifting at a department store, in accordance with a company rule which made criminal misconduct, on or off duty, subject to discipline. Although the amount involved was small and the stewardesses were not prosecuted, their commission of a criminal act while wearing their uniforms not only tarnished the company's public image but led to serious embarrassment and inconvenience for two other stewardesses who were shopping in the same store and were mistakenly identified as the guilty pair and apprehended by store officials later that day.[102]

---

[101]*New York State Dep't of Correctional Servs.*, 69 LA 344, (Kornblum, 1977). In *U.S. Air, Inc.*, 91 LA 6 (Ables, 1988), a flight attendant's conviction of off-duty possession of a controlled substance (Percoset) was held to be cause for discharge, even though the attendant was placed on probation. The airline's rules allowed discharge for serious misdemeanors, the attendant failed to use the employee assistance program, and grand jury and FAA investigations into airline-employee drug use created a sufficient nexus between the off-duty conduct and the airline's business.

[102]*American Airlines, Inc.*, 71-2 ARB ¶8497 (Turkus, 1971). See also the following cases in which identification of the misconduct with the company was held to justify discharge: *Bay Area Rapid Transit Dist.*, 79-1 ARB ¶8015 (Koven, 1978) (arrest of security officer for drawing gun on and engaging in altercation with stranger); *Cameron Iron Works*, 73 LA 878 (Marlatt, 1979) (sale of stolen property); *Southern Bell Tel. & Tel. Co.*, 75 LA 409 (Seibel, 1980) (obscene phone calls to company customer by outside repairman); *Polk County, Iowa*, 80 LA 639 (Madden, 1983) (correction officer's conviction for drunk driving). But in *Eastern Air Lines, Inc.*, 64 LA 828 (Wyckoff, 1975), a pilot's off-duty arrest for assault while under the influence of marijuana and alcohol did not justify his discharge for bringing discredit on the employer, since the incident received no publicity and took place 3,000 miles from his home base. The lack of any adverse effect also led to the grievant's reinstatement in *K.L.M. Royal Dutch Airlines*, 66 LA 547 (Kupsinel, 1975) (possession of marijuana); *Indian Head, Inc.*, 78-2 ARB ¶8319 (Rimer, 1978) (possession of marijuana); *Fairmont Gen. Hosp.*, 91 LA 930, 88-2 ARB 8556 (Hunter, 1988) (shoplifting); *Lockheed Aeronautical Sys. Co.*, 92 LA 669 (Jewett, 1989) (off-duty sale of marijuana); and *W. R. Grace & Co.*, 93 LA 1210 (Odom, 1989) (arrest for possession of cocaine with intent to sell, conviction of possession of drugs and paraphernalia). In *Fairmont General Hosp., supra*, the arbitrator found that a long suspension was justified because by shoplifting the employee, a nurse, violated the implied covenant of good faith and fair dealing in her employment contract with the hospital.

"Behavior renders employee unable to perform his duties or appear at work, in which case [discipline] would be based on inefficiency or excessive absenteeism." *Drunk driving:* An employee's drunk driving conviction did not in itself justify discharge, an arbitrator found, since he did not operate a motor vehicle in the course of his work as a laborer, and the company had never put employees on notice that a drunk driving arrest off premises would lead to discharge. Nevertheless, some discipline was called for. The employee was incarcerated following his arrest and not only missed work but failed to call in to say he would be absent, in violation of a company rule.[103]

"Behavior leads to refusal, reluctance or inability of other employees to work with him." *Assault with a deadly weapon:* An employee who attacked his wife with a knife, and who had previously served time for another serious crime, was discharged because the company decided that keeping him on the job would run the risk that he might engage in violent behavior on the job, a risk that it was obligated to avoid in the interest of maintaining safe working conditions. The arbitrator sustained the company's action.[104]

The presence of any of the foregoing conditions makes criminal activity a reasonable cause for discharge or discipline. In judging situations of this type, most arbitrators have held that discipline is justified, even where no adverse impact has

---

[103]*Lamb Glass Co.*, 32 LA 420 (Dworkin, 1959). See also *National Screw & Mfg. Co.*, 33 LA 735 (Dworkin, 1959) (fact that police advised employee to remain at home while rape charges were being investigated did not excuse his failure to report to work); *Ampco Pittsburgh Corp.*, 75 LA 363 (Seinsheimer, 1980) (being jailed on manslaughter charge rendered employee not available for work and absent without proper cause); *Boston Edison Co.*, 89-2 ARB ¶8310 (Bornstein, 1988) (company could deny employee six-month leave of absence to serve alcohol-related jail sentence and discharge him for absenteeism). In *New York Dep't of Correctional Servs.*, 87 LA 165 (Babiskin, 1986), the discharge of two officers observed "snorting" cocaine was upheld not because they were prevented from working but because their behavior called into question their fitness to perform their duties. Similar result in *Wayne State Univ.*, 87 LA 953 (Lipson, 1986) (possession of cocaine). And in *CSX Hotels, Inc.*, 93 LA 1037 (Zobrak, 1989), the arbitrator upheld the discharge of an employee who stole tires from a nearby service station because the employee had access to guest rooms in the hotel.

[104]*Albritton Eng'g Co.*, 66-2 ARB ¶8552 (Hughes, 1966). In *Alabama Power Co.*, 88 LA 425 (Baroni, 1987), the arbitrator held that it was reasonable for a company to discharge an employee arrested in a highly publicized drug raid in part because of the publicity and also because coworkers expressed concern about working with him in a hazardous setting. See also *Pearl Brewing Co.*, 48 LA 379 (Howard, 1967) (supervisors' concern that return to work of employee charged with widely publicized violent crime would lead to altercations with other employees and stated fear of giving him orders were valid grounds for discharge).

actually materialized, if there is a strong likelihood of harm to the employer's business,[105] or if the grievant's misconduct is very serious or closely related to the nature of his job.[106]

But where the harm to the company's business is only potential, some arbitrators have held that the company must produce concrete evidence, e.g., that the grievant's criminal act will hurt its reputation or will cause other employees to refuse to work with him or her.[107] It is not enough merely to predict that the company will suffer.

> *Arbitrator Turkus:* The right of management to suspend or discharge an employee for conduct away from the plant which is neither work connected nor work related is dependent upon the readily adverse effect of that conduct, if any, upon the employer's business or its plant operations.
>
> Mere surmise, conjecture or speculation as to the adverse effect upon its operations or its business because of the nature *per se* of the alleged misconduct, is insufficient.[108]

> *Arbitrator Nicholas:* [I]n order to satisy the just cause standard in a discharge case tied to off-duty misconduct, Management . . . must show that said actions significantly affected the employee's work life relative to his performance and/or usefulness in the workplace. Such a showing may be made via the presentation of evidence which clearly reveals that Company's name and reputa-

---

[105]See, e.g., *Great Atl. & Pac. Tea Co.*, 45 LA 495 (Livengood, 1965) (bootlegging); *Union Oil Co.*, 87-2 ARB ¶8360 (Doering, 1987) (sale of drugs off company property; no need to wait for activity on company property); *College of St. Scholastica*, 96 LA 244 (Berquist, 1991) (arrest on charge of domestic abuse and prior conviction of criminal sexual conduct; strong likelihood college would be held civilly liable in event of misconduct toward female students).

[106]E.g., *Inspiration Consolidated Copper Co.*, *supra* note 100 (employees convicted of stealing property similar to company's product); *Great Scot Food Stores, Inc.*, 73 LA 147 (Porter, 1979) (food-stamp fraud related to employee's job as meat cutter).

[107]E.g., *Michigan City Educ. Ass'n*, 89-1 ARB ¶8169 (Eagle, 1989), where the discharge of a school teacher after he was convicted of drunk driving, public intoxication, and resisting arrest was held not for just cause. There had been no adverse effect on his job, his jail time coincided with school holidays and weekends, and any negative impact on the school system or the community was speculative and not based on concrete evidence.

[108]*Raytheon Co.*, 66 LA 677 (1976) (indictment for second-degree murder). Perhaps even more stringent was the test applied by the arbitrator in *City of Columbus, Ohio*, 88-1 ARB ¶8196 (Miller, 1988). A fireman who pled guilty to mailing obscene materials was discharged under a rule that forbade any act "which tends to bring into disrepute the Division of Fire." Reducing the discharge to an eight-month suspension, the arbitrator noted that although the public knew of the situation, the employee's conviction was not due to violent behavior, so he was not a threat to the public. Moreover, he had a good 13-year employment record, and he was under psychiatric care for obsession with obscene materials.

tion in the community has been dealt a detrimental blow; that the perception and regard for Company's product has been lessened; or that the employee's ability to perform in the workplace and/ or with his fellow employees has been impaired . . . .[109]

EXAMPLE: A lineman for a public utility was discharged after being convicted of second-degree manslaughter—killing in self-defense. The lineman shot the victim, a friend of his, at a time when the two men had been drinking heavily and after the friend had threatened to kill him and had reached for his own gun. The employer contended that discharge was necessary because keeping the lineman on the job would cause hostility in the community and because fellow employees would be afraid to work with him.

Proof was the crucial factor in the arbitrator's decision. When an employee commits a violent crime such as manslaughter, an employer has good reason to be concerned that he might again become violent on the job, or that employees might be afraid to work with him. But in this case the evidence undercut the persuasiveness of that normally reasonable concern. The shooting had been accidental; leading citizens who knew the lineman testified that they believed he had paid his debt to society, that they would trust him in their homes, and that general community sentiment favored his return to the company. That testimony, coupled with his 34 years of good service, persuaded the arbitrator to reinstate the lineman without back pay.[110]

5. Reasonable Rules Unreasonably Applied

The Basic Test

Arbitrator King: If reasonable regulations are unreasonably interpreted or applied, the result is the same as if the regulations were unreasonable on their face.[111]

Arbitrator Dash: Employees can be expected to respond much more favorably to a rule that is enforced with reasonable recogni-

---

[109]*Amoco Oil Co.*, 91 LA 158, 163 (1988) (cocaine possession).

[110]*Alabama Power Co.*, 66 LA 220 (Caraway, 1976). See also *Par Beverage Corp.*, 35 LA 77 (Schmidt, 1960) (assault with deadly weapon); *Lockheed Aircraft Corp.*, 69-2 ARB ¶8836 (Foster, 1969) (arrest for rape); *John Morrell & Co.*, 90 LA 38 (Concepcion, 1987) (possession of drugs).

[111]*Aro, Inc.*, 64-2 ARB ¶8500, 4778 (1964) (negligence).

tion of the variety of acts against which the rule is directed than they can to a rule which is enforced with absolute rigidity regardless of the situation involved.[112]

Six Unreasonable Applications of Reasonable Rules

1. Application of the Rule Does Not Serve the Purpose of the Rule. When the application of a reasonable rule is challenged, the key question usually is whether the purpose or intent of the rule is reasonably fulfilled in the particular context in which the employer seeks to apply it.

> **EXAMPLE:** For several years an employer had had a rule requiring employees to wear safety glasses in the factory area during working hours. Then, as part of a tightening up on enforcement of the rule, the employer notified the union that employees would be required to wear glasses on their lunch breaks as well as when actually working. There was no cafeteria or break area on company premises; if employees chose not to leave the plant, they ate their lunches anywhere on the premises. The union protested that the glasses were uncomfortable and that applying the rule to lunch periods, when no machinery was operating, was unreasonable.

The employer's rule was a reasonable one, but inspection of the factory areas convinced the arbitrator that if no machinery was operating near an employee there was little danger. Thus it was unnecessary to make employees wear the heavy glasses continuously throughout a long day.[113]

What the company should have done here was figure out what was a "safe" distance from machinery. Requiring the wearing of glasses within that distance would reasonably have fulfilled the purpose of protecting employees' eyes from hazards.

Purpose likewise was the test of whether a rule was reasonably applied where two employees were discharged for violating

---

[112]*Pennsylvania Greyhound Bus Co.*, 18 LA 400, 403 (1952) (intoxication).

[113]*Bauer Bros. Co.*, 48 LA 861 (Kates, 1967). Safety rules commonly pose application problems of this kind, as illustrated by *Allied Chem. Corp.*, 74 LA 412, 417 (Eischen, 1980), where the arbitrator found that a new rule requiring all employees to be clean shaven was "divorced from the underlying rationale and justification which gives it validity, i.e., a demonstrated actual or potential need to wear a respirator." The employer's "bare assertion" that all employees would have occasion to wear respirators either in routine work or in emergencies was not supported by solid evidence; thus the rule was not properly applied to employees who did not work in designated respirator areas. See also *U.S. Steel Corp.*, 66-3 ARB ¶9039 (Dybeck, 1966) (safety glasses rule).

a no-gambling rule after they had made an oral bet on company premises. "Obviously, the Company is not concerned with the moral implications of a bet between two employees on the World Series. What it is concerned about, however, is a regular practice of betting on Company time or property which leads to lost time and bad feeling between employees." The employees were reinstated with back pay.[114]

2. Rule Is Applied to Employees in a Discriminatory Manner. A reasonable rule may also be unreasonably applied if the employer applies it to some employees but not to others. Thus, where a rule that prohibited radio playing was enforced at only one of the company's several plants, the arbitrator concluded that the application was discriminatory. There was no convincing evidence that radio playing presented safety problems or interfered with production only at the one plant.[115] Similarly, a rule forbidding bargaining-unit employees to smoke or eat at their work stations was found to be unreasonable since it was not applied to non-bargaining-unit employees who had equal opportunity to contaminate delicate equipment.[116]

3. Rule Is Applied in an Arbitrarily Restrictive Manner. In many instances, a rule that is reasonable on its face is interpreted too narrowly, with no accommodation to the circumstances in which it is applied. A case in point is presented by a contract provision stating that employees must dress "within the bounds of good taste" and in conformance with "the standards of the general

---

[114]*Lockheed Aircraft Corp.*, 13 LA 433, 438 (Aaron, 1949). See also *Trane Co.*, 12 LA 559 (Graff, 1949) (rule against defacing company property not properly applied to smearing of grease on men's room screen, since little damage was done and acts were committed in spirit of horseplay); *Cranston Print Works*, 36 LA 179 (Maggs, 1960) (rule prohibiting falsification of time card not properly applied absent intent to defraud company); *Badger Concrete Co.*, 68-2 ARB ¶8509 (Krinsky, 1968 (rule requiring employees to be clean shaven for reasons of safety and sanitation not properly applied to nonproduction employees); *Wilkinsburg-Penn Joint Water Auth.*, 73-1 ARB ¶8117 (Kates, 1973) (rule requiring employees to reside within employer's service area not properly applied to clerical employee, since office employees not subject to emergency call); *Contico Int'l*, 93 LA 530 (Cipolla, 1989) (discharge reduced to suspension where employee found sleeping during slack time had been working more than 60 hours per week for more than a month).

[115]*Anaconda Aluminum Co.*, 51 LA 281 (Dolson, 1968).

[116]*Aro Corp.*, 66 LA 928 (Lubow, 1976). In *Union Sanitary Dist.*, 79 LA 193 (Koven, 1982), application of a no-smoking rule to employees in one building but not another was found to be arbitrary and discriminatory, where the purpose of the rule was to protect the rights of nonsmokers, who worked in both buildings. See also *City of Racine*, 77-1 ARB ¶8143 (Schoenfeld, 1977) (no-tank-top rule improperly applied to some cemetery workers but not to others who performed similar work).

business community in similar office settings." The employer interpreted that provision to mean that male employees had to wear neckties. An employee who was disciplined for not conforming argued that "good taste" did not necessarily demand a tie, and he produced evidence that ties were not always worn in similar office settings. The arbitrator agreed, also pointing out that a flamboyant costume that *included* a loud tie might on occasion be in poor taste.[117]

4. Discipline Is Imposed Under a Rule That Has Nothing To Do With Discipline. Rules and regulations that are not disciplinary in nature generally cannot be applied for disciplinary purposes. An employee who missed more than 18 months of work because of serious illness was terminated because the pension plan required retirement board approval of a leave of absence lasting more than one year. The contract's disciplinary provisions, however, placed no limit on length of sick leave, leading the arbitrator to hold: "This penalty, in the context of its usage, affects the employee's rights under the Company's voluntary fringe benefits package and cannot possibly be stretched or twisted to cover or include disciplinary action such as loss of seniority."[118]

5. Compliance With the Rule Is Impossible.

> *Arbitrator Lilly:* The right and duty to establish meaningful rules . . . should also be measured by whether or not such rules and procedures can be accomplished by the employee with the means and tools at hand to enable him to carry out his appointed duties.[119]

That proposition is the key to a case in which an employee failed to comply with a company rule requiring the immediate removal of a door plate after the unloading of a railroad car. The company had neither provided him with the necessary equipment to do the job himself nor given him the authority to direct a fellow employee who worked with that equipment to

---

[117]*Social Sec. Admin.*, 67 LA 766 (Smith, 1976). Similarly, in *Monroe Concrete Co.*, 56 LA 15 (Weckstein, 1971), a rule requiring employees to present a neat appearance was applied too restrictively to an employee who wore a clean and closely trimmed beard. In *Mississippi Valley Gas Co.*, 71-1 ARB ¶8359 (Nicholas, 1971), a rule requiring maintenance employees to live in the employer's headquarters area was unreasonably applied when the employer defined "headquarters area" arbitrarily in terms of county boundaries and not actual distance from the service area.

[118]*Great Atl. & Pac. Tea Co.*, 48 LA 910 (Keefe, 1967).

[119]*Gulf Printing Co.*, 61 LA 1174, 1178 (1974).

take care of the job for him.[120] In another graphic example of the same principle, discipline for violation of a rule requiring employees to remain at their work stations until the sound of the quitting bell was set aside. The reason: Neither the employee in question nor anyone else could hear the bell over the high noise level in the plant.[121]

6. Employees Are "Off the Clock." The question of whether a plant rule may be applied when employees are on company premises but "off the clock"—during breaks or at other nonwork times— is closely related to questions involving the reasonableness of rules specifically applicable to break-time activity. (See above, p. 114.) The difference is that it is the reasonableness not of the rule itself that is in question but of the application of a reasonable rule when no work is being performed.

The safety-glasses rule cited above is one example of an arbitrator's finding that applying a rule during breaks was not reasonable. The basic criterion in this and similar cases is by now a familiar one: To what if any degree is the employer's business or the employer-employee relationship affected.

> **EXAMPLE:** A bus company had a rule prohibiting drivers from being under the influence of alcoholic beverages on company property. After a long night's drive, one driver checked in, went to a local VFW hall, where he had a sandwich and two bottles of beer, and then returned to the company-owned dormitory provided for the drivers. A supervisor learned he had been drinking, and the driver later was fired for being under the influence on company premises. The union protested that, although the company certainly had the right to prevent its drivers from driving while intoxicated, it was an "unsupportable use of management's prerogatives" to apply its no-alcohol rule so as to interfere with employees' private lives.

The arbitrator disagreed with the union, at least in part. The rule was reasonable to the extent that it prevented the riding public from encountering a tipsy driver and thereby losing confidence in the company. But he agreed that in this case the rule was not reasonably applied. The driver, even if

---

[120]*Id.*

[121]*Visador Co.*, 73 LA 578 (Seifer, 1979). See also *Weatherhead Co.*, 56 LA 159 (Maxwell, 1971) (rule requiring employees to produce doctor's certificate for even one-day absence was unreasonably harsh, since obtaining certificate in many circumstances might be impossible); *General Elec. Co.*, 74 LA 125 (Clark, 1979) (grievant's discharge for not working at his assigned task overturned because necessary tools not available).

intoxicated, was not on company property to which the public was admitted, nor was he on duty at the time. Some sort of discipline was justified; but discharge was too severe a penalty, since the risk to the company's business was minimal.[122]

But every off-the-clock case is treated on its own facts.

EXAMPLE: An employee had a little too much to drink one night and, as a lark, entered company property without authorization and drove his motorcycle through the plant. The employer fired him for violating rules against appearing on company premises under the influence and against horseplay. The union contended that, because the employee was not working at the time, his action was "outside the course and scope of his employment" and the employer had no right to discipline him.

In contrast to the preceding case, this grievant's behavior had an immediate and serious impact on the employer. His caper not only posed a danger to employees and to the employer's product (plate glass) but "was calculated to impair and to undermine the authority of management in its relationship with its employees." Discharge was not an unreasonable penalty.[123]

Rules That Invite Unreasonable Application

Rules That Are Vaguely Worded. Any work rule potentially may be applied unreasonably. Some rules, however, by their very phrasing tend more than others toward arbitrary, or discriminatory, application. The chief problem is that the rule is phrased vaguely, and the circumstances under which it is to be applied

---

[122]*Pennsylvania Greyhound Bus Co.*, 18 LA 400 (Dash, 1952). See also *Williams Bros. Markets*, 64 LA 528 (Combs, 1975) (discharge not justified where grievant was observed kissing store's produce manager in break area, since conduct was not so open and notorious as to affront fellow workers or customers).

[123]*Pittsburgh Plate Glass Co.*, 67-2 ARB ¶8559 (Dworkin, 1967). See also *Glass Containers Mfrs. Inst.*, 70-1 ARB ¶8140 (Dworkin, 1969), where the arbitrator upheld the application of plant rules prohibiting immoral acts on company property, as well as improper conduct during nonwork hours that affected an employee's job, to an employee's showing up at a softball game wearing a sweatshirt bearing the words "fuck you." The game took place at a company-owned recreational facility, and the arbitrator rejected the union's argument that an employee is exempt from discipline during off hours. See also *AMF Lawn & Garden Div.*, 64 LA 988 (Wyman, 1988) (drinking beer in company parking lot during meal break cause for discharge); *Marathon Petroleum Co.*, 93 LA 1082 (Marlett, 1989) (grievant subject to discharge for having loaded handgun and several half-empty bottles of alcoholic beverages in car on company parking lot). For citations to other cases holding that off-duty employees have a general obligation to obey plant rules, see F. ELKOURI & E. A. ELKOURI, HOW ARBITRATION WORKS 658 (4th ed. 1985).

are not clearly spelled out. Following are three examples of work rules reflecting that problem.

> *Substantial reasons for absence—who decides?* An unwritten policy required employees who sought permission to leave work early to substantiate their reasons for leaving, and left it to individual supervisors to decide whether proof was to be supplied in advance or when an employee returned to work (or even whether it was to be required at all). Such a policy is unreasonable, the arbitrator found, because "it is susceptible to whimsical application, and can be invoked simply because a Foreman might not like an employee."[124]

> *Resignation after marriage—under what circumstances?* The statement in a company booklet that it "may be necessary" for an airline flight attendant to resign if she married another company employee "leaves the enforcement of the policy at whim." Since the policy did not make clear what circumstances would make resignation necessary, it was "fatally uncertain and illusory" and unenforceable.[125]

> *Too long in the rest room—what's a good excuse?* At issue was a rule limiting the number of minutes an employee might spend in the rest room and providing that discipline would be imposed for exceeding that limit if the foreman decided the employee had no valid excuse for longer use. The limit was reasonable in itself, the arbitrator found, but the rule was unreasonable because it did not define what was a good excuse. Leaving the definition up to individual foremen invited arbitrary and discriminatory administration of the system.[126]

Rules That Quantify Misconduct. Unreasonable application is often a problem when an employer uses strictly numerical measures of substandard productivity or performance—units of output or numbers of errors—and of other types of misconduct that are easily quantifiable. Such standards are not customarily re-

---

[124]*McLouth Steel Corp.*, 64 LA 1216 (Keefe, 1975). See also *Charley Bros. Co.*, 84-1 ARB ¶8128 (Hunter, 1984), in which a proposed rule regarding overtime notification was found to be unreasonable. The rule provided that a message could be left at a phone number supplied by the employee, but it did not state how a senior employee was to exercise his option to refuse or accept overtime work if a family member answered the phone, or how a junior employee was to avoid being penalized if he did not receive a message or if his family refused overtime work on his behalf.

[125]*Western Air Lines, Inc.*, 70-1 ARB ¶8120 (Wyckoff, 1969).

[126]*Detroit Gasket & Mfg. Co.*, 27 LA 717 (Crane, 1956).

garded as arbitrary or unreasonable in themselves; problems that develop ordinarily stem from inflexible administration.[127]

The following three cases offer garden-variety examples of how "the numbers" work or do not work.

> *How many operating errors?* To measure and penalize substandard peformance, a company had a three-step plan that provided for a warning for an employee's first operating error, a three-day suspension for the second error, and discharge for the third error. That plan replaced an earlier one under which neither supervisor nor employees could predict what penalty might be imposed for unacceptable work performance. When the grievant was discharged for his third operating error, he protested that his performance was improving and that his supervisor did not adequately train him for some of his assignments.

The arbitrator did not question the company's right to adopt the three-step plan, nor did he question the advantages of predictability. But, he said, "that goal in itself within the framework of sound industrial relations is an incomplete goal since 'uniformity' must operate within more basic considerations of fairness, equity, and nondiscrimination."

Examining the facts of this particular case, the arbitrator asserted that quality as well as quantity must be taken into account to meet the requirements of reasonable cause. The company did not allow for the fact that the grievant's three errors were successively less serious and less costly to the company. Moreover, the company itself contributed to his inadequacies by failing to train him adequately for the jobs in which he made his errors. Hence the discharge was not justified.[128]

> *How many trips to the rest room?* When a time and motion study revealed that employees were slowing down the production line by visiting the rest room in large numbers, the company decided that chickens moving along the processing line could not wait. A 20-trip limit was placed on the number of rest-room trips an employee might take between scheduled breaks in a four-week period. The union protested that such a limit was unfair.

---

[127]An example is provided by rules concerning wage garnishments. Arbitrator Daugherty pointed out, in *Alcan Co.*, 67-2 ARB ¶4679 (1967), that a policy that provides for automatic discharge after a fixed number of garnishments may not be sufficiently flexible to protect employees from mistaken or illegal attachments.

[128]*Chevron Chem. Co., Ortho Div.*, unpublished opinion (Koven, 1967).

Emergency rest-room trips may not seem susceptible to the numbers format. Nevertheless, the arbitrator agreed with the company that the right to make such trips at any time was not absolute. The limit of 20 was reasonable on its face, he found, pointing out that (1) the number had not been picked arbitrarily but was consistent with medical opinion and (2) exceptions were provided for in extenuating circumstances, e.g., certain illnesses.

There was a catch, however. The rule was not being administered reasonably, since the extenuating circumstances for which it provided were not recognized in practice by management, and the opinion of a female supervisor was arbitrarily overruled by a male supervisor with no concern for employees' needs. The arbitrator directed the company to apply the rule flexibly by giving fair consideration to mitigating circumstances.[129]

> *How many warnings justify discharge?* Company rules provided that continued misconduct resulting in four warnings in a 12-month period would result in discharge. The grievant's poor tardiness record earned him three warnings, all advising him that if he did not reduce his tardiness level to 5 percent he would be fired. He collected a fourth warning not long thereafter, but not for tardiness—he was caught out of his work area without permission and then two days later failed to show up at a safety meeting he had been directed to attend. The company fired him in accordance with the four-warning rule.

The arbitrator revoked the grievant's discharge because the fourth warning did not satisfy the notice test. The first three warnings were all directed toward his tardiness problem; he had never been told explicitly that violation of some other rule also would lead to discharge. On the larger question of whether the four-warnings rule was reasonable, the arbitrator quoted an unpublished decision by Arbitrator Louis Yagoda as follows:

> I find such a policy to be too mechanistic and superficial as an automatic justification. Surely, some difference must be made by such factors as the nature and degree of the offenses for which the warnings had been given and such other factors as length of service of the employee involved.
>
>   I do not believe that a mandate is imposed on the arbitrator to support management solely because it has been "consistent"

---

[129]*Cagle's Poultry and Egg Co.*, 73 LA 34 (Roberts, 1979).

when that "consistency" embraces strict arithmetical quantity . . . rather than evaluation of the quality of the offenses, separately and cumulatively.[130]

Problems have also arisen when employers have decided to play "by the numbers" in formulating rules to control absenteeism and tardiness.[131] In question here are so-called no-fault absence policies under which employees are penalized for being absent or tardy a fixed number of times (whether a "time" is defined as a day, part of a day, or two or more consecutive days).

No-fault policies that operate "by the numbers" are often challenged on the ground that they are arbitrary, since they do not take into account the different reasons for which employees may be absent or late. Employees whose absences are beyond their control (as in the case of illness) are penalized in the same manner as those who malinger.

Do arbitrators agree that no-fault policies are in principle unreasonable? As a rule, no. Some arbitrators have ruled that such plans are unreasonably rigid,[132] but most have allowed them to stand for the following reasons:

- Although the purely mathematical character of no-fault plans makes them appear to be arbitrary from one perspective, in another sense they actually eliminate arbitrary

---

[130]*General Elec. Co.*, 69 LA 707, 711 (Jedel, 1977).

[131]For a comprehensive discussion of arbitrators' approaches to cases involving absenteeism, see H. Block & R. Mittenthal, *Absenteeism*, ARBITRATION 1984 77–108 (Proceedings of the 37th Annual Meeting, National Academy of Arbitrators 1985). No-fault plans are discussed *id.* at 94–104.

[132]E.g., Arbitrator Herman, in *Hoover Ball and Bearing Co.*, 66 LA 764, 768 (1976): A plan which penalizes absenteeism and tardiness . . . is proper and should be supported. However, the plan must take into consideration the human factor as well as the plant production requirements. An employee should not be penalized because he is absent for medical reasons . . . at least not until the absence becomes so protracted and excessive that the Company may properly terminate the employee. . . . An arbitrary hard and fast procedure may simplify administration, but it does not offer the reasonableness and fairness which the collective bargaining agreement contemplates.
A similar conclusion was reached in *Standard Transformer Co.*, 51 LA 1110 (Gibson, 1968). In *Union Camp Corp.*, 91 LA 749 (Clark, 1988), the arbitrator found a no-fault policy unreasonable because it did not give employees a reasonable opportunity to improve their attendance records by perfect attendance. On this basis he refused to uphold the discharge of an employee who was discharged for being eight minutes late— his seventh violation in 12 months—even though he had had a perfect record for seven months. In *St. Joseph Mercy Hosp.*, 87 LA 529, 532-33 (Daniel, 1986), the arbitrator found a no-fault policy unreasonable because of its "unrelenting progression through the disciplinary steps without regard whatsoever for the reason why the employee is absent from work."

individual supervisors make subjective decisions about which absences should be excused and which should not.[133]

- Even under contracts or company rules which provide for excused absences, the employer is not necessarily prevented from adopting a plan which sets an upper limit on the number of absences the company will tolerate.[134]
- Where a particular employee is discharged or otherwise disciplined under a no-fault plan, the employer's action is still subject to the standard of just cause.[135]

EXAMPLE: An employee began to feel severe pain in her arm and shoulder and had some medication brought to her from home. She tried to continue working but became too dizzy and uncoordinated to so so. The company nurse recommended that she go to the hospital; finding no one to drive her, she went home instead. Later that afternoon she was able to get to the hospital, where the doctor gave her some new medication and told her to go home and rest. When she called the company the next day, she was told that she had been discharged, since her early departure counted as her seventh "occurrence" within a 12-month period under a no-fault absence control program. The program also provided that an absence for hospital confinement would not count as an occurrence.

This case puts no-fault absence rules and just cause squarely up against each other. Expecting the employee to remain at work solely to avoid the seventh charge was unreasonable, said the arbitrator, since her foreman and the nurse both agreed

---

[133]*Kinnear Corp.*, 56 LA 325 (Seinsheimer, 1971:
The Company's explanation that the new system does away with having Foremen determine whether an employee's excuse . . . is legitimate or not is, from my many years' experience in the industrial field, a sensible and logical approach and certainly not unreasonable.
See also *American Standard*, 30 LA 231 (Thompson, 1958); *University of Chicago Hosps.*, 95 LA 286 (Goldstein, 1990).

[134]*Cannon Elec. Co.*, 46 LA 481 (Kotin, 1965); *Westinghouse Elec. Corp.*, 47 LA 464 (Stouffer, 1966); *DAP, Inc.*, 84 LA 459 (Shieber, 1984); *Associated Wholesale Groceries*, 89 LA 1144 (Berger, 1985); *Philip Morris U.S.A.*, 94 LA 91 (Dolson, 1989).

[135]Arbitrator Cohen, in *Park Poultry, Inc.*, 71 LA 1, 78-2 ARB ¶8420 (1978): "Violation of the policy is not *prima facie* cause for discipline or discharge. Were that so, [sections of the agreement] providing for 'reasonable cause' for discipline along with the grievance and arbitration procedures, would be meaningless." See also *University of Chicago Hosps.*, *supra* note 133. In *The Maccabees*, 27 LA 99 (Smith, 1956), defining "chronic tardiness" as a fixed number of instances was found to be reasonable in principle, but the number selected by the employer was too drastic a change from past practice, and the new policy was held to be unreasonable on that basis.

that she could not perform any work and needed immediate medical attention. Had she been admitted to the hospital that afternoon, no charge would have been made. "In my judgment," the arbitrator stated, "discharge for 'reasonable cause' cannot depend on such arbitrary finite distinctions." He reinstated the employee without back pay.[136]

That a program designed to curb excessive absenteeism is superficially reasonable will not save it if it is flawed by internal inconsistencies that might have obviously unfair results.

> **EXAMPLE:** Plagued for many years with absenteeism and tardiness problems, a company tried plan after plan to get the situation under control. Finally it instituted a system of progressive discipline under which absences accumulated by an employee up to a certain point were charged against him and made subject to increasing penalties no matter what their cause; absences thereafter might be charged or not charged, depending on whether the employee had a legitimate excuse, such as illness.

"This does not appeal to reason," the arbitrator said. For management to take excuses into account only in the final stages could mean a better deal for an employee who malingered than for an employee who was genuinely ill for the first three steps (and got no consideration) but whose two subsequent absences were not "excused." Stated another way, the threshold for consideration of excuses in this program was arbitrary. "In determining in a given case whether an employee's absence constitutes cause for discharge, he is reasonably entitled to a review of the aggregate of the incidents which together are deemed to constitute causes."[137]

Finally, no-fault programs have been held to be unreasonable where they are in conflict with any provision of the con-

---

[136]*Park Poultry, Inc., supra* note 135, at 8. In *Forest City Dillon Core Sys., Inc.*, 84-1 ARB 8092 (Strasshoffer, 1983), the arbitrator found a proposed absence-control program unreasonable because it did not make allowance for unanticipated emergencies and certifiable illness and penalized a tardiness of one minute the same as a full day's absence. See also *Kaiser Aluminum and Chem. Corp.*, 68-2 ARB ¶8606 (Hebert, 1968), and cases cited in note 135 *supra*. But see *DAP, Inc., supra* note 134 (discretion to distinguish between justifiable and unjustifiable absences vested in management, so employer may refuse to accept medical reasons for absences); *Hughes Aircraft Co.*, 92 LA 634 (Richman, 1989) (charging employee for absences caused by breakdown of company-sponsored van pool not improper, since company is not guarantor of prompt arrival of van pool and participation in pool is voluntary).

[137]*Sylvania Elec. Prods., Inc.*, 32 LA 1025 (Wallen, 1958).

tract.[138] In other words, the numbers used to define excessive absenteeism and tardiness under no-fault systems are viewed by arbitrators as norms; they are not "written in stone."

III. Some Conventional "No-Win" Arguments on Reasonableness

From Management's Side of the Table

The following arguments why a rule is reasonable are often made by the employer, but not one of them, standing alone, is likely to persuade an arbitrator if the rule is unreasonable when judged by the criteria set forth above.

"The rule gets results." Commenting on a new absence control policy, the arbitrator noted: "The fact that the Company said the policy had reduced absenteeism by 17% does not impress me from the standpoint of reasonableness. It could do that and still be unreasonable."[139]

"The rule is easy to enforce." That the company had problems policing its old personal-phone-call rule, which allowed employees to use the phone only in emergencies, did not justify the adoption of an arbitrary and unreasonable rule under which employees were docked 15 minutes' pay for even a short emergency call. The arbitrator said:

> Difficulties of enforcing reasonable rules in a reasonable fashion do not, I think, justify the abdication of managerial authority to impose appropriate discipline in favor of a system of absolute and—often enough—unwarranted penalties. No one ever claimed that the management of a work force was an easy job.[140]

"The rule hasn't hurt anyone yet." The employer adopted a new rule requiring employees to get a special pass before going to the medical department. Although that rule was in conflict with the contract, the employer argued that it was reasonable because no employee had been prevented from getting needed medical attention. The arbitrator rejected that argument, pointing out that the pass system might not have been given a real test.

---

[138]See *Sweco, Inc.*, 73 LA 684 (Hardbeck, 1979); *Central Tel. Co. of Va.*, 68 LA 957 (Whyte, 1977); *County of Appanoose*, 92 LA 246 (Gallagher, 1989).

[139]*Miami-Carey Co.*, 73-1 ARB 8102, 3403-3404 (Seinsheimer, 1973).

[140]*Dover Corp.*, 69 LA 779, 781 (Edes, 1977).

It could be that no employee has [applied for a pass] under conditions that were not arguably an emergency, or that supervisors have exercised restraint pending clarification of the validity of the requirement. Also, the well recognized principle that an employee is expected to work and grieve would serve as an admonishment to most employees that they should comply with the new procedure pending clarification of its validity.[141]

"The rule is common in the industry." Rules that are common in an industry are not necessarily reasonable for a particular plant in that industry. "The arbitrator must decide on the validity of *these* rules under *this* collective bargaining agreement between the particular parties to this grievance."[142]

"Without this rule, some people might cause problems." A rule requiring employees to stand during their "piece" (coffee) breaks was held to be unreasonable where there was no evidence that sitting during breaks would interfere with production. "The evidence indicated that the Company's objection to sitting was based on the assumption that employees were more likely to loaf on the job if they sat down while eating their piece than if they stood." Even if some employees were more apt to loaf if they sat, "it would . . . be improper to order that all employees stand while eating their piece merely because a few employees might take advantage of the situation."[143]

From the Union's Side of the Table

The union sometimes makes one of the following futile arguments as to why a rule is unreasonable:

"There was a better way to do it." Requiring employees to sign and return a copy of a new rule barring unauthorized visitors was not unreasonable, the arbitrator found.

> Although it has been suggested by the Association that the Company could have utilized other methods to bring the rule to the attention of the employees, such would not abrogate the right of the company to select the medium which in its judgment and direction would best accomplish its objective.
>
> The right of the employer to make and enforce rules and regulations . . . includes the right to exercise this authority in an

---

[141]*Bucyrus-Erie Co.*, 69 LA 970, 974 (Fleischli, 1977).
[142]*United Baking Co.*, 43 LA 337, 338 (Kreimer, 1964).
[143]*Ross Clay Prods. Co.*, 64-3 ARB 8933, 6230 (Kabaker, 1964).

effective and practical manner, thereby according some latitude and discretion as regard the form and manner to be its objective.[144]

"The abuse the rule is meant to cure isn't all that widespread." The arbitrator was not impressed by a union protest that a rule requiring all employees to sign out and sign in when making trips to the rest room was designed to prevent abuses by a relatively small number of employees.

It is of the essence of a shop rule or a disciplinary regulation that it should have general application. It is sufficient if the rule is designed to cope with a situation which can reasonably be said to require correction; it is not necessary that a situation become chaotic as a result of widespread abuses before measures may be taken to eliminate it.[145]

III. Challenging Reasonableness

When Does the Union Have to Register Its Protest?

Can the union protest the reasonableness of a company rule without waiting for an employee to be actually disciplined for violating it? There are two views on this question.

"He Who Hesitates Is Lost"

Arbitrator Schmidt: [T]he grievance procedure is directed toward promoting orderly and prompt settlement of disputes to the end that there be just administration of the Agreement . . . undisturbed, to the extent possible, by unresolved employee complaints. To require employees to wait until a regulation, which they object to, should be enforced by disciplinary measures, before they can have a decision by an arbitrator on the validity of such regulation, would not be consonant with the intent of the grievance and arbitration procedures.[146]

Many arbitrators agree with that view, and the company may face tough sledding if it takes the position that grievances over rules are out of bounds.

---

[144]*Metromedia, Inc.*, 46 LA 161, 165-66 (Dworkin, 1965).
[145]*Detroit Gasket & Mfg. Co.*, 27 LA 717, 719 (Crane, 1956). The same argument was raised and rejected in *Columbian Rope Co.*, 7 LA 450 (McKelvey, 1947) (smoking, fighting).
[146]*Linde Co.*, 34 LA 1, 6 (1959) (safety rules).

EXAMPLE: When an employer announced a new point system for controlling excessive absenteeism, the union protested that under the new program employees might be subject to discipline for absences that would have been excused under customary tests of reasonableness. The employer argued that the grievance was not arbitrable because, under the grievance procedure, a grievance could arise only with respect to interpretation, application, or violation of the contract—none of which was put in issue by the adoption of the new absence program. The time to grieve, in its view, was when someone was disciplined under the program.

The arbitrator disagreed. His reasoning:

One must assume that a program adopted by the company will be enforced. Otherwise, adoption of such a program is a *pro forma* useless act. A violation of the Agreement, therefore, could be anticipated from the enforcement of the program.[147]

The practical advantages and limitations of challenging rules "in the abstract" are generally set forth as follows:

No risk of waiver for the union. Protesting the reasonableness of a rule as soon as it is announced eliminates the possibility that an arbitrator might decide that, by failing to grieve promptly, the union waived its right to protest at a later time.

A form of "declaratory relief." Both parties may benefit from having the reasonableness of a rule weighed by an arbitrator when it is first adopted, since disputes over the rule's application down the line may be avoided if the parties know in advance where they stand.

Limits to what an arbitrator can decide. There are limits, however, to what can be accomplished by challenging rules in principle. When an arbitrator is asked to decide whether a rule is reasonable *per se*, he or she can only give a "yes" or "no" answer or, at most, make some general observations. "The Arbitrator acts as a reviewing agent, as a censor, and can point out and declare that which is beyond the limits of propriety. The Arbitrator cannot sit down and pencil and impose language on the parties."[148]

Disputes may still arise. Even if the arbitrator finds that a rule is reasonable in principle, every situation in which the rule may

---

[147]*Cannon Elec. Co.*, 46 LA 481 (Kotin, 1965).
[148]*United-Carr Tenn.*, 59 LA 883, 886-87 (Cantor, 1972) (unilateral adoption of company rules).

be applied cannot be anticipated. Grievances may therefore still arise in particular cases where employees are disciplined.[149]

"He Who Hesitates Is Better Off"

But what if the union does not file a grievance when a rule is posted? Does its failure to do so mean that it has accepted the rule as valid? In general, the answer is no.[150] In fact, many arbitrators take the view that a rule is appropriately challenged only "in the particular." The courts, too, have said that disputes are more properly decided when the facts present what is called a "justiciable controversy" than in the abstract.

> *Arbitrator Platt:* Grievance determination, in order to be effective, should rest on facts or conclusions drawn from facts and not on speculative or hypothetical situations. The question of whether a rule is fair and reasonable cannot be confidently determined except in the context of a concrete case and upon consideration of the specific circumstances of a particular case in which the rule is invoked and applied.[151]

Platt went on to suggest that waiting to protest rules "in the particular" is especially necessary where the language of the rule is vague and ambiguous. Otherwise, "in attempting to construe it we would increase the chances of our overlooking or misinter-

---

[149]*Associated Wholesale Groceries*, 89 LA 1144, 1147 (Berger, 1985) (no-fault policy): A conclusion that the policy is reasonable in the abstract . . . would not preclude the filing of a future grievance claiming that an individual case of discipline pursuant to the policy was not supported by just cause. This is because a rule may be valid in general terms, but yet be unfairly applied to a particular employee.

[150]See, e.g., *Wilkinsburg-Penn Joint Water Auth.*, 73-1 ARB ¶8117, 3451 (Kates, 1973):

The fact that the Union has known that the Employer for the past 10 years has been requiring new employees to sign the residency agreement, without any grievances from the Union or Union members, has not . . . barred the Union from attacking the validity of that prior agreement in the very first case in those 10 years (the instant case) in which that private agreement has been used as a ground of discharge of a Union member with seniority.

In *Peoples Gas Light and Coke Co.*, 73 LA 357 (Gundermann, 1979) (break-time activity), even the fact that the union had dropped a prior grievance protesting the reasonableness of a new rule *per se* did not preclude it from arguing that the rule was unreasonable when the company at a later time suspended three employees for violating it, since the union had made clear to the company that it was not acquiescing in the rule and the rule had its first impact when the three grievants were disciplined. See also *J. Weingarten, Inc.*, 77-1 ARB ¶8050 (Helburn, 1977) (use of obscene language to customer).

[151]*Trans World Air Lines*, 47 LA 1127, 1130 (1967).

preting facts and issues which, though not appearing of record, may well be in real controversy."

The rule Platt was asked to judge in the abstract illustrates the kind of roadblocks an arbitrator can encounter if he or she is asked to decide the question of reasonableness outside the context of an actual situation. The rule required a flight attendant to resign if she adopted a child but did not set forth any criteria as to what constituted "adoption"—whether only legal adoption was intended or whether the rule might also apply to an attendant who assumed care of a child without legally adopting it or to one who married a man with children from a previous marriage. "All these and other questions which readily come to mind are important in any effort to construe the rule and its reasonableness. Yet no grievance before us reflects any factual situation from which an answer to the above question can be derived."[152]

Another example is provided by the unilateral addition by a company of a urinalysis drug screen to government-mandated physical examinations that its drivers were required to undergo. A union objection to this change in working conditions was rejected by the arbitrator on the ground that the union had previously waived its right to bargain over the issue. However, the arbitrator further determined that questions concerning the reasonableness of testing conditions—the drug-testing guidelines, whether a second test would be required if the first test result was positive, and whether independent corroborating evidence would be needed to insure reliability of the test—could be decided only when a particular driver was disciplined for testing positive.[153]

One caveat: If it chooses not to challenge a rule when it is first adopted, the union must be careful that it does not allow any kind of past practice to develop which might suggest that it has accepted the rule as reasonable. For example, if employees

---

[152]*Id.* at 1131. See also *Budd Co.*, 67 LA 130 (Howard, 1967) (adoption of new rules):

> Whether a given rule is vague cannot be answered in a vacuum but only within the context of the specific circumstances in which the Company sought its implementation through the assessment of discipline. ... Otherwise the arbitrator becomes a legislator of plant rules rather than an interpreter of the validity of particular discipline under the just cause standard. The Union has not shown any rule to be patently unreasonable under any and all circumstances.

[153]*Fleming Foods of Mo.*, 89 LA 1292 (Yarowsky, 1987).

are disciplined under the rule and the union does not protest, it may be considered to have waived its right to complain about the rule at a later date (assuming, of course, that the circumstances are substantially the same).[154]

The Doctrine of Self-Help and its Exceptions

"Work Now, Grieve Later"

> *Arbitrator Shulman:* Some men apparently think that, when a violation of contract seems clear, the employee may refuse to obey and thus resort to self-help rather than the grievance procedure. That is an erroneous point of view.
>
> In the first place, what appears to one party to be a clear violation may not seem so at all to the other party. Neither party can be the final judge as to whether the contract has been violated. The determination of that issue rests in collective negotiation through the grievance procedure.
>
> But, in the second place, and more important, the grievance procedure is prescribed in the contract precisely because the parties anticipated that there would be claims of violations which would require adjustment. That procedure is prescribed for all grievances, not merely for doubtful ones.[155]

"Work now, grieve later"—if any principle of contract administration deserves to be carved in stone, this is almost surely

---

[154]As in *Federal Paper Bd. Co.*, 60 LA 924 (Porter, 1973), where one factor in the arbitrator's decision upholding a company rule on garnishments was that the union had not protested any of 38 previous terminations under the rule; and *Carondelet Coke Corp.*, 88-1 ARB ¶8084 (Miller, 1988), where the arbitrator ruled that the union's failure to object to a unilaterally adopted drug-testing policy or to process grievances over seven discharges under the policy barred it from challenging the policy when it finally did get around to arbitrating the discharge of a worker who tested positive; the only issue at that point, he said, was whether the policy had been applied reasonably. See also *Fleming Foods of Mo.*, *supra* note 153 at 1294:

> [T]he Union, *in not demanding bargaining*, waived its right to do so. It had notice of the intended new policy and notice of the date of implementation. It, therefore, had the "burden of demanding bargaining if it wished to preserve its right to bargain about the decision (to require a drug screen) and the effect of such decision upon the employees' terms and conditions of employment."

(quoting *U.S. Lingerie Corp.*, 170 NLRB 750, 751-52, 67 LRRM 1482 (1968)). However, agreements the company may have made with individual employees as to their acceptance of any rules or working conditions, if inconsistent with the contract, have been held not to be binding on the union. See discussion and citations in *Allegheny Airlines, Inc.*, 67-1 ARB ¶8244 (Kelliher, 1967) (no-marriage rule), and *Wilkinsburg-Penn Joint Water Auth.*, *supra* note 150.

[155]*Ford Motor Co.*, 3 LA 779, 780-81 (1946).

it. Employees who believe that a work order, assignment, or company rule is improper may not take matters into their own hands. They must accept the assignment, or carry out the order or obey the rule, and then turn to the grievance procedure for relief.[156] Three arbitrators explain why:

> *Arbitrator Platt:* It must be recognized by all employees that Management's authority derives from its responsibility to produce and manage and that the rights of Management would be meaningless if workers had the right to reject its authority in the plant.[157]

> *Arbitrator Shulman:* [A]n industrial plant is not a debating society. Its object is production. When a controversy arises, production cannot wait for exhaustion of the grievance procedure. While that procedure is being pursued, production must go on. And someone must have the authority to direct the manner in which it is to go on until the controversy is settled. That authority is vested in supervision.[158]

> *Arbitrator McCoy:* The grievance procedure, ending when necessary in arbitration, is set up for the express purpose of providing means, times and places for proper argument and disposition of disputes, thus eliminating the need for such forms of "self-help" as strikes, slowdowns, refusal to obey orders, and even unseemly argument on the plant floor.[159]

---

[156]Arbitrator Roberts, in *Kast Metals Corp.*, 70 LA 278, 282 (1978), stated the principle thus: "The usual rule is that if an employee challenges the propriety of a rule or a work direction, it is his duty to perform the work direction and grieve later over the propriety of that work direction." In *Johnson Controls, Inc.*, 92 LA 449 (Mayer, 1989), the arbitrator upheld the suspension of an employee who refused to obtain a doctor's certificate supporting his claimed illness, whether or not the employer had a right to require the certificate. The employee violated the obey-now, grieve-later rule and thereby lost his right to a review on the merits. For an extensive review of arbitration cases on the subject of self-help, see *California Processors, Inc.*, 56 LA 1275 (Koven, 1971). See also F. ELKOURI & E. A. ELKOURI, HOW ARBITRATION WORKS 199–203 (4th ed. 1985).

[157]*Wolverine Shoe & Tanning Corp.*, 18 LA 809, 812 (1952).

[158]*Ford Motor Co.*, *supra* note 155. More recently, Arbitrator Roberts, in *Kast Metals Corp.*, *supra* note 156, stated similarly,
> If employees were permitted to challenge the propriety of a work direction or order and not to carry it out until the propriety of that order had been resolved, chaos would result. Production could not be maintained and there would be a consequent loss not only of profit to the Company but of the Company's very ability to pay wages to the members of the bargaining unit.

[159]*Sheller Mfg. Corp.*, 34 LA 689 (1960). In the same vein, Arbitrator Shulman in *Ford Motor Co.*, *supra* note 155: "To refuse obedience because of a claimed contract violation would be to substitute individual action for collective bargaining and to replace the grievance procedure with extra-contractual methods."

Self-Help Versus Insubordination

Self-help and insubordination overlap to a considerable degree, insofar as both involve the refusal of an employee to comply with a directive of management; the differences between them are not hard and fast. But one factor that frequently distinguishes them is the employee's motivation.

Self-Help. Take the case of an employee who refuses to put on a pair of protective gloves in accordance with a new safety rule because he or she believes that wearing gloves will make it harder to control the machine and thereby create more hazards than the gloves guard against. Or take the employee who ignores a new rule that limits washup time to five minutes at the end of the shift because employees in that department have been permitted for many years to head for the locker room whenever their work was completed.

In both instances what is bothering the employees is their conviction that the company is trying to make them do something it has no right to require under the contract. Their beef, one might say, is institutional rather than personal. It is not directed at a particular supervisor. There is no disrespect or intimidation involved. The employees are not trying to challenge any individual's authority—only management's authority with respect to some particular contractual right.[160]

Insubordination. In cases involving insubordination, as the term is commonly used, the personal element is often at the heart of the problem. An employee who is directed to work Saturday overtime on short notice, for example, thinks his foreman has been picking him for all the most inconvenient assignments and blows up, yelling at the foreman in front of the crew that he will not show up another Saturday.

With insubordination, a question of management's rights under the contract may lie behind the employee's refusal to do something. Then again, the employee may have no complaint under the contract at all, but refuses an order out of frustration, resentment, hostility, or the desire to show independence. Even if the employee honestly believes he or she has a legitimate grievance, those subjective factors also are present.

---

[160]*Albertson's Inc.*, 65 LA 1042, 1047 (Christopher, 1975): "The term 'self-help' generally refers to a refusal to carry out a work order or directive on grounds, whether real or imagined, that the order violates the Contract or is otherwise improper."

Summary: Two Different "Flavors." The flavor of insubordination
is defiance of proper authority,[161] while the flavor of self-help is
the conviction that one is right and is entitled to say so. By
resorting to self-help, an employee is using the wrong method
to challenge the reasonableness of a management directive—
something he or she has a right to do by using the grievance
procedure.

What we might call simple self-help, because it lacks added
attractions such as disrespect or defiance, is frequently not penalized as severely as insubordination.[162] But unless one of the
following exceptions is present, discipline is likely to be upheld
when an employee bypasses the grievance procedure—even on
the most principled of grounds—to challenge a rule or work
order.

Exceptions to Self-Help Rule

Two classic exceptions to the self-help rule have been accepted by virtually all arbitrators. Employees are not obliged to
work now and grieve later if obedience would endanger their
health and safety or if the order requires the performance of
an illegal act.[163] Beyond these two "classics," there is no hard

---

[161]*National Carbide Co.*, 24 LA 804 (Warns, 1955), cited in *Stroh Brewery Co.*, 85 LA
89 (Boyer, 1985): "Insubordination is generally understood to mean a deliberate and
wilful refusal to carry out a proper order. Such refusal may be by words or action."
Some arbitrators expand this definition to include the use of profanity toward, cursing,
and threatening a supervisor, as in *La Victoria Foods, Inc.*, 89-2 ARB ¶8487 (Prayzich,
1989), citing *Marshall Brass*, 78 LA 806 (Keefe, 1982), and *General Portland, Inc.*, 81 LA
230 (Flannagan, 1983). See also W. B. Nelson, *Insubordination: Arbitral "Law" in the
Reconciliation of Conflicting Employer/Employee Interests*, 35 LAB. L.J. 112–22 (1984).

[162]*E.g.*, in *Wolverine Shoe & Tanning Co.*, *supra* note 157, the arbitrator concluded
that discharge was too severe for an employee who violated a rule against parking on
certain streets outside the plant:

[H]e apparently became suddenly obsessed with the notion that the rule was illegal
and decided to contest it not only on his own behalf but on behalf of all the other
employees. Although he obviously chose the wrong method by which to test out
the validity of the rule, I am convinced that he was sincere in his beliefs and that
he foolishly assumed the role of martyr in his anxiety to prove that Management
was in error.

And in *Ingalls Shipbuilding Corp.*, 39 LA 419, 430 (Hebert, 1962), the arbitrator
concluded that

the violations of this rule by the employees . . . was in fact designed to obtain a
test of the Union's position through the grievance procedure and arbitration. The
Arbitrator feels, therefore . . . that it would be unduly harsh to treat the rule
violations here as that kind of a willful violation or independent insubordination
which normally should result in sustaining the disciplinary action on that ground.

[163]Arbitrator Silver, in *Central Contra Costa County Sanitation Dist.*, 93 LA 801
(1989):

[W]hen an employee refuses a work-related order, he or she may not contest a

and fast list. Arbitrators have sometimes recognized other exceptions that offer a kind of safe conduct out of occupied territory—territory over which management holds sway by virtue of accepted principles of management rights.[164]

The Safety Exception.

Arbitrator McCoy: An employee is under no duty to obey an order which would endanger his life or health.[165]

EXAMPLE: While out on a service call to a customer, an employee slipped on the ice and injured his back. About nine months after he returned to work, he was assigned a job he refused to perform because, on the basis of his doctor's diagnosis, he believed the strain would aggravate his back injury. The following day he was again directed to do the job, and again he refused. He was then suspended indefinitely because the employer believed that he should at least have attempted the job. Its own physician had cleared him to return to work, and it thought the job was no more strenuous than his routine duties.

The arbitrator reasoned as follows:

The principle applicable here is that an employee may refuse to carry out a particular work assignment, if at the time he is given

---

discharge for insubordination by challenging the reasonableness of the order. . . .
The only recognized exception . . . is when the order would place the employee's health or safety in imminent danger.
See also *Pilgrim Liquor, Inc.*, 66 LA 19 (Fleischli, 1975) (work unsafe or beyond employer's authority); *Kast Metals Corp.*, 70 LA 278 (Roberts, 1978) (illegal act; safety hazard; irreparable harm to employee or others); *Atlantic Richfield Co.*, 70 LA 707 (Fox, 1978) (health hazard; criminal act; performance by skilled worker of work wholly unrelated to craft; order contrary to arbitration award).

[164]Arbitrator Volz, in *Ashland Oil, Inc.*, 91 LA 1101, 1103 (1988) (short notice of mandatory overtime, refusal to accept reasonable excuse):
The justifications for refusal or failure to obey a supervisory directive to perform work are few in number. One is where the directive is unclear and does not sufficiently inform the employee as to what he or she is to do, when, and how. . . . A second justification for not obeying a work order is where the assignment involves an undue threat to the employee's safety or health not inherent in the usual duties of his or her job. . . . A third justification applies if the work order requires the commission of an immoral or illegal act. . . . Finally, . . . that Management in utilizing mandatory overtime must accept reasonable excuses advanced by the employee."
Illustrating the last-named exception is *Hawkeye Chem. Co.*, 89-1 ARB ¶8253 (Traynor, 1988), where the arbitrator disapproved the suspension of a maintenance worker who refused a direct order to work overtime. The employer's long-established practice was to assign overtime work to the employee having the fewest overtime hours; the grievant was not at the bottom of the list, and there was sufficient time for the company to assign the work to a qualified employee with less overtime. Thus, the order was unreasonable, and the grievant did not have to obey it.
[165]*Dwight Mfg. Co.*, 12 LA 990, 996 (1949).

the work assignment, he reasonably believes that by carrying out such work assignment he will endanger his safety or health. . . . In the case of dispute . . . the question to be decided is not whether he actually would have suffered injury but whether he had a reasonable basis for believing so.

In the grievant's case, the arbitrator found, the decisive facts were these: He had undeniably sustained a serious back injury; his doctor had advised him to avoid heavy lifting and other strenuous exertion; the job he was assigned to was more strenuous than his normal job duties, which he had learned to perform in a manner that minimized back strain; and even the company's own medical experts declined to testify with certainty that he would not have hurt his back again.

This classic self-help case was therefore decided on the basis of two principles: (1) The grievant had a reasonable basis for believing that carrying out his assignment would injure him; and (2) he was not obligated to attempt the job to see what would happen. The principle that an employee must obey a reasonable rule or order was thus outweighed by the risk of injury.[166]

The Not-Job-Related Exception.

Arbitrator McCoy: Nor is [an employee] under any duty to obey an order which is quite clearly and indisputably beyond the authority of Supervision to issue.[167]

---

[166]*Laclede Gas Co.*, 39 LA 833, 839 (Bothwell, 1962). *Peoples Natural Gas Co.*, 88-1 ARB ¶8140 (Sherman, 1988), provides a good example of the line between a reasonable and an unreasonable refusal to work. Pipeline workers were wrongfully suspended, the arbitrator found, for refusing to work on a cold and snowy morning, since they reasonably believed conditions were dangerous; but by afternoon the snow had melted, the weather had improved, and the employer was justified in requiring the grievants to work. See also *Kaiser Aluminum and Chem. Corp.*, 92 LA 367 (Corbett, 1989), in which the arbitrator upset the discharge of a woman who refused to work a double shift. She had been ill the previous day and might have been unable to work another shift safely. But a suspension was held proper because the employee failed to tell her foreman of her legitimate health concern and to contact the union steward.

In some instances, arbitrators have held employees to the more stringent requirement that not only must there be a reasonable fear of imminent danger but the danger actually must exist. For extended discussions of standards that may be applied, see F. ELKOURI AND E. A. ELKOURI, HOW ARBITRATION WORKS 713–24 (4th ed. 1985); J. M. Smith, *Arbitrating Safety Grievances: Contract or Congress?* 33 LAB. L.J. 241–43 (1982); L. Drapkin, *The Right to Refuse Hazardous Work After* Whirlpool, 4 INDUS. REL. J. 29–60 (1980). Cases in which an employee's self-help defense was not accepted include *American Welding & Mfg. Co.*, 47 LA 457 (Dworkin, 1967); *Hoerner Waldorf Co.*, 70 LA 335 (Talent, 1978); *Atlantic Richfield Co.*, 70 LA 707 (Fox, 1978).

[167]*Dwight Mfg. Co., supra* note 165.

McCoy offers the example of a supervisor ordering an employee to shine the supervisor's shoes. Orders of this kind are related not to the employee's work but to the supervisor's personal convenience, and as such are clearly unacceptable. But some orders, even though work-related, are so clearly outside management's purview that an employee need not obey them. An example is a case in which a supervisor sought to add a new assignment to an employee's other job duties. When the employee protested, the supervisor admitted that the company had not complied with a contract provision requiring it to give the union seven days' notice of changes in a job or work assignment. Since the supervisor knowingly gave the employee an order for which he had no contractual authorization, the employee's refusal to carry it out was justified.[168]

The Grievance-Processing Exception.

Arbitrator Koven: Some arbitrators have recognized other possible exceptions to the duty to obey orders, as where the order violates the rights or domain of the Union itself as by interfering with the Union's contractual right to investigate and process grievances . . . or where the order interferes with the employee's proper use of the grievance procedure.[169]

EXAMPLE: While talking to several employees about their complaint that overtime was being unequally distributed, the foreman hinted that he believed one particular employee was behind all the agitation. When the foreman called that employee in to discuss the matter, the latter, who had been warned about the foreman's "hints," refused to say anything unless a steward was present. The foreman rejected his request. Shortly thereafter both men were summoned to the superintendent's office to have the matter out. Again the employee refused to discuss things without union representation, and this time he was fired for insubordination.

The arbitrator's view: The employee was entitled under the contract to be represented by the union. When the employer

---

[168]*Id. Ironrite, Inc.*, 28 LA 394, 397 (Haughton, 1956): "Another modification of the general [self-help] principle would be when a skilled craftsman is assigned to work *wholly* different and unrelated to his classification." See also *Titanium Metals Corp.*, 55 LA 690 (Block, 1970) (employee entitled to refuse assignment to carry out trash since for six years she had been exempt from that task); *San Diego Gas & Elec. Co.*, 57 LA 821 (Leonard, 1971) (order to shave beard not work assignment); *Pilgrim Liquor, Inc., supra* note 163 (requiring employee to provide personal information on applications for fidelity bonds exceeded employer's authority); *Mark Twain Indus., Inc.*, 74 LA 441 (Stix, 1979) (employer may not require performance of non-bargaining-unit work).

[169]*California Processors, Inc.*, 56 LA 1275, 1283 (Koven, 1971).

denied him that right, his refusal to obey the order to discuss the matter was a justifiable exception to the self-help rule.

> The purpose of this exception reveals why it is recognized. In the first place, the Company order was not a work direction to the employees. Thus, refusal to obey the order did not disrupt production. . . .
>
> Secondly, and more specifically, if there were not such an exception to the 'obey and grieve later' principle, a company could continue to order an employee not to assert his rights under the grievance procedure. Then the company could discharge him for insubordination for defying the order. The employee could not obey the order and grieve later . . . because the company could also deny him the right to grieve later.[170]

To state it another way, the right to grieve later is nonexistent if the order which the employee must obey now is an order not to use the very procedure to which he is supposed to resort. The following case shows a similar "Catch 22" at work.

> **EXAMPLE:** Shortly after learning that a probationary employee had been terminated, a shop steward requested permission from the foreman to check out of his department to investigate the matter. The foreman refused, informing the steward that because the probationer had no rights under the contract there could be no grievance, and walked away. The steward checked his contract anyway and began writing up a grievance for the probationer. When the foreman returned, he ordered the steward back to work. The latter replied that he had two jobs—one on production and the other as the union's representative on the job—and that he intended to continue his work on the probationer's behalf. The foreman thereupon fired him for insubordination.

Here's how the arbitrator saw the situation:

> There is a clear distinction between the case of a supervisor telling an employee to go back to his job, and a supervisor telling the Union to stop investigating a grievance. . . . If [the steward] could rightly be penalized it would put the entire grievance machinery, set up by agreement at the highest levels, at the mercy of supervisors, with the possibility of great harm to the parties, even to a

---

[170]*Braniff Airways, Inc.*, 27 LA 892, 900 (Williams). Related cases include *The Arcrods Co.*, 39 LA 784 (Teple, 1962); *City of Port Huron, Mich.*, 68-2 ARB ¶8788 (Keefe, 1968); and *Southern Cal. Edison Co.*, 61 LA 453 (Block, 1973), all dealing with an employee's right to refuse to meet with the employer on disciplinary matters without union representation; and *G. C. Murphy Co.*, 79-1 ARB ¶8212 (Kossoff, 1979) (refusal to sign for rule booklet without being allowed to consult union).

complete breakdown of the grievance machinery. The Company is in the anomalous position here of asking that a rule be laid down that a steward must rely upon a grievance machinery that is even then under attack and being violated.[171]

The No-Possible-Remedy Exception. Another exception to the self-help rule is sometimes said to arise where the nature of the order is such that compliance would result in an irreparable injury which no possible later remedy could redress.[172] Of course, whether an arbitrator would decide that an injury is really irreparable depends on his view of the particular facts.

> **EXAMPLE:** About two weeks before a week-long union conference they had been delegated to attend, two employees requested the industrial relations manager for leaves of absence for that purpose. A few days later one of them asked the chief clerk not to schedule him to work during the week of the conference, and the clerk approved his leave after consulting with the front office. The second employee, on the other hand, failed to alert the clerk to his plans. When he told the foreman the Friday before the conference that he was going to take the week off, the foreman said no because a backlog of orders had developed and he could not be spared. This employee attended the conference anyway, first calling in sick and subsequently telling the employer that he needed time off to handle a family emergency outside the state. The company fired the employee for absence without permission, falsifying reports, and excessive absence after he was spotted at the conference hotel. The union protested that he had permission to be off work and that it would have been futile for him to grieve the foreman's refusal to let him go because by the time the grievance had been processed the question of attending the conference would have become moot.

The arbitrator agreed with the union—in principle—concluding that the right of self-help was implicit in the contract provision requiring the company to grant leaves of absence to a reasonable number of employees for union business. Otherwise, the union would have no practical remedy if the company unjustifiably denied an employee's request for a leave. Given the facts of this case, though, that principle did not help the grievant. Why? Because he did not meet the adequate-notice require-

---

[171]*International Harvester Co.*, 16 LA 307, 310-11 (McCoy, 1951).
[172]*Skenandoa Rayon Corp.*, 18 LA 239 (Justin, 1952).

ment of the contract; falsified the reasons for his absence; and had had prior disciplinary difficulties.[173]

The no-possible-remedy exception applies primarily where a unique event is involved. Take the case of a library employee who used mace and his flute as weapons to aid two women under attack by two men in the library foyer, despite being ordered by a superior to cease and desist. The arbitrator rescinded his suspension for insubordination and violation of city emergency rules. Rather than being charged with insubordination, he said, the employee should have been commended for his heroic act.[174]

Many disputed orders and assignments have some element that is not fully subject to remedy. Consider the case of the truck driver who, after being involved in a minor accident, was fired for refusing to submit to a drug test. The arbitrator found that, since the employer had no reason to suspect that the driver was under the influence, the test requirement was arbitrary and unreasonable. In this situation, he held, the driver's right to privacy overrode the obey-now, grieve-later doctrine, especially since the driver would have had to release testing-agency personnel from any liability for consequences of the testing procedure.[175]

---

[173]*Colorado Fuel and Iron Corp.*, 68-1 ARB ¶8157 (Koven, 1967). Other cases on the same subject include *Bethlehem Steel Co.*, 11 LA 629 (Shipman, 1948) (taking vacation despite last-minute denial of vacation request, where employee had made vacation plans and would have suffered financial loss to postpone trip); *Electro Metallurgical Co.*, 22 LA 684 (Shister, 1954) (time off for union business).

[174]*City of Berkeley*, 93 LA 1161 (Riker, 1989). A variant of "irreparable injury" was present in *Albertson's, Inc.*, 65 LA 1042 (Christopher, 1975). The grievant refused to divest himself of a financial interest in a business that his employer believed to be a competitor; requiring him to give up his investment and then file a grievance was unreasonable. See also *Kaiser Steel Corp.*, 31 LA 567 (Prasow, 1958) (no reasonable remedy for grievants if they had worked Christmas and New Year's Eves as ordered).

[175]*Tribune Co.*, 93 LA 201 (Crane, 1989); to the same effect, *Utah Power and Light Co.*, 94 LA 233 (Winograd, 1990). In *EZ Communications, Inc.*, 91 LA 1097 (Talarico, 1988), the arbitrator made an exception to the work-now, grieve-later rule in the case of a female newscaster who walked off the job. She had been the target of a two-year campaign of lewd, outrageous on-air remarks by two disk jockeys, culminating in the use of her name in a vile joke. This was degrading, humiliating, and a serious invasion of her personal rights and dignity, the arbitrator stated, and to require her merely to file a grievance would have been unreasonable. But see *Vista Chem. Co.*, 92 LA 328 (Duff, 1989), in which the arbitrator upheld a substance-abuse policy allowing searches of employees clothing upon reasonable suspicion, where the searches were permitted only to the extent necessary to insure safe and productive conduct of the employer's business. Employees could challenge the propriety of searches through the grievance procedure, he noted, and the possibility that employees would improperly be subjected to humiliation and indignity was not sufficient to deprive the employer of so fundamental a weapon.

The Shift in the Burden. The "safe conducts" represented by the foregoing exceptions to the self-help rule do not come free. The "cost" to the employee is that when he relies on one of these exceptions to escape penalty, the burden shifts to him to prove that his conduct was justified. If he cannot, the mere claim of exceptional circumstances will not help.[176]

---

[176]Thus, in connection with the employee who takes time off for union business, the arbitrator noted in *Colorado Fuel and Iron Corp.*, *supra* note 173, at 3542: "[T]he principle of self-help is subject to the condition that once any particular grievant engages in self-help he also assumes the risk that he can justify the leave which he took pursuant to the Contract." And where the safety exception is concerned, the employee, according to the arbitrator in *Laclede Gas Co.*, *supra* note 166, at 839, "has the burden, if called upon, of showing by appropriate evidence that he has a reasonable basis for his belief."

Chapter 3

Investigation

"Did the Employer, before administering the discipline to an employee, make an effort to discover whether the employee did in fact violate or disobey a rule or order of management?"

Arbitrator Gentile: "Just cause" is a multi-faceted consideration which has been applied by Arbitrators to fact portraits in various ways. A thread which runs through these numerous decisions is the concept that the Company make a full, fair and objective investigation in order to be satisfied that the charged individual is in fact guilty of the offense or breach.[1]

Arbitrator Erbs: [W]hen the discipline or discharge is invoked the Company bears the burden of the responsibility of having considered any and all facts, from whatever source, that could have an influence on the extent of the discipline.[2]

A timely, thorough investigation of suspected misconduct is important to management for two self-evident reasons:

Fair play. Due process requires that an employee be informed promptly, and in reasonable detail, of the charges (or possible charges) against him and given the chance to tell his side of the story. If the company fails to let the employee defend himself, or bypasses other avenues of investigation, whatever

---

[1]*Dow Chem. Co.*, 60 LA 703, 706–07 (1973) (strike-related misconduct).

[2]*Missouri Research Laboratories*, 55 LA 197, 209 (1970) (abusive language). See also *Hilo Coast Processing Co.*, 84-1 ARB ¶8111 (Gilson, 1983) (grievant found to be guilty of falsification reinstated without back pay because employer failed to make adequate investigation of factors bearing on appropriate penalty).

159

penalty has been imposed is likely to be reduced by an arbitrator, even if the employee is clearly guilty.[3]

Sufficient proof. A faulty and inadequate investigation often produces faulty and inadequate proof. A thorough investigation may elevate assumptions and suspicions to the status of proof; avoid reliance on hearsay and other "lightweight" or "non-weight" evidence; prevent later-discovered evidence from being thrown out on the ground that it was irrelevant to the actual decision; or provide the "extra ingredient" that tips the scales in the company's favor.

Consider the case of the bus driver who was ordered to undergo a drug-screening test or face discharge, simply because he had been identified by two coworkers as possibly having a drug problem. The order was improper, the arbitrator held, because the employer acted on the basis of the allegations with no firsthand knowledge or evidence that the driver, a 10-year employee with an unblemished record, ever used drugs on the job or was under their influence when he arrived at work.

> The employer never made any independent investigation to verify or find support for these allegations. It never confronted Grievant with this information and asked for his side of the story. It never so much as asked either of the employees who had done the finger pointing what was the basis for their beliefs. . . . Of course, it may be that a rumor has some basis in fact, but without inquiry, without posing the simple question "How do you know?" there is no real way of ascertaining if there is any merit to the rumor and if further investigation is warranted.[4]

The basic purpose of an investigation is to find out, in Daugherty's words, "whether the employee did in fact violate or disobey a rule or order of management." It is thus concerned mainly with problems of adequate proof, but the quality of the investigation may be critical to meeting one or more of the other tests as well. Thus, the pivotal factor in evaluating disciplinary action may be whether management determined that the grievant had adequate notice of the consequences of his or her mis-

---

[3]*E.g.*, in *Southern Cal. Edison Co.*, 88-1 ARB ¶8129 (Collins, 1987), the company's failure to prove it conducted a proper investigation caused the arbitrator to reduce a five-day suspension for sleeping on the job to a written reprimand. Such an investigation, he held, is an essential element of just cause.

[4]*Trailways, Inc.*, 88 LA 1073, 1081 (Goodman, 1987). See also *Foster Food Prods.*, 88 LA 337 (Riker, 1986) (working elsewhere while collecting Worker's Compensation); *Snyder Gen'l Corp.*, 88 LA 1153 (Bard, 1987) (unsupported allegations of malingering).

conduct;[5] whether the grievant's alleged misconduct was investigated as thoroughly as similar misconduct engaged in by other employees;[6] or whether the investigation revealed all factors bearing on the appropriate penalty for the misconduct in question.[7]

Whereas the company bears the burden of proving that the grievant committed the offense with which he or she is charged, and that the penalty was appropriate, it is the union (or the grievant) that has the burden of proof with respect to the investigation. That is, the company is not required to prove that it made a proper investigation; the grieving party must show that the employer failed to do so.[8]

I. Investigation and Proof

What the company needs to prove in a particular case, and therefore what it needs to investigate, depends on what type of misconduct is involved. Theft is a good example. To catch a thief requires proof of the following elements: (1) personal property belonging to the company or to another employee (2) must be taken (3) by trespass (4) with the intent to steal.[9]

---

[5]As in *Howard Indus.*, 86-1 ARB ¶8559 (Taylor, 1986) (leaving work without permission), where the employment administrator discharged the grievant on the basis of a foreman's statement as to what the grievant had been told without himself talking to the grievant).

[6]See, e.g., *Allegheny Ludlum Steel Corp.*, 84 LA 476, 480 (Alexander, 1985) (investigation failed to identify grievant as alcoholic entitled to rehabilitation, contrary to general policy statement calling for diagnosis and treatment of alcoholism); *Hollywood Park*, 84 LA 902 (Draznin, 1985) (failure to interview others involved in incident leading to discipline suggested bias); *Santa Clara County*, 88 LA 1226 (Concepcion, 1987) (supervisor's failure to investigate thoroughly as well as fairly was disparate treatment).

[7]See, e.g., *Olin Corp.*, 86 LA 1096, 1098 (Seidman, 1986) (company's failure to consider mitigating circumstances "fatally flawed its decision and made it unjust and procedurally infirm"); *Hilo Coast Processing Co., supra* note 2.

[8]Arbitrator Ash, in *Angelus Sanitary Can Mach. Co.*, 68 LA 973, 975 (1977):

It has been widely held in arbitration of discharges that management has the burden of proving that the alleged offense is a just cause for discharge and that the employee was in fact guilty of the violation. Given the establishment of these two premises, the burden of proof properly shifts to the Grievant to prove . . . there was not a fair investigation and hearing.

See also *Bi-State Dev. Agency*, 84 LA 427 (Heinsz, 1985) (failure by bus driver to make assigned runs).

[9]See, e.g., *Imperial Glass Co.*, 61 LA 1180, 1183 (Gibson, 1973):

[I]t is well recognized that larceny or theft is the taking and carrying away of personal goods of another of any value, from any place, with the intent to steal the same. . . . The elements of the offense are (1) personal goods of another must be involved; (2) the goods must be taken without the consent of the other; (3) there must be some asportation; (4) both the taking and the asportation must be

Investigation into a case of suspected theft would thus logically focus on obtaining evidence with respect to these elements, with special emphasis on the ones that are in dispute.

Or take a case of suspected intoxication. To prove that an employee is intoxicated, the employer needs to establish that some combination of the accepted behavioral symptoms of intoxication (i.e., the odor of alcohol, slurred or thick speech, red or bloodshot eyes, uncoordinated movements) is present, so its investigation would be directed to obtaining credible reports concerning the employee's appearance and behavior. Requesting that the employee take a blood test might be necessary if, for example, the employee makes a plausible claim that his symptoms were caused not by drinking but by medication.

But whatever type of misconduct is involved, an investigation that satisfies the requirements of proof has three earmarks—all sides to the dispute have been considered, all relevant evidence has been obtained, and the investigation has been timely.

All Sides to the Dispute Must Be Considered

Must Company Talk to Grievant?

Is talking to the grievant an essential ingredient of an acceptable investigation? Technically, no—at least, not unless the contract requires it. But in practice, from a good investigatory stance (and from the stance of providing due process, as discussed in the next section), the answer is yes.

> *Arbitrator Lilly:* While nothing in the agreement specifically spells out the requirement that the Company must solicit and inquire of the grievant regarding the facts which affect the grievant's continued employment . . ., it is basic to the fact finding process to inquire of those who should best know what happened with respect to those facts.[10]

---

with an intent to steal or *animus furandi, i.e.,* an intent to deprive the owner of his property permanently.

[10]*Gulf Printing Co.*, 61 LA 1174, 1179 (1974) (damage to company property). Arbitrator Dobry, in *Bismarck Food Serv., Inc.*, 88-1 ARB ¶8104, 3509 (1987) (drinking beer): "[T]he employer decided to discharge the employees without discussing the matter with them, or seeking their explanation. This amounts to a failure to fairly and objectively investigate, one of the procedural elements of just cause for discharge." See also *Aeroquip Corp.*, 85-1 ARB ¶8031 (Roumell, 1984) (fighting). Cases in which a failure to interview the grievant has been found insufficient to disturb a discharge because the failure was held not to have prejudiced the grievant include *Shepard Ambulance, Inc.*, 85-2 ARB ¶8336 (Krebs, 1985) (intoxication), and *Greyhound Food Management*, 89 LA 1138,

What Was the Reason? One risk the employer runs if it decides on disciplinary action without hearing the grievant's side of the story is that it may find itself taking action on an incomplete set of facts.[11] Many common categories of misconduct logically invite inquiry into the reason for the misconduct, and without such inquiry an investigation is likely to be regarded as incomplete or unacceptable. It is not enough to show that someone refused a work order. Why should this person, an employee of 19 years who never before has refused to do what he had been asked to do, now refuse to accept a proper work assignment?[12] Or why is it that another employee did not accept the overtime work?[13] Or why did someone else not report for work?[14] Or why did several employees walk off the job one afternoon?[15]

Why the grievant did what he or she did inevitably relates to the gravity of the misconduct and therefore to penalty and to possible corrective action.[16] In the case of the refusal of the

---

1144 (Grinstead, 1987) (pilferage of 58-cent can of orange juice). In *Husky Oil Co.*, 85-2 ARB ¶8459 (Watkins, 1985) (racial slurs), an investigation that did not include an interview of the grievant was described as "imperfect but acceptable," in part because the grievant had been warned that one more misstep would result in his discharge.

[11]*E.g., Philco Corp.*, 45 LA 437 (Keeler, 1965) (profanity); *Amoco Chem. Corp.*, 70 LA 504 (Helburn, 1978) (substandard performance); *Apollo Merchandisers Corp.*, 70 LA 614 (Roumell, 1978) (rudeness to customers); *Arizona Aluminum Co.*, 82-1 ARB ¶8212 (Sass, 1982) (damage to company property); *Times Mirror Cable Television of Springfield, Inc.*, 86-2 ARB ¶8372 (Berns, 1986) (drug abuse).

[12]*Artco-Bell Corp.*, 61 LA 773 (Springfield, 1973). The point that inquiry is especially called for when an employee's supposed misconduct is conspicuously out of character was made even more directly by the arbitrator in *United Parcel Serv.*, 72 LA 1069, 1072 (White, 1979), where the grievant was fired for on-the-job intoxication even before the results of a company-ordered blood test were in:

His supervisors must have recognized that Grievant's claimed conduct was strange, uncharacteristic and a radical departure from his known life style. Still they did not wait until the final verdict was in before deciding to fire him. That decision was admittedly made before Grievant was taken to the hospital, and without waiting to talk with Grievant in his recovered moments.

Among many other cases where discipline for insubordination has been struck down because management did not ask why, see *Smith Cabinet Mfg. Co.*, 68-2 ARB ¶8376 (Geissinger, 1968) (refusal to perform what grievant believed to be additional work); *Atlantic Richfield Co.*, 70 LA 707 (Fox, 1978) (refusal to see company doctor because of religious beliefs).

[13]*United Tel. Co. of Fla.*, 61 LA 443 (Murphy, 1973).

[14]*Southern Cal. Edison Co.*, 89-1 ARB ¶8149 (Horowitz, 1989). See also *Bethlehem Steel Co.*, 31 LA 797 (Valtin, 1958); *Appalachian Regional Hosps., Inc.*, 70-2 ARB ¶8515 (Reid, 1970); *A. E. Staley Mfg. Co.*, 61 LA 125 (Traynor, 1973); *Dubuque Lorenz, Inc.*, 66 LA 1245 (Sinicropi, 1976); *St. Charles Furniture Corp.*, 70 LA 1099 (Fitzsimmons, 1978).

[15]*Phelps Dodge Aluminum*, 52 LA 375 (Howlett, 1969).

[16]*United Tel. Co. of Fla.*, supra note 13, at 447: "[I]t is not only what an employee did that is important; why he did it may minimize the gravity of what he did and thus bear directly upon what corrective action is appropriate."

work assignment, for example, if the foreman had asked the employee why he did not want to perform the assignment instead of ordering him to punch out immediately, he would have learned the reason for the refusal: The employee had suffered a bronchial attack the night before and was afraid that the dust and fumes from the paint shop would aggravate his condition. Under these conditions, discharge for insubordination was too harsh a penalty.[17]

Or take the employer that discharged an employee for not reporting for work in response to a call-in. Had it looked into the matter, it would have discovered that there was confusion about the reporting time; the employee came in too early and was unable to get through the plant gates, so, after waiting in the parking lot for nearly a half hour, he left. Viewing the current offense in combination with prior rules violations, the company determined to discharge him and turned a deaf ear to his protest that he had reported and could prove it. Ordering his reinstatement, the arbitrator observed: "Generally speaking, arbitrators overturn terminations on this factor [failure to investigate] alone."[18]

Even in a simple and straightforward case where everything points to an employee's guilt, what amounts to "probable cause"

---

[17]In *Gulf Printing Co.*, 61 LA 1174 (Lilly, 1974), the grievant allegedly violated a company rule by failing to remove a dock plate immediately after a railroad car was unloaded, causing considerable damage. The grievant claimed at the hearing that he had not complied with the rule because he had not been provided with the proper equipment and the damage was done after he left the dock to find a forklift driver to do the job—a fact the company could have learned if anyone had questioned the grievant before he was discharged. See also *International Harvester Co.*, 12 LA 1190 (McCoy, 1949) (was failure to follow instruction intentional?); *Sherwin-Williams Co.*, 56 LA 101 (Sullivan, 1971) (why did grievant strike foreman?); *Demby Rod and Fastener Mfg., Inc.*, 70-1 ARB ¶8293 (Daugherty, 1969) (why did verbal altercation take place?); *Ryder Truck Rental, Inc.*, 82-1 ARB ¶8186 (Allen, 1982) (was property damage willful?); *Concrete Pipe Prods.*, 91 LA 405 (Williams, 1988) (why did grievant fail to report as scheduled?).

[18]*Concrete Pipe Prods. Co.*, *supra* note 17, at 408. In *U.S. Steel Corp.*, 29 LA 272 (Babb, 1957), two truck drivers were fired solely because the company that leased trucks to their employer reported that they had "confessed" to swindling the lessor in connection with gasoline credit card purchases. From that report the employer, without troubling to ask the drivers whether the charges were true and whether their confessions had been freely given, jumped to the erroneous conclusion that a court had found the drivers guilty of larceny. Needless to say, both drivers were reinstated. See also *City of Cocoa*, 95 LA 425 (Seidman, 1990) (improper to discharge grievant for falsification of employment application, where company acted on basis of hearsay allegation that grievant had been convicted of felony rape when in fact conviction was for misdemeanor of sexual misconduct and grievant believed record had been expunged and statute of limitations had expired).

may not be enough to satisfy just cause standards. A good example is a case in which a nurse called in at 9 a.m. to say that she was too sick to work, then was seen by her supervisor that evening at a high school football game, and was fired without further investigation. What the employer thought was probable cause for discharge turned to be only "probable cause in a hurry." The nurse explained at the hearing that she had rested and taken medication all day, and felt well enough in the evening to accompany her son to his first high school football game. These facts were as consistent with innocence as with guilt, in the arbitrator's view, and the nurse prevailed.[19]

Needless to say, part of giving the grievant a chance to explain means that his or her explanation has to be considered seriously and not merely brushed off.

> **EXAMPLE:** Three times one night the web—i.e., the paper going through the printing press—broke, stopping production each time. When the foreman looked into the problem, one of the employees told him that he saw another employee "knock the web out" on one occasion. The foreman stationed himself on a walkway above the latter employee and saw his hand come through the web at one edge. He confronted this employee immediately and accused him of intentionally breaking the web. The employee was subsequently discharged.

But what did the foreman really see? Fixated on the idea that he had seen the grievant break webs before, and disturbed by the evening's production interruptions and by the report he had received, he made up his mind that the grievant must be the cause of the breakages and that his conduct must have been deliberate. But at a meeting held after the incident, the grievant explained that he was only trying to straighten the web by "flipping" the edges. Nevertheless, all the foreman would say (though he admitted that "flipping" the web was a common practice) was that there was no use in the grievant's lying—"I saw you do it!"

The problem: The foreman was not about to let anything the grievant had to say upset the conclusion to which he had already jumped. Because he was unwilling to listen or give the grievant a reasonable opportunity to explain, and because the

---

[19]*Appalachian Regional Hosps., Inc.*, 70-2 ARB ¶ 8515 (Reid, 1970).

grievant's explanation was plausible, the arbitrator put the grievant back to work.[20]

Was the Employee on Notice? Aside from the customary notice
problems (e.g., whether notice was understandable, specific
enough, in an acceptable form, and the like), investigation may
be needed to put to rest the preliminary question of whether
the employee was given any notice at all that the misconduct
could lead to discipline.

For example, just cause standards were held to have gone
by the board in a case where the company failed to find out
whether the employee had been aware that the conduct for
which he was discharged was prohibited. The employee's supervisor did not personally investigate his suspected misconduct, as
the agreement required, but instead referred the case to the
Postal Inspection Service for disciplinary action on the prema-
ture assumption that the employee had violated a federal postal
law. Had the supervisor questioned the grievant first, he would
have heard the explanation that later came out at the arbitration
hearing, namely, that the employee had never been explicitly
told that his misconduct (which involved backdating the postmark on a piece of personal mail) could result in discharge.[21]

Questioning Other Witnesses

Proof of misconduct falls short in many cases where more
thorough efforts by the employer to question all witnesses about
the events in dispute might have produced enough evidence by
way of corroboration for the employer to prevail.[22]

---

[20]*Dayton Newspapers, Inc.*, 70-2 ARB ¶8813 (McIntosh, 1970). The company's
investigation was also found to be deficient in *A. O. Smith Corp.*, 66-1 ARB ¶8025
(Daugherty, 1965), where the general foreman acknowledged that he had made up his
mind to terminate the grievant, and had even had the discharge papers prepared,
before hearing the grievant's explanation of why he had left his work area. See also *Goss
Co.*, 52 LA 201 (Sullivan, 1969) (employer took at face value complaint by employee
that grievant had encouraged him to restrict production); *Southwest Airlines Co.*, 89-1
ARB ¶8019 (Williams, 1988) (grievant given insufficient notice of fact-finding meeting;
no consideration of possible extenuating reasons for grievant's excessive idle time).
[21]*U.S. Postal Serv.*, 62 LA 293 (Killion, 1974).
[22]The failure to make a thorough investigation may not hurt the company's case
if it is nevertheless able to produce convincing evidence. See, e.g., *Washington, D.C.,
Publishers Ass'n*, 67-1 ARB ¶8060 (Whyte, undated) (employer's failure to investigate
supervisor's report not prejudicial, since there were no witnesses and no suggestions
were made as to what additional evidence investigation might have disclosed); and
McConway and Torley Corp., 67-2 ARB ¶8441 (Shister, 1967) (two supervisors' testimony
that grievant was sleeping was more credible than grievant's uncorroborated denial).

EXAMPLE: Consistent with a custom whereby employees brought in pastries and other snacks to share among themselves, a loaf of banana bread appeared one day in the unloader shack. After eating some of the bread, two employees experienced "strange sensations" and reported the matter to the company the next day. A check of some crumbs left in the shack revealed that the bread contained marijuana. Responsibility for the bread was subsequently laid at the door of a third employee, the grievant, on the basis of the following evidence:

(1) One of the employees who ate the bread stated that several employees (whose names he did not recall) told him that the bread had been brought in by the grievant.

(2) The second complainant remembered that the grievant invited him to have a piece of the bread.

(3) According to the employer, the grievant, when confronted, did not deny bringing in the bread but only made some comments about possible trouble with the police. At the hearing, however, the grievant claimed that he said he had nothing to do with the banana bread.

Did the employer's investigation produce convincing evidence of the grievant's guilt? The information that he had brought in the banana bread was only hearsay, and that he had invited an employee to have a piece established only that he knew the bread was in the shack, not that he necessarily had put it there. As for the implied "confession by silence" he gave when questioned, the grievant later repudiated it. His discharge was overturned.[23]

The employer's problem was that it stopped its investigation prematurely. "More probative facts" might have been produced, the arbitrator pointed out. For example, the employer did not try to determine the names of those who claimed to know that the bread belonged to the grievant. It did not interview employees who frequented the unloader shack to determine whether they had seen the grievant leave the bread there.[24] And it did

---

[23]*Hilo Coast Processing Co.*, 77-2 ARB ¶8453 (Tsukiyama, 1977). See also *Ryder Truck Rental*, 84-1 ARB ¶8002 (Murphy, 1983)(grievant prejudiced at predischarge hearing by failure of any party to discuss circumstances of fight with the one witness who observed entire incident); *General Tel. Co.*, 87-2 ARB ¶8340 (Collins, 1986) (investigation incomplete because of failure to interview essential witnesses).

[24]The company was also charged with the affirmative duty to determine whether any witnesses were present as an essential part of its investigatory efforts in *Spartan Printing Co.*, 50 LA 1263 (Bernstein, 1968). See also *Olin Mathieson Chem. Corp.*, 51 LA 97 (Daugherty, 1968) (failure to interview two witnesses who grievant claimed would confirm he was not smoking in boiler room); *Modern Automotive Servs., Inc.*, 69-2 ARB ¶8708 (Kennedy, 1969) (eyewitnesses to fight not questioned to determine who started

not obtain a signed statement from the grievant as confirmation of his supposed "confession."

Then there was the employer who had had persistent problems with employees drinking on their lunch hours. One afternoon, a group of eight employees returned from lunch an hour late, and their foreman smelled alcohol on the breath of one of them. The foreman assumed that all eight had been drinking and hence were not in a safe condition to resume work, and sent them home for the balance of the day. Other facts were ignored: Witnesses testified that some of the employees had drunk two or three glasses of beer at lunch but that some had had nothing to drink; and that their late return was caused not by drinking and carousing but by the unusually large number of patrons who had crowded the local tavern for its St. Patrick's Day corned beef special. Said the arbitrator: "The mere fact that one employee had the smell of alcohol on his breath is not an indication that he specifically was incapable of performing work and certainly there is no evidence of the condition of the other employees. The employer simply has not met any reasonable burden of proof in this regard."[25]

The employer may need to exercise some imagination and initiative in getting information from witnesses in certain situations. Take a case where an employee produced a doctor's excuse to show that he missed work because he was sick and not because he was on strike. The employer doubted the validity of the excuse and suspended him along with other employees for participating in the work stoppage. But going forward on the basis of doubts was unacceptable, the arbitrator found. The employer could have checked directly with the employee's doctor to find out whether he had been ill that day, asking the employee to waive confidentiality if necessary. Had he con-

---

it); *Gilman Paper Co.*, 61 LA 416 (Murphy, 1973) (reliance on statement of witness whose testimony proved to be equivocal coupled with failure to question two other employees who could have supplied additional evidence); *Oil City Hosp.*, 78-1 ARB ¶8082 (LeWinter, 1978) (coworkers of nurses' aide not questioned as to whether they heard her use abusive language to patient); *W-L Molding Co.*, 72 LA 1065 (Howlett, 1979) (personnel director refused shop steward's request that she question witnesses to grievant's alleged attack on vending machine because "I have my own witnesses"); *General Elec. Co.*, 74 LA 125 (Clark, 1979) (abuse of company time).

[25]*Automotive Pattern Co.*, 77-2 ARB ¶8435, 4862-63 (Daniel, 1977). See also *Inland Mills, Inc.*, 42 LA 840 (Davey, 1964) (sleeping on the job); *Great Atl. & Pac. Tea Co.*, 45 LA 968 (Volz, 1965) (theft); *East Ohio Gas Co.*, 62 LA 90 (Edes, 1973) ("sick-out"); *Pillsbury Co.*, 67 LA 601 (Levy, 1976) (misuse of sick leave); *Trailways, Inc.*, 88 LA 1073 (Goodman, 1987) (refusal to take drug test).

sented, "the Company might have obtained facts which would have supported the excuse or supported its disciplinary action. Instead of this, the Company was satisfied to do no more than to present to the Board an aura of suspicious circumstances. . . ."[26]

The Importance of Follow-Up

The requirement that an investigation be reasonably complete also means that the employer needs to take necessary follow-up measures, especially if its initial investigation leaves unsettled questions or produces contradictory versions of what took place.

> **EXAMPLE:** On Monday morning a grocery store supervisor informed the acting manager about a complaint lodged against one of his employees by a customer the previous Saturday evening. The gist of it was that the employee, one of two who were cleaning up some milk spilled by the customer's wife, had referred to her as "that bitch there." The acting manager interviewed the employee, who protested that all he said was, "That old lady knowed better than to spill the milk." His co-worker confirmed his story. Later that day the customer returned to the store and told the acting manager directly that the employee had called his wife an "old whore." The employee was thereupon fired.

The arbitrator noted:

> Such contradictions are neither unknown nor unusual, particularly in discharge cases. For a variety of reasons, each party has a different view of the events leading to discharge. There is, however, a distinction which may properly be made between cases where differences remain for the arbitrator to resolve, even after complete investigation by the company, and the instant case.

Both the grievant and his coworker said the grievant did not utter any profanity about the customer's wife. Moreover, the supervisor's hearsay version of the exact words used by the grievant was in conflict with the words the customer said the grievant used. Yet the acting manager did not continue his investigation by requestioning either the grievant or the supervisor to try to resolve the discrepancy, but accepted the customer's

---

[26]*U.S. Steel Corp.*, 40 LA 598, 602 (Seitz, 1963). In *Pottsville Area School Dist.*, 91 LA 515 (Mayer, 1988), the arbitrator held that the company's failure to interview the supervisor of two employees disciplined for "goofing off," or to involve the supervisor in the investigation, was evidence of a failure to make a proper or sufficient investigation.

complaint at face value. The arbitrator revoked the grievant's discharge, explaining that he was "unwilling to provide answers where such answers might have been provided in response to a more thorough investigation."[27]

This case raises another point about the necessity of questioning all witnesses to misconduct. For an employer to accept a customer's complaint on its face, without checking it out, is to ask for trouble. Although there may be reluctance to embroil a customer in an employer-employee dispute, an employer cannot rely on the maxim that "the customer is always right" to justify discipline without adequately investigating the truth of the customer's claims.[28] As stated by the arbitrator:

> The Company clearly has a responsibility to its customers to provide a store which is free from harassment by Company personnel. The Company also has a responsibility to its employees to administer discipline in a fair and impartial manner. Difficult as it may be, these responsibilities must be balanced.[29]

---

[27]*J. Weingarten, Inc.*, 77-1 ARB ¶8050, 3225 (Helburn, 1977). The necessity of follow-up is also highlighted in *Oil City Hosp.*, *supra* note 24, where the patient who complained that a nurse's aide had used abusive language toward her was not re-interviewed, even though details of the written statement that she provided at a later date did not jibe with her initial complaint; the grievant denied all her allegations and said she had her own witness; and there was some doubt as to whether the patient could actually have heard what she reported hearing from her own room. In *Pipe Coupling Mfg., Inc.*, 68-1 ARB ¶8088 (McDermott, 1967), an investigation that was limited to one phone call to an employee's home to find out if he was sick in bed as he claimed was not a sufficient basis on which to discharge him for unauthorized absence, especially since the company's only evidence that he was not sick was a hearsay report that he had "gone off to Canada with a lady." See also *Durham Hosiery Mills*, 24 LA 356 (Livengood, 1955) (more careful investigation would have established that one of two supposed felony "convictions" that led to grievant's discharge was only finding of probable cause); *Michigan Standard Alloys, Inc.*, 53 LA 511 (Forsythe, 1969) (no evidence that two unnamed employees who accused grievant of carrying gun "had been closely interrogated" by management following supposed incident); *Donaldson Co.*, 60 LA 1240 (McKenna, 1973) (arson; careful questioning of witnesses required to determine credibility).

[28]A case in point is *Reliance Universal, Inc.*, 68-1 ARB ¶8027 (Alexander, 1967) in which the discharge of a truck driver was overturned because the company accepted at face value a customer's complaint that he had caused considerable trouble by wandering through the customer's plant, starting uncomplimentary rumors about its business image, and undermining its employees' morale. The company made no attempt to determine exactly what the driver said or did that prompted the customer's protest, despite the fact that his codriver confirmed his statement that he had done nothing improper or out of the ordinary. See also *G. Heileman Brewing Co.*, 54 LA 1 (Solomon, 1969) (insubordination); *Alpha Beta Markets, Inc.*, 70-1 ARB ¶8034 (Guild, 1969) (rudeness to customer).

[29]*J. Weingarten, Inc.*, *supra* note 27.

All Documentary, Physical, and Medical Evidence Must Be Obtained

In his hot pursuit of facts, Sherlock Holmes tells us that it "is an axiom of mine that the little things are infinitely the most important"[30] and concludes that "[t]here is nothing more deceptive than an obvious fact."[31] The "little things" and "obvious facts" often are present in investigations in which documentary, physical, or medical evidence might play a part. When such readily available and obvious evidence is overlooked or disregarded or perhaps in some cases consciously ignored, an arbitrator may conclude that the investigation was incomplete or shabby and consequently sustain the grievance in whole or in part.

> **EXAMPLE:** In an effort to end an epidemic of thefts of jewelry and other valuables from its warehouse, the employer dusted a container of watches with a special powder. Supervisors watched as an employee entered the truck in which the container had been placed and disappeared from view. When he emerged a few minutes later, traces of powder were found on his hands and the watches were missing from their container. No one else was seen in the vicinity of the truck, and the employer concluded that this employee must have been the thief even though supervisors who searched him when he left the truck found no watches on his person.

The circumstances were suspicious indeed. But the employer overlooked one possibility: The truck was not searched carefully to see if the employee had concealed the watches somewhere inside. If that physical evidence had been located, the employer would have had the goods on the employee, both figuratively and literally. As it was, the arbitrator was left with a reasonable doubt as to who the culprit was.[32]

More "little things" and "obvious facts":

A brief scuffle. Two employees had a brief scuffle on the production line and were fired. The shift supervisor vaguely recalled that the employees had been previously warned about excessive fraternizing on the line and thereupon fired them. Result: Their dis-

---

[30]Sir A. Doyle, *A Case of Identity,* 1 The Complete Sherlock Holmes 217 (1905).
[31]*Id., The Boscombe Valley Mystery,* at 229.
[32]*Aldens, Inc.,* 77-1 ARB ¶8013 (Seitz, 1976).

charges were converted to disciplinary suspensions because "it is quite clear that he did not review their records, nor did he separate fact from gossip."[33]

A traffic accident. The employer reviewed reports filed by some employees, but not other reports, about a traffic accident. The police report was considered, but it was only hearsay and contained unverified accounts of the incident. Result: To consult just some of the reports was not enough. The grievant was reinstated with back pay.[34]

A fire in a locker. Two employees were charged with starting a fire in the maintenance shanty. Without taking a close look at the scene, the company rejected out of hand their story that they had discovered the fire in a locker shortly after they reported to work, kicked the lock off, and removed the burning contents but had been unable to extinguish the blaze. Instead, the company believed the fire investigator, who stated that the fire had started not in the locker but elsewhere in the building. The missing link: No one thought to examine the physical evidence that could have settled the matter—that is, no one looked at the locker (whose location the employees had pinpointed) to see if it was still locked. Result: reinstatement with full back pay.[35]

A case of sore ankles. An employee refused to work overtime, claiming he could not work in the cold boning room because his ankles were sore. The foreman, suspicious, fired him. The arbitrator pointed out that the employer could easily have determined whether the foreman's suspicions had any substance. "It could have had the company nurse look at his ankles. Swelling and discoloration would have been evident if his assertions were true. Lack of such symptoms would have deflated his excuse. Unfortunately, the Employer did not bother to determine the truth of the Grievant's assertion. . . ."[36]

---

[33]*Aerosol Techniques, Inc.*, 48 LA 1278 (Summers, 1967). Other cases involving failure to check personnel records in a timely manner are cited in Ch. 5, p. 251.

[34]*Hertz Corp.*, 78-1 ARB ¶8086 (Fox, 1978). See also *Armak Abrasives Div.*, 60 LA 509 (Hertz, 1973) (no attempt to obtain court records to establish facts of employee's prior criminal conviction).

[35]*U.S. Steel Corp.*, 78-2 ARB ¶8365 (Gootnick, 1978). See also *Carus Chem. Co.*, 70-2 ARB ¶8492 (Anrod, 1970) (equipment used to run defective product not inspected to make sure grievant's error, not mechanical failure, was responsible); *Formica Corp.*, 79-1 ARB ¶8012 (Keefe, 1978) (no attempt to retrieve cans guard believed contained beer and grievants later claimed contained soda pop); *Pettibone Ohio Corp.*, 72 LA 1144 (Feldman, 1979) (no search of grievants' lockers or vehicles for physical evidence to corroborate undercover agent's claim of marijuana smoking).

[36]*Hygrade Food Prods. Corp.*, 69 LA 414 (Harter, 1977). See also *Packaging Corp. of Am.*, 51 LA 127 (Davey, 1968), where the foreman merely assumed the grievant was malingering when he asked to go home early, and neither sent him to the company nurse to have his complaints verified nor questioned him in any detail; *Snyder Gen'l*

Sober or soused? Several witnesses reported that an employee had exhibited slurred speech, an unkempt appearance, and other signs of intoxication. The employee denied that she was drunk and blamed her symptoms on medication. She asked for a blood alcohol test but the employer said no. She prevailed because the employer could have put to rest the question of whether she was drunk, and therefore she was entitled to the benefit of the doubt.[37]

Investigation Must Be Pursued in a Timely Manner

Investigation Should Precede Discipline

No one would seriously argue that it is sound practice for the company to discipline without making an investigation. However, it is sometimes argued that where a grievance procedure is in place, an investigation can wait until a formal grievance has been filed and the issue joined. That view is by and large rejected (subject to certain exceptions[38]) for reasons enumerated by Arbitrator Kates:

Corp., 88 LA 1153 (Bard, 1987), where the company cancelled an employee's medical leave when it learned he had attended a fishing tournament and then fired him when he failed to return, without attempting to determine whether the employee had violated the terms of his leave or whether his leave request was a sham. But in *P. N. Hirsch & Co.*, 60 LA 1335 (Bothwell, 1973), the company was not required to obtain a medical report on the employee's condition where the causes of disability (cirrhosis of the liver and other complications of chronic alcoholism) were already known and the employee's ability to perform his job was best determined by actual observation. On medical evidence generally, see M. HILL, JR. & A. V. SINICROPI, EVIDENCE IN ARBITRATION 166–80 (2d ed. 1987).

[37]*Park Haven Care Center, Inc.*, 79-2 ARB ¶8238 (Fitzsimmons, 1979). In *Poly Tech, Inc.*, 91 LA 512 (Gunderson, 1988), an employee fired for bringing three cans of beer to work was ordered reinstated by the arbitrator. The supervisor who apprehended the employee failed to establish that the cans were not empty (as the employee later claimed), did not seize them, and gave the employee no chance to state his case. The company then discharged the employee without investigating further. Thus it failed to meet its burden of proof.

[38]Exceptions to this general rule have been made by arbitrators where the contract expressly provided for a hearing or review after communication of the company's decision or the filing of a grievance; see, e.g., *Hawaiian Airlines, Inc.*, 70-2 ARB ¶8563 (Tsukiyama, 1970). On the other hand, a contract requirement that the employer investigate, review the facts and circumstances, or hold a hearing before imposing discipline will carry special weight with the arbitrator. See, e.g., *Hayes Mfg. Co.*, 17 LA 412 (Platt, 1951); *Decor Corp.*, 44 LA 389 (Kates, 1965); *Trans World Airlines*, 56 LA 82 (Gilden, 1971); *Railway Employees' Dep't, AFL-CIO*, 69-1 ARB ¶8230 (Sembower, 1968). The arbitrator in *Hayes Mfg. Co.* commented:

> The obligation thus imposed upon management to consider the matter with the plant committee before placing the discharge into effect is on a par with an employee's obligation under the contract not to take the law into his own hands but to submit any grievance he may have against management for joint settlement under the grievance procedure. And no one will deny that it is just as necessary, in the field of industrial relations, for a management to adhere to contract proce-

Judgment. Investigation before discipline "tends to diminish the likelihood of impulsive and arbitrary decisions by supervisors and permits tempers to cool and deliberate judgment to prevail;

Carefulness. "it encourages careful investigation of the facts by both the Company and the Union;

Hearing. "it provides an opportunity whereby the accused may be heard;

Completeness. "it permits the presentation, sifting and weighing of all relevant factors;

Penalty. "it provides an opportunity to measure the proposed penalty against the alleged offense in the light of grievant's history, the past treatment by the employer of similar offenses, and other relevant circumstances;

Mitigating factors. "it permits consideration of apologies, regrets, and other mitigating circumstances;[39]

Rehabilitation. "and enables the parties to consider rehabilitation possibilities."

In conclusion, Kates commented as follows:

In my opinion, the fact that the discharge was subsequently reviewed through the grievance proceedings . . . does not cure the previous omission of such due process. The attitudes of the parties after an actual discharge notice has been given and a grievance filed and processed ordinarily cannot possess the same elements of elasticity as before the discharge. The Company is more likely to feel compelled to support a supervisory discharge deci-

---

dures as it is for the employees and the union to do so."
17 LA at 418.

[39]In *Southern Cal. Rapid Transit Dist.*, 93 LA 20 (Christopher, 1989), the arbitrator ruled that a bus driver was improperly discharged for testing positive for marijuana following his involvement in an accident, even though testing positive was a dischargeable offense under the company's drug policy. The parties' contract, he noted, required "fair and equitable" handling of discipline matters based on "proper cause." He inferred from this that the company must make a full and fair investigation to determine whether any mitigating facts are present in the triggering incident or in the employee's overall employment record. In the absence of such facts, discharge for a first offense of drug use would be proper; but in this case the driver had an exemplary employment record, and there was no evidence that drug use played any part in the accident or, indeed, that he was at fault in any way. See also *Indianapolis Power & Light Co.*, 88 LA 1109 (Volz, 1987) (discipline for threatening behavior reduced because of mitigating facts brought out at hearing but not discovered during company's investigation).

sion already made than the mere suggestion of a discharge not yet effectuated.[40]

Several other benefits might be added to Kates's list of reasons why an investigation should precede disciplinary action:

A posture of fair dealing. Investigation before disciplinary action not only helps get all the facts but lets employees know that the company is acting in good faith and intends to be fair. In this sense, investigation is a favorable influence upon the continuing relationship between the parties.[41]

Unpleasant surprises. Facts in the grievant's favor that are not brought out in its investigation are likely to emerge as unpleasant surprises for the employer at the arbitration hearing.[42]

Credibility problems. Failure to make a timely investigation

---

[40]*Decor Corp., supra* note 38, at 391. See also *Aerosol Techniques, Inc., supra* note 33: "The action, once taken, loads the scales with a desire to justify, and short of arbitration the burden is put on the employee and the Union to persuade the Company that the employee is entitled to his job back." In *Hertz Corp., supra* note 34, at 3409, the arbitrator put it this way:

It would appear to this Arbitrator that the Company in effect told the grievant that he would get his day in court through the grievance procedure after the exaction of the disciplinary measure. When this latter does in fact occur, as it appears to have done in the instant case, there usually results in excessive hardening of positions as well as difficulty in the procurement of witnesses by the Grievant.

And see *Ekstrom, Carlson & Co.*, 55 LA 764 (Davis, 1970) (profanity toward supervisor).

[41]Considerations of that kind were present in *Artco-Bell Corp.*, 61 LA 773, 783 (Springfield, 1973), where the company did not investigate the employee's reasons for refusing a work assignment. In the arbitrator's words:

In view of the foreman's statement [that he would quit] if the grievant were reinstated, there is left in the arbitrator's mind the strong impression that the Company did not particularly want the grievant back on the job and therefore did not take any action that might lead to his return. The evidence clearly shows that other employees have been allowed to change their minds about quitting. . . . Also other employees have been given an opportunity to produce a doctor's certificate to verify a physical disability. Why not the grievant?

See also *National Gallery of Art*, 91 LA 335 (Craver, 1988) (unfair to discharge employee for using abusive language without investigating circumstances and considering penalties meted out in similar situations); *Hollywood Park*, 84 LA 902 (Draznin, 1985) (failure to interview all participants in incident leading to grievant's termination suggests bias against grievant).

[42]*E.g.*, in *Gem Indus. Contractors Co.*, 89 LA 1087 (Wolk, 1987), the company discharged an employee on the basis of a report that he had "failed the urine test" required by a utility for which the company was performing work or that he had refused to take the test. What came out at the hearing—and what the company would have learned if had investigated the matter—was that the employee had "bashful kidneys" and was unable to urinate in the presence of others. He offered to take a blood test instead, but the utility's testers would not allow this alternative, and he was barred from the utility's premises. Since the employee was blameless, the arbitrator ordered his reinstatement.

often puts the arbitrator in "the difficult position of determining which of the two parties is telling the truth."[43] In other words, if the employer does not probe to uncover all the relevant facts, it may boil down to one side's word against the other's when the case reaches arbitration.

An unwelcome liability. Finally, if it "shoots from the hip" and is proved wrong in the grievance procedure or at the arbitration hearing, the company may find itself saddled with uncomfortably large back-pay and other costs—an obligation it might have avoided if it had asked questions first.[44]

Investigation Should Be Made Promptly

Again, no one would seriously argue that it is sound practice to drag one's heels in making an investigation. But sometimes promptness becomes a problem when the employer does not recognize that particular situations call for hot pursuit of the smoking gun.

EXAMPLE: Because supervisors had been finding empty beer cans and other indications that alcohol was being consumed in the plant, the employer stationed observers at the entrances to keep an eye out for employees who might be bringing alcohol back with them after lunch. The stakeouts appeared to pay off when two supervisors spotted three employees leaving the parking lot carrying paper bags. Before they reached the plant entrance they deposited the bags in some weeds and proceeded inside. The supervisors retrieved the paper bags, which contained cans of beer, and the employees subsequently were suspended. The grievants claimed, when questioned the following day, that they knew nothing of any beer. Two of them said their bags contained cigarettes and bowling clothes for an after-work game, and that they brought the bags into the plant. Two other employees testified that they saw one of the employees carrying a paper bag past their machines.

---

[43]*Aeroquip Corp.*, 85-1 ARB ¶8031, 3130 (Roumell, 1984) (fighting).

[44]In *Gem Indus. Contractors Co., supra* note 42, not only was the employee awarded full back pay, but the arbitrator suggested that the remedy should include reimbursement to the union for the costs of psychiatric evaluation and the psychiatric testimony presented at the hearing as well as payment of the cost of the entire arbitration proceedings. See also *National Gallery of Art, supra* note 41, at 338, where the arbitrator awarded the grievant partial back pay because the agency "should not be rewarded for its clear failure to carefully investigate the relevant circumstances before it formulated its disciplinary proposal."

Faced with a direct conflict in testimony, the arbitrator looked elsewhere for a basis to decide the case and found it in the company's lack of reaction to events as they were unfolding. The supervisors did not stop the grievants as soon as they entered the plant to ask them about the suspect bags. Had they done so, "[w]hether or not the grievants had bags (of beer? of bowling clothes and cigarettes?) with them before and/or after they entered the plant would not now be one of the subjects of contradictory testimony." If the grievants were guilty, the company would have had the proof it needed. This case illustrates the proposition that "if weaker and less satisfactory evidence is offered when it was within the power of the party to produce stronger and more trustworthy evidence, the evidence should be viewed with distrust."[45]

If investigation is delayed and serious misconduct is in issue, arbitrators have been known to infer that whatever the employee may have done, it probably was not as grave as the company later tried to make out.[46] In other cases memories have

---

[45]*Okonite Co.*, 74-2 ARB ¶8525, 4951 (Ludlow, 1974). A similar situation was presented in *Poly Tech, Inc., supra* note 37, where a supervisor failed to seize beer cans brought to work by an employee and thus was unable to establish that the cans were not empty, as the employee later claimed. Cases involving drinking and intoxication especially require prompt investigation because the "evidence" of an employee's physical symptoms tends to disappear quickly. See, e.g., *St. Louis Diecasting Corp.*. 69-1 ARB ¶8163 (Erbs, 1968) (supervisor waited to confront grievant with accusation that he had been drinking until after lunch, when food could have covered up any alcohol smell). But see *Kellogg Co.*, 93 LA 884, 892 (Clarke, 1989), where the arbitrator held that a three-month delay between an episode of on-duty pot smoking and the beginning of disciplinary proceedings did not invalidate the grievant's discharge, even though it deprived him of the opportunity for a defense based on a drug screen, where the delay was caused by the employer's desire to preserve the anonymity of its undercover agent. "[W]hat constitutes a fair procedure must be determined in light of all the circumstances existing at the time. . . . The Company has not only the right but the obligation to provide all of its employees as safe a working environment as it can reasonably do so."

[46]Thus in *Spartan Printing Co.*, 50 LA 1263, 1265 (Bernstein, 1968), the arbitrator commented:

No investigation of the asserted insubordination was made during the shift in which it was supposed to have taken place. Although the Grievant was allegedly refusing orders and threatening supervisors with bodily harm, he was permitted to continue at his work for almost five hours without surveillance. [The supervisor] did not even report the matter to the foreman in charge of the shift for almost half an hour. Moreover, the foreman in charge did not feel that the problem warranted either an immediate investigation or a call to the department superintendent, although he clearly had the authority to do both.

In *Sahara Hotel*, 76-2 ARB ¶8410 (Koven, 1976), the arbitrator found that it was unlikely the grievant was as intoxicated as the employer later claimed, since her supervisor ordered her to go on working even after he first suspected she might have been drinking. See also *St. John's Episcopal Hosp.*, 87-2 ARB ¶8350 (Brown, 1987) (four- or five-day delay in reporting verbal threats made seriousness questionable).

faded,[47] or, as shown in the following examples, delay has caused the company to miss the chance to gather evidence that by its very nature is available only at a particular time and place.

> *Was the grievant malingering?* The evidence was in conflict as to whether the grievant had gone to the first aid station to have his eye cleaned out, as he claimed, or whether he had been malingering, as his foreman suspected. Another employee testified that he had watched the grievant being treated; but the foreman asserted that while he had been at the first aid station, the grievant was just standing around. The first aid attendant did not recall even seeing the grievant there. What should the foreman have done?

The foreman should have talked to the grievant. In addition to noting reasons why the attendant might not have remembered, the arbitrator asked:

> Why did not [the foreman] question the grievant in the First Aid Room or immediately after he stepped out the door concerning the reason for his presence there? Had he done so, he could have confronted him with the First Aid Attendant and thereby better established whether the latter had seen and treated the grievant. It must also be remembered that the grievant and [the attendant] were not brought together for purposes of positive identification before the discharge decision was made.

As a result, the conflict was decided in the grievant's favor.[48]

> *Did the grievant spray the paint?* The grievant was suspected of spraying the cars of "scabs" with paint as he walked a picket line. But numerous placard-carrying pickets stood between the grievant and company observers, obscuring their view of the grievant. What could they have done?

Someone should have followed the grievant.

---

[47]*E.g., Apollo Merchandisers Corp.*, 70 LA 614 (Roumell, 1978), where the arbitrator found that a sales clerk who was confronted about customer complaints only long after the fact did not have an opportunity to defend herself because she could not be expected to remember the specific incidents.

[48]*National Carbide Co.*, 49 LA 692, 697 (Kesselman, 1967). The foreman's failure to ask questions on the spot also hurt the company in *Artco Bell Corp., supra* note 41. Because the company did not learn until after the employee's discharge that he had refused an assignment to work in the wood shop allegedly for health reasons, it cut off the possibility of getting solid evidence that the excuse was invalid. If the company had asked the employee to produce medical confirmation of his condition and the employee was unable to do so, the company would have had a strong case.

Furthermore, considering the obvious trauma surrounding this entire situation, it seems to the Arbitrator the security employees lacked perceptivity, and prudence as well, when they failed to take photos at the scene (they had the equipment to do so), or why they did not keep Grievant under very close scrutiny until the police arrived, so Grievant, if he had a spray can, would be apprehended with the evidence."

Result: an incomplete investigation, and a grievant put back to work.[49]

Was the clerk rude to a customer? Two customers complained to the grocery store manager about a clerk's discourteous conduct. The clerk was not confronted by either of the customers, nor was he allowed to give his version of what took place. What should the manager have done?

The manager should have brought the customers face to face with the clerk. The way the arbitrator saw the evidence, it was possible that the clerk's supposed affronts did not take place as charged but were exaggerated. Instead of arranging a confrontation when the complaints were first lodged, the manager allowed his "witnesses" to vanish without attempting to find out what really had taken place. Result: an inconclusive investigation and no just cause.[50]

II. Investigation and Due Process

Due Process—An Industrial Version

The renowned arbitrator and former labor secretary Willard Wirtz has often been quoted as saying, "To speak of 'due process of arbitration' is to risk a seeming confusion of terms. For 'due process' is a symbol borrowed from the lexicon of law and therefore suspect in this shirt-sleeves, seat-of-the-pants,

---

[49]*McDonnell Douglas Astronautics Co.*, 74 LA 726 (Hardy, 1980). Another strike case is *Briggs Mfg. Co.*, 74 LA 877 (Welch, 1980), where the company failed to identify the active participants in a strike because it did not ask for the names of employees who were assembled outside the gate or even those who entered the plant to speak with the plant manager.

[50]*Alpha Beta Markets, Inc.*, 70-1 ARB ¶8034 (Guild, 1969). In *J. Weingarten, Inc.*, 77-1 ARB ¶8050 (Helburn, 1977), the discharge of a grocery-store employee for using abusive language to a customer was reversed because the company failed to resolve discrepancies between the customer's and employee's versions of what took place.

look!-no-hands business of arbitration."[51] Wirtz was expressing the view widely held among arbitrators that the complex due process protections that individuals are afforded in judicial proceedings under the Constitution and the law are out of place in disciplinary proceedings.

Nevertheless, arbitrators with few exceptions[52] have taken the position that the employer must observe certain basic standards of fairness in its dealings with employees—what has been called an "industrial version" of due process[53] or an employee's "industrial civil rights."[54] The rationale has been stated thusly by Arbitrator Dworkin:

> The procedural aspect of just cause is not dogmatic ritual. Its object is to postpone a penalty until thorough consideration takes place—to prevent supervisors from making bottom-line decisions before they know the knowable facts and have a chance to reflect. Who is to say that Grievants would not have been treated to greater moderation if the Superintendent had investigated and considered before reacting?[55]

The basic due process rights to which an employee who is accused of misconduct is entitled include:

---

[51]According to Wirtz, due process in arbitration and at the work place "is not a set of rules at all, at least not any particular set of rules, and is much more than a 'legal' doctrine. I think of 'due process' as being the exercise of any authority with a 'due' regard to the balancing of the two kinds of interests, individual and group interests, that are involved in every situation arising in a complex society." *Due Process of Arbitration*, THE ARBITRATOR AND THE PARTIES 1, 2 (Proceedings of the 11th Annual Meeting, National Academy of Arbitrators 1958).

[52]*E.g., American Hoist & Derrick Co.*, 53 LA 45 (Stouffer, 1969), where the arbitrator held that the contract is the only source of such due process rights as the right of an employee to be heard before discipline is imposed. See also *Johnson Controls, Inc.*, 85 LA 594 (Garnholtz, 1985), where the arbitrator found that the parties' contract left it up to the company to determine what evidence it needed to discharge an employee and that the company's failure to conduct an investigation did not violate any due process rights of the employee.

[53]Arbitrator Kelliher, in *Flintkote Co.*, 59 LA 329, 330 (1972): "While this Arbitrator does not believe that all of the complexities of due process that exist in judicial proceedings are equally applicable in arbitration matters, certain 'basic notions of fairness or due process' must be followed." Arbitrator Berman, in *DeVry Inst. of Technology*, 87 LA 1149 (1986): "Basic considerations of due process would require the employer to: (1) notify the charged employee of the charges against him; (2) inform him of the nature of the evidence in its possession so that he might respond to it; and (3) commence and complete the investigation within a reasonable period, at the conclusion of which the charges will be dropped or the employee will be disciplined" (footnotes omitted).

[54]S. Bernstein, *Workshop on Chicago Tripartite Committee Report*, PROBLEMS OF PROOF IN ARBITRATION 129 (Proceedings of the 19th Annual Meeting, National Academy of Arbitrators 1967).

[55]*Meyer Prods., Inc.*, 91 LA 690, 693 (1988) (fighting).

- the right to be informed of the charges;
- the right to confront accusers;
- the right to answer charges; and
- the right to counsel (i.e., to union representation).

That list should be lengthened, in the view of some arbitrators, to include the constitutional rights against self-incrimination (Fifth Amendment) and unreasonable search and seizure (Fourth and Fourteenth Amendments), as discussed further below.

Due process in disciplinary cases has been discussed by numerous authorities.[56] This chapter deals solely with the principal due process issues that come up within the context of investigation. (A remaining due process matter, an employee's right to be told what he is accused of, is covered in Chapter 5.)

Remedy for Due Process Violations. Does an employer's failure to provide due process mean that discipline will be overturned by an arbitrator? Not necessarily. Some arbitrators have taken the position that, although the employer has an obligation to respect the due process rights of employees, a failure to do so should not be ground for overturning or modifying disciplinary action unless the employee's interests have been—or at least may have been—prejudiced in some way.[57]

---

[56] In addition to Wirtz, *supra* note 51, see R. W. FLEMING, THE LABOR ARBITRATION PROCESS 165–98 (1965); H. T. Edwards, *Due Process Considerations in Labor Arbitration*, 25 ARB. J. 141–47 (1970); R. L. Hogler, *Industrial Due Process and Judicial Review of Arbitration Awards*, 31 LAB. L.J. 570ff (1980); R. L. Miller, *Worker Privacy and Collective Bargaining*, 33 LAB. L.J. 154–68 (1982); FAIRWEATHER'S PRACTICE AND PROCEDURE IN LABOR ARBITRATION 267–309 (R. J. Schoonhoven, ed., 3d ed. 1991); R. L. Hogler, *Taracorp and Remedies for Weingarten Violations: The Evolution of Industrial Due Process*, 37 LAB. L.J. 403–11 (1986); M. HILL, JR., & A. V. SINICROPI, EVIDENCE IN ARBITRATION 229–72 (2d ed. 1987).

[57] Arbitrator Marlatt, in *Cameron Iron Works*, 73 LA 878 (1979):

The essential question for an arbitrator is not whether disciplinary action was totally free from procedural error, but rather whether the process was fundamentally fair. [The arbitrator] must find in order to overturn the employer's action on procedural grounds, that there was at least a possibility, however remote, that the procedural error may have deprived the grievant of a fair consideration of his case.

See also *Michigan Dep't of Social Servs.*, 84-1 ARB ¶8145 (Borland, 1984) (withholding identities of key witnesses against grievant until hearing not ground for overturning discipline, since grievant not disadvantaged); *U.S. Postal Serv.*, 88 LA 825 (Nolan, 1987) ("Before a small procedural error will be held to invalidate a disciplinary action the Union must show it was 'harmful'—that is, that in some significant way it led Management to an erroneous decision or prejudiced the Grievant's position."); *Safeway Stores, Inc.*, 93 LA 1147 (Wilkinson, 1989) (failure to interview grievant or his physicians before discharging him for malingering did not invalidate discharge, since further investigation would only have confirmed employer's belief that discharge was justified).

Where the arbitrator finds that a grievant guilty of misconduct otherwise meriting discharge was denied due process—in the case of the "pragmatist," to the point where the grievant's interests were prejudiced—a common remedy is reinstatement without back pay, sometimes with an admonition to the grievant that he or she is being given an undeserved last chance.[58] On the other hand, arbitrators occasionally have opted for back pay in varying amounts without reinstatement.[59] One arbitrator, in a case where the grievant had been proved guilty of misappropriation of funds but had been the victim of serious procedural defects, offered the employer a choice of remedies—reinstatement without back pay or back pay without reinstatement. The grievant's usefulness as an employee might have been ended, he stated, and it was up to the employer to determine whether this was so.[60]

Right to Answer Charges and Time of Hearing

One of the indispensable due process rights that have been imported from the criminal law and incorporated into "industrial due process" is the right of an employee who is accused of misconduct to answer the charges.[61] Arbitrators have stressed

---

[58]*E.g., Otero County Hosp. Ass'n*, 83 LA 98 (Finston, 1984) (poor attitude, uncooperativeness); *Lockheed Corp.*, 83 LA 1018 (Taylor, 1984) (insubordination; abusive language); *United Press Int'l*, 88-2 ARB ¶8421 (Witney, 1988) (assaulting coworker); *Meyer Prods., Inc.*, 91 LA 690 (Dworkin, 1988) (fighting).

[59]*E.g., Southwest Airlines*, 80 LA 628 (King, 1983) (back pay awarded up to time when proper investigation established just cause for discharge); *State Paper & Metal Co.*, 88-1 ARB ¶8112 (Klein, 1987) (back pay from date of discharge to date of hearing where contract provided that no employee would be discharged without hearing); *Chromalloy Am. Corp.*, 93 LA 828 (Woolf, 1989) (back pay from date of discharge to close of arbitration hearing, since grievant not informed of specific charges against him prior to hearing).

[60]*Virgin Islands Water & Power Auth.*, 89 LA 809 (Watkins, 1987).

[61]Only in the very exceptional case has an employer been held to be justified in undertaking an investigation into misconduct without informing the suspect. Such a case was *National Labor Relations Bd.*, 74 LA 518 (Draznin, 1980), involving a field examiner with the National Labor Relations Board who was accused by the responding party of engaging in collusion with the charging party in a case he had been assigned to investigate. Although the union protested that the examiner was entitled to be informed that a serious charge had been made against him, the arbitrator accepted the employer's argument that secrecy was required by the very nature of the alleged misconduct, since if the examiner knew of the investigation and were guilty, he might conspire further with the charging party to cover up his misconduct. Another situation that may justify a failure to inform the target of an investigation of the charges is where the company has evidence of criminal activity on company premises, such as drug dealing or gambling. See note 45 *supra*.

that an employer's failure to give an employee a fair hearing as part of its investigation is a due process violation as well as a matter of inadequate fact finding.[62]

> *Arbitrator Murphy:* In addition to a valid substantive basis, disciplinary actions must conform to procedural fairness, sometimes referred to as "industrial due process." This requires a full and fair investigation of the facts and circumstances surrounding the employee conduct, and normally will include an opportunity for the employee, before the Company makes its final decision, to offer any denials, explanations or justifications which may be relevant.[63]

The right of an employee to present witnesses, which is closely related to the right to speak on one's own behalf, has also been upheld as a fundamental due process right in a number of cases,[64] as has the right of an employee to have access to damaging information in the possession of the company.[65]

---

[62]E.g., *U.S. Steel Corp.*, 29 LA 272 (Babb, 1957) (swindling company that leased trucks to employer); *Phelps Dodge Aluminum*, 52 LA 375 (Howlett, 1969) (walking off job); *Osborn & Ulland, Inc.*, 68 LA 1146 (Beck, 1977) (various infractions, including smoking on sales floor, wandering into unauthorized areas, excessive use of telephone); *St. Charles Furniture Corp.*, 70 LA 1099 (Fitzsimmons, 1978) (absenteeism); *Ryder Truck Rental, Inc.*, 82-1 ARB ¶8186 (Allen, 1982) (destruction of company property); *Otero County Hosp. Ass'n*, 83 LA 98 (Finston, 1984) (poor attitude, uncooperativeness); *McCartney's, Inc.*, 84 LA 799 (Nelson, 1985) (absenteeism); *Federal Mogul Corp.*, 86 LA 225 (Blinn, 1985) (delay in obtaining leave extension); *United Press Int'l, supra* note 58. However, in *Dierbergs Market*, 93 LA 1113, 1117 (Yarowsky, 1989), the arbitrator held that the company's failure to inform the grievant of the charges against her and give her an opportunity to explain did not invalidate her discharge for "grazing" (eating snack-bar food without paying for it). The grievance procedure, he said, adequately protects the interests of a grievant; in the public sector, he added, "this failure would clearly invalidate the disciplinary proceedings."
[63]*United Tel. Co. of Fla.*, 61 LA 443, 447 (1973). Arbitrator Taylor, in *Lockheed Corp.*, 83 LA 1018, 1023 (1984):

> Management did not give the Employee at least a chance "to tell his side of the story" before the discharge decision was made. This is one of the basic principles of due process and whereas Management undoubtedly felt it had all the evidence it needed to support the termination, basic principles of fairness would indicate that the accused be given "his day in court." It is important that the "day in court" be given *before* a decision to impose discipline is made.

[64]*E.g., Hudson and Manhattan R.R. Co.*, 38 LA 641 (Seidenberg, 1962) (negligence); *Bethlehem Steel Corp.*, 54 LA 361 (Porter, 1969) (striking another employee).
[65]In *Social Sec. Admin.*, 86 LA 1205, 1211 (Kubie, 1986) (unsatisfactory performance), the arbitrator held that the grievant had a right to inspect the employer's original files to determine whether the mistakes with which he was charged were really significant. He further ruled that the hour's time allowed on the eve of the hearing to inspect a large box of 250 forms was "patently insufficient." "I deem this unconscionable procedure inconsistent with the entire nature of the arbitration process." In *Regional Transp. Dist.*, 90 LA 27 (Yarowsky, 1987) (sobriety test), the arbitrator held that due process was denied a grievant who was refused a copy of a report that converted a urine

Arbitrators in many cases have taken what might be called a hard-line approach to the question of timing, holding that an employee must be given an interview or hearing before any discipline is imposed, and that due process is not satisfied even if he gets a chance to tell his story after disciplinary action has been taken.[66] Due process, according to this approach, is not merely a matter of technicalities, but serves to insure that discipline will be imposed only on the basis of all the facts and with adequate cause.[67] A predisciplinary hearing or interview also allows the union to represent the employee at an early stage; this further assures full consideration of the employee's rights, as well as the needs of both parties in the collective bargaining process.

Due process rights, in other words, are important in themselves. A decision by an arbitrator to revoke or reduce discipline because the grievant was not given a predisciplinary hearing, or some other due process right (e.g., the right to union representation, which is treated in the next section), serves as "notice" to the employer that due process is an integral part of just cause, and that observing employees' due process rights is an obligation that flows from the collective bargaining relationship.[68]

---

test to an equivalent blood alcohol level. The grievant, he stated, had a right to receive this information promptly in order to contest his discharge.

[66]Arbitrator Kelliher in *Flintkote Co., supra* note 63, at 330: "The value of such a hearing both to the Company and the Grievant is fully recognized. The purpose cannot be served by an ex post facto determination as to whether the Grievant was 'prejudiced' by the lack of 'due process.'" Application of this principle may be seen in, *e.g., Pennsylvania Dep't of Public Welfare,* 86 LA 1032 (Spilker, 1986) (leaving work after collapse of ceiling); *Sun Valley Bus Lines,* 87 LA 195 (D'Spain, 1986) (leaving passenger at bus stop); *Meyer Prods., Inc.,* 91 LA 691 (Dworkin, 1988) (fighting); *Chromalloy Am. Corp., supra* note 59 (threatening supervision). In *Tucson Unified School Dist.,* 89-1 ARB ¶8236 (White, 1989) (theft), the arbitrator overturned a discharge because the grievant was not given an opportunity to respond to additional information received by the company between the disciplinary interview and the issuance of the termination letter.

[67]See *Osborn & Ulland, Inc., supra* note 62, in which the employee was discharged without hearing solely on the basis of unsupported complaints by her supervisor, who she claimed was angry because she had rejected his persistent sexual advances. See also *Penn-Dixie Cement Co.,* 29 LA 451 (Brecht, 1957), where the employer discharged the grievant upon hearing that he had been arrested on a burglary charge, only later looking for reasons to support its impulsive action.

[68]In *Chromalloy Am. Corp., supra* note 59, the arbitrator, having found the grievant guilty of flagrant misconduct, declined to order reinstatement but awarded the grievant back pay from the date of his discharge to the close of the arbitration hearing because the company failed to tell him what he was charged with or give him opportunity to tell his side of the story. The arbitrator concluded her opinion as follows:

The arbitrator reminds both parties, [the grievant], and all others who learn of this decision that this remedy is ordered to encourage the Company in its adherence to

Other arbitrators have taken a more pragmatic view of due process, declining to alter a penalty unless an employee has been demonstrably disadvantaged or prejudiced by not being given a hearing until after discipline has been imposed.[69] This approach to due process places more emphasis on the end result of disciplinary action, and on whether justice has been served in the case of an individual grievant, rather than on the process by which disciplinary decisions are made.

"Practicalities" have also governed in cases where, for example, an employer has made up its mind that discharge is called for but has not actually implemented the decision before hearing the employee's story;[70] and where the employer told a number of employees they were to be suspended and that the length of the suspensions would be decided after the hearings had been held.[71]

Must Employee Cooperate With Company's Investigation?

Whether an employee is obligated to cooperate with a company's investigation of suspected misconduct depends primarily upon whether constitutional privileges against self-incrimination (Fifth Amendment) and unreasonable search and seizure (Fourth and Fourteenth Amendments) guaranteed to individuals as citizens carry over to the workplace and apply to them as

---

the procedural elements of just cause. The ordering of this remedy does *not* reflect any approval of [the grievant's] statements or justification of his behavior.

[69]*E.g., St. Regis Paper Co.*, 74 LA 1281 (Kaufman, 1980) (although "better course" would have been for company to have heard his side, company had convincing evidence of grievant's guilt and outcome would have been the same); *Southern Bell Tel. & Tel. Co.*, 75 LA 409 (Seibel, 1980) (grievant had chance to defend himself in court and at arbitration hearing; no contention that he was prejudiced by company's failure to question him earlier); *Kidde, Inc., Weber Aircraft Div.*, 86 LA 681, 86-1 ARB ¶8200 (Dunn, 1985) ("harmful error" found in failure to obtain grievant's side of story; hence, reinstatement without back pay ordered); *U.S. Postal Serv.*, 88 LA 825, 831 (Nolan, 1987) ("Before a small procedural error will be held to invalidate a disciplinary action the Union must show it was 'harmful'—i.e., that in some significant way it led Management to an erroneous decision or prejudiced the Grievant's position.").

[70]*Baumfolder Corp.*, 78 LA 1060 (Modjeska, 1982) (reporting to work under the influence).

[71]*Equitable Gas Co.*, 75 LA 853 (Duff, 1980). Although the letter to the employees indicated a "predisposition" as to management's view of their involvement in an illegal work stoppage, the decision to suspend them had not been "etched in stone," and no chilling effect on the employees' ability to defend themselves at the future hearings was demonstrated.

employees.[72] There is a division of opinion on this question among arbitrators.[73]

Majority View: Employee Has Duty to Cooperate

Most arbitrators take the position that an employee must answer questions put to him in the course of an investigation and submit to reasonable searches. Constitutional privileges, in this view, do not affect the duty to cooperate.[74]

> *Arbitrator Dworkin:* [A]n employee owes a duty to cooperate with management in investigation of matters within its legitimate concern. While in a criminal case an employee may remain silent, and need not testify against himself, the employment relationship is not governed by these principles. The grievant was duty-bound to answer inquiries on the part of members of management, forthrightly and truthfully.[75]

Reasons cited by arbitrators in support of the duty to cooperate include the following:

Constitutional protections out of place in the industrial setting. Constitutional privileges under the Fifth, Fourth, and Fourteenth Amendments have their origin in concerns about the abuse of governmental power and the need to protect individuals against the power of the state; thus they are properly invoked only against the government, and have no place in the industrial setting.[76]

---

[72]Arbitrator McGury, in *Simoniz Co.*, 44 LA 658, 660 (1964): "The dilemma is often presented . . . between implementing the obviously legitimate right, concern and duty, of the Company to make an exhaustive investigation of all the facts surrounding the theft of a substantial amount of Company property, while protecting the rights of employees and citizens to be free from unreasonable search and interrogation, or the humiliation caused by the implicit suggestion of dishonesty."

[73]A useful review of the issues involving constitutional rights at the workplace include R. L. Miller, *Worker Privacy and Collective Bargaining*, 33 Labor L.J. 154–68 (1982). The issue also is discussed in *Hearing*, Arbitration 1982 143–48 (Proceedings of the 35th Annual Meeting, National Academy of Arbitrators 1983); and Arbitration 1988 184–87 (Proceedings of the 41st Annual Meeting, National Academy of Arbitrators 1989).

[74]In addition to the citations in note 73 *supra*, see W. W. Wirtz, *Due Process in Arbitration*, The Arbitrator and the Parties 19 (Proceedings of the 11th Annual Meeting, National Academy of Arbitrators 1958); Fleming, *supra* note 56 at 182ff; Edwards, *supra* note 56, at 142; R. L. Hogler, *Industrial Due Process and Judicial Review of Arbitration Awards*, 31 Labor L.J. 796 (1980).

[75]*Babcock & Wilcox Co.*, 60 LA 778, 783 (1972) (refusal to answer questions concerning possession of marijuana).

[76]See comment by John E. Dunsford on J. Getman, *What Price Employment? Arbitration, the Constitution, and Personal Freedom*, Arbitration—1976 76ff (Proceedings of the 29th Annual Meeting, National Academy of Arbitrators 1976); *Lockheed Aircraft Corp.*, 27 LA 709 (Maggs, 1956) (drinking and possession of alcohol); *Northwest Airlines, Inc.*,

Industrial penalties not as serious as criminal penalties. Discharge has been characterized by some as "economic capital punishment," a phrase which suggests that there is an analogy between the criminal and industrial systems of justice. However, even the extreme penalty of discharge is not commensurate with the penalties that the state can impose; loss of freedom is more serious than loss of a job.[77]

Guilt not the bottom line. Industrial discipline is not to be viewed "primarily as a question of penalty for misconduct, but as a problem of whether or not, all things considered, the individual has proved an unsatisfactory employee."[78]

No right to a particular job. "[W]hile everyone has a right to all constitutional protections, he does not have a right to a particular job. It is felt that there are circumstances where an employee cannot contemporaneously fully enjoy all of his constitutional rights, and full freedom from company discipline."[79]

Duty to cooperate a "quid pro quo." In an important sense, the employee's obligation to cooperate with an investigation is a logical correlative—a kind of *quid pro quo*—of management's obligation to conduct an investigation.[80] To put this another way, it would be unreasonable to hold management to the duty of conducting a thorough investigation and, at the same time, to tie its hands by allowing employees to refuse to participate.

---

56 LA 837 (Wyckoff, 1971) (alcohol violation); *Weirton Steel Co.*, 68-1 ARB ¶8249 (Kates, 1968) (theft); *Orthodox Jewish Home for the Aged*, 91 LA 810 (Sergent, 1988) (assault and robbery).

[77]A. H. Stockman, comment on W. W. Wirtz, *supra* note 74 at 39-40.

[78]J. Hill, cited by Wirtz, *supra* note 74, at 19.

[79]*Aldens*, 58 LA 1213, 1215 (McGury, 1972) (theft). The arbitrator went on to point out:

> The contract for wages carries with it the restriction, and even complete suspension of many individual rights during working hours. An employee is fettered in many ways while on company time. Accordingly, we do not hold that all of the rights of a criminal defendant automatically extend to a grievant in a disciplinary case.

[80]Arbitrator Johnson, in *St. Luke's Hosp.*, 93 LA 1241, 1245 (1989):

> While the hospital is committed to thoroughly investigate the facts upon which disciplinary action is premised, it cannot be accountable for knowledge not available to it. The aggrieved has a corresponding duty to diligently present all pertinent information which may affect a disciplinary decision. It is the grievant who must bear the consequences of a failure to pursue and present all corroborating information.

See also *Dover Corp.*, 78-2 ARB ¶8465 (Haemmel, 1978) (sexual advances to female employee; grievant tied company's hands by refusing to meet with its representative); *Ralston Purina Co.*, 75 LA 313 (Brown, 1980) (company had no means of verifying grievant's statement denying responsibility for telephoned bomb threats because he refused to name individuals who he claimed were responsible).

Both sides to a disciplinary dispute have mutual obligations with respect to determining all the facts and circumstances, which reflect the parties' mutual rights and responsibilities within the collective bargaining relationship.[81]

An employee's duty to cooperate applies not only when his own conduct is being investigated, but when another employee is under suspicion. Arbitrators have expressed sympathy for the employee who is asked to give evidence against a fellow employee, but have held that reluctance to act as an "informer" does not excuse him from the duty to cooperate.

> *Arbitrator Jones:* [A]s on-duty employees, being questioned about the conduct of other on-duty employees, they were obligated to respond honestly and in good faith, even if they found the uninvited and unwanted situation of witnessing and reporting—"informing"—to be distasteful or embarrassing to them. Unlike kids on the street or late night movie heroes, employees are not entitled to refuse to "tell on" co-workers who have violated such a serious work rule as forbids alcoholic drinking by employees while on duty.[82]

Arbitrators who subscribe to this "majority view" have held that the company may justifiably require an employee to cooperate in an investigation in the following ways:

- Answer questions in connection with suspected misconduct;[83]
- Submit to a search of his person, lunch box, purse, locker, etc.;[84]

---

[81]"The relationship of labor and management is not an isolated, impersonal affair comparable to that of prosecutor and defendant, but an ongoing collaborative enterprise with its own unique texture." Dunsford, *supra* note 76, at 78.

[82]*Pacific Southwest Airline*, 70 LA 205, 213 (1977). See also *Simoniz Co.*, *supra* note 72, at 663: "The assumed desire not to help convict a fellow-employee of wrongdoing, which had already adversely affected all concerned, is not to be given precedence over the grievant's duty to his employer who was not guilty of wrongdoing and who was making a legitimate and necessary inquiry." See also *Templet Mfg. Co.*, 36 LA 839 (Feinberg, 1961) (leaking information to competitor); *Dow Badische Co.*, 67 LA 611 (Sickles, 1976) (damaging company property). In *South Chicago Community Hosp.*, 84-1 ARB ¶8299, 4326 (Cox, 1984) (accessory to theft), the arbitrator went a step further by stating: "I find that there is a duty for an employee to inform his employer when he acquires knowledge of a crime either through an admission or actual observance." On the basis of this reasoning, he upheld the suspension of an employee for failing to inform the company that a coworker was stealing film.

[83]See, e.g., cases cited in note 80 *supra*.

[84]*Weirton Steel Co.*, 68-1 ARB ¶8249 (Kates, 1968) (possession of stolen property); *Champion Spark Plug Co.*, 68 LA 702 (Casselman, 1977) (drinking of alcohol); *Formica Corp.*, 79-1 ARB ¶8012 (Keefe, 1978) (possession and drinking of alcohol); *Issacson Structural Co.*, 72 LA 1075 (Peck, 1979) (possession of marijuana); *Georgia Power Co.*, 93

- Provide other relevant evidence as the particular situation demands;[85]
- And in some cases, submit to fingerprinting,[86] medical examination, or sobriety, drug, or other test.[87]

Most arbitrators who take the majority view make no distinction between misconduct that is purely "industrial" in nature (e.g., alcohol violations, horseplay, absenteeism, and the like) and offenses that could lead to criminal prosecution.[88]

Minority View: No Duty to Cooperate

This view, which has been taken by relatively few arbitrators, may be summed up as follows:

> *Arbitrator Fitzgerald:* [A]n employee does not lose the basic constitutional rights which a citizen enjoys, merely because the employee is exercising those rights within an industrial setting.[89]

LA 846 (Holley, 1989) (drugs and alcohol). In *Dow Chem. Co.*, 65 LA 1295 (Lipson, 1976) (suspicion of theft; refusal to show guard identification card), the arbitrator pointed out that even the Constitution prohibits only *unreasonable* searches and seizures.

[85]*E.g.*, in *Trans World Airlines, Inc.*, 46 LA 611, 612 (Wallen, 1965), a flight attendant was returned to work, but without back pay, after she refused to lift the back of her hair in order to demonstrate that she was not wearing a wig in violation of a company rule. The arbitrator expressed the view that "management must be accorded the right to verify compliance with clothing, hair length and appearance regulations in a manner which imposes no unreasonable or undignified demands on the employee." In *Niemand Indus., Inc.*, 88-1 ARB ¶8070 (Sergent, 1987), the arbitrator denied back pay to an employee who refused to provide documents and information sought in informal discovery or to comply with a subpoena and directives issued by the arbitrator. See also *Rexall Drug Co.*, 65 LA 1101 (Cohen, 1975) (right to require employee to authorize inquiry into criminal record); *City of Detroit*, 68 LA 848 (Roumell, 1979) (right to require verification of illness).

[86]*Colgate-Palmolive Co.*, 50 LA 441 (Koven, 1968) (courts have found no constitutional privilege against submitting to fingerprinting, photography, measurement, or speaking or writing for identification purposes).

[87]See discussion in Part III of this chapter.

[88]Exceptions to this position include *Thrifty Drug Stores, Inc.*, 68-2 ARB ¶8628 (Jones, 1968) (refusal to answer questions in connection with theft investigation); *Imperial Glass Co.*, 61 LA 1180 (Gibson, 1973) (evidence obtained by police in unlawful search not considered by arbitrator). Arbitrator Brisco made the point in *Phillips Painting Contractors*, 72 LA 16 (Brisco, 1978), that state statutes (California is cited) may extend the privilege against self-incrimination to arbitration hearings and other noncriminal proceedings.

[89]*Abex Corp.*, 79-2 ARB ¶8614, 5747 (1979). Other cases in this line are cited in R. L. Miller, *Worker Privacy and Collective Bargaining*, 33 LABOR L.J. 156 (1982). See also *King Co.*, 87-2 ARB ¶8410 (Bard, 1987) (vandalism), in which a refusal to cooperate with an investigation was held justified on the ground that requiring cooperation was an attempt by the employer to shift the burden of proof. The arbitrator cited *Exact Weight Scale Co.*, 50 LA 8 (McCoy, 1967) (work for competitor), in support of this proposition.

The model of the employer-employee relationship that this position reflects tends to be that of the citizen's adversarial relationship to the state, rather than that of two parties to a collective bargaining agreement with its continuing relationship and mutual rights and obligations.

Take an example that highlights the difference in the majority and minority positions. An employee knows the identity of a fellow employee who has physically assaulted a supervisor, but refuses to tell the employer what he knows because he is afraid he may implicate himself. To uphold his right to remain silent would impair the employer's ability to run its business, a "majority view" arbitrator might well reason. Obviously, supervisors must be able to do their jobs without fear of being "jumped" any day in the parking lot.[90] By contrast, the "minority view" tends to give greater weight to the constitutional rights of the employee than to the business needs of the employer when the two conflict.

Some cases in which arbitrators have upheld an employee's right to refuse to cooperate with an employer's investigation have been decided not on the basis of constitutional protections but in reference to notice. In an exceptional and frequently discussed case, the arbitrator found that the employer had no right to order the grievant to empty his pockets (which it had reason to believe contained a pistol). The reason: The employer did not have a rule providing for personal searches during working hours, and a rule that allowed the employer to search employees' possessions upon leaving the plant was found not to apply.[91] Other arbitrators have suggested that searches (and, by implication, other forms of cooperation with an investigation) can be required only if the requirement to cooperate has been negotiated by the parties[92] or has become an established working condition by virtue of past practice.[93]

Limits on Employer's Right to Require Cooperation; Probable Cause

Even to arbitrators who hold the majority view on an employee's duty to cooperate, the company cannot subject employ-

---

[90]Arbitrator Lipson, in *Dow Chem. Co.*, 65 LA 1295, 1298 (1976), adopted a similar position with respect to searches: "Were the view to be adopted that an employee may leave a plant, concealing anything that he wishes, even under the most suspicious circumstances, without either interference or search, companies would be utterly defenseless in resisting theft. Obviously, industry could not function under such restrictions."

[91]*Scott Paper Co.*, 69-2 ARB ¶8470 (Williams, 1969).

[92]*Abex Corp.*, *supra* note 89.

[93]*Comco Metal Prods., Inc.*, 58 LA 279 (Brown, 1972) (alcohol violation).

ees to questioning or searches whenever, and in whatever manner, it wishes. A condition of requiring an employee to cooperate with an investigation is that the matter be of legitimate concern to the employer.[94] As Arbitrator Jones has stated, "The parameters of legitimate inquiry are set by the employment relationship." He continued:

> Job-related conduct of the employee and fellow workers is within the area of the permissible, whereas prying into subjects of a personal nature or concerning conduct that is not job-related is foreclosed. Nor is there any license to conduct interviews in a manner coercive or demeaning to the employee.[95]

A basic limit on the company's right to require employees to cooperate with an investigation is that there must be strong specific reasons for the questioning, search, test, or other form of cooperation sought. This is roughly analogous to "probable cause" in the law.[96] In the view of some arbitrators, however, "probable cause" has a different and less stringent meaning in the industrial setting than in criminal law. One arbitrator has stated in a case involving drug testing that there must be "strong

---

[94]*E.g., Lockheed Aircraft Corp.*, 27 LA 709 (Maggs, 1956) (alcohol on company premises was proper subject of management concern and not inquiry into employee's personal affairs); *Rexall Drug Co.*, 65 LA 1101 (Cohen, 1975) (drug company's inquiry relating to employee's use of drugs and criminal record was reasonable and not invasion of privacy since drug business is unusually susceptible to criminal involvement); *Bi-State Dev. Agency*, 88 LA 854 (Brazil, 1987) (employer entitled to obtain information from grievant's physician as to whether prescribed medication could have resulted in positive test result for marijuana since grievant had suggested this possibility as defense to charge of drug use).

[95]*Pacific Southwest Airline*, 70 LA 205, 213 (1977). Jones discusses the "reasonable relationship to the enterprise" test further in *Evidentiary Concepts in Labor Arbitration: Some Modern Variations on Ancient Legal Themes*, 13 UCLA L. REV. 1286ff. (1966). In *Skaggs-Stone, Inc.*, 40 LA 1273, 1279 (Koven, 1963), the arbitrator, while confirming the employer's right to question an employee accused of participating in warehouse thefts, overturned his discharge for refusing to answer because the company's interrogation methods were "accusatory, and not directed toward gaining information beyond these accusations." See also *Union Plaza Hotel*, 88 LA 528 (McKay, 1986) (refusal to provide urine specimen while under observation).

[96]The probable-cause analogy is drawn in *Champion Spark Plug Co.*, 68 LA 702, 705 (Casselman, 1977) (alcohol violation):

> In criminal cases, an officer who has probable cause to believe a felony has been committed and probable cause to believe that a specific individual committed such a felony, may arrest the individual and search him in connection with the arrest. There is no constitutional protection against such a search. . . . The right of Management to fairly operate its business without undue impediment must be balanced against the right of employees to continue to enjoy their civil rights to the fullest. However, the two will clash and in the factual setting of this case, it is not inappropriate to treat a supervisor by analogy to a peace officer in the plant setting.

linkage" between evidence of the presence of drugs and the employee before testing can be required. But to establish such linkage, he said, does not require a showing of probable cause under the Fourth Amendment standard.[97]

Probable cause in an industrial setting is illustrated by the following case:

> **EXAMPLE:** As the foreman entered an employee's work bay, he noticed another employee hovering near the entrance, about 15 or 20 feet from the employee's machine, appearing (the foreman thought) to be very nervous. The foreman approached the employee and saw him carefully transfer "a material that looked like chewing tobacco—dark brown and stringy" from one container to another. Believing the material to be marijuana, the foreman asked the employee what he was doing. The employee placed both containers in his shirt pocket and answered, "Nothing." Even after the foreman offered to leave the room and let the employee show a steward what he had put in his pocket, the employee declared that a person does not lose his rights as a citizen just because he is on the job and that he did not have to submit to a search. Management disagreed, and discharged him.

In dealing with the employee's refusal to submit to a search, the arbitrator focused on the underlying question of where to put the burden of proof, since the company had satisfied its initial responsibility of making a *prima facie* case that what was in the employee's pocket was marijuana.

> In such a case it is appropriate to place the burden upon the employee to rebut the *prima facie* case by giving an explanation of his conduct and demonstrating the fallacy or at least a weakness in the *prima facie* case. [The employee] refused to do this, and the *prima facie* case remained against him. . . .

The employee's testimony that the substance he was pouring into a container was sunflower seeds, not marijuana, just did not wash. It was unlikely that he would have used the meticulous

---

[97]*Georgia Power Co.*, 93 LA 846 (Holley, 1989). The arbitrator cited earlier decisions involving the same parties by Arbitrators Hoyt Wheeler and Ferrin Mathews which also dealt with the question of when drug tests could be required. Arbitrator Wheeler, like Arbitrator Holley, found that a drug-detection dog's sensing of the presence of marijuana in an employee's vehicle provided reasonable cause to require the employee to take a drug test. Arbitrator Mathews held that it did not, but his decision was overturned by a federal district court. *Georgia Power Co. v. Electrical Workers (IBEW), Local 84*, 707 F. Supp. 531, 130 LRRM 2419 (1989)) For additional discussion of the probable-cause standard in the industrial setting, see R. DeCresce, DRUG TESTING IN THE WORKPLACE (1989).

care noted by the foreman if he were just pouring something with as little value as sunflower seeds. And his coworker was more likely to have moved far away from a forbidden transaction, to a location where he could serve as lookout, than from an innocent one. Both employees' actions, then, were fatally suspicious and gave strong probable cause to believe that the transaction involved some kind of drug, probably marijuana. Thus, the employer was justified in discharging him for refusing to be searched.[98]

Whether the employer has probable cause to require an employee to cooperate with an investigation depends on the particular facts, as the following two cases of theft illustrate.

> *A fishing expedition?* The employee worked near where the thefts apparently occurred, had worked long enough at the plant to be familiar with the operation, and was in a position to use his truck to remove company products if he chose to do so. The employer sought to interrogate the employee but the union resisted, claiming the investigation was really an improper "fishing expedition."

Not at all, said the arbitrator. "The management did not single out this grievant, or any other employee, nor did they indiscriminately interview all of the employees. . . . [A] reasonable analysis was made and only the parties who were in a position to have some knowledge were interrogated."[99]

> *A "special powder."* The employer showed that a special powder placed on hidden company product by an outside investigation agency had been found on two suspects' persons. Moreover, company product identical to that which had been hidden were discovered in the back of a garage where one of two suspects was apprehended and in a trash buggy located in a basement area from which the other suspect was observed emerging; and in the same trash buggy, an unusual type of wrist band identical to that worn by the latter suspect was found. Could the suspects be required to be fingerprinted?

In order to justify an investigation, the arbitrator said, only reasonable (or probable) cause need be shown. The facts here

---

[98]*Issacson Structural Co.*, 72 LA 1075, 1078-79 (Peck, 1979).

[99]*Simoniz Co.*, 44 LA 658, 660 (McGury, 1964). The arbitrator clarified one important point thusly: "This is not to say that because the grievant was near the apparent location of the theft, that it may be fairly inferred that he was probably guilty of complicity in the theft. However, it is to say that his location was a legitimate basis for selecting him as one of the persons to be interrogated."

were enough to establish cause to believe that the suspects might have engaged in misconduct, and thus to warrant taking their fingerprints.[100]

Three Possible Results of Refusal to Cooperate

May Add to Proof of Guilt. If an employee suspected of misconduct has been asked to cooperate in an investigation, refusal to cooperate may be viewed by the arbitrator as indirect evidence of guilt (on the theory that the employee would have reason to withhold evidence only if it would be damaging).[101]

Even arbitrators who take the position that an employee has a constitutional right to refuse to testify about matters that might be used against him or her in a criminal prosecution have pointed out that an employee who remains silent may become subject to disciplinary action almost by default. In a case where two grievants who had been discharged for the strike-related destruction of company property refused to testify at the arbitration hearing because criminal charges on the same matter were pending against them, the arbitrator did not question their right to assert the constitutional privilege against self-incrimination. But he found that the effect of their silence was to leave the company's *prima facie* case against them unrebutted,

---

[100]*Colgate-Palmolive Co.*, 50 LA 441 (Koven, 1968). In *Aldens, Inc.*, 73 LA 396, 398 (Martin, 1979), the arbitrator held that in the absence of an established rule arbitrary personal searches of company employees would be improper, but "there is no need for any rule to authorize a personal search of an employee who patently has something unusual carried in an unusual place. It is not customary for people to have square bulges under their pants leg, and it would be a clear dereliction of duty for a guard to observe such a condition and do nothing about it." See also *Lockheed Aircraft Co.*, 27 LA 709 (Maggs, 1956), where hearsay reports by company guards that an employee was implicated in bringing a bottle of whiskey onto company premises justified the employer is requiring the employee to answer its questions about the incident (though the reports themselves did not establish his guilt); *Dow Chem. Co.*, *supra* note 90, where two employees wearing "bulging" jackets gave a guard reasonable cause to require them to unzip by refusing to explain their appearance.

[101]See R. W. FLEMING, THE LABOR ARBITRATION PROCESS 182 (1965); and R. L. Miller, *Worker Privacy and Collective Bargaining*, 33 LABOR L.J. 156 (1982). In *U.S. Steel Corp.*, 40 LA 598, 602 (Seitz, 1963) (work stoppage), the arbitrator found that a refusal to cooperate might show "the absence of good faith and credibility." See also *St. Luke's Hosp.*, 93 LA 1241, 1245 (Johnson, 1989) (leaving post), where the arbitrator ruled that a six-month delay by the grievant in identifying an eye witness to her alleged misconduct "renders his testimony at the Arbitration proceedings suspect. The trustworthiness of the evidence is undermined by the inexplicable failure of the grievant to immediately name an individual capable of verifying her version of events."

noting, "The plea of privilege does not supply proof. . . ." Their discharges were sustained.[102]

May Affect the Remedy. Even if there is insufficient proof of misconduct to justify the action taken by the employer, lack of cooperation can affect the remedy to which a noncooperating employee is entitled.

> **EXAMPLE:** A customer accused one of the employer's drivers of ramming his truck into its loading dock and breaking the dock plate. The driver became excited and began to talk incoherently. Concluding that the driver had been drinking, the customer called the employer. When company officials arrived, they too noted the driver's rapid, disjointed, and slurred speech, and a supervisor directed him to take a sobriety test. If he refused, he was told, his refusal would be taken as proof of intoxication and he would be discharged. The driver nevertheless refused. The union argued that the driver was not intoxicated and that his refusal to take a sobriety test was due not to fear that he could pass it but to fear that he was being framed.

Refusal to take a sobriety test often justifies an inference that the employee is under the influence. But in this case, the arbitrator found, the driver was understandably suspicious of the motives of both the company and its customer because both were guilty of jumping to conclusions about the dock plate accident and his alleged drunkenness. Thus, while his refusal to be tested added some weight to the shaky evidence that he was under the influence, it was not enough to prove his guilt.

The remedy, though, was another matter. The driver, though entitled to reinstatement, rated no back pay for the following reason:

> When one of the foremost purposes of the sobriety test provision is to provide a method for a quick and definitive resolution of the intoxication issue, an employee who defeats that purpose by refusing to take that test ought not to be able to collect back pay during the delay which he himself has caused.[103]

---

[102]*Southern Bell Tel. & Tel. Co.*, 26 LA 742, 746 (McCoy, 1956). A similar result was reached in *United Parcel Serv., Inc.*, 45 LA 1050 (Turkus, 1965). See also *St. Luke's Hosp., supra* note 101, at 1245: "It is the grievant who must bear the consequences of a failure to pursue and present all corroborating information."

[103]*Blue Diamond Co.*, 66 LA 1136, 1142 (Summers, 1976). The arbitrator continued: "The employee's loss of pay during this period was the result of his action; he and not the employer had the ability to avoid that loss. The underlying principle here is the same as the one which requires an employee who is wrongfully discharged to seek other work to mitigate the damages." A similar conclusion was reached in an earlier, frequently

May Be Regarded as Misconduct in Itself. In many cases arbitrators have upheld the company's right to discipline or discharge an employee for refusing to cooperate with a legitimate investigation.[104] Refusal to cooperate is sometimes viewed as insubordination by employers and arbitrators even though the customary elements of insubordination—namely, a refusal to obey a clear, bona fide work order after a clear warning of the consequences of refusing—are often not present.

The main reason for this view is that the right to require cooperation in investigations of suspected misconduct is considered by management to be essential to the running of its business. In a case where the employee argued that he was not guilty of insubordination for refusing to open his sweater (under

---

cited case, *Exact Weight Scale Co.*, 50 LA 8, 9 (McCoy, 1967), where the grievant was reinstated, but without back pay, following his refusal to tell the company whether he was working a second job for one of its competitors: "All he had to do was to say that he was not violating the rule and had never violated it. By maintaining his silence until he got on the witness stand, he contributed to his own damages." See also *Monarch Mach. Tool Co.*, 51 LA 391 (Sembower, 1968), where grievant's "flip" statement, "You can't pin anything on me," instead of an outright denial of responsibility, led the arbitrator to deny his claim for overtime lost as a result of an improper disciplinary transfer; *Niemand Indus., Inc.*, 88-1 ARB ¶8070 (Sergent, 1987), where the arbitrator denied back pay to an employee who had been improperly discharged because she refused to provide documents and information sought in informal discovery or to comply with a subpoena and directives issued the the arbitrator; *Templet Mfg. Co.*, 36 LA 839 (Feinberg, 1961) (refusal to tell who was leaking information to competitor); *Babcock & Wilcox Co.*, 60 LA 778 (Dworkin, 1972) (refusal to answer questions on coworker who damaged company property); *Dow Badische Co.*, 67 LA 611 (Jones, 1976) (refusal to name coworker who damaged company property); *Pepsi Cola Bottling Co. of San Diego, Inc.*, 93 LA 520 (Randall, 1989) (company lacked required probable cause for testing order, but back pay denied because grievant knew he could have challenged validity of order after complying).

[104]Following are some of the cases in which discharge has been sustained: *Issacson Structural Co., supra* note 98 (possession of marijuana; refusal to empty pockets); *Lockheed Aircraft Corp., supra* note 100 (drinking and possession of alcohol; refusal to answer questions); *Simoniz Co., supra* note 99 (refusal to cooperate with theft investigation); *Champion Spark Plug*, 68 LA 702 (Casselman, 1977) (refusal to allow personal search; drinking alcoholic beverages); *Furr's, Inc.*, 88 LA 175 (Blum, 1986) (discharge justified for lying during investigation); *Philadelphia Gas Works*, 89-2 ARB ¶8481 (Simpkins, 1989) (failure to provide urine sample for unannounced drug test attributed to fear of testing positive). Lesser penalties were held to be proper for refusing to cooperate in, *e.g.*, *Freightliner, Inc.*, 53 LA 274 (Lindel, 1969) (discharge too harsh for refusal to answer foreman's questions about attitude); *Comco Metal Prods., Ltd.*, 58 LA 279 (Brown, 1972) (drinking and possession of alcohol; suspension appropriate for refusal to reveal contents of purse); *Rexall Drug Co.*, 65 LA 1101 (Cohen, 1975) (suspension, not discharge, proper for refusal to answer questions about drug use and refusal to authorize inquiry into police record); *Hollytex Carpet Mills, Inc.*, 79-1 ARB ¶8181 (Anderson, 1979) (insufficient harm to company's operation to justify discharge for giving false information in theft investigation); *Koppers Co.*, 76 LA 175 (Amis, 1981) (five-day suspension proper for conspiring to obstruct company's investigation of sabotage).

which his foreman had reason to believe he had concealed a liquor flask) because the order to "open up" was not a job assignment, the arbitrator responded, "Obviously any order directed to normal requirements of plant order, discipline or work are proper. . . ."[105]Refusal to cooperate is also related to insubordination in that management authority is challenged when an employee refuses to answer questions or otherwise to provide needed information.[106] Discipline for noncooperation has been justified on the ground that it reflects an indifference to company rules and to the employer's legitimate need, for example, to keep the work place free from drugs.[107]

Another approach is reflected in a case in which an employee was discharged for lying when she was questioned about a glass door she had broken. The arbitrator upheld her discharge under a company rule covering acts of dishonesty. Management, he said, has a right to expect an employee to tell the truth when it is investigating an act of misconduct.[108]

Must a Union Representative Be Allowed at Predisciplinary Interview?

The *Weingarten* Rule

In 1975 the U.S. Supreme Court put its stamp of approval on an employee's right to union representative in an investigatory interview, even before formal grievance machinery is set in motion. The Court held in *J. Weingarten v. NLRB*[109] that an employee has the right under Section 7 of the National Labor

---

[105]*Champion Spark Plug, supra* note 104.

[106]*Freightliner, Inc., supra* note 104.

[107]*Issacson Structural Co., supra* note 98.

[108]*Furr's, Inc., supra* note 104. In *King Co.*, 87-2 ARB ¶8110 (Bard, 1987) (damage to property), on the other hand, the arbitrator held that a work rule forbidding "lying to the employer" could not be used as an additional basis for discipline of an employee who lied during an investigation.

[109]420 U.S. 251, 88 LRRM 2689 (1975). In *Weingarten*, the employer operated a chain of retail stores in which the sales personnel were represented by a union. A sales person was summoned to the store manager's office, where she was confronted by the store manager with allegations of theft of store merchandise. She made numerous fruitless requests to have a union representative present. After the interview the employee reported the actions of the employer to several union representatives. Even though no discipline was imposed, the union filed charges with the NLRB alleging that the employer's denial of the employee's requests was a violation of §8(a)(1) of the NLRA. The board upheld the charge and ordered the employer to honor such requests in the future.

Relations Act to refuse to meet with management at an investigatory interview unless a union representative is present, where the employee "reasonably believes the investigation will result in disciplinary action" and where he requests representation.[110] The term "investigatory interview" means an interview in which the interviewer is attempting to gather information from the employee regarding a problem, rather than merely informing the employee of some predetermined discipline.[111]

Among the reasons in support of its decision, the Supreme Court noted that its holding

> gives recognition to the right [of representation] when it is most useful to both employee and employer. A single employee confronted by an employer investigation to determine whether certain conduct deserves discipline may be too fearful or inarticulate to relate accurately the incident being investigated, or too ignorant to raise extenuating factors. A knowledgeable union representative could assist the employer by eliciting favorable facts, and save the employer production time by getting to the bottom of the incident occasioning the interview.[112]

---

[110]For discussion of the *Weingarten* decision, see W. B. Nelson, *Union Representation During Investigatory Interviews*, 31 ARB. J. 181–90 (1976); P. N. Erickson, Jr., & C. E. Smith, *The Right of Union Representation During Investigatory Interviews*, 33:2 ARB. J. 29–35 (1978); D. M. Cohen, *The Right of Representation: Weingarten and the Federal Employee*, 30 LAB. L.J. 10–19 (1979); R. L. Hogler & G. Maloney, *Developments in the Right of Representation During Investigatory Interviews*, 7 EMPLOYEE REL. L.J. 224–34 (1981); L. H. Silverman & M. J. Soltis, *Weingarten: An Old Trumpet Plays the Labor Circuit*, 32 LABOR L.J. 725–35 (1981); A. R. Tuttle, *Weingarten Rights and the Nonunion Employee*, 19 NEW ENG. L.J. 867ff (1983–84); M. J. Fox, Jr., L. Baldwin, Jr., & T. Fox, *The Weingarten Doctrine*, 40:2 ARB. J. 45ff (1985); R. L. Hogler, *Taracorp and Remedies for Weingarten Violations: The Evolution of Industrial Due Process*, 37 LAB. L.J. 403–11 (1986); N. Orkin & L. Schohmeyer, *Weingarten: Rights, Remedies, and the Arbitration Process*, 40 LAB. L.J. 594–602 (1989).

[111]*Baton Rouge Water Works Co.*, 246 NLRB 995, 103 LRRM 1056 (1979). In *Deaconess Medical Center*, 87-1 ARB ¶8085 (Robinson, 1986), the arbitrator defined the term as "the asking of questions by one person of another person. . . . The adjective *investigatory* implies that the interview must be part of an effort to obtain information." For further discussion of the distinction between an investigatory interview and a disciplinary proceeding, see J. Fanning, *National Labor Relations Board v. J. Weingarten, Inc.—An Overview of the Development and Application of the NLRB Section 7 Right to Representation*, 5 W. NEW ENG. L. REV. 21–30 (1982).

[112]88 LRRM at 2693. Following *Weingarten*, the Third Circuit, in *E. I. du Pont de Nemours & Co. v. NLRB*, 724 F.2d 1061, 115 LRRM 2153 (3d Cir., 1983), upheld an NLRB ruling that under §7 even a nonunion employee has the right to assistance from a coworker in an investigatory interview. In *E. I. du Pont de Nemours & Co. v. NLRB*, 707 F.2d 1076, 113 LRRM 3241 (9th Cir., 1983), the Ninth Circuit held that a nonunion employee's request for the presence of a coworker at an interview with his employer did not meet the concerted-activity requirement of §7. The *Weingarten* rationale, it said, could not be extended to the nonunion setting in the absence of evidence that the employee's coworkers shared the same concerns or would provide the requested assis-

The Court noted further that "the well established current of arbitral authority" had been in the direction of permitting representation at early stages, even where the contract did not explicitly spell out such a right.[113] It added, however, that the employer has no duty to bargain with a union representative who attends an interview; the representative is there to advise the employee and as an observer only.

What are the employer's rights if the employee demands representation and the employer does not wish to permit it? In that situation, the Court said, the employer may insist that the employee choose between an interview without representation and no interview at all; and if the employee chooses the latter, the employer is free to continue its investigation and act on the basis of whatever information it has "without such additional facts as might have been gleaned through the interview."[114]

The *Weingarten* rule and the Board's clarifications have been consistently viewed as minimum standards by arbitrators since 1975.[115] So most disputes about an employee's right to representation at an investigatory interview turn, not on the existence of the right itself, but on whether the *Weingarten* rule is properly applied in particular situations.

Applicability of *Weingarten;* Three Key Tests

Does the Employee Have a Reasonable Basis to Believe That Discipline May Result? The *Weingarten* rule clearly comes into play when

---

tance. These factors could be presumed, the court noted, in the case of union-represented employees.

[113]88 LRRM at 2695. The NLRB has made a number of clarifications that restricted the application of the *Weingarten* doctrine: (1) An employee cannot refuse to report to a supervisor without a union representative unless he or she has a "reasonable fear" that discipline may result from the interview. (2) An employee cannot refuse to be questioned or instructed about work performance without a union presence, even if such questioning necessarily carries a threat of discipline upon a refusal to comply. (3) The right to representation does not apply to "run of the mill" shop floor conversations. (4) An employee cannot refuse to attend a meeting if he or she is told in advance that there will be no interrogation at the meeting.

[114]88 LRRM at 2692. The quoted language is from the Board's decision in *Quality Mfg. Co.*, 195 NLRB 195, 79 LRRM 1269 (1972).

[115]See. e.g., *Auburn Faith Community Hosp., Inc.*, 66 LA 882 (Killion, 1976) (complaints about staffing); *Social Sec. Admin.*, 68 LA 197 (Lubow, 1977) (substandard job performance); *Ward La France Truck Corp.*, 69 LA 29 (Levy, 1977) (unauthorized possession of company property); *South Central Bell Tel. Co.*, 71 LA 174 (Wolff, 1978) (work stoppage); *VRN Int'l*, 75 LA 243 (Vadakin, 1980) (secret taping of grievance meeting); *Dep't of the Air Force*, 75 LA 994 (Hart, 1980) (grooming); *Renaissance Center Partnership*, 76 LA 379 (Daniel, 1981) (carrying unauthorized passengers, other violations); *Maui Pineapple Co.*, 86 LA 907 (Tsukiyama, 1986) (sleeping on duty); *Hughes Aircraft Co.*, 86

the employer tells an employee explicitly that it intends to question him or her in connection with potential disciplinary action.[116] The harder cases are those in which nothing is said about discipline directly, but the employee nonetheless claims a "reasonable belief" that the employer had discipline in mind. (A "reasonable belief" test was applied by arbitrators even before *Weingarten* where the right to representation was in issue.[117])

> **EXAMPLE:** A new supervisor was heartily resented by the employees under him for being a stickler about details and schedules. One day, after he heard an employee making some sarcastic remarks about him to other employees in the lunch room, the supervisor decided he had to do something about the employee's uncooperative attitude and told him to report to his office. When the employee showed up, accompanied by his shop steward, the supervisor explained that this was just a counseling session; that he had no intention of taking any disciplinary action; and that the steward's presence was unnecessary.
>
> After the steward left, the supervisor and the employee discussed matters amicably, but things heated up when the supervisor turned to the employee's attitude toward supervision. The employee told the supervisor that respect had to be earned, and the latter responded, "You're just asking for trouble—you could use some self-control." The employee, taking the supervisor's words as a threat of disciplinary action, got up to leave. The supervisor insisted that he was not excused and could be disciplined if he left. Nevertheless, the employee took off and was subsequently reprimanded for insubordinate conduct in failing to follow the supervisor's directions.

Did *Weingarten* apply? The key question was "whether [the employee] had a reasonable belief that the counseling session was the first stage of some disciplinary action against him." The arbitrator took into account three factors: First, the employee had done nothing to get the supervisor down on him; his re-

---

LA 1112 (Richman, 1986) (insubordination); *Trailways, Inc.*, 88 LA 941 (Heinsz, 1987) (intoxication); *Arkansas Power & Light Co.*, 92 LA 144 (Weisbrod, 1989) (theft); *Macmillan Bloedel Containers*, 92 LA 592 (Nicholas, 1989) (alcohol and drug use and possession).

[116]The Ninth Circuit (covering, generally, the West Coast) held in *Pacific Tel. & Tel. Co. v. NLRB*, 711 F.2d 134, 113 LRRM 3529 (9th Cir. 1983), that *Weingarten* requires the employer to give the employee advance notice of the subject matter of an interview and a chance to confer with a union representative before the interview takes place.

[117]*Erickson and Smith, supra* note 110, discuss the pre-*Weingarten* application of the reasonable belief test; for cases, see, e.g., *Valley Iron Works*, 33 LA 769 (Anderson, 1960) (insubordination); *Southern Cal. Edison Co.*, 61 LA 453 (Block, 1973) (absenteeism).

marks in the lunch room may have been somewhat disrespectful but were in the nature of "grousing," and the employee was not aware that the supervisor had overheard them. Second, the supervisor expressly told the employee that discipline was not the purpose of their talk. Third, the supervisor stuck to his promise and did not try to convert the counseling session into an occasion for discipline.

The supervisor's admonition that the employee could be heading for trouble if his attitude did not change could not "by any stretch of the imagination" be considered discipline; in fact, it was designed to prevent the employee from continuing a course of conduct that might lead to discipline in the future, and offered no threat of immediate discipline. The supervisor's cautionary words bring to mind the famous common law case on assault in which the court ruled that the defendant's statement "If it were not assize time, I would hit you" was not a threat of assault because there was no threat of immediate bodily harm. Indeed, it was just the opposite—since it was assize time, the speaker was actually assuring his listener that he was not intending to assault him. "In short, then, if [the employee] really believed that he was going to be disciplined at the counseling session, such belief had absolutely no rational basis in fact." Under these circumstances, *Weingarten* did not apply. The employee's refusal to continue the discussion was therefore not justified, and his reprimand was allowed to stand.[118]

The reasonable belief test was passed, however, in a case where a supervisor told five employees that he wanted to talk to them individually about their complaints of unequal overtime distribution. By the time he got to the grievant, the word was out that the supervisor had concluded that it was the grievant who was causing all the trouble. Under these circumstances, the grievant had reason to fear that discipline was hanging over his head and was justified in refusing to talk to the supervisor unless a union representative was present.[119]

Other factors that have supplied a reasonable belief that an interview might lead to discipline are an employee's knowledge that he has disobeyed work orders;[120] his recent involvement in

---

[118]*Vulcan Materials Co.*, 68 LA 1305 (Marlatt, 1977).
[119]*Braniff Airways, Inc.*, 27 LA 892 (Williams, 1957).
[120]*The Arcrods Co.*, 39 LA 784 (Teple, 1962); *Dep't of the Air Force*, 75 LA 994 (Hart, 1980).

some incident about which there has been a dispute;[121] and conflicting statements by different supervisors as to whether the company was contemplating discipline.[122] In the *Weingarten* case itself, the Supreme Court noted that since the employee knew she was suspected of theft, and since the contract made dishonesty cause for discharge without notice, she had clear reason to believe that her interview might result in discharge.[123]

Where a supervisor expressly informs an employee that an interview is not for disciplinary purposes, arbitrators have held that the employee should accept that assurance.[124] But as one arbitrator pointed out, "[s]uch assurances [are], of course, self-serving, and the Company could not convert a disciplinary session to a counseling session by the simple process of labeling it as the latter at the outset."[125] If the employer were to change course in mid-stream, making it clear once the employee was in the office that discipline could follow, the employee at that point would become entitled to representation.

Likewise, if something an employee said in a meeting that he or she had been assured would not lead to discipline should later be used to support a disciplinary penalty, a persuasive case could be made that the penalty should be set aside on the ground that the employee might not have made a disclosure if the union had been present. Something of that sort happened in a case where the employer took notes of an ostensibly nondisciplinary meeting and then placed the notes in the employee's personnel file. The notes were "the equivalent of a warning letter," the arbitrator decided, "in contravention of management's promise not to discipline." He directed the employer to remove the "warning" from the employee's file.[126]

Does the Interview Come Under Any of the Exclusions to the Weingarten Rule? The *Weingarten* rule, it has been held, "applies to an interview in which possible wrongdoing on the part of an employee is not established and the facts have to be ascertained."[127] Inter-

---

[121]*Valley Iron Works, supra* note 117.

[122]*Southern Cal. Edison Co., supra* note 117.

[123]88 LRRM at 2691.

[124]*Hoerner Waldorf Corp.*, 70 LA 335 (Talent, 1978); *VRN Int'l, supra* note 115; *Southern Cal. Edison Co., supra* note 117; *Twin Coast Newspapers*, 89 LA 799 (Brisco, 1987).

[125]*Vulcan Materials Co., supra* note 118.

[126]*Social Sec. Admin., supra* note 115.

[127]*Atlantic Richfield Co.*, 81-1 ARB ¶8261, 4165 (Barnhart, 1981) (insubordination). See also *Oklahoma City Air Logistics Center*, 79-2 ARB ¶8360, 4512 (Moore, 1979) (safety

views, discussions, and other types of encounters in which an employee is not asked to supply information, or in which discipline is not in prospect, normally do not create a right of representation.[128] The following are common types of encounters that have been excluded under *Weingarten*:

Work orders and instructions. The Supreme Court noted this exclusion in *Weingarten* when it quoted with approval an NLRB finding that the right to representation does not apply "to such run-of-the-mill shop-floor conversations as, for example, the giving of instructions or training or needed corrections of work techniques. In such cases there cannot normally be any reasonable basis for an employee to fear that any adverse impact may result from the interview. . . ."[129]

Discipline becomes a relevant concern in this type of situation only if the employee should challenge the propriety of the supervisor's work order and threaten to disobey. But the basic premise of "work now and grieve later" is that production must go on. An employee is not entitled to call in a steward to discuss a disputed work order unless some overriding health and safety issue is involved or the contract allows union intervention in that type of situation.[130] What if the discussion ends with the employee saying, "No way I'll do that job"? The right to representation would arise at the point when the employer asks questions about the reasons for the refusal in contemplation of some

---

violation): "The right to Union Representation arises when the significant purpose of the interview is to obtain factors to support disciplinary action that is probable or being seriously considered."

[128]*American Can Co.*, 57 LA 1063 (Kerrison, 1971) (insubordination). In *Deaconess Medical Center*, 88 LA 44 (Robinson, 1986), the arbitrator held that a nurse suspected of drug and alcohol abuse was not entitled to have union representation at an interview in which the supervisor asked no questions and made no job threats but merely sought her written consent to be subjected to random blood and urine tests, where the contract, like the *Weingarten* rule, limited the right to representation to "investigatory interviews." In *Brunswick Corp.*, 89-1 ARB ¶8193 (Ipavec, 1988), the arbitrator ruled that the refusal to comply with an employee's request for union representation during a confrontation between the employee and a supervisor was not improper, where the confrontation was not intended to be disciplinary in nature. The fact that an oral reprimand was subsequently issued to the employee, in the arbitrator's view, was irrelevant to the original intent. See also *Shell Oil Co.*, 84 LA 562 (Milentz, 1985) (search of grievant's car in company parking lot not an occasion for representation); *Southern Cal. Edison Co.*, 86 LA 888 (Weiss, 1986) (discussion with grievant to determine how accident took place not an "investigatory interview").

[129]88 LRRM at 2691.

[130]*Marion Power Shovel Co.*, 66-2 ARB ¶8566 (Klein, 1966) (insubordination).

disciplinary penalty, but not until then.[131] The right to representation has also been rejected where a supervisor discussed a late
return from lunch with a group of employees;[132] and where a
supervisor informed the grievant that she was suspended for
refusing to carry out an assignment.[133]

Counseling and correction. Interviews that are solely for the
purpose of counseling an employee, for example, about how he
or she might improve job performance, or for exploring in a
corrective, nonpunitive spirit what might be the reasons for an
attendance problem, perhaps, or a lackluster attitude, also fall
outside the scope of the *Weingarten* rule.[134] As one arbitrator put
it, "There must be a clear-cut distinction between discipline (in
which the Union is involved) and corrective supervision (in
which the Union has no business). . . ." In the case at hand, the
supervisor's warning that if the grievant did not shape up he
could be heading for trouble was intended not as discipline, but
to avoid discipline by encouraging the grievant to mend his
ways.[135]

When a blood alcohol or drug test is being administered. The
following case raises the question of whether an employee may

---

[131]This was the situation in *St. Regis Paper Co.*, 71 LA 740, 743 (Williams, 1978),
for example, where the arbitrator responded to the union's contention that the grievant
was entitled to call a steward when her foreman told her that if she left work early she
would be charged with an unauthorized absence by characterizing what took place

> as an attempt by the foreman to direct the work force and manage the plant. It
> was not an investigation of a situation. On the contrary, the foreman had given
> instructions, and the Grievant was failing to follow them. It is true that to the
> extent of being required to leave the plant she was disciplined; however, the fact
> remains that once her insubordinate attitude had been expressed, the question
> of whether or not she should have been required to leave would be the subject of
> a grievance and an investigation would be made by the person who had the
> authority to discipline.

[132]*Appalachian Power Co.*, 75 LA 911, 913 (Andrews, 1980). "The supervisor merely
told him what was expected of him in the future," the arbitrator commented.

[133]*Atlantic Richfield Co.*, *supra* note 127, at 4165. The arbitrator noted: "The act of
suspension can hardly be said to be an investigatory interview." In *Baton Rouge Water
Works Co.*, 246 NLRB 995, 103 LRRM 1056 (1979), the NLRB held that *Weingarten*
rights do not apply to a meeting that is convened *solely* for the purpose of informing
the employee of, or acting upon, a previously made disciplinary decision.

[134]*E.g., VRN Int'l*, 75 LA 243 (Vadakin, 1980), where a supervisor called an
employee into his office to try to determine the reasons for her frequent complaints
about her assigned work and for her poor attendance, in an attempt to "reach" her
rather than to penalize her. Note, however, that this exception may become irrelevant
if the contract goes beyond *Weingarten* in providing representation rights. In *De Bourgh
Mfg. Co.*, 86 LA 1263 (Jacobowski, 1986) (absenteeism), the arbitrator overturned a
discharge for absenteeism in part because the company failed to allow union representation at a counseling session although the contract provided for such representation.

[135]*Vulcan Materials Co.*, 68 LA 1305 (Marlatt, 1977) (poor attitude).

refuse to take a blood alcohol test unless a union representative is present. It also illustrates how other kinds of due process considerations often are joined to *Weingarten* problems.

EXAMPLE: As a bus driver was preparing to begin his first run, his foreman climbed aboard and leaned over the driver to inspect the schedule posted on the dashboard. As he did this, the smell of alcohol assailed him, and he took the driver with him to the office to wait for the superintendent. The driver protested that he only had had a couple of beers with his dinner and was not drunk. He also asked repeatedly to be allowed to call the union and to use the restroom. The foreman, however, would not allow him to do either until the superintendent arrived, telling him that the latter might want him to take a blood alcohol test and that urinating might render a test inaccurate. An hour later the superintendent arrived and accompanied the driver to the hospital for the test. The driver again asked that the union be called; this time the superintendent tried but could not reach any union representative.

Did the driver have a right to call the union in the foreman's office? Many arbitrators would say no. Under *Weingarten*, the right to representation arises only when an interview might lead to discipline. An alcohol or drug test might well lead to discipline, but it is not an "interview" in the sense that any discussion takes place, and for that reason it has been held that a union representative's presence is not required.[136]

The question still remains, however, whether an employee has the right to confer with a union representative before agree-

---

[136]*Bethlehem Steel Corp.*, 55 LA 994 (Seward, 1970). In *Public Serv. Elec. & Gas Co.*, AAA Case No. 345 (Nicolau, 1987), however, the arbitrator held that an employee ordered to submit to urine testing in accordance with the company's drug abuse policy was entitled to have a union representative present when he gave a urine sample. He stated:

It is quite true that an interview is normally thought of as involving a verbal interchange between employer and employee. But the essence of an interview, verbal or otherwise, is to elicit information through and by means of an employee's participation. That, in my view, is what took place here and the fact that little was said or that questions were posed in written form rather than orally does not change the nature of what occurred or convert it into a "pure search."

See also *Birmingham-Jefferson County Transit Auth.*, 84 LA 1272 (Statham, 1985), where the arbitrator held that a grievant was not entitled to union representation at an interview in which she was told she must take a physical examination including a drug screen or be discharged. The nature of the interview was not fact finding, he reasoned, but was simply to give direction. In *Deaconess Medical Center*, *supra* note 128, the arbitrator found the grievant not entitled to union representation at an interview in which the supervisor sought her written consent to be subjected to random blood and urine tests, without asking questions or making job threats.

ing or refusing to take a sobriety or drug test. According to one arbitrator, an interview at which an employee was requested to take such a test was an investigative interview, and the employee had a right to representation. "At a minimum," the arbitrator noted, " [the representative] would have been another witness to corroborate the condition of the Grievant."[137] The bus driver in the case above had special reason to want to call his representative, not only to consult about the blood alcohol test but to get free from the kind of "house arrest" under which the foreman had overzealously and unjustifiably placed him.[138]

Where employees have tested positive in a drug-testing program, subsequent interviews at which their fate is determined surely would qualify as "investigatory interviews" triggering *Weingarten* rights, since discipline would be all but inevitable. One arbitrator has said that even if an employee does not request the representation to which he or she is entitled, "such independent Union representation would improve on the neutrality of the proceedings. Thus, the introduction of such Union representation is strongly encouraged and should be provided; but, the absence thereof does not . . . invalidate (or render unreasonable) the testing process itself."[139]

Questioning by law enforcement authorities, not by company. The usual question in investigatory interviews is whether an employee's rights as a citizen apply at the work place. One employee turned this around by claiming his right as an employee to have a union representative present when police questioned him about bomb threats on company property. The union argued that the *Weingarten* rule applied but the arbitrator disagreed, since the meeting with the police "was not a 'company conference'"; it was not until the company initiated its own investigation of the bomb threats that the grievant's *Weingarten* rights came into play.[140]

Has the Employee Actually Requested Representation? Under *Weingarten*, an employee must clearly request that a union representative be present. An employer does not have an affirmative duty under *Weingarten* to offer to call a union representative on an

---

[137]*Trailways, Inc.*, 88 LA 941 (Heinsz, 1987). See also *City of Milwaukee*, 78 LA 89 (Yaffe, 1982).
[138]*Alameda-Contra Costa Transit Dist.* (Koven, 1982), unpublished opinion.
[139]*Dow Chem. Co.*, 91 LA 1385 (Baroni, 1989).
[140]*Ralston Purina Co.*, 75 LA 313, 320 (Brown, 1980).

employee's behalf or to advise an employee that he has the right to representation in an investigatory interview.[141] The claims of numerous grievants that they were denied their *Weingarten* rights have failed because they did not request representation when they were interviewed.[142] One arbitrator also held that a proper request was not made where the grievant only asked her supervisor if someone was going to be called in and dropped the subject when the supervisor said no.[143]

Who Is a Proper Representative Under *Weingarten?*

An employee's *Weingarten* rights do not include un- restricted freedom of choice in selecting a representative at an

---

[141]The contract or company policy may place this duty on the employer; see, e.g., *General Tel. Co. of Cal.*, 82-1 ARB ¶8198 (Roberts, 1982) (drinking on break). So may the arbitrator himself, as reflected in the following comment by Arbitrator Weisbrod, in *Arkansas Power & Light Co.*, 92 LA 144, 150 (1989):

> I concur with many arbitrators who hold employers to a higher standard than the strict requirements of *Weingarten* and who require that Union representatives be present whenever an employer seeks to interrogate an employee on a matter that could lead to discipline, whether or not the employee himself has the knowledge to demand representation.

In *Immigration and Naturalization Serv.*, 86-1 ARB ¶8124, 3539 (Bailey, 1985), the arbitra- tor, while noting that a grievant had not requested representation, added: "If manage- ment's failure to inform the grievant of his right to have a union representative reason- ably might have made any substantial difference in this case, I would be inclined to set aside his suspension. But I don't believe it did." See also *Golden Nugget Hotel*, 89-1 ARB ¶8079 (Hardbeck, 1988) (discharge for distributing confidential personnel information reduced to four-week suspension in part because company failed to tell grievant of right to have union representative present during investigatory interview); *H. J. Heinz Co.*, 95 LA 82, 88 (Ellmann, 1990), quoting from arbitrator's dissent in *City of Southfield*, 177 Merc. 330 ("it is essential that an employee be informed of his right to union representation, and his right to consultation with a knowledgeable union representative prior to the interview"); *General Dynamics Convair Div.*, 95 LA 500 (Jones, 1990) (im- proper to detain and interview employee suspected of bringing marijuana onto company property without union representation, even though employee did not request repre- sentation).

[142]See *Angelica Corp.*, 62 LA 1227 (Bryan, 1974) (drunk driving arrest); *Commercial Nat'l Bank*, 67 LA 163 (Lubow, 1976) (misappropriation of funds); *Library of Congress*, 73 LA 1092 (Aronin, 1979) (reading on the job); *Renaissance Center Partnership*, 76 LA 379 (Daniel, 1981) (carrying unauthorized passengers and other violations); *Calcasieu Parish Police Jury*, 86 LA 350 (Nicholas, 1985) (negligence); *Tampa Elec. Co.*, 88 LA 791 (Vause, 1986) (sexual harassment).

[143]*VRN Int'l*, 75 LA 243 (Vadakin, 1980). The NLRB has ruled that once a request for representation is made, it need not be repeated. In *Lennox Indus., Inc.*, 244 NLRB 607, 102 LRRM 1298 (1979), an employee requested representation on the plant floor and repeated the request at the interview that followed, where it was ignored. The Board held that a *Weingarten* violation occurred as soon as the interview began without a representative present. In *Southwestern Bell Tel. Co.*, 227 NLRB 1223, 94 LRRM 1305 (1976), the Board ruled that the remark "I would like to have someone . . . that could explain to me what is happening" was all that was needed to bring *Weingarten* rights into play.

investigatory interview. The NLRB has ruled that an employer
was not required to postpone an interview merely because a
particular union representative was unavailable, where the employee could have picked another representative who *was* available.[144] The Board further held that, if no union representative
was available, the employee could not insist on a union representative when a fellow employee attended and competently participated in an interview;[145] and that an employer could lawfully
deny a request for the presence of an attorney made by several
employees who were being interviewed before undergoing polygraph examinations.[146]

A shop steward whom the employer seeks to interview is
entitled to request that another union representative be present.
Although an employee who is a union representative is likely to
know what rights the contract provides, "[t]he person being
disciplined is likely to be in a stressful situation and unlikely to
afford himself proper representation."[147]

The Right to Representation, *Weingarten* Aside

The *Weingarten* decision clearly settled the question of
whether an employee has a right to union representation under
the circumstances set forth above, namely: (1) where the employee has a reasonable belief that the interview in question
could result in discipline; (2) where the purpose of the interview
is to obtain facts that the company might consider in deciding
whether some penalty will, in fact, be imposed; and (3) where
the employee has requested that the union be present.

But what if these three tests are not strictly met. Are there
circumstances in which an arbitrator might still uphold the right
to representation? Consider the following situation: Two employees are spotted by the plant superintendent getting coffee
from a vending machine. As they head back to their work stations, the superintendent stops one of them and reminds him
that he had previously been advised that employees were not to
go to the coffee machine in pairs or groups. The employee
insists that his meeting with his coworker was accidental and

[144]*Coca-Cola Bottling Co. of Los Angeles*, 227 NLRB 1276, 94 LRRM 1200 (1977).
[145]*Crown Zellerbach, Inc.*, 239 NLRB 1124, 100 LRRM 1092 (1978).
[146]*Consolidated Casinos Corp. v. NLRB*, 266 NLRB 988, 113 LRRM 1081 (1978).
[147]*Commercial Nat'l Bank*, 67 LA 163, 165 (Lubow, 1976). This holding followed
the position taken by the NLRB in *Keystone Consol. Indus., Keystone Steel & Wire Div.*, 217
NLRB 995, 89 LRRM 1192 (1975).

the discussion escalates from there, with the superintendent rebuking the employee loudly and angrily for not doing his job properly and the employee defending his record. After some time the employee asks for his steward, and the superintendent replies, "First you are going to listen to me, and then after I am done with you, you can have your union representative." The employee files a grievance protesting the superintendent's refusal to allow him representation.

If the *Weingarten* rule were strictly applied, the employee's grievance might well go down the drain. His encounter with the superintendent was not clearly for "investigatory" purposes as contemplated by *Weingarten*, since he was not actually questioned but simply was given a piece of the superintendent's mind. The discussion might be said to have had a corrective flavor, in that the superintendent reminded the grievant about the coffee break rule and advised him that his production needed improvement. But no discipline was mentioned, and none was imposed as a result of the discussion. Thus under a strict construction of *Weingarten*, a plausible case could be made that the grievant had no right to union representation then and there but, if he thought he had a grievance, should have waited to get the union involved.

But *Weingarten* is not necessarily the only source of an employee's right to union representation. Prior to the *Weingarten* decision, arbitrators found representation rights in two other sources:

The Constitution. In a controversial case,[148] Arbitrator Jones cited the Supreme Court's *Miranda* decision in support of the proposition that an employee is entitled to union "counsel" whenever he is being questioned in connection with suspected misconduct, just as a criminal suspect need not agree to questioning unless his attorney is present. But the application of *Miranda* to the industrial world has received little support. Most arbitrators and other authorities hold to the position (discussed in the foregoing section) that constitutional privileges do not apply at the work place, especially in the private sector.[149]

The intent of the contract. A more popular approach has been through the contract itself. According to some arbitrators, the

---

[148]*Thrifty Drug Stores Co.*, 68-2 ARB ¶8628 (1968).
[149]See FAIRWEATHER'S PRACTICE AND PROCEDURE IN LABOR ARBITRATION 274–75 (R. J. Schoonhoven, ch. ed. 1991); H. T. Edwards, *Due Process Considerations in Labor Arbitration*, 25 ARB. J. 150ff, 163ff (1970).

collective bargaining agreement gives an employee the right to have the union present when a dispute arises over his rights under that agreement, or even where a discussion with management might lead to a dispute. In addition, a few arbitrators have held that the recognition clause implies the right to representation,[150] and others have found that right to go along with coverage by a collective bargaining contract containing a grievance procedure.[151]

Certainly an employee is entitled to union representation once a grievance is filed, the latter line of reasoning typically runs, and "grievance" should be interpreted broadly as any dispute or complaint that might conceivably be the subject of a grievance. Furthermore, having a steward present in the early stages of a dispute may make the collective bargaining relationship function more smoothly by facilitating the settlement of some disputes before they become formal grievances.[152]

How does this affect the coffee-machine situation described above? The contract provided that when a grievance arose, the foreman had to send for a steward if the grievant requested one; it defined a grievance as "any difference that may arise between the parties" on matters covered by the contract. The grievant and the superintendent certainly had such a difference,

---

[150]See F. ELKOURI & E. A. ELKOURI, HOW ARBITRATION WORKS 173 (4th ed. 1985). This interpretation of the recognition clause is subject to dispute, however; see, e.g., *E. I. du Pont de Nemours & Co.*, 29 LA 646 (Gregory, 1957) (discussion of possible disciplinary action not an attempt to negotiate); *F. W. Dwyer Mfg. Co.*, 69-1 ARB 8361 (Bothwell, 1968) (disciplinary matters covered by management rights clause and not subject to collective bargaining; right to representation arises only when grievance has been filed).

[151]*Auburn Faith Community Hospital, Inc.*, 66 LA 882, 895 (Killion, 1976):
Where the contract provides that an employee may be assisted or represented by a representative of the Association "at any step in the Grievance procedure," the arbitrator construes the language to mean that a [grievant] has the right to be represented at *any* time during the Grievance procedure if she so desires. . . . This is so because, apart from specific contract language, an employee, by just being employed under a union contract, is accorded this right.

[152]Arbitrator Heinsz, in *Trailways, Inc.*, 88 LA 941, 947 (Heinsz, 1987) (alcohol and drug test): "At a minimum, [the union representative] would have been another witness to corroborate the condition of the Grievant." See also *North Am. Aviation, Inc.*, 22 LA 310 (Blair, 1953) (unauthorized possession of company property); *Caterpillar Tractor Co.*, 44 LA 647 (Dworkin, undated); *Marion Power Shovel Co.*, 66-2 ARB ¶8566 (Klein, 1966) (insubordination); *Sterling Drug, Inc.*, 68-1 ARB ¶8358 (Stein, 1968) (absenteeism); *Dow Chem. Co.*, 68-2 ARB ¶8647 (Davis, 1968) (early quitting). However, where the contract stated specifically that an employee might be represented *after* he has filed a grievance, the contract has controlled; see, e.g., *City of Port Huron, Mich.*, 68-2 ARB ¶8788 (Keefe, 1968) (rudeness); *W. R. Grace & Co.*, 63 LA 138 (Caraway, 1974) (insubordination). See also W. B. Nelson, *Union Representation During Investigatory Interviews*, 31 ARB. J. 181–90 (1976)

the arbitrator found, even though no discipline had been imposed and no formal grievance had been filed. "The employee was the object of severe criticism and censure," he pointed out, and by a powerful member of upper management. He was charged with breaking the rule against socializing and congregating with fellow employees at the coffee machine; the conversation became heated and generated other charges concerning his work performance. In short, the employee had every reason to believe that the superintendent was getting ready to throw the book at him, and he was within his rights to want his steward present before the matter escalated any further. The grievance was therefore sustained.[153]

This pre-*Weingarten* case could have the same result today as in 1962, when the dispute took place, if the arbitrator looked beyond the relatively restrictive *Weingarten* tests and took the not-uncommon view that an employee has a right to representation in situations not contemplated by *Weingarten* that flow from the contract.

In the same vein, consider another set of facts that, strictly speaking, were not encompassed under *Weingarten*: Five employees were suspended after they insisted on consulting a union representative before they signed a receipt for an instruction booklet setting forth new procedures and providing that deviation from the procedures could lead to discipline. No "interview" was involved, and none of the employees was threatened with discipline. Nevertheless, the arbitrator, citing the necesssity of balancing the legitimate interests of both parties, found that the grievants' refusal to sign was justified. They reasonably believed, he pointed out, that signing for the new rules might put their jobs in jeopardy at some future time, and that their interests could be protected only if they were allowed to obtain the union's advice. The company would not have been prejudiced by allowing the grievants to consult the union, since no interference with production would have taken place; and if the employees ultimately had agreed to sign, only a slight delay would have resulted. The grievants' suspensions were therefore invalidated.[154]

Some arbitrators view the requirement that an employee be given union representation as not only a matter of due process. The presence of a union representative keeps the employer's

---

[153]*Caterpillar Tractor Co., supra* note 152.
[154]*G. C. Murphy Co.*, 79-1 ARB ¶8212 (Kossoff, 1979).

fact-finding procedures open and above board and protects the employer from later charges by the union that, for example, the employee was subject to coercion.

> **EXAMPLE:** When a supervisor implicated himself and others in an epidemic of thefts in the warehouse, the company began an investigation which included interrogations of the employees named by the supervisor. Two of the employees asked to have their union representatives called, but the company said no. They answered questions anyway and, like the supervisor, implicated the grievant. He refused to say a word unless the union was present and was fired for theft along with several others.

The employer's refusal to permit a union representative to be present when the two employees were interrogated directly affected the credibility of those two witnesses against the grievant. If an employer's fact-finding procedures are significantly flawed, the arbitrator noted, the "facts" produced are suspect. The union charged, and the arbitrator agreed, that the two employees might have "confessed" to their own involvement in the thefts and given evidence against the grievant because interrogators led them to believe that coming clean might save their jobs and avoid criminal prosecution. Denial of their request for a union representative also contributed to an atmosphere of unfair compulsion in which the two employees might have been induced to make false statements. For that reason, the arbitrator decided, the two employees' evidence against the grievant could not be considered reliable, and because the supervisor's testimony also was suspect, the grievant was reinstated with full back pay.[155]

A similar conclusion was reached in another case where denial of representation "cast a shadow" over an interview in which the employee admitted that she had stolen money from the company. Her later testimony that she was very upset about the accusations, that the company had promised her immunity from prosecution if she confessed, and that she lied to put the matter to rest was therefore believable.[156]

Remedy When Right to Representation Has Been Violated

The issue of an employee's right to union representation in pre-disciplinary interviews under *Weingarten* typically comes before an arbitrator in one of two ways:

---

[155] *Thrifty Drug Stores Co.*, 68-2 ARB ¶8628 (Jones, 1968).
[156] *Pick-N-Pay Supermarkets, Inc.*, 52 LA 832 (Haughton, 1969).

Employee Disciplined for Refusing to Meet With Management Because Steward Not Present. Arbitrators have frequently set aside[157] or at least reduced[158] a penalty on the theory that an employee cannot properly be disciplined for asserting legitimate rights under the collective bargaining agreement. The right to refuse to participate in a disciplinary interview without a steward present has also been construed as one of the exceptions to the "self-help" rule.[159]

Note, however, that the employee may be putting his or her job on the line by defying an order to meet with a supervisor or other member of management. The NLRB has held that the reasonable belief test is a highly subjective one;[160] that is, it is the employee's determination of whether discipline is likely to be imposed that is controlling. But the Board also has said that *Weingarten* rights come into play at the commencement of a predisciplinary interview, not when the employee is told to come to a meeting.[161] Citing this ruling, an arbitrator held that an employee was properly discharged for insubordination after he walked away from a manager when told to go to his office, where the manager merely wanted the employee to complete an accident report and did not intend even to accompany the employee to the office.[162]

---

[157]Discharge was set aside and the grievant reinstated with full back pay in, *e.g., Braniff Airways, Inc.,* 27 LA 892 (Williams, 1957) (overtime distribution), and *American Enka Corp.,* 68-2 ARB ¶8558 (Pigors, 1967) (peeping into women's restroom). Suspensions and reprimands were revoked in *Valley Iron Works,* 33 LA 769 (Anderson, 1960) (insubordination); *The Arcrods Co.,* 39 LA 784 (Teple, 1962) (refusal to attend meeting with company officials); *G. C. Murphy Co., supra* note 154; *Dep't of the Air Force,* 75 LA 994 (Hart, 1980) (grooming); *Pacific Bell,* 92 LA 127 (Oestreich, 1989) (questions about performance).

[158]In the typical "split decision" case, the grievant has been found to have been at least partially responsible for his difficulties. See, e.g., *Sterling Drug, Inc., supra* note 152 (discharge justified had company not violated employee's right to representation); *Dow Chem. Co., supra* note 152 (past uncooperative attitude and refusal to leave plant when directed); *Southern Cal. Edison Co.,* 61 LA 453 (Block, 1973) (absenteeism).

[159]*Southern Cal. Edison Co., supra* note 158; *Braniff Airways, supra* note 157.

[160]*Quality Mfg. Co.,* 195 NLRB 197, 79 LRRM 1269 (1972), *enforced in part,* 481 F.2d 1018, 83 NLRB 2817 (4th Cir., 1973).

[161]*Roadway Express,* 246 NLRB 1127, 103 LRRM 1050 (1979).

[162]*Twin Coast Newspapers,* 89 LA 799, 804 (Brisco, 1987). There was a dispute as to what the manager said to the employee, but the arbitrator found the manager's version ("I need for you to go to my office") more credible than the employee's version ("I'd like to talk to you in my office"). He was motivated to this conclusion in part by the grievant's record of "seeming to enjoy keeping his supervisors off balance, so that they never knew when he was going to respond negatively to their instructions, curse them, or ignore them."

Employee Disciplined After Meeting With Management Even Though Request for Union Representation Denied. The typical case is where the foreman calls in an employee to discuss a poor attendance record, expecting to impose a disciplinary suspension. The employee asks that a shop steward be called in, and the foreman denies the request. The employee then answers the foreman's questions but fails to provide acceptable reasons for the absences and is suspended. The employee protests, either in a grievance or later at the arbitration hearing, that the suspension was not warranted and, furthermore, that *Weingarten* rights were denied. What an arbitrator would do about that due process violation depends on which of several variations the case presents.

Was the request really made? Sometimes the employer flatly asserts that the employee did not ask that a union representative be called. In that case, the question becomes one of credibility. If the arbitrator believes the employer, the representation issue may be pursued no further; if he believes the grievant, or if he holds the view that the employer was obligated to inform the grievant of his right to representation (see note 142 above), one of the other variations comes into play.

The employee's original misconduct is proved. The question of remedy for *Weingarten* violations comes into focus when the arbitrator decides that the misconduct for which the employee was disciplined was proved, but that his *Weingarten* rights were violated. In this situation, arbitrators are split between the same "hard line" and "pragmatic" camps as they are for other due process violations (e.g., an employer's failure to give an employee a hearing before taking disciplinary action). To the pragmatist, whether the *Weingarten* violation should be reflected in the outcome depends on whether the grievant was actually prejudiced by the denial of his request for union representation.[163] In such a case the arbitrator would find precedent in

---

[163]If, for example, the employee said nothing damaging during an "improper" interview with the foreman, the pragmatist would tend to uphold discipline despite the due process violation on the theory that the company should not be penalized for what was merely a technical violation. *E.g.*, in *U.S. Sugar Co.*, 84-1 ARB ¶8161 (Hanes, 1984) (falsification of worker's compensation claim), the arbitrator ruled that any violation of *Weingarten* rights was irrelevant because the company's decision to discharge was not based on facts gained through its interview with the grievant. See also *Millington Plastics Div. of Worthington Indus.*, 87-2 ARB ¶8425 (Duda, 1987) (grievant not disadvantaged by denial of union representation); *Macmillan Bloedel Containers*, 92 LA 592 (Nicholas, 1989) (*Weingarten* violation overlooked because of time invested by both parties and good proof offered by company).

NLRB holdings that where clear misconduct has been proved, disciplinary action should not be disturbed and only a cease and desist order is appropriate.[164]

To a hard liner, on the other hand, a *Weingarten* violation requires that discipline be set aside or at least reduced on the theory that where due process is in issue, the means are as important as the ends. Thus, in a case where the employer granted the grievant's request for representation only after she had already been questioned about violating a rule against drinking on her lunch break, the arbitrator set aside her suspension. "Management may not now seek to invoke one Company policy in a circumstance where another equally relevant Company policy [i.e., to call in the union] was violated by a supervisor."[165]

The employee's misconduct is not proved. Following the principle "if no infraction is proved, no penalty is just," an arbitrator could reinstate the grievant with back pay without referring at all to *Weingarten* rights if the company failed to prove misconduct. Could any additional remedy—for example, damages—be awarded to remedy a *Weingarten* violation? In this case even the

---

[164]See, e.g., *Kraft Foods*, 251 NLRB 598, 105 LRRM 1233 (1980); *NLRB v. Southern Bell Tel.*, 676 F.2d 449, 110 LRRM 2880 (11th Cir. 1982); *NLRB v. Consolidated Food*, 694 F.2d 1070, 112 LRRM 2683 (6th Cir. 1982); *Taracorp Inc.*, 273 NLRB 221, 117 LRRM 1497 (1984). The Eighth Circuit, in *NLRB v. Potter Elec. Signal Corp.*, 600 F.2d 120, 101 LRRM 2378 (8th Cir. 1979) invoked §10(c) of the NLRA in denying enforcement to a make-whole remedy for two employees terminated for fighting who were denied union representation. Section 10(c) provides that "[n]o order of the Board shall require the reinstatement of any individual as an employee who has been suspended or discharged, or the payment to him of any backpay, if such individual was suspended or discharged for cause." The Sixth, Seventh, and Ninth Circuits subsequently adopted the Eighth Circuit's view. *General Motors Corp. v. NLRB*, 674 F.2d 576, 109 LRRM 3345 (6th Cir. 1982); *NLRB v. Illinois Bell Tel. Co.*, 674 F.2d 618, 109 LRRM 3244 (7th Cir. 1982); *Pacific Tel. & Tel. Co. v. NLRB*, 711 F.2d 134, 113 LRRM 3529 (9th Cir. 1983). For a discussion of a trend toward narrowing of the scope of *Weingarten*, see B. Heshizer & R. Downing, *The Contracting Weingarten Doctrine: NLRB Policymaking in a Politicized Environment*, 36 LAB. L.J. 707–15 (1985).

[165]*General Tel. Co. of Cal.*, 82-1 ARB ¶8198 (Roberts, 1982) (drinking during break). See also *Maui Pineapple Co.*, 86 LA 907 (Tsukiyama, 1986) (discharge upheld, but one month's pay awarded for *Weingarten* violation); *Amstar Corp.*, 89-1 ARB ¶8075 (Feigenbaum, 1987) (abusive conduct provoked by supervisor's refusal to allow grievant to consult union representative before answering question about whether he would work overtime; hence penalty reduced); *Golden Nugget Hotel*, 89-1 ARB ¶8079 (Hardbeck, 1988) (failure to tell grievant of representation rights, together with facts that grievant did not benefit from misconduct and had 24 years of good service, warranted reducing discharge to four-week suspension); *Arkansas Power & Light Co.*, 92 LA 144, 89-2 ARB ¶8362 (Weisbrod, 1989) (reinstatement without back pay because of denial of representation); *H. J. Heinz Co.*, 95 LA 82 (Ellmann, 1990) (discharge set aside, but four-month suspension imposed for "abysmal record of absenteeism").

hardest of hard liners would follow the general rule that an arbitrator does not have the authority to award damages or other type of remedy that goes beyond making the grievant whole for an unjust dismissal unless the contract expressly permits such remedy.

But take another possibility—the company fails to prove that the employee is guilty of theft, but the arbitrator finds proof of the lesser misconduct of taking company property without proper authorization, for which some penalty less than discharge is appropriate; and the employee's *Weingarten* rights were violated. In this situation, the arbitrator reinstated the grievant with full back pay in part because of the *Weingarten* violation.[166]

Company's Obligation to Investigate Criminal Misconduct

An exception to the rule that the company needs to investigate suspected misconduct has sometimes been made where the misconduct in question is criminal in nature and prosecution has been undertaken by law enforcement authorities. As discussed in Chapter 5, the company has two choices when an employee has been arrested for the same misconduct for which it seeks to impose discipline. It may elect to discharge him without waiting for his case to be decided in court, or it may suspend him pending final court action.

If immediate discharge is the choice, the company has the same obligation to investigate the suspected misconduct as it has in any disciplinary situation. Arrest or indictment, standing alone, does not prove that an individual is guilty, and discharge cannot be supported unless investigation by the company has produced convincing evidence that the charges against the employee are valid.[167]

If the company elects to postpone disciplinary action until a court finds the grievant guilty or innocent, on the other hand,

---

[166]*Tucson Unified School Dist.*, 92 LA 544, 89-1 ARB ¶8236 (White, 1989). Other factors considered by the arbitrator were that the grievant was discharged on the basis of the investigatory interview rather than his hearing a week later and that he had a 15-year unblemished record and a reputation for honesty.

[167]*Lone Star Gas Co.*, 56 LA 1221 (Johannes, 1971). See also cases cited in Ch. 5, note 175.

it may reasonably argue that investigation is more appropriately handled by law enforcement authorities.

> *Arbitrator Koven:* [A] distinction must be made between an employer's responsibility to investigate allegations of non-criminal employee misconduct and its undertaking of independent inquiries into serious criminal charges. An employer who launches independent inquiries of this latter type treads on delicate ground indeed.
>
> If its inquiries tend to exculpate the accused employee, no damage may be done. But if the employer uncovers information that supports the charges, the prejudicial effects upon a pending criminal proceeding are potentially serious, and an employer should not be required by an arbitrator to take such risk.[168]

In such cases the job of investigating the serious criminal charges (e.g., selling narcotics) and protecting the individual's constitutional rights belongs to law enforcement officials and to the accused's legal counsel, not to the employer.[169] Of course, every case turns on its own facts. If under the facts of a particular case an employer can obtain relevant information without compromising the rights of the accused employee—if credible eyewitnesses to the alleged misconduct are available for questioning, for example—an arbitrator might find that the employer was obligated to investigate the matter at least to that extent.[170] Independent investigation by the company may also be required if there is a long delay in the employee's case coming

---

[168]*Armstrong Rubber Co.* (1980), unpublished opinion.

[169]For a holding to this effect, see *National Steel Corp.*, 60 LA 613, 618 (McDermott, 1973), involving the suspension of two employees and discharge of a third for drug-related violations:

> Furthermore, in a matter of this sort there is not much in the way of an independent investigation that can be conducted by the Company. Such investigation is the responsibility of law enforcement authorities, and it must be conducted in accordance with constitutional rights of the individuals involved. Therefore, the failure of the Company to carry out an extensive independent investigation cannot serve as a bar to prevent it from taking immediate action against employees indicted for possession with the intent to sell marijuana. Suspension of such employees is a proper action pending determination of their guilt.

[170]*A. S. Abell Co.*, 39 LA 859 (Strong, 1962) (gambling). In *Whirlpool Corp.*, 90 LA 41 (Holley, 1987), the arbitrator ruled that a company improperly suspended an employee who had been arrested and charged with aggravated assault because it failed to investigate sufficiently to determine whether a suspension was justified. The assault, which the employee admitted, occurred off company property, and the arbitrator held that the company was required to determine whether it generated adverse publicity or had an adverse effect on the company or on employee safety.

to trial. The rationale is that while a short suspension pending court action may be justified, indefinite suspension is tantamount to discharge and cannot be sustained without at least some evidence of guilt.[171]

There is yet another consideration. If the grievant is convicted of criminal misconduct, but is not given a lengthy jail sentence, the conviction may or may not justify converting a suspension to discharge. Take a case where the grievant was convicted of the felony of "gross sexual imposition," whereupon the company terminated him. Noting that the company's rules listed conviction of a felony as among the reasons for "disciplinary action up to and including discharge (depending upon Management's judgment of the seriousness of the offense and other relevant factors)," the arbitrator held that the employer was required to make an independent investigation to determine whether what the grievant did was just cause for discharge; it could not adopt a *per se* rule that conviction of a felony was itself ground for discharge since its own rules required it to exercise judgment as to the seriousness of the offense. Since no such investigation was made, the grievant was reinstated, though without back pay.[172]

III. Investigative Techniques

When a company embarks upon an investigation of suspected misconduct, all the normal ways of eliciting information from employees are available to it. However, certain techniques have sometimes been claimed by grievants and their unions to infringe upon the due process rights of employees. These techniques include the use of alcohol and drug tests, lie detector tests, electronic or camera surveillance, and undercover

---

[171]*New York Shipbuilding Co.*, 22 LA 851 (Dash, 1954) (gambling); *Plough, Inc.*, 54 LA 541 (Autrey, 1970) (strike-related violence).

[172]*Bard Mfg. Co.*, 91 LA 193 (Cornelius, 1988). The arbitrator noted that the employer could have avoided the predicament in which it found itself by discharging the employee for unexcused absence while he was in jail prior to his release on probation after four months. In other words, the employer could have fired the employee for absenteeism, but not for the conviction as such. See also *Federal Prison Sys.*, 92 LA 261 (Shearer, 1989), in which the arbitrator ruled that the discharge of a correctional officer following his conviction for disorderly conduct was not for just cause, where management made no independent investigation and the conviction was reversed on appeal.

agents.[173] How arbitrators have ruled on claims of this nature is the subject of this part.

Alcohol and Drug Tests

Given the potentially serious consequences in the work place of alcohol and drug use, arbitrators have tended to uphold the right of an employer to adopt reasonable policies aimed at curbing such use on the job or under circumstances that might be expected to affect job performance.[174] In the application of such policies, employees often are required to undergo alcohol and/or drug testing in certain situations—for example, when they show signs of being under the influence of alcohol or drugs or when they are involved in accidents.

Whether a test requirement is reasonable often comes down to a matter of balancing the company's legitimate concerns for its business and the employee's right of privacy.

> *Arbitrator Ross:* Obviously, the goal of controlling drug and alcohol abuse in and outside the workplace is laudable, and rules promulgated to achieve such a goal may be sufficiently related to a legitimate business purpose so as to be reasonable even if such rules are invasive. As always, it comes down to the balancing of rights, duties and responsibilities. It is the duty of an employer to provide a safe working environment for its employees. It is also the responsibility of employees to come to work unimpaired and free from the effects of alcohol and drugs. To insure that these duties and responsibilities are carried out, it may be necessary to trample upon the privacy rights of an individual for the benefit and good not only of the business but of other employees and the public at large.[175]

---

[173]As to the admissibility and credibility of evidence gained by means of these techniques, see Ch. 5. The use by employers of various techniques, including those discussed in this part, is discussed in R. I. Lehr & D. J. Middlebrooks, *Work-Place Privacy Issues and Employer Screening Policies*, 11 EMPLOYEE REL. L.J. 407–21 (1985–86); W. E. Hartsfield, *Suggestions for Investigating Employee Misconduct*, 31:2 PRAC. LAW. 11–27 (1985); D. W. MYERS & P. S. MYERS, *Arguments Involving AIDS Testing in the Workplace*, 38 LAB. L.J. 582–90 (1987); J. D. Bible, *When Employers Look for Things Other Than Drugs: The Legality of AIDS, Genetic, Intelligence, and Honesty Testing in the Workplace*, 41 LAB. L.J. 195–213 (1990).

[174]See Ch. 2, pp. 102, 104. For management, union, and neutral perspectives on the use of alcohol and drug tests, see W. A. McHugh, Jr., W. J. Goldsmith, & L. D. Clark, *Substance Abuse: The Problem That Won't Go Away*, ARBITRATION 1987, 67–106 (Proceedings of the 40th Annual Meeting, National Academy of Arbitrators 1988).

[175]*Stone Container Corp.*, 91 LA 1186, 1190–91 (1988).

In the case before him, Arbitrator Ross held that mandatory drug testing as a technique for investigating all industrial accidents requiring medical attention was unreasonable and violative of just cause requirements. Such testing might be justified to pin down or at least eliminate a possible cause of an accident resulting in severe injury, he noted. But in the case of minor accidents causing minor injury where no blame could be attached, requiring a drug test was seen as invasive and violative of the basic privacy of the employee tested. "Again, it is a matter of balancing rights, duties and responsibilities and interests."[176]

The problem in this case was that the company required testing whether or not it had reason to believe that alcohol or drug use was a factor in an accident. The same consideration impelled an arbitrator to hold that a drug screening program applied without regard to evidence of impairment was highly invasive of personal privacy. However, he added, "employees who show the slightest sign of drug-related effects should and must be subject to investigation."[177] The arbitrator in another case, where the contract provided for testing to determine whether an employee was under the influence of alcohol or drugs but did not specify what evidence of intoxication or drug

---

[176]*Id.* See also *Southern Cal. Rapid Transit Dist.*, 89-1 ARB ¶8117 (Jones, 1988), in which the arbitrator held that a fair and impartial investigation was precluded by a policy providing for automatic discharge of a bus driver who tested positive, where testing was required of any driver involved in an accident involving injury or property damage, regardless of fault. For discussions of the privacy, due process, and other considerations involved in the use of alcohol and drug testing as an investigative technique, see T. S. & R. V. Denenberg, *Employee Drug Testing and the Arbitrator: What Are the Issues?* 42:2 ARB. J. 19–31 (1987); J. D. Bible, *Employee Urine Testing and the Fourth Amendment*, 38 LAB. L.J. 611–40 (1987); B. Heshizer & J. P. Muczyk, *Drug Testing at the Workplace: Balancing Individual, Organizational, and Societal Rights*, 39 LAB. L.J. 342–57 (1988); D. L. Casey, *Drug Testing in a Unionized Environment*, 13 EMPLOYEE REL. L.J. 599–613 (1988); D. A. Simpson, *Does a Drug-Free Federal Workplace Also Mean a Fourth Amendment Free Workplace?* 40 LAB. L.J. 547–66 (1989).

[177]*Day & Zimmermann, Inc.*, 88 LA 1001, 1008 (Heinsz, 1987). Said the arbitrator:
[I]n cases involving public employees, almost all courts have determined that random, mandatory drug testing is unconstitutional as an unreasonable search and seizure under the Fourth Amendment. In this case the Grievant, as a private employee, is not directly subject to such constitutional guarantees. However, Arbitrators have always considered the just cause protection of collective bargaining agreements to include basic notions of due process as to individual employee rights and protection against unreasonable employer action.

In *Trailways, Inc.*, 88 LA 1073, 1080 (Goodman, 1987), the arbitrator held that it was improper to require a bus driver to undergo drug testing because of unsubstantiated charges of two coworkers. "[A]n employee does not somehow abandon his right of privacy at the doorstep of the employer's premises." See also Ch. 5, p. 275.

use was required to justify testing, offered the following prescription:

> [I]t is beyond doubt that the demand for testing cannot be arbi-
> trary, capricious, malicious, or discriminatory. At the other ex-
> treme, it cannot be seriously suggested that supervisors who sus-
> pect drug use be held to specialized knowledge on the effects of
> drugs, alcohol, and other mind-altering drugs. . . . Instead, the
> standard is one of reasonableness and good faith; the contract
> allows the Company to demand an employee to undergo drug/
> alcohol screening tests whenever a responsible supervisor has an
> honest reasonable suspicion that an employee may be under the
> influence of alcohol or drugs.[178]

The nature of the particular test the employer requires may
have a bearing on whether or not the test requirement meets the
just cause standard. Requiring employees to submit to urinalysis
was held to be improper because the test did not distinguish
between on- and off-duty marijuana use and could not conclu-
sively show that employees testing positive had used drugs while
on the job. "The principal inquiry to be made in examining the
question of reasonableness is whether there is a 'reasonably
discernible' connection between employee activities and the Employer's business." In other words, this particular testing requirement was unreasonable, even though there was evidence
of on-premises sale and use of drugs, because the employer
failed to show a connection between off-duty use of marijuana
and business operations.[179]

The conditions of testing, too, may be an important factor

---

[178]*Roadway Express, Inc.*, 87 LA 224, 229 (Cooper, 1986). In *Deaconess Medical
Center*, 88 LA 44 (Robinson, 1986), the arbitrator ruled that a nurse's history of drug
use gave the employer sufficient reason to require her to undergo periodic drug tests.
Given the nature of the nurse's duties and the potential for serious injury or even loss
of life, it was not necessary for the employer to await some suspicious action by the
nurse to require testing. See also *Potomac Elec. Power Co.*, 88 LA 290 (arrest three days
earlier for possession of marijuana, PCP, and drug paraphernalia gave employer just
cause to require drug-screening test upon return to work, even though employee gave
no evidence of impairment).

[179]*CFS Continental, Inc.*, 86-1 ARB ¶8070, 3297 (Lumbley, 1985). The test given
was the combination emit/thin layer chromatography test, which, the arbitrator said,
could show no more than that the employee had used marijuana within the preceding
30 days; active use, according to expert testimony, could have been shown only by a
blood or tissue test. See also *Texas Utils. Generating Co.*, 84-1 ARB ¶8025 (Edes, 1983),
where an order to submit to testing was held to be improper because the test result, if
positive, would have shown only that the grievant had used marijuana, not that he had
used it as an employee on company property.

in determining the reasonableness of alcohol or drug testing. Where an employee suspected of drug abuse refused to provide a urine specimen for a drug-screening test while under a nurse's observation, the arbitrator found her discharge improper even though the employer had a right to require monitoring of the testing procedure. The problem was that the employee was wearing a leotard and would have had to disrobe almost completely to provide the specimen, and the nurse refused her request for a robe. The employer exceeded its rights, in the view of the arbitrator, in demanding that the employee provide the specimen in an unusually embarrassing manner.[180]

Lie Detector Tests

Under the Employee Polygraph Protection Act of 1988 (EPPA),[181] the use of lie detector or polygraph tests by employers has been greatly restricted. Thirty-one states and the District of Columbia have laws either prohibiting or regulating the use of polygraph tests by employers.[182] These laws, like negotiated collective bargaining contracts, are unaffected by the EPPA to the extent that they are more restrictive; however, the EPPA does preempt laws or agreements that would restrict testing by the federal government or by defense or FBI contractors.[183] The law bars an employer from requiring an employee to submit to polygraph tests except where the employer is engaged in "an on-

---

[180]*Union Plaza Hotel*, 88 LA 528 (McKay, 1986).

[181]Pub. L. No. 100–347, June 27, 1988, 102 Stat. 646 (Title 29, §2001 *et seq.*). For a discussion of the law and its implications, see J. L. Cross, *The Employee Polygraph Protection Act of 1988: Background and Implications*, 40 Lab. L.J. 663–71 (1989). For a statistical analysis of how arbitrators have handled cases involving polygraph tests, see *The Truth About Arbitrators' Treatment of Polygraph Tests*, 42:4 Arb. J. 23–32 (1987). The subject of polygraph evidence and right of the employer to require employees to undergo testing is discussed in M. F. Hill, Jr., & A. V. Sinicropi, Evidence in Arbitration 199–228 (2d ed. 1987). See also J. B. Dworkin & M. M. Harris, *Polygraph Tests: What Arbitrators Need to Know*, 41:1 Arb. J. 23–33 (1986); K. Janisch-Ramsey, *Polygraphs: The Search for Truth in Arbitration Proceedings*, 41:1 Arb. J. 34–41 (1986); R. B. Jacobs & C. S. Koch, *Polygraph Testing: Weighing the Risks*, 14 Employee Rel. L.J. 203–22 (1988); J. W. Jones, P. Ash, & C. Soto, *Employment Privacy Rights and Pre-Employment Honesty Tests*, 15 Employee Rel. L.J. 561–75 (1990).

[182]These states are Alaska, California, Connecticut, Delaware, Georgia, Hawaii, Idaho, Illinois, Iowa, Kansas, Maine, Maryland, Massachusetts, Michigan, Minnesota, Montana, Nebraska, Nevada, New Jersey, New Mexico, New York, Oregon, Pennsylvania, Rhode Island, Tennessee, Utah, Vermont, Virginia, Washington, West Virginia, and Wisconsin. See BNA's Fair Employment Practices Manual, §§453, 455, 457, for more recent information.

[183]EPPA, §10.

going investigation involving economic loss or injury to the employer's business, such as theft, embezzlement, misappropriation, or an act of unlawful industrial espionage or sabotage." Even then, the employer must show that the employee had access to the property in question and have a reasonable suspicion that the employee was involved in the incident being investigated.

The law does not apply to government at any level or to any company that is a national defense or FBI contractor. There also are exemptions for the drug industry as to employees who have direct access to controlled substances, and for the private security industry as to employees directly involved in protecting facilities that affect the public safety.

The law states that results of a polygraph test, whether in connection with an ongoing investigation or within the private security industry, may not be used as the sole basis of an adverse employment action; there must be additional supporting evidence. Employees undergoing testing have the right to terminate a test at any time; they may not be asked any question that might be degrading or needlessly intrude on their privacy, or any question related to religious, racial, or union beliefs. After testing, an employee must be provided with a copy of any conclusion reached by the examiner and a copy of the questions and the charted responses.

Apart from legal restrictions, the use of lie detector tests as a means of investigation may be of limited value to an employer from a discipline standpoint, since "the overwhelming weight of arbitral authority is that the test results should be given little or no weight in arbitration."[184] Nevertheless, such tests have frequently been used by employers in the investigation of employee misconduct, not necessarily in the expectation that the results will be put in evidence in arbitration but as a means of obtaining information which, together with other evidence, will point the way to the proper resolution of a disciplinary problem.

Reasons for using lie detector tests as an investigatory tool have been summarized as follows by Arbitrator Laughlin:

> First, there is always the chance that the test may exonerate the grievant. . . .
> Second, if the result of the test should be adverse to the grievant, it might induce him to confess. . . .
> Third, even if the result of the test has no evidential value in a subsequent proceeding, it might provide the Employer with

---

[184]F. ELKOURI & E. A. ELKOURI, HOW ARBITRATION WORKS 315 (4th ed. 1985).

an argument to justify its own action in taking disciplinary action, particularly in an otherwise close case. . . .

Fourth, if the result of the test should prove adverse to the grievant, even if of little value in a subsequent proceeding, the Company's supervisors even if they chose not to discipline the grievant, would have reason to keep him under a legitimate surveillance to guard against such further acts.

Finally, in view of the developing change of attitude, an arbitrator, in a grievance proceeding based upon a discharge, might accept and credit the result of the polygraph test. Thus, if the tests can be accepted as reliable, and not barred because of policy objections, the Employer has legitimate reasons for desiring to know the results of a polygraph test.[185]

The employer's right to require an employee to take a lie detector test, with discharge the penalty for refusal, has been upheld by some arbitrators, usually but not always because the employee or the union had explicitly or implicitly agreed to testing.[186] More often, however, refusals to submit to testing have been excused by arbitrators, sometimes even in the presence of a prior agreement to be tested.[187] In a case where an employee

---

[185]*Bowman Transp.*, 61 LA 549, 557 (1973). The "developing change of attitude" discerned by the arbitrator referred to his perception that lie detector test results were coming to be viewed as more reliable and trustworthy. If there was a trend in this direction it was not a pronounced one, and it is no longer in evidence. See, e.g., E. A. Jones, Jr., *"Truth" When the Polygraph Operator Sits as Arbitrator (or Judge): The Deception of "Detection" in the "Diagnosis of Truth and Deception,"* TRUTH, LIE DETECTORS, AND OTHER PROBLEMS IN LABOR ARBITRATION 75–152 (Proceedings of the 31st Annual Meeting, National Academy of Arbitrators 1979). See also Ch. 5, p. 273.

[186]In *Orthodox Jewish Home for the Aged*, 91 LA 810, 816 (Sergent, 1988), the arbitrator found that a nursing home, as a private employer, had the right to require an employee to submit to a polygraph test on the ground that the constitutional protection against self-incrimination applies only to state action and is not recognized in labor arbitration. The compelling interest of the employer, he stated, took precedence over the employee's right of privacy. However, since there were legitimate questions about the employer's right to require the test, the arbitrator held that the employee should not have been discharged for refusing to be tested but should either be discharged for his alleged misconduct—assault and robbery—or offered another opportunity to take the test. See also *Warwick Elecs., Inc.*, 46 LA 95 (Daugherty, 1966) (plant guards could be compelled to take tests because labor contract required them to cooperate fully in any investigation of theft or other security matter); *Bowman Transp. Co., supra* note 185 (company may compel grievant to take polygraph test if there is plausible showing that employee committed seriously dishonest acts); *Grocers Supply Co.*, 75 LA 27 (Williams, 1980) (prehire agreement to take test enforced); *City of Carrolton*, 90 LA 276 (Stephens, 1988) (police officer properly discharged, even though refusal to take lie detector test was based on erroneous advice of counsel, where civil service rules granted police chief authority to order test).

[187]E.g., *Lag Drug Co.*, 39 LA 1121 (Kelliher, 1962) (grievant not bound by promise on employment application to submit to lie detector tests); *Buy-Low, Inc.*, 77 LA 380 (Dolnick, 1981) (prehire agreement to submit to testing unenforceable after probation-

voluntarily submitted to a lie detector test but then terminated it after learning that he was considered to have lied in the first part of the test, the arbitrator ruled that he was free to terminate the test at any time without prejudice to himself. His action, therefore, did not establish his guilt.[188]

The unreliability of lie detector tests was cited by an arbitrator as ground for denying a grievant the right to demand that he be given a lie detector test. The grievant had twice tested positive for marijuana but maintained that he had not used the drug and demanded that he be given a lie detector test. The company refused this demand and discharged him. Upholding the discharge, the arbitrator held that polygraph test results would be meaningless, given "the overwhelming trend of arbitral opinion" that they are inadmissible as evidence.[189]

Electronic and Camera Surveillance

"Management is properly concerned with the employee's work performance, what he does on the job and whether he obeys the plant's rules and regulations."[190] One of the principal duties of supervision is to observe employees in their performance of their assigned tasks. But does management's proper concern extend to the use of surveillance devices such as television cameras and tape recorders?

> *Arbitrator Mittenthal:* One of the supervisor's principal functions is to observe employees at work. Surely, such supervision cannot be said to interfere with the an employee's right of privacy. The same conclusion should apply in this case. For all the Company has done is to add a different method of supervision to the receiving room—an electronic eye (i.e., the television camera) in

---

ary period); *Leggett & Platt, Inc.*, 85-1 ARB ¶8288, 4118 (Heinsz, 1987) ("[u]nder the overwhelming weight of arbitral authority, employees are not to be penalized for refusal to take lie detector tests"); *Houston Lighting & Power Co.*, 87 LA 478 (Howell, 1986) (refusal to take lie detector test not refusal to cooperate with company's investigation).

[188]*Mississippi Power Co.*, 90 LA 220 (Jewett, 1987).

[189]*Texas City Refining, Inc.*, 89 LA 1159 (Milentz, 1987).

[190]*FMC Corp.*, 46 LA 335, 338 (Mittenthal, 1966) (use of closed-circuit television to monitor employees). For a discussion of the considerations involved in various methods of workplace monitoring, see M. L. Greenbaum, *Employee Privacy, Monitoring, and New Technology*, ARBITRATION 1988 163–96 (Proceedings of the 41st Annual Meeting, National Academy of Arbitrators 1989). See also P. A. Susser, *Electronic Monitoring in the Private Sector: How Closely Should Employers Supervise Their Workers?* 13 EMPLOYEE REL. L.J. 575–98 (1988).

addition to the human eye. Regardless of the type of supervision (a camera, a supervisor, or both), the employee works with the knowledge that supervision may be watching him at any time. He has a much better chance of knowing when he is being watched where there is no camera. But this is a difference in degree, not a difference in kind. For these reasons, I find there has been no interference with the employee's right of privacy.[191]

A telephone company's use of remote listening devices to monitor telephone operators' performance was upheld by the arbitrator. The union argued that information gathered by secret and remote means should not be used for disciplinary purposes. The arbitrator's answer was that this argument was "more pertinent for collective bargaining than to the arbitral forum."[192]

Use of Undercover Investigators

An employer may resort to an undercover investigation when it receives reports of the sale of drugs on its premises. So, too, may retailers or restauranteurs that suspect employees of dishonesty. And it is common for transportation companies to use "spotters"—trained employees of independent investigating companies who board vehicles anonymously—to check and report on drivers' fare-collection practices. In all these cases claims may be made that employees' due process rights have been violated.

In a case where the city police department had received information from various sources that a drug problem existed

---

[191]*FMC Corp.*, 46 LA 335, 338 (Mittenthal, 1966). See also *Cooper Carton Corp.*, 61 LA 697 (Kelliher, 1973) (installation of television cameras to permit vice president and production manager to observe operations being run by foreman); *Colonial Baking Co.*, 62 LA 586 (Elson, 1974) (TV camera installation approved for security purposes only). In *EICO, Inc.*, 44 LA 563 (Delany, 1965), on the other hand, the arbitrator directed the removal of television cameras installed by a company. Basing his decision on a maintenance-of-working-conditions clause in the contract, he found that installation of the cameras "vitally affected the employees' working conditions" and imposed an "appreciable and intolerable burden" on them. He added, "I do not base my opinion on the Union's argument of the employees' legal 'right of privacy,'" though "this argument cannot be totally overlooked. . . ."

[192]*Michigan Bell Tel. Co.*, 45 LA 689, 695 (Smith, 1965).

in its plant, the arbitrator held that the company had "a right, even a duty," to investigate. Dealing in drugs, he said, does not take place in an open and notorious manner but is furtive and secret. While employees may report drug activity, they usually do so anonymously; rarely do they come forward to give evidence. Thus, "[t]he Company cannot be faulted for having hired an undercover agent to determine the extent of the drug problem, and identify the persons involved."[193]

The use of "spotters" as an investigatory technique was approved by Arbitrator Hildebrand for the following reasons:

1. control over bus drivers is essential for the safety of the public and protection of company property, and the spotter system provides the only practical means by which supervision can exert its responsibility in the transit industry;
2. open identification of the spotters would destroy the effectiveness of the system;
3. the spotters, unlike ordinary employees, were trained observers taught to be accurate and objective, having no personal contacts with the employees and having no incentive to falsify facts;
4. the spotters' reports were prepared before the decision to discipline was made;
5. there was no tangible basis for believing that the company was biased against the grievant.[194]

Complaints that the use of unidentified observers to keep watch on employees is an improper form of investigation have been treated unsympathetically by arbitrators. In a case where a transit company hired an outside auditing company to check on fare-collection practices, the arbitrator held that the use of spotters "is a matter that lies squarely within the exercise of Management's prerogatives. . . ." He further ruled that what the spotters were doing—boarding buses and offering operators incorrect fares, passes, and transfers—was not entrapment.

---

[193]*Burger Iron Co.*, 92 LA 1100, 1108 (Dworkin, 1989). See also *Tarmac Virginia*, 95 LA 813, 818 (Gallagher, 1990) ("use of undercover investigative reports through spotters or agents disguised as co-workers appears to be an accepted method for the detection of more clandestine violations of plant rules") (with many additional case citations).

[194]*Los Angeles Transit Line*, 25 LA 740, 744-45 (1955).

Where spotters are merely boarding buses and offering improper fares in an attempt to detect improper fare collection by Operators, it cannot be said that instigation or wrongful conduct was seen on the part of the spotters. . . . Thus, it must be held that Grievant was not "entrapped" by Management's surveillance program. . . .[195]

---

[195]*Metropolitan Transit Auth.*, 88 LA 361, 365-66 (Nicholas, 1987). See also *Kroger Co.*, 40 LA 316 (Reid, 1963) (use of anonymous checkers to follow and report on work of delivery truck drivers did not put drivers under "intolerable strain"); *Transit Auth. of River City*, unpublished opinion (Allen, 1986) (surveillance program involving use of spotters upheld).

Chapter 4

Fair Investigation

"Was the Employer's investigation conducted fairly and objectively?"

What Constitutes a Fair Investigation

Many readers of Arbitrator Daugherty's seven tests have wondered why Daugherty made "fair investigation" a test separate from "investigation." From a general point of view, the question of what makes an investigation "fair," as well as complete, timely, and the like, raises a number of issues concerning what employee rights the company is obliged to respect—for example, protections against self-incrimination and unreasonable searches; the right to be heard; the right to confront one's accusers; and the right to union representation. These issues were discussed in Chapter 3.

However, Daugherty had something specific in mind that relates to the psychology of decision making and to the way in which management delegates authority for conduct of investigations. As he explained in his "Notes" to Question IV:

> Note 1: At said investigation, the management official may be both "prosecutor" and "judge" but he may not also be a witness against the employee.
>
> Note 2: It is essential for some higher, detached management official to assume and conscientiously perform the judicial role, giving the commonly accepted meaning to that term in his attitude and conduct.
>
> Note 3: In some disputes between an employee and a management person there are no witnesses to an incident other than the two immediate participants. In such cases, it is particularly important that the management "judge" question the manage-

ment participant rigorously and thoroughly, just as an actual third party would.

What these notes add up to is this:

- For an investigation to be successful (from the point of view of both proof and due process), it must be objective.
- For it to be objective, someone from management must make sure that as much available evidence as possible is collected and that evidence gets a careful look, not from a partisan, management-oriented perspective but from the perspective of a disinterested third party.
- For a disinterested evaluation to be conducted, some management official other than the supervisor who imposed discipline is generally required.

Everyone sometimes misperceives or misjudges a situation or makes a mistake. And few people are so objective that they are aware (or if aware, will admit) that they might be wrong in a particular instance. The thrust of Daugherty's Notes 1 and 2 is that the supervisor who has been an employee's accuser, or has produced evidence against the employee, may be too caught up in defending a position—even in saving face in some cases— to be the best judge. That is especially true if the discipline-provoking incident was a heated one; it is very hard for someone to be objective when things are tense and confused, hardest of all when that someone is emotionally involved.

How the grievance procedure should function as an integral part of fair investigation was expressed in these terms by Arbitrator Jones:

> The purpose of the negotiated Step II and III hearings is to enable a dispassionate and objective review of the disciplinary decision of an immediate supervisor by members of higher management, sufficiently remote from the occasion as to have no compelling psychic stake in its resolution. Those occasions for possible recognition by a relatively objective person of an over-reaching supervisorial error, an inadequate marshaling of the facts, an overblown assessment of the significance of the circumstances, or a need for the application of progressive discipline in the interests of both of the Hospital and of the affected employee in rehabilitation rather than termination.[1]

---

[1]*Capitol Hill Hosp.*, 93 LA 947, 952 (1989) (walking off job). The arbitrator who focused more on the result of the disciplinary process than on the means of reaching that result might take a somewhat flexible approach to the fair investigation test. In *Pan Am Support Servs.*, 89-1 ARB ¶8306 (Odom, 1988) (use of offensive language at training

Failure to Investigate Fairly

Arbitrators commonly cite two kinds of management failure in the area of fair investigation.

The Foregone Conclusion

> "I'll be judge, I'll be jury," said cunning old Fury; "I'll try the whole cause, and condemn you to death."[2]

In the normal course of things, the condition that "a second opinion" be provided is fulfilled where the personnel manager or other higher management representative is responsible for making final decisions on disciplinary cases that are referred to him from below. But where a single supervisor has the authority to function as witness, prosecutor, and final judge, the outcome is often a foregone conclusion, and whatever investigation is made might as well not have taken place at all.

EXAMPLE: On a day when the grievant was assigned to the job of capping fiber drums with metal tops, his foreman noticed that two or three of the tops had been damaged by excessively hard blows from a mallet and that one drum had been damaged by being shoved or kicked. Making no further investigation, the foreman fired the grievant.

Once the case reached arbitration, the outcome was all but inevitable. The foreman thought that his eyes told him everything he needed to know and made no attempt, even by talking to the grievant, to find out if his conclusion was correct or if there was some reasonable explanation for the grievant's actions. And, what is to the point here, neither did anyone else. Since the foreman's treatment of the incident was never reviewed, his mishandling of the incident by failing to question

---

sessions), for example, the arbitrator took the position that the disciplinary process is not necessarily fatally poisoned merely because the reviewing manager begins with the belief that the grievant is guilty. It must be shown, or at least be inferrable, he said, that the grievant's interests were harmed by the prejudgment. This, essentially, is an application of the "pragmatic" approach (as distinct from the "hard line" approach) mentioned in Ch. 3, p. 184.

[2]L. CARROLL, ALICE'S ADVENTURES IN WONDERLAND, Ch. 3 (1865).

the grievant was never corrected. The arbitrator overturned the grievant's discharge on the basis of that due process violation.[3]

The possibility that, without the intervention of someone from upper management in the disciplinary process, an employee can become the victim of a single supervisor's prejudice or animosity is underscored in a case where a female meat wrapper was discharged for mismarking the prices on two packages of meat. The decision to discharge her was made solely by the head meat cutter, who on several occasions had expressed his dissatisfaction about having to work with a woman, and whose objectivity was therefore highly suspect.[4]

An employee might also be the victim of a supervisor's mistakes if, for example, the supervisor who was responsible for the training later fires the employee for poor work performance. If the employee claims he or she did not receive adequate preparation, the union would have a persuasive argument that the supervisor was hardly in a position to make an objective decision as to whether the employee was entirely at fault.

Half Measures

The fair investigation test suggests that the role of the upper management official is comparable to that of the arbitrator to the extent that both function as fair and objective reviewers of evidence. But the manager has an additional task that the arbitrator does not have. Assuming that his or her review discloses some defect in a subordinate's handling of the case, the manager may be able to save the day by investigating further and coming up with additional evidence before final disciplinary action is taken. If the defect is allowed to stand, on the other hand, the employer's case may simply slide from bad to worse,

---

[3]*Grief Bros. Cooperage Corp.*, 42 LA 555 (Daugherty, 1964). Due process also fell by the wayside in *Railway Employees' Dep't, AFL-CIO*, 69-1 ARB ¶8230 (Sembower, 1968), in which a supervisor who initiated complaints about an employee's careless work and was the subject of a cross-complaint by her subsequently presided over the hearing in which her case was considered; refused to be cross-examined by her union representative; and made the final decision that she would be discharged. See also *Demby Rod and Fastener Mfg. Co.*, 70-1 ARB ¶8293 (Daugherty, 1969) (verbal altercation); *Sherwin-Williams Co.*, 56 LA 101 (Sullivan, 1971) (assault on foreman).

[4]*Shop Rite Foods, Inc.*, 67 LA 159 (Weiss, 1976). See also *Amoco Chem. Corp.*, 70 LA 504 (Helburn, 1978) (sex discrimination complaint, not substandard performance, real reason for discharge).

frustrating the whole purpose of the manager's participation in the decision-making process.

> **EXAMPLE:** When an employee refused an assignment to work in the wood shop, his foreman fired him without even asking him the reason for his refusal. The vice president for personnel testified at the hearing that he "tried more or less to investigate actually what happened," and that he pulled the employee's medical record when the latter claimed that he had refused the job because he was afraid that dust and fumes in the wood shop would aggravate his bronchial condition. Finding no mention of a bronchial condition, he sent the employee packing.

In the arbitrator's view, the vice president blew it. His follow-up to the foreman's nonexistent investigation was half-hearted at best. He did not, as might reasonably have been expected, talk to the employee himself to try to discover the discrepancy between the employee's explanation and the medical record, although the fact that the employee had always been a cooperative employee who had never before challenged a work assignment should have told him that a thorough inquiry was in order. Nor did he ask the employee for a doctor's verification that he was ill, although he conceded it was company policy to do so. The foreman's initial decision was essentially rubber-stamped, and as a result the arbitrator returned the employee to work.[5]

The fairness problem is compounded when the higher-ups who approve a disciplinary recommendation without giving the matter fresh consideration turn out to be the reviewing authorities when a grievance is filed. Take the case of the nurse in the "float pool"—meaning that she was subject to being assigned anywhere in the hospital—who was discharged for refusing an assignment and leaving the hospital. The two managers who approved her termination never spoke with her but took the position that, as an experienced nurse, she knew that walking

---

[5]*Artco-Bell Corp.*, 61 LA 773 (Springfield, 1973). A similar situation was presented in *Howard Indus.*, 86-1 ARB ¶8132 (Taylor, 1986), where an employee was discharged for leaving the plant without permission. The employment administrator, who made the discharge decision, never spoke with the employee but relied solely on a brief report from a foreman. Because of this lack of procedural fairness, the discharge was reduced to a 30-day suspension. See also *VA Medical Center*, 88 LA 752 (Ludolf, 1987) (manager who issued reprimand relied on subordinates' investigation without talking with grievant); *Universal Foods Corp.*, 84-1 ARB ¶8087 (Belcher, 1984) (sales manager should have been accompanied by grievant or union steward during investigation of substandard performance to avoid hazard of offering hearsay evidence).

off the job was ground for discharge. They also were the hearing officers, respectively, at second and third steps of the grievance procedure. In ordering the nurse's reinstatement (though without back pay), the arbitrator had these comments:

> Those reviewing officials have prejudged the matter by authorizing a termination based on factual assumptions accepted by them to be true at the time. Extensive experience (as well as plain common sense) counsels that the psychology of the situation militates against any realistic prospect of a fresh review and change of mind and reversal of the decision. It is unlikely for hearing officers in those circumstances to be objective in their review, regardless of their good faith intention, even self-confidence, to be so. In making realistic judgments, they normally have to cope with their quite natural inclinations to give support to and uphold the decisions of their supervisors. It simply overloads the circuits of objectivity to expect them as well to be prepared readily to reverse their own prior judgments to support a supervisor's recommended discipline.[6]

"My Supervisor, Right or Wrong"

Arbitrators do not always come out and say it, but at the bottom of many cases where upper management has made only a lukewarm review of the evidence, or has rubber-stamped a decision made by a subordinate without even going through the motions of an objective evaluation, is the attitude that upper management is going to back up its supervisors' decisions, right or wrong.

> *Arbitrator Seitz:* Not infrequently, an employee is discharged because a supervisor has used bad judgment or because a personnel decision was made in haste or in the heat of controversy. Tribal loyalty then encourages the employer to support a questionable initial decision through the grievance steps and in arbitration, even though second thoughts, more careful consideration, and later developed facts indicate that disciplinary suspension would

---

[6]*Capital Hill Hosp.*, *supra* note 1, at 952–53. What might be called playing with loaded dice was also seen in *Montana Educ. Ass'n*, 89-1 ARB ¶8211 (McCurdy, 1988). There the head cook was the target of a removal petition submitted by parents. The school's investigation consisted of an open survey of the parents by a superintendent who had received a disciplinary letter for a serious verbal altercation with the cook on school grounds. This investigation struck the arbitrator as "bumbling, bizarre and biased." See also *City of Balch Springs*, 84 LA 268 (Nelson, 1985) (demotion for cursing and losing temper; same individual served as accuser, investigator, jury, and judge).

be more just, fair and consonant with the pattern of discipline in the plant.[7]

Upper management may well have its reasons for backing up a supervisor in a case that is almost sure to be a loser if it goes to arbitration. Just as a union on occasion needs to press bad grievances for "political" reasons—to demonstrate its zeal to the membership, or to satisfy an insistent grievant—"politics" may also prompt management to endorse a dubious decision to show its support for the particular supervisor or as a demonstration of strength to supervisors who think the employer is too "soft."[8]

Making a "back up" decision is management's prerogative. Doing so need not cause a serious problem as long as management recognizes the back-up decision for what it is—a show of solidarity with those "in the trenches." But the employer should not be outraged if an arbitrator shoots it down because he or she had to answer no to Daugherty's Question 4, or because upper management's hands-off policy left the company with a less than overwhelming cause from an evidentiary standpoint.

It is where management tries to hold on to two contradictory goals (i.e., to support its supervisor, right or wrong, and at the same time to win every case) that it is likely to find itself with unrealistic appraisals of the merits of particular cases; a distorted view of what the arbitration process can accomplish; and an adversarial stance vis-á-vis the union that exceeds the bounds of normal conflict and adversarial realities.

Finally, it goes without saying that anyone from upper management who tries to make an effective evaluation of a disciplinary case will be hamstrung if the supervisor who started the ball rolling does not supply him all the available relevant information. Thus there was no way for the higher-ups to pursue the investigation of an incident in which an employee was accused of smoking in an off-limits area, where his foreman reported

---

[7] *Substitution of Disciplinary Suspension for Discharge (A Proposed "Guide to the Perplexed" in Arbitration),* 35 Arb. J. 27–28 (1980).

[8] See the comments of C. W. Ahner, *Arbitration: A Management Viewpoint,* THE ARBITRATOR AND THE PARTIES 80 (Proceedings of the 11th Annual Meeting, National Academy of Arbitrators 1958). ("The company president may recognize that a plant manager has made a wrong and potentially dangerous decision, but finds it unpolitic not to back him up. Similarly the plant manager may prefer to let the *arbitrator* make it clear to his foreman that he is wrong."); and of S. BERNSTEIN, *Chicago Panel Report,* DECISIONAL THINKING OF ARBITRATORS AND JUDGES 80 (Proceedings of the 33rd Annual Meeting, National Academy of Arbitrators 1981).

the evidence against him but did not mention that the employee had denied the charge and claimed to have two witnesses who would testify in his favor. His discharge was overturned because Daugherty's Questions 3 and 4 were answered in the negative.[9]

A supervisor might hold back what he or she knows in order to make some points with the higher-ups by giving them what appears to be an open-and-shut case. Or maybe there was something wrong with the way the supervisor handled the situation initially, and he or she is trying to cover this up. Then again, a supervisor may let upper management down simply because he or she is not alert enough or well trained enough to conduct an adequate investigation when it is necessary. Whatever the reason, the result is the same: Upper management cannot (even with the best intentions) review the case objectively because it does not get the information it needs.

---

[9]*Olin Mathieson Chem. Corp.*, 51 LA 97, 68-2 ARB ¶8630 (Daugherty, 1968).

Chapter 5

Proof

"At the investigation did the company 'judge' obtain substantial evidence or proof that the employee was guilty as charged?"

Arbitrator Witney: As countless arbitration decisions demonstrate, in a disciplinary case the employer bears the burden of proof. In short, the employer must supply convincing evidence that the employee committed the offense for which he was discharged. It is up to the employer to prove the employee "guilty"; and not the employee who must prove himself "not guilty."[1]

Arbitrator Burke: A discharge cannot be based upon conjecture, surmise, suspicion, or anything but hard, material, and known facts.[2]

Once the company has thoroughly investigated all the facts—and once someone from management has taken a good, objective look at those facts—the question is whether there is sufficient proof that the employee committed the misconduct with which he is charged. To put it mildly, proof is indispensable. Whatever an arbitrator's approach to just cause happens to be, proof that the employee really "did it" is a rock-bottom requirement for discipline to pass arbitral review. As one arbitrator has put it, "If no infraction has been proved, then no penalty is just."[3]

---

[1]*Midwest Tel. Co.*, 66 LA 311, 314 (1966) (low productivity).
[2]*Borden's Farm Prods., Inc.*, 3 LA 607, 608 (1945) (dishonesty).
[3]*Arizona Aluminum Co.*, 82-1 ARB ¶8212 at 3975 (Sass, 1982) (damage to company property).

237

As stated above by Arbitrator Witney, the company bears the burden of proof in a disciplinary case, since it is accusing the employee of failing to meet his or her job responsibilities. This is in marked contrast to grievances which claim that the company has failed to carry out *its* contractual responsibilities— for example, by failing to observe seniority in a layoff situation or to distribute overtime equally; in such cases the union bears the burden of proof. This is not to say, however, that the burden of proof in a discipline case is entirely one-sided.

> *Arbitrator Dworkin:* It is well recognized that the Company bears the initial evidentiary responsibility in a discharge case. It must establish that the aggrieved employee committed the offense(s) charged, that the misconduct warranted severe discipline, and that the contractual prerequisites were observed in substance as well as in form. But the burden of proof is not one-sided, stable, or unvarying. It shifts from time to time, especially when mitigating factors are raised.[4]

In the case before him, Arbitrator Dworkin found that the company had amply proved unacceptable attendance, but the union had not met its burden of establishing that the mitigating factors alleged—alcoholism and marital difficulties—were the cause of the grievant's attendance problems or, if the cause, justified upsetting the action taken by the company. He therefore upheld the grievant's discharge.[5]

Proof is a topic of enormous proportions—too large to be treated exhaustively in this chapter. But certain aspects of proof are closely tied to just cause considerations and need to be taken up here. For example, the requirement that the company must prove that an employee has committed the misconduct in question:

- protects the employee from arbitrary, capricious, or discriminatory discipline, since the company cannot use pretexts or trumped-up charges to cover up reasons for discharge that would not pass just cause tests;

---

[4]*Goodyear Tire & Rubber Co.*, 92 LA 91, 95 (1988) (absenteeism caused by alcohol and marital problems). Arbitrator Fox, in *St. Charles Grain Elevator Co.*, 84 LA 1129, 1132 (1985) (firing shotgun at administrative building): "Management has the initial burden to justify its action. Once this burden has been shouldered, the burden of the affirmative passes to the Union which must, if it is to prevail, either successfully refute Management's case of establishing 'just cause' or else prove mitigating circumstances." As to the shifting burden of proof in group misconduct cases, see below, p. 286.

[5]*Goodyear Tire & Rubber Co.*, 92 LA 91, 95 (1988).

- prevents supervisors or even other employees with personal grudges from getting the employee fired merely by making accusations of wrongdoing;
- ensures due process by giving an employee a fair opportunity to offer a defense, since there is a specific charge and specific evidence the employee can respond to.

EXAMPLE: An audit of a union's books revealed a shortage of over $100,000, a one-month test period showing about $7,000 missing for that month alone. As a result, the financial secretary resigned under a cloud. His two clerical assistants refused to quit and were fired for gross negligence on the theory that intuition alone should have told them that funds were missing.

The key question: What proof did the employer submit to support its charge? The answer: not one iota! The arbitrator concluded: "What the [employer] has seen fit to do is transfer the negligence of their elected officials, trustees and others to the shoulders of these two grievants and now seeks to foist its own shortcomings on them." Both grievants were reinstated with back pay.[6]

Because the company has the burden of proof, a minimum requirement is that its case must rest on facts that, taken as a whole, rise to the level of some recognized, objective standard of proof.

Arbitrator Chapman: [An arbitrator] is concerned with careful analysis of the evidence, his evaluation of the truthfulness of the witnesses and the nature of the charge made against the grievant. This can vary from case to case.

After considering these matters and anything else relevant, he makes an honest judgment as to whether or not the discharge was for proper cause and, whether his decision is based on "beyond a reasonable doubt," "preponderance of the evidence," "clear and convincing proof," or any other measurement, it is how the particular arbitrator views the case. His rationale, of course, must be presented and be reasonable to protect the integrity of the decision.[7]

---

[6]*United Brotherhood of Carpenters and Joiners,* 57 LA 17, 20 (Rohman, 1971).

[7]*General Tel. Co. of Ky.,* 77-2 ARB ¶8578, 5537(1977) (sabotage). Another formulation: "Although there was extensive argument by both parties as to the appropriate standard of proof, the fact remains that under *any* standard of proof, the Arbitrator must be sure in his own mind that the evidence proves what the Employer claimed." *Modine Mfg. Co.,* 90 LA 189,194 (Goldstein, 1987) (marijuana use).

It is highly important that the arbitrator and the employer speak the same language with respect to the criteria by which the evidence and proof are evaluated. Any disagreement as to whether misconduct has been proved in a particular case should come down to differences as to interpretation of facts rather than differences as to the standards used to evaluate those facts. If, for example, an employer should argue (as some still do) that it does not have the burden of proof or the burden of going forward in the case of a discharge for theft, it would not be speaking the language of anyone in the arbitration business.

Another example arose with respect to the proper quantum of proof in a theft case. The arbitrator said essentially that he and the employer were in separate worlds. He was, he said, "not particularly impressed by the Employer's contention that the Employer was merely obligated to prove the Grievant's guilt by a preponderance of the evidence," where the grievant had been discharged for deliberately giving false information during a lie detector test, thereby interfering with the employer's investigation into an alleged theft.[8]

The employer can ask itself, as the party with the burden, whether instead of proof it is offering up a sure loser from a parade of pseudo-proofs that cannot measure up to any acceptable standard. It does this when it serves up a mishmash of suspicions,[9] assumptions,[10] possibilities,[11] unsupported opin-

---

[8]*Hollytex Carpet Mills, Inc.*, 79-1 ARB ¶8181, 3761 (Anderson,1979).

[9]*State of Conn. Dep't of Corrections*, 81-2 ARB ¶8597, 5605 (Murphy, 1981 (abuse of sick leave): "However justified the employer's suspicions, they are not facts . . . ." *Templet Mfg. Co.*, 36 LA 839, 841 (Feinberg, 1961) (disloyalty): "The circumstances were, at the most, merely suspicious." *Carus Chem. Co.*, 70-2 ARB ¶8492, 4616 (Anrod, 1970) (negligence): "The most that can be said in favor of the Company is that there exists a suspicion that the Grievant was at fault. . . . But mere suspicious circumstances are insufficient convincingly to prove the Grievant's alleged guilt." *National Metal & Steel Corp.*, 86 LA 217, 219 (Rothschild, 1985): "Suspicions are not a proper basis for demotion." *City of Middletown, Ohio*, 93 LA 1085, 1088 (Duff, 1989): "[S]uspicion is no substitute for proof."

[10]*Alameda-Contra Costa Transit Dist.*, 76 LA 770, 771 (Koven, 1981) (moonlighting): "'Assumption' of guilt is not sufficient basis to impose any penalty, let alone the penalty of discharge." *U.S. Postal Serv.*, 89 LA 495, 500 (Nolan, 1987) (off-duty misconduct): "[A]n employer will automatically assume some harm from every employee's breach of the law, even if the public is unaware or unconcerned. For that reason presumptions should be used only in the clearest of cases; in all others the employer must supply some credible evidence of a connection between the offense and the job."

[11]*Farm Pac Kitchens, Inc.*, 72-1 ARB ¶8358, 4253 (Sartain, 1972) (sabotage, slowdowns): "[W]hen an employee's work record and important aspects of his future well-being are at stake, being merely possibly or likely true is not enough." *Whirlpool Corp.*, 58 LA 421, 426 (Daugherty, 1972): "[T]he verdict should not have been based on just possibilities."

ions,[12] and funny coincidences.[13] Thus, if all the employer has going for it is one or more of these flimsy substitutes, even the strongest showing of good faith cannot make up for the absence of solid proof.[14]

I. What Must Be Proved: Three Requirements

In the context of just cause, the company's proof is subject to three basic requirements, all of which operate to ensure that the case the company proves is one against which the employee in jeopardy will have a fair chance to defend himself.

1. A Proper Charge

The company's obligation to prove its case starts out when it decides exactly what case it intends to prove. The charge against an employee must meet two criteria: First, the charge must be reasonably clear and specific—that is, the nature of the misconduct in question must be explicitly identified. Second, it must be made known to the employee before discipline is imposed.

> **EXAMPLE:** On a day following an unauthorized work stoppage in the mill, the employer notified two employees of its intent to discharge them for violating a contract provision that prohibited engaging in, encouraging, or sanctioning a strike. The union protested at the subsequent discharge hearing that the reason given for the employer's action was inadequate to explain why, out of 1,500 employees who participated in the work stoppage, these two men were singled out for discharge. Without knowing exactly what they were supposed to have done, it pointed out, they could not defend themselves.

---

[12]*Midwest Tel. Co.*, 66 LA 311, 315 (Witney, 1976) (low productivity): "Though the judgment or opinions of supervision deserve consideration, they are not of much evidentiary value unless supported by objective evidence."

[13]*U.S. Steel Corp.*, 40 LA 598, 604 (Seitz, 1963) (work stoppages): "When a medical excuse, *prima facie* valid, was given to it, the circumstances did not justify reliance on what the Company regarded as a 'funny coincidence.'"

[14]*Ames Harris Neville Co.*, 42 LA 803, 805 (Koven, 1964) (dishonesty): "We know that the Company made every effort to produce the grievant's accusers and the fact that they could not be produced is not chargeable against the good faith of the Company. However, despite this diligence, no conclusion is possible but that the Company failed to produce sufficient evidence to connect the grievant with the charged misconduct."

The problem with the charges against the employees was that a violation of the no-strike clause could involve many different acts of misconduct, ranging from simple participation in the work stoppage to the more serious offenses of encouraging or leading other employees to strike. The employer refused to say exactly what these two employees had done. The effect of that ambiguity was to deny them due process. Said the arbitrator:

> An employee who does not know of what he is accused can obviously not defend himself against the accusations. If he is to have a "reasonable opportunity" to present evidence in his behalf, he must be given at least some idea of the acts, events or issues to which his evidence should relate.[15]

Even if management properly charges an employee with misconduct and subsequently imposes discipline, its case may not stand up in arbitration if it turns out that something else was really bugging the company. Take the case of an Air Force employee who was discharged for failing to request leave on a day when she said she did not feel well. The arbitrator found that even this relatively minor transgression, when considered in the light of her poor employment record, ordinarily would have warranted severe discipline. However, the agency admitted that the employee's having gone public with charges of fraud and waste against management was an important factor in the decision to fire her. Said the arbitrator, "the fact that the 'whistle blowing' played a significant role so taints the Agency's stated justification for removing Grievant as to render that stated basis invalid." He ordered the agency to reinstate the employee with back pay.[16]

---

[15]*Bethlehem Steel Co.*, 29 LA 635, 640 (Seward, 1957). That it is not enough to get specific at the arbitration hearing was stressed by the arbitrator. Charges need to be made and evidence presented before discharge, "while Management's mind is still open, while it is still weighing the facts and while appeals to its discretion are still possible." *Id.* at 642. See also *Pillsbury Co.*, 67 LA 601 (Levy, 1976) (grievant discharged merely on basis of "posted rules" and not given chance, prior to termination, to confront the supervisor and discuss facts); *City of Detroit*, 79-2 ARB ¶8533 (Roumell, 1979) (delay in telling grievant reasons for his suspension—drinking on duty and allowing prisoners to leave cells to perform homosexual acts—until 30 days after discipline was imposed prevented facts from being discovered and denied grievant due process); *Champion Spark Plug Co.*, 93 LA 1277 (Dobry, 1989) (mere listing of rules allegedly violated did not satisfy contractual requirement that union be given "reasons for such actions . . . at the time such action is taken," especially since employer knew exactly what charges it wished to level).

[16]*Air Force Logistics Command*, 84 LA 108, 112 (Shearer, 1985).

2. *Proof of the Misconduct Charged*

Proof of Misconduct, but Not the Misconduct Charged

In some cases the original penalty (whether discharge or suspension) cannot be sustained because the offense that prompted it has not been proved. Only some lesser degree of misconduct has been established.

> *Arbitrator Maggs:* When a company bases its dismissal of an employee upon a charge that he committed an offense of one kind, proof that the employee committed another offense different in kind or not connected with the offense charged does not constitute a showing of just cause for the discharge.[17]

> **EXAMPLE:** During his three years of employment, an employee worked only 69 40-hour weeks and was tardy 82 times. Many of his absences were excused because they were due to illness or other legitimate reason. The employee received only a single warning slip, pursuant to a company rule that provided for a series of graduated penalties for poor attendance. Finally the employer discharged him—for deliberately restricting output, an offense that under the rules called for immediate discharge.

The employer had proof of misconduct—but not proof of the charge on which the discharge was based. The employee's absentee record was indeed terrible, but there was no way it could be interpreted as a deliberate restriction of production, misconduct that implies an act such as sabotage, a sitdown strike, or loafing. And in any case, the employer did not demonstrate how many of the absences were excused or unexcused, so that the extent to which the employee might have been "shirking" was not established. As a result, he was reinstated to his job.[18]

---

[17]*Cranston Print Works*, 36 LA 179, 185 (1960) (punching another employee's time card). He added, however:

> But proof that the employee committed what is in substance the offense charged, though it should have been labelled or characterized differently, may constitute just cause for the discharge or for a lesser penalty if the employee has not been unfairly handicapped in the presentation of his challenge to the discharge by the erroneous label or characterization of his misconduct.

[18]*Titus Mfg. Co.*, 50 LA 133, 135 (Hughes, 1968). Backpay, however, was not awarded. Although the grievant's poor absence record, together with other evidence that he was often uncooperative about providing medical verification of his illnesses when requested to do so, could not serve as a basis for discharge, the arbitrator found it relevant to the remedy to which he was entitled. See also *Dunham Bush, Inc.*, 80-1 ARB ¶8053 (Fasser, 1979), where an employee who was intoxicated, became ill, and fell asleep in his car shortly after punching in was discharged for sleeping on the job. The arbitrator reduced the penalty to a three-day suspension (the penalty provided by the employer's rules for a first offense of intoxication) since it was not proved that the employee was sleeping, at least in the sense that he made a deliberate choice to sleep instead of work.

Other such examples include the following:

Gross negligence versus simple carelessness. The employee was careless in continuing to operate a machine that was putting out defective work, but the evidence did not prove her guilty of "gross negligence." There was no showing that the injury to the company was serious, that the customer was delayed or inconvenienced, or that the mistake was costly.[19]

Fraud versus carelessness. The extreme inaccuracy of lab test results reported by an employee established that he had been careless but not that he was guilty of fraud. There was no evidence that he had failed to perform the tests and had deliberately submitted bogus results.[20]

Criminal behavior versus neglect of duty. The employee was guilty of neglect of duty when he sold drugs on company time, but he was not guilty of criminal activity. The pills he was selling were not classified as controlled substances.[21]

Insubordination versus threatening language. A machine operator who shook his finger at a supervisor and said "Don't fuck with me" was not guilty of a serious form of insubordination and should not have been discharged. What he did was more akin to using threatening language, the penalty for which was suspension, according to the employer's rules.[22]

---

[19]*Riverside Book Bindery , Inc.*, 38 LA 586 (McKelvey, 1962). See also *Mead Corp.*, 89-2 ARB ¶8367 (Haemmel, 1989), in which a seven-day suspension was reduced to a reprimand on the basis of findings that the grievant was guilty only of negligence, not gross negligence, and that his supervisor was guilty of gross negligence in failing to advise him of equipment changes that resulted in leakage of a contaminating fluid; *Inco Alloys Int'l, Inc.*, 91 LA 1126 (Kilroy, 1988), in which absences coupled with unacceptable or sham excuses were held to be an absence problem subject to progressive discipline, not punishable as "improper conduct" or "violation of other common-sense standards of conduct." In *Hess Oil Virgin Islands Corp.*, 89-1 ARB ¶8096 (Hunter, 1988), the arbitrator held that a charge of gross negligence does not fit the contractual nature of employment relations. The question, he said, is whether the grievant violated his implied contractual duty to perform his assignment in a good, workmanlike manner.

[20]*National Lead Co.*, 35 LA 939 (Roberts, 1960). Similarly, in *Panhandle Eastern Pipeline Co.*, 88 LA 725 (Yarowsky, 1987), an employee who falsely stated on his wife's medical claim that she was not insured through her own employer was found to have been careless and inattentive but not guilty of fraud; and in *Firestone Tire & Rubber Co.*, 93 LA 381 (Cohen, 1989), an employee who made several errors and omissions on an employment application was found to be guilty of carelessness rather than falsification of the application.

[21]*Todd Pacific Shipyards Corp.*, 72 LA 1022 (Brisco, 1979). A similar case is *Phelps Dodge Aluminum Prods. Corp.*, 52 LA 375 (Howlett, 1969), where the evidence showed that the grievants had left work early without permission, but not that they had acted in concert so as to have engaged in an illegal walkout.

[22]*Alumax Aluminum Corp.*, 92 LA 28 (Allen, 1988). See also *Salt River Project*, 92 LA 97 (Koven, 1988), in which the arbitrator overturned the discharge for insubordination of an employee suspected of being intoxicated who refused to submit to a fitness-

Proof of Misconduct, But Only in Part

Frequently the company proves only part of what it needs to prove in a discipline case. Three areas typically cause problems.

Something Less Than All the Elements. In proving misconduct, all elements of the transgression must be established before the charge can be considered proved. Theft is a good example. The company must prove not only that the grievant took property that did not belong to him but also that he had an intent to steal the property.[23] A mere showing that company property has somehow found its way into an employee's locker, or into his car, is not sufficient to prove a charge of theft.[24]

Proof of more than one element is also required in other types of misconduct. For example:

Insubordination. A refusal to follow a direct, valid work order is only half the story. There must also be proof that the employee was given clear prior warning of the consequences.[25]

"Totality of misconduct." A poor prior work record does not justify discharge without proof that the employee committed

---

to-work evaluation. He pointed out that the contract said the employer might presume that the employee was impaired, not that he was insubordinate.

[23]*Southern Cal. Edison Co.*, 61 LA 803, 807 (Helbling, 1973): "The commission of [theft] and the existence of criminal intent must both be proved by accurate, reliable and credible evidence which does not permit of an honest doubt . . . ." *Grant Hosp.*, 88 LA 587, 590 (Wolff, 1986): "In requiring proof of 'intent to steal,' arbitrators are not simply applying criminal law requirements for theft but common, everyday understandings." See also *Cincinnati Gas & Elec. Co.*, 90 LA 841 (Katz, 1988) (consumption of customer's soft drinks by meter reader); *Ohio Dep't of Mental Health*, 93 LA 377 (Goldstein, 1989) (unauthorized possession of company property). For a contrary view, holding that not every element of theft need necessarily be proved, see *Northview Village*, 95 LA 401 (Cipolla, 1990) (falsification of time card).

[24]On the other hand, proof of intent to steal without an actual taking of company property was held sufficient to justify discharge in *Pennzoil Prods. Co.*, 86 LA 877 (Stoltenberg, 1986). A truck driver was shown to have made an unauthorized trip for the express purpose of stealing diesel fuel from a company vehicle, even though he did not actually remove fuel from the vehicle. Whether his failure to complete the theft resulted from an "attack of conscience," as he claimed, or from the arrival of a state trooper, the arbitrator found cause for discharge in the driver's having made the unauthorized trip with the intent to steal the fuel.

[25]See, e.g., *Micro Precision Gear & Mach. Corp.*, 31 LA 575 (Young, 1958). In *International Salt Co.*, 88-1 ARB ¶8118 (Brannon, 1987), an employee who defied a telephone order to report for his designated shift because he had consumed alcohol and was unfit to work was found not to have been guilty of insubordination. It was unclear whether the employee had hung up without telling his supervisor of his condition or whether the supervisor had hung up, thereby preventing the employee from giving his reason. The arbitrator gave the employee the benefit of the doubt on the theory that the company had the burden of proving insubordination.

the final act of misconduct which the employer considered the last straw.[26]

Off-premises misconduct. Not only must the commission of the act in question be proved, but also some effect on the employer's business must be established.[27]

Exaggeration by the Company. Where the employer discharged an employee under a contract provision stating that the "flagrant violation" of safety rules could lead to discharge, the arbitrator agreed that violations had been proved, but not "flagrant" violations.[28] In another case the employer charged the employee with being absent "many times without reason," but it had proof of only one such incident.[29]

Whatever Is Claimed Must Be Proved. If the employer relies on an employee's history of misconduct to justify a stiff penalty like discharge, it should be prepared to produce solid proof that his or her record is as bad as it claims (not just a bald assertion that "we've had problems with him before" or the like).

Paradoxically, there are times when the company does not have to prove as much as it may think. Take on-the-job intoxication. All that the company has to prove is that a suspected employee is under the influence; it does not normally have to prove that he is "falling down drunk" to justify discipline. Or consider chronic absenteeism. The question of intent—an essential element of theft and other acts of dishonesty—is irrelevant if an employee's attendance has become so irregular that he is a liability to the company. It does not matter whether he has been malingering or whether he genuinely has health problems.

Proof of Something, But Not Misconduct

To be penalized for something, an employee must be charged with and proved guilty of a specific kind of misconduct.

---

[26]*Turco Mfg. Co..* 74 LA 889 (Penfield, 1980); *Ogden Food Serv. Corp.,* 75 LA 805 (Kelman, 1980).

[27]*Raytheon Co.,* 66 LA 677 (Turkus, 1976) (indictment for second degree murder).

[28]*West Va. Pulp & Paper Co.,* 10 LA 117 (Guthrie, 1947). See also *Ralston Purina Co.,* 88-1 ARB ¶8039 (Roumell, 1987), in which the grievant's suspension for leaving the job without permission was held to be improper since the employee had advised management that he was leaving, even though he did not wait for a response. The company had bound itself to handle such cases as unauthorized absences and had initially treated this incident as such an absence. It could not later impose a penalty for a different offense, in the arbitrator's view.

[29]*Ohmstede Mach. Works, Inc.,* 60 LA 522 (Marlatt, 1973).

Without misconduct, there can be no violation and, obviously, no punishment; and the most airtight proof is entirely beside the point. "If no infraction has been proved, then no penalty is just."[30]

The following cases of "mistaken identity" involve situations in which what appeared to be misconduct at first glance turned out to be something less.

> *Watching TV, but no dereliction of duty.* An employee was found watching TV while on duty, but there was no showing that he was doing anything other than what he was supposed to do—i.e., stand by for emergency calls. Since the company had no rule against watching TV under these circumstances, and since there was no specific type of misconduct that could be charged, proof that the employee was actually watching TV was irrelevant.[31]

> *Unfriendly coworkers, but nothing more.* Storeroom employees no longer wanted to work with an employee after he was accused of participating in a theft of company property by two recent dischargees. But no proof of his guilt was produced, thus leading the arbitrator to invalidate the transfer of the employee to another, less desirable job "simply to mollify the feelings of fellow employees who may not like [him]."[32]

> *Damage to company property, but no carelessness.* A hot metal bar was damaged when an employee dropped it. But no proof was provided that he had been careless, and the arbitrator was persuaded that he would not have been suspended if no damage had resulted when he dropped the bar—"hence the discipline was based on chance rather than error." There was proof of dropping something, but not proof of misconduct.[33]

3. Proof of Charge Made at Time of Discharge

The third requirement is that the company must prove the charge it made when it discharged the employee;[34] it cannot

---

[30]*Arizona Aluminum Co.*, 82-1 ARB ¶8212, 3975 (Sass, 1982) (damaging company property).

[31]*City of Cleveland, Ohio*, 71 LA 1041 (Siegel, 1978).

[32]*Monarch Mach. Tool Co.*, 51 LA 391, 396 (Sembower, 1968).

[33]*Tennessee Forging Steel Corp.*, 69-1 ARB ¶8282, 3967 (Owen, 1968). To the same effect, see *U.S. Immigration & Naturalization Serv.*, 84 LA 830 (Gwiazda, 1985) (no proof that damage to company vehicle was caused by grievant's negligence); *Olin Corp.*, 64 LA 56 (Jacks, 1975) (no proof grievant's statements were part of concerted plan to limit production); *Decor Corp.*, 44 LA 389 (Kates, 1965) (notification that legal action was pending against employee for nonpayment of bills not actual garnishment notice).

[34]In *Defense Mapping Aerospace Agency*, 88-1 ARB ¶8168 (Kubie, 1987), the employer was held to be required to prove *all* charges against the grievant. The charges were unauthorized possession of intoxicants in his work area, drinking on the job,

change the charge or add charges after the event. Problems with this requirement typically occur in one of the following three ways:

Postdischarge complaints—when the employer discharges an employee for one reason and then cites additional misconduct that occurred prior to discharge in support of its action.

Postdischarge evidence—when, following discharge, the employer comes up with additional evidence to support its action.

Postdischarge misconduct—when an employee engages in misconduct after discharge that the employer seeks to use as an additional reason why the discharge should be sustained.

Postdischarge Complaints

Arbitrators expect that the charge for which the company offers proof will be the charge for which discipline was originally imposed—not something the company cites for the first time at the arbitration hearing.

> *Arbitrator Armstrong:* In a discharge case, an Employer cannot bring up at the arbitration hearing new and additional grounds for discharge of which the grievant and the Union are unaware. The reason for this rule is to prevent unfair surprise to the Union and the grievant.[35]

> **EXAMPLE:** Over a year before, a meter mechanic for a taxicab company, at the request of the company's former management,

---

violation of alcohol regulations, and falsification of a material fact in connection with the investigation of the incident. The arbitration submission stated the issue as whether discipline for these offenses was for just cause. Given this submission, the arbitrator said, the employer had to prove all four charges to prevail. In *Denman Rubber Mfg. Co.*, 88-1 ARB ¶8228 (Pincus, 1987), on the other hand, proof that the grievant falsified his time card was held to be all that was required to justify the grievant's discharge. It was unnecessary, the arbitrator held, to consider a second charge, that the grievant had left the plant without permission.

[35]*Golden Grain Macaroni Co.*, 86 LA 1260, 1262–63 (1986)(gross negligence). Similarly, Arbitrator Howlett, in *Price Bros. Co.*, 61 LA 587, 589 (1973) (off-premises misconduct): "Generally, arbitrators hold that an employer may not present evidence of alleged offenses which were not specified as reasons for the discharge when notice was given." Arbitrator Guthrie, in *West Va. Pulp & Paper Co.*, *supra* note 28, at 118: "It seems clear that the discharge here involved must stand or fall upon the reason given at the time of discharge. . . . If the company was acting on the basis of other or additional considerations when it discharged the aggrieved employee, then, the official discharge should have so stated." Again: "The determination of reasonable cause must be made as of the time when disciplinary action was taken. Theoretically, time should be made to stand still." *Penn-Dixie Cement Corp.*, 29 LA 451, 457 (Brecht, 1957) (off-premises misconduct). Elkouri and Elkouri discuss postdischarge charges in How ARBITRATION WORKS 675–77 (4th ed. 1985).

had cooperated in "rigging" the cab meters so that customers were charged for more miles than the cabs actually traveled. When one of his former supervisors, who had since moved to a rival firm that wanted the company's franchise, got wind of what had happened and asked the mechanic for a written statement, he was glad to oblige. An investigation by the city got under way, and the mechanic was questioned by the company's attorney. He denied that he had given any written statement or that he had been offered a job with the competitor in exchange for that statement. About a month later, however, in his testimony before a city board, he admitted having given the written statement. The next day he was fired for making untruthful statements to the company's attorney. At the arbitration hearing, the company added another charge, namely, that the mechanic was guilty of attempting to trade company secrets for personal benefit.

Arbitrator Jones agreed with the union that this was "a material and disallowable change of ground" for the discharge, citing the same due process considerations as Arbitrator Seward emphasized when he required the company to formulate its charges clearly and explicitly (see p. 242 above):

> The company, not the Union, set the context in which this grievance proceeded to arbitration. . . . The preparation of Grievant's case, and the possibilities for its settlement short of arbitration, depend on the direction given it by the employer's stated justification for his action.
> In this case, this was clearly a carefully stated reason for discharge. It should not now be ballooned into a far reaching inquiry into the implications of the tension between employer-employee loyalty and the duty of disclosure of criminal acts owed to the community by its citizens.[36]

Adding additional charges after discharge has taken place is a common occurrence, and just as common are objections by the union that such charges are irrelevant. Even if an arbitrator

---

[36]*Yellow Cab Co. of Cal.*, 44 LA 175, 182 (Jones, 1965). Arbitrator Clark, in *General Elec. Co.*, 74 LA 125, 128 (1979) (abuse of company time): "There are serious questions of whether the company can shift the grounds for discharge in an arbitration to a claim that was not alleged or explored in prior grievance proceedings because of the lack of notice to the grievant as to the precise nature of the defense he must erect." See also *U.S. Steel Corp.*, 55 LA 677 (Wolff, 1970) (charge changed from being "unfit" to work to intoxication); *Beck's Transfer, Inc.*, 71-2 ARB ¶8490 (Witney, 1971) (dishonesty); *Tam O'Shanter Country Club*, 86-1 ARB ¶8238 (Borland, 1986) (evidence of prior criminal conviction and falsification of employment application not admitted); *Pittsburgh Press Club*, 89 LA 826 (Soltenberg, 1987) (sexual harassment complaint could not be added to charge of offensive behavior toward customer).

admits postdischarge complaints into the record, he will give them little weight—except perhaps for purposes of remedy, as discussed below.

Why Postdischarge Complaints Are Made. Typically charges get tacked on or changed after the fact as a result of one of three types of management blunder—the "false start," the "belated record check," and the "whitewash."[37]

The "false start" occurs when the company finds that the evidence does not support its original charge, and it brings in another charge to shore up its shaky position.

> **EXAMPLE:** A wire service newsman refused to tell a congressional committee whether a statement on his employment application that he was not a member of the Communist Party was true or false, citing his Fifth Amendment right to remain silent about the matter. His employer discharged him for intentionally creating a doubt about the honesty of the answer on his employment application. Later the employer made the additional argument that the newsman's testimony and subsequent discharge had received considerable publicity. Discharge, it contended, was necessary to protect its reputation for unbiased reporting of the news. Could that additional complaint be used to justify the newsman's discharge?

The arbitrator found it easy to believe that the newsman's outspoken public stand on a controversial subject might be taken by the public to mean that his news reporting would lack objectivity. As a result, although he had every right to assert his constitutional privileges, his usefulness to the employer as a disinterested news reporter had been compromised, which in principle was cause for discharge.

But the reason given for the newsman's discharge was that he had intentionally created doubts about his honesty. The employer produced no proof whatsoever of that charge. If the evidence in support of the original ground for discharge is inadequate, even the most solidly proved charge, added later,

---

[37]For other cases involving postdischarge charges, in addition to those cited below, see *Forest Hill Foundry, Inc.*, 1 LA 153 (Brown, 1946) (insubordination); *Price Bros. Co.*, *supra* note 35; *General Elec. Co.*, 74 LA 125 (Clark, 1979) (abuse of company time); *Owens-Illinois, Inc.*, 79-2 ARB ¶8518 (Witney, 1979) (insubordination, profanity).

cannot save the day for the company. The newsman's discharge was therefore set aside.[38]

The "belated records check" occurs when the company waits until after discharge to take a look at the employee's record.

This situation is classic: After firing someone, the employer goes into the personnel file and discovers all manner of past misconduct that it then tries to use to reinforce the original basis for discharge.

> *Arbitrator Burke:* Th[e] question is: Did the company have definite and concrete proof upon which it could make a proper determination at the time it discharged him, or did it act first and then proceed to fine comb his record for material to sustain it? The former is the proper way of proceeding, and the latter is unfair and unwise. . . . The only relevant evidence are the facts which the person making the discharge was in possession of at the time he acted.[39]

EXAMPLE: After it discovered that a truck driver had claimed reimbursement for a towing fee that he had not paid, the employer fired him for dishonesty. It then studied his record and found evidence that he had cheated on his expenses on many other trips. In response to the union's claim that it had undertaken a "witch hunt" to support an infirm discharge, the employer argued that the prior incidents all were relevant to its charge that the driver was dishonest.

Who was right? At the time of the driver's discharge, "dishonesty" referred to the towing fee episode and not any of the prior incidents. Moreover, even after the employer came up with the extra charges, it did not disclose the fruits of its postdischarge investigation to either the driver or the union, seriously prejudicing the union's ability to produce evidence to disprove the new allegations. The postdischarge charges were therefore

---

[38]*United Press Ass'n,* 22 LA 679 (Spiegelberg, 1954). See also *Anvar Indus. Inc.,* 72-2 ARB ¶8516 (Kossoff, 1972) (charge of possession of alcohol changed to drinking when employer realized discharge for first offense of possession was not permitted by contract).

[39]*Borden's Farm Prods., Inc.,* 3 LA 607 (Burke, 1945) (dishonesty). For a rare exception to this principle, see *Harshaw Chem. Co.,* 32 LA 23 (Belkin, 1958) (insubordination), where the arbitrator reasoned that "fairness and equity" required him to consider the grievant's entire work record, even though it was not cited on his discharge notice, and that it was up to the union to offer evidence that the foreman who discharged the grievant did not know about his past misconduct, or was not thinking about it, when he made his decision.

thrown out, and because the arbitrator judged that a five-year employee did not deserve to be discharged for cheating the employer out of $5, the driver was reinstated (though without back pay).[40]

The "whitewash" exists where an employee has been discharged impulsively, often when tempers were flaring, and the employer later tries to put together a respectable case for its action.

> *Arbitrator Brecht:* A discharge or disciplinary action cannot be said to be based on reasonable or just cause if, after it is taken on impulse, a search for reasons is made that seemingly would justify the action. This is a form of rationalizing disciplinary action that is completely unjustified.[41]

> **EXAMPLE:** A noisy exchange of words ensued after an automobile mechanic complained to his foreman about being directed to change the oil in a customer's car, an assignment he had repeatedly protested in the past. When the general manager approached him later to find out what had happened, the mechanic launched into a new tirade, telling the general manager, "I won't change oil for anybody and what are you going to do about it, fire me?" "That's right," replied the general manager and, when the mechanic came back with an obscene suggestion, did indeed fire him. At the hearing, the company argued that the mechanic's carrying on a loud argument with the foreman within earshot of customers was bad for customer relations. It also ran through a catalog of past misdeeds (including unauthorized absences and abusive language) to convince the arbitrator that the last incident was the straw that broke the camel's back.

The arbitrator took a different view of the case. The general manager was not thinking about the mechanic's past offenses when he told him to hit the road; he acted in anger and exasperation at the man's refusal to do any more oil changes and at his

---

[40]*Beck's Transfer, Inc.*, 71-2 ARB ¶8490 (Witney, 1971). Similar cases include *Dubuque, Lorenz, Inc.*, 66 LA 1245 (Sinicropi, 1976), where the arbitrator refused to take into account charges that the grievant was flippant toward fellow employees, defiant toward supervision, frequently absent from her work station, and disruptive of other employees' work because the only stated reason for her discharge was excessive absenteeism; *Unimart, Div. of Food Giant Markets, Inc.*, 49 LA 1207 (Roberts, 1968), where prior written warnings concerning, *inter alia*, taking excessive time for lunch and breaks and giving a customer improper advice about the exchange of merchandise were not considered when the grievant was discharged. See also *West Va. Pulp & Paper Co.*, *supra* note 28; *General Controls*, 34 LA 432 (Roberts, 1960) (inciting slowdown); *Abilene Flour Mills Co.*, 61-1 ARB ¶8049 (Granoff, 1960); *American Airlines, Inc.*, 46 LA 737 (Sembower, 1966) (unauthorized absence).

[41]*Penn-Dixie Cement Corp.*, *supra* note 35, at 457.

challenge to do something about it. The mechanic deserved discipline for his outburst, but an employee with long seniority and developed skills should not lose his job solely because a management official loses his temper.[42] The ostensible reason for discharge becomes no reason at all according to just cause standards if the real reason is to be found in someone's emotional reaction and is attributable to personalities rather than to principles.

Where the employer shifts ground at the hearing and seeks either to add to or change the charges, the arbitrator may suspect that the employer itself had doubts as to whether its original charges would stand up. New charges may also lead the arbitrator to suspect that the real reason for the grievant's discharge was not the one cited.

Take a case where the employer originally fired an employee for giving false information about his prior work experience, then later added the charge that he had falsified his arrest record by claiming to have been arrested for possession of marijuana when his real crime was the felonious sale of that drug. The employer's "change of plea," so to speak, led the arbitrator to suspect that the real reason for the discharge remained unstated. The original charge was not serious enough to warrant termination, he found; and if the employer had taken the employee's arrest record seriously, it would have raised that charge immediately, not as an afterthought. "There is a difference between a cause for discharge and a pretext for it. The evidence tends to exhibit not the former, but the latter. . . . Hence, the arbitrator is left with no information which permits him to identify a proper cause for the Grievant's discharge."[43]

---

[42]*Woodward's Spring Shop, Inc.*, 63 LA 367 (Pincus, 1974). Similar is *U.S. Borax and Chem. Corp.*, 63-2 ARB ¶8668, 5198 (Singletary, 1963), where the employee was fired on the spot after he refused to accept a written warning from his supervisor about sleeping on the job. Although the company argued that his discharge was justified because he had been warned previously about sleeping, the arbitrator found that he was not finally fired for sleeping (as demonstrated by the fact that only a written warning had been prepared), but on the supervisor's momentary impulse. "In spite of the fact that the grievant was almost certainly at fault, the arbitrator does not believe that the company can fire a man on impulse, and then look back for grounds to support the discharge."

[43]*Armak Abrasives Div.*, 60 LA 509, 511 (Hertz, 1973). For a variation on the same theme, see *Texstar Corp., Transtemp Div.*, 69-1 ARB ¶8328 (Larson, 1968), where the employer abruptly fired an employee after he had filed two successful grievances about improper work assignments and only later stated that the real problem was the supervisor's inability to organize the work under his jurisdiction and his attempt to shift the blame to his subordinates.

Exceptions to the "No New Complaints" Rule. Where arbitrators have allowed new complaints to be added to the original cause for discharge, the reason generally has been that the employer brought up the new matter sufficiently in advance of the hearing to give the union a fair opportunity to develop a response—in other words, because due process was substantially satisfied.[44] Another basis for adding new charges is a past practice on the part of the parties of taking postdischarge complaints into account.[45]

The best the company can reasonably hope for if it brings in additional charges after discharge is that, if the discharge is set aside, the arbitrator will take the after-the-fact allegations into account in deciding whether back pay is called for. The theory is that even if postdischarge complaints are not relevant to just cause, they can serve as evidence about the quality of the grievant's past record, which is a major factor that arbitrators consider in determining the remedy. Thus, if postdischarge complaints are proved, the misconduct in question often leads the arbitrator to withhold some or all of the back pay to which the grievant would otherwise be entitled.[46]

Back Pay Without Reinstatement. In a few situations, arbitrators have gone even further and directed the unusual remedy of

---

[44]*E.g.*, *Wagner Elec. Co.*, 61 LA 363 (Ray, 1973), where the company abandoned its original ground for the grievant's discharge, excessive absenteeism, but the arbitrator nonetheless allowed it to proceed on the basis of a subsequent allegation that she had also falsified her production records. The reason for not allowing new grounds, he observed, is to prevent unfair surprise to the union and grievant at the arbitration hearing. Here, however, the alleged false accounts were thoroughly discussed at a grievance meeting months before arbitration, and the union was given ample opportunity to prepare a defense. See also *DeVry Inst. of Technology*, 87 LA 1149 (Berman, 1986) (unprofessional conduct).

[45]In *Safeway Stores, Inc.*, 75 LA 430 (Winograd, 1980), the company was permitted at the hearing to withdraw the charge that the grievant had been absent without leave for three days and to substitute the charge that his persistent medical problems had raised his absentee rate unacceptably. He had been aware throughout the grievance proceedings that his entire medical record was at issue; furthermore, the company had followed a longstanding practice, accepted by the union, that only one reason for discharge could be stated in discharge notices, even though other reasons might apply and could be aired in the course of the grievance procedure. See also *Lyon, Inc.*, 24 LA 353 (Alexander, 1955) (substandard performance; falsification of job application).

[46]See, e.g., *Int'l Shoe Co.*, 7 LA 941, 943 (Whiting, 1947)(absenteeism): "The fact that other cause for discharge did exist . . . obviates any valid claim for pay for time lost." In *Unimart, Div. of Food Giant Markets, Inc.*, *supra* note 40, at 1210, the arbitrator held that past infractions which were not considered at the time the grievant was discharged "may be given weight when determining the appropriate degree of discipline." See also *Rotor Tool Co.*, 49 LA 210 (Williams, 1967) (profanity); *Gardner Denver Co.*, 51 LA 1019 (Ray, 1968) (immoral conduct).

back pay without reinstatement, chiefly where the postdischarge complaint is so serious that it would be unrealistic to put the employee back to work. That was the case, for example, where an employee was fired for willfully obstructing the company's investigation into thefts at the plant. That charge did not stand up; nevertheless, after discharge but before the hearing, a court found the employee himself guilty of the theft. Even though theft was not the original reason for discharge, the arbitrator allowed the discharge to stand because the trust on which the employer-employee relationship is founded had been destroyed.[47]

The most common situation in which reinstatement has been ruled out as essentially useless is where the added reason for discharge is serious "and would be good reason for another discharge immediately following a reinstatement by the arbitrator." Thus it would have been futile to reinstate a grievant whose discharge for participating in a wildcat strike was defective, but who after discharge was found to have lied on his employment application to cover up his criminal record and a prior discharge for strike activities.[48]

Postdischarge Evidence

Some might say that as between postdischarge complaints and postdischarge evidence there is a distinction without a difference. And perhaps they would be right, because evidence the employer produced to support its case after an employee had already been fired has been resisted by arbitrators more often than not. There is, however, a clear distinction to be drawn between postdischarge evidence that supports the charge for which the grievant was discharged and such evidence that relates

---

[47]*Hollytex Carpet Mills, Inc.*, 79-1 ARB ¶8181 (Anderson, 1979). See also *Sunshine Specialty Co.*, 55 LA 1061 (Levin, 1970), where the arbitrator found that a discharge for belligerence toward fellow employees and poor production was not for just cause because the grievant had been unfairly singled out for discipline; but in view of a later-discovered, proved allegation that the grievant had once struck a janitor, a much older man, the remedy was back pay without reinstatement; *Telewald, Inc.*, 39 LA 183, 187 (Daugherty, 1961) (fighting), where previous incidents of violence which the company turned up when it investigated the grievant's record after discharge were found by the arbitrator to "establish a . . . pattern of behavior that the Arbitrator judges would be unreasonable, through reinstatement, to ask the company to continue to live with."

[48]*Pullman-Standard*, 47 LA 752 (McCoy, 1966).

to a different charge.[49] Evidence in the latter category is routinely excluded unless one of the exceptions discussed above applies. Whether arbitrators will admit evidence in the former category depends on several factors, including whether the arbitrator is acting as a reviewer or as a trier of fact; whether admitting the evidence would be unfair to either party; the character of the evidence, especially whether it is adverse to or favors the grievant; and whether it could have been brought to light prior to discharge with due diligence on the part of the party now seeking to present it.

Where arbitrators view themselves as reviewers rather than as triers of fact, they undertake to determine whether the company acted properly in discharging the grievant, based on the record the company had when it took action. This view is reflected in the following comment:

> *Arbitrator Daniel:* An employer not only has the obligation . . . of proving just cause for its action but also must do so on the basis of the facts and evidence it knew of at the time the decision was made. An employer may not buttress its basis for disciplinary action . . . by submitting evidence and documentation which it has secured afterward. To be specific, such a case should be treated by the arbitrator as if it were being heard on the very day that the disciplinary action was taken.[50]

---

[49]Arbitrator Cheney (chairman of the Vermont Labor Relations Board), in *Vermont Dep't of Social Welfare,* 86 LA 324, 327 (1986) (divulging confidential information):
> [W]e draw a distinction between evidence gathered after discharge which supports the reason given for discharge . . . and evidence gathered after a discharge to add an entirely new offense. The latter is clearly inappropriate. . . . However, with regard to post-dismissal evidence supporting the stated reasons for disciplinary action, we believe the relevant consideration is really one of fairness and surprise.

To the same effect, *San Gamo Elec. Co.,* 44 LA 593 (Sembower, 1965); *DeVry Inst. of Technology, supra* note 44. Evidence obtained following discharge is discussed in Fairweather's Practice and Procedure in Labor Arbitration 259–62 (R. J. Schoonhoven, ch. ed., 3d ed. 1991); M. F. Hill, Jr., & A. V. Sinicropi, Evidence in Arbitration 305–33 (2d ed. 1987); and F. Elkouri & E. A. Elkouri, How Arbitration Works 302–04 (4th ed. 1985).

[50]*Rochester Community Schools,* 86 LA 1287, 1290 (1986). In the case before him, which concerned an employee who was found to be playing softball while supposedly disabled, the arbitrator found that the company had sufficient evidence of misconduct to act when it did. He then gave consideration to later-obtained evidence, on the theory that
> [o]nce the employer has satisfied [its] burden of proof, then it may introduce supporting evidence of the same nature revealing the totality of the grievant's conduct. This may be allowed for a number of reasons: to test the credibility of the grievant, to emphasize the knowing and intentional repetition of acts of misconduct and generally to depict the egregious character of the misconduct in

Arbitrators of this persuasion may receive postdischarge evidence into the record and credit it for purposes of corroboration. But if sufficient evidence was not present at the time of discharge, after-the-fact additions cannot be expected to make up for the original lack of just cause.[51] Admission of postdischarge evidence, in this view, operates primarily in the service of a consideration subscribed to by many arbitrators—namely, let in everything including the kitchen sink "for what it's worth," as they say.

Later-discovered evidence against the grievant gets especially short shrift if it is clear that the employer could have come up with it earlier but failed to do so (i.e., by dragging its feet in its investigation),[52] or that the employer was making an eleventh-hour attempt to impress the arbitrator.[53] But the fact that it was not available at an earlier time, so that inadequate investigation cannot be blamed for its delayed production, does not transform adverse evidence from unacceptable to acceptable.[54]

---

response to any assertion that the disciplinary penalty is too severe."
See also *Penn-Dixie Cement Corp.*, 29 LA 451 (Brecht, 1957) ("Only if the facts as they existed at the time of discharge lead to reasonable inferences in support of that discharge can the conclusions based on those inferences be said to comprise just or reasonable cause."); *Georgia-Pacific Corp.*, 93 LA 754, 758 (Ipavec, 1989) ("A review of just and proper cause must be limited to the information available to the Company when it made its decision.").

[51]Even in cases where some weight has been given to postdischarge evidence, arbitrators have been at pains to point out that the company had good reason earlier to believe what the later evidence served to confirm. In *American Air Filter Co.,*, 64 LA 899 (Young, 1975), where the company learned only after the grievant's discharge that he had been selling far more scrap than he could have come by innocently, the arbitrator used this piece of evidence to sustain the discharge on the theory that the company must have known earlier that such large quantities were missing. In *New York Tel. Co.*, 66 LA 1037 (Markowitz, 1976), the company had some reliable evidence that the grievant was intoxicated, and for that reason the arbitrator accepted as further evidence the result of a blood alcohol test which the company received after the discharge.

[52]On the other hand, the mere fact that the employer continues its investigation after discharge does not in itself prove that the predischarge investigation was inadequate or that sufficient proof of misconduct was not present at the time of discharge. (*Pacific Tel. & Tel. Co.*, 45 LA 655 (Somers, 1965) (unauthorized possession of company property).

[53]"[E]vidence gathered to support an action after the fact is of dubious value," the arbitrator found in *Allied Aviation Servs. Co.*, 71-1 ARB ¶8016 (Leventhal, 1970), commenting on written statements, secured after the grievant's discharge, purporting to show that the grievant had a poor attitude and history of defiance toward supervision.

[54]In *Owens-Illinois, Inc.*, 79-2 ARB ¶8518 (Witney, 1979) (insubordination, profanity), the arbitrator refused to consider testimony that after the shop steward's discharge, productivity on his shift increased and fewer grievances were filed by the employees he had represented; and in *Reliance Universal, Inc.*, 68-1 ARB ¶8027 (Alexander, 1967), where the grievant was discharged for poor customer relations, the arbitrator paid no

Take the case of a moonlighting bus driver who was discharged because his primary employer suspected him of working his second job on days when he called in sick. The second employer's personnel records, which were subpoenaed for the arbitration hearing, produced concrete evidence that the driver had been claiming sick leave under false pretenses. But that postdischarge evidence did not change the fact that at the time of discharge the employer was operating solely on the basis of suspicion and thus did not terminate the driver for just cause.[55] An employer's after-the-fact attempts to round up evidence against an employee, like its attempt to add new complaints after discharge, might suggest to the arbitrator that the company wanted to get rid of the employee all along but had no good reason for doing so.

> **EXAMPLE:** An employee who had taken a day off to get married was arrested on the way home on suspicion of burglary because his car fitted the description of a vehicle spotted at the scene of the crime. The police did not have enough evidence to hold him, however; charges were dropped, and he was released late the next day. The employee returned to work and told his foreman about the incident. Two hours later he was called in to the general foreman's office and asked if he was running a house of prostitution on the side. According to the employer, he said yes; the employee claimed he denied it, and only said he knew where he could find prostitutes. The general foreman told him, "You are not the kind of person I want around here," and fired him for immoral conduct. Management's next step was to question the employee's fellow workers. One of them claimed that about a month earlier, the employee had solicited him on behalf of one of his prostitutes, and others reported that the employee displayed pictures of nude and scantily dressed women on his locker.

---

attention to notices from the company's customers that the grievant would not be allowed to service their accounts, since those notices were received after the discharge. In a case where the grievant was later convicted on a morals charge that was related to the incident for which he was fired, the conviction was not considered relevant by the arbitrator (although it became the occasion for a second discharge upon his reinstatement). *Northwest Airlines, Inc.*, 69-1 ARB ¶8122 (Rohman, 1968); followed in *Northwest Airlines, Inc.*, 53 LA 203 (Sembower, 1969). See also *Brass-Craft Mfg. Co.*, 36 LA 1177 (Kahn, 1961) (falsification of work records).

[55]*Alameda-Contra Costa Transit Dist.*, 76 LA 770 (Koven, 1981). See also *Goddard Space Flight Center*, 91 LA 1105 (Berkeley, 1988), where evidence that the grievant used drugs and introduction of another employee to drug use was held to be inadmissible, since it came to light well after the decision to terminate the grievant was made and could not have affected the decision.

The arbitrator was not seduced by all this. It simply was not believable that the employee would have admitted so readily that he moonlighted in the business of prostitution. And other than that "admission," the company's only evidence was the coworker's statement that he had been solicited, which had to be discounted for two reasons: Not only did the company not have that evidence in hand when it fired the employee, but it was unlikely that the coworker would have kept the information to himself for so long a period, if in fact it was true.

The arbitrator therefore concluded that the alleged immoral conduct was not the real basis for the company's decision. It was only after the general foreman learned that the employee had been arrested on suspicion of burglary that he decided the latter had to go and began building a case against him, despite the fact that the charge had been dropped. Observing that "[i]t is difficult to imagine a clearer case of prejudgment of an employee," the arbitrator ordered reinstatement with full back pay.[56]

Where New Evidence May Play a Role. Arbitrators have sometimes found it appropriate to admit and give full weight to postdischarge evidence, as long as doing so was not unfair to the other party, even to the point of reopening a hearing that had already been completed. One arbitrator set forth the following standards for reopening a hearing to let in new evidence:

1. The request to reopen the hearing must precede the arbitrator's final award. . . .
2. The proffered evidence must not have been available with due diligence at the time of the hearing. . . .
3. The proffered evidence must be pertinent. . . .
4. The proffered evidence must be likely to affect the outcome. . . .
5. Admission of the new evidence must not improperly prejudice the other party. . . . Of course the delay and expenditures required because of a new hearing will cause some harm, as will the increased chance of losing the case, but these prejudices are not improper. Moreover, those detriments are outweighed by the desirability of a complete chance for each party to present its case so that the arbitrator can make a knowledgeable decision.[57]

---

[56]*Gardner Denver Co.*, 51 LA 1019, 1023 (Ray, 1968).
[57]*Westvaco, Va. Folding Box Div.*, 89-1 ARB ¶8072, 3373-74 (Nolan, 1988) (abuse of sick leave). See, to the same effect, *Madison Inst.*, 18 LA 78 (Levy, 1952) (unilateral change in seniority rules); *Borden Co.*, 33 LA 302 (Morvant, 1959) (termination of

Evidence Favorable to Grievant. Greater receptiveness to postdischarge evidence may be shown when the evidence is favorable to the grievant. The arbitrator's task in evaluating a discharge is to determine whether the company acted properly in terminating the employee. Postdischarge evidence against the grievant is often viewed as irrelevant because, being unknown to the employer, it could not have influenced the termination; but such evidence in the grievant's favor casts doubt on the employer's action even though the employer was unaware of the evidence. Especially if the company could have discovered the evidence sooner by more diligent investigation, favorable evidence is likely to find its way in.

Take the case of the employee whose failure to pay a ticket he received while driving a leased vehicle resulted in the suspension of his driver's license, which in turn caused his discharge under a company rule providing for suspension pending termination in the event of license suspension or revocation. It turned out that the employee thought the leasing company had paid the ticket, and upon being discharged he took care of it and had his license reinstated.

The arbitrator pointed out that the postdischarge evidence became known to management before the discharge was submitted to arbitration, so there was no element of surprise in the grievant's introduction of the evidence. Moreover, had the company conducted its own investigation before discharging the grievant, the evidence likely would have surfaced earlier. The arbitrator therefore held the evidence admissible, and the grievant was reinstated with back pay to the date the company became aware that his driving privileges had been restored.[58]

---

seniority); *Gateway Prods. Co.*, 61-3 ARB ¶8629 (Marshall, 1961) (change in washup rule); *General Foods Corp.*, 85-1 ARB ¶8051 (Abernethy, 1964) (withholding of medical information); *Savannah Maritime Ass'n*, 88-1 ARB ¶8035 (Baroni, 1987) (payment methods). In *Naes Mobile Cleaning*, 89-1 ARB ¶8122 (Ross, 1988) (negligence, dishonesty), the arbitrator ruled that ordering the reinstatement, even without back pay, of a grievant found to have been improperly discharged for refusing to pay for damage to company equipment would have been "ludicrous," in view of postdischarge evidence showing that the grievant had been pocketing money made on company time with company equipment, a cause for immediate dismissal.

[58]*Group W Cable of Chicago*, 93 LA 789 (Fischbach, 1989). See also *Borden Co.*, *supra* note 57, at 307 ("allowances should be made which would protect the less astute and permit him to present his case to the best of his ability and leave him with the feeling that he has had his full day in court"); *Oxford Chems., Inc.*, 84-1 ARB

Credibility. Evidence turned up after an employee's discharge that tended to discredit previous statements he or she had made is likely to be admitted "for credibility purposes" or "for impeachment purposes." In such situations, it may carry significant weight.[59]

Remedy. Like postdischarge complaints, postdischarge evidence may be taken into account when remedy is being considered. In the case of the moonlighting bus driver cited above, to take a typical example, the evidence produced at the hearing that the driver had been working a second job while claiming sick leave from the company justified denial of any back pay, since the postdischarge evidence convincingly established that he was guilty of the charges against him.[60]

To take another example, this time dealing with evidence in the employee's favor: Although the company acted reasonably and in accord with the evidence at hand when it discharged an employee for being absent without explanation for seven straight days, subsequent medical reports showed that he was suffering from mental illness at the time of his discharge. The arbitrator concluded that the employee's seniority should be restored and his termination converted to sick leave.[61]

¶8277 (Holley, 1984) (court reversal of criminal conviction held ground for reopening of hearing); *Washington Public Power Supply Sys.*, 89-1 ARB ¶8214 (Tilbury, 1989) (fact that company reduced time security guards were required to spend at isolated post was factor to be considered in determining whether discharge for sleeping on duty was justified).

[59]As in *Mintz Co.*, 79-1 ARB ¶8038 (Cohen, 1978), where the credibility of the grievant's denial that he had stolen large amounts of company product was damaged irretrievably by evidence that he had threatened a fellow employee upon learning that the employee had been subpoenaed by the company to testify against him. See also *Westvaco, Va. Folding Box Div.*, *supra* note 57; *Rochester Community Schools*, *supra* note 50.

[60]*Alameda-Contra Costa Transit Dist.*, *supra* note 55. See also *Rochester Community Schools*, *supra* note 50.

[61]*Spaulding Fibre Co.*, 21 LA 58 (Thompson, 1953). See also *Husky Oil Co.*, 65 LA 47 (Richardson, 1975) (grievant's postdischarge revelation that excessive absences were caused by long-term mental depression led arbitrator to recommend reemployment); *Samuel Bingham Co.*. 67 LA 706 (Cohen, 1976) (medical report that grievant's epilepsy was sufficiently under control to allow him to work with reasonable safety considered by arbitrator even though company did not have benefit of report when it discharged him).

Postdischarge Misconduct

> *Arbitrator Kates:* As a general rule, occurrences subsequent to a discharge may not properly be taken into account in an arbitration involving the propriety of that discharge.[62]

Typical examples of postdischarge misconduct include the employee who, upon hearing that he has been fired, loses his temper and slugs the supervisor who has given him the bad news; or who broods about his discharge at the local bar and returns to the plant looking for his supervisor, disrupting production; or who tells lies during a grievance hearing. The principle that "the clock stops with discharge," which excludes postdischarge complaints about predischarge misconduct from consideration by arbitrators, has been applied to postdischarge misconduct as well, on the theory that whatever happens after discharge is irrelevant to whether just cause was present when the company acted.[63]

Exceptions to the "No Postdischarge Misconduct" Rule. Arbitrators have made exceptions to that principle, relying on one or more of the following reasons:

Res gestae (part of the total picture)—or, to quote Arbitrator Kates once again, where "the subsequent occurrences are so closely related to the event or events leading to the discharge as . . . to constitute an extension or continuation or integral part thereof."[64]

---

[62]*Cadillac Plastic & Chem. Co.*, 58 LA 812, 814 (1972)(horseplay, profanity).

[63]*E.g.*, in *Pacific Gas & Elec. Co.*, 88 LA 749 (Koven, 1986), the arbitrator ruled that a grievant's postdischarge arrest for drug possession was not relevant to the question of whether his discharge for refusing to take a drug test was justified. The company sought to make an issue of the arrest to show both that the grievant had violated a promise to maintain a drug-free life style and that he had lied at the arbitration hearing about his past use of drugs. The arbitrator held, however, that since the arrest occurred after discharge, it shed no light on the grievant's use of drugs before discharge; and that whether he lied at the hearing was irrelevant to his refusal to take a drug test. Similarly, in *Care and Emergency Ambulance Co.*, 89-1 ARB ¶8146 (Price, 1988), the arbitrator held that threatening and abusive behavior following discharge was not a reason for upholding the grievant's discharge, especially where no notice had been given that his behavior would be an issue at the hearing. But see *Niemand Indus., Inc.*, 89-1 ARB ¶8152 (Biblin, 1988), where verbal abuse of a supervisor and hitting him in the leg with a glue pot following discharge, and returning to the plant and assaulting a fellow employee, were held to be ground for discharge, even if the original ground was not valid.

[64]*Cadillac Plastic & Chem. Co.*, *supra* note 62, at 814.

EXAMPLE: A salesman in a men's clothing store was informed by the district manager that he was being fired for a "bad audit"—his books did not match up with actual inventory. Upon hearing the news, the salesman exploded, threatening to beat up or kill the manager, raising his fists, and finally chasing the manager into another office. The bad-audit charge subsequently failed because, as it turned out, the company had made a procedural mistake, and the union argued that because the salesman's other misconduct came after the fact, no grounds for discharge remained.

In the arbitrator's view, the subsequent events counted.

[T]he Grievant's assault upon the Supervisor was so immediate to and contemporaneous with the abortive discharge that it cannot be deemed "post-discharge conduct" in a time sense. Nor is the assault a separate unrelated and *post factum* event that the employer is attempting to use to determine the existence of the original cause of discharge. It arose out of and was a definite part of that discharge event.

Thus, as an "independent basis of just cause for termination," the assault charge passed muster.[65]

There are many variations on this theme, such as a case where an employee showed up to pitch a baseball game at a company-owned recreational facility wearing a sweatshirt bearing obscene language. Following his discharge for that peccadillo, the employee returned to the plant without authorization and told his foreman that if he found out who had turned him in, the foreman had better let the informer know that he "had had it." A month later, he returned again, fled from supervisors trying to escort him off the premises, and was arrested for criminal trespass. The arbitrator rejected the union's argument that these later events were irrelevant to the discharge.[66]

The employment relationship does not necessarily end with discharge. Another theory under which a postdischarge event can become relevant and perhaps decisive is that the employment

---

[65]*White Front Stores, Inc.*, 61 LA 536 (Killion, 1973). Similar reasoning applicable to a longer time frame was seen in *Bib Bear Stores*, 90 LA 634, 88-1 ARB ¶8199 (Ross, 1988), where the grievant after being discharged without proper cause went to two of the company's stores and harassed and threatened a store manager and other employees over a period of several months. The arbitrator found that this conduct was intolerable and made it unnecessary for the company to reinstate the grievant. *Niemand Indus., Inc., supra* note 63, is to the same effect. But see *Care and Emergency Ambulance Co., supra* note 63.

[66]*Glass Container Mfrs. Inst.*, 53 LA 1266, 1274 (Dworkin, 1969).

relationship has not ended until an employee has fully exhausted the grievance machinery, up to the point at which the arbitrator renders his decision. Thus, whatever misconduct the employee engages in after discharge and before termination becomes "final, final" is considered to be part of the employment relationship. A grievant who exacerbates the original record cannot expect to be protected from the consequences.[67]

Serious postdischarge misconduct may irreparably damage the employer-employee relationship. To take a graphic example from Arbitrator Kates, "if a man were unjustly discharged and thereafter deliberately blew up the plant, surely he ought not to be reinstated."[68] Where postdischarge misconduct is so serious that it would warrant another discharge if the grievant were put back to work, the act of reinstatement has been considered futile.[69]

Postdischarge Misconduct and Remedy. Even if postdischarge misconduct is not serious enough to justify discharge on its own, or is found to be irrelevant to the original bill of complaint, it still (like other postdischarge matters) may have a bearing on the

---

[67]Where the company's original basis for discharge is a nullity, the grievant is "still in the status of being an employee and subject to rules governing the employer-employee relationship." *White Front Stores, Inc., supra* note 65 at 538. Accordingly, misconduct in which he engages after discharge becomes part of his employment record as a whole. See also *Glass Container Mfrs. Inst., supra* note 66, at 1274 ("habitual disregard for rules and regulations demonstrates a disposition that militates against reinstatement"); *Link-Belt Co.*, 17 LA 224, 226-27 (Updegraff, 1951) ("[A]n employee has rights and privileges in respect to grievance procedure after he has been notified of the determination of the employer to terminate him. If he would avail himself of such procedure, however, he must so conduct himself as to justify his return to the payroll."); *Interstate Bakeries Corp., Dolly Madison Cake Div.*, 64-3 ARB ¶9139 (Williams, 1964) (breach of trust); *Meadowbrook United Super Market*, 66-3 ARB ¶8860 (Elkouri, 1966) (leaving work).

[68]Kates explains further, in *Columbus Show Case Co.*, 65-1 ARB ¶8347, 4269 (1965) (no smoking):

It is my view that events like these, occurring after a discharge, are not relevant upon the question of the justness of the previous discharge. However, it is my further opinion that, in considering matters of reinstatement and back pay, account may be taken of the employee's actions subsequent to his discharge insofar as they may relate to his fitness for employment, and as they bear upon the effect of reinstatement on plant morale, discipline, efficiency and the like.

[69]E.g., *Auburn Faith Community Hosp., Inc.*, 66 LA 882, 897 (Killion, 1976), where the grievant, a highly trained nurse, walked off the job on her last day of work, leaving an intensive care unit in charge of an unqualified employee. "Thus, we have a situation where the Employer could in the event that the Grievant were to be reinstated, again discharge her on the claimed ground that her March 14–15 conduct proved her to be incorrigible." See also *Link-Belt Co.*, 17 LA 224 (Updegraff, 1951); *Naes Mobile Cleaning, supra* note 57.

remedy to which the grievant is entitled, since it tells something about what could be expected of the grievant in the future.[70]

EXAMPLE: Learning that an employee had been selling and installing telephones on the side, his employer, a telephone company, fired him for acting "to the detriment of the company and its reputation." It developed, however, that he had pursued his sideline outside the company's franchise area and that the company had no specific rule covering such activity of which the employee was aware. Accordingly, an arbitrator ruled, he should not have been fired. Following his discharge, however, the employee made attempts to prevent witnesses from testifying at the arbitration hearing. These attempts, the arbitrator found, were relevant to the remedy to which he was entitled. He directed the parties to confer on the remedy for 10 days, at the end of which, if necessary, he would decide what was appropriate.[71]

Postdischarge "good conduct." The proposition that what an employee does after discharge is relevant to the remedy may also apply where the employee has engaged in "good conduct" following termination. The typical case involves the employee who is discharged for chronic alcoholism and who, after discharge, turns over a new leaf, attends AA meetings regularly, gets medical help, signs on for counseling, and appears at the arbitration as a "new man" or "new woman." In such a case, the arbitrator might well take the postdischarge conduct into account and commute the employee's penalty from discharge to a disciplinary suspension without back pay.[72]

Such an award says, "The grievant is not entitled to back pay"—because he or she gave the employer good cause for

---

[70]As in *Metal Specialty Co.*, 43 LA 849, 852 (Volz, 1964), where the arbitrator found that subsequent picketing by employees who had been discharged for walking off the job "is only relevant on the question of mitigation or aggravation." Although the arbitrator found in *Catholic Press Soc'y, Inc.*, 40 LA 641, 650 (Gorsuch, 1963), that the grievant's discharge "was a 'fait accompli' and has to stand on its own bottom," his participation in a chapel meeting the following day to protest his discharge, in violation of the contract, "is of importance in considering the penalty which should be equitably imposed upon the Grievant." See also *Pittsburgh Standard Conduit Co.*, 33 LA 807 (McCoy, 1959) (wildcat strike).

[71]*Continental Tel. Co. of Va.*, 86 LA 274 (Rothschild, 1985).

[72]E.g., *Texaco, Inc.*, 42 LA 408 (Prasow, 1963); Chrysler Corp., 40 LA 935 (Alexander, 1963); *Pacific Northwest Bell Tel. Co.*, 66 LA 965 (Harter, 1976); *Northwest Airlines, Inc.*, 89 LA 943 (Nicolau, 1984). Not all arbitrators would agree, however, that rehabilitation undertaken after discharge should have a bearing on the grievant's penalty. See *Armstrong Furnace Co.*, 63 LA 618 (Stouffer, 1974); *Int'l Nickel Co.*, 68-2 ARB ¶8593 (Klamon, 1968); *Ambrosia Chocolate Co.*, 88-2 ARB ¶8508 (Briggs, 1988); *Duquesne Light Co.*, 92 LA 907 (Sergent, 1989); *Georgia-Pacific Corp.*, 93 LA 754 (Ipavec, 1989).

discharge in the first place—"but is nevertheless entitled to reinstatement"—because the conduct following discharge gives good reason to believe he or she will shape up in the future. To put it another way, if after discharge the grievant gets it all together, it could be that the employer's original judgment was mistaken—the grievant was not beyond rehabilitation and could still be a valuable employee.

Although most cases in which rehabilitation after discharge leads to reinstatement involve alcoholics or, occasionally, drug abusers, the issue can arise with respect to any type of misconduct that stems from a "condition" subject to "cure" rather than from willful misconduct. Wage garnishments offer one example; if, after discharge, the grievant makes arrangements to pay creditors and takes effective steps to put his or her financial house in order, such "good conduct" might reasonably be accepted as evidence that if reinstated the grievant will not give the employer further problems.[73] Absenteeism offers another; if an employee's poor attendance resulted from an illness that has since been cured, and if the employee's work record was acceptable except for the attendance problem, an arbitrator might find a reasonable basis for reinstatement.

II. Proof and Evidence

How Much Evidence Is Required

How much evidence should be required by the arbitrator in evaluating the facts in disciplinary matters—especially in cases

---

[73]*Delta Concrete Prods. Co.*, 78-2 ARB ¶8435 (Bailey, 1978). In *Amoco Oil Co.*, 61 LA 10 (Cushman, 1973), the fact that the grievant attempted suicide and sought treatment in a psychiatric hospital the day after his discharge helped convince the arbitrator that the threats of violence against members of management for which he was fired had been irrational and caused by the combined effects of alcohol and paranoia. He was reinstated without back pay, on condition that he continue medical treatment. Similarly, in *Philco Corp.*, 43 LA 568 (Davis, 1964), and *National Steel Corp.*, 66 LA 533 (Traynor, 1976), employees diagnosed following discharge as suffering from mental illness were allowed to return to work when they responded to treatment. But in *General Tel. Co. of Ind.*, 88-1 ARB ¶8222 (Goldstein, 1988), evidence of rehabilitation was not viewed as a mitigating factor in the case of a "peeping Tom" who was fired for using company vehicles and access to apartments by reason of his job to engage in voyeuristic acts. The grievant underwent psychotherapy to cure his aberrant behavior and sought reinstatement on that basis. The arbitrator, however, saw a big difference between an alcoholic and someone with a chronic mental condition such as voyeurism. The employer's exposure to liability because of the grievant's actions, he said, precluded any consideration of his postdischarge behavior.

involving discharge—is the subject of much controversy.[74] Some have argued that a different quantum of proof should be applied depending on the nature of the offense. This is particularly true of discharge cases alleging theft or other criminal misconduct, in which arbitrators have often applied the criminal standard, proof beyond a reasonable doubt.[75] Even as to cases involving serious misconduct, however, a lower standard, clear and convincing evidence, has its fair share of adherents.[76] And some arbitrators view the civil law standard, preponderance of the evidence, as appropriate even in cases of serious misconduct because of the difference between arbitration and the judicial system.[77] Note, however, that it is not always easy to tell exactly what standard is being applied. Thus, in a case involving alleged overcharging of customers by a cocktail waitress, the arbitrator observed:

> A charge of dishonesty is, of course, a very serious matter. A high standard of proof is obviously therefore required. The preponderance of the evidence in this case clearly supports the position of the Company and therefore the discharge must be upheld and the grievance denied.[78]

---

[74]For a sampling of the literature on this subject, see M. Talent, *Quantum of Proof—Arbitration*, 41 J. Mo. Bar 387–92 (1985); L. Farley & J. Allotta, *Standards of Proof in Discharge Arbitration: A Practitioner's View*, 35 Lab. L.J. 424–34 (1984); *Burden of Proof*, Arbitration 1982 133–37 (Proceedings of the 35th Annual Meeting, National Academy of Arbitrators 1983). Quantum of Proof is also discussed in M. F. Hill, Jr., & A. V. Sinicropi, Evidence in Arbitration 32–39 (2d ed. 1987).

[75]E.g., *Fruehauf Trailer Co.*, 21 LA 832 (Murphy, 1954); *Kroger Co.*, 25 LA 906 (Smith, 1955); *Aladdin Indus., Inc.*, 27 LA 463 (Holly, 1956); *Dockside Mach. & Boilerworks, Inc.*, 55 LA 1221 (Block, 1970); *Owens-Corning Fiberglas Corp.*, 56 LA 608 (Moore, 1971); *Southern Cal. Edison Co.*, 61 LA 803 (Helbling, 1973); *Interstate Brands*, 87-2 ARB ¶8355 (Castrey, 1986); *Monsanto Chem. Co.*, 88-1 ARB ¶8287 (Maniscalco, 1988); *Arkansas Power & Light Co.*, 92 LA 144 (Weisbrod, 1989).

[76]E.g., *Chrysler Corp.*, 12 LA 699 (Wolff, 1949) (gambling); *International Harvester Co.*, 21 LA 428 (Platt, 1953) (intentional slowdown); *Bell Helicopter Co.*, 69-2 ARB ¶8608 (Abernethy, 1969) (drug possession or sale); *Mastic Corp.*, 86-1 ARB ¶8217 (Nathan, 1986) (theft); *American Steel Foundries*, 94 LA 745 (Seidman, 1990) (attempted theft).

[77]E.g., *Daystrom Furniture Co.*, 65 LA 1157 (Laughlin, undated) (theft); *County of Martin, Fairmont, Minn.*, 87-2 ARB ¶8328 (Flagler, 1987) (theft); *GAF Bldg. Materials Corp.*, 89-1 ARB ¶8004 (Abrams, 1988) (sabotage). In *Daystrom*, the arbitrator reinstated the grievant because guilt was not proved beyond a reasonable doubt, but denied back pay on a preponderance-of-the-evidence standard.

[78]*Holiday Inn—Duluth*, 86-1 ARB ¶8232, 3995-96 (1986). Or take *N.S.K.*, 88-1 ARB ¶8169 (Grossman, 1988):
Clear and convincing proof means proof beyond a reasonable, well founded doubt. Proof which should leave no reasonable doubt in the mind of the trier of fact concerning the truth of the matter in issue. . . . [I]t is an intermediate burden or degree of proof being greater than by the preponderance of the evidence, but

In any event, "[t]here is no controlling authority on this question . . . ."[79] And none of the standards has a definite objective set of criteria. In the last analysis, regardless of how the quantum of proof is characterized, its application is up to the individual arbitrator. As Arbitrator Block has observed:

> In weighing the evidence, . . . the Arbitrator sees no reason to adopt a Courtroom criterion as to the quantum of proof required. He seeks only to determine whether the evidence is convincing to him that the Company did or did not have "just and sufficient cause" to discharge the Grievant for the alleged act of theft.[80]

Circumstantial Evidence

The best way to prove misconduct, of course, is to produce credible witnesses who actually saw it happen. This is "direct" evidence. But direct evidence often is not available, and in such cases the employer must rely on "circumstantial" evidence— indirect evidence inferred from circumstances that appear to lead to only one conclusion. To the person in the street, circumstantial evidence is highly suspect and is not to be believed or trusted. But the courts and arbitrators view it otherwise. Though they may differ in the value they give to circumstantial evidence, for the most part arbitrators regard such evidence as fully acceptable. A panel of the National Academy of Arbitrators placed its stamp of approval upon circumstantial evidence in the following endorsement:

> Circumstantial evidence may have as much probative value as testimonial [direct] evidence. It should be received and it should be given such weight as it may deserve, considered in context with all evidence offered.[81]

---

not requiring the degree of certainty as is necessary in the standard beyond a reasonable doubt.

[79]*Federal Compress and Warehouse Co.*, 75 LA 217, 221 (Howell, 1980).

[80]*Flintkote Co.*, 49 LA 810, 814 (1967). Similarly, Arbitrator Kates in *Weirton Steel Co.*, 50 LA 103, 106 (1968) (theft): "My view is that if an arbitrator is convinced, after considering all the relevant competent evidence, that an alleged offense has occurred, he may so find without consciously applying any particular rule as to degree of proof." See also *Bi-State Dev. Agency*, 88 LA 854, 860 (Brazil, 1987) (decisions have been based upon "evidence that persuaded the arbitrator that the company had good cause to take the action for the conduct alleged").

[81]Problems of Proof in Arbitration 98 (Proceedings of the 19th Annual Meeting, National Academy of Arbitrators 1966).

Another panel of the Academy summarized the view that circumstantial evidence can be as good as or better than direct evidence in this observation:

> Since "direct" evidence may be falsified due to the commission of perjury by witnesses, it is not necessarily more probative than circumstantial evidence. Indeed, the latter may be more reliable than so-called "direct" evidence to the degree that close reasoning by inference in a particular situation may actually weave a tighter factual web often less subject to the diversion of doubts of credibility than is true where reliance must be had solely on the "I seed him do it" kind of direct evidence.[82]

The problem with circumstantial evidence is that the weight it deserves is a matter of judgment and depends on many different factors, especially its quality and quantity and the availability of direct evidence. Consider these caveats put forth by arbitrators:

> *Arbitrator Daniel:* "Circumstantial evidence" is perfectly acceptable provided that it is reasonable, logical, and fairly excludes the possibility of some other explanation being likely.[83]

> *Arbitrator McDermott:* If two or more alternatives are possible and the sequence of evidence is such that it can lead to any one of them, then . . . a case based on circumstantial evidence must fail.[84]

> *Arbitrator Summers:* [Circumstantial evidence] requires that in weighing the evidence, all of the circumstances be carefully weighed. The catch-word "circumstantial evidence" only cautions us to beware of piecing together a picture from parts of the available evidence, and overlooking other parts which cannot fit that picture.[85]

---

[82]*Id.* at 192. Arbitrator Keefe, in *American Motors Corp.*, 52 LA 709 (1969): "This is not to say that the matters cannot be decided on circumstantial evidence. Indeed, an individual charged . . . with murder, can be convicted by the weight of such evidence, when the individual is found, beyond reasonable doubt to have been guilty." Arbitrator Hoh, in *Consolidation Coal Co.*, 87 LA 729, 735 (1986) (marijuana use): "Circumstantial evidence can be utilized to satisfy a party's burden of proof by inference from those circumstances proven. Since direct evidence of a fact or occurrence is frequently unobtainable, arbitrators often decide cases on the basis of circumstantial evidence . . . ." See also *Brown Shoe Co.*, 16 LA 461 (Klamon, 1951) (gambling); *Lone Star Steel Co.*, 48 LA 949 (Jenkins, 1967) (strike in violation of contract); *Western Airlines, Inc.*, 66 LA 1165 (Christopher, 1976) (theft); *Hoover Universal, Inc.*, 73 LA 868 (Gibson, 1979) (marijuana possession); *Wisconsin Dep't of. Health & Social Servs.*, 84 LA 219 (Imes, 1985) (patient abuse); *Southwestern Bell Tel. Co.*, 84 LA 583 (Penfield, 1985) (tampering with computers).
[83]*Brooks Foundry, Inc.*, 75 LA 642, 643 (1980) (marijuana use).
[84]*City of Pittsburgh*, 71-1 ARB ¶8146 (1971).
[85]*New Haven Trap Rock Co.*, 66-1 ARB ¶8082, 3294 (1965) (sabotage).

Arbitrator Duff: [An arbitrator in using circumstantial evidence] must exercise extreme care so that by due deliberation and careful judgment he may avoid making hasty or false deductions. If the evidence producing the chain of circumstances pointing to [guilt] is weak and inconclusive, no probability of fact may be inferred from the combined circumstances.[86]

At least one arbitrator has taken the position that, although circumstantial evidence is valid, "[t]he extreme penalty of discharge cannot and should not be based on inference."[87]

A compelling reason for accepting circumstantial evidence is that for some kinds of misconduct, it may well be the only evidence that is available. Theft is a good example. Cases of theft that become the subject of grievances and arbitrations usually have the following three features in common:

- Typically, the culprit is not caught red-handed. The "smoking gun" cases are rare.
- Most involve pilferage, although the stakes occasionally are much greater.
- The threshold question is almost invariably who did it. But hard on the heels of this inquiry is the question of *intent*—that is, even assuming the grievant took the articles in question, whether he actually intended to steal them.[88]

Thus, in order to prove an employee guilty of theft, the company must prove that he or she both took the articles in question and intended to keep them.[89] Now and again it may be

---

[86]*South Penn Oil Co.*, 29 LA 718, 721 (1957) (intoxication on job).

[87]*Radio Corp. of America*, 39 LA 621, 624 (Scheiber, 1962) (gambling). See also *Stokely-Van Camp, Inc.*, 59 LA 655 (Griffin, 1972) (changing time cards), where the arbitrator, in sustaining the grievance, emphasized that the employer had failed to provide direct proof.

[88]Arbitrator Wolff, in *Grant Hosp.*, 88 LA 587 (1986):

[A]n employee cannot be guilty of theft absent an intent to steal. . . . [I]n requiring proof of "intent to steal," arbitrators are not simply applying criminal law requirements for theft but common, everyday understandings. . . . In seeking other employment it would be impossible for Grievant to satisfactorily explain to a prospective employer that her past employer discharged her for theft even though it didn't believe she intended to steal.

See also *City Utils. of Springfield*, 92 LA 515 (Erbs, 1989) (discharge reduced to suspension where no clear proof grievant intended to convert company pipe to her personal use).

[89]See, e.g., *Safeway Stores, Inc.*, 55 LA 1195 (Jacobs, 1971); *Stant Mfg. Co.*, 67-1 ARB ¶8322 (Larkin, 1967); *General Tel. Co. of Southwest*, 79 LA 102 (Holman, 1982); *Panhandle E. Pipeline Co.*, 88 LA 725 (Yarowsky, 1987). However, *Pennzoil Prods. Co.*, 86 LA 877, 880 (Stoltenberg, 1986), makes the point that, while there can be no theft without intent, a showing of intent to steal may be sufficient to warrant discipline even in the absence of an actual taking:

able to do this by means of credible eye witnesses and direct testimony. But if this is not possible—and usually it is not—the case must be pieced together from persuasive circumstantial evidence and compelling inferences drawn from such evidence.

Cases involving concerted action are like theft cases in that they almost always must be proved by means of circumstantial evidence. The same is true of cases involving an individual slowdown or sabotage.

> *Arbitrator McCoy:* Because of the secret nature of the offense [instigation of a strike] . . . proof is extremely difficult. It does not follow from this that proof may be dispensed with or that mere suspicious circumstances may take the place of proof. . . .
>
> But I think it does follow that something less than the most direct and the most positive proof is sufficient; in other words, that, just as in cases of fraud and conspiracy, legitimate inferences may be drawn from such circumstances as a prior knowledge of the time set for the strike. . . .
>
> But . . . suspicious circumstances, in combination, and especially in the case of known leaders in the union's affairs, may be sufficient to convince the reasonable mind of guilt.[90]

> *Arbitrator Platt:* Because of its very nature, a charge of intentional slowdown is, of course, often difficult to prove by direct evidence; hence it may be established by circumstantial evidence.
>
> But the necessity for relying upon inferential proof does not eliminate the requirement for clear and convincing proof to establish that the offense charged was committed.[91]

Both of these arbitrators recognized the pivotal role played by circumstantial evidence in cases involving concerted action. Note that in neither case was there application of a standard of proof beyond a reasonable doubt; Platt spoke of "clear and convincing proof," while McCoy referred to evidence "sufficient to convince the reasonable mind of guilt."[92]

The fact that no product of any amount was removed does not serve to offset the fact that this act was one of theft. Indeed, that was the purpose of [grievant's] being there; that was the purpose of his physical actions; and that was the purpose of his pre-planned trip . . . . Had the Grievant's attack of conscience occurred prior to his arrival [at the scene of the planned theft of fuel], he would not have become a thief. . . . Accordingly, there exists no basis to modify the Company's discharge penalty."

[90] *Stockham Pipe Fittings Co.*, 4 LA 744 (1946) (strike in violation of contract).

[91] *International Harvester Co.*, 21 LA 428 (1953) (slowdown).

[92] See *infra,* under "Proving Group Misconduct," for the proof problems presented by cases involving concerted action.

Direct Evidence and Credibility

The Shulman Rationale

Direct evidence gives the arbitrator a different kind of problem—credibility. It often happens that the story told by the grievant cannot be reconciled with the supervisor's version of the same incident. Given that both appear to be telling the truth, that there are no other witnesses, and that no facts disprove or contradict their respective versions, who is to be believed? The answer given many years ago to this question by Arbitrator Harry Shulman is that the supervisor is to be believed.[93]

Why is this so? Because the employee has an *interest* to protect—namely, his job. Such an interest "is cause for suspicion and tends to weaken credibility"[94] because, "when an employee's job is at stake, his testimony generally is an exercise in self absolution."[95] Thus, under the Shulman rationale, the supervisor and not the grievant would tend to be credited if most—not necessarily all—of the following conditions are satisfied: (1) the supervisor has nothing immediately to gain or lose in the case; (2) there are no facts to suggest the supervisor is mistaken; (3) there is no evidence of bad feeling or ill will (or bias, malice, jealousy, anger, etc.) on the part of the supervisor toward the grievant; and (4) the supervisor's version is not incredible.[96]

The Shulman rationale has its critics among arbitrators

---

[93]*Ford Motor Co.*, 1 ALAA ¶67,244, p. 67620 (1954). Cited variously in arbitration literature and throughout cases, e.g., *Western Condensing Co.*, 37 LA 912 (Mueller, 1961); *United Parcel Serv., Inc.*, 66-2 ARB ¶8703 (Dolson, 1966); *Riley-Stoker Co.*, 63 LA 581, 74-2 ARB ¶8434 (Shister, 1974); *Motor Transp. Co.*, 76 LA 958 (Talent, 1981); *Bismarck Food Serv., Inc.*, 88-1 ARB ¶8104 (Dobry, 1987).

[94]R. Mittenthal, *Credibility—A Will-o'-the-Wisp*, Truth, Lie Detectors, and Other Problems in Labor Arbitration 68 (Proceedings of the 31st Annual Meeting, National Academy of Arbitrators 1979).

[95]*Kraft Foods, Inc.*, 73 LA 493, 495 (Rose, 1979). For reasoning that goes beyond the Shulman rationale in preferring supervisor over grievant testimony, see *Standard Oil Co. (Ind.)*, 19 LA 795 (Naggi, 1952):

> To rule against management in a case based solely on the personal testimony of a member of the supervision staff as against the personal testimony of two employees could very well, in the future, jeopardize the responsibility vested in those who direct and supervise.

[96]*Ford Motor Co., supra* note 93. Accord, *Pennsylvania Greyhound Lines, Inc.*, 19 LA 210 (Seward, 1952); *American Motors Corp.*, 52 LA 709, 69-2 ARB ¶8504 (Keefe, 1969). See also *General Elec. Co.*, 40 LA 1084 (Crawford, 1963); *Billingsley, Inc.*, 48 LA 802 (Krimsly, 1967); *Grand Union Co.*, 48 LA 812 (Scheiber, 1967); *St. Louis Diecasting Corp.*, 69-1 ARB ¶8163 (Erbs, 1968); *Lake Orion Community Schools*, 73 LA 707 (Roumell, 1979); *Maui Pineapple Co.*, 86 LA 907 (Tsukiyama, 1986); *Georgia-Pacific Corp.*, 89-1 ARB ¶8194 (Sergent, 1989).

(and understandably even more so among union people). One arbitrator—in an opinion in which he ultimately found the supervisor's testimony more believable than the grievant's—had this to say:

> *Arbitrator Dworkin:* The [Shulman] theory does afford a mechanical method for assessing truthfulness. But it is grossly unfair and contrary to the most fundamental precepts of what arbitration is, how it works, and what it is supposed to achieve.
>
> In short, this mechanism for finding "truths" is a canard which ought to be summarily dismissed from arbitral thinking. What it says to a union and a grievant is, "You are going to lose if your evidence and testimony differs from what the company presents." It makes that statement even before the employer's first witness testifies; before the controversy begins to unroll. It flies in the face of the universal understanding that management, not the bargaining unit, carries the burden of proof in a dispute over discipline. It undermines arbitration as an impartial instrument for preserving industrial peace.[97]

Polygraph Tests and Credibility

A federal law, the Employee Polygraph Protection Act of 1988, limits employers' use of polygraph or lie detector tests as a means of uncovering misconduct, as do laws in a majority of the states.[98] Nevertheless, there are situations—in particular, cases of suspected theft—in which it is still possible for management to gather evidence in the form of polygraph test results. How do arbitrators view such evidence?

The answer is that they usually regard it as too weak to stand by itself and entitled to little or no weight except, perhaps, to corroborate other evidence or as one way of assessing credibility. One of the strongest opponents of polygraph evidence is Arbitrator Edgar A. Jones, Jr., who has summed up his views as follows:

> [T]he conclusion is compelling that no matter how well qualified educationally and experientially may be the polygraphist, the results of the lie-detector tests should routinely be ruled inadmis-

---

[97]*Cincinnati Paperboard Corp.*, 93 LA 505 (1989). For other cases reflecting some or all of these criticisms, see *Poloron Prods. of Pa., Inc.*, 23 LA 789 (Rosenfarb, 1955); *Giant Food, Inc.*, 72 LA 281 (Fields, 1979); *FMC Corp.*, 73 LA 705 (Marlatt, 1979); *Standard Oil of Ohio*, 75 LA 588 (Kindig, 1980); *Kidde, Inc., Weber Aircraft Div.*, 86 LA 681, 86-1 ARB ¶8200 (Dunn, 1985); *Town of Melbourne Beach*, 91 LA 280 (Frost, 1988).

[98]See Ch. 3, p. 222.

sible. The polygraph is treacherous in its applications to innocent employees ensnared in circumstances suggesting their guilt, and this because of its unreliability. It is . . . improperly preemptive of the act of judgment of the arbitrator on the issue of credibility. Indeed, the irony is that the more capable and experienced the polygraphist may appear as an observer of credibility, the more intrusively, and therefore improperly, preemptive of the arbitrator's exercise of the discretion of the office of trier of fact are the test results apt to be. And, of course, the less competent the polygraph operator, the more obviously does unreliability escalate as the polygraphist is demonstrated to be incompetent to make sensitive subjective judgments personally required in the situation."[99]

A respectable minority of arbitrators, nevertheless, view polygraph evidence not only as admissible but entitled to be given significant weight. Arbitrator Abrams sums up the case for admitting polygraph evidence as follows:

It is difficult to see why polygraph evidence should be automatically inadmissible in labor arbitration. Such results should be considered as just another piece of information an arbitrator might find useful in determining the credibility of witnesses. The question then is what weight the evidence should receive. . . . [T]here is the risk that it will be given more weight than it warrants, and the arbitrator must guard against that. The polygraph is *not* an easy way out. It is best used to supplement other evidence already in the record of the case.[100]

---

[99]E. A. Jones, Jr., *"Truth" When the Polygraph Operator Sits as Arbitrator (or Judge): The Deception of "Detection" in the "Diagnosis of Truth and Deception,"* Truth, Lie Detectors, and Other Problems in Labor Arbitration 151 (Proceedings of the 31st Annual Meeting, National Academy of Arbitrators 1979). Cases finding polygraph evidence inadmissible or entitled to no weight include *American Maize Prods. Co.*, 45 LA 1155 (Epstein, 1965); *Ramsey Steel Co.*, 66-1 ARB ¶8310 (Carmichael, 1966); *Bowman Transp. Co.*, 59 LA 283 (Murphy, 1972); *Kisko Co.*, 75 LA 574 (Stix, 1980); *Transit Management of Tucson, Inc.*, 81-2 ARB ¶8334 (Hildebrand, 1981); *Reynolds Metals Co.*, 85 LA 1046 (Taylor, 1985); *Deer Lakes School.* 94 LA 334 (Hewitt, 1989). See also H. A. & T. M. Theeke, *The Truth About Arbitrators' Treatment of Polygraph Tests*, 42 Arb. J. 23-32 (1987), in which the authors present the results of statistical analyses showing that polygraph evidence was either ruled inadmissible or given little or no weight in 74% of reported decisions between 1958 and 1984.

[100]*City of Miami*, 92 LA 175, 180, 89-2 ARB ¶8357 (1989) (attempted sale of drugs by police officer). The arbitrator added this caution in a footnote: "Of course, before admitting the evidence the arbitrator must be fully satisfied that the person administering the polygraph was skilled in the task and followed standard procedure in administering the test." In *A.R.A. Mfg. Co.*, 87 LA 182 (Woolf, 1986), the arbitrator's reason for giving little weight to polygraph evidence was the unavailability of the polygraph examiner for questioning.

As this comment suggests, even arbitrators who look with some favor upon polygraph evidence are unwilling to give it a paramount role in the determination of a grievant's guilt or innocence. Its proper role, they have said, is to supplement or corroborate other evidence,[101] or as a test of the credibility of the grievant or some other witness.[102]

Drugs and Alcohol and Evidence

Special evidentiary problems are presented by situations in which employees are disciplined for the possession or use of alcohol or drugs in the workplace environment. These include the evidence needed to prove that an employee is under the influence of or impaired by alcohol or drugs; the evidence needed to require that an employee undergo an alcohol or drug test; and the validity of test results in proving prohibited alcohol or drug use.[103]

Evidence of Impairment or Being Under the Influence

Arbitrators agree that lay observations by supervisors or others are admissible to prove that an employee is under the influence of alcoholic beverages. Intoxication is one of the few areas where nonexpert, lay opinion is admissible as evidence, not only in arbitration proceedings but in courts of law in many states as well. It may be true, as one arbitrator has commented, that "the determination of whether or not an employee was 'under the influence' of alcohol is never an easy task."[104] Nevertheless, a supervisor's judgment as to whether an employee is under the influence will normally be admitted and given

[101]E.g., American Maize Products Co., 56 LA 421 (Larkin, 1971); Bowman Transp. Co., 64 LA 453 (Hon, 1975); Nettle Creek Indus., 70 LA 100 (High, 1978); Knit-Rite, Inc., 84-1 ARB ¶8195 (Madden, 1983); Avis Rent A Car Sys., Inc., 85 LA 435 (Alsher, 1985).
[102]E.g., Daystrom Furniture Co., 65 LA 1157 (Laughlin, undated); Georgia-Pacific Corp., 84-2 ARB ¶8541 (Seidman, 1984); Avis Rent A Car Sys., Inc., supra note 101; City of Miami, supra note 100. In Daystrom Furniture, the arbitrator stated (at 1162):
    It has long been the view of this arbitrator that polygraph tests are more useful in verifying the truthfulness of testimony than in detecting its unreliability. From that point of view the term truth verifier would be more apt than lie detector.
[103]For more detailed treatment of this area, see T. S. & R. DENENBERG, ALCOHOL AND DRUGS: ISSUES IN THE WORKPLACE Chs. 4–6 (1983); M. F. HILL, JR., & A. V. SINICROPI, EVIDENCE IN ARBITRATION Ch. 11 (2d ed. 1987). See also A. M. KOVEN & S. L. SMITH, ALCOHOL-RELATED MISCONDUCT Ch. 5 (1984).
[104]General Felt Indus., Inc., 74 LA 972, 975 (Carnes, 1979).

considerable weight by an arbitrator *if* formed on the basis of specific, complete, and credible observation of the employee's behavior and appearance. In fact, in most cases involving discipline for intoxication that come before arbitrators, the company's proof consists of supervision's *observations* of what the grievant said or did, on the basis of which the supervisor formed an *opinion* that the grievant was under the influence.[105] The critical question then is whether the testimonial evidence is sufficient to convince the arbitrator that the company has met its burden of proof.[106]

The case against the grievant is strengthened if the company has breathalyzer or blood test results showing the presence of alcohol in the grievant's system. However, blood alcohol content (BAC) standing alone often has been viewed as insufficient to show that the grievant was under the influence *unless* the parties had previously agreed upon what BAC would prove intoxication.[107] Urine test results have even less validity in themselves because urinalysis does not reliably establish blood alcohol content.[108]

Proving that an employee is under the influence of an illegal drug is a more difficult problem because the physical manifestations are less pronounced than in the case of alcohol

---

[105]See, e.g., *Hi-Life Packing Co.*, 41 LA 1083 (Sembower, 1963); *Blaw-Knox Co.*, 66-2 ARB ¶8532 (Wood, 1966); *F. and M. Schaeffer Brewing Co.*, 68-2 ARB ¶8739 (Seidenberg, 1968); *City of Buffalo*, 59 LA 334 (Rinaldo, 1972); *Sherwin-Williams Co.*, 66 LA 273 (Rezler, 1976); *Tennessee River Pulp & Paper Co.*, 68 LA 421 (Simon, 1976); *Freightliner Corp.*, 79-1 ARB ¶8300 (Rose, 1979); *Bi-State Dev. Agency*, 88 LA 854 (Brazil, 1987).

[106]E.g., in *General Dynamics Corp.*, 91 LA 539 (Marcus, 1988), the fact that the grievant smelled of alcohol, spoke in a raised voice, and had elevated blood pressure and bloodshot eyes was found insufficient to show that he was under the influence of alcohol, where he showed no signs of physical impairment and the company had not defined "under the influence." See also *Western Air Lines, Inc.*, 37 LA 130 (Wyckoff, 1961) (flight attendant's disheveled appearance not proof of preflight drinking); *Reliance Elec. Co.*, 76-2 ARB ¶8446 (Gibson, 1976) (shaking and poor coordination possibly due to exposure to cold and unexpected rainstorm); *General Felt Indus., Inc., supra* note 104 (boisterousness not accepted as proof of intoxication).

[107]See, e.g., *Kaiser Steel Corp.*, 31 LA 832 (Grant, 1958); *Northrop Worldwide Servs., Inc.*, 64 LA 742 (Goodstein, 1975); *Hayes Albion Corp.*, 76 LA 1005 (Kahn, 1981); *Ohio Ferro-Alloys Corp.*, 82-2 ARB ¶8480 (Odom, 1982). Cases accepting test results as proving intoxication because the term "under the influence" had been defined in advance in terms of specific test levels include *Sperry Rand Corp*, 59 LA 849 (Logan, 1972); *Day & Zimmermann*, 75 LA 699 (Sisk, 1980). In *Pittsburg & Midway Coal Mining Co.*, 91 LA 431 (Cohen, 1988), the arbitrator accepted a BAC of 0.10, the state intoxication standard, as proving intoxication and upheld discharge because of the hazardous working conditions in the coal-mining environment.

[108]See *Chase Bag Co.*, 88 LA 441 (Strasshofer, 1986); *Regional Transp. Dist.*, 90 LA 27 (Yarowsky, 1987).

intoxication. The mere possession or use of drugs at the work-place often is ground for discharge whether or not impairment is proved. Proof of impairment is nevertheless important be-cause test results showing the presence of an illegal drug do not reveal when the drug was ingested. If the grievant smoked pot or used cocaine while off duty, the company may have no ground for imposing discipline unless it can show that the griev-ant's work performance was affected.[109]

Test results alone have been held in many cases to be insuf-ficient to prove impairment.[110] On the other hand, where an employee refused to submit to a test when supervision suspected him of being under the influence of marijuana, the arbitrator found just cause for discharge in the combination of the supervi-sor's observations and the refusal to be tested.[111]

Evidence Needed to Require Test

Unless the contract spells out the circumstances in which management may require an employee to submit to testing, the company may have a hurdle to surmount in proving that an employee is under the influence of alcohol or drugs. That is, the company needs proof that it had good reason to believe the individual was impaired in some way; otherwise, any discipline it imposes upon the individual, whether because of a refusal to undergo testing or positive test results, may not stand up.

> **EXAMPLE:** When a public utility lineman behaved erratically on the job, followed unsafe work procedures, and was absent from the job for several days without permission or notice, manage-ment suspected drug use and instructed him to undergo a drug-

---

[109]See, e.g., *Kroger Co.*, 88 LA 463 (Wren, 1986), where the grievant was discharged on the basis of clear evidence that he had used cocaine on the morning in question. The arbitrator, noting that the grievant performed his work satisfactorily throughout the day, reinstated him without back pay because there was no evidence that his performance was impaired. However, reinstatement was on a last-chance basis, conditioned on the grievant's submitting to up to six drug tests during the ensuing six months, with nongrievable discharge the penalty for testing positive.

[110]E.g., *Boone Energy*, 85 LA 233 (O'Connell, 1985); *Georgia-Pacific Corp.*, 86 LA 411 (Clarke, 1985); *Orange County Transit District*, 89 LA 544 (Brisco, 1987); *Phoenix Transit Sys.*, 89 LA 973 (Speroff, 1987); *Bowman Transp.*, 90 LA 347 (Duff, 1987); *Stanadyne*, 91 LA 993 (Fullmer, 1988); *United Technologies Carrier*, 92 LA 829 (Williams, 1989).

[111]*Sun Chem. Corp.*, 88 LA 633 (Murphy, 1986). See also *Uniroyal Goodrich Tire Co.*, 93 LA 893 (Dworkin, 1989) (company entitled to rely on believable observations when employee refuses to submit to drug test.

screening examination. When he tested positive for marijuana, the lineman was fired.

The union argued that the company had no basis for requiring the lineman to take the drug test, but the arbitrator thought otherwise. While agreeing that there must be "some degree of cause" before an employer may require an employee to be tested, the arbitrator found such cause in the lineman's on-the-job behavior, his absence without notice, and the fact that he had used drugs in the past.[112]

Validity of Test Results

Apart from the question of whether alcohol or drug test results, alone or in combination with other evidence, are proof of misconduct, arbitrators often are faced with union challenges to the results themselves—that is, whether the results are valid indicators of the grievant's condition. The claim has often been made that the content of a particular blood or urine specimen was irrelevant because there was no proof that it was the grievant's.

> *Arbitrator Miller:* The most important element of any drug testing program is the chain of custody of the sample being tested. If a secure, verifiable chain of custody is not present, no amount of screening or drug testing, simple or sophisticated, will prove anything.[113]

The elements involved in establishing a proper chain of custody were set forth as follows by Arbitrator Huffcutt:

> Chain of custody does not consist exclusively of a series of entries marching up and down sheets of paper introduced to prove the integrity of the specimen. It consists as well of all the facts and circumstances and people behind and among the entries. . . .
> It is essential, too, to emphasize . . . that the evidence that must be tracked and identified and its integrity proven is R's

---

[112]*Georgia Power Co.*, 87 LA 800 (Byars, 1986). In *Morton Thiokol, Inc.*, 89 LA 572 (Nicholas, 1987), the arbitrator held that a foreman's belief that he smelled alcohol on the grievant's breath was not reasonable cause to order the grievant to submit to a breathalyzer test and that, accordingly, the grievant's refusal was not cause for discharge. But the grievant's resort to self-help made a two-week suspension proper. See also *Utah Power and Light Co.*, 94 LA 233 (Winograd, 1990) (poor attendance record was not reasonable cause to require grievant to submit to drug test). For other cases dealing with reasonable cause for requiring an alcohol or drug test, see Ch. 3, p. 219.

[113]*Carondelet Coke Corp.*, 88-1 ARB ¶8084, 3408 (1988).

urine—not the specimen bottle and not the labels on the bottle—
only the urine. . . .

Assurance of an unbroken chain also demands proof that
the conduct of the entire collection process was so supervised and
observed by responsible people that there was no likelihood of
chicanery. Monitoring the custodian of the evidence, of course,
would have provided a strong link in the chain.[114]

It should be added, however, that absolute certainty is not
required in establishing a secure chain of custody.[115] In the
words of the Denenbergs:

> The criterion would seem to be whether a reasonable amount
> of diligence and normal care were taken in the handling and
> processing of the sample. Good faith handling is presumed unless
> there is evidence to the contrary, and the company's burden of
> proof does not necessarily include the burden of affirmatively
> demonstrating the security of the sample at every stage of the
> chain of custody.[116]

III. Keeping Proof Personal: Guilt By Association and Group Misconduct

Arbitrator Summers: Our industrial life has no place for concepts
of group guilt. Certainly, "just cause" for discipline requires clear
proof of individual guilt. . . . No man can be found guilty and
subjected to discipline unless there is clear proof that he as an
individual acted wrongfully.[117]

---

[114]*Department of the Army*, 91 LA 137, 147–48 (1988). The arbitrator found the
grievant's discharge improper not only because the chain of custody was faulty but also
because the urinalysis that purportedly showed the presence of marijuana constituted
an unreasonable search under the Fourth Amendment. Other cases in which chain-of-
custody problems were largely responsible for the overturning of discharge include
Holliston Mills, Inc., 60 LA 1030 (Simon, 1973); *Pacific Motor Trucking*, 86 LA 497
(D'Spain, 1986); *Roadway Express, Inc.*, 87 LA 1010 (D'Spain, 1986); *Amalgamated Transit
Union*, 87-2 ARB ¶8510 (Speroff, 1987); *Metropolitan Transit Auth.*, 93 LA 1214 (Baroni,
1990).
[115]As stated by the arbitrator in *Arkansas Power & Light Co.*, 88 LA 1065, 1071
(Weisbrod, 1987), "under any procedure a mistake is possible; however, it is also my
opinion based on the testimony of the expert witnesses that AP&L exerted a reasonable
effort to insure the quality of the drug testing procedures." See also *Cessna Aircraft Co.*,
52 LA 764 (Altrock, 1969) (no reason to believe company would have contaminated
drinking cup before sending it to independent laboratory for testing).
[116]T. S. & R. DENENBERG, *supra* note 103, p. 77.
[117]*New York Tel. Co.*, 69-2 ARB ¶8680, 5310 (1969) (sabotage). Summers continued:
Guilt by association is an odious doctrine which has no place in a society which
values the worth and dignity of the individual, and it is the recognition of this
worth and dignity of the individual which collective bargaining seeks to bring to
industrial life.

Guilt by Association

The idea of guilt by association so outrages the American sense of justice that it may seem surprising that it even comes up in arbitration. But the problem is not unusual. It arises when the only "evidence" against an employee is his or her relationship to some other individual and this evidence is elevated to proof of guilt. There are two typical variations on this theme.

The "Wrong Place at the Wrong Time"

The classic guilt-by-association scenario: A is accused of misconduct; B is somehow associated with A; therefore, B is guilty, too.

> **EXAMPLE:** During a company stakeout of a parking lot prompted by problems with theft and use of intoxicants, security personnel searched an employee's pickup truck, which he had just parked in the lot, and found a paper bag containing marijuana on the front seat. The employee admitted the marijuana was his and agreed to resign. The grievant was a passenger in the truck. This, coupled with the fact that two weeks earlier a "roach clip" (device for holding a marijuana cigarette) was spotted by guards in the grievant's own truck, led the company to fire the grievant as well.

There was no proof that the grievant even knew the marijuana was in the truck, let alone that he was involved in any plan to distribute it or intended to use it on company premises. The prior incident with the roach clip might have caused the company to suspect that the grievant was involved; but suspicion is not proof, and therefore the discharge was faulty.[118]

In another case, an employee was fired after he was observed standing outside a phone booth while a good friend and fellow employee was calling in a bomb threat to their employer. The arbitrator refused to sustain his discharge and reinstated him with back pay.[119]

---

[118]*Whirlpool Corp.*, 65 LA 386 (Gruenberg, 1975).

[119]"[W]e cannot sustain the ultimate industrial penalty on the basis of guilt by association. We cannot permit the strong suspicions to suffice. Even at the risk of allowing possibly 'guilty' persons to retain their jobs, we cannot permit possibly innocent persons to incur drastic punishment." *Eastern Associated Coal Co.*, 66 LA 1063 (Lubow, 1976). See also *Excelsior Truck Leasing Co.*, 71 LA 470, 471–72 (Votaw, 1978), where an employee whose time card had been punched for him without his knowledge was improperly discharged "on the specious assumption that a worker would not risk clocking another's time card unless the other had specifically asked him to do so . . . ."

Someone Did It—But Who?

An industrial crime has been committed. A, B, C, D, and E all could have done it. Or maybe only one or more of the five were guilty. The company cannot pinpoint the guilty person or persons and as a consequence disciplines all five.[120]

> **EXAMPLE:** Acts of sabotage had plagued the final assembly line for several weeks. Carburetor mechanisms had been closed so the engines would not run; grease had been placed on starter cords; toilet paper had been stuffed into engines. The line where the incidents occurred was in a clearly defined area where 12 employees worked; all could have been involved. When there was a new series of incidents on the heels of the foreman's warning that the trouble had better stop, the whole line was sent home for the day.

As the arbitrator put it, "There is only one question . . . and that is whether the company has a right to discipline 12 persons in a group without reasonable proof that all were positively guilty of the actions involved. This raises a very fundamental principle. Can the innocent be punished with the guilty?" His answer was no, and all 12 employees were awarded pay for their lost time.[121]

> *Arbitrator Kelliher:* It is contrary to the basic philosophy of Anglo-Saxon jurisprudence that any person shall be found guilty of an offense merely because some other person or persons in their identifiable group may have committed an offense. . . . Merely because one has the "opportunity to be guilty" does not mean that he is guilty.[122]

---

[120]Arbitrator Marshall, in *Evinrude Motors Co.*, 36 LA 1302, 1303 (1961) (faulty work): "The essential problem here is one of the appropriateness of group disciplinary action, where there is a conceded culprit in the group, but because of the nature of the offense and the circumstances surrounding it, it is not possible to 'finger' the real offender."

[121]*Quick Mfg., Inc.*, 45 LA 53, 55–56 (Gross, 1965). See also *Joerns Healthcare, Inc.*, 94 LA 17 (Kessler, 1989) (improper to discipline 32 workers because three were guilty of vandalism, where many of the 32 were not in a position to know who the guilty parties were).

[122]*Dirilyte Co. of Am., Inc.*, 25 LA 639, 640 (1955), where a group of six inspectors was given a final warning notice for approving an abnormal amount of defective work. In *Southern Ohio Canal Co.*, 76-2 ARB ¶8608, 7043 (Ipavec, 1976), where all nine members of a work crew were suspended after they left their foreman behind in the mine, the arbitrator found similarly that

> the Company may not discipline an entire group of employees because of a wrongful action which may have been committed by one or more of the group, but in all probability less than all members of the group. . . . [I]f it could have been shown . . . that each of the . . . nine grievants . . . deliberately did nothing to prevent the mantrip from leaving the section without the foreman; then, the entire group would properly be disciplined; however, the evidence was not

Separating the sheep from the goats, then, is an affirmative duty that management cannot avoid where discipline is contemplated. The difference between proof and nonproof in group discipline situations may be simply a matter of the company's making a serious effort to discover who is guilty and who is not—that is, a matter of investigation.

> **EXAMPLE:** A group of employees returned to work an hour late from lunch. The company had had persistent problems with drinking on lunch breaks, and when the foreman smelled alcohol on the breath of one of them, he sent the whole group home on the assumption that none of them was in any condition to work. He did not smell anyone else's breath, did not ask others if they had been drinking, and did not look for other symptoms of intoxication.

Had he done so, he might have come up with evidence against individuals that would have supported the company's charge. But convicting the whole group on evidence that only one member had had a drink did not meet just cause standards.[123]

It is true that in other situations it may be difficult or impossible to prove a case against specific individuals. Sabotage is a good example, as Arbitrator McCoy observed years ago, "because of the secret nature of the offense."[124] But the fact that proof is hard to come by does not let the company off the hook. Arbitrator McCoy again: "It does not follow from this that proof may be dispensed with or that mere suspicious circumstances may take the place of proof . . . ."[125]

But what if the employer, plagued by what is thought to be

---

persuasive in that regard . . . .

See also *New York Tel. Co., supra* note 117; *Goodyear Tire and Rubber Co.*, 71-2 ARB ¶8458 (Jaffee, 1971) (sabotage); *Arizona Aluminum Co.*, 82-1 ARB ¶8212 (Sass, 1982) (damaging company property); *Oshkosh Truck Corp.*, 79-1 ARB ¶8253 (Kossoff, 1979) (graffiti); *Silva Harvesting, Inc.*, 81-2 ARB ¶8575 (McKay, 1981) (insubordination).

[123]*Automotive Pattern Co.*, 77-2 ARB ¶8435 (Daniel, 1977). See also *East Ohio Gas Co..* 62 LA 90, 95 (Edes, 1973), where the employer made no attempt to investigate the claims by several employees that they had missed work on the day of a work stoppage because of legitimate illness, and was "not receptive to facts which might separate the innocent from the offenders." In *Quick Mfg., Inc., supra* note 121, at 56, the arbitrator pointed out that the company had not "exhausted all means of determining the guilty individuals by the use of modern investigative methods, including checks for fingerprinting."

[124]*Stockham Pipe Fittings Co.*, 4 LA 744 (McCoy, 1946).

[125]*Id.* Or, in the words of Arbitrator Edes, in *East Ohio Gas Co., supra* note 123, at 95: "The innocent cannot be lumped together with the guilty. This is not permissible even where it is difficult to differentiate between the two."

group misconduct, gets the goods on a particular employee and lowers the boom? Is the employer in the clear? The following case suggests that, if there is reason to believe that others are involved, the employer would do well to look beyond the tree to see if it can locate the forest.

EXAMPLE: A rash of harassing telephone calls was the signal for the employer's investigative machinery to swing into action. Zeroing in on one man it suspected, the employer arranged things so that only he had access to a particular phone, had the line monitored, and made a record of the harassing calls. On the basis of this evidence, it fired the man.

Not good enough, in the arbitrator's view. Although the employer proved by clear and convincing evidence that the man had made harassing phone calls, it made no showing that he made *all* such calls. Some members of management, moreover, testified that they did not believe this man was the only culprit. In view of this fact and the man's 14 years of good to excellent service, the arbitrator reduced the penalty to a 30-day suspension.[126]

One situation in which the company may be able to discipline just some of those guilty of group misconduct is where the misconduct takes the form of a strike or slowdown in violation of the contract. Arbitrators have sometimes held that the sole question in reviewing discipline for violation of a no-strike clause is whether the grievant was a participant.[127] The more common view is that "an employer may discharge some, but not all, participants in a wildcat strike, but that the basis for selecting those to be discharged must be reasonable."[128] In particular, arbitrators have held it proper to focus upon the leaders of wildcat strikes and impose lesser penalties, or none at all, on those who merely participated.[129]

---

[126]*Southern Ohio Coal Co.*, 88-2 ARB ¶8502 (Zobrak, 1988).

[127]*Acme Boot Co.*, 52 LA 1043 (Oppenheim, 1969); see also *The Randall Co.*, 66-2 ARB ¶8692 (Wissner, 1966).

[128]*Rust Eng'g Co.*, 89 LA 1296 (Gallagher, 1987). See also *Kaye-Tex Mfg. Co.*, 36 LA 660 (Horlacher, 1960); *Philips Indus., Inc.*, 45 LA 943 (Stouffer, 1965); *Permall, Inc.*, 48 LA 257 (Krimsly, 1967). Many additional citations are given in F. ELKOURI & E. A. ELKOURI, HOW ARBITRATION WORKS 685–86 (4th ed. 1985).

[129]See, e.g., *Alside, Inc.*, 33 LA 194 (Teple, 1959); *American Radiator & Standard Sanitary Corp.*, 37 LA 401 (Volz, 1961); *Drake Mfg. Co.*, 41 LA 732 (Markowitz, 1963); *General Am. Transportation Corp.*, 42 LA 142 (Pollack, 1964).

Proving Group Misconduct

Group discipline is proper where the involvement of all members of the group can be proved. Most cases where group responsibility becomes an issue involve concerted action such as sabotage, slowdowns, and work stoppages. Proof supporting group discipline in this type of case is supplied when the only logical conclusion is that everyone in the group must have participated in the misconduct or at least must have known what was going on.

The "Must Have Participated" Test

Meeting this test requires the presentation of convincing circumstantial evidence that everyone in the group must have contributed to the misconduct.

> *Arbitrator Williams:* To sustain disciplinary action against the group of employees, a concert of activity must be shown sufficient to implicate all members of the group; otherwise, group discipline cannot be justified.[130]

> **EXAMPLE:** Shortly after beginning the production of a new product, the employer conducted a time study and concluded that too few units were coming off the line. A new standard, about 50 percent higher than the old one, was announced to the crew, with a warning that layoffs would follow if it was not met. That same day production was down substantially, and observers noticed that wasted time for the line as a whole exceeded the norm by 27 percent. The entire crew was laid off for one day, and the union protested on the ground that the employer had failed to prove that everyone was guilty.

The arbitrator's analysis identified several key factors often seen in concerted-action cases of this type.

(1) *Balanced line* (or *integrated line*): The 15 grievants worked together as a unit, each one functioning as an essential part of the whole and having equal responsibility for the final product.

(2) *Group standard*: The standard against which the employer measured the grievants' productivity was based on the sum total of their normal capacities to perform as a unit.

(3) *No bottlenecks*: There was no bottleneck or irregularity at

---

[130]*Westinghouse Elec. Co.*, 48 LA 211, 213 (1967) (defective production).

any particular point on the line, so there was no basis for a claim that one individual was responsible and others were not. Thus, no one had to see anybody do anything for group discipline to be upheld, since the evidence established that all members of the group worked so closely together as a team that the slow-down could not have taken place without everyone's cooperation. Discipline was therefore sustained.[131]

Just being there was enough to satisfy the arbitrator that discipline was justified in another case. The employer reprimanded five members of an eight-man crew for being away from the job after discovering them in a restroom filled with cigarette smoke. The arbitrator viewed it as immaterial that the employer made a hasty decision without conducting a good investigation. No doubt there were varying degrees of guilt, he said, but each employee at least showed bad judgment and thus earned a reprimand.[132]

If the employer makes a convincing case that the group as a whole was responsible, the burden shifts to the union to prove that particular individuals in the group were not involved.[133] Even where the evidence is overwhelming that concerted action has taken place, as Arbitrator Jenkins explains,

> it is always possible that some individual employee may have been genuinely ill, or may have been faced with circumstances which required him to "report off" from work, and that his action in so doing would appear to be, but not actually be, in the furtherance of a common object or design.[134]

[131]*Whirlwind, Inc.*, 68-2 ARB ¶8525 (Solomon, 1968). To the same effect, *Kennecott Copper Corp.*, 41 LA 1339 (Dykstra, 1963) (slowdown). But where the facts indicated that all crew members' contributions to the job were not relatively equal, or that some were not in a position to produce defective work, group discipline has not been upheld. See *Westinghouse Elec. Co.*, supra note 130; *Buddy L Corp.*, 49 LA 581 (McIntosh, 1967) (low production); *U.S. Steel Corp.*, 49 LA 1236 (McDermott, 1968) (slowdown). *Silva Harvesting, Inc.*, supra note 122, represents a "mixed" result. The company's evidence fell short of proving that every member of a 19-man crew knowingly disobeyed an order to work overtime or be discharged and so was guilty of flagrant insubordination; nevertheless, all were guilty of leaving work early without permission and deserved some penalty. Reinstatement without back pay was the award.
[132]*Niemand Indus., Inc.*, 89-2 ARB ¶8404 (Giblin, 1989).
[133]In *U.S. Rubber Co.*, 66-1 ARB ¶8239 (Dworkin, 1966), the arbitrator found that where the circumstantial evidence warranted the inference that all three grievants had been smoking in an off-limits area as the company claimed, they had a duty to appear at the hearing either to testify on their own behalf or to identify the violator or violators. Since they did not appear, the company's case stood unrebutted, and the discipline was upheld.
[134]*Lone Star Steel Co.*, 48 LA 949, 951 (1967).

Nevertheless, the employer need not prove that each and every individual who missed work during a "sick-out" or other form of work stoppage was not sick or did not have some other good reason for being out.

> [E]ach employee must present to [the employer] probative, credible, and convincing proof that bona fide reason for his absence did in fact exist. Failing such proof his grievance will be denied.[135]

Just one caveat: The "shifting burden" applies only where the company has produced convincing evidence that some form of *group* misconduct has occurred and the question is which, if any, of the individuals was not a participant. It does not apply where individual misconduct has occurred and the question is "who done it?" In such cases the basic principle remains: "It is up to the employer to prove the employee 'guilty'; and not the employee who must prove himself 'not guilty.'"[136]

Illustrating this point is a case in which the employer knew that one of two employees must have damaged the outer wall of the plant by carelessly backing a trailer into it. The employer disciplined both of them, contending that their joint discharge was necessary because neither would admit having caused the damage. The arbitrator saw it differently:

> In effect, the Company seems to be arguing that the burden of proof should shift to the individuals in this case to prove their innocence. However, our civilized system of justice does not recognize such a shift in the burden of proof particularly where, as here, the innocent person is not shown to have any information at their disposal which would resolve the dilemma . . . .

He went on to point out that if the company had recognized its obligation to carry the burden of proof, it might have investigated the matter more thoroughly and come up with evidence

---

[135]*Id.* Similarly, Arbitrator Statham in *Veterans Admin.*, 85 LA 272, 277 (1985): Based upon the circumstantial evidence available, a presumption arose that the employees were engaging in a sick out, and the burden of proof, therefore, shifted to the employees to establish a clear, convincing and a preponderance of the evidence that they were incapacitated and not engaging in a concerted sick out. For a case in which the burden of proof was not met, see *Southern Cal. Permanente Medical Group*, 89-2 ARB ¶8557 (Christopher, 1989), in which credible reports that employees planned a sick-out plus inability to produce evidence of claimed illnesses in the form of doctors' certificates were held to justify the conclusion that the employees were guilty.

[136]*Midwest Tel. Co.*, 66 LA 311 (Witney, 1976) (low productivity).

against the guilty party. If not, "then our system of justice requires that the deed go unpunished."[137]

The "Must Have Known" Test

This test requires evidence showing that all employees disciplined at least knew about the misconduct.

> *Arbitrator Jaffee:* If we assume that one (undisclosed) man (or more than one but less than the group) is guilty, it is improper to discipline all unless it is found that the others knew who was guilty but concealed this knowledge from the Company.[138]

Involved here is a kind of "constructive knowledge"— knowledge that is imputed to an individual because the circumstances are such that he must have known. Guilty knowledge, if proved—not just suspected—can justify discipline on either of two counts, or both, depending on the circumstances: (1) as a refusal to cooperate in a legitimate investigation; and (2) as misconduct in itself. Of these two possibilities, the first is the more common,[139] but sometimes they coexist.

Here is a case in point: After a prolonged period in which rocks were thrown into a plant, everyone working in the area was suspended, even though the employer could not identify any of the rock-throwers. The arbitrator found it impossible to believe that any of the crew could have been ignorant of what was going on, and group discipline was amply justified. By refusing to assist the employer in its attempt to separate the innocent from the guilty, "the 'innocent' have chosen to not only stand with the guilty as a group but have also failed to follow [the safety rule] 'Look out for the other man as well as yourself.'" That is, nonthrowers in the group (if indeed there were any)

---

[137]*Arizona Aluminum Co.*, 82-1 ARB ¶8212, 3975 (Sass, 1982).

[138]*Goodyear Tire and Rubber Co.*, 71-2 ARB ¶8458 (Jaffee, 1971) (sabotage), at 5032.

[139]See, e.g., *Koppers Co.*, 76 LA 175, 177 (Amis, 1981), where the arbitrator found that responsibility for an act of sabotage could not be definitely pinned on any member of a five-man crew; nevertheless, "by their silence those members not directly involved are guilty of conspiring to obstruct the company's investigation of the matter, and they, too, deserve a penalty." See also *Marhoefer Packing Co.*, 70-2 ARB ¶8556, 4826 (Sembower, 1970): "The refusal of members of a crew or team to 'tell' on the others who may be the source of error may be individually admirable. . . . But at the same time there has to be a specific claim of invalidity of disciplinary action for any recovery to be granted." Employees' duty to cooperate in a company investigation is discussed further in Ch. 3, p. 185.

were guilty of allowing a serious safety hazard to continue unchecked by not helping to put a stop to the mischief.[140]

Some Alternatives to Group Discipline

Sometimes the employer can solve a problem without running afoul of just cause standards by resorting to something that, strictly speaking, is less than discipline.

Transfer. Where the evidence established that one of 43 central office employees was responsible for an act of sabotage, the company was justified in transferring all 43 out of that office even though it could not prove who was responsible.

> The company was not imposing discipline but simply making a business judgment as to the necessity and method of protecting its operations. The most evidence which it needed for this purpose, when no disciplinary action was taken, was that kind of evidence upon which reasonable men make such business judgments.[141]

Cleaning Duty: When the company's efforts to determine who was responsible for recurring outbreaks of offensive graffiti on its washroom walls failed, it attacked the problem by assigning all nonmaintenance employees, in alphabetical order, to take turns cleaning the washroom. While the arbitrator agreed that wholesale discipline may not be imposed as a way of pressuring employees to police one another's behavior, in this situation the cleaning job was not a disciplinary penalty, properly speaking, but a work assignment permitted under the contract.[142]

IV. Proof of Criminal Misconduct

Responsibility for Proving Criminal Misconduct

Where an employee is arrested for committing a crime, either on or off company premises, management is faced with

---

[140]*Empire-Reeves Steel Corp.*, 64-2 ARB ¶8537 (Childs, 1964).

[141]*New York Tel. Co.*, 69-2 ARB ¶8680, 5312 (Summers, 1969).

[142]*Oshkosh Truck Corp.*, 79-1 ARB ¶8253 (Kossoff, 1979) (graffiti). In *New York Tel. Co.*, *supra* note 141, the transfers brought no monetary loss to the affected employees, since all transfers were within the same classifications, and the new assignments were not inherently more undesirable than the employees' old jobs. In *Oshkosh*, the arbitrator cited the absence of monetary loss, the fact that no notations were made in employees' personnel files, the nondiscriminatory application of the assignments, and the legitimate business need involved (janitors could not remove the graffiti and perform their regular duties as well).

a question that does not arise in connection with any other type of misconduct, namely, whose job is it to determine innocence or guilt?

> **EXAMPLE:** An employee is arrested while at work by two police officers for failing to appear in court to answer for three traffic violations. Before leaving company premises, the officers search the employee and discover in his pockets two tightly rolled cigarettes, a small brass pipe, and four aluminum-foil-wrapped plugs of "greenish vegetable matter." The following day the employee is charged with possession of marijuana and hashish.

What now? If the company concludes that the offense in question calls for discipline (which in this type of case is usually discharge), can it undertake to prove a case against the employee as it would if he were charged with noncriminal (industrial) misconduct and impose discipline accordingly? The answer is yes.

Or, can the company leave the matter of proof in criminal cases to the courts and reserve final decision on discipline until the verdict is in? The answer again is yes.

Each of these options reflects a distinct view of the relationship between the criminal justice system and the industrial justice system. Each also presents its own problems of proof.

Independent Action by the Employer

This option leans toward the view that the two systems of justice, criminal and industrial, are largely independent of one another and that management can (and wherever possible should) act without waiting for the legal process to wend its way to its own conclusion.

> **EXAMPLE:** Continuing the earlier example, upon receiving the results of police lab tests confirming the arresting officer's visual identification of the drugs, the company decides to fire the employee for violating its rule prohibiting possession of narcotics on company property. Three days later a hearing is held on a motion to suppress the evidence against the employee on the ground that the search was illegal. That motion is granted, and the charges are dropped. The employee files a grievance protesting that his discharge was not for just cause.[143]

---

[143]*Babcock & Wilcox Co.*, 60 LA 778 (Dworkin, 1972). See also *Hennis Freight Lines*, 44 LA 711, 714 (McGury, 1964), in which criminal charges had been dismissed, even though the grievants had confessed to theft of company property, because the evidence was illegally obtained. Said the arbitrator: "The grievants have a procedural right not to be convicted of a crime because of the methods of arrest used by the police, but they

Under these circumstances, must the company defer to the court's ruling, likewise drop the charges, and reinstate the employee? To put it another way, does the dropping of charges preempt company proof of the employee's guilt? Two arguments are often made by unions that the answer to those questions should be yes.

Double jeopardy—that is, a person cannot be tried twice for the same offense.

Res judicata—that is, the merits of the same case cannot be relitigated, once a decision has been made.

But arbitrators do not normally accept these arguments.

Arbitrator Autrey: Although a felony conviction of an employee might be a basis for disciplinary action, it is well established that an employer is not bound by the finding of a criminal court on the guilt or innocence of an employee.[144]

The same holds true for an arbitrator who may hear the case at a later time.[145] Among the reasons for the view that an

---

do not have the substantive right to prevent the Company from knowing the facts and acting on their knowledge in a reasonable manner."

[144]*Meyer's Bakery of Blytheville, Inc.*, 70-2 ARB ¶8582, 4912 (1970) (possession of restricted drugs). Similarly, Arbitrator Turkus in *Service Trucking Co.*, 41 LA 377, 379 (1963) (theft): "The acquittal of the criminal charge is not conclusive or 'res judicata' of a subject matter which was in dispute between the same parties . . . ." To the same effect, *Allied Chem. Corp.*, 50 LA 616, 618 (1968) (theft); *Sahara Coal Co., Inc.*, 89-1 ARB ¶8207 (Suardi, 1989). The double jeopardy argument is discussed in Fairweather's Practice and Procedure in Labor Arbitration 301–04 (R. J. Schoonhoven, ed., 3d ed. 1991).

[145]*New York State Dep't of Correctional Servs.*, 69 LA 344, 349 (Kornblum, 1977) (calling in false alarm to police): "[T]he broad consensus of arbitral awards in labor disciplinary cases is that neither criminal acquittals *nor convictions* of the affected employees are *per se* binding on the arbitrator under the collective agreements." To the same effect, *Babcock & Wilcox, supra* note 143; *United Parcel Serv.*, 67 LA 861 (Lubow, 1976) (assault on supervisor); *Lockheed Corp.*, 75 LA 1081 (Kaufman, 1980); *Muskegon Heights Police Dep't*, 88 LA 675 (Girolamo, 1987) (officer's abuse of ex-spouse). Arbitrator Alexander, in *Chrysler Corp.*, 53 LA 1279, 1282 (1969) (malicious destruction), made clear that the inapplicability of *res judicata* holds true not only for criminal trials but for other types of proceedings as well:

[I]t is well established that in the absence of a contrary stipulation by the parties, determinations by other tribunals of issues arising on the same facts are not binding on arbitrators. Thus a ruling by a Worker's Compensation Board as to eligibility for benefits, or by courts of law as to criminal or civil responsibility, do not by themselves foreclose an arbitrator from proceeding to judgment on issues submitted to him on the basis of evidence and arguments presented to him.

To the same effect, *ITT Continental Baking Co.*, 79 LA 166 (Modjeska, 1982) (notification of illness); *Pacific Towboat & Salvage*, 88 LA 907 (Perone, 1987) (negligent damage to property); *Interstate Brands Corp.*, 87-2 ARB 8444 (Draznin, 1987) (tardiness); *Eastern Air Lines, Inc.*, 88-2 ARB 8364 (Jedel, 1987) (misuse of company computer); *Grinnell Corp.*, 92 LA 124 (Kilroy, 1989) (absenteeism).

employer is not bound by the results of a criminal trial are the following:

> *Different parties.* "The parties to the two proceedings are not the same. The parties to the criminal case were the Commonwealth of Pennsylvania and the dischargee, X. The parties to the arbitration are the Company and the Union."[146]

> *Different standards of proof and evidence.* "[L]eaving aside the matter of the identity of the parties, the issues and the requisite measure of proof, etc., in the usual course are not the same in criminal cases as distinct from those simply involving the employer–employee relationship."[147]

> *Different decision-maker.* "When the parties bargained for the arbitration process to resolve their disputes, they did not bargain for a jury of lay persons to do so."[148]

> *Finally, different issues:* "Unlike a criminal trial, the typical discharge arbitration is not a means of determining the guilt or innocence of the accused."[149]

To expand on the last point, what the employer must prove is somewhat different from what must be proved in court. In criminal proceedings, the state must prove not only that the accused committed a certain act but that he had criminal intent—a guilty state of mind. Without that element of proof, the case against him fails. In the disciplinary context, however, even if all the elements of a crime cannot be demonstrated, some penalty (even if not discharge) may still be justified if some form of wrongdoing (even if not criminal) can be proved.

---

[146]*Allied Chem. Corp.*, *supra* note 144, at 618.

[147]*Id.* See also *San Francisco Sheriff's Dep't*, 90 LA 154, 158 (Riker, 1987): "The criminal matter and the [arbitration] hearing while they arise from the same set of facts take different paths to reach their objectives. One being the difference in the level of proof from proof beyond a reasonable doubt in the criminal matter to that of a preponderance of evidence in the civil." *FAA*, 93 LA 41 (Allen, 1989), represents another situation in which criminal and industrial justice diverge. The grievant was convicted of drunk driving, but his conviction was overturned on appeal because the lower court failed to make a timely submission to the appellate court. The arbitrator held that the company was nevertheless entitled to act on the basis of the conviction.

[148]*United Parcel Serv.*, *supra* note 145, at 867. The arbitrator also commented that "[t]he criminal system of trial by one's peers has built into it the community's prejudices, and a host of other factors which make it different from the system of industrial arbitration."

[149]A. M. Ross, comment on S. N. Kadish, *The Criminal Law and Industrial Discipline as Sanctioning Systems: Some Comparative Observations*, Labor Arbitration—Perspectives and Problems 146 (Proceedings of the 17th Annual Meeting, National Academy of Arbitrators 1964).

For example, an arbitrator, after studying the trial record and hearing evidence on his own, concurred with the decision of a court that the grievant had not committed the crimes with which he was charged—assault and battery with intent to ravish and indecent assault—in a legal sense. Nonetheless, the evidence indicated that he had made indecent advances of some kind toward the passenger who filed the complaint. Some penalty was in order, and reinstatement without back pay was the award.[150]

The employer, on the other hand, has to prove one element with which the court is not concerned at all, namely, that an employee's criminal misconduct has had, or might reasonably be expected to have, an adverse impact on its business. (See Ch. 2, p. 127, for the relevant criteria.) Without that element of proof, no penalty can be justified, even if the act itself has been proved beyond the shadow of a doubt.[151]

From a management perspective, because the double-jeopardy and *res judicata* principles do not apply, the company does not have to wait for the court to dispose of criminal charges before it can take disciplinary action.[152]

Potential Problems When Employer Acts Independently

When the company decides to proceed with disciplinary action without waiting for the court, it signs on for two potential problems.

---

[150]*Philadelphia Transp. Co.*, 49 LA 606 (Gershenfeld, undated). See also *Harker Paint and Varnish Co.*, 63 LA 308 (Erbs, 1974), where dismissal of criminal charges led to the grievant's reinstatement, but the arbitrator withheld some back pay on the ground that he had admittedly had amphetamines and sleeping pills in his possession while driving a company vehicle.

[151]*U.S. Postal Serv.*, 89 LA 495, 500 (Nolan, 1987) (sexual battery): "Employers have no general authority to punish employees for off-duty misconduct, even illegal misconduct. To the contrary, they may discipline employees only when the misconduct has some significant effect on the employer." The arbitrator went on to say that an employer will automatically assume some harm from every breach of law by an employee. "For that reason, presumptions should be used only in the clearest of cases; in all others the employers must supply some credible evidence of a connection between the offense and the job." See also *Muskegon Heights Police Dep't, supra* note 145; *Wells Aluminum Moultrie, Inc.*, 89-1 ARB ¶8047 (Haemmel, 1988) (guilty plea to child molestation not cause for discharge, where some doubt as to actual guilt and no proof conviction had detrimental effect on company operations or image).

[152]The argument that an arbitrator cannot properly make a finding on an employee's guilt or innocence until final disposition of concurrent criminal proceedings was made by the union in *Continental Paper Co.*, 16 LA 727, 729 (Lewis, 1951). The arbitrator rejected that argument, concluding, in view of the company's evidence concerning the grievants' gambling activities, "it appears wholly unwarranted to require the employer to retain in his service these men until the wheels of the criminal process, over which the employer exercises no control, grind on to their ultimate outcome." See also *Continental*

Obtaining Sufficient Proof.

> **EXAMPLE:** Concluding the above drug fact situation, the company decides to hold the line on the employee's discharge for possession of drugs on company property. When the case comes to arbitration, the company argues that the employee was clearly in violation of a posted company rule because (1) suspicious substances were found on his person on company property; and (2) laboratory analysis confirmed that the substances were narcotics.

But the arbitrator saw things differently. "There is here absent direct evidence, of a persuasive and convincing character that the material, or substances the grievant had in his possession were narcotics, either marijuana or hashish." Why that failure of proof? The arresting officer admitted he was not certain about his visual identification of the substances. And although the lab report was introduced in evidence, the two technicians who performed the tests were not called to testify and thus were not subject to cross-examination concerning their qualifications, competence, and findings. "Thus, although circumstances are here present that suggest possession of prohibited narcotics on company property, the relevant facts are not of a convincing character or sufficient to support the penalty of discharge."[153]

Employer's Decision May Not Be Final. When the employer chooses to "act now," it is saying that it can function independently of the criminal justice system. Notwithstanding that determination to proceed on its own, a subsequent decision by the court may turn out to have an effect if the case goes to arbitration. Although arbitrators agree in theory that they are not bound by court determinations as to a grievant's guilt or innocence, what the court has done may affect the arbitrator in one of the following ways:

- *Admissible for a limited purpose.* "The only exception to [the principle that criminal proceedings are irrelevant to arbitration] is in the area of statements, or admissions, made by a party during the course of a criminal proceeding, such as a confession, or plea of 'guilty.' Although such statements are not controlling, they are admissible

---

Baking Co., 88 LA 1142 (Statham, 1987) (drug trafficking); *Burger Iron Co.*, 92 LA 1100 (Dworkin, 1989).

[153]*Babcock & Wilcox*, 60 LA 778 (Dworkin, 1972).

in an arbitration proceeding as admissions against interest."[154]

- *Admissible for all purposes.* "The Impartial Chairman is persuaded that the Company's position with regard to the independence of the arbitration forum *vis-á-vis* the Courts is basically sound. . . . However, . . . the court decision finding X not guilty on two counts while not binding here may appropriately be introduced into the arbitration hearings in support of the Union position."[155]
- *Persuasive—as long as . . . .* "Although the acquittal is not conclusive as *res judicata*, it must manifestly be given due and serious consideration in a case where both proceedings, namely the criminal case and the arbitration, involve the identical offense and in each proceeding it is requisite that guilt be established beyond a reasonable doubt."[156]

The result of a criminal court proceeding is a form of postdischarge evidence which arbitrators do not welcome into the record with open arms.[157] But there are two reasons why

---

[154]*Id.* at 782. In *Hennis Freight Lines*, 44 LA 711 (McGury, 1964), the arbitrator ruled that evidence relating to the grievants' confession of theft could be considered by the company and the arbitrator, even though the grievants were acquitted of theft charges and the evidence was suppressed as having been illegally obtained. Said the arbitrator: "The grievants have a procedural right not to be convicted of a crime because of the methods of arrest used by the police, but they do not have the substantive right to prevent the Company from knowing the facts and acting on their knowledge in a reasonable manner."

[155]*Philadelphia Transp. Co.*, *supra* note 150, at 607–08. In *Muskegon Heights Police Dep't*, *supra* note 145, the arbitrator ruled that, although a not-guilty verdict is not binding in arbitration, it increases the employer's burden of persuasion.

[156]*Allied Chem. Corp.*, *supra* note 144, at 619. The arbitrator found that where the proofs offered in both proceedings are the same, the effect of a not-guilty verdict is to create a reasonable doubt as to the dischargee's guilt. He distinguished *Allied* from *Service Trucking*, *supra* note 144, on that basis, finding that in *Service*, since the trial record was not introduced in evidence, he had no way to determine whether the evidence and arguments before the jury had been the same as those before him at the hearing. He therefore gave no weight to the grievants' acquittal on a theft charge and upheld their discharges. Lack of information about the basis for the grievant's acquittal was also cited by the arbitrator in *Chrysler Corp.*, *supra* note 145, in refusing to be bound by that determination. See also *Michigan Power Co.*, 68 LA 183, 187 (Rayl, 1977) (distribution of drugs), where it was ruled that dismissed charges could not be held against the grievant because he had been discharged solely on the basis of his arrest, and the company produced no independent proof of his guilt.

[157]In *National Screw & Mfg. Co.*, 33 LA 735, 740 (Dworkin, 1959), the arbitrator stated:

At most, the subsequent conviction and particularly the admission of guilt at the trial, could be considered as corroborative evidence bearing upon the company's initial appraisal of the employee's conduct. It cannot, however, serve to provide

arbitrators are more likely to be receptive to verdicts of guilt or innocence than to other varieties of postdischarge evidence.

An overlap of standards. In the area of criminal activity, the community's standards of justice cannot easily be kept separate from "industrial justice," and in at least some cases must be respected. As one arbitrator noted, "[t]he basic consideration in this forum is the employee-employer relationship as described by the collective Agreement. However, the overlap of societal values cannot be ignored."[158]

Guilty verdicts especially put the arbitrator on the spot. Where the nature of the offense does not justify discharge, the arbitrator's job is relatively simple, since the question then becomes what, if any, lesser penalty is appropriate. (This assumes, of course, that the grievant is not sentenced to a jail term that would make him unavailable for work.) But what if an employee is charged with stealing from the employer and fired; the arbitrator finds that the employer did not have adequate proof of his guilt at the time of discharge; but, following discharge, a court finds him guilty of (or he pleads guilty to) the theft?

A "societal imperative." To put it bluntly, is the arbitrator going to return a convicted felon to work solely because proof was belated? Almost certainly not, and in the few cases where this problem has arisen, arbitrators have dealt with what might be called the "societal imperative" with a flexible use of the remedy power. Thus, where there was no just cause at the time of the grievant's discharge but he later pled no contest to a charge of stealing from the employer, the arbitrator found that the appropriate remedy was back pay from the date of discharge to the date his guilt became clear. But reinstatement was not required.[159]

---

justification for discipline retroactively in the absence of the existence of "just cause" prior to the discharge.

[158]*Michigan Power Co.*, *supra* note 156, at 185. Similarly, in *Kennecott Copper Co.*, 38 LA 93, 98 (Wyckoff, 1962) (slowdown): "[A]s a practical matter the jury verdict of acquittal reflects standards of justice prevalent in the . . . community which should not be lightly disregarded."

[159]*Hollytex Carpet Mills, Inc.*, 79-1 ARB ¶8181 (Anderson, 1979). The length to which arbitrators have gone to accommodate both strict just cause standards and community standards is illustrated by *Lone Star Gas Co.*, 56 LA 1221 (Johannes, 1971). There the arbitrator found there was no just cause for the grievant's arrest for incest, since the company had no proof that the charge was true. But, he reasoned, the company would have had just cause to suspend the grievant as a result of his arrest, pending trial, and

Leaving It to the Courts

The other option open to the employer when an employee is charged with committing a crime is to defer final decision concerning discharge, and instead to suspend the employee pending court resolution. Advocates of the "suspend pending" option cite three reasons for taking this approach.

(1) *Problems of proof.* Especially where the alleged offense was committed off company premises, the employer may not be in a position to prove its case because the necessary evidence may be in the hands of law enforcement authorities. In a leading case, the arbitrator tied the appropriateness of a suspension to the difficulty management may have in conducting an investigation that, in his view, is properly a public responsibility.[160]

(2) *Problems of self-incrimination.* An employee facing criminal charges may be understandably reluctant to answer questions concerning his alleged misconduct before his case comes to trial (and, indeed, his attorney may instruct him not to answer such questions).[161]

(3) *Safeguards on both sides.* Suspension "protects the company against having a potential criminal in its employ during the period while he is awaiting trial, and at the same time protects the interests of the employee should he be acquitted of the charges."[162]

In part, an employer's decision not to "go it alone" may be a pragmatic one—if evidence is unavailable, it may have no reasonable alternative. But decisions to suspend the employee pending judicial determination may also reflect an attitude that in cases where state and employer authority overlap, the legal

---

then to terminate him with no back pay upon his conviction. His award achieved the same result—discharge effective when the grievant was found guilty; no compensation for any period of time.

[160]*National Steel Corp.*, 60 LA 613 (McDermott, 1973). See also *News Syndicate Co.*, 43 LA 511, 514 (Berkowitz, 1964) (gambling); *New York Times Co.*, 29 LA 442 (Seitz, 1957) (gambling).

[161]*New York Times Co.*, supra note 160; *Par Beverage Corp.*, 35 LA 77 (Schmidt, 1960). See also *Service Trucking Co.*, 41 LA 377, 379 (Turkus, 1963) (theft):

A mere "nodding" acquaintance with the trial of a criminal case would indicate the wisdom and providence of avoiding an arbitration hearing with its far less stringent evidentiary procedures and the subjection of the defendant (grievant) to an intensive and binding cross-examination in advance of the determination of the criminal case.

[162]*Par Beverage Corp.*, supra note 161. See also *Safeway Stores, Inc.*, 82-1 ARB ¶8207 (Phelan, 1982) (distribution of illegal drugs).

system is best equipped to carry the ball and management should keep hands off.

There is just one objection: Does not suspension before trial run counter to the presumption under law that an individual is innocent until proved guilty? There are two views.

Minority report. "[S]uspension solely on the basis of indictment must be held to represent that an employee is guilty until proven innocent, a principle, of course contrary to a basic tenet of our code of justice."[163]

Majority report: "[A]n employer who suspends an employee in such a situation is not deciding whether the employee is guilty or innocent without due process but is exercising a managerial right to protect its employees and to lessen possible adverse effects on its business."[164]

Arbitrator Livengood summed up the majority position. "In fact, I do not regard this as a disciplinary case at all."[165] Similarly, Arbitrator Rayl observed that "such a suspension is not disciplinary but a precautionary administrative procedure to eliminate a potential detriment or impairment of the company's business."[166] In another case, the arbitrator likened suspension pending trial to a situation in which an employee is suspended for noncriminal misconduct pending full investigation by the company, where the offense of which he is suspected is serious and his continued employment involves certain risks.[167] A conditional suspension for the purpose of protection, not punishment, does not require the degree of proof that is required for discharge. Some say that "reasonable suspicion" is enough.[168]

Three Conditions for "Suspend Pending." When the company chooses to suspend an employee pending legal action, three conditions ordinarily come into play.

(1) If it decides to suspend an employee on the basis of arrest or indictment, leaving the job of establishing guilt or innocence to the court, management has elected to abide by

---

[163]*Brown & Williamson Tobacco Co.*, 62 LA 1211, 1212 (Davis, 1974) (possession and sale of cocaine). The arbitrator went on to add that suspension pending trial "is, in spirit, exactly contrary, too, to our bail system. Bail is devised to prevent a member of society from suffering until he is proven guilty." *Id.* at 1213. To the same effect, *Times Mirror Cable Television of Springfield, Inc.*, 86-2 ARB ¶8372 (Berns, 1986).

[164]*Ampco Pittsburgh Corp.*, 75 LA 363, 366 (Seinsheimer, 1980) (manslaughter).

[165]*Great Atl. & Pac. Tea Co.*, 65-2 ARB ¶8753 (undated).

[166]*Michigan Power Co.*, *supra* note 156, at 187.

[167]*New York Shipbuilding Corp.*, 22 LA 851, 859 (Dash, 1954) (gambling).

[168]*Id.*

what the court decides. So if the verdict is not guilty, the company would be required not only to reinstate the employee but in many cases to compensate him for his lost time.[169] A guilty verdict with a sentence of probation may have the same effect.[170]

(2) Management must prove that keeping the employee on the job pending trial would have an adverse impact on its business.

> *Arbitrator Turkus:* Mere surmise, conjecture or speculation as to the adverse impact upon its operations or its business because of the nature *per se* of the alleged misconduct is not enough.[171]

(3) Suspension pending determination of guilt or innocence may be permissible for only a limited time unless management has evidence that misconduct was committed. One premise operating here: Whether or not a suspension is called disciplinary,

---

[169]Arbitrator Davis, in *Brown & Williamson Tobacco Co.*, *supra* note 163, at 1213: "The arbitrator believes that if the company is going to apply its rule as it did in the B case [*i.e.*, suspend solely on the basis of an arrest] then it must regularly expect to make restitution for a subsequently proven unwarranted economic punishment." Arbitrator Koven, in *Lucky Stores, Inc.*, 59 LA 559, 562 (1972) (sale of drugs): "[T]he employer bears the burden of the consequences when it is ultimately established that the employee is innocent of the charge for which he was arrested and then suspended." See also *Air France*, 71 LA 1113 (Turkus, 1978) (stealing mail bags); *Federal Prison Sys.*, 92 LA 261 (Shearer, 1989) (correctional officer whose suspension was converted to discharge upon conviction for off-duty misconduct entitled to reinstatement with back pay when conviction reversed on appeal). There have been a few exceptions to this rule, *e.g.*, *Great Atl. & Pac. Tea Co.*, *supra* note 165, and *Pearl Brewing Co.*, 48 LA 379 (Howard, 1967). In *Muskegon Heights Police Dep't*, 88 LA 675, 678 (Girolamo, 1987) (abuse of ex-spouse by police officer), the arbitrator held that he was not bound by the jury's not-guilty verdict because the issue and the parties were not the same. But he added that "a determination of innocence in the criminal forum does increase the Employer's burden of persuasion that discharge is warranted."

[170]The theory, as expressed in *Linde Co.*, 37 LA 1040, 1043 (Wyckoff, 1962) (possession of narcotics), is that "[t]he grant of probation was an inseparable element of the conviction," representing the court's determination that the individual is a safe and useful member of society, and that reinstatement must follow as it would if he were found innocent. See also *Inspiration Consolidated Copper Co.*, 60 LA 173 (Gentile, 1973). But *contra*, see *National Steel Corp.*, *supra* note 160, where the arbitrator found that the company was not obligated to reinstate a grievant who pleaded guilty to the sale of marijuana, despite the granting of probation, in view of the seriousness of that crime.

[171]*Raytheon Co.*, 66 LA 677 (1976) (shooting death). See also *U.S. Postal Serv.*, 89 LA 495, 500 (Nolan, 1987) (child abuse): "[A]n employer will automatically assume some harm from every employee's breach of the law, even if the public is unaware or unconcerned. For that reason presumptions should be used only in the clearest of cases; in all others the employers must supply some credible evidence of a connection between the offense and the job." Having said this, however, the arbitrator nevertheless upheld the suspension of an employee arrested for sexual battery because the contract permitted suspension upon a showing of "reasonable cause to believe" the employee was "guilty of a crime for which a sentence of imprisonment can be imposed." The arrest itself, he reasoned, provided reasonable cause.

the employee is left in "economic limbo," without means of support, for a considerable period of time—a loss for which even an eventual award of back pay might not fully compensate. Maybe his car has been repossessed; perhaps the bank has foreclosed on his house.

Another premise: The employer has other options. It can, for example, conduct its own investigation to determine the employee's guilt and impose discipline on that basis.

> *Arbitrator Statham:* There is no limitation of the management rights clause or language in the Agreement which restricts the Company right to conduct a hearing in a different forum than a criminal court. In fact, it is not uncommon for a Company to conduct an investigation for industrial theft, not prosecute the employee, but make a determination as to the employee's guilt or innocence of the crime.[172]

If an investigation does not turn up sufficient evidence of guilt or proves to be impracticable, the employer can return the employee to work until a court renders its verdict, at which time cause for discharge or other discipline may exist.[173] That was the view taken in one case where the arbitrator held that suspension on the basis of suspicion should not extend "beyond that point in time that is reasonably necessary to permit the company either to determine the facts of the case that give rise to the suspicion or to conclude that it is impossible to obtain sufficient facts to terminate the suspension in the form of some exact disciplinary act."[174]

Employer Versus the Courts: A Final Word

If what has just been discussed has a familiar ring, it is because the reasoning takes us back full circle to the "act now" option and the notion that the job of proving cause for discipline belongs to the employer, not the courts. But if the decision to "suspend pending" will not necessarily get the employer off the hook, on what basis can management decide which option to follow? In fact, it is partly a matter of philosophy and partly a matter of practicalities.

---

[172]*Continental Baking Co.*, 88 LA 1142, 1146 (1987) (drug trafficking).

[173]*Plough, Inc.*, 54 LA 541 (Autrey, 1970) (strike-related violence); *News Syndicate Co.*, *supra* note 160; *New York Times Co.*, *supra* note 160; *City of Flint, Mich.*, 69 LA 574 (Bowles, 1977)

[174]*New York Shipbuilding Corp.*, *supra* note 167.

The "act now" option. If the employer, on its own, can come up with sufficient evidence to prove that the employee committed the offense of which he or she has been accused, there is no reason why the employer cannot act, if it wishes.

The "suspend pending" option. But if the employer does not have proof and cannot reasonably get it, suspension is the only realistic course. If a grievance is filed, the employer risks having its decision reversed by an arbitrator who is unsympathetic toward indefinite suspensions, especially if it appears that returning the employee to the job would not involve significant risk to the employer. But the employer is still no worse off than if it had discharged the employee without proof and had had that decision reversed, since the bottom line, in terms of what an arbitrator can direct as a remedy, is the same: reinstatement of the employee, with or without back pay.

Arrests and Indictments as Proof

Failures of proof occur most commonly when management jumps to conclusions and takes an employee's arrest or indictment as proof that a crime was committed.

> *Arbitrator Schmidt:* It is not open to question that the mere fact that a person is charged . . . with the commission of a crime, does not tend to establish his guilt. Under our system of criminal law he is protected by a presumption of innocence in the criminal proceedings until his guilt is proved by proof beyond a reasonable doubt under procedures which conform to the principle of due process of law. While it is true that this legal presumption does not apply in civil proceedings nor, necessarily, in determining the propriety of a discharge under a collective bargaining agreement, it is equally true that the charge itself cannot be used as a basis for inferring or presuming the guilt of the person charged . . . .[175]

---

[175]*Par Beverage Corp.*, 35 LA 77, 80 (Schmidt, 1960): "The one consistent factor in almost all of the cases reviewed was that the arrest and/or indictment for the commission of a crime was not sufficient to justify discharge." *A. S. Abell Co.*, 39 LA 859, 862 (Strong, 1962) (gambling, tax code violations): "An indictment is merely an accusation; it is proof of nothing." (*Raytheon Co., supra* note 171) See also *Yellow Cab Co.*, 55 LA 590 (Helbling, 1970) (assault); *Lone Star Gas Co.*, 56 LA 1221 (Johannes, 1971) (incest). Exceptions to this principle are rare and involve unusual situations; *e.g.*, in *Wheaton Indus.*, 64 LA 826 (Kerrison, 1975), the arbitrator upheld the grievant's discharge and indictment for his arrest for possession of heroin with intent to sell where the employer had a consistent past practice, never previously challenged by the union, of discharging employees indicted for possession of narcotics.

In other words, the company needs to go beyond the fact of the arrest to reliable evidence that the employee committed the act in question. If it is going to assert the right to make a determination of the facts, independent of the legal determination, it must also assume the responsibility of investigating and proving its case by just cause standards. The close connection between investigation and proof is once again emphasized.

> **EXAMPLE:** Company officials learned from a newspaper report that an employee had been arrested and charged with shooting and wounding a bartender. The newspaper stated that the employee had admitted the shooting. The employer called the police and was told that the employee had left the bar to obtain a gun, returned, and shot the bartender after an argument. It concluded, on the basis of both the shooting incident and prior episodes in which the employee had threatened coworkers, that he was too violent a character to keep on payroll and fired him.

The employer investigated the incident to the extent of calling the police; but that was it. The "evidence" that this investigation produced was "not only hearsay but . . . double hearsay." No information was presented as to the basis upon which the police made their statements; no showing was made that any of them had been present when the alleged crime was committed; no opportunity was afforded the employee or his representative to test the accuracy of their statements by cross-examination.

Even if the hearsay tended to establish that the employee did the shooting, the arbitrator pointed out, it shed no light upon the circumstances in which the deed was done, for example, whether the shooting was self-defense. The employee was therefore reinstated with back pay.[176]

A guilty plea is another matter. An employee may argue that he pleaded guilty to a charge only to avoid a hassle, to save legal expenses, or because his lawyer advised him to, and so his plea does not prove a thing. Arbitrators have held, however, that "it is not possible to go beyond such a plea,"[177] and that a "voluntary plea of guilty, understood by a respondent, admits all the facts sufficiently pleaded in an indictment and is as con-

---

[176]*Par Beverage Corp.*, *supra* note 175.

[177]*Northwest Airlines, Inc.*, 53 LA 203, 206 (Sembower, 1969) (immoral conduct).

clusive as a verdict . . . ."[178] In all but exceptional cases, then,[179] guilty pleas have been accepted at face value as proving the charges. Pleas of *nolo contendere* (no contest), although not actual admissions of guilt, have been given similar effect by some arbitrators.[180]

---

[178]*U.S. Steel Corp.*, 29 LA 272, 277 (Babb, 1957) (larceny); *Westlake City School Dist.*, 94 LA 373 (Graham, 1990) (grand theft); *Washington Area Transit Auth.*, 94 LA 1172 (Garrett, 1990) (drug possession). But see *Emhart Packaging Group*, 88 LA 51 (Rothschild, 1986), in which the arbitrator found that a grievant's guilty plea to charges of possession of marijuana did not in itself provide just cause for discharge for violation of a rule against possession of nacotics on company property. He noted that the plea was entered four months after the discharge; that the employee might have been motivated by a desire to avoid a jail term (he was fined and placed on probation); and that no evidence of possession was produced at the arbitration hearing.

[179]As in *Tibbetts Plumbing-Heating Corp.*, 46 LA 124 (Stouffer, 1966) (indecency), where the grievant tried to withdraw his guilty plea, claiming he had been illegally trapped and pressured by an enforcement officer into confessing. A court had denied his request, and the matter was still on appeal to a higher court.

[180]*Great Scot Food Stores, Inc.*, 73 LA 147 (Porter, 1979)(food stamp fraud); *Hollytex Carpet Mills, Inc.*, 79-1 ARB ¶8181 (Anderson, 1979) (theft); *Southern Bell Tel. & Tel. Co.*, 75 LA 409 (Seibel, 1980) (obscene telephone calls); *Alpha Beta Co.*, 91 LA 1225 (Wilmoth, 1988). In *Reed Mfg. Co.*, 88-2 ARB ¶8587, on the other hand, the arbitrator held that a *nolo contendere* plea entered by a striker who assaulted a temporary replacement could not be equated to a guilty plea. He pointed out that the striker, who had been reinstated after a two-week suspension without being told that his job was in jeopardy, had entered the plea on the advice of counsel and might not have done so had he known it would result in his discharge.

Chapter 6

Equal Treatment

"Has the employer applied its rules, orders and penalties even-handedly and without discrimination to all employees?"

Arbitrator McDermott: Discrimination against an individual occurs when it is shown that there is unequal treatment of that employee as against others.[1]

Arbitrator Peck: Discrimination in its pejorative or prohibited sense consists of the treatment of persons who should be treated equally upon the basis of an irrelevant factor.[2]

"Discrimination," according to its general dictionary definition, means treating some things or some people differently from others. Especially since the passage of Title VII of the 1964 Civil Rights Act,[3] however, the term "discrimination" in common usage has taken on the more specific and more provocative connotation of difference in treatment because of certain factors, most often race and sex but also union activity, age, national origin, religion, and disability.

Title VII, which prohibits discrimination in employment on the basis of race, sex, national origin, and religion, has led to many changes in the status of minorities and women at the

---

[1]*Vulcan Mold & Iron Co.*, 70-1 ARB ¶8117, 3411 (1969) (shift-swapping).

[2]*University Parking, Inc.*, 57 LA 876, 879 (1971) (job performance). Arbitrator Taylor, in *Cities Serv. Co.*, 87 LA 1209, 1212 (1986) (sex discrimination): "In the field of industrial relations to discriminate in employment means to treat Employees differently on a basis other than individual merit."

[3]42 U.S.C. §2000e *et seq.*

303

workplace (even though the change for many has not gone far enough). In that process, Title VII has focused a spotlight not only on objective conditions of employment but on the subjective attitudes concerning race and sex that play a part in practically all employment discrimination claims.

The term "discrimination" in the context of just cause, however, is not restricted to discrimination because of Title VII-type factors. It refers to unequal treatment for any reason, as the following hypothetical example illustrates.

> **EXAMPLE:** Of the 250-odd employees working in the most highly skilled and highly paid classifications, only a handful are blacks. One of these, who made it by dint of hard work and night classes and was promoted to his job as a result of a complaint he filed with the EEOC after he had initially been passed over in favor of a white applicant, has a run-in with his foreman shortly after he takes over his new assignment. The foreman, who believes black employees are troublemakers who try to "make it" on the basis of race alone, is the one who initially refused this particular black his promotion.
>
> Claiming that the black employee has misinterpreted the blueprint for the assembly he is working on, the foreman says sarcastically, "I guess you still have one or two things to learn before you're ready to take over my job," and adds that he intends to give him a "write-up" for his error. He then tells another employee, who is white, to find a shop steward. The black employee grabs the other employee's arm, shouting, "I don't need a union—I haven't done anything!" The white employee responds with a right to the chin, yelling "No nigger lays a hand on me, boy," and a fight ensues.
>
> As a result of the episode, the black employee is fired and the white employee is sent home for the day. The black files a grievance claiming that both his discharge and the reprimand that set events in motion were racially motivated—part and parcel of the company's hostility toward blacks in general and of the foreman's desire to make things tough for blacks in particular.

The foregoing example makes the point that discrimination in disciplinary matters may be at the same time both simpler and more complex than it first appears. It is easy to see how attitudes on both sides, the black employee's as well as the foreman's, made it almost inevitable that the black employee would claim he was a victim of racial discrimination. The foreman was resentful of black employees generally and felt threatened by blacks like this one who were skilled and ambitious and on their way up the job ladder—who might eventually pass him on that ladder and become his boss without (he thinks) really deserving it. He also had particular reason to resent this employee, whose promotion he opposed. Thus the foreman was wide open to the charge that he was out to get the black employee and would seize upon any excuse to discredit him or send him packing. (It is even possible, under the circumstances, that this foreman might unconsciously "see" nonexistent flaws in this employee's work or exaggerate minor faults, with the hidden agenda of vindicating his original judgment about the black's lack of ability.)

As for the black employee, he was sensitive to racial prejudice and did not hesitate to make waves about treatment he believed to be unfair. His complaint of discrimination to the EEOC was found to be valid. So it is not surprising that he believed racial motivation was behind his reprimand and discharge. (It is even possible that he might have unconsciously tended to downplay any error he might have made, or to find excuses for his error, as a way of "defending" that belief.)

Thus, to these two individuals, the racial attitudes that underlay the facts of the case and gave the incident its emotionally charged character might have appeared to be what the case was really about. But in arbitration, attitudes alone do not decide cases. When it comes to just cause discipline, the critical question with respect to discrimination is not what a single supervisor or the company collectively feels about blacks, women, or Hispanics but whether a particular black, woman, or Hispanic has been treated differently from other employees—that is, whether he or she was subject to disparate (unequal) treatment—the key term.

If disparate treatment is proved, it is superfluous to prove that the motivation was improper in Title VII terms. Thus, in deciding whether the black employee's "write-up" for a performance error was discriminatory, arbitrators do not ask whether his foreman resented his promotion; they ask whether the company proved that an error was made, and then whether other employees were similarly reprimanded for errors of the same sort. If other employees had received the same treatment, no discrimination was involved in this reprimand. If, on the other hand, errors made by other employees of any race had been overlooked, chances are that an arbitrator would invalidate the reprimand, not because the recipient was black but simply because he had been treated more severely than others without any valid, work-related basis. The matter, then, is one of discrimination in a just cause sense rather than discrimination in a Title VII sense.

What about the discharge? Assuming that the two employees had comparable work records and lengths of service, it would follow that the black employee's discharge was discriminatory. True, he "started" the fight by grabbing the white employee's arm. But instead of backing off, the white employee responded with a racial slur and an aggressive physical attack that went beyond either self-defense or responding in kind. Responsibility for the ensuing scuffle was therefore more or less equal, and more or less equal penalties were called for—not discharge for one and only a suspension for the balance of the day for the other.

Again, an arbitrator would not have to get to the question of whether the black employee was treated more harshly because he was black. The fact of unequal treatment stands on its own, and most cases that involve discrimination have nothing to do with race, sex, or other Title VII-type claims but present problems like inconsistent enforcement of company rules and (an important area) union activity.

Unlike the other just cause tests, equal treatment is not a self-contained test but draws its essence from one or more of the other tests. That is, disparate treatment arises when the grievant has been treated unequally with respect to notice, the application of a rule, or investigation, proof, or penalty. Take, for example, the case of an alcoholic who was discharged for poor attendance. The employer was unaware of her problem because, the arbitrator found, it failed to make any meaningful investigation of what lay behind her absenteeism. This was not consistent with the employer's general policy statement calling for identification of and assistance to employees with drinking problems and constituted disparate treatment.[4]

---

[4]*Allegheny Ludlum Steel Corp.*, 84 LA 476 (Alexander, 1985). Other cases in which disparate treatment was found because the employer's investigation was less thorough than in other cases include *Hollywood Park*, 84 LA 902 (Draznin, 1985) (propensity toward violence); *Santa Clara County*, 88 LA 1226 (Concepcion, 1987) (sexual harassment). In *Lucky Stores*, 88 LA 841 (Gentile, 1987), the employer's failure to investigate to determine whether there were other positions suitable for an employee who, because of religious scruples, refused to sell lottery tickets was a violation of its duty to make reasonable accommodation to the employee's religious convictions.

I. Disparate Treatment and Inconsistent Enforcement

In common usage the terms "discrimination" and "disparate treatment" are often used interchangeably. "Discrimination" is susceptible of several connotations and can be taken to mean that management has it in for a particular employee or "that there is a lack of reasonable uniformity in meting out punishment for a particular offense,"[5] but the same is true of the term "disparate treatment." Though some have sought to distinguish between the two terms by saying that "discrimination" conveys the thought of being singled out[6] while "disparate treatment" implies comparing one individual with another (or failing to do this) followed by the treatment of that individual to his disadvantage,[7] the distinction is of little practical use because no such clear distinction is evident in most cases.

A more useful distinction is to apply "discrimination" to unfavorable treatment of an individual because he or she happens to be a member of a particular group and "disparate treatment" to less favorable treatment accorded to an individual not because he or she is part of any group but because some rule or policy was applied differently or not applied at all. But whether

---

[5]*R. Herschel Mfg. Co.*, 47 LA 20, 26 (Sembower, 1966) (absenteeism). In *Overhead Door Co.*, 70 LA 1299, 1302 (1978) (absenteeism), Arbitrator Dworkin put it this way: "Discrimination exists when an employee is unreasonably and without privilege subjected to treatment or discipline which is different in quality or amount than that which should be anticipated by other employees under similar circumstances. Discrimination may never be presumed."

[6]*American Meat Packing Co.*, 79 LA 1327, 1332 (Malinowski, 1982) (suspicion of theft, drinking, marijuana use):

As to matters of drinking and smoking marijuana on the job, the Arbitrator finds that even if these charges were to be accepted as having been proved, the plain fact is that the undercover agent and W agreed that everyone at the plant did it. That being the case, the Arbitrator holds the Company's decision to discharge Grievants was discriminatory as they were unfairly singled out for such conduct.

See also *Lockheed Aircraft Corp.*, 13 LA 433 (Aaron, 1949) (bookmakers discharged but not bettors); *Anaconda Aluminum Co.*, 51 LA 281 (Dolson, 1968) (ban on radios); *Lozier Corp.*, 74 LA 475 (Murphy, 1980) (haphazard enforcement of spitting rule). The notion of "scape goating" came up in *Monroe County Sheriff's Dep't*, 80-2 ARB ¶8403, 4810 (McDonnell, 1980) (termination of jailhouse cook by new county administrator): "The term 'scapegoat' ... is a harsh term and implies that the grievant has been consciously singled out by the County to be punished." The arbitrator found no evidence of "any such vicious intent"; nevertheless, the fact that other employees were not penalized for their part in throwing an unauthorized party with public funds amounted to selective discipline which led to the grievant's reinstatement.

[7]*Kimberly Clark Corp.*, 71-2 ARB ¶8562 (Ipavec, 1971) (group discipline; production standards, unsatisfactory work); *Toledo Molding & Die Corp.*, 88 LA 937 (Ipavec, 1987) (drugs and alcohol).

called discrimination or disparate treatment, unequal treatment at bottom results from the inconsistent enforcement of work rules and disciplinary policies.

In "disparate treatment" cases, the grievant's claim may be that he or she has been disadvantaged because other employees are currently being treated[8] or in the past were treated[9] in a more favorable manner; or that what was previously acceptable conduct on the grievant's part has somehow become unacceptable.[10]

In "discrimination" cases, the grievant may be experiencing less favorable treatment because he or she is a member of a particular group.[11] The groups usually thought of are those

---

[8]See, e.g., *Rotor Tool Co.*, 49 LA 210 (Williams, 1967) (shop talk and profanity common among employees and supervisors alike); *U.S. Steel Corp.*, 53 LA 1241 (McDaniel, 1969) (use of profanity toward supervisors); *Modern Automotive Servs., Inc.*, 69-2 ARB ¶8708 (Kennedy, 1969) (fighting); *National Grocers Co., Ltd.*, 57 LA 637 (Weathergill, 1971) (drinking beer during lunch break); *Manistee Drop Forge Corp.*, 62 LA 1164 (Brooks, 1974) (insubordination, refusal to wear protective ear muffs); *Whirlpool Corp.*, 65 LA 386 (Gruenberg, 1975) (possession of marijuana); *Clark Equip. Co.*, 77-2 ARB ¶8443 (Allen, 1977) (eating and drinking on job); *Jessup Door Co.*, 75 LA 478 (Brooks, 1980) (walking off job); *U.S. Pipe & Foundry Co.*, 84-1 ARB ¶8050 (Williams, 1983) *Champion Int'l Corp.*, 84-1 ARB ¶8217 (Mathews, 1984) (shift preference); *Zenith Elecs. Corp.*, 88 LA 157 (Doering, 1986) (off-duty, off-premises fighting); *City of Houston*, 87-2 ARB ¶8575 (Williams, 1987) (false claim for court pay); *Wagner Castings Co.*, 89-2 ARB ¶8577 (Talent, 1989) (altering medical statement).

[9]*Harshaw Chem. Co.*, 46 LA 248, 251 (Volz, 1966):
Neither the grievant nor his Union had notice that fighting, regardless of its severity, would result in discharge. In fact, in all previous cases the participants had received 10-day suspensions except in one instance where drinking on the job was involved.
See also *Telewald, Inc.*, 39 LA 183 (Daugherty, 1961) (fight outside plant); *Unimart Div. of Food Giant Markets, Inc.*, 49 LA 1207 (Roberts, 1968) (display of obscene drawings); *Stauffer Chem. Co.*, 69-1 ARB ¶8329 (Hayes, 1968) (sleeping on duty); *O'Brien Corp.*, 77-2 ARB ¶8405 (Wright, 1977) (incompetence); *General Cable Corp.*, 72 LA 975 (Watkins, 1979) (dress code violations); *Hooker Chem. Co.*, 74 LA 1032 (Grant, 1980) (marijuana); *Day & Zimmermann/Basil Corp.*, 84-1 ARB ¶8267 (Kanowitz, 1984) (felony convictions); *Johnson Controls, Inc.*, 84 LA 659 (Imundo, 1985) (violation of ICC off-duty regulations); *General Bag Corp.*, 86 LA 739 (Klein, 1985) (negligence); *Beverly Enters.*, 86-1 ARB ¶8102 (Nelson, 1985) (use of toxic cleaning substances); *Merced Irrigation Dist.*, 86 LA 851 (Riker, 1986) (conviction of drug offenses); *Nuodex, Inc.*, 87 LA 256 (Millious, 1986) (absenteeism); *Westinghouse Elec. Corp.*, 91 LA 685 (Talarico, 1988) (assaulting coworker); *Chicago Transit Auth.*, 89-1 ARB ¶8129 (Goldstein, 1988) (violation of last-chance agreement).

[10]*Rochester Tel. Corp.*, 45 LA 538 (Duff, 1965) (obscene language); *Milwaukee & Suburban Transp. Corp.*, 48 LA 98 (Somers, 1967) (negligence in allowing robbery to take place); *Triple E Corp.*, 52 LA 1296 (Sembower, 1969) (dishonesty, "banking" production); *M. Pascale Trucking, Inc.*, 59 LA 47 (Rodio, 1972) (moonlighting).

[11]See, e.g., *Lynchburg Foundry Co.*, 64 LA 1059 (Coburn, 1975) (employees on one shift sent home for refusing to wear safety shoes, on another shift merely warned); *Union Sanitary Dist.*, 79 LA 193 (Koven, 1982) (smoking prohibited in one building but not in another).

based upon age, sex, race, color, religion, national origin, and union affiliation or activity, which are dealt with in Part II of this chapter. But discrimination may be based upon groupings having nothing to do with these characteristics, such as hourly versus salaried employees, supervisors versus employees, one classification versus another classification, some strikers versus other strikers, and the like.

Thus, for example, foremen were allowed to bring soft-drink containers into a certain area despite a rule forbidding such conduct, but an employee was not allowed the same convenience; as a result, his discharge was invalidated.[12] Similar reasoning was applied where an airline's supervisors, but not its bargaining unit employees, were permitted to take bouillon packets and other foodstuffs for their own use, despite a rule prohibiting all employees, bargaining unit or not, from taking company property; the grievant's defense of inconsistent enforcement was upheld.[13] The fact that two groups of employees are treated differently does not mean that a claim of discrimination or disparate treatment will stand up, however. The critical question is whether there is a valid reason for the unequal treatment.

EXAMPLE: Employees in the foundry area were constantly exposed to airborne lead particles during working hours. As a result of new and tougher OSHA standards on lead exposure, the employer adopted a new rule prohibiting employees from eating or drinking in the foundry. One employee continued to eat on the job and was threatened with discipline as a result. He then complied with the new rule, but filed a grievance protesting that the rule was discriminatory because it did not apply to supervi-

---

[12]*Kast Metals Corp.*, 70 LA 278 (Roberts, 1978). Similarly, in *National Gallery of Art*, 91 LA 335, 338 (Craver, 1988) (use of profanity), the arbitrator observed: "So long as the National Gallery tolerates such inappropriate behavior by its supervisory personnel, it does not have the right to impose a different standard upon its rank-and-file employees." See also *Michigan Dep't of Corrections*, 93 LA 339 (Knott, 1989) (discharge of security officer for breach of security reduced to suspension in part because supervisor guilty of similar violation had only been reprimanded).

[13]*Pan Am. World Airways, Inc.*, 70-2 ARB ¶8802 (Koven, 1970). Similarly, in *U.S. Steel Corp.*, 57 LA 302 (Freund, 1971), to discipline only tenders for installing an alarm system that warned of the approach of supervisors was discriminatory, where there was strong reason to believe that helpers also were guilty. See also *Anaconda Aluminum Co.*, 51 LA 281 (Dolson, 1968) (no justification for permitting radio playing at one company plant but not another). In *LNP Corp.*, 88 LA 1031 (Tripp, 1987), on the other hand, the arbitrator declined to address claims of unfairness in the application of a drug-screening program to employees but not to management personnel on the ground that he did not have jurisdiction over persons not in the bargaining unit.

sors, whom he had frequently seen consuming food and drink they were carrying from the lunch area to their offices.

Although the arbitrator found the grievant's irritation understandable, he pointed out that employees were exposed to lead continuously throughout the day; supervisors, on the other hand, spent most of their working hours outside the foundry area, and occasionally sipping coffee as they passed through the foundry did not pose as great a risk as regular snacking in a lead-contaminated work environment. For that reason, it was neither unreasonable nor discriminatory for the employer to apply the new rule to employees but not to supervisors.[14]

The nature of an employee's work may provide justification for what might appear to be disparate treatment. Thus, arbitrators have decided that police officers may be held to a higher standard than others when it comes to truthfulness.[15] Arbitrators have also held that union officials have a greater responsibility than ordinary employees to avoid engaging in a slowdown or work stoppage[16] and should normally be held to a higher standard with respect to honesty, integrity, and adhering to rules of conduct.[17]

Typically, a defense based upon inconsistent enforcement involves one of the following situations:

- Where a rule has not been enforced, a practice has developed that is in conflict with the rule, and an employee is claimed to have violated the rule. The practice develops because the rule has been inconsistently applied for any of a variety of reasons, or because the rule is unclear and ambiguous or has not been adequately communicated to the employees.[18]

---

[14]*Anderson Elec. Connectors*, 75 LA 214 (Hardin, 1980).

[15]*Washington Metro. Area Transit Auth.*, 84 LA 292 (Tharp, 1985) (improper conduct). See also *City of Pomona*, 84 LA 1118, 1123 (Collins, 1985), in which the arbitrator, in upholding the suspension of a police officer found to have used unnecessary and excessive force in apprehending and arresting a suspect, stated that "police officers, empowered by the State to use force against other human beings, are properly held to a high standard of conduct in such situations."

[16]*Weyerhaeuser Co.*, 89-1 ARB ¶8066 (Allen, 1988).

[17]*Morton Thiokol*, 93 LA 434 (Allen, 1989).

[18]*Lockheed Corp.*, 75 LA 1081 (Kaufman, 1980):

The Arbitrator does not mean to say that the Company actually condoned the smoking of marijuana during the lunch break. . . . However, what counts when it comes to enforcing Company rules is the impact of the Company's inaction upon the employees, not the Company's motivation. As the Union points out, the

- Where no rule exists and a practice develops permitting certain conduct (or even misconduct). At some point the employer seeks to put a stop to the practice and does so by disciplining or firing some employee.[19]
- Where the employer attempts to change practice by establishing a new rule or policy on the subject.

How Inconsistent Enforcement Comes About

A Failure of Supervision

Inconsistent enforcement commonly results from the employer's failure to enforce a rule uniformly,[20] often because it has failed adequately to communicate either the rule or the conditions under which the rule will be enforced.[21] Sometimes

---

practical effect, despite the posted rules, was that the employees "looked upon the lots as sanctuaries for this relaxation."

See also *Automotive Pattern Co.*, 69 LA 424 (Daniel, 1977) (drinking, late return from lunch break); *Collins Packing Co.*, 84-1 ARB ¶8035 (Modjeska, 1983) (insubordination); *Van Nuys Communication Co.*, 84 LA 881 (Gentile, 1985) (no-relatives policy); *Frito-Lay, Inc.*, 86 LA 420 (Daniel, 1985) (dishonesty); *U.S. Army Corps of Eng'rs*, 86 LA 939 (O'Grady, 1986) (seat-belt rule).

[19]*E.g.*, *Anchor Hocking Glass Corp.*, 67-1 ARB ¶8209 (Stouffer, 1967), where the company's suspension of the grievant for "running bad ware" was approved even though there were no plant rules on standards of production and even though other members of the grievant's crew were disciplined less severely. See also *Southland Corp.*, 84-1 ARB ¶8133 (Marcus, 1984), in which the discharge of three route salesmen was overturned, even though their actions ordinarily would have been just cause for discharge, because pocketing cash payments from customers was a common practice known to and condoned by the company.

[20]*E.g.*, *Gallagher Co.*, 46 LA 882, 884 (Gross, 1966), where the evidence disclosed "rather loose enforcement" of the contractual three-day-absence rule, with some employees reporting in to a company executive, others merely leaving word with the telephone operator, and still others requesting and being granted leave after the fact when they brought in doctors' notes upon return to work. "Thus the arbitrator finds that the Company, while it has a perfect right to set forth the reasonable and fair conditions of the enforcement of Section 10, is required to do so uniformly and to give fair warning of its intent so to do . . . ." See also *Fawn Eng'g Co.*, 63 LA 1307 (Fitch, 1974) (employer tolerated laxity concerning rule that employee get foreman's approval before leaving work); *Freightliner Corp.*, 79-1 ARB ¶8300 (Ross, 1979) (intoxication) (penalties need not be identical but pattern of consistency should be readily discernible); *Montcalm County Road Comm'n*, 94 LA 45 (Daniel, 1989) (inconsistent and unfair enforcement of seat-belt rule).

[21]As in *Lawrence Bros., Inc.*, 28 LA 83 (Davis, 1957), where the employer never told employees that its rule stating that females "should" wear jeans would be enforced for reasons of decorum as well as safety, and had not enforced the rule uniformly. In *Russell Stanley Corp.*, 66 LA 953, 955 (Kornblum, 1976), the grievant's discharge for painting the words "paz" (peace), "amor" (love), and "hermanos" (brothers) on the frame of a door was set aside because the walls were covered with a wide variety of graffiti. "What occurred here was primarily due to a failure by management to

inconsistent enforcement arises out of poor supervision (such as when a foreman boozes with employees and then imposes discipline for drinking[22]) or by an employer's "policy of leniency"[23] (such as when management closed its eyes to the grievant's previous "juvenile behavior"[24]). It may well be that the disparate treatment is not intended, but intent is irrelevant; it is the impact on the employee that counts.[25] Oft-quoted is the following statement on lax enforcement of rules:

> Arbitrators have not hesitated to disturb penalties, assessed without clear and timely warning, where the employer over a period of time has condoned the violation of the rule in the past—lax

---

communicate distinctly and directly to its employees how gravely it viewed the subject of impermissible markings on the walls of its plant." See also *McCormick & Baxter Creosoting Co.*, 55 LA 1274 (Jacobs, 1971) (drinking on duty); *Copaz Packing Corp.*, 84-1 ARB ¶8067 (Imundo, 1983) (conditions of strike settlement).

[22]As in *Foremost-McKesson, Inc.*, 69-1 ARB ¶8405 (Chalfie, 1969) (falsification of production records), in which an atmosphere of "goofing off" had been generated by poor supervision and the employees had not only been allowed but encouraged to fall into poor work habits. *Chicago Mastic Co.*, 53 LA 428 (Kelliher, 1969) (leaving work early, failure to punch time card), is similar. Discharge was converted to a suspension because the supervisor had almost never disciplined employees for prior violations, although he knew of them, and did not warn them that they could be discharged. By way of remedy, the arbitrator ordered the immediate posting of a notice stating an intention to enforce the rule strictly in the future.

[23]*Durham Hosiery Mills*, 24 LA 356, 360 (Livengood, 1955): "[T]he Company's past practice fails to establish discharge as the uniform and consistent penalty for fighting, and, to the contrary, indicates that heretofore an extremely lenient view has been taken as to altercations among employees." In *Bay Area Rapid Transit Dist.*, 92 LA 444 (Koven, 1989), the discharge of an employee who was unable to perform her duties because she was in a cocaine-induced stupor was found improper in view of the employer's practice of trying to rehabilitate employees with drug problems. The misconduct was extremely serious, but the arbitrator reasoned that the employee deserved a second chance because she had sought and completed treatment following her discharge and had an 11-year unblemished record. See also *Ed Friedrich, Div. of AIC Corp.*, 45 LA 517 (Larkin, 1965) (killing of fellow employee; employer had policy of leniency for fighting outside plant); *Gallagher Co.*, supra note 20.

[24]*Rochester Tel. Corp.*, 45 LA 538, 540 (Duff, 1965) (obscene language):
> Where a Company has taken a lenient attitude toward misbehavior of an employee over a period of time, and does not impose any substantial punishment on him to convince him of the necessity to reform, it would not be just to permit such infractions to be accumulated and made the basis for a discharge.

[25]An example of such lack of intent is provided by *Solar Turbines, Inc.*, 85 LA 525 (Kaufman, 1985). The grievant was fired under a company rule that provided for immediate discharge for threatening other employees. However, in a prior case an employee who struck a fellow worker—also cause for immediate discharge under the same rule—was not disciplined because the victim was unwilling to pursue the matter, leading the arbitrator to hold that sustaining the discharge would "make for a result that smacks of disparate treatment."

enforcement of rules may lead employees reasonably to believe that the conduct in question is sanctioned by management.[26]

EXAMPLE: Five bus drivers were suspended for wearing black nationalism buttons bearing the words "Free Angela Davis"—a black activist—while on the job. The wearing of such buttons was not strictly prohibited by the dress regulations (which prohibited only political campaign buttons); and the wearing of a variety of other buttons and badges—such as Knights of Columbus badges and St. Patrick's Day shamrocks—had been tolerated. The suspensions touched off a wildcat strike, and the drivers were discharged.

The arbitrator ordered that the drivers be reinstated. The dress code, he found, was "so incomplete that it [failed] to meet the requirements of enforceability."[27] But it was not the dress code or its incompleteness that gave rise to the defense of inconsistent enforcement, since if there had been no practice (permissible or not permissible) there could have been no problem of inconsistent enforcement. Thus, strictly speaking, it is not the rule, even if vague or uncertain, that gives rise to the inconsistent enforcement defense, but rather the practice under that rule.[28]

Some of the inconsistent enforcement cases boil down to a matter of simple fairness, as where an employee is disciplined in order to set an example for others,[29] or where management

---

[26]F. ELKOURI & E. A. ELKOURI, HOW ARBITRATION WORKS 683–84 (4th ed. 1985). Cited, *e.g.*, in *Gallagher Co.*, *supra* note 20, and *Chicago Mastic Co.*, *supra* note 22, which also quotes L. STESSIN, EMPLOYEE DISCIPLINE (1960):

> But as in most other areas of arbitration of discharge and discipline cases, arbitrators, before upholding management in any action, must have assurances that the insubordinate act was deliberate, not merely technical and *that the employee was on notice, at least by virtue of a past practice of rule enforcement, that he was inviting discipline by his recalcitrant attitude.* (Emphasis by arbitrator.)

[27]*Port Auth. of Allegheny County*, 71-2 ARB ¶8694, 5646 (Duff, 1971).

[28]For an example, see *Kimberly-Clark Corp.*, 87-2 ARB ¶8315 (Ratner, 1987). Although there was a rule restricting coffee drinking to break times, it was honored more in the breach than in the observance. When one supervisor enforced the rule by pouring the grievant's coffee down the drain, the grievant became enraged and punched the supervisor in the face. Despite this extreme misconduct the arbitrator reduced the grievant's punishment from discharge to suspension because his reaction was provoked by the unequal treatment.

[29]*Triple E Corp.*, 52 LA 1296, 1300 (Sembower, 1969) (dishonesty, "banking" production):

> The making of the Grievant as "an example" in order finally to eliminate "banking" in this plant is not consonant with the basic ends of justice which do not make exemplary employees "fair game" for that kind of rectification. In our society we do not accept the destruction of a worthy individual as a fit "sacrifice" to achieve such a desirable end.

"gets tough" with an employee after past tolerance and condonation.[30] It may be that the grievant's discharge is the first ever
for the misconduct in question: "In mitigation, there were 35
employees ready and willing to testify that 'this type of horseplay' has gone on since the plant first started up . . . . This was
the first discharge of its kind under the contract . . . ."[31] Other
cases give the employer no points for stoically putting up with
a particular grievant; to the contrary, such "long-suffering . . .
tends to make it more difficult—rather than less—to evaluate
the fairness of [the employer's] decision to put an end to the
relationship when it did."[32]

New Rules, Policy Changes, Revival of Old Rules

Inconsistent or lax enforcement in reference to notice has
been discussed in Chapter 1. The matter of forewarning is much
emphasized as a precondition for discipline, and arbitrators
tend to be rather demanding on this score. The minimum requirement is that whatever is being prohibited must be pro-
claimed clearly and loudly for all affected employees to hear.
Thus, an employee who spends a few moments on the job
reading a magazine cannot be punished if there is no known
rule prohibiting engaging in personal pursuits during working
hours and no one has previously been penalized for doing such
personal things as showing family photographs to one another.[33]

---

[30]*Rexall Drug Co.*, 65 LA 1101 (Cohen, 1975) (garnishments) (unfair to invoke
previously unenforced rule on now-and-then basis). See also *The O'Brien Corp.*, 77-2
ARB ¶8405 (Wright, 1977) (incompetence, inefficiency); *Stevens Shipping & Terminal
Co.*, 70 LA 1066 (Hall, 1978) (unauthorized absence); *American Hoechst Corp.*, 84-1 ARB
¶8143 (Marlatt, 1984) (incompetence, inefficiency).

[31]*Universal Match Corp.*, 42 LA 184, 186 (Coffey, 1963) (horseplay). See also *Ball
Corp.*, 74-1 ARB ¶8050 (Shanker, 1974) (absenteeism); *Ohio Power Co.*, 64 LA 934 (High,
1975) (dishonesty); *Werner-Continental, Inc.*, 72 LA 1 (LeWinter, 1978) (absenteeism).

[32]*Michel Warehousing Corp.*, 67 LA 565, 570 (Mallet-Prevost, 1976) (negligence,
absenteeism). The arbitrator further stated:

> [T]he Company's rule or policy about using the IN and OUT doors was so loosely
> administered that it was neither fair nor reasonable for the Company to make a
> violation of the rule the basis for a discharge, without issuing a more clear-cut
> statement of it or a warning to the employees that a serious penalty would follow
> future violations.

See also *Hammermill Paper Co.*, 58 LA 145, 147 (Reid, 1972) (absenteeism): "[P]er-
haps the Company had unconsciously by its attitude created the reasonable impression
with the Grievant that it was so long suffering in fact that the Grievant was led to believe
the situation would never end in discharge."

[33]*Litton Indus., Inc.*, 62 LA 1195 (Karasick, 1974). See also *Dubuque Lorenz, Inc.*, 66
LA 1245 (Sinicropi, 1976) (tardiness applied differently in grievant's case than on prior
occasions); *Copaz Packing Corp.*, 84-1 ARB ¶8067 (Imundo, 1983) (disparate treatment

Inconsistent enforcement claims may be generated when the employer institutes a new rule for the purpose of changing an existing practice or puts out a "change in policy" or takes an existing but dormant rule and attempts to "revitalize" it. Can the employer do this? Of course it can. But, as emphasized in Chapter 1, the employer cannot put a halt to an existing practice or bring an old rule back from the dead without giving notice of its determination to make a change.[34] Such notice "unrings the bell," so to speak, where there is a history of lax enforcement.[35] For example, haphazard enforcement of a plant rule barring washing up on company time did not mean that a company could not reprimand employees whom it had warned individually not to wash up before the whistle sounded. In other words, any implication that the rule would not be enforced was cancelled by the giving of individual notice that future violations would lead to discipline.[36]

Sometimes when a new plant rule is put into effect, or the company tries to tighten enforcement of an old rule, the union may not argue in terms of lax or inconsistent enforcement (though in effect it amounts to that) but may take the position that working conditions have been unilaterally changed.[37] "Lax enforcement," strictly speaking, connotes failure by the em-

---

in application of strike-settlement agreement); *Menasha Corp.*, 90 LA 427 (Clark, 1987) (only one other discharge for poor attendance in preceding 10 years).

[34]*Genest-Midwest, Inc.*, 67-2 ARB ¶8569, 4994) (Allman, 1967) (drinking on duty, overstaying break): "The Company has the right to take steps to tighten discipline, but . . . when the Company has tolerated a condition and decides to end its toleration, there must be some indication of the change in policy." See also *Kansas Power & Light Co.*, 87 LA 867 (Belcher, 1986), where the employer was not permitted to expand its no-fault absenteeism policy to include paid sick leave because it had not counted such leave in the past.

[35]Examples where management has been able successfully to resurrect an old rule include *Fairbanks Morse, Inc.*, 47 LA 224 (Fisher, 1966) (notice of absence), and *Hartman Elec. Mfg. Co.*, 48 LA 681 (Dyke, 1967) (eating at work). In *Pacific Northwest Bell Tel. Co.*, 48 LA 498 (Lovell, 1967) (taking coins from pay telephone), and *Memphis Light, Gas and Water Div.*, 77-1 ARB ¶8202 (Flannagan, 1977) (reconnecting personal utility service without authorization), the grievant's defense that other employees had been penalized less severely for the same misconduct failed because the prior incidents had taken place before the employer issued a notice that future violations would lead to discharge.

[36]*Goslin-Birmingham, Inc.*, 69-1 ARB ¶8406 (King, 1969). See also *Sanyo Mfg. Corp.*, 85 LA 207 (Kelliher, 1985), where written warnings given to employees who returned late from their breaks were approved, despite a pattern of past inconsistent enforcement, since management had twice advised employees that plant rules would be strictly enforced.

[37]For discussion of changed working conditions, past practice, and management's right to make new work rules in the context of reasonable rules, see Ch. 2, pp. 91–99.

ployer to do something that it ought to have done with respect to misconduct. "Change in working conditions," in contrast, implies that the employer is trying to take away something to which employees have acquired a legitimate right over time.

The change-in-working-conditions argument is generally rejected when made in a lax-enforcement context, as in the case where the employer put into effect a new rule prohibiting employees from bringing into the work area soft drinks in cans and other disposable containers. The arbitrator held that "[t]he previous permission to bring soft drink containers to the work area must be regarded not as a condition of employment but as a matter which management saw fit to tolerate under the conditions of the old plant but found impractical and had the right to change under conditions in the new plant."[38]

The distinction between tightening up on enforcement of the rules and changing a condition of employment was summed up as follows by Arbitrator Raymond Roberts:

> When management exercises its prerogative to promulgate a particular work rule, it does not express a mutual assent that adherence to that particular work rule or practice is to become binding in the sense of the binding past practice which is a condition of employment. Instead, management evidences thereby an expression of its retention of its right to make reasonable work rules and to change and modify them from time to time as conditions and reasonable business objectives require.

> Accordingly, a practice which is permitted by a particular work rule or which is allowed to grow up in the absence of a work rule is a present manner of doing things which management retains the right to change. It does not evidence assent to a binding past practice which is a condition of employment. The significance of management's exercise of its work rule promulgation authority,

---

[38]*Kast Metals Corp.*, 70 LA 278 (Roberts, 1978). Arbitrator McCoy, in *Esso Standard Oil Co.*, 16 LA 73, 74 (1951) (right to change work schedule):

The mere failure of the Company, over a long period of time, to exercise a legitimate function of management, is not a surrender of the right to start exercising that right. If a company had never, in 15 years under 15 contracts, disciplined an employee for tardiness, could it thereby be contended that the company could not decide to institute a reasonable system of penalties for tardiness? Mere nonuse of a right does not entail loss of it.

See also *Nabisco Brands, Inc.*, 86-1 ARB ¶8198 (Allen, 1986), in which it was held that a 20-year practice of exceeding break allowances did not prevent the employer from enforcing contractual limits, since the employer from time to time had sought to stop the abuse through warnings and the recent imposition of discipline. However, in recognition of past laxity, the arbitrator ordered that prior disciplinary action be rescinded.

or its permissiveness in such circumstances, is not an assent to a binding practice but only an assent that management presently approves that manner of doing things.[39]

But let's say the company seeks to revitalize a grooming rule that has fallen into disuse. Say it has tolerated beards but now decides to do so no longer. Can it reassert the rule and enforce it? The union may argue that the employees have acquired a "benefit" by the company's failure to enforce the no-beard rule and that the employer may not now cancel it. Is that argument valid?

An arbitrator is likely to say no. He would probably find no binding past practice—that, in the words of one,

> there is no cause to find that management has waived its right to revitalize the disputed rule .... [I]t is doubtful that the Company's actions in allowing beards in the past may properly be characterized as a "benefit" or "past practice," as suggested by the Union. ... Rather, the facts must be seen for what they are; management has been undeniably lax in enforcing an existing rule. One may justifiably require that the employees receive adequate notice as to its prospective application. ... But there is no reason to conclude, assuming an otherwise valid rule, that management has forever foregone its right to enforce this aspect of the grooming policy.[40]

But suppose the arbitrator found there was indeed an established past practice. Would the employer still have been precluded from resurrecting its prohibition on the wearing of beards? This arbitrator still said no. He noted that circumstances

---

[39]*Kast Metals Corp.*, *supra* note 38, at 281. To similar effect, see *Ford Motor Co.*, 19 LA 237, 241-42 (Shulman, 1952) (refusal of work assignment):

> But there are other practices which are not the result of joint determination at all. They may be mere happenstance, that is, methods that develop without design or deliberation. Or they may be choices by Management in the exercise of managerial discretion as to the convenient methods at the time. In such cases there is no thought or obligation or commitment to the future. Such practices are merely present ways, not prescribed ways, of doing things. The relevant item of significance is not the nature of the particular method, but the managerial freedom with respect to it. Being the product of the managerial determination in its permitted discretion, such practices are, in the absence of contractual provision to the contrary, subject to change in the same discretion.

The abuse of a benefit has also been held to justify management's making new rules or enforcing old ones; see cases cited in Ch. 2, p. 96.

[40]*Hughes Air Corp.*, 72 LA 588, 589 (Bloch, 1979), citing *Great Atl. and Pac. Tea Co.*, 57 LA 789 (Casselman, 1971), *San Diego Gas and Elec.*, 57 LA 821 (Leonard, 1971), and *City of E. Detroit*, 61 LA 485 (Kelman, 1973), all grooming rule cases.

had changed—the employer had changed its uniforms and its slogan to present a more conservative image to the public—and that it had a right to abandon the prior practice. For additional support for the proposition that a rule may be revitalized in the face of contrary past practice, one need only turn to Arbitrator Mittenthal.

> One must consider, too, the *underlying circumstances* which give a practice its true dimensions. A practice is no broader than the circumstances out of which it has arisen, although its scope can always be enlarged in the day-to-day administration of the agreement. No meaningful description can be made without mention of these circumstances. For instance, a work assignment practice which develops on the afternoon and night shifts and which is responsive to the peculiar needs of night work cannot be automatically extended to the day shift. The point is that every practice must be carefully related to its origin and purpose.[41]

Past Practice and the Single Supervisor

Two separate but related questions that come up from time to time are these: Can a single supervisor establish a binding past practice? Can a single past event make a binding past practice? The answer to both questions: Yes, depending on the circumstances.

> **EXAMPLE:** The employer appeared to have an open-and-shut case that an employee had been drinking and became intoxicated on the job. He admitted having drunk some of the two quarts of wine and a six pack of beer that he had purchased during his lunch hour, and a doctor's examination established that he was under the influence. The employer discharged him, pointing to the no-alcohol rule written into the most recent contract as proof of the seriousness of its effort to stamp out on-the-job drinking. The employee claimed, however, not only that his fellow employees had been drinking regularly on the job but that the foreman had imbibed right along with the crew and shared some of the beer and wine on the day in question. The foreman admitted this was true.

Unquestionably, the arbitrator found, the contract language prohibiting drinking gave clear and unambiguous notice

---

[41]*Id.* at 589, quoting R. Mittenthal, *Past Practice and Administration of Bargaining Agreements*, ARBITRATION AND PUBLIC POLICY 33, (Proceedings of the 14th Annual Meeting, National Academy of Arbitrators 1961) (emphasis in original).

to employees that management did not condone drinking. Nevertheless, the foreman's drinking along with the employees could not be overlooked. What the employee did was wrong, but his infraction was excused because he and others in effect had the foreman's blessing. "Notwithstanding the fact that the foreman was guilty of the most wrongful violation of his duty and responsibility as a Company supervisor, the Company is bound by his conduct in supervising Grievant and the other employees involved." The employer was therefore held responsible for establishing the practice at least for this employee and this grievance.[42]

Whether a single event can amount to a binding past practice is also a matter of context. Such a circumstance occurred when the employer prohibited the use of the same company signs in a current stoppage that had been used by the union during a previous wildcat strike without penalty. No notice prohibiting the use of the signs for that purpose had been issued in the interim. The only relevant history thus was the prior event, so that event was the controlling past practice for the current event.[43]

Safety Rules: Sometimes an Exception

The customary view on inconsistent enforcement of safety rules is that "[w]here safety rules have not been vigorously enforced and where repeated breaches of these rules have been condoned or ignored by foremen or other first level management, even limited suspensions have been mitigated."[44] Indeed,

---

[42]*Luck Mining Co.*, 69-1 ARB ¶8050 (Hayes, 1968). Other cases in which a single supervisor was held to have created a binding past practice include *Labor Standards Ass'n, Gimbel Bros.*, 61-3 ARB ¶8899 (Di Leone, 1961) (drinking on job); *Misco Precision Casting Co.*, 40 LA 87 (Dworkin, 1962) (card playing); *William Feather Co.*, 68 LA 13 (Shanker, 1977) (moonlighting, conflict of interest).

[43]*Public Tel. and Tel. Co.*, 69-2 ARB ¶8537 (Koven, 1969). Other "single event" cases include *Lucky Stores, Inc.*, 42 LA 837, 840 (Koven, 1964) (insubordination): "More important, however, is that such picture taking by management though it occurred only once, provides some allowance for the confusion which apparently was generated in the grievant's mind on the right to take photographs"; *Northwest Eng'g Co.*, 72 LA 486 (Grabb, 1979) (grievant allowed to go on working without safety glasses).

[44]*Eberle Tanning Co.*, 78-2 ARB ¶8316, 4513 (Dean, 1978) (negligence, carelessness). See also *Alan Wood Steel Co.*, 3 LA 557, 559 (Brandschain, 1946): "Thus, we have a situation where the repeated breach of the rule, if it existed, established a practice, which the workers may have been justified in believing was proper because of the failure of the employer to enforce the rule."

management may itself become partly responsible for any harm that is traceable to its lax enforcement.[45]

> *Arbitrator Dean:* The rationale for this past practice proposition is twofold. First, an employee cannot be held to a certain safety standard if he entertains doubts as to the true meaning or importance of the safety rule because of lax enforcement and condonation of unsafe activity. Second, management cannot impose severe punishment on an employee where it is partly responsible for the safety violation . . . since to do so would force the employee to shoulder all the guilt himself.[46]

But there is a second view. That view urges that consistent past enforcement of rules established for the purpose of protecting employees' health and safety and not for disciplinary purposes is not required. This puts safety rules in a special category that is insulated from the defense of inconsistent enforcement. "If a safety and health rule is reasonable, and as long as inconsistencies in rule application did not work to entrap a worker, . . . standards for rule review usually applied in discipline cases do not strictly apply."[47]

Can Rule Enforcement Be Too Consistent?

Some cases have emphasized that consistency and uniform enforcement of rules, if pushed too far, are bound to result in application of the rules (even admittedly reasonable rules) too mechanically and inflexibly.

> **EXAMPLE:** A punch press operator is caught in the locker room by his foreman with a bottle of gin in his hand. He has been previously warned about drinking on the job, and the employer fires him. The union produces evidence that employees in the shipping department have been caught drinking on the job and have been sent home or suspended instead of being discharged.

On this one the arbitrator went along with the company. "There remains one important aspect raised by the Union—lack of uniformity of disciplinary punishment within the plant for alcohol related offenses. . . . The existence of exceptions

---

[45]*Allis Chalmers Mfg. Co.*, 8 LA 177 (Kelliher, 1947); *Coleman Co.*, 54 LA 281 (Springfield, 1970); *McCormick & Baxter Creosoting Co.*, 55 LA 1274 (Jacobs, 1971).

[46]*Eberle Tanning Co.*, supra note 44, at 4514.

[47]*J. R. Simplot Co.*, 77-1 ARB ¶8272, 4178 (Conant, 1977) (plant rule prohibiting facial hair).

does not move me to throw out the rule. The Company's election to recognize individual or unusual circumstances when assessing penalties is no argument that [the grievant] has been treated unfairly." The arbitrator then went on to observe:

> We worship consistency and uniformity of discipline to create predictability and to prevent the intrusion of prejudice and caprice into the process. . . . [A]n inflexible, mechanical application even of reasonable and negotiated rules and penalties would be unacceptable to the Union as well as the Company beyond the shortest of operating periods.

In this case, what the union's argument failed to take into account was that the punch press operator's job was one of the most dangerous in the industry, and even a minor error or momentary lapse of attention could result in serious injury to the operator himself or to a coworker. Since the operator's use of alcohol posed significantly greater hazards than alcohol use by shipping employees, then, penalizing the former more harshly was reasonable.[48]

How, then, can an employer individualize discipline and at the same time achieve uniformity? Here is the recipe provided by Arbitrator Jonathan Dworkin:

---

[48]*Jehl Cooperage Co.*, 75 LA 901, 903 (Odom, 1980). To the same effect, Arbitrator Kates in *Abex Corp.*, 47 LA 441, 443 (1966) (doctor's clearance required for return to work):

> I do not doubt that reasonable exceptions resulting from special circumstances would not necessarily taint the enforceability of a rule or prove wrongful discrimination. But the propriety of particular exceptions in individual cases ought to be clearly established, and the extent or variety of such exceptions ought not to be such as to show wrongful discrimination.

Again, Arbitrator Stouffer in *American Hoist & Derrick Co.*, 53 LA 45, 58 (1969) (strike in violation of contract):

> The Union argues that enforcement of rules and assessment of discipline must be exercised in a consistent manner. Stated differently, all employees who engage in the same type of misconduct must be treated essentially the same unless reasonable basis exists for variation in the assessment of punishment. . . . [W]hile absolute consistency has been said to be an impossibility, that fact should not excuse random and completely inconsistent disciplinary practice. However, where reasonable basis for variations in penalties assessed do exist, they will be permitted.

See also *Bethlehem Steel Co.*, 29 LA 635 (Seward, 1957) (strike activity) (different penalties for same offense permissible if reasons for making distinctions are "sound and just"); *Iowa Pub. Serv. Co.*, 78-1 ARB ¶8134 (Sinicropi, 1978) (selective discipline of strikers acceptable if selection not capricious); *Freeman United Coal Co.*, 84-1 ARB ¶8266 (Roberts, 1984) (right to punish drinking on duty not lost by reason of past leniency). The fact that one employee "confesses" misconduct and implicates another, however, has been held not to justify significantly different penalties; see *Browning-Ferris Indus. of Ohio, Inc.*, 77 LA 289 (Shanker, 1981) (drinking on duty).

The answer lies in recognizing enforcement as a two-step process. To be evenhanded, an employer must avoid arbitrarily singling out some violators, and prohibited conduct is to be consistently answered. An employer cannot legitimately select an individual or a group for discipline to set an example for the rest of the workforce; it cannot create scapegoats.

The second step of the process occurs once it is established that an employee's misconduct merits disciplinary response. At that point, the employer must assess the person, his/her service record, and other mitigating (or exacerbating) elements.[49]

The Comparability Issue

For a defense of inconsistent enforcement to be successful, the misconduct for which the grievant was disciplined must be similar to the misconduct he or she claims was winked at in the past or is being overlooked now. For example, in a case where the grievant was discharged for attempting to steal a large quantity of scrap metal, his claim that other employees had taken pieces of cable and other scrap without being disciplined failed as an inconsistent enforcement defense. The employer may have acquiesced in a certain amount of "pilfering," the arbitrator commented, but it never had let any employee get away with theft on the scale attempted by the grievant.[50]

Another case in which superficially similar misconduct was found not comparable to earlier, tolerated errors was that of a television station employee who mistakenly loaded the first reel of Part 5 of a miniseries instead of Part 2, and was suspended for two days as a result. The union argued that other employees had made similar errors and had not been disciplined. Finding no disparate treatment, the arbitrator pointed out that the grievant's error occurred during prime time and was evident to millions of viewers; the earlier errors were not so noticeable and

---

[49]*Goodyear Tire & Rubber Co.*, 86-1 ARB ¶8230, 3988 (1986) (excessive break time).

[50]*U.S. Steel Corp.*, 48 LA 1114 (Mittenthal, 1967). See also *Worthington Corp.*, 47 LA 1170) (Livengood, 1966) (grievant's absentee record far worse than those of employees treated more leniently); *White Pine Copper Co.*, 63-2 ARB ¶8548 (Larkin, 1963) (alcohol-related misconduct compounded by insubordination); *Louisville Cooperage Co.*, 70-2 ARB ¶8652 (Volz, 1970) (different degrees of participation in the offense must be recognized); *Cadillac Plastic & Chem. Co.*, 58 LA 812 (Kates, 1972) (grievant's horseplay more serious in that it was intentional and accompanied by profanity); *Citizens Gas & Coke Util.*, 84-1 ARB ¶8258 (Kates, 1984) (three of five employees who falsely claimed unemployment benefits entitled to more lenient treatment because they made restitution); *Group W Cable of Chicago*, 87-2 ARB ¶8447 (McAlpin, 1987) (sleeping on job more serious where it presents danger to safety of employee or to company equipment).

were not on prime time, when an operator may properly be held to a duty of greater care.[51]

Drug problems and consequent disciplinary action frequently give rise to charges of disparate treatment. It may be claimed on behalf of a grievant discharged for drug use, for example, that other employees have been offered rehabilitation, and this may indeed be viewed as evidence of disparate treatment.[52] Or it may be argued that the possession of drugs is a less serious offense than using them on company property. In a case involving a rule which stated that reporting to work under the influence of or possessing or using alcohol or drugs on company property was "non-excusable," Arbitrator Nicholas held that the employer must prove two things to justify penalizing use more severely than mere possession: (1) that use of drugs within the plant represents a greater risk to employees' health and safety than mere possession; and (2) that the charged employee did, in fact, use drugs in the plant. Finding the employer's proof lacking on both counts, he set aside the discharge of an employee charged with smoking marijuana on company property where another employee had merely been reprimanded for selling "speed pills" within the plant.[53]

Another offense that is highly likely to spark charges of disparate treatment is that of fighting. If one of two employees who engage in fisticuffs on company property is discharged whereas the other is not, the dischargee is almost sure to lodge

---

[51]*WGN Continental Broadcasting Co.*, 88-2 ARB ¶8500 (Kossoff, 1988).

[52]As in *Navistar Int'l Corp.*, 88 LA 179 (Archer, 1986), where the employee was found to have suffered disparate treatment in being discharged for reporting to work under the influence of alcohol since employees represented by a different union had consistently been given an opportunity for rehabilitation and reinstatement. See also *Boise Cascade Corp.*, 90 LA 791 (Nicholas, 1988). In *Kansas City Cold Storage*, 94 LA 777 (Madden, 1990), on the other hand, the arbitrator upheld the denial of sick pay to an admitted cocaine addict who was hospitalized in a drug-treatment program, even though the employer had granted sick leave for absences in connection with alcohol-abuse treatment.

[53]*Owens-Corning Fiberglas Corp.*, 86 LA 1026 (1986). In *Standard Oil Co.*, 89 LA 1155 (Feldman, 1987), the arbitrator found no disparate treatment in the discharge of an employee who had been discharged after pleading no contest to charges of drug trafficking, even though the employer had reinstated several other employees convicted of felonies, where the employer regarded the other felonies as less serious and it had never reinstated a drug trafficker. See also *Potomac Elec. Power Co.*, 88 LA 290 (Feigenbaum, 1986), where the discharge of a grievant after charges of possession of marijuana on company property were dropped was held not to be disparate treatment, even though a fellow employee had not been discharged when charges of theft were similarly disposed of. The company believed the coworker innocent, the arbitrator noted, but had no such belief in the case of the grievant.

a claim of disparate treatment. One arbitrator has held flatly, however, that the concept of disparate treatment is not applicable to cases of fighting. Arbitrators, he said, customarily treat such cases on the basis of relative culpability.[54] This arbitrator's approach is illustrated by a case in which the employer discharged two employees who engaged in horseplay and fighting. The arbitrator upheld the discharge of one because he ignored a management order to "stay put" and struck the second employee with sufficient force to cause injuries requiring medical treatment. The discharge of the second employee was held not justified, however, although he initiated the horseplay, because he took no further aggressive action and obeyed the managerial order.[55]

Individual Circumstances

Finally, in deciding what is the appropriate penalty for one employee compared to another, the employer may be expected to take into account an employee's past record[56] as well as his prospects for future improvement.

---

[54]*General Metals Prods. Co.*, 87-2 ARB ¶8503 (Canestraight, 1987).

[55]*Valentec-Kisco Co.*, 89-1 ARB ¶8059 (Canestraight, 1988). As a corollary, many cases stand for the proposition that employees who are equally guilty in a fighting incident should receive equal penalties; see, e.g., *Stedman Mach. Co.*, 85 LA 631 (Keenan, 1985). In *General Mills, Inc.*, 92 LA 969 (Dworkin, 1989), the arbitrator ruled that, given a policy of discharging only the aggressor in a fight, it was improper for the employer to discharge both participants where it could not determine which was the aggressor. He opted instead for a 30-day suspension. The basis for the decision, however, was not disparate treatment but lack of just cause. See also *Farmbest, Inc.*, 44 LA 609 (Karlins, 1965).

[56]E.g., *City of Auburn*, 72 LA 626 (Silver, 1979), where prior infractions justified an officer's 15-day suspension for leaving his police car unattended, even though officers with him received only two- or three-day suspensions, since their records were clean. To similar effect, see *Major Safe Co.*, 76-2 ARB ¶8642 (Weiss, 1976) (punching out before lunch break):

> There is no requirement—in criminal law or in labor law—that a second offender must be treated in the same manner as a first offender. . . . As a matter of fact, the entire concept of progressive discipline is based on increasing the severity of the penalty for the employee who continues to violate his responsibilities toward his employer.

See also *Ocean Spray Cranberries, Inc.*, 68-1 ARB ¶8252 (Sembower, 1968) (grievant properly discharged for intoxication, while drinking companion only suspended, where grievant had recently been disciplined for drinking); *Rohr Industries, Inc.*, 88 LA 703 (Ross, 1987) (intoxication) (27 years' seniority and agreement to enter rehabilitation program justified differential treatment). In *City of Detroit*, 88-2 ARB ¶8340 (Brown, 1988), the proposition that seniority is a mitigating factor was turned on its head when a rookie officer claimed that she should have been punished less severely than her partner, a 10-year veteran, because the latter bore greater responsibility as the senior officer for a failure to follow proper procedures. The arbitrator rejected this claim,

Employers are not required to apply identical disciplinary measures for like offenses. The employer may properly consider whether more lenient discipline may serve the desired purpose of correction so that the employment relationship may be salvaged. The Union indeed, would be the last to argue that the Company ought to fire everybody who commits a serious act of misconduct.[57]

As Arbitrator Kesselman has pointed out, "each employee is unique and what may help in one case may not help in another."[58]

Is the fact that an employee is an alcoholic a "special circumstance" that ought to be given consideration in fixing his or her penalty for violating a rule? In a case involving an airline pilot who was discharged for violating a rule forbidding the use of alcohol within 24 hours of a flight, Arbitrator Nicholau held that it is. It was argued that consideration of the pilot's alcoholism would establish a dual standard and that nonalcoholic rule-breakers could thereafter complain of disparate treatment. The arbitrator responded that a wide variety of factors may be taken into account in considering reinstatement and that a diagnosed alcoholic is clearly in a recognized, distinguishing medical category. This pilot, he noted, had an unblemished 16-year record, his conduct was an unavoidable consequence of alcoholism, he had exhibited a consistent pattern of recovery during the two years following his discharge, and other alcoholic pilots had been given opportunities to requalify for flying. Reinstatement (without back pay) was ordered at such time as the pilot was certified by federal authorities as qualified to resume flying.[59]

holding that both officers bore equal responsibility, and equal penalties were appropriate.

[57]*Baker Marine Corp.*, 77 LA 721, 725 (Marlatt, 1981) (marijuana). See also *National Hose Co.*, 73 LA 1048, 1049 (Robins, 1979) (refusal of overtime):

The Arbitrator does not find that the failure of a Company to apply identical disciplinary action to all employees . . . can be considered to be prohibited disparate treatment. . . . The Union talks of inequitable treatment, but nothing could be more inequitable than to ignore an employee's length of service, past record with the employer or prior disciplinary record.

In *Pacific Bell*, 87-2 ARB ¶8582 (Oestreich, 1987), the arbitrator cited language problems as a factor in mitigation of allegedly dishonest acts committed by key punch operators. Because of their difficulty with the English language and cultural adaptation, he said, they deserved the benefit of the doubt as to whether they fully understood company policy.

[58]*Sperry Rand Corp.*, 70-1 ARB ¶8149, 3521 (1969) (absenteeism).

[59]*Northwest Airlines*, 89 LA 943 (1984). The arbitrator's award was vacated by the U.S. District Court for the District of Columbia (633 F.Supp. 779, 122 LRRM 2311), but reinstated by the U.S. Court of Appeals for the District of Columbia, which ruled

On the other hand, a union's argument in another case that the employer knew of the grievant's alcoholism and should have forced treatment upon him before his absenteeism was out of hand got nowhere with the arbitrator. The employer was not obligated to impose treatment, and since the employee did not seek it, his discharge was sustained. Two employees who were not discharged for similar misconduct *did* seek treatment, so the arbitrator rejected the claim of disparate treatment.[60]

Proving Inconsistent Enforcement

Obviously a binding past practice cannot be based on conduct that is contrary to the company's instructions and outside the company's knowledge.[61] And all would agree that "[t]here is a vast chasm between surmise, guess, and suspicion, and factual knowledge thereof."[62] But "a practice, to constitute a binding 'local working condition,' need not be accompanied by *express* consent or agreement on the part of Supervision. . . . [I]n the case of a practice so long continued and so widespread, Supervision's awareness—even if not directly proved—must reasonably be presumed."[63]

Yet, as Arbitrator Mittenthal has observed, "[t]o allege the existence of a practice is one thing; to prove it quite another."[64]

---

that the award was not contrary to public policy (808 F.2d 76, 124 LRRM 2300 (1987)). The U.S. Supreme Court declined to review the appeals court's decision (128 LRRM 2296 (1988)).

[60]*Lily-Tulip, Inc.*, 87-2 ARB ¶8434 (Garnholtz, 1987). In *Regional Transp. Auth.*, 94 LA 489 (Fullmer, 1990), a driver who was subjected to a mandatory postaccident drug test was found to have been the victim of disparate treatment, where three other drivers who had been involved in accidents had not been subjected to such testing. Accordingly, the arbitrator said, the driver's discharge for testing positive for cocaine was without just cause, even though the driver acknowledged using cocaine off duty.

[61]*Allied Chem. Corp.*, 68-1 ARB ¶8020 (Feinberg, 1967) (length of off-premises lunch break).

[62]*Northwest Airlines, Inc.*, 1975 ARB ¶8207 (Turkus, 1975) (drinking within 24 hours of flight time).

[63]*Bethlehem Steel Co.*, 33 LA 374, 375-76 (Valtin, 1959) (length of lunch period). See also *Eberle Tanning Co.*, 78-2 ARB ¶8316, 4514 (Dean, 1978) (negligence, carelessness): "[W]here, as here, supervisory personnel had knowledge of safety violations and even committed violations themselves, management will be presumed to have knowledge of these acts and to have participated in the safety violations."

[64]R. Mittenthal, *Past Practice and Administration of Bargaining Agreements*, ARBITRATION AND PUBLIC POLICY 35 (Proceedings of the 14th Annual Meeting, National Academy of Arbitrators 1961). On the burden of proof falling upon the party claiming a past practice, see F. ELKOURI & E. A. ELKOURI, HOW ARBITRATION WORKS 439 (4th ed. 1985).

In order to prove the existence of a practice, it must be demonstrated that in fact certain kinds of activities have been going on. Where drinking is in question, for example, to prove inconsistent enforcement the union must show that the company knew that drinking was prevalent in the plant and did nothing to stop or penalize the employees involved, despite the existence of a no-drinking rule. In other words, it must be shown that prohibited activity took place with the company's "permission," even if that permission was given not explicitly but only by management's closing its eyes. An example of such permission is provided by a case where the foreman in charge of the night shift was fully aware that the grievants indulged in card playing during their rest period and occasionally played a hand himself.[65]

But what if company officials swear up and down that they knew of no drinking incidents and the union cannot show that any supervisor knew of or condoned drinking? Suppose further that the union *can* prove that drinking has been going on to such an extent that it is hard to believe that management did not know. The "should have known" test is then applicable. When there is clear evidence of widespread violation of a rule, it is reasonable to conclude that the employer "should have known" or "must have known" what was going on. In other words, the employer can be said to have "constructive knowledge" of the practice in question.[66]

---

[65]*Misco Precision Casting Co.*, 40 LA 87 (Dworkin, 1962). See also *U.S. Borax and Chem. Corp.*, 70-1 ARB ¶8435, 4425 (Miller, 1970) (insubordination): "[T]he Company also failed to offer adequate proof that members of management had not known men were reading unauthorized material and winked at it." Lax-enforcement defenses failed, however, in *Allied Maintenance Co.*, 12 LA 350 (Feinberg, 1949), where the company denied tolerating alcohol at any time and union witnesses refused to name supervisors who they claimed had supplied drinks to them; and in *Sealright Co.*, 72-1 ARB ¶8349 (Goetz, 1972), where supervisors were unaware that employees other than the grievant had refused to wear hair nets.

[66]"Constructive knowledge" can also be imposed upon the union and/or the grievant, as in *Baer Bros.*, 16 LA 822, 824 (Donnelly, 1951) (applicability of shift premiums to watchmen): "The claim of the Union that it did not know that the Company was not paying the shift bonus is not strongly persuasive. . . . [I]n the absence of any protest over this long period of time it must be presumed that both the Union and the Company considered that the provisons of the Agreement were being carried out." See also *Friden, Inc.*, 52 LA 448, 449 (Koven, 1969) (unsatisfactory work record) ("rules were posted in a conspicuous place and . . . [the grievant] is charged with constructive knowledge"); *Coleman Co.*, 54 LA 281 (Springfield, 1970) (placing fire bomb on company premises); *Memphis Light, Gas and Water Div.*, 77-1 ARB ¶8202, 3886 (Flannagan, 1977) (unauthorized reconnection of utility services) ("knowledge is imputed to an employee when he reasonably should know of the rule").

EXAMPLE: The grievant's defense for being drunk on the job was that other employees had done the same. The union could not prove that any supervisor ever saw employees drinking. But the employer admitted that janitors often found empty liquor bottles in the trash.

Under these circumstances, could the employer be charged with knowledge of the extent to which drinking was taking place in the plant? Yes, said the arbitrator, concurring (reluctantly) with the union that

> the rule against drinking had not, prior to [the grievant's] termination, been enforced with that degree of effectiveness and consistency which might fairly have been regarded as a clear indication to Grievant, or any other employee, that one more drinking episode would warrant discharge.

Moreover, since the company had clear evidence of misconduct (such as the empty bottles in the trash) and made no investigation as to who was drinking when, where, and under what circumstances, the conclusion follows that in effect the company condoned the drinking.[67]

II. Arbitration and Title VII of Civil Rights Act

Impact of Title VII on Arbitration

A Collision Course

After Title VII of the Civil Rights Act was passed by Congress in 1964, many authorities expressed concern that the new legislation might "place employment discrimination law on a collision course with some of the basic principles of the labor legislation which preceded it."[68] Under the Taft-Hartley Act of 1947, and subsequently under the U.S. Supreme Court's celebrated *Steelworkers Trilogy*, national labor policy strongly endorsed the private settlement of employment disputes through the grievance machinery of the collective bargaining agreement. After Title VII, however, an employee who believed himself to be the victim of prohibited discrimination could pursue his claim

---

[67]*Ward Furniture Mfg. Co.*, 63-2 ARB ¶8826, 5662 (Boles, 1963).
[68]W. B. Gould, *Judicial Review of Employment Discrimination Arbitrations*, LABOR ARBITRATION AT THE QUARTER-CENTURY MARK 114-15 (Proceedings of the 25th Annual Meeting, National Academy of Arbitrators 1973).

through the machinery of the Equal Employment Opportunity Commission (EEOC) and the courts as well as through the contract grievance procedure and arbitration.

As a result, it was widely asked whether arbitration could remain a viable forum for resolving employment discrimination claims. Many labor relations experts argued that the courts offered employees a better chance for an adequate hearing because arbitration lacks the elaborate procedural safeguards and discovery procedures that may be required in a complex discrimination case.

Certain "institutional" drawbacks of arbitration as a method of deciding discrimination cases were also pointed out. An individual employee may be unable to obtain adequate representation if his union has itself been guilty of discriminatory practices and policies (the problem of "fair representation"). And even if it is not deliberately racist or sexist, the union may have problems in pressing the Title VII rights of an individual employee if those rights are in conflict with the interests of a majority of union members. The most common example is when a seniority system comes into collision with an affirmative action program that favors the advancement of minority group members or women.

Critics contended further that many arbitrators lack the necessary expertise in the difficult legal issues that discrimination may present, especially in areas where the law itself is unsettled. Sexual harassment and some other types of sex discrimination cases are frequently given as examples.

The Impact of *Alexander v. Gardner-Denver Co.*

In the years immediately following the passage of Title VII, the courts were divided on the question of whether an employee who took a discrimination case to arbitration and lost had the right to take another crack at the employer by filing suit under Title VII. That question was finally settled when the Supreme Court issued its landmark decision in the case of *Alexander v. Gardner-Denver Co.*[69]

The facts in *Gardner-Denver* were simple. Complainant Alexander, a black, was discharged for allegedly producing too much waste and filed a grievance. At the arbitration hearing

---

[69]415 U.S. 36, 7 FEP Cases 81 (1974). The text of the decision is reprinted in B. L. SCHLEI & P. GROSSMAN, EMPLOYMENT DISCRIMINATION LAW 1075–83 (2d ed. 1983).

Alexander contended for the first time that his race was the real reason for his discharge and that he did not trust the union to press his case. The arbitrator found no racial basis for the discharge and concluded that it was for proper cause.

While his grievance was being processed, Alexander filed a claim with the EEOC under Title VII. Some time after the arbitrator issued his decision, the EEOC, too, found that there was no basis for the discrimination charge. Nevertheless, Alexander went on to file suit in district court. Ruling against Alexander, both the district court and the court of appeals relied on the fact that his racial discrimination claim had already been raised and rejected in arbitration. In taking his claim to arbitration, they ruled, he had made a final and binding election of remedies and was therefore precluded from suing the company under Title VII.

The U.S. Supreme Court disagreed. The Court took the position that an employee's rights as an individual under Title VII are separate and distinct from his collective rights under the contract and that an individual's rights may not be adequately protected under collective processes where discrimination is charged. For that reason the Court ruled that submission of a grievance to arbitration under a nondiscrimination clause is not a binding waiver of subsequent court action under the election-of-remedies doctrine. An employee is entitled to a trial *de novo* under Title VII, should he fail to prevail in arbitration—that is, he is entitled to a "second bite at the apple."

The Court's decision in *Gardner-Denver* set off a new wave of concern that arbitration was finished as far as discrimination cases went. It was predicted that employers would be discouraged from arbitrating discrimination grievances, knowing that they might have to start again from the beginning if the grievant lost his case. However, these predictions have not been borne out by events. Few attempts have been made to bar grievances involving discrimination; on the contrary, there has been a trend for employers and unions to write stronger contract language on discrimination in the wake of *Gardner-Denver*. In many instances the parties have contractually committed themselves to abide by the intent of Title VII and other federal and state laws on discrimination.

There has also been a tendency to bring arbitration proceedings closer to court proceedings in discrimination cases. Favorable response has been given to suggestions that the arbitrator and parties place the same kind of emphasis on procedural safeguards that a litigant could expect in court—that transcripts be taken, that arbitrators become more familiar with Title VII case law in order to make their decisions as consistent with court rulings as reasonably possible, and that the grievant be represented by his or her own counsel.

If arbitration proceedings are closer to court proceedings, the reasoning runs, the arbitrator's decision will be more likely to be accepted as final, since the grievant will have less reason to expect a different result from a suit under Title VII if the arbitrator uses the same standards as a court would apply. Moreover, if the grievant should choose to take his "second bite" in court, the court would be more likely to take the arbitrator's finding into account, in accordance with the much-discussed footnote 21 to the *Gardner-Denver* decision, wherein the Court set forth several conditions under which an arbitrator's decision might properly be given "great weight."[70]

That arbitrators and judges need not end up far apart, especially in areas like discharge and discipline where law and contract are not normally in conflict, is illustrated by the fate of the *Gardner-Denver* case itself. Following the Supreme Court's ruling, complainant Alexander took the merits of his discharge to court. The conclusion was the same as the arbitrator's. The evidence established that Alexander had been producing more waste than other employees, as the employer claimed, so that a proper basis for discharge was present.[71]

---

[70]Footnote 21:

> Relevant factors include the existence of provisions in the collective bargaining agreement that conform substantially with Title VII, the degree of procedural fairness in the arbitral forum, adequacy of the record with respect to the issue of discrimination, and the special competence of particular arbitrators. Where an arbitral determination gives full consideration to an employee's Title VII rights, a court may properly accord it great weight. This is especially true where the issue is solely one of fact, specifically addressed by the parties and decided by the arbitrator on the basis of an adequate record.

However, the Court went on to make clear that it did not intend in footnote 21 to be letting a deferral rule in by the back door. "But courts should be ever mindful that Congress, in enacting Title VII, thought it necessary to provide a judicial forum for the ultimate resolution of discriminatory employment claims. It is the duty of courts to assure the full availability of this forum."

[71]For a survey of the views of labor lawyers on the impact of *Gardner-Denver* on the arbitration of discrimination grievances, see M. M. Hoyman & L. E. Stallworth, *Arbitrating Discrimination Grievances in the Wake of Gardner-Denver*, 106:2 MONTHLY LAB. REV. 3–10 (1983). See also L. D. Clark & B. A. Bush, *Arbitration of Employment Discrimination Claims: A Need for Statutory Reform*, 11 THURGOOD MARSHALL L. REV. 47–64 (1985); W. A. Carmell & P. A. Westerkamp, *Arbitration of EEO Claims a Decade After Gardner-*

Title VII Requirements Versus Just Cause Requirements

Just Cause and Title VII Compared

Discipline and discharge is one area in which the goals of Title VII and the goals of collective bargaining are usually not in conflict. For that reason, neither Title VII nor *Gardner-Denver* had as unsettling an effect upon disciplinary disputes as it did, for example, in the area of seniority, where contractually established lines of job preferment were often found by the courts to perpetuate discrimination by reason of race or sex or both.

Just cause, in fact, goes beyond the requirements of Title VII in the sense that it offers protection against disparate treatment to all employees, not just to members of the protected groups that Title VII covers. The principles upon which disciplinary cases were decided in arbitration remained fundamentally the same, with the notable exception of reasonable accommodation to an employee's religious practices.

Title VII affected discipline cases most conspicuously by placing them in a new and more highly charged context. Allegations such as "They got down on me because I'm black," or "They just don't want women in this plant," began to play a more prominent part in grievances. Such allegations assumed new meaning for employers as well as employees in the Title VII era, since they potentially represented charges of violation of federal law as well as of the collective bargaining agreement.[72]

One respect in which arbitration and court proceedings differ has to do with what must be proved and who must do the proving.

In court, Title VII has been interpreted to hold that an

Denver, 12:1 EMPLOYEE REL. L.J. 80–97 (1986); D. R. Willig, *Arbitration of Discrimination Grievances: Arbitral and Judicial Competence Compared*, ARBITRATION 1986: CURRENT AND EXPANDING ROLES 101–20 (Proceedings of the 39th Annual Meeting, National Academy of Arbitrators 1987).

[72]As Arbitrator J. Earl Williams commented in *Gulf States Utils. Co.*, 62 LA 1061, 1062 (1974) (job qualifications):

> While it has always been true that an employer's action is subject to being overruled in arbitration if the action is arbitrary, capricious, or discriminatory, Title VII has unavoidably become a part of the definition of discrimination in the industrial relations context. . . . Regardless of the facts of the case, when a charge of discrimination is made by a member of a group protected by public law, the environment for the hearing changes immediately, and a case that might have normally been considered routine can become extremely important.

employer has the right to discharge an employee for any reason, good or bad, as long as the reason is not the employee's race, sex, or other protected characteristic. According to principles set forth by the Supreme Court in *McDonnell Douglas Corp. v. Green*,[73] the employee has the initial burden of proof. He or she must produce evidence of disparate treatment from which it may be inferred that there was a causal connection between the discharge and the employee's race, sex, etc. The employer is considered to have rebutted that inference if it articulates a legitimate, nondiscriminatory reason for the discharge. It is then up to the employee to prove that that reason was in fact a pretext.

In arbitration, the burden of proof, as in any discharge or discipline case, initially falls upon the employer. If the employer establishes that it had a bona fide, work-related reason for the discipline, the presumption is that there was no bias or prejudice.[74] At that point the union must assume the burden of going forward and of proving that other employees have not been

---

[73]411 U.S. 792, 5 FEP Cases 965 (1973).

[74]Arbitrator Pedrick, in *Borg-Warner Corp.*, 15 LA 308, 313 (1950) (leaving work without permission):

> Since the Arbitrator has concluded that the incident . . . was, in light of [the grievant's] past record, "cause" for discharge under the contract, the Union's contention that the discharge was prompted by anti-Negro, anti-Union bias loses most of its force. Under the contract neither [the grievant's] face nor his Union status protected him from discharge for cause.

In *Gulf States Utils. Co.*, *supra* note 72, a case where the grievant protested that his demotion for inability to perform his job was an act of discrimination, the arbitrator commented (*id.* at 1091): "Unfortunately, there are examples where some have considered the fact that a person is a member of a protected class, and also failed to achieve an employment objective, to be *ipso facto* racial discrimination." In holding that demotion was proper and nondiscriminatory if an employee did not possess the necessary qualifications, he cited the Supreme Court's opinion in *Griggs v. Duke Power Co.*, 401 U.S. 424, 3 FEP Cases 175 (1971): "Congress did not intend by Title VII . . . to guarantee a job to every person regardless of qualifications. . . . Discriminatory preference for any group, minority or majority, is precisely and only what Congress has proscribed." See also *Del Monte Corp.*, 71 LA 96 (Griffin, 1978) (assault on supervisor, threats). Even where he went so far as to recommend that an entry be made on a supervisor's personnel record to show that he had a "proclivity towards racial bias," based on demeaning remarks he had made to the grievant, the arbitrator in *Northrop Corp.*, 65 LA 400, 404 (Rose, 1975), went on to state, "This cannot alter the weight of the evidence which substantially supports the Company decision. The probative evidence shows that the grievant lacked the necessary qualifications to perform his assignments satisfactorily." Similarly, in *Alameda-Contra Costa Transit Dist.*, 76-1 ARB ¶8221 (Koven, 1976), a statement by a supervisor that he "would 'bury' the black drivers 'one by one'" was insufficient to establish that the employer had fired the grievant because of his race, where there was convincing proof that he had committed an act of theft.

penalized, or have been penalized less severely, for the same misconduct or that some mitigating factor such as harassment accounts for the grievant's misconduct.[75]

Subliminal Considerations in Race and Sex Cases

If the existence of unequal treatment leads to a finding that just cause was lacking, making it unnecessary for the arbitrator to decide whether the reason for the unequal treatment was the grievant's race or sex, why do express claims of racial and sex discrimination come up time after time in discipline cases? A major reason is that, from the perspective of both the grievant and the employer, considerations are involved apart from the question of whether or not there was just cause.

Employee's Point of View. The hypothetical case set forth in the introduction to this chapter makes the point that blacks who are sensitive to racial bias to the extent that they have previously taken legal action to protect their rights would naturally want to stand up for their dignity as well as get their jobs back.[76] Similar concerns about dignity and self-worth also lurk below the surface of many sex discrimination claims.

Sensitivity to prejudice plays a part even in some cases where no evidence of bias is present. Take a case where a black employee, disciplined for failing to carry out his foreman's instructions, complained that what the employer really wanted was that he be more subservient because he was black. Said he: "Doing your job in this department, you must also be like a bootlicker or something. You must smile and bow your head and all this unnecessary foolishness. . . ." No evidence was found that he was asked to behave differently from white employees

---

[75]Arbitrator Griffin, in *Aggregates & Concrete Ass'n of N. Cal.*, 69 LA 439, 448 (1977) (failure to report availability for work): "In a straightforward discharge case, the burden of proof lies squarely with the moving party/employer. The defense of racial discrimination is, however, an affirmative one in which the burden of persuasive proof shifts to Complainant/Grievant." Similarly, Arbitrator Koven, in *Alameda-Contra Costa County Transit Dist.*, *supra* note 74: "We know that the District bears the burden of proving to a moral certainty a charge that an employee has been dishonest. . . . As to the charge of discrimination, the Union has the burden in this respect."

[76]In the same vein is *Cocker Mach. and Foundry Co.*, 70-2 ARB ¶8628, 5087 (Currier, 1970) (profanity), where the arbitrator expressed the belief that the grievant, who had been terminated twice previously and restored to his job both times after he complained to the EEOC, "honestly felt, reasonably or not, that he was singled out by [the foreman] for adverse treatment."

in any way.[77] But it is not surprising that a black who has experienced racial prejudice all his life might be more sensitive than a white to supervisors' requests that he be pleasant and cooperative.

One sometimes encounters minority employees who carry "racial chips" on their shoulders[78] or employees who have a hard time facing up to their own faults and choose to believe that they are victims of racial or sex bias and not their own misconduct.[79] For some grievants, then, bias on the part of management is the obvious "why" behind the employer's actions, and their feelings about their race or sex are indelibly stamped on their quarrels with management.

If a grievant feels strongly that discrimination is present, the union will almost always try to prove discrimination. Ever since the U.S. Supreme Court's decision in *Bowen v. U.S. Postal Service*,[80] unions have been particularly sensitive about their exposure to damages if they are found to have breached their duty of fair representation and are therefore likely to carry forward discrimination claims with great vigor.[81]

Management's Point of View. In theory, if the employer has proved just cause for discipline, it may not need to rebut any allegations of discrimination the union might make. But in practice few employers will stand by quietly while their employment policies or the attitudes of individual supervisors are publicly labeled "racist" or "sexist." A failure to answer discrimination charges may make it hard for supervisors to function effectively at the workplace and may encourage the filing of new complaints of

---

[77]*General Foods Corp.*, 53 LA 291 (House, 1969) (poor attitude).

[78]See, e.g., *American Enka Corp.*, 54 LA 562 (Steele, 1969) (insubordination, profanity).

[79]As in *South Bend Tool & Die Co.*, 68 LA 536 (Traynor, 1977) (totality of misconduct).

[80]459 U.S. 212, 112 LRRM 2281 (1983).

[81]The Court relied on *Vaca v. Sipes*, 386 U.S. 171, 64 LRRM 2369 (1967), the Court's lead case on the duty of fair representation, and the subsequent case of *Hines v. Anchor Motor Freight*, 424 U.S. 554, 91 LRRM 2481 (1976), in holding that a union may be liable for damages resulting from its refusal to process a grievance. Some of the sting may have been taken out of this decision by *Air Line Pilots v. O'Neill*, 136 LRRM 2721 (1991), in which the Supreme Court ruled that a union's actions may be considered "arbitrary," and thus in violation of its duty of fair representation, only if its behavior is so far outside a "wide range of reasonableness" as to be irrational. The Court held that the union's negotiation of a back-to-work agreement which allowed the airline to disregard the seniority of returning strikers, resulting in discrimination between striking and nonstriking pilots in the allocation of vacant positions, was well within this "wide range of reasonableness."

discrimination. Furthermore, the employer, like the union, is likely to be looking over its shoulder in the direction of the federal court building, concerned to protect the record in case a separate legal proceeding by the grievant is waiting in the wings.

How Arbitrators Handle Claims of Race or Sex Discrimination

As a "creature of the parties," the arbitrator is in a unique position and, in cases of race or sex discrimination, is subject to mutually exclusive implied pressures from two directions. On the one hand, he or she is drawn to avoid a direct confrontation with the question of whether race or sex was the real reason for discipline if the case can be decided strictly on just cause principles. On the other hand, pressures are generated to meet such questions head-on.

There are three reasons why an arbitrator might tend to avoid dealing directly with charges of Title VII discrimination.

Reluctance to "point a finger." In the minds of many arbitrators, an express finding that an employer discriminated against an employee because of race or sex may carry with it more general and more provocative implications than a finding that the employer violated the just cause provision of the contract. A finding of discrimination may be construed not only as a statement about what the employer did in this one case but as a judgment that the employer has discriminatory policies.

A good analogy is how one says that someone has been untruthful. Stating merely that a person did not tell the truth on a particular occasion leaves open the possibility that he or she is a model of probity as a general rule. Calling that person a liar, on the other hand, implies a negative judgment about his or her character, and for that reason the label "liar" is one that arbitrators—like most other people—avoid. Similarly, arbitrators are reluctant to pin the "scarlet R" of racism or the "scarlet S" of sexism on an employer, even by implication, if this can be avoided.

The parties' continuing relationship. One reason why an arbitrator might steer clear of a finding that tends to label the employer as one who discriminates is that tensions at the workplace might be exacerbated by such a finding.

The arbitrator's continuing relationship with the parties. An arbitrator might also be concerned about the effect upon his or her own acceptability of attacking questions of race and sex discrimination head-on, since name-calling may not sit well with some of those who do the selecting.[82]

These disincentives to confront discrimination charges directly explain in part why some critics have asserted that the courts are a more appropriate forum than arbitration for discrimination complaints. A judge, who does not serve at the parties' pleasure and will almost surely never see them again, has no reason to consider anything but the issues at hand.[83] Yet, however strong the temptation may be to stay away from potentially sticky issues, arbitrators are also pushed to deal directly with race and sex for the following reasons:

Silence does the parties no favors. The arbitrator who ducks the question of discrimination leaves the parties exactly where they were on an issue that may be of considerable importance to them. It has been argued that if discriminatory intent is obvious, both the grievant and the union are entitled to have the arbitrator say so, in order to deter further acts of discrimination. That is especially true in cases where the employer has disciplined an employee in retaliation for complaints about discrimination—retaliation that violates express provisions of Title VII and strikes at the heart of contractual grievance procedures.[84]

---

[82]A finding by Margaret Oppenheimer and Helen LaVan that arbitrators are more likely to find sex bias than race discrimination may be explained in part by acceptability considerations. Charges of sex discrimination, while equally serious as a matter of public policy, do not have for the public generally the same moral stigma or incendiary potential as race discrimination charges. Sex discrimination may be understood as "part of the game," especially by more conservative male managers and by male-dominated unions. *Arbitration Awards in Discrimination Disputes: An Empirical Analysis,* 34 ARB. J. 12–16 (1979).

[83]A. Blumrosen, *Labor Arbitration, EEOC Conciliation, and Discrimination in Employment,* 24 Arb. J. 94 (1969):

Arbitrators are "neutral" only as between company and union. When a third interest arises, the arbitrator will side with the company and union to promote collective bargaining relationships. The instinct, self-interest and the training of the arbitrator as well as the body of law surrounding his work, all call out for him to accept that position which will secure the assent of both union and management. Union and management want him to operate within the framework of contractual principles which *they* have established, rather than range over their relationship with a roving commission to implement federal legislative policy.

[84]For a typical "retaliation" case, see *Amoco Chems. Corp.,* 70 LA 504 (Helburn, 1978) (absenteeism, job performance). See also *Shop Rite Foods, Inc.,* 67 LA 159 (Weiss, 1976), where statements by the head meat cutter that he did not know why he had to work with the grievant, and his attempts to dissuade her from filing EEOC charges, helped persuade the arbitrator that she had been discharged because of her efforts to

By the same token, it is said, if the absence of discriminatory intent is obvious, it is only fair that the arbitrator make that clear, so that the employee will not be encouraged to appeal to the courts or return to the workplace with the same suspicions. That is especially true in the rare case where the arbitrator believes that the grievant is charging discrimination in bad faith for the purposes of self-aggrandizement or simple trouble-making.[85]

The arbitrator may have no choice if the issue is put directly. On occasion, a violation of the contract's no-discrimination clause is specifically cited in the grievance, and the question of discriminatory intent must be addressed. Also, because they are usually not protected by the just cause provisions of the contract, probationary employees can be terminated at the company's discretion for any reason *except* unlawful discrimination, so that charges of race or sex bias often are at the heart of probationers' grievances.[86]

Common Types of Discrimination Claims

Race or Sex Was the Real Reason for Discipline.

Arbitrator Yarowsky: If it is found that the reasons given for the personnel action were a sham or mere window-dressing, of course the discharge will not be permitted to stand. It would be repugnant to the preemptive Federal law guaranteeing to all minorities the right to equal treatment in the employment relation and, in addition, it could not be based on "reasonable cause" as contemplated by . . . the Agreement.[87]

---

get the company to adopt nondiscriminatory policies toward female employees, not because of her alleged mispricing of meat. But in *Rim & Wheel Serv., Inc.*, 65 LA 631 (McIntosh, 1975), the grievant's claim of retaliation was rejected since the company did not become aware of the charge he had filed with the Civil Rights Commission until after the insubordinate outburst that led to his discharge.

[85]As in *United Aircraft Corp.*, 55 LA 484 (Turkus, 1970), where the arbitrator upheld the grievant's discharge for insubordination after he persistently refused to change a shirt on which he had written charges against the company that the arbitrator found were intended to provoke racial conflict at the plant, not to further fair employment practices. See also *New York Tel. Co.*, 55 LA 525 (Friedman, 1970) (charging employer with pursuing racist policies).

[86]For cases involving the discharge of probationary employees, see *Food Employers Council, Inc.*, 64 LA 811 (Jacobs, 1975); *Amoco Tex. Refining Co.*, 71 LA 344 (Gowan, 1978); *Paccar, Inc.*, 72 LA 769 (Grether, 1979) (all unsatisfactory work).

[87]*Whitaker Cable Corp.*, 63 LA 1262, 1264 (1974) (failure to report absence).

Where the grievant charges that the real reason for his or her discharge or other discipline was race or sex (or in some cases complaints about race or sex discrimination), the employer's main problem of proof is the customary one: to prove that misconduct took place. Even evidence of animosity will not as a rule influence the arbitrator's decision if good business-related cause for discipline (that is, cause unrelated to Title VII factors) has been securely established. Under such circumstances, a charge of discrimination normally is irrelevant. But if the call is a close one, a strong showing by the union on the discrimination issue may become a factor that tips the scales in the grievant's favor.

> **EXAMPLE:** A black truck driver who also was a union steward prepared a detailed charge of racial discrimination against the employer which he read to a supervisor when he arrived at work. The same evening he was discharged after three supervisors came to the conclusion that he was under the influence of alcohol, even though he protested that the symptoms of "intoxication" were attributable to flu, for which he had been taking several drugs, and to exhaustion from working a heavy overtime schedule.

If the company had had solid proof that the grievant was under the influence, the arbitrator would have had no problem sustaining his discharge. But the evidence on that critical point was equivocal. The arbitrator accepted the supervisors' testimony that the grievant had shown several symptoms of intoxication. At the same time, he thought it plausible that those symptoms might have been innocently produced by the combination of illness, medication, and a small amount of alcohol that the grievant had consumed before starting work that night.

Against the background of claim and counterclaim the grievant's discrimination complaint loomed large, the arbitrator commenting, "I am not convinced that it had no effect." Certainly the timing was suspicious. Furthermore, there was uncontradicted testimony that when the grievant read his charge, one of the supervisors who observed him "drunk" stated that he likely would not be around to see the outcome of his charges.

> I am . . . convinced that had the company not had an impermissible urge to rid itself of Grievant, it would have taken a more judicious approach to the problem that would have resulted in discipline less than discharge. Motivations of this nature are so unacceptable that actions reasonably suspected of being produced by them must be undone."

The grievant was reinstated, but back pay was not awarded since he was guilty at least of a culpable mixing of alcohol and medication.[88]

Race or Sex Was Reason for Unequal Penalties. One of the most common defenses raised by the grievant in Title VII-type cases is that the penalty imposed for misconduct was unfairly severe solely because of race or sex considerations. Such cases normally are decided according to the general principle that governs all disparate-penalty cases: If the evidence establishes that penalties for the same misconduct, under similar circumstances, have been reasonably consistent, the grievant's claim will fail.[89] On the other hand, if the grievant's penalty was disproportionately harsh in comparison with penalties imposed on other employees, it will be reduced on that basis alone.[90] In either case the

---

[88]*United Parcel Serv.*, 72 LA 1069, 1072-73 (White, 1979). In *San Mateo County Restaurant-Hotel Owners Ass'n*, 59 LA 997 (Kenaston, 1972), the doubtful credibility of employer witnesses, plus reported statements by the grievant's supervisor that he did not like female bartenders, created "a strong possibility" that the underlying reason for the grievant's discharge was her sex, not her bartending. In *Arkansas Power & Light Co.*, 62 LA 25, 28 (Woodward, 1973) (rudeness to customers, other misconduct), the arbitrator commented, "While the burden of proof is on the grievant to prove that his discharge was caused by racial discrimination and not by the flagrant misconduct of which he was guilty, it is important for a company to avoid even the appearance of impropriety with respect to racial discrimination." Accordingly, evidence that there was a "general atmosphere of racial discrimination" in the grievant's department helped give him the benefit of the doubt that his discharge was unduly harsh.

[89]As in *Whitaker Cable Corp.*, *supra* note 87, where company records showed that around the same time the grievant was discharged for being absent for three consecutive days without calling in, 15 other employees, of whom 11 were white, were discharged for the same offense. There was no evidence that any employee, white or black, had received a lesser penalty for this offense; employees cited by the union as having received only warnings, or as having been excused because of extenuating circumstances, had been disciplined under a rule concerning excessive absenteeism. In *Agrico Chems. Co.*, 55 LA 481 (Greene, 1970), although other employees had disobeyed supervisors' orders without being discharged, one employee had not been as flagrantly defiant and belligerent as the grievant and the other had reason to believe that compliance would have endangered his safety. The arbitrator noted further that lighter penalties had been given to other black employees for similar offenses, producing the conclusion that the employer was not out to get the grievant solely because he was black. See also *Armstrong Cork Co.*, 58 LA 303 (Geissinger, 1972) (absenteeism); *National Airlines*, 61 LA 680 (Cushman, 1973) (absenteeism, falsifying time card); *A. O. Smith Corp.*, 75 LA 439 (Petrie, 1980) (theft).

[90]As in *Aerojet Liquid Rocket Co.*, 75 LA 255 (Wollett, 1980), where the arbitrator found that supervisors were inconsistent generally in their treatment of employees who reported to work under the influence of alcohol; *Anaconda Aluminum Co.*, 62 LA 1049 (Warns, 1974) (excessive personal telephone calls); *Gold Star Prods.*, 82-2 ARB ¶8609 (Roumell, 1982) (carelessness).

framework is not discrimination in Title VII terms, but the elements of just cause in reference to disparate treatment.[91]

Only in unusual circumstances is the question of the grievant's race or sex addressed directly by the arbitrator, as in one case where the grievant specifically claimed that the contract's no-discrimination clause had been violated,[92] and in the following case which had a rather special wrinkle.

> **EXAMPLE:** A white woman who tried to take a pillow from a black woman and called her a "bitch" was assaulted by the black. Both women were fired. The employer contended that the white woman's discharge was justified, even though she struck no blow herself, because there had been a good deal of racial tension at the plant following a fight two months earlier that started when a white woman called a black woman names. Under Title VII, the employer argued, it had an affirmative obligation to keep the workplace free of racial tension and intimidation. It had to discharge the white woman to make it clear that provocative behavior would not be tolerated.

Did the arbitrator buy this argument? No, based on considerations of both fact and fairness. As to the facts, the arbitrator was not convinced that racial antagonism was as intense or as widespread as the company represented. He also accepted the grievant's testimony that she had not intended to provoke the black woman but merely said "Oh, bitch!" in frustration during

---

[91]*American Hoechst Corp.*, 84-1 ARB ¶8143, 3663 (Marlatt, 1984), provides a striking example of this point. The arbitrator rejected the employer's explanation of why newspaper reports of the grievant's work as a black activist were kept in his file with these words:

> I am struck by the testimony . . . that they were "proud of" the Grievant's achievements in the N.A.A.C.P. . . . If the truth were known, the Grievant's supervisors probably received the news of his militant activities with the same degree of enthusiasm as a letter carrier would feel upon learning that a Doberman pinscher on the route had graduated top in its class from Attack Dog School. . . . The clipping in the Grievant's file could have but one possible message, and that message came across loud and clear: "Watch this guy—he is a troublemaker."

Nevertheless, the basis on which the arbitrator directed that a reprimand for "goofing off" be removed from the grievant's file was that he had been unfairly singled out for punishment—i.e., that he was the victim of disparate treatment.

[92]*Lianco Container Corp.*, 60 LA 938 (Dugan, 1973), where the grievant complained that other employees had been given only two-week suspensions, as opposed to his own 45-day penalty, for drinking on company property. The arbitrator disagreed with the company's contention that those employees' misconduct was sufficiently different to justify the lighter penalties. Since all those employees were white, whereas the grievant was black, he inferred that the company had been guilty of racial discrimination and reduced the grievant's suspension to two weeks.

their argument over the pillow, which she thought belonged to her.

As to fairness, the arbitrator declared himself to be "not unmindful of the racial sensitivity" that led the employer to make a strong show of nondiscrimination by treating the two employees alike. However, he noted, "[d]ue consideration to the sensitivities of race relations must not lead to actions which are unfair to individual employees." The grievant's misconduct was not as serious as the black woman's, and called for a penalty less than discharge. She could not be made a sacrificial offering to better race relations just because she happened to be white.[93]

Harassment as Mitigation. A claim of harassment as mitigation presents a type of "but for" situation. The grievant does not deny engaging in whatever misconduct is charged, but claims there would have been no misconduct if he or she had been left in peace; harassment, the argument runs, kept the grievant from doing the job properly (or, perhaps, from learning the job). The burden of proving a claim of this sort falls upon the union, and a strong showing is normally required if the claim of harassment is to prevail.

The elements of proof likely to be required by an arbitrator are the following: (1) The union must produce credible evidence that the grievant was actually harassed, verbally or physically. (2) It must show that the harassment was of a continuing nature and not a matter of a few isolated incidents. (3) The harassment must have been either directly work-related (for example, a supervisor or coworker refusing to assist or cooperate with the grievant in his work), or the harassment must have been such as would have upset the "reasonable man." (4) Either the harassment must have been carried out by supervisors or, if fellow employees are the culprits, the grievant must have reported the harassment to management.[94]

---

[93]*Borg Instruments*, 73-2 ARB ¶8561, 5120 (Somers, 1974). For other "reverse discrimination" cases, a rare animal in the discipline area, see *Struck Constr. Co.*, 74 LA 369 (Sergent, 1980), where a white employee was discharged so the company could hire a minority employee to meet its affirmative action obligations; *P.D.I., Inc.*, 88-2 ARB ¶8436 (Dworkin, 1988), where the discharge of a white employee who cursed a black coworker after suffering abuse and threats for two days was found to have been improperly based on a desire to avoid the appearance of racial discrimination rather than on just cause.

[94]See *Amoco Chems. Corp.*, *supra* note 84; *Amoco Tex. Refining Co.*, *supra* note 86 (Gowan, 1978). In the latter case the arbitrator was impressed by the company's showing that the grievant had demonstrated only marginal ability even early in her training before the harassment began, and that she had failed to utilize available study areas

The last requirement presupposes that the employer can be held responsible only for harassment of which it had knowledge—at least constructive knowledge—and therefore a reasonable opportunity to prevent.[95] It also implies that an employee who is subjected to harassment has a responsibility to try to put a stop to it, even if bringing certain incidents to the employer's attention may cause embarrassment and even if the grievant fears that other employees will retaliate with stepped-up harassment.

Despite the difficult problems of proof involved, claims of harassment as mitigation are sometimes successful.

> **EXAMPLE:** A black working foreman at one of the employer's bakeries was transferred to a new location after that bakery closed. Eight months later the employer demoted him to the job of first baker, contending that he had not managed his department properly and pointing to such problems as product shortages, lack of cleanliness, and excessive overtime. The union protested the demotion on the ground that the employees in the department resented working for a black foreman and deliberately caused problems, such as adulterating the sugar used in baking, scrawling derogatory remarks on the foreman's time card, and leaving him notes containing racial slurs. At least two employees had admitted their racial hostility. To convey the message that racial prejudice would not be tolerated, a supervisor had held meetings with employees and notices were posted, but to no avail.

The employer's evidence that production had suffered under the black foreman was clear; but so was union evidence

---

where she would have been left alone. On the EEOC's guidelines on sexual harassment, see D. E. Ledgerwood & S. Johnson-Dietz, *The EEOC's Foray Into Sexual Harassment: Interpreting the New Guidelines for Employer Liability*, 31 LAB. L.J. 741–44 (1980). On issues involving sex harassment generally, see M. L. Greenbaum & B. Fraser, *Sexual Harassment in the Workplace*, 36:4 ARB. J. 30–41 (1981); R. W. Schupp, J. Windham, & S. Draughn, *Sexual Harassment in Its Social and Legal Contexts*, 7 EMPLOYEE REL. L.J. 567–86 (1982); P. Linenberger, *What Behavior Constitutes Sexual Harassment?* 34 LAB. L.J. 238–47 (1983); K. Jennings & M. Clapp, *A Managerial Tightrope: Balancing Harassed and Harassing Employees' Rights in Sexual Discrimination Cases*, 40 LAB. L.J. 756–64 (1989). The other side of the sex harassment coin—discharge of a male employee for engaging in sexual harassment—is discussed in M. Marmo, *Arbitration Sex Harassment Cases*, 35 ARB. J. 35–40 (1980).

[95] In *Amoco Tex. Refining Co.*, *supra* note 86, the arbitrator adopted the even more stringent requirement that for a claim of harassment to succeed, it must be shown that the company not only knew about but "condoned, endorsed or encouraged" the acts of which the grievant complains. By contrast, a factor diluting the grievant's claim of sexual harassment in *Union Carbide Corp.*, 74 LA 532 (Taylor, 1980) (failure to pass progress tests), was company evidence that it had "immediately and effectively" remedied the situation whenever an incident of harassment was brought to its attention.

that workers in the department were hostile and refused to cooperate with him. He had had no trouble at the old location, and management had enough confidence in his abilities to transfer him to a new supervisory job. The employer had the responsibility to intervene, and what it had done was not enough. Evidently it had not, for instance, considered transferring uncooperative employees or assigning the foreman to another store in a supervisory capacity. For that reason, the demotion was held to be improper.[96]

Provocation as Mitigation. Where provocation is put forward as a mitigating factor, the misconduct is usually a physical assault or verbal outburst of some kind, and the grievant's defense is that he or she was goaded into misbehaving by a racial slur or other display of antagonism. The outcome in such cases normally depends on two or possibly three factors. First, the union must establish that provocative behavior took place.[97] Second, the behavior must have been offensive enough to account for the grievant's reaction.[98] The possible third factor is that where the "provocateur" is a fellow employee and not a supervisor, the propriety of the grievant's penalty often depends on whether the other employee also was disciplined.[99]

Inadequate Training as Mitigation. A claim of inadequate training because of race or sex may be made when the grievant was discharged for poor performance. The employer's job here is to produce convincing evidence that the training given the grievant was comparable to that afforded to other employees. Lack of equal training is a form of disparate treatment to the extent that it places an employee at a disadvantage in relation to other employees, and evidence of prejudice based on race or

---

[96]*Albertson's, Inc.*, 59 LA 1119 (Edelman, 1972).

[97]*Singer Controls Co. of America*, 70-2 ARB ¶8760 (Hon, 1970) (striking coworker).

[98]In *Union Camp Corp.*, 71 LA 886, 889 (Duff, 1978), the grievant's complaints of persecution were dismissed by the arbitrator as having been "vaguely dredged up" long after the alleged events took place. "If there was any meat or substance to his allegations . . . it should have been flushed out by direct, timely complaint; to now belatedly raise these claims indirectly, as a sort of afterthought defense of provocation, is an extremely ineffective way to assert contractual rights against racial discrimination." The arbitrator concluded further that the grievant had injected his claim of persecution into the case precisely because he was aware that his battery upon another employee had been unprovoked.

[99]As in any case where there is fault on both sides.

sex may help convince an arbitrator that the grievant's learning opportunities were limited by the employer.[100]

What Weakens a Discrimination Claim

Whatever form an employee's discrimination claim happens to take, the employer's chances of surviving it are enhanced if the claim is defective for any of the following reasons:

- The claim is first raised late in the game—at the arbitration hearing, for example—rather than in the original grievance.[101]
- The charge is vague as to the exact nature of the alleged bias and unsupported by specific incidents.[102]
- The grievant has substantial seniority, and it is not apparent why the employer would now be "out to get" him or her.[103]
- The supervisor accused of bias belongs to the same Title VII group as the grievant.[104]

---

[100]In *Basic Vegetable Prods., Inc.*, 64 LA 620 (Gould, 1975), evidence that the employer was reluctant to place a woman in the job of crew leader buttressed testimony that the grievant had not received the same instruction and assistance as male employees typically received; that she had been warned about her performance problems only shortly before she was removed from the job; and that she was not allowed the full 60-day trial period provided for in the contract. For cases in which the arbitrator upheld the employer on the equal-training issue, see *Simoniz Co.*, 70-1 ARB ¶8179 (Traynor, 1969); *Imperial Sugar Co.*, 70-1 ARB ¶8219 (Shearer, 1969); *Amoco Chems. Corp.*, 70 LA 504 (Helburn, 1978); *Texas Utils. Generating Co.*, 71 LA 1205 (Mewhinney, 1979); *Union Carbide Corp.*, 74 LA 532 (Taylor, 1980). In *Texas Utilities*, the arbitrator found that the grievant lacked the basic verbal and quantitative skills necessary to learn the job of mechanic's helper, but that the employer had no existing program to teach any employee those skills and no contractual obligation to establish such a program.

[101]*Agrico Chem. Co.*, 55 LA 481 (Greene, 1970) (insubordination); *Aggregates & Concrete Assn. of Northern Cal., Inc.*, 69 LA 439 (Griffin, 1977) (failure to report availability for work); *VRN Int'l*, 74 LA 806 (Vause, 1980) (unsatisfactory performance).

[102]*Knight Newspapers, Inc.*, 58 LA 446 (Platt, 1972) (incompetence); *National Airlines*, 61 LA 680 (Cushman, 1973) (absenteeism, falsifying time card); *VRN Int'l, supra* note 101; *U.S. Customs Serv.*, 82-1 ARB ¶8073 (Kanowitz, 1981) (sexual harassment); *Lady Baltimore Foods, Inc.*, 83 LA 945 (Mikrut, 1984) (poor performance); *Rockwell Int'l Corp.*, 84 LA 496 (Feldman, 1985) (low productivity); *Rust Eng'g Co.*, 86-1 ARB ¶8010 (Whyte, 1985) (possession and use of drugs).

[103]*ITT Rayonier, Inc.*, 65 LA 1122 (Hardy, 1975) (profanity, reading on job); *Rust Eng'g Co., supra* note 102.

[104]*Colgate-Palmolive Co.*, 64 LA 397 (Allen, 1975) (insubordination); *FSC Paper Co.*, 65 LA 25 (Marshall, 1975) (obscene language); *Del Monte Corp.*, 71 LA 96 (Griffin, 1978) (threats, assault on supervisor). In *Colgate*, the arbitrator asked: "While one Negro could oppressively discriminate against another black, would it be racial discrimination? Looking at an analogous situation, if a white oppressively discriminates against another white, do we consider that racial discrimination?" 64 LA at 403. The arbitrator in *Del Monte* (71 LA at 100) found it "a psychological possibility that a black man could be anti-

- Evidence that a particular supervisor was biased is hearsay;[105] is conflicting;[106] refers only to generalized attitudes;[107] or rests on isolated statements made in the past.[108]
- The grievant has had difficulty with supervisors other than the one he has accused of being prejudiced against him.[109]
- There is no evidence that other members of the grievant's Title VII group have been discriminated against.[110]
- Prior EEOC complaints or other discrimination actions against the employer by this grievant (possibly even by other employees) have been resolved in the employer's favor.[111]
- The grievant was replaced, following termination, by another individual from the same Title VII group.[112]

Statistics that show a decrease in the number of minority members employed may form the basis of an affirmative action complaint concerning hiring practices. Standing alone, however, they do not prove that the employer resorted to unjust discharge to reduce its ranks of minorities or women.[113]

Discriminatory Work Rules

"Sex Plus"

"Sex plus" cases come about (in the words of Schlei and Grossman) "where an employer classifies employees on the basis

---

black," but found no evidence of any discriminatory "Uncle Tom" mentality in the case before him.

[105]*American Sugar Co.*, 52 LA 1228 (Whyte, 1969) (insubordination).

[106]*Intalco Aluminum Corp.*, 66 LA 155 (Burke, 1976) (unauthorized absence).

[107]*Borg-Warner Corp.*, 15 LA 308 (Pedrick, 1950) (leaving work without permission); *Intalco Aluminum Corp.*, supra note 106; *Lady Baltimore Foods, Inc.*, supra note 102. Arbitrator Burke, in *Intalco*, at 157:

> [T]he important point here is not what was said, but what was done. The law does not speak to opinion, or attitude or sentiment—it speaks only to actions or behavior. It seeks to prevent action which mitigates [sic] against equal opportunity in employment. It does not and can not seek to control beliefs and bias and prejudice—these dehabilitating [sic] phenomena exist only in the mind, and as long as they are not translated into behavior, the law does not, and cannot apply.

[108]*Gold Star Prods.*, 82-2 ARB ¶8609 (Roumell, 1982).

[109]*Del Monte Corp.*, supra note 104.

[110]*Intalco Aluminum Corp.*, supra note 106.

[111]*Allied Thermal Corp.*, 54 LA 441 (Altieri, 1970) (absenteeism).

[112]*Taft Broadcasting Co.*, 69 LA 307 (Chaffin, 1977) (insubordination).

[113]*Food Employers Council, Inc.*, 64 LA 811 (Jacobs, 1975) (unsatisfactory work); *Alameda-Contra Costa Transit Dist.*, 76-1 ARB ¶8221 (Koven, 1976) (theft).

of sex *plus* another characteristic."[114] The most common type of "sex plus" complaint occurs when a male employee protests that a hair-length requirement violates his Title VII rights because females are not subject to the same requirement. Neither the courts nor arbitrators have accepted the proposition that hair-length requirements constitute sex discrimination within the meaning of either Title VII or just cause. One commentator has explained:

> Congress, in passing Title VII, attempted to assure individuals equal employment opportunities irrespective of sex; the Act was not designed to prevent an employer from promulgating reasonable employment requirements designed to enhance the public image of its business. . . . Where the appearance regulations of an employer are reasonably drawn and are not used as a subterfuge to exclude members of one sex from employment, a violation of the Act should not be found merely because of minor differences between requirements for male and female employees.[115]

The courts have reasoned that "distinctions in employment practices between men and women on the basis of something other than immutable or protected characteristics do not inhibit employment *opportunity*."[116] An individual's sex is a protected characteristic because it is normally regarded as unchangeable. A male employee's right to wear a certain hair style (or beard, sideburns, etc.) is not protected by Title VII, on the other hand, because it can be readily changed to meet an employer's grooming standards.[117] Arbitrators have consistently agreed, deciding the reasonableness of hair rules, as discussed in Chapter 2, on the basis of whether they are justified by business necessity.[118]

---

[114]B. L. SCHLEI & P. GROSSMAN, EMPLOYMENT DISCRIMINATION LAW 403 (2d ed. 1983).

[115]H. B. Golden, *Sex Discrimination and Hair-Length Requirements Under Title VII of the Civil Rights Act of 1964—The Long and Short of It*, 25 Lab. L.J. 351 (1974). For other surveys of the hair cases, see R. Valtin, *Hair and Beards in Arbitration*, LABOR ARBITRATION AT THE QUARTER-CENTURY MARK 235–52 (Proceedings of the 25th Annual Meeting, National Academy of Arbitrators 1973); P. F. Zeigler, *Employer Dress and Appearance Codes and Title VII of the Civil Rights Act of 1964*, 46 S. CAL. L. REV. 965–1002 (1973).

[116]*Willingham v. Macon Tel. Publishing Co.*, 507 F.2d 1084, 9 FEP Cases 189 (5th Cir. 1975); see SCHLEI & GROSSMAN, *supra* note 114, at 413.

[117]Although the condition of being married or having children, two factors that can figure in "sex plus" cases, is "mutable" in the sense that one's race or sex is not, courts have held that those conditions cannot "readily" be changed as hair style can. For that reason, discrimination for "sex plus" on either of those grounds can exist under Title VII. See I. Kovarsky & V. Hauck, *The No-Spouse Rule, Title VII, and Arbitration, 32* LAB. L.J. 366–74 (1981).

[118]*E.g., American Buslines, Inc.*, 1975 ARB ¶8013 (Gentile, 1975). See also *Allied Employers, Inc.*, 55 LA 1020 (Kleinsorge, 1970); *Arrow Redi-Mix Concrete, Inc.*, 71-1 ARB ¶8252 (Fleischli, 1971); *Big Star No. 35*, 73 LA 850 (Murphy, 1979).

Sex might creep in, however, if the evidence showed that while one sex was subject to a particular dress or grooming standard, the other sex was not subject to any appearance standards whatsoever. One employer, for example, required male employees in the data processing department to wear neckties to work, whereas women in the same department were allowed to wear whatever they pleased, including tank tops, jeans, and other casual clothing. After viewing a sampling of the employees' customary attire, the arbitrator described the women's wear as "swinging with the times," while "[t]he male employees . . . were required to comply with a tradition, lost in antiquity, of wearing a necktie." Citing EEOC guidelines as well as just cause criteria for reasonable rules, he concluded that male employees were being discriminated against on the basis of "sex plus" in being subject to a substantially different mode of dress from their female peers.[119]

But take another case in which a male attendant at a nursing home announced that he intended to have sex-change surgery in about two years' time. With his doctor's concurrence he asked that he be treated as if he were a woman until then, and be allowed to wear a female attendant's uniform, in order to prepare himself psychologically for the change. The nursing home went along with him, but when three years passed with no sex change, management directed the attendant to resume wearing a male uniform. When he refused, he was discharged.

Were the attendant's Title VII rights violated because he was required, as a male, to wear one type of uniform when female attendants wore another type? For three years the employer had been extremely accommodating, not only allowing him to wear a female attendant's uniform but also giving him separate changing space because he would not use the men's locker room and female employees refused to accept him in their locker room. But patients as well as employees have feel-

---

[119]*Union Tribune Publishing Co.*, 70 LA 266, 268 (Richman, 1978). The concept of "sex plus" has been extended by one U.S. court of appeals to a race discrimination situation. The court found that black females were a distinct subgroup protected by Title VII, so that where discrimination against black females is claimed, the fact that black males or white females are not subject to the same discrimination is irrelevant. *Jeffries v. Harris City Community Action Ass'n*, 615 F.2d 1025, 22 FEP Cases 974 (5th Cir. 1980. Another example of "race plus" would be a company's prohibition of the wearing of "Afro" hair styles by black men. Some EEOC decisions have held that an "Afro" cut may be a protected characteristic because it is widely understood to be an expression of racial pride.

ings and rights, the arbitrator found, and among their rights is that of knowing the sex of employees who treat them. When it became apparent that the attendant would remain anatomically male, the employer acted reasonably in putting an end to a situation that had caused inconvenience and confusion for at least some patients.

This case stands squarely for the proposition, endorsed by the courts, that "distinction in dress is not by itself discriminatory where employment opportunities of one sex are unaffected and no particular burden is placed on one sex (or any group of employees) as opposed to the other sex (or different group of employees)." Here, both sexes were subject to uniform requirements; these requirements placed no greater a burden on males than on females; and the reason for the different uniforms was not arbitrary and capricious. The requirement that the male attendant wear a male uniform thus was nondiscriminatory. By way of remedy, the arbitrator ruled that the attendant could be reinstated without back pay if he agreed to wear the uniform intended for his "then anatomical status."[120]

Other Types of Discriminatory Work Rules

Some rules on their face apply to all employees equally, but are claimed by the union to affect one sex, race, or other protected group more severely than other types. The bulk of these rules put in issue the employer's duty to accommodate to an employee's religious practices, as discussed in the next section. But some involve other groups protected by Title VII.

EXAMPLE: The employer had a rule stating that all employees required by OSHA to wear respirators must be clean shaven. An employee who suffered from a skin condition common to black males which prevented him from shaving with a razor was to be moved to another job because management decided that an electric shaver would not shave him closely enough for the respirator to seal properly. When the employee protested, he was suspended for two days.

Did the application of the "razor shaved" rule to this employee violate his Title VII rights? Said the arbitrator: "A rule or policy that requires employees to shave by razor or depilatory even for a safety purpose is subject to a serious question of

---

[120]*Greater Harlem Nursing Home*, 81-2 ARB ¶8314, 4387 (Marx, 1981).

discrimination since it can act to disqualify an otherwise qualified black from employment solely on the basis of a genetic character- istic peculiar to his race . . . ." For that reason the employer was obligated to conduct tests to determine whether the employee could achieve a tight seal on his respirator in some way that would not require shaving with a razor. If OSHA standards could be met only by razor shaving, then enforcing the razor- only rule against this employee would be justified, on the princi- ple that Title VII rights must give way when safety is a compel- ling concern.[121]

This case stands for the proposition that even where an immutable racial characteristic is involved, there is no discrimi- nation if a clear business necessity can be established—a conclu- sion that some courts have reached.[122] The business-necessity test applies also in cases involving sex and national origin, where minimum height or weight requirements may operate to ex- clude women, Asians, and Hispanics.

Here are three more situations in which a rule applies to all employees equally on its face, but the union argued nevertheless that the rule was discriminatory. All involve the same basic principle.

Sex. A rule made both males and females subject to maximum weight limits. When a woman was discharged for being over- weight, the union protested that the rule was discriminatory be- cause it was more difficult for women to meet a weight limitation than it was for men. Did the union prevail?[123]

Religion. The employer had a rule requiring all employees, re- gardless of sex, to wear pants as a safety measure to prevent injuries to the legs. One woman protested that her civil rights were being violated by the pants-only requirement because her religious beliefs prevented her from wearing men's clothing. Did she have a valid discrimination claim?[124]

Race: The employer adopted a new rule requiring all production employees to punch a special time clock on their way to and from the bathroom. The union challenged the rule's validity partly on the ground that 90 percent of the production employees were

---

[121]*Niagara Mohawk Power Corp.*, 74 LA 58, 62-63 (Markowitz, 1980).
[122]SCHLEI & GROSSMAN, *supra* note 114, at 290–91.
[123]*American Airlines, Inc.*, 68 LA 527 (Turkus, 1977).
[124]*Colt Indus.*, 71 LA 22 (Rutherford, 1978).

black, while all office employees, to whom the rule did not apply, were white. Was the union's challenge on target?[125]

In all three cases, the rule was held by the arbitrator to be reasonable, and discipline under the rule to be grounded in just cause. In each case the inherent reasonableness of the rule, under the business-necessity test, outweighed whatever discriminatory impact the rule might have had. In the weight-limit case, the employer had a legitimate need to have its flight attendants project "a trim, effective appearance"; in the safety case, the employer established that only pants could protect the legs effectively against spattering acids and other work-related hazards; and in the case of the bathroom time clock, the arbitrator accepted employer testimony that different working conditions justified the use of different methods of monitoring bathroom-visit abuse for the two groups.

Religion and Reasonable Accommodation

EEOC Guidelines: Source of Employer's Duty to Accommodate

Title VII prohibits discrimination based on religion as well as race, sex, color, and national origin but does not elaborate on what the term "religion" might encompass. It was the EEOC in its 1966 guidelines that formally announced that religious practices as well as beliefs are protected by Title VII and that even a work requirement that is nondiscriminatory on its face can have a discriminatory result if an employee cannot comply with it without compromising his or her religious convictions. An example is the case of an employee who, like other employees, is required to work on the Sabbath, which his religion prohibits.[126]

The EEOC further determined that an employer has a duty to accommodate to an employee's religious needs—within certain limits. In the 1966 guidelines, the Commission required accommodation that could be made "without serious inconve-

---

[125]*Cagle's Poultry and Egg Co.*, 73 LA 34 (Roberts, 1979).

[126]For a general overview, see M. Hill, *Reasonable Accommodation and Religious Discrimination Under Title VII: A Practitioner's Guide*, 34 ARB. J. 19–27 (1979); J. M. Hecker, *Accommodation of an Employee's Religious Practices Under Title VII*, Univ. of Ill. L.F. 867–94 (1976); B. W. Wolkinson, *Title VII and the Religious Employee: The Neglected Duty of Accommodation*, 30 ARB. J. 89–113 (1975). See also SCHLEI & GROSSMAN, *supra* note 114, at Ch. 7, and 61–72 (Five-Year Cum. Supp.).

niences" to the employer; amended guidelines in 1967 changed the quoted language to "undue hardship."[127]

The reaction of the courts to the EEOC's position was mixed; the frequently cited *Dewey v. Reynolds Metals Co.*[128] held that prohibition of religious discrimination under Title VII did not extend to policies under which all employees were equally treated, such as uniform overtime requirements; in effect, then, the EEOC's reasonable-accommodation requirement was cancelled out. Other courts agreed. However, in 1972, Congress put an end to the uncertainties when it added section 701(j), which made the duty to accommodate part of the law:

> The term "religion" includes all aspects of religious observance and practice, as well as belief, unless an employer demonstrates that he is unable to reasonably accommodate to an employee's religious observance or practice without undue hardship on the conduct of the employer's business.

Arbitral Views on Reasonable Accommodation

Before section 701(j) was added to Title VII, an employee who was discharged or suspended for refusing to work on the Sabbath, or for failing to comply with some other employment obligation on religious grounds, had little chance of convincing an arbitrator that the company should have made allowance for his religious needs, unless it had made a practice of excusing other employees in the past or some other factor within traditional just cause criteria required that accommodation be made.[129]

Arbitrator Volz stated the paradox this way: "Generally, the application of a rule uniformly to all employees is not discrimination whereas excusing some employees therefrom may be."[130] Or as Arbitrator Gilden commented in an earlier case upholding the discharge of a grievant for refusing to report for Saturday work:

> What [the grievant] is asking for is a unique kind of treatment applicable to him and not to others who may have different, but

---

[127]The guidelines are discussed in Wolkinson, *supra* note 126, at p. 94ff. For the text of the 1967 version, see *American Forest Prods.*, 65 LA 650, 651 (Jacobs, 1975).

[128]429 F.2d 324, 2 FEP 687 (6th Cir. 1970).

[129]Wolkinson, *supra* note 126, traces arbitral views on this subject from an historical perspective, beginning at p. 91.

[130]*A. O. Smith Corp.*, 58 LA 784, 789 (1972).

equally valid, reasons for avoiding their work schedule. To adopt
a special rule excepting [the grievant] from working his work
schedule would be unfair to all other employees, and discriminatory against them.[131]

Once accommodation became settled law, however, arbitrators began falling in line with the EEOC and the courts. In a
case where the grievant had lost his seniority after refusing to
accept recall to a shift that would have prevented him from
attending twice-weekly evening Bible classes, Arbitrator Jacobs
found:

> Article 9(d) [providing that laid-off employees forfeit seniority if
> they do not accept recall] . . . is a neutral and non-discriminatory
> provision. It is necessary and important to the protection of the
> rights of both the Employees and the Company and, accordingly,
> should be strictly construed. It cannot, however, be construed in
> such a fashion as to violate rights guaranteed by Title VII of the
> Civil Rights Act of 1964.[132]

Although cases to the contrary can be found,[133] arbitrators
since 1972 have increasingly held employers to the duty of
accommodation, citing the law, the no-discrimination clause of
the contract, or both.[134] In the process, "nondiscrimination" has
come to mean something more subtle than merely the uniform
application of company policy. Arbitrator Volz explains as
follows:

> [D]ue to variations in religious beliefs, the uniform application of
> a general rule may have the effect of treating employees differ-
> ently, where some of them, due to strong beliefs, are placed in
> the dilemma of compromising their beliefs or violating the rule.
> While it may be said that a woman has a constitutional right to her
> religion but not a constitutional right to a job with the particular

---

[131]*John Morrell & Co.*, 17 LA 280, 282 (1951). For other representative cases from
the pre-1972 era, see *Combustion Eng'g, Inc.*, 49 LA 204 (Daugherty, 1967) (stressing the
"chaos" that could result if individual employees could refuse to work when legitimately
scheduled by management); *Avco Corp.*, 69-2 ARB ¶8602 (Turkus, 1969).

[132]*American Forest Prods. Corp.*, *supra* note 127, at 654.

[133]E.g., *Kentile Floors, Inc.*, 66 LA 933 (Larkin, 1976) (enforcement of Civil Rights
Act is matter for EEOC); *Acme Markets, Inc.*, 165 AAA 18 (Koretz, 1972).

[134]Arbitrator Rehmus, in *Norris Indus.*, 68 LA 171, 174 (1977):
Article 2 of the parties' bargaining Agreement provides that neither the Company
nor the Union will discriminate against any employee on account of religion,
among other factors. I have no doubt that this language must in light of recent
court decisions cited by the Union be construed to impose on the parties an
affirmative duty to accommodate to an employee's religious beliefs.

employer, reasonableness suggests that an accommodation should be sought . . . .[135]

Preconditions for Accommodation

The duty to accommodate will be enforced only if certain conditions are met. The job of establishing that those conditions are present begins with the employee, who must normally satisfy three requirements.

Employee's Religion Is Legitimate One. In practice, disagreement about whether an employee's beliefs and observances are legitimately "religious," and therefore protected, is rare. The courts have been liberal in this respect, and no organization that refers to itself as a church or religious group is likely to be disqualified by an arbitrator, except in the unlikely case that it was concocted by the grievant for his own purposes.[136]

Employee's Belief Is Sincerely Held. The question of whether an employee is really serious about his or her professed religious beliefs is one that the arbitrator is unlikely to tackle except in unusual cases where the grievant's lack of sincerity is clear.

> **EXAMPLE:** A grievant refused to work overtime on his Sabbath, which was Saturday. The evidence showed that he had worked Saturdays without comment during his probationary period; that at times he had given the company reasons other than his faith for Saturday absences; and that he had brought up his religious scruples as the real reason he could not perform Saturday work only after he had been reprimanded for absenteeism.

In the arbitrator's words: "Such demonstrated bad faith on the part of Grievant seriously dilutes his otherwise valid and very

---

[135]*A. O. Smith Corp.*, *supra* note 130.

[136]See H. T. Edwards & J. H. Kaplan, *Religious Discrimination and the Role of Arbitration Under Title VII*, 69 Mich. L. Rev. 599–654 (1971); *Toward a Constitutional Definition of Religion*, 91 Harv. L. Rev. 1056–89 (1978). Where an employee belongs to no established religious organization but nonetheless claims to hold certain religious beliefs, the EEOC has applied the test used by the courts in cases where an individual seeks exemption from military service as a conscientious objector, *i.e.*, whether his belief is, to quote the U.S. Supreme Court, a "sincere and meaningful belief which occupies in the life of its possessor a place parallel to that filled by the God of those admittedly qualifying for the exemption . . . ." (*United States v. Seeger*, 380 U.S. 163 (1965)) This test is cited by Arbitrator Randall in *Alameda-Contra Costa Transit Dist.*, 81-1 ARB ¶8002, 3014–15 (1980).

important claim that the Company reasonably accommodate a religious practice which was of the utmost importance to him."[137]

Religious Requirement Really Exists. Whether the employee's religion really prohibits what he or she says it prohibits is a much more common bone of contention than either of the two foregoing conditions. It comes up frequently in cases involving work on the Sabbath, since not every religion imposes a prohibition on Sabbath work. Where, for example, an employee refused to work on Sundays because, according to him, the Roman Catholic Church forbade Sunday work, his case fell flat because (1) that church does not forbid Sunday work; (2) the grievant could satisfy his obligation to attend religious services by attending mass on Saturday or on Sunday evening;[138] (3) although in theory the grievant might have the right to impose on himself more stringent spiritual standards than his church required, the fact was that his priest did not recognize him as a regular churchgoer;[139] and (4) the grievant made no inquiry about possible Sunday work when he was hired, thus implying that the problem was not uppermost in his mind.[140]

The Employer's Rights: The Undue-Hardship Test

Once the foregoing three criteria have been satisfied, the employer has a duty—but not an unconditional duty—to accommodate to the employee's religious practices. According to both EEOC guidelines and the 1972 amendments to Title VII, accommodation need be made only if it can be achieved "without undue hardship" to the employer. Both arbitrators and the courts have placed the burden on the employer to prove any

---

[137]*Weyerhaeuser Co.*, 70 LA 1123, 1127 (Shearer, 1978). See also *Alameda-Contra Costa Transit Dist.*, *supra* note 136, where employer witnesses testified credibly that they had several times seen the grievant driving her bus without wearing the hair-covering turban that she claimed her Black Muslim faith required her to wear at all times; and *Building Owners and Managers Ass'n*, 67 LA 1031 (Griffin, 1976).

[138]See *J. Schoeneman, Inc.*, 69 LA 325 (Oppenheimer, 1977), where the arbitrator upheld the grievant's discharge for attending a two-week religious school program, after the company denied his leave application, even though attendance was required of him as an Elder in his Jehovah's Witness congregation, since he could have attended the same program later in the year.

[139]See also *Kentile Floors, Inc.*, *supra* note 133, where the grievant took an unauthorized leave of absence to attend a conference to raise funds for an educational institution. Even though the college in question was church-affiliated, the arbitrator found that attendance at the conference was not a religious practice in the same sense as a religious service.

[140]*Building Owners and Managers Ass'n*, *supra* note 137.

undue-hardship claim with hard evidence that extra costs or other problems would result from accommodation. Speculation by the employer that accommodation to an employee's religious needs might cause it undue hardship at some future date is not enough to justify a refusal to accommodate.

> *Arbitrator Dunsford:* [S]uch an approach would reduce the standard of reasonable accommodation to a nullity, since by definition there will be no need to accommodate an employee unless there is the prospect of a conflict. . . . If the standard of reasonable accommodation is to have any substance at all, it must at least mean that the Company will endeavor to work out conflicts in concrete situations rather than to seek ideal assurance that a particular assignment of an employee will never entail a conflict in the future.[141]

In the following survey of the two areas in which religion–job conflicts crop up most frequently—work scheduling and dress rules—however, it will become clear that in deciding what constitutes undue hardship, arbitrators have generally taken the position that just cause contemplates accommodation to an employer's business needs as well as the religious needs of the employee.

Work-Scheduling Cases. By far the greatest number of reasonable-accommodation disputes come about when an employee is disciplined for refusing to work on the Sabbath (either as part of the normal work schedule or as required overtime) or on some other occasion when there is a conflict with religious obligations—Bible classes,[142] church conferences,[143] religious schools,[144] special services,[145] and the like.

---

[141]*U.S. Steel Corp.*, 70 LA 1131, 1138 (1978).

[142]*Norris Indus.*, *supra* note 134, at 175, in which the arbitrator rejected the employer's argument that its obligation to accommodate the grievant's religious needs was limited to Sabbath observances, commenting,

> I cannot wholly agree with this position, for to do so would allow the Company to assume the role of a Pontius Pilate. The relevant [EEOC] guidelines and [court] cases emphasize Sabbath observance, but they do not eliminate the need to take account of other religious observances. I conclude that such accommodation is appropriate here, though perhaps not as great an obligation as for a Sabbath.

The arbitrator in *J. Schoeneman, Inc.*, *supra* note 138, also rejected the employer's contention that Title VII protects only Sabbath observances.

[143]*Armstrong Rubber Co.*, 58 LA 143 (Williams, 1972).

[144]*J. Schoeneman, Inc.*, *supra* note 138.

[145]*Kuhlman Elec.*, 81-2 ARB ¶8372 (Archer, undated).

In its decision in *Trans World Airlines v. Hardison*,[146] the Supreme Court laid down two basic limits to accommodation in work scheduling cases.

(1) Neither the employer nor the union may be required in the interest of accommodation to take any steps that are inconsistent with an otherwise valid collective bargaining agreement or that violate the seniority rights of other employees.

(2) The company may not be required to bear a significant cost in accommodating a religious employee, for example, by having to call in a higher-paid supervisor or to pay premium wages to another available employee.[147]

How these limits are applied depends upon the particular facts, as the following examples show:

> **EXAMPLE NO. 1:** An employee asked to be let off early every Wednesday evening in order to attend Bible class. The employer refused and, when she took off early one night without permission, discharged her for insubordination. Factors that the arbitrator took into account:
>
> - Not enough qualified substitutes were available to cover the employee's job every Wednesday.
> - When the employee left early, the remaining employees produced at only 71 percent of capacity, proving that she was needed.
> - The company demonstrated its good faith by allowing the employee to leave early on Wednesday when she was not absolutely needed.
> - The employee always was given advance notice when she was required to work Wednesday evening and could have arranged to attend Bible class at another nearby church on Wednesday morning.

In his decision, the arbitrator acknowledged the company's needs, agreeing that to allow the employee to leave early every Wednesday was too great a hardship. Nevertheless, he decided that the employee deserved one more chance to comply with the company's requirements and reinstated her without back

---

[146]432 U.S. 63, 14 FEP Cases 1697 (1977).

[147]The scope of the the the duty to make work-schedule accommodations is discussed in B. L. SCHLEI & P. GROSSMAN, EMPLOYMENT DISCRIMINATION LAW 236–39 (2d ed. 1983), and 67–68 (Five-Year Cum. Supp.). See also *U.S. Steel Corp.*, *supra* note 141, at 1135ff; *Quality Transparent Bag, Inc.*, 81-2 ARB ¶8496 (Heinsz, 1981); *Kuhlman Electric,*, *supra* note 145.

pay on condition that she agree to work full shifts whenever required.[148]

> **EXAMPLE NO. 2:** When an employee bid into a sanitation department job, she informed the employer that she could not work Sundays because her Old Orthodox faith strictly prohibited Sabbath work. The employer returned her to production, and she protested that her Title VII rights had been violated. The relevant factors included the following:
>
> • Regular Sunday work for the sanitation crew was necessary to keep the plant clean for food processing scheduled the other six days during harvest season.
> • High turnover in the sanitation department due to the employment of much casual labor required the employer to be strict about Sunday work.
> • Although the production job to which the employee was transferred carried a lower rate, she had not taken advantage of opportunities to bid for higher positions following her transfer.

In this situation, the arbitrator held that the employee's transfer was proper, and the employer was under no further duty of accommodation.[149]

> **EXAMPLE NO. 3:** An employer adopted a rotating schedule that sometimes required two Orthodox Jews to work between sundown Friday and sundown Saturday, their Sabbath. Both were discharged when they refused the Sabbath work assignment. The circumstances were these:
>
> • The new schedule was necessary to cope with an upswing in production.
> • The two employees both worked in highly skilled classifications, and their presence was required on every shift.
> • Substitutes were rarely available, and the use of substitutes would impair production efficiency.

Given these facts, the arbitrator found, the employer could not reasonably be required to excuse the two employees whenever their schedule called for Sabbath work. Yet the employer failed in its obligation to accommodate the two, for it did not

---

[148]*Norris Indus.*, *supra* note 134.

[149]*General Foods Corp.*, 72 LA 505 (Conant, 1979). For other cases in which the employer met its duty of accommodation, see *Avco Corp.*, 69-2 ARB ¶8602 (Turkus, 1969); *Walker Mfg. Co.*, 60 LA 525 (Simon, 1973); *J. Schoeneman, Inc.*, *supra* note 138; *Weyerhaeuser Co.*, *supra* note 137; *Quality Transparent Bag, Inc.*, *supra* note 147.

consider transferring them to other positions in which Sabbath work would not be required or from which they could be excused, if necessary, without undue interference with operations. The parties were directed to explore the feasibility of a transfer.[150]

> **EXAMPLE NO. 4:** Suspended for excessive absenteeism, the grievant claimed the employer had improperly refused to excuse his absences when he took time off to preach at funeral services for members of his congregation. These were the relevant factors:
>
> - There would have been no added cost to the company in allowing the employee time off because it had a pool of employees who substituted for absentees and were paid at comparable rates.
> - The employer did not allow the employee to use vacation days for funeral absences, nor had it counseled him about the possibility of transferring to another shift that would have involved fewer schedule conflicts.
> - The employee had shown his willingness to compromise by agreeing to give up his practice of assisting ministers from other congregations and to limit his preaching to funerals within his own congregation. He also agreed to take only half days off when he was needed to preach.

In the arbitrator's view, the employer made no showing of undue hardship. The employer was directed to rescind the employee's three-day suspension and to make reasonable accommodation to his religious practices.[151]

> **EXAMPLE NO. 5:** A corrections officer who was a Seventh Day Adventist performed his assigned tasks on Friday evening, his Sabbath, for some 18 months before he began to have guilt pangs. After much soul-searching and discussions with his pastor, he refused to work on Fridays when the rotating schedule required him to do so and was suspended indefinitely for insubordination. Key factors were these:
>
> - The officer had done his best to swap shifts with other employees but had been unable to do so. He also had offered to

---

[150]*U.S. Steel Corp.*, *supra* note 141. See also *American Forest Prods. Corp.*, 65 LA 650 (Jacobs, 1975), where the employer was not permitted to terminate the seniority of an employee who refused recall to a shift that conflicted with Bible class, since there were other employees on the seniority list who were willing to work that shift and no cost or production problems would have resulted from allowing the grievant to remain on the seniority list until another opening came up.

[151]*Kuhlman Elec.*, *supra* note 145.

reimburse the employer for any additional costs it might incur
by allowing him to be off.
- He was willing to change shifts but had insufficient seniority to
  do so.
- The employer had a "float pool" of officers without regular
  assignments who could fill in for him.

The arbitrator reinstated the officer with back pay, less
compensation for any Friday he would not have worked for
religious reasons during the suspension period. The officer's
proposal, he said, would "allow him to worship without violating
the rights of anyone else and at no cost to the Department. I can
fathom no reason why his approach should not be adopted."[152]

Dress-Rule Cases. The second major group of disputes concerning
reasonable accommodation can be traced to the Biblical injunction against wearing the other sex's clothing, which is strictly
observed by some religious groups.[153] Most pants-only rules are
adopted for safety reasons and present little difficulty. Once it
has been established that it is reasonable and necessary, according to criteria discussed in Chapter 2, an employee can be
required to comply with a pants-only rule unless she can offer
an acceptable alternative to pants that protects the legs equally
well.[154] It is by giving employees a fair opportunity to come up
with substitute leg covering that the employer satisfies its duty
of reasonable accommodation.[155]

In one case of this type, a hospital began requiring all
operating room personnel to wear a new type of pants uniform,
among other new measures adopted to reduce the danger of
infection to patients in its operating area. The requirement was
reasonable, the arbitrator found, since research persuasively
established that pants were more effective than the old scrub

---

[152]*Dep't of Correctional Servs.*, 92 LA 1059, 1063 (Babiskin, 1989). In *New York Dep't
of Environmental Conservation*, 87 LA 848 (Babiskin, 1986), a forest ranger who refused
on religious grounds to work Saturdays was given 30 days by the arbitrator to choose
one of three alternative positions offered by the employer which would not require
Saturday work. The arbitrator found that the employer had "bent over backwards" to
accommodate the grievant, but that the latter had sought accommodation regardless of
cost or inconvenience to the employer or coworkers.

[153]"A woman shall not wear anything that pertains to a man, nor shall a man put
on a woman's garment; for whoever does these things is an abomination to the Lord
your God." Deuteronomy 22:5.

[154]*A. O. Smith Corp.*, 58 LA 784 (Volz, 1972); *Colt Indus.*, 71 LA 22 (Rutherford,
1978).

[155]In *A. O. Smith Corp.*, *supra* note 154, the grievants were given a chance to come
up with alternative protective clothing.

gowns in channeling tiny particles of shedding skin to the floor. The arbitrator gave the grievant the chance to design a modified gown that would achieve the same result. When she was unable to do so, he approved her transfer to another department where pants were not required.[156]

Where considerations other than safety are behind a pants-only rule (or other dress rule to which an employee objects on religious grounds), the employer must demonstrate that the type of clothing required is reasonably required for its operations—that is, the familiar business-necessity test is applied.[157]

Religious Accommodation and Arbitration: Summary

The employer cannot avoid the duty of accommodation by arguing that even if accommodating would not be a hardship, other employees might clamor for similar treatment that would cause a serious problem.

> *Arbitrator Dunsford:* No doubt the number of employees seeking such special treatment on religious grounds does affect the ability of the Company to find accommodation for them all, and on a proper showing the Company may certainly rely on that factor.[158]

But the showing mentioned by Dunsford normally is possible only after the employer has made an effort to accommodate the employees requesting special treatment. Mere guesswork as to what might occur is not sufficient.

Sometimes a claim of failure to accommodate to religious practices is based upon the fact that accommodation has been made for other employees—what might be called "disparate accommodation." An example is where a Jewish employee who was discharged for refusing to work Saturdays complained that Christian employees were routinely excused from work to at-

---

[156]*Hurley Hosp.*, 70 LA 1061, 71 LA 1013 (Roumell, 1978) (the second cite is to a proceeding required to decide whether the garment designed by the grievant met the employer's sanitation standards). In *Alameda-Contra Costa Transit Dist.*, 81-1 ARB ¶8002 (Randall, 1980), the duty of accommodation was put in issue by a female employee's claim that her Black Muslim faith prohibited her from wearing a standard bus driver's cap and required that she wear a turban that covered her hair entirely. The arbitrator acknowledged the importance to the employer of having its drivers wear a clearly identifiable uniform. However, she did not reach the question of whether an exception should be made; the grievant had been seen without her turban on several occasions, leading to the conclusion that she did not take her religion's turban-only injunction as seriously as she claimed.

[157]See Ch. 2, p. 110.

[158]*U.S. Steel Corp.*, 70 LA 1131, 1138 (1978).

tend Sunday church services.[159] Such a complaint is not fundamentally a matter of Title VII rights; it goes to the just cause
principle that what applies to one employee must apply to all
unless different treatment can be justified on some reasonable
basis.

> *Arbitrator Heinsz:* It is true that most arbitrators require that Com-
> pany practices and discipline be uniform. . . . However, where a
> reasonable basis for variations exists in a policy or penalty, most
> arbitrators will permit such differences notwithstanding charges
> of disparate treatment.[160]

In the case mentioned above of the Jewish employee who
refused to work on Saturday, he was unwilling to work at all on
Saturday, whereas the Sunday chuchgoers asked only that they
be allowed to report late; furthermore, Saturday was a regular
work day, whereas Sunday work was required only occasionally.
Thus, the conditions under which the Sunday churchgoers requested accommodation were significantly different, and the
"disparate accommodation" was justified.[161]

Another employee who was denied permission to attend
church on Good Friday complained that employees in other
departments had been accommodated. The evidence showed,
however, that the machines operated by those other employees
could be shut down for a short period without any problem,
while in the grievant's department the manufacturing process
could not be interrupted without significant loss of time and
material. Again, different circumstances justified treating the
grievant differently from the other operators.[162]

The cases discussed above all emphasize that reasonable
accommodation cases call for a balancing of interests: the em-

---

[159]As in *Weyerhaeuser Co.,* 70 LA 1123 (Shearer, 1978).

[160]*Quality Transparent Bag, Inc., supra* note 147, at 5181.

[161]*Weyerhaeuser Co., supra* note 159.

[162]*Quality Transparent Bag, Inc., supra* note 147. In *General Foods Corp., supra* note
149, some employees had been excused from Sunday work for family events and other
reasons, as the grievant claimed, but only on an intermittent basis; no one else had been
granted the full exemption from working Sundays that the grievant was seeking. In *J.
Shoeneman, Inc.,* 69 LA 325 (Oppenheimer, 1977), other employees had been given
leaves of absence for religious reasons, but all during "slow" production periods, not
during the peak season when the grievant wanted time. In *Norris Indus.,* 68 LA 171
(Rehmus, 1977), although some supervisors had adjusted some employees' work schedules so that they could participate in bowling leagues, the evidence showed that the
company had stopped that practice as soon as the union complained about it.

ployee's right to follow his or her religious convictions, and the employer's right to run its business efficiently. An employee has the right, as an individual, to practice religion as his or her conscience dictates, but not an absolute right to a particular job. By law, the employer must do what it reasonably can to accommodate religious needs, but if accommodation causes real problems that could be eliminated or alleviated by compromise on the employee's part, the employee cannot expect to be kept on if he or she refuses to meet the employer half way. Thus, reasonable accommodation may be a matter of mutual effort— both sides may have to give a little to make accommodation work.[163]

Reasonable Accommodation and the Disabled

Until fairly recently, the concept of reasonable accommodation was applied almost exclusively in the context of religious discrimination. But since passage of the Rehabilitation Act of 1973, as amended,[164] and the adoption of federal orders and regulations under that Act, the concept of accommodation has been extended to the needs of disabled individuals, at least those working for the Federal Government or employers contracting with the government.[165]

---

[163]See, e.g., *Reynolds & Reynolds Co.*, 63 LA 157 (High, 1974), involving a Jehovah's Witness who attended religious gatherings two evenings a week. When the employer began scheduling required overtime that extended the work day beyond 6 p.m., he began leaving work before quitting time and was warned, suspended, and finally discharged in rapid succession. The employee claimed that if he worked until six o'clock he would not have time to make the one-hour drive from the plant to his home, prepare himself spiritually, eat dinner, pick up other family members, and get to church in time for the service.

Should the employer have accommodated this employee's religious needs? Perhaps, if there had been a clear and irreconcilable conflict between his overtime work schedule and his religious obligations. But by asking for time not only to attend church but also to attend to personal matters such as picking up his mother-in-law, the employee went too far. Furthermore, he admitted he could fulfill his obligations even though he arrived after the meeting had begun, but he felt he should be punctual. Clearly, the arbitrator found, the employee was unwilling to make any adjustments that might have permitted him to fulfill both his religious and his employment obligations. Instead, he left the matter of accommodation entirely to the employer. Under these circumstances, his discharge was sustained.

[164]29 U.S.C. §791 *et seq.*

[165]Amended §503 of the Rehabilitation Act provides:

Any contract in excess of $2,500 entered into by any Federal department or agency . . . shall contain a provision requiring that, in employing persons to carry out such contract the party contracting with the United States shall take affirmative action to employ and advance in employment qualified handicapped persons as

Like victims of race or sex discrimination, disabled employees of covered employers have recourse to the grievance procedure to pursue their right to accommodation.[166] For the most part, discrimination against the disabled arises at the hiring stage. However, just cause discharge may become an issue under any of the following circumstances: where an individual becomes disabled (often because of injury, industrial or otherwise) after being hired; where a preexisting condition deteriorates after hiring; or where changed job requirements make it more difficult for a disabled individual to perform the job.

At one time the question of whether accommodation—for example, by means of transfer to a light-duty assignment—instead of discharge should be attempted depended almost entirely on whether the contract expressly required such accommodation.[167] The Vocational Rehabilitation Act, however, injected a new basis upon which an arbitrator might direct that accommodation be made.

> **EXAMPLE:** When a paraplegic was hired as a clerk typist in the employer's data processing center, she informed management that she would need to take time off for medical reasons and was told that would be no problem. However, soon after she began work, she suffered a series of ailments related to her paraplegia until she was missing 31 percent of her work days. She was counseled and warned and finally discharged about seven months after she had been hired.

Was accommodation to this employee's health problems required of the employer? The arbitrator's starting point was the familiar undue-hardship test.[168] A 31-percent absence rate

---

defined in Section 706(7) of this title."
Section 504 prohibits discrimination against disabled persons in any program or activity receiving federal financial assistance.

[166]See *Bay Area Rapid Transit Dist.*, 79 LA 1171 (Koven, 1983), in which the question of whether the employer could be required to make reasonable accommodation to disabled employees was determined to be arbitrable based on the theory that an arbitrator may consider federal law as a guide and on language in the contract prohibiting discrimination because of handicap.

[167]B. W. Wolkinson, *Arbitration and the Employment Rights of the Physically Disadvantaged*, 36:1 ARB. J. 23–30 (1981). For an example of accommodation required by the contract, see *K-P Mfg. Co.*, 74 LA 1046 (Grabb, 1980) (industrial injury; reassignment of grievant to job within physical capacity).

[168]29 C.F.R. 1613.704: "An agency shall make reasonable accommodation to the known physical or mental limitations of a qualified handicapped applicant or employee unless the agency can demonstrate that the accommodation would impose an undue hardship on the operation of its program."

was higher than the employer could reasonably be expected to tolerate, he found, especially since the grievant was one of only a handful of employees in a busy office and her many absences caused serious difficulties.

If the evidence had stopped there, just cause for discharge probably would have been found. But it did not. The employer fired the grievant without making any investigation into the circumstances underlying her attendance problems. Had it done so, it would have learned that the end was in sight. The particular medical problems causing most of the grievant's absences were well on their way to being cleared up. According to her doctor, her future absences could be expected to total no more than 14 days per year, close to the sick leave allowance and therefore certainly a tolerable level of absence. Even that, the arbitrator found, should be stretched somewhat to accommodate to the grievant's disability, perhaps by allowing her to use some of the annual leave provided by the contract.

Moreover, the employer could have helped the grievant prevent some of her absences. One of her problems was a skin condition aggravated by prolonged sitting. The grievant testified that if she could take an hour for lunch instead of half an hour, making up the time after work, and if a couch could be provided, her condition would improve.

The employer protested that it would incur extra expense by having someone work overtime to supervise the grievant, but admitted that an employee could work an hour or two without supervision. "There is no doubt," the arbitrator noted, "that permitting her a special shift . . . would cause some inconvenience and perhaps expense to the agency, but the statute protects against undue hardship, not against any hardship caused by efforts to accommodate." The grievant was reinstated with back pay.[169]

Again, as in accommodation cases involving religion, what is needed is a balancing of a disabled employee's right to work and the employer's right to manage the business efficiently.

III. Arbitration and the National Labor Relations Act

The Bargaining Contract and the National Labor Relations Act

The problem of alleged discrimination because of union activity is similar in several respects to the problem of discrimina-

---

[169]*Fleet Combat Training Center, Pac. Agency,* 82-1 ARB ¶8099, 3482 (Ross, 1981).

tion on the basis of race, sex, and other Title VII factors. Most collective bargaining agreements contain a clause prohibiting discrimination because of union activity. Even in the absence of such a clause, the just cause provision has been interpreted as prohibiting discharge or discipline motivated by an employee's efforts on behalf of the union.[170] Anti-union discrimination is also covered by section 8(a)(1) of the National Labor Relations Act (NLRA), which makes it an unfair practice for an employer to interfere with, restrain, or coerce employees in the exercise of the right to organize for collective bargaining purposes; section 8(a)(3), which prohibits discrimination in regard to hire, tenure, or any condition of employment to discourage or encourage membership in a labor organization; and section 8(b)(2), which prohibits the union from causing an employer to discriminate against an employee in violation of section 8(a)(3).

Because of this overlap between contract and law, arbitrators hearing grievances that involve union discrimination charges must decide whether they should confine themselves to interpreting contract language or follow the requirements of the NLRB as interpreted by decisions of the NLRB and the courts.[171] This question of contract versus external law is the same issue that arose when Title VII was passed in 1964.

The overlap between contract and the NLRA also presents the employee with the choice whether to pursue his or her claim through the grievance procedure and arbitration, or to file an unfair labor practice with the NLRB, or both. There are, however, major differences between the Title VII overlap cases and the NLRA overlap cases. Among the most notable is the preferred status that arbitration has historically been accorded by the courts as a mechanism for dispute settlement in union discrimination cases. In *Alexander v. Gardner-Denver Co.*,[172] the U.S. Supreme Court openly expressed doubt whether an employee's Title VII rights could be adequately protected by arbitration, and for that reason the Court gave employees the right to press Title VII-type discrimination claims in the courts as well

---

[170]In *Dow Jones & Co.*, 70 LA 375 (Kornblum, 1978), the employer's argument that the grievant could not raise a claim of union discrimination because the contract contained no specific no-discrimination clause was rejected by the arbitrator, who held that discipline because of union activity would violate the just cause provision.

[171]For a review of the approaches arbitrators have taken to this question, see F. ELKOURI & E. A. ELKOURI, HOW ARBITRATION WORKS 384–87 (4th ed. 1985).

[172]415 U.S. 36, 7 FEP Cases 81 (1974).

as in arbitration. No comparable skepticism about arbitration as an appropriate forum has been voiced by the courts in NLRA-type cases.

One reason is that the NLRA itself, although it retains for the Board the ultimate authority to decide whether the Act has been violated, encourages (in section 173(d)) the final settlement of disputes by means of negotiated grievance procedures. Another reason is that in most cases anti-union discrimination presents no conflict between an individual's rights and the union's interests. Indeed, such discrimination is a direct threat to the union's security, as well as to the grievant's job, so the union may be expected to give the grievant the best representation it can. The exception arises in cases in which the grievant's activities are not on behalf of the recognized bargaining agent but are directed towards unseating the incumbent leadership or to getting another union installed.

Then, too, the factors that may inhibit an arbitrator from making explicit findings about race or sex discrimination are not likely to be present in disputes involving union discrimination; to say that an employer is antagonistic to the union ordinarily is not as incendiary as saying that it discriminates on the basis of race. Moreover, the very nature of the collective bargaining relationship is adversarial, so that an arbitrator's finding that an employer seized upon some pretext to get rid of a militant shop steward who had been flooding the grievance procedure might be regarded in some measure as just "part of the game."

The Doctrine of Deferral to Arbitration

For these and other reasons, the NLRB, with the courts' approval, has in many cases deferred to arbitration in matters that are susceptible to resolution in both forums. The Board's "deferral doctrine" has changed over the years, but it was pushed to its outer limit in 1971 with *Collyer Insulated Wire Co.*[173] There the Board held that it would temporarily defer action even where the parties had not proceeded to arbitration, as long as there was a grievance procedure that might reasonably be expected to lead to settlement or a decision by the arbitrator that would meet the following standards, as enunciated in the

---

[173]192 NLRB 837, 77 LRRM 1931 (1971).

earlier case of *Spielberg Mfg. Co.*:[174] (1) all parties had agreed to be bound by the award; (2) the proceedings before the arbitrator had been fair and regular; and (3) the arbitrator's conclusions were "not clearly repugnant to the purposes and policies of the Act." However, the Board said it would retain jurisdiction to take further action if (1) the dispute was not resolved amicably or submitted promptly to arbitration or (2) there was a showing that the grievance procedures were not fair and regular or reached a result that was repugnant to the Act.[175]

Collyer generated a wave of discussion concerning the wisdom of the NLRB's deferral policy. Protests were heard that the *Collyer* doctrine operated to compel the parties to arbitrate even in cases where both might believe that the Board was a preferable forum for their dispute. The argument was also made that arbitrators to whom cases were deferred (or "Collyered," in the phrase that was quickly coined) would be under greater pressure to rule on violations of the NLRA as well as on contract violations, since review of their awards by the Board was not only possible but probable.

Whether in response to these protests or for other reasons, the Board beginning in 1977 began restricting the application of the *Collyer* doctrine. However, in 1984, the Board, noting that it had "worked well," ruled that the *Collyer* doctrine "deserves to be resurrected and infused with renewed life."[176] Thus, under current NLRB policy, the Board will defer to arbitration not only in cases involving allegations of unilateral action by the employer on a matter subject to bargaining (the issue in *Collyer*) but also in discharge and other types of cases.[177]

Impact of Deferral on Arbitration

How has the Board's deferral policy affected arbitration, particularly in reference to disputes involving just cause and anti-union discrimination?

In the years following *Spielberg*, the NLRB's deferral policy was taken by many (though not all) arbitrators as an implied

---

[174]112 NLRB 1080, 36 LRRM 1152 (1955).

[175]*Collyer Insulated Wire Co.*, 192 NLRB 837, 77 LRRM 1931 (1971).

[176]*United Technologies*, 268 NLRB 557, 115 LRRM 1049, 1051 (1984).

[177]For a full review of the *Collyer* doctrine and the Board's policy of deferring to arbitration, see THE DEVELOPING LABOR LAW Ch. 20 (C. J. Morris, ed., 2d. ed. 1983), and 1982–1988 Supp.

mandate to take the NLRA into account when deciding grievances that also potentially involved unfair labor practices.

> *Arbitrator Wallen:* [The *Spielberg* doctrine] places on arbitrators an
> especial responsibility, in a case where an allegation of discrimina-
> tion appears to be other than wholly capricious, to make certain
> that Management's actions are completely free from discrimina-
> tory taint and, it seems to us, to resolve doubts on this score in
> favor of upholding the purposes of the Act.[178]

Collyer, as already suggested, gave many arbitrators a new
impetus to attempt to conform their decisions, not only to the
purposes of the NLRA, but also to the NLRB's prevailing standards for interpreting the Act's requirements. That was true,
for example, in a case where the grievant was discharged for
calling his supervisor a liar and a fool in the course of a grievance
meeting. The arbitrator, noting that the Board might reverse
his decision if he did not take NLRB standards into account,
relied on Board rulings in deciding that because the grievant
had been acting in his role as union representative, his activity
was protected and his discharge for insubordination should be
set aside.[179]

In view of the current policy of the Board to give full

---

[178]*Hoague-Sprague Corp.*, 48 LA 19 (1967) (insubordination). See also *In the Round
Dinner Playhouse, Inc.*, 55 LA 118 (Kamin, 1970) (discharge for being too old for chorus
line); *Shields & Terrell Convalescent Hosp.*, 56 LA 884 (Heilbrun, 1971) ("best course for
arbitrators in determining allegations of employment discrimination is to use the same
standards applied by the [NLRB]"); *Roanoke Iron & Bridge Works, Inc.*, 75 LA 917
(Boetticher, 1980) (hiring of nonunion employee); *Chamberlain Group, Inc.*, 88-1 ARB
¶8226 (Woolf, 1988) (applying statutory standards to unilateral implementation of no-
fault absence policy not beyond arbitrator's authority).

[179]*Owens-Illinois, Inc.*, 79-2 ARB ¶8518 (Witney, 1979). Other post-*Collyer* cases in
which the NLRA and/or NLRB standards are expressly taken into account include
Southern Cal. Edison Co., 61 LA 453 (Block, 1973) (refusal to participate in investigatory
interview without union representation); *Dura Containers, Inc.*, 67 LA 82 (Maslanka,
1976) (safety rule violations); *Ozark Border Elec. Coop.*, 67 LA 438 (Maniscalco, 1976)
(refusal of work assignment); *Theo. Kupfer Iron Works, Inc.*, 67 LA 1203 (Gundermann,
1976) (libeling employer); *Redfield Co.*, 69 LA 1024 (Aisenberg, 1977) (strike misconduct); *Chamberlain Group, Inc.*, 88-1 ARB ¶8226 (Woolf, 1988) (holding that
the arbitrator should interpret the contract, see *Kings Command Meats, Inc.*, 60 LA 491
(Kleinsorge, 1973) (low productivity); *Farmer Bros Co.*, 64 LA 901 (Jones, 1975) (refusal
to work new schedule), noting that an award couched in statutory terms might be subject
to reversal in the courts on the ground that the arbitrator had exceeded his authority
under the contract; *Western Mass. Elec. Co.*, 65 LA 816 (Summers, 1975) (unilateral
suspension of employee purchase plan). In *American Mach. and Foundry, Inc.*, 63 LA
1138 (Serot, 1974), the arbitrator interpreted the *Collyer* doctrine to mean that an
arbitrator should give full consideration to the facts underlying both the grievance and
the unfair labor practice charge but should not necessarily decide whether the law had
been violated.

credence to the *Collyer* doctrine, it seems likely that many arbitrators will continue to look to the Act and to the views of the Board in discrimination cases on the theory that, whatever the Board's policy on deferral, an arbitrator's decisions should be consistent with the relevant labor law.[180] Arbitrator Reginald Alleyne has pointed to four major reasons why the grievant may be well-advised to resort to arbitration rather than to the NLRB:[181]

(1) In arbitration, the burden of proof is on the company; in unfair labor practice matters, the General Counsel of the NLRB has to assume the burden of proving that disciplinary action was discriminatory.

(2) An arbitrator can find there was no just cause for discipline on any one of a number of grounds (lack of notice, an unreasonable rule, insufficient proof of misconduct, etc.). The Board can find for the complaining employee on only one basis, that the employer was motivated specifically by that employee's union activity.[182]

(3) An arbitrator has more flexibility with respect to remedy than does the NLRB. If the Board finds that all essential elements of a violation were not present, it will normally dismiss the charge and the employee is back where he or she began. An arbitrator who reached the same conclusion that union discrimination was not proved might nevertheless reduce discharge to some lesser penalty if, for example, the penalty was too harsh under customary just cause standards for the misconduct in question.

(4) Finally, arbitrators and the Board typically consider

---

[180]For a comprehensive discussion of the NLRB's deferral policy, see C. J. Morris, *NLRB Deferral to the Arbitration Process: The Arbitrator's Awesome Responsibility*, ARBITRATION 1984 51–76 (Proceedings of the 37th Annual Meeting, National Academy of Arbitrators 1985). See also D. E. Ray, *Individual Rights and NLRB Deferral to the Arbitration Process: A Proposal*, 28:1 B.C. L. REV. 1–18 (1986); M. W. Jeanette, *NLRB Policies Concerning Deferral to Arbitrators*, 38 LAB. L. REV. 348–59 (1987).

[181]R. Alleyne, *Courts, Arbitrators, and the NLRB: The Nature of the Deferral Beast*, DECISIONAL THINKING OF ARBITRATORS AND JUDGES 249–51 (Proceedings of the 33d Annual Meeting, National Academy of Arbitrators 1981).

[182]Arbitrator Jones observed in *Farmer Bros. Co., supra* note 179, at 905:

As in many labor-management situations, this contract and statute are almost wholly duplicative. By necessary implication, if not expressly, collective agreements, every bit as much as statute, typically proscribe anti-union disciplinary actions discriminating against employees because of their union acts or views. But anti-union discrimination, comprised of purposeful acts having foreseeable consequences, difficult of proof and even more so of defense, need not be ruled upon here since there are alternative dispositive grounds in the collective agreement which govern this case.

the same elements in deciding whether proof of discrimination because of union activity was present in a particular case. So in this respect the grievant loses nothing by going to arbitration.

What Proves Anti-Union Discrimination

Arbitrators agree that if an employee engages in misconduct, being a union activist does not offer him or her protection from discipline. Some like to say that when charges of anti-union discrimination come into the picture, "it becomes necessary for the Arbitrator to examine the evidence with special care,"[183] or that "added caution" is required,[184] or that "the responsibility of his task is increased,"[185] or that the employer shoulders "an exceptional burden."[186] What this really means is hard to pin down, however, since an arbitrator should weigh the evidence with great care in any discharge or discipline case. The decisive factor is whether the employer proved that misconduct was committed.[187] As in any disciplinary case, if no misconduct is proved, no discipline is proper, and it is not necessary for the union to prove that the real reason for the employer's action was anti-union animus.

If, on the other hand, the employer produces convincing evidence of misconduct, then the burden shifts to the union to prove that anti-union animus was the real reason for the grievant's discipline.[188] Arbitrators sometimes have gone further, however, and adopted the "dual motive" standard of the NLRB,

---

[183]*Cook Paint and Varnish Co.*, 63 LA 230, 233 (Erbs, 1974) (poor attitude).

[184]*Crowell-Collier Broadcasting Corp.*, 65-2 ARB ¶8739, 5710 (Jones, 1965) (poor performance).

[185]*Underwood Glass Co.*, 70-2 ARB ¶8577, 4896 (Caraway, 1970) (substandard performance).

[186]*W. R. Grace & Co.*, 62 LA 779, 783 (Boals, 1974) (absenteeism).

[187]Cases in which the company satisfied its burden, thereby diluting union charges that anti-union animus was the motive for its action, include *Atlantic Broadcasting Co.*, 20 LA 7 (Bailer, 1953) (tardiness, neglect of duty, dress rule violations); *Kroger Co.*, 24 LA 48 (Holly, 1954) (accident record); *Buick Youngstown Co.*, 41 LA 570 (Dworkin, 1963) (gross negligence); *Intalco Aluminum Corp.*, 70-1 ARB ¶8043 (Stoll, 1969); *Underwood Glass Co.*, *supra* note 185; *King's Command Meats, Inc.*, *supra* note 179; *American Mach. & Foundry, Inc.*, *supra* note 179; *Univ. of Cal., Berkeley*, 93 LA 450 (Wilcox, 1989) (absenteeism, failure to obey order).

[188]See, e.g., *Sinclair Refining Co.*, 63-2 ARB ¶8632 (McGury, 1963) (uncooperative attitude); *Feather-Lite Mfg. Co.*, 62 LA 305 (Williams, 1974) (low productivity); *Humko Sheffield Chem.*, 66 LA 1261 (Ross, 1976) (insubordination); *Genuine Parts Co.*, 66 LA 1331 (O'Neill, undated) (dishonesty); *City of W. Palm Beach*, 69 LA 1157 (Remington, 1977) (poor attitude).

holding that even if misconduct was committed, and even if the penalty was reasonable on its face, no discipline can be sustained if anti-union motivation played a part.[189]

Standing alone, neither the fact that an employee has engaged in militant activity on the union's behalf[190] nor the fact that the employer has shown itself to be hostile to the union[191] is enough to prove anti-union discrimination. Some combination of the following four elements normally must be present: (1) evidence of union activity;[192] (2) lack of good cause for discipline;[193] (3) expressions of antagonism by management;[194] and (4) a close connection between the timing of disciplinary action and the union activity.

EXAMPLE NO. 1: A few months after she was hired to sing and dance in the chorus at a musical comedy theater, an employee

---

[189]*E.g., Safeway Stores, Inc.*, 44 LA 889 (Block, 1965) (other employees penalized far less severely for refusing to work overtime); *Hoague-Sprague Corp., supra* note 178 (leadership in recent strike found to be reason for discharge rather than suspension); *Grand Auto Stores*, 54 LA 766 (Eaton, 1970) (misrepresenting reason for leaving work); *Kisco Co.*, 75 LA 574 (Stix, 1980) (insubordination).

[190]*American Mach. & Foundry Co., supra* note 179.

[191]*Cooper Thermometer Co.*, 45 LA 1182 (Johnson, 1966) (transfer).

[192]Arbitrator Heinsz, in *A.R.A. Mfg. Co.*, 85 LA 549, 552 (1985) (excessive breaks): "This inference of discrimination was supported by the Company's position that the Grievant had filed too many grievances against the Company. It is clear that the discipline of employees for filing or processing grievances is generally held to be a violation of Section 8(a)(1) of the [NLRA]." Evidence that the grievant has been unusually litigious in pursuing union business, as in *Safeway Stores, Inc., supra* note 189, or that he has shown a quick temper in discussions with management, as in *Feather-Lite Mfg. Co., supra* note 188, has been considered a reason why an employer might have wanted to get a union representative off its back.

[193]*E.g.*, in *Crowell-Collier Broadcasting Co., supra* note 184, where the allegedly poor ratings that led to a radio disk jockey's discharge (according to the employer) proved to be no worse than those of any of his coworkers, and the only conclusion the arbitrator could come to was that the employer was listening to the grievant's on-air voice through the static of a bitter strike in which he had participated the year before. See also *Sinclair Refining Co., supra* note 188; *Russell Aluminum Corp.*, 56 LA 543 (Simon, 1971) (absence rule applied inflexibly to grievant but not to others); *Playboy Clubs Int'l, Inc.*, 59 LA 805 (Keefe, 1972) (only grievant singled out to have "Bunny image" evaluated); *Feather-Lite Mfg. Co., supra* note 188 (no proof that grievant and not other employees responsible for low production); *Thunderbird Inn*, 77 LA 849 (Armstrong, 1981) (inadequate performance).

[194]*E.g., Grand Auto Stores*, note 189 above (grievant told company would get rid of her if she did not keep her nose out of union matters); *Dura Containers, Inc.*, 67 LA 82 (Maslanka, 1976) (grievant warned he was filing too many grievances and, upon asking whether management was threatening his job, told he could "take it any way he wanted"); *Thunderbird Inn, supra* note 193 ("There could be no more positive statement of intent to discharge the Grievant than the supervisor's statement: 'I told you if you went to the Union, I would be mad and I am mad. Furthermore, I am going to harass you right out of here.'").

was elected Chorus Deputy and promptly embarked on an active campaign to resolve employees' many complaints about such matters as unpaid overtime claims and safety and sanitation issues. The attitude of the theater owner toward her soon changed from cordiality to chilliness, and he was heard making remarks about "troublemakers" and "agitators." Nevertheless, the employee persisted in her efforts to get the owner to address the employees' grievances. When he took no action, she called the situation to the attention of the union's regional office, which wrote to the owner insisting that the contract be honored. A few days later the employee was informed that she was being terminated because she was too old to perform her duties.

Discrimination, or rapid aging? The owner discharged the employee so quickly after he received the union's letter, the arbitrator found, that he would have had to come forward with substantial evidence to prove that the coincidence of the two events was merely fortuitous. But was there such evidence? The owner's assertion that the employee was too old for the chorus line was hard to swallow, given the fact that she had been hired just eight months earlier and her talents as a singer and dancer had been recognized by management. Furthermore, the owner admitted that he had fired her in part because she had been "disrespectful"—by which he meant that she had insisted that he pay contractual overtime. Thus all four elements of proof were present in this textbook case, and the conclusion was clear: The employee was discharged not because of any deficiencies in her performance but because of her union activity.[195]

EXAMPLE NO. 2: A supervisor who had temporarily taken over as production superintendent directed an employee to fill in for a welder who had become ill. The employee, who was the chief shop steward on his shift, had filed a grievance a year earlier over his right to work in the welder classification and, as a result of negotiation between the parties, had waived his right to that job in return for a lump-sum settlement. Believing he was thus prevented from doing welding work, the steward told the supervisor about the settlement, which came as news to the latter. After checking with higher-ups, the supervisor again directed the employee to do the job, and later in the day wrote up a warning slip reprimanding the steward for not obeying immediately. For good measure he added two more warnings about production errors made by the steward that day and a few days earlier.

---

[195]*In the Round Dinner Playhouse, Inc.*, 55 LA 118 (Kamin, 1970).

Were the warnings justified? The earlier grievance settlement gave the steward good reason to question the supervisor's order, and he had a right as a union representative to try to resolve the matter under a contract provision stating that the foreman and the steward should try to settle disputes whenever they arose. The most likely scenario, the arbitrator said, was that the supervisor, who was "on trial" in his temporary role as superintendent, perceived the steward's question as a challenge to his authority and then sought to vindicate that authority with the salvo of warning notices. The warning about the steward's refusal to take over the welder's job was therefore unjustified, and it was highly unlikely that the two other warnings would have been issued without the first. The timing was suspicious; the errors in question were minor; and no other employee had even been given a formal warning for similar mistakes. All three warnings were therefore set aside.

This case makes the point that a supervisor does not necessarily have to be a rabid union hater to be guilty of discrimination for union activity. Evidently this supervisor was too insecure in his new role to accept the fact that the steward, too, had authority as the union's representative, and to realize that the steward's legitimate exercise of that authority was not aimed at him personally.[196]

Proof That Fails to Make the Grade

Often the union makes the claim that one or more of the four elements used to prove anti-union discrimination is present. But what the union asks the arbitrator to accept as proof may be one of the following conditions that fall short of hard evidence that the grievant's discharge directly resulted from his or her union activity.

Antagonistic Statements. Statements by management that supposedly prove a desire to "get" the grievant often do not live up to their billings. Typically, the union will rely on statements such as "The union is no good," or "Everyone who supports the union ought to be fired."[197] Statements like these are certainly evidence that management has little use for the

---

[196]*Detroit Steel Joint Co.*, 66-2 ARB ¶8465 (Kallenbach, 1966).
[197]*Firestone Tire & Rubber Co.*, 33 LA 206 (McCoy, 1959) (demotion for incompetence).

union; but they fail as proof of anti-union discrimination because they do not amount to specific threats against the grievant's job. Standing alone, angry discussions,[198] remarks about the grievant's union activism,[199] or casual remarks about the grievant's union connections[200] are insufficient to prove discrimination.

Extent of Union Activity. Proof of anti-union discrimination often falls short, too, because the grievant's union activity turns out to be so low-key that it is hard to understand why the employer would be concerned about it. The grievant's claim that management resented his militant pro-union activity lost its force, for example, when the evidence showed that his record as a shop steward had been uneventful;[201] that his criticisms of management had been "minimal";[202] or that he had not been a leader in a recent organizing campaign and that other employees who also had merely supported the union were still on the job.[203] Then, too, if the employer had no knowledge that the employee was active on the union's behalf, bias can hardly have been the reason for discipline.[204]

Timing Is Remote. Ordinarily, when discipline follows closely upon an employee's involvement in union activities that anger the employer, discrimination is a distinct possibility. However, considerations of timing can work to dilute discrimination claims as well as to support them. For example, where the employer had expressed dissatisfaction with an employee's work prior to union elections in which the employee was involved, no connection between his union activity and his

---

[198]*Kroger Co.*, 24 LA 48 (Holly, 1954) (accidents).

[199]*Ogden Defense Depot*, 1975 ARB ¶8253 (Richardson, 1975) (promotion).

[200]*Sabine Towing and Transp. Co.*, 79-1 ARB ¶8104 (Bailey, 1979) (negligence).

[201]*Illinois Consol. Tel. Co.*, 70-2 ARB ¶8452 (McGury, 1970) (transfer).

[202]*21 Brands, Inc.*, 71-1 ARB ¶8168 (Kesselman, 1970) (improper attitude, uncooperativeness).

[203]*Firestone Tire & Rubber Co.*, supra note 197. The union's failure to produce evidence that other shop stewards were harassed by the employer helped persuade the arbitrator that the grievant's union activity was not the reason for his low job ratings in *Standard Oil Co. of Cal.*, 43 LA 529 (McNaughton, 1964), while in *Intalco Aluminum Corp.*, 70-1 ARB ¶8043 (Stoll, 1969), the evidence showed that the grievant had had less responsibility in connection with bitter negotiations than other union leaders who had been discharged without protest from the union, and was no longer a union officer at the time of his termination.

[204]*Shields & Terrell Convalescent Hosp.*, 56 LA 884 (Heilbrun, 1971) (failure to perform assigned duties).

demotion could be inferred.[205] In another case, the arbitrator found it hard to believe that a union steward's strike activities were the reason for his discharge when the strike had taken place more than two years earlier and his career as a steward since then had been uneventful.[206]

---

[205]*Cook Paint & Varnish Co.*, 63 LA 230 (Erbs, 1974).
[206]*Illinois Consol. Tel. Co.*, *supra* note 201.

Chapter 7

Penalty

"Was the degree of discipline administered by the Employer in a particular case reasonably related to (a) the seriousness of the employee's *proven* offense, and (b) the record of the employee in his service with the Employer?"

Arbitrator Dworkin: Inherent in the contractual provision that an employee may be disciplined for just cause is the fairness and reasonableness of the penalty.[1]

Arbitrator Platt: Indeed, it is an essential element of "just cause" that the penalty in a discipline case be fair and reasonable and fitting to the circumstances of the case. For although an employee may deserve discipline, no obligation to justice compels imposition of the extreme penalty in every case or a penalty that is more severe than the nature of the offense requires.[2]

Of all the just cause tests, it is the manner in which the parties approach the matter of penalty that tells the most about their overall relationship. Is the list of offenses for which summary discharge is the penalty long or short? Is the penalty system mechanical and rigid, or do the parties take a more flexible, "seat of the pants" approach? Are warnings put in writing and placed in personnel files, or do they tend to be oral and more in the nature of counseling than formal reprimands? At what point in the disciplinary process is suspension applied? The answers to these and similar questions convey a good deal about the kind of relationship the parties have.

The penalty system also reflects the demands of the particular industry. Take an obvious example relating to "the seri-

---

[1]*Davis Fire Brick Co.*, 36 LA 124, 127 (1960) (negligence).
[2]*Wolverine Shoe & Tanning Corp.*, 18 LA 809, 812 (1952) (violation of parking rule).

ousness of the employee's proven offense"—one of the just cause factors that affect the penalty, according to Arbitrator Daugherty. In most workplace environments, the first violation of a no-smoking rule would not be serious enough to warrant summary discharge; but that same violation might well warrant sending an employee down the road in a chemical plant where there was a high risk of fire or explosion. Similarly, drinking on the job typically leads to more severe penalties in industries such as transportation and mining than in businesses where the consequences of alcohol-related accidents are not so potentially serious.[3]

I. Penalty: In Theory

The concept of industrial penalty stems from two sources— the judicial system, with its heavy emphasis on criminal law, and the collective bargaining relationship. Those two influences may receive greater or lesser emphasis, depending on such factors as the particular industry and the parties involved—their history, their problems, the state of their relationship, and the like.

Influence of the Criminal Law

The industrial justice system is heavily influenced by several assumptions that underlie the criminal justice system—for example, that punishment is necessary to convince the lawbreaker that his conduct was wrong and that he must mend his ways in the future; that the punishment of criminal offenders serves as a deterrent to others who might break the law;[4] that punishment serves to protect society from individuals who have committed crimes against persons or property; that punishment may be mitigated if it can be proved that an individual was not acting

---

[3]See, e.g., *Pacific Greyhound Lines, Inc.*, 25 LA 709 (Lennard, 1955); *Asarco, Inc.*, 76 LA 163 (Grooms, 1981); *Cities Serv. Co.*, 77 LA 1180 (Brisco, 1982); *Consolidation Coal Co.*, 82-2 ARB ¶8605 (Sass, 1982).
[4]As argued by the employer, *e.g.*, in *Interchemical Corp.*, 48 LA 124, 131 (Yagoda, 1967).

with criminal intent when he broke the law or was not responsible for his actions because of insanity.[5]

The criminal law influence is apparent, for example, in the widespread acceptance of suspension, with the loss of earnings it entails. No one would seriously argue that punishment at the workplace should be retributive, or that the principle of "an eye for an eye" has any place in the industrial penalty system. Suspension is advocated on the ground that it serves more effectively than a mere warning to convince an employee that he must shape up or risk discharge.

But loss of earnings is undeniably a punishment, even though the expressed purpose may be corrective rather than retributive. As one arbitrator has put it, suspension "serves notice *punitively*" that misconduct will not be tolerated.[6] Another arbitrator has taken the position that for some employees the shame of being penalized with reprimands and suspensions, and having those penalties known to other employees, is necessary to correct their behavior. An employee who is not made to feel guilty, according to this arbitrator's view, has no reason to believe he or she has done anything wrong and therefore has no reason to improve in the future.[7]

> *Arbitrator Howlett:* Perhaps an arbitrator may be forgiven if he muses concerning yesteryear in "Merrie England," when pickpockets and other petty thieves were called upon to "ride a cart up the heavy hill," there to "hang from Tyburn tree." We have learned that these excessive penalties for minor offenses did not decrease the crime rate or improve public morals and civic responsibility of the citizens of London and the English shires. The principle is as applicable to industrial enterprises.[8]

---

[5]The classic discussion of the influence of the criminal law on industrial penalties is S. H. Kadish, *The Criminal Law and Industrial Discipline as Sanctioning Systems: Some Comparative Observations*, Labor Arbitration—Perspectives and Problems 125–44 (Proceedings of the 17th Annual Meeting, National Academy of Arbitrators 1964), with comments by A. M. Ross, J. F. E. Hippel, and B. Diamond. The threefold purpose of industrial discipline as set forth by Arbitrator Howlett in *Spartan Stores, Inc.*, 33 LA 40, 41 (1959), reflects the criminal law model: "(1) to teach an employee that his actions are wrong and must be corrected . . . ; (2) to penalize or punish an employee for his wrongdoing; and (3) to furnish an example to other employees so that they will learn that they must not be guilty of the same failures."

[6]*General Tel. Co. of Cal.*, 44 LA 669, 672 (Prasow, 1965) (safety rule violation).

[7]J. J. Justin, How to Manage With a Union 399ff (1969).

[8]*Phelps Dodge Aluminum Prods. Corp.*, 52 LA 375, 378 (1969) (leaving plant without permission).

Influence of Collective Bargaining Relationship

The second source of the concept of industrial penalty is the collective bargaining relationship. The characteristics of this relationship give the individual penalty system its tone and shape. Within this framework, the following factors are influential:

Rehabilitation. The purpose of disciplinary penalties is corrective and rehabilitative rather than punitive—penalties serve to impress upon employees that obeying reasonable rules is one of their obligations under the collective bargaining relationship, and to make them better employees.[9] From this assumption flows the concept of progressive or corrective discipline.

A prominent management attorney has gone so far as to suggest that punitive elements within a disciplinary system should be entirely eliminated and that the traditional graduated penalty system of progressive discipline should be replaced by a series of "decisional conferences" in which supervisors advise employees of their deficiencies and ask them to reaffirm their desire to remain with the company and to commit themselves to obeying the rules in the future. Such a system, the author proposed, would better reflect the voluntary nature of the employer-employee relationship than the traditional "coercive" penalty system.[10]

Continuing relationship. What the penalty system will be is affected decisively by the parties' continuing relationship. For example, the penalty in a particular case depends not only on

---

[9]See, e.g., *Lawrence General Hosp.*, 55 LA 987 (Zack, 1970) (unsatisfactory performance), and other cases cited in note 25 infra. In *Western Insulated Wire Co.*, 45 LA 972, 974 (1965), Arbitrator Jones pointed out that the distinction in the criminal law between felonies and misdemeanors is likewise geared toward rehabilitation rather than punishment *per se,* since for misdemeanors

more typically, there is no actual imprisonment, but instead, suspended sentences and probation are imposed in an effort to rehabilitate the person. Quite likely, the sentence, on a first offense as here (given the 16 years of employment without blemish on his record), would be a suspended one (that is, no time in jail, and quite possibly also only a token monetary penalty imposed of the $500 maximum possible).

Emphasizing that rehabilitation and punishment should go hand in hand is *Connecticut-American Water Co.*, 89-2 ARB ¶8554 (Berger, 1988), where the arbitrator revoked a one-day suspension for a safety violation because the management official who spotted the violation (failure to wear safety goggles) did not call it to the grievant's attention. Management's duty to promote safe practices, the arbitrator said, obligated the official to correct the condition, not merely report it.

[10]J. R. Redeker, Disciplinary Policies and Procedures 33ff (1983).

an assessment of the employee's past and future with the company but on what is justified in the light of how the company has treated other employees in the past and what precedential effect the penalty might have on future disciplinary actions.

"Guilt" not necessarily the issue. Under the criminal law, intent is an important factor in determining the penalty. It is exactly the opposite with many types of industrial misconduct. The classic example is chronic absenteeism, for which management's right to discharge is customarily upheld, even if the cause of absence is illness or other condition beyond the individual's control. Substandard performance is another example. Guilt or innocence is not the issue in cases of this type, in which misconduct typically involves failure to perform affirmative duties required by the employer-employee relationship (to show up promptly and regularly, to meet reasonable standards of production, and the like), rather than engaging in prohibited misconduct.[11]

The parties' power positions. The respective power positions of the two parties have a direct impact on the shape and form of any penalty system. At one time the Teamsters were able to gain a provision in the over-the-road trucking agreements that permitted an employee whom the employer sought to discharge for reasons other than theft, gross insubordination, or chronic alcoholism to remain on the job and continue to draw pay until his or her grievance had been heard and an arbitration had taken place. (More recent agreements provide, instead, an expedited arbitration system to assure prompt resolution of grievances over discharges and suspensions.)

As another example, take the case of a rule stating that discharge will be the penalty for even a first offense of failing to report for work on time without a valid excuse. In the airline industry, such a strict rule is generally accepted by unions because the nature of the business requires that schedules be rigorously observed. In an industry where time is not so critically a factor, the same rule might be on the books because the union

---

[11]Disciplinary penalties, up to and including discharge, have been characterized as management's recourse when an employee does not hold up his end of the employment bargain, e.g., by showing up regularly for work, by following supervisors' instructions, by complying with reasonable rules of on-the-job conduct. (As a balancing factor, if management fails to live up to the employment bargain, the employee has the grievance procedure available.) See A. M. Ross, *supra* note 5, at 146; and R. I. Abrams, *A Theory for the Discharge Case,* 36:3 ARB. J. 25 (1981).

lacked the muscle to eliminate or modify it at the bargaining table.

In sum, the purpose of penalties from a criminal law perspective tends to be defensive; that is, penalties have the negative purpose of keeping misconduct at bay. From the collective bargaining perspective, penalties have the more "affirmative" function of effectuating the respective rights and obligations of the parties with a central emphasis on the goal of rehabilitating the employee.

Is Discharge "Economic Capital Punishment"?

The differences between the criminal law and collective bargaining influences are highlighted in the perennial debate over whether the characterization of discharge as "economic capital punishment" (or "industrial capital punishment") is a meaningful one. That many persist in so describing it illustrates the strong hold the criminal law model has on the concept of industrial penalty.[12] Discharge, the logic runs, is the most extreme penalty the employer can impose, since it irrevocably terminates an individual's employment, cuts off his income, deprives him of all the seniority and other benefits he has accumulated in the course of his employment, and often jeopardizes his chances of finding another job. The implication is that discharge—and perhaps even disciplinary penalties short of dis-

---

[12]*E.g.*, *Sterling Drug, Inc.*, 67 LA 1296, 1299 (Draper, 1976) (terms of reinstatement violated by alcoholic): "Discharge in industrial life is comparable to the electric chair in criminal law. In the first case, a man's work life is terminated; in the second, his physical life is terminated." *Western Insulated Wire Co.*, 45 LA 972, 974 (Jones, 1965) (pilferage):

> It may be helpful to think by analogy of the criminal law for the moment. Whatever may be the validity of the generalization that equates a discharge with capital punishment, it is certainly the reality here that to uphold Grievant's discharge would be, in all probability, to condemn him to unemployment for . . . his [few] employable years.

Discounting the relevance of such concerns is *Thomas Steel Strip Co.*, 87 LA 994, 999 (Feldman, 1986) (testing positive for marijuana):

> While the employee may be in need of employment and while the lack of work may place a grievous financial hardship upon the grievant and his family and while good employment is difficult to find, the fact of the matter is, these economic problems are not viable defenses to disciplinary activity under the terms of the instant contract. These financial problems should have been thought of by the grievant prior to his activity, which activity was detrimental to his perpetuating his employment at this facility.

charge—should be imposed only if the employer proves misconduct beyond a reasonable doubt.[13]

But the "economic capital punishment" view (which Arbitrator Aaron once described as "the historic conquest of common sense by rhetoric"[14]) has been attacked by critics who have
used arguments grounded in the criminal law as well as in
collective bargaining. They argue that the concept is either useless or unrealistic or both. Even in criminal law terms, it is
pointed out, the analogy falls apart because loss of a job is not
nearly as serious a penalty as loss of life, or even loss of freedom.[15] Undeniably there is a stigma attached to having been
fired from a job; but the stigma of a criminal conviction is
patently greater still.

Moreover, critics argue that the "economic capital punishment" view ignores the crucial difference that in the criminal
justice system the parties are the individual and the state, engaged in a one-time encounter, whereas in the industrial justice
system the parties are the company and the union, who must
continue to deal with each other.

> *Arbitrator Aaron:* Those who are prone indiscriminately to apply
> the criminal law analogy in the arbitration of all discharge cases
> overlook the fact that employer and employee do *not* stand in the
> relationship of prosecutor and defendant. It cannot be empha-
> sized too often that the basic dispute is between the two principals
> to the collective bargaining agreement, that is, the company and
> the union. At stake is not only the matter of justice to the individ-
> ual employee, important as that principle is, but also the preserva-
> tion and development of the collective bargaining relationship.[16]

The preservation and development of the collective bargaining relationship, as Aaron sees it, requires that management's need to run its business profitably be included in the
equation with an employee's rights when penalty is being decided upon. As an example, Aaron points out that many of-

---

[13]The implications of the "economic capital punishment" theory were discussed
(and rejected) in B. Aaron, *Some Procedural Problems in Arbitration*, 10 VAND. L. REV. 740
(1957).

[14]*Id.*

[15]A. H. Stockman, commenting on W. W. Wirtz, *Due Process of Arbitration*, THE
ARBITRATOR AND THE PARTIES 39–40 (Proceedings of the 11th Annual Meeting, National
Academy of Arbitrators 1958).

[16]Aaron, *supra* note 13, at 741. Aaron's and other arguments why the "economic
capital punishment" analogy is misapplied in the industrial setting are reviewed by P.
Prasow & E. Peters, ARBITRATION AND COLLECTIVE BARGAINING 240ff (1970).

fenses—sleeping, for example—are difficult to prove beyond a reasonable doubt; yet management could not hope to run its business efficiently if it could not penalize employees for sleeping on the job. The "economic capital punishment" view does not easily accommodate collective bargaining considerations of this kind.

Basic Definitions

Penalty Versus Remedy

Although penalty and remedy are two sides of the same coin, etymologically (the supervisor's) "penalty" has its origins in pain,[17] whereas (the arbitrator's) "remedy" is that which tends "to bring back health."[18] "Penalty" is defined as "a punishment imposed for breach of law, rule, or contract" as well as "a loss, disability, or disadvantage of some kind, either ordained by law to be inflicted for some offense, or agreed upon to be undergone in case of violation of a contract . . . ." "Remedy" serves as "a means of counteracting or removing an outward evil of any kind; reparation; redress; relief."[19]

Summary Discharge Versus Progressive Discipline

As one of the first to analyze the concept of progressive discipline (a term used interchangeably with "corrective discipline" and, less frequently, with "graduated discipline," "constructive discipline," and "constructive progressive discipline"), Arbitrator McCoy in 1949 defined progressive discipline as follows:

> [T]he Company imposes a mild penalty for a first offense, a somewhat more severe penalty for a second, etc., before abandoning efforts at correction and resorting to discharge. . . . The theory is that this is in the interest of both management and employees. . . . I might hold a discharge without any prior discipline whatever proper in the case of some offenses; in the case of other offenses it might be held that discharge did not become

---

[17]W. W. Skeat, A Concise Etymological Dictionary of the English Language 381 (1980); E. Partridge, Origins—A Short Etymological Dictionary of Modern English 463, 480 (1966).

[18]Partridge, *supra* note 17, at 393, 558; Skeat, *supra* note 17, at 441.

[19]Oxford English Dictionary (1971).

reasonably necessary for a long time and after many fruitless efforts at correction.[20]

In the same case, McCoy pointed out that corrective discipline is intended to be applied to conduct that was *malum prohibitum* rather than *malum in se*, to use a distinction in the criminal law—bad only because prohibited, not bad in itself. Later, he articulated this distinction in "industrial justice" terms in the following language, which is often quoted in connection with progressive discipline:

> (1) those extremely serious offenses such as stealing, striking a foreman, persistent refusal to obey a legitimate order, etc., which usually justify summary discharge without the necessity of prior warnings or attempts at corrective discipline;
> (2) those less serious infractions of plant rules or of proper conduct such as tardiness, absence without permission, careless workmanship, insolence, etc., which call not for discharge for the first offense (and usually not even for the second or third offense) but for some milder penalty aimed at correction.[21]

This basic division often is reflected in contract provisions or company rules that set up two parallel penalty systems, one covering offenses calling for summary discharge and another providing for progressive discipline for less serious misconduct.[22]

Manifestly, the subject of penalty is not open for discussion where summary discharge is the established penalty for particular misconduct by way of contract or past practice, or because the conduct is so obviously unacceptable (*malum in se*) that the employer-employee relationship cannot be repaired. In other words, if an offense calls for summary discharge and if all

---

[20]*International Harvester Co.*, 12 LA 1190, 1193 (1949). The topic of summary discharge and progressive discipline has received extensive treatment from arbitrators and others in the labor relations field. See, e.g., F. ELKOURI & E. A. ELKOURI, HOW ARBITRATION WORKS 670–73 (4th ed. 1985).

[21]*Huntington Chair Corp.*, 24 LA 490, 491 (1955). An excellent restatement of the same two-part division of misconduct with respect to penalty appears in *R. E. Phelon Co.*, 75 LA 1051, 1053 (Irvings, 1980) (unauthorized absence). See also *American Motors Corp.*, 52 LA 709 (Keefe, 1969); *Bay Area Rapid Transit Dist.*, 80-2 ARB ¶8612 (Koven, 1980) (cumulative misconduct); *Mallinckrodt, Inc.*, 80 LA 1261 (Seidman, 1983) (marijuana use).

[22]Among many other cases, see, e.g., *Babcock & Wilcox Co.*, 41 LA 862 (Dworkin, 1963) (absenteeism); *J. Weingarten, Inc.*, 77-1 ARB ¶8050 (Helburn, 1977) (use of improper language to customer); *Western Auto Supply Co.*, 71 LA 710 (Ross, 1978) (hiding in storage closet).

the elements of proof of that offense have been satisfied, the question is a closed issue, although confrontations may take place over whether in the particular circumstances the misconduct was serious enough to fit into the summary discharge category.[23] Modification of the summary discharge penalty can come about not by an attack on the appropriateness of the penalty itself but only if unusual mitigating circumstances can be proved. However, where an offense calls for something less than summary discharge, the subject of penalty remains very much open to discussion and inquiry.

Progressive Discipline

Conceptual Underpinnings of Progressive Discipline

A number of propositions are identified with progressive discipline. Underlying all systems of progressive discipline is the notion that a discipline and discharge program above all must be fair and just on both a substantive and a procedural or due process level. Arbitrator Platt has expressed another consideration as follows:

> [I]t is not socially desirable that disciplinary penalties for industrial offenses be regarded strictly as punishment for wrongdoing. Rather, the object of the penalty should be to make employees recognize their responsibilities so that they might become better workers in the future.[24]

Arbitrator Alexander developed Platt's point further:

> To draw an analogy from the criminal law, corrective discipline is somewhat like a habitual offender statute. It presupposes that the primary purpose of punishment is to correct wrong-doing rather than to wreak vengeance or deter others. Corrective discipline assumes that the employer as well as the employee gains more by continuing to retain the offender in employment, at least for a period of future testing, than to cut him from the rolls at

---

[23]*E.g.*, in *T. W. Recreational Servs.*, 93 LA 302 (Richard, 1989), the arbitrator rejected the employer's assertion that a bus driver was guilty of "gross negligence" in causing a one-vehicle accident that resulted in some $20,000 property damage and minor injury to a passenger. His analysis showed the driver to be guilty of at most simple negligence, an offense calling for progressive discipline; that the consequences were serious was irrelevant.

[24]*The Arbitration Process in the Settlement of Labor Disputes*, 31 J. Am. Judicature Soc'y 58 (1947).

the earliest possible moment. . . . If a continuing level of employment is assumed, the discharged employee must be replaced by
another. Normal hiring procedures provide little guarantee that
the new hire will be a perfect citizen . . . .[25]

Another principle underlying progressive discipline is that
the "punishment should fit the crime."[26] "[O]nce the misconduct
has been proved, the penalty imposed must be fairly warranted
and reasonably calculated to eliminate or correct the offensive
conduct."[27] It has been emphasized that punishment should be
based on the employee's actions, not on the consequences of
those actions.[28]

But when rehabilitation fails, discharge can then follow.[29]

---

[25]*Concepts of Industrial Discipline*, MANAGEMENT RIGHTS AND THE ARBITRATION
PROCESS 79–81 (Proceedings of the 9th Annual Meeting, National Academy of Arbitrators 1956), cited in *American Int'l Aluminum Corp.*, 48 LA 283, 287 (Howlett, 1967). The
rehabilitative purpose of progressive discipline is strongly emphasized in *Victory Markets,
Inc.*, 84 LA 354 (Sabghir, 1985): "Progressive discipline is not simply an escalator to
crucify an employee. Through it an employer must demonstrate an honest and serious
effort to salvage rather than savage an employee. To hold otherwise distorts, demeans
and defeats the goals underlying the concept of progressive and corrective discipline."
See also *Bell Aircraft Corp.*, 17 LA 230 (Shister, 1951) (disrupting operations); *Rochester
Tel. Co.*, 45 LA 538 (Duff, 1965) (use of obscene language); *Lawrence Gen'l Hosp.*, 55 LA
987 (Zack, 1970) (unsatisfactory performance); *Louisville Cooperage Co.*, 70-2 ARB ¶8652
(Volz, 1970) (draining untaxed whiskey out of barrels); *Armstrong Cork Co.*, 71-1 ARB
¶8242 (Wolf, 1971) (absenteeism due to alcoholism); *Ohio Power Co.*, 64 LA 934 (High,
1975) (dishonesty); *Warren Assemblies, Inc.*, 93 LA 521 (Roumell, 1989) (leaving post
without permission), among many other cases.

[26]*R. E. Phelon Co.*, 75 LA 1051, 1053 (Irvings, 1980) (unauthorized absence)
("disciplinary penalty imposed must fit the seriousness of the offense"); *Grand Haven
Brass Foundry*, 68 LA 41, 43 (Roumell, 1977) (threatening personnel director) ("parties
have codified in their agreement a policy that the degree of penalty should be in keeping
with the seriousness of the offense"); *Noranda Aluminum, Inc.*, 81-1 ARB ¶8091 (Ross,
1980) (taking coins from vending machine).

[27]*Capital Airlines, Inc.*, 25 LA 13, 16 (Stowe, 1955) (misuse of sick-leave privilege):
"One of the primary purposes of discipline in the industrial relations field is to bring
about improvement. It is, therefore, axiomatic that the degree of penalty should be
in keeping with the offense, and should be designed primarily to bring about such
improvement." See also *Bay Area Rapid Transit Dist.*, *supra* note 21 (cumulative misconduct).

[28]*T. W. Recreational Servs., Inc.*, *supra* note 23. The arbitrator reversed the discharge
of a bus driver whose negligence resulted in some $20,000 damage to his bus and minor
injury to a passenger. Discipline may be based on an unsafe act, he said, but not on the
consequences of that act, which in this case he found to be ordinary negligence, not
gross negligence. In a superficially similar case, *Celanese Trucking Div.*, 90 LA 819 (Nolan,
1988), the arbitrator upheld the discharge of a truck driver whose actions caused damage
amounting to about $100,000. Although here, too, the arbitrator found only simple
negligence, the driver had received counseling, several warnings, and a suspension
relating to his driving practices, and this record persuaded the arbitrator to approve
the discharge.

[29]See, e.g., *Pratt & Whitney Aircraft Group*, 91 LA 1014 (Chandler, 1988) (poor
performance), where the arbitrator held that, if an employee does not respond to

The purpose of progressive discipline is not only the rehabilitation of the employee and the prevention of continued misconduct, but also "the protection of the right of the Company to sever completely its relationships with any employee who by his total behavior shows himself to be irresponsible."[30]

What Arbitrators Consider in Applying Progressive Discipline

This said, the question then becomes, how do arbitrators apply these foundational concepts of progressive discipline in practice? Is there some rhyme and reason, some pattern of reasonable expectancy, when an arbitrator reviews a penalty in which progressive discipline is in issue?

Arbitrators routinely experience a multiplicity of parties, histories, relationships, and situations, and as a consequence are called upon to review all kinds of disciplinary and penalty systems. Thus, what arbitrators look for where progressive discipline and penalty systems become an issue is what is appropriate in the particular situations that confront them—in other words, they take a pragmatic approach. When it comes to progressive discipline, arbitrators, like the leprechaun in *Finian's Rainbow*, tend to fondle the hand at hand.

Requirements of Contract Language. Considerations involving contract language are always likely to occupy center stage. If the contract expressly requires progressive discipline, an arbitrator

---

progresssive discipline, management "may conclude on a non-arbitrary or capricious basis, that rehabilitation is an impossibility and is then at liberty to dismiss the employee before all progressive disciplinary steps normally taken are concluded."

[30]*Bell Aircraft Co.*, 17 LA 230, 233 (Shister, 1951) (refusal to carry out supervisor's direction). According to Arbitrator J. Dworkin, discharge should be regarded as separate and distinct from progressive discipline. His reasoning, as set forth in *Red Cross Blood Serv.*, 90 LA 393, 397 (1988) (poor performance):

> Discharge and suspension are separate, distinct penalties. Suspensions are corrective measures, designed to rehabilitate a miscreant employee; to restore him/her to acceptable levels of production and/or behavior. Discharge, on the other hand, is the severance of an employment relationship. . . . In other words, discharge is designed to abolish the employment relationship; disciplinary suspension is designed to improve it.

The distinction may appear to be sophistry. However, the contract before the arbitrator specified discharge as the penalty for a third rule violation within a 12-month period. The grievant had committed three violations, and the employer argued that since it could discharge the grievant, it could suspend him for two months. The arbitrator rejected that argument, holding that the purpose of a suspension must be corrective and that a suspension of more than 30 days is punitive rather than corrective. He therefore cut the suspension to 30 days, "the longest conceivable period consistent with the Employer's corrective-discipline philosophy."

will obviously follow the contract. "The past practice of summary discharge referred to by the Company in its closing statement cannot modify the unambiguous contractual language requiring progressive discipline."[31] Even contract language stating, for example, that "an employee shall be liable to disciplinary action, including layoff or termination," and that employees may be discharged for repeated violations of plant rules, has been relied upon by arbitrators as evidence that the parties themselves intended progressive discipline to be applied.[32] The just cause provision, too, has been held in itself to incorporate some form of progressive discipline.[33]

On the other hand, lack of any reference in the contract to progressive discipline has been the basis upon which a few arbitrators have refused to set aside discharge.

> *Arbitrator Whyte:* While concepts of corrective (in contrast to punitive) discipline have merit, it is an arbitrator's function to interpret collective bargaining agreements, not advise company and union what should be in them. It is one thing to determine whether or not a contract permits discharging an employee under given circumstances. It is entirely another matter for an arbitrator to conclude that an employee's discharge violated a contract because of something not in the contract. The latter approach has the effect of rewriting the contract for the parties or, if not that, of adding something to the contract.[34]

Contract language has also controlled the manner in which progressive discipline is to be administered. The contract may, for example, spell out specific steps for progressive discipline, with which arbitrators are reluctant to tamper. Thus, where the contract required only that the company give at least one written warning to an employee prior to discharge or suspension, the

---

[31]*White Mfg. Co.*, 74 LA 1005 (LeBaron, 1980) (check-cashing operation on company property), quoting in support R. W. FLEMING, THE LABOR ARBITRATION PROCESS (1965): "Most arbitrators conclude that failure to comply with a contractual procedure will affect the degree of penalty which is appropriate, but not necessarily vitiate the action in its entirety."

[32]*Stuck Mould Works, Inc.*, 70 LA 1103, 1110 (Dyke, 1978) (low productivity).

[33]See cases cited in F. ELKOURI & E. A. ELKOURI, HOW ARBITRATION WORKS 672 (4th ed. 1985).

[34]*Aro, Inc.*, 47 LA 1065 (1966). See also *Tex-A-Panel Mfg. Co.*, 62 LA 272 (Ray, 1973) (no requirement in contract that progressive discipline be applied for unsatisfactory work performance; discharge upheld); *Union Carbide Corp.*, 46 LA 195 (Cahn, 1966) (arbitrator will not require progressive discipline not mandated by contract). In *Union Carbide*, as in many other cases, the question was whether suspension, rather than warnings only, was required prior to discharge.

arbitrator rejected the union's contention that a verbal warning would have been more appropriate for a first safety rule violation. Considering the seriousness of the matter, "the written warning to Grievant was not excessive nor an abuse of discretion."[35]

Another case in point is that of a school district that sent a letter to a teacher stating that failure to follow the district's rules of conduct "will result in discipline up to and including discharge." Progressive discipline under the contract consisted of four steps—oral reprimand, written reprimand, suspension, and discharge. Since no oral reprimand had preceded the letter, the arbitrator reasoned that the letter was not part of progressive discipline. Indeed, he regarded it as an improper attempt to bargain individually with the teacher as to the matters in question.[36]

Contract Language and the Test of Reasonableness. While the letter of the contract has customarily been followed by arbitrators, contract language dealing with discharge and progressive discipline has also been subjected to tests of reasonableness, in part because the just cause provision itself puts forward competing claims.

> **EXAMPLE NO. 1:** A wrapper in a supermarket's meat department with seven years' seniority was given a warning when she put the wrong price on a package of meat. When she did this again a short time later, she was discharged. The contract stated that no employee might be discharged without just cause and required at least one warning notice prior to suspension, discharge, or other disciplinary action.

The literal requirement of the contract might have been followed, the arbitrator found, but "[t]he Company misreads Article 5 of the collective bargaining agreement when it argues that it has free rein to discharge any employee committing his second offense. Just cause is required." In the wrapper's case the punishment just did not fit the crime. She was a long-service

---

[35]*Grain Processing Corp.*, 82-1 ARB ¶8229 (Thornell, 1982). See also *American Petrofina Co.*, 61 LA 861 (Marlatt, 1973) (absenteeism) (company may not bypass step in contract's progressive discipline system).

[36]*Rockford School Dist.*, 88-2 ARB ¶8367 (Traynor, 1987) (improper behavior by teacher toward student). See also *Simplex Prods. Div.*, 91 LA 356 (Byars, 1988) (failure to send warning letters under progressive-discipline policy showed company did not intend to apply notification rule).

employee, only small amounts of money were involved, and no customer complaints resulted from her errors. While the contract required that an employee be given at least one warning notice, just cause required that this grievant be given more than that: another warning or, at most, a suspension.[37]

EXAMPLE NO. 2: Shortly after he complained that other employees had been performing duties belonging to his classification, an employee refused to carry out his foreman's work order and was discharged for insubordination. The union claimed the discharge was improper because under the contract that penalty was specified for four offenses that amounted to violations of the contract within an 18-month period; the employee's act of insubordination was only his third violation. The penalty schedule, the union argued, applied to all offenses, "regardless of their character or degree of malignity."

The union had a point, the arbitrator noted, when it said that all acts of misconduct at variance with the employment relationship can in some sense be construed as contract violations. Nevertheless, the union's interpretation of the contract was too narrow, since it could mean that an employee would have to commit (for example) four acts of physical violence before the employer could expel him from the plant. Furthermore, to uphold the union's interpretation would "substantially dilute" not only the management rights clause but also management's contractual right to discharge employees "for just and proper cause." The employee's misconduct amounted to an act of flagrant insubordination for which discharge was appropriate.[38]

---

[37]*Shop Rite Foods, Inc.*, 67 LA 159, 162 (Weiss, 1976). In *Tokheim Corp.*, 62 LA 1040, 1042 (Edes, 1974), the arbitrator found that giving the grievant a written warning for a first offense of unexcused absence under the progressive discipline system was unreasonable even though dangerous road conditions were not an accepted excuse for absence:

> The whole purpose of corrective discipline . . . is that the employee will heed the lesser discipline and take the action necessary to avoid the harsher consequences. But it makes no sense and does violence to basic concepts of equity to mete out discipline in regard to conduct which the employee cannot correct or take any action whatsoever to avoid.

See also *Warren Assemblies, Inc.*, 92 LA 521 (Roumell, 1989) (leaving post without permission): "Corrective discipline is not to be applied in lock step. Each situation must be considered and the rule of reasonableness applied."

[38]*Alliance Mach. Co.*, 48 LA 457 (Dworkin, 1967). Other cases in which arbitrators have held that one or more steps in a system of progressive discipline may be bypassed if the misconduct is very serious include *City of Appleton*, 62 LA 342 (Lee, 1974) (abuse of sick leave); *Active Indus., Inc.*, 62 LA 958 (Ellmann, 1974) (absenteeism, malingering); *United Parcel Serv., Inc.*, 67 LA 861 (Lubow, 1976) (assault on supervisor); *Viking Fire*

Contract provisions that allow the company to discharge employees summarily for certain enumerated offenses, but require progressive discipline for others, have been relied upon by arbitrators in many cases as a guide to the parties' intentions.[39] But such provisions, too, have been found to have been unreasonably applied where the employer tried to elevate some act of misconduct into the "summary" category when it really did not belong there. A hotel bellman's profane outburst, for example, was found to have resulted from momentary and extreme frustration when his supervisor refused to help him find a personal possession he urgently needed; it could not reasonably be construed as "willful misconduct," which was cause for summary discharge under the contract.[40] In another case, the arbitrator rejected the employer's argument that hiding in a storage closet was comparable to sleeping on the job, which called for summary discharge. Hiding, he reasoned, was more akin to "willful idleness," an offense which the contract made subject to progressive discipline."[41]

Established Policy and/or Past Practice. Some situations can be judged in terms of the parties' own actions regarding disci-

---

Protection Co., 74 LA 947 (Pollard, 1980) (insubordination, violation of safety procedures); *R. E. Phelon Co.*, 75 LA 1051 (Irvings, 1980) (leaving work area without authorization); *Interstate Brands-Four S*, 76 LA 415 (Adler, 1981) (leaving early).

[39]E.g., *J. Weingarten, Inc.*, 77-1 ARB ¶8050 (Helburn, 1977), where the grievant's discharge for using obscene language to a customer was not sustained in part because that offense was not included in the list of offenses made subject to summary discharge. In *Airco, Inc.*, 62 LA 1103 (Traynor, 1974), the arbitrator set aside the grievant's summary discharge for insubordination and intimidating his supervisor because those offenses were not included in the contract's "summary discharge list." To uphold discharge, he said, would amount to impermissible amending of the contract; only in an extreme case would the arbitrator be justified in upholding discharge for a nonlisted offense. For other cases advocating strict adherence to the contract, see, e.g., *Morton Frozen Foods*, 61 LA 98 (Barnhart, 1973) (insubordination); *Von's Grocery Co.*, 1975 ARB ¶8186 (Christopher, 1975) (failure to record sale); *Browning-Ferris Indus. of Ohio, Inc.*, 77 LA 289 (Shanker, 1981) (drinking on duty).

[40]*MGM Grand Hotel*, 76-1 ARB ¶8197 (Koven, 1976).

[41]*Western Auto Supply Co.*, 71 LA 710 (Ross, 1978). See also *Precision Extrusions, Inc.*, 61 LA 572 (Epstein, 1973) (violation of safety rule not a "wanton or malicious" violation of major shop rule); *Manistee Drop Forging Corp.*, 62 LA 1164 (Brooks, 1974) (intentional violation of safety rules not punishable as insubordination); *Solano Contract Warehouse Corp.*, 80-1 ARB ¶8065 (Koven, 1979) (failing to follow common sense safety precautions not recklessness or willful negligence); *Hoover Co.*, 82-2 ARB ¶8524 (Dean, 1982) (improper language and sexual suggestions to female employee not actual sexual activity or demand). But in *Anchor Supply Co.*, 69 LA 655 (Witt, 1977), the arbitrator found that deliberate falsification of a time card, which was not on the list of summary-discharge offenses in the contract, was tantamount to theft, which *was* on that list; discharge was upheld. Other cases where the grievant was found to have committed less

pline—that is, whether the employer has followed its own schedule of penalties or past practice. For example, even though the grievant had reached the point where the employer's progressive-discipline schedule provided for discharge, the arbitrator set aside his discharge because other employees had been treated more leniently for offenses no less serious than those of the grievant. The arbitrator viewed the grievant's rule violation—sleeping on the job—as a minor transgression under the circumstances. But even if the employer's schedule were accepted at face value, he said, the employee should not have been discharged because the schedule had not been applied consistently.[42] Thus, "once guidelines are established and publicized, only under 'extraordinary circumstances' may an employer disregard his own guidelines. Otherwise, the guidelines would be meaningless."[43]

Uniformity Versus Individuality. Ordinarily one would think that it is impossible to treat all employees in the same way and at the same time treat them differently—to enforce a progressive discipline system uniformly, yet at the same time recognize each individual as unique, so that the length and quality of his or her service and other relevant considerations play a part in determining the appropriate penalty.

Arbitrators manage to reconcile these two seemingly contradictory propositions by reasoning along these lines: "Management must be permitted to exercise its judgment as to the proper discipline to impose as long as it does not discriminate against a particular employee. If progressive or corrective discipline is used, then this method must be applied in all cases."[44] For

---

serious misconduct than that alleged by the company are discussed from the standpoint of proof in Ch. 5, p. 243.

[42]*Essex Industrial Chems.*, 88 LA 991 (Cluster, 1987). See also *Pyrene Mfg. Co.*, 9 LA 787, 788 (Stein, 1948) ("The Company must either use its warning system or abandon it. . . . Where a warnings system is in effect, the workers have a right to be warned . . . ."); *F. W. Stock & Sons*, 78-1 ARB ¶8158 (Beitner, 1978) (discharge reduced to suspension because company had applied progressive disciplinary system to others for similar offenses); *Ryan Aeronautical Co.*, 39 LA 58 (Spaulding, 1962) (altercation with foreman); *R. Herschel Mfg. Co.*, 47 LA 20 (Sembower, 1966) (absenteeism); *Southwest Elec. Co.*, 54 LA 195 (Bothwell, 1969) (carrying unauthorized passengers); *O'Brien Corp.*, 77-2 ARB ¶8405 (Wright, 1977) (inefficiency, incompetence); *Wolf Mach. Co.*, 72 LA 510 (High, 1979) (various infractions); *Zapata Indus., Inc.*, 76 LA 467 (Woolf, 1981) (insubordination); *Metal Container Corp.*, 81-2 ARB ¶8609 (Ross, 1981) (tardiness).

[43]*Metal Container Corp.*, *supra* note 42, at 5652.

[44]*Sperry Rand Corp.*, 70-1 ARB ¶8149, 3521 (Kesselman, 1969) (absenteeism). Arbitrator Kerrison stated the same principle in *Electric Hose and Rubber Co.*, 47 LA 1104 (1967) (unauthorized absences): "While this does not mean that all must be judged by

example, if long service is considered as a mitigating circumstance in the case of one employee, it should be a mitigating circumstance for all.

> *Arbitrator Seward:* Included in the concept of "just cause" is the principle that the Company's right to discipline or discharge must be exercised justly and consistently; that the distinctions which it draws between employees in the imposition of penalties must be reasonable and fair. The Umpire has previously held—and he here repeats—that the Company need not penalize *all* employees who are guilty of an offense if it is to penalize *any* of them. But he also holds that if the Company is to select some employees for discipline and let others off scot-free (or if it is to impose heavy penalties on some and lighter penalties on others) it must—if it is to meet the standard of "just cause"—show that its reasons for making such distinctions were sound and just.[45]

Mitigation and Its Opposite, Aggravation. The factor that plays the leading role in balancing the need for uniformity against the need to treat employees as individuals is the length and quality of an employee's work record. A Niagara of cases stands for the proposition that an employer may justifiably impose a lesser penalty on an employee with long, creditable service than on an employee whose service is short or whose work record is poor.[46]

---

the same standards as interpreted by giving the same penalties for the same offense at all times, regardless of extenuating circumstances, it does mean that all must be judged by the same standards as such, and that rules must apply equally to all." See also *Interchemical Corp.*, 48 LA 124 (Yagoda, 1967) (refusal to perform work); *Gerstenlager Co.*, 66-1 ARB ¶8331 (Teple, 1966) (tardiness); *Group W Cable of Chicago*, 87-2 ARB ¶8447 (McAlpin, 1987) (sleeping on job); and cases cited in Ch. 6, pp. 325–27.

[45]*Bethlehem Steel Co.*, 29 LA 635, 643 (1957) (discharge of union officers for illegal work stoppage). The question of selective discipline and penalty is an ever-present issue in cases involving strikes, picketing, illegal walkouts, slowdowns, etc. See the following cases for treatment of this problem: *Stockham Pipe Fittings Co.*, 4 LA 744 (McCoy, 1946); *McInerney Spring & Wire Co.*, 21 LA 729 (Howlett, 1953); *McLouth Steel Corp.*, 24 LA 761 (Bowles, 1955); *American Radiator & Standard Sanitary Corp.*, 37 LA 593 (McCoy, 1961); *Ford Motor Co.*, 64-1 ARB ¶8128 (Platt, 1963); *Phillips Indus.*, 66-1 ARB ¶8042 (Stouffer, 1965); *Trane Co.*, 71-1 ARB ¶8089 (Turkus, 1971); *Aladdin Indus., Inc.*, 61 LA 896 (Hilpert, 1973); *Abex Corp.*, 68 LA 805 (Richman, 1977); *Cecil I. Walker Mach. Co.*, 78-1 ARB ¶8004 (Hunter, 1977); *Clinton Corn Processing Co.*, 71 LA 555 (Madden, 1978), with many additional citations; *Electrocast Steel Foundry, Inc.*, 78-2 ARB ¶8492 (Larkin, 1978); *Celotex Corp.*, 79-2 ARB ¶8506 (Murphy, 1979).

[46]Recent decisions in point include *Air Treads, Inc.*, 86 LA 545 (Allen, 1986) ("blatant insubordination"); *Deer Lake School Dist.*, 94 LA 334 (Hewitt) (pilferage); and cases cited in notes 47 and 48 *infra*. But see *W. R. Grace Co.*, 86 LA 999 (Galambos, 1986) (tampering with company records), holding that an arbitrator may not reduce a penalty because of the grievant's long and satisfactory service "in the absence of any provisions in the Agreement regarding degrees of discipline." For citations to many other cases weighing the effect of past record on penalty, see F. ELKOURI & E. A. ELKOURI, *supra* note 33, at 679–81.

Not only is an employee with long service presumed to be capable of satisfactory performance if given the opportunity; because such an employee has a greater stake in his job, he is entitled to greater consideration than someone who has been around only a short time and has less to lose.[47] Indeed, the administration of a disciplinary system without making allowances for long service has often led to the overturning of discharge decisions.[48]

Other factors that may warrant giving an employee a lesser penalty than would otherwise be justified include provocation;[49] contribution by management to the misconduct;[50] absence of

---

[47]*I. Schumann & Co.*, 65 LA 674 (Cohen, 1975) (refusal to work overtime); *Pacific Tel. & Tel. Co.*, 73 LA 1185 (Gerber, 1979) (intoxication, other violations). But see *Industrial Phosphating Co.*, 87 LA 877 (Daniel, 1988) (abusive language): "Simply because the grievant is a short term employee does not mean that he loses equal standing with other employees to require that the employer treat him fairly and justly in terms of discipline."

[48]*Olin Corp.*, 86 LA 1096, 1098, 86-1 ARB ¶8248 (Seidman, 1986) (sleeping on job):

> [B]efore invoking terminal discipline the Company must consider the employee's entire past record with respect to work performance, attendance, and discipline and give it appropriate weight in determining whether discharge, or some lesser discipline, should be meted out .... The company's failure to do so, and its affirmative policy not to do so, have fatally flawed its decision and made it unjust because procedurally infirm.

In *Armstrong Cork Co.*, 71-1 ARB ¶8242, 3811 (Wolf, 1971), where the employer followed its progressive discipline system to the letter, giving the grievant repeated warnings and progressively more severe penalties for his absenteeism, the arbitrator noted: "Its actions were impeccable except in one respect. ... The punishment was applied mechanically without sufficient regard for the circumstances surrounding the event and the individual." What were those circumstances? Most conspicuously, the grievant had been employed for 14-1/2 years and had a good record. See also *Shepard Niles Crane & Hoist Corp.*, 71 LA 828, 831 (Alutto, 1978) (absenteeism and tardiness):

> [A]n employee found asleep on the job, but possessing an unblemished 20-year work history should certainly be treated differently than an employee with four years seniority and a history of disciplinary problems. It is circumstances such as these that appear to explain discrepancies in the severity of disciplinary action taken against the grievant and other employees.

[49]*E,g,, Reynolds Metals Co.*, 55 LA 1168 (Block, 1971) (grievant "erred greatly" in refusing supervisor's order to leave office, but supervisor's "offensive tongue lashing," which included use of racial epithets, was "highly provocative factor"); *Industrial Phosphating Co.*, supra note 47 (grievant's resort to abusive language not excusable, but fact that grievant had been victim of several payroll errors was "degree of provocation"); *Kimberly-Clark Corp.*, 87-2 ARB ¶8315 (Ratner, 1987) (insubordination); *Warren Assemblies, Inc.*, 92 LA 521 (Roumell, 1989) (supervisor's having discharged grievant without reasonable cause viewed as provocation for profane outburst).

[50]*Golden Operations, CWC Castings Div. of Textron, Inc.*, 80-2 ARB ¶8543, 5433 (Ipavec, 1980), in which management, upon discovering that employees had been concealing beer on the premises, kept watch on the hiding place and waited until an employee retrieved and drank some beer before acting. "When a Company has knowledge or could reasonably foresee that a violation of the Company's rules is about to

intent to commit serious misconduct;[51] absence of hazards or
other aggravating circumstances;[52] language difficulties;[53] and
acute personal problems such as chronic alcoholism and mental
illness.[54] With particular reference to alcoholism and drug
abuse, however, several arbitrators have held that rehabilitative
efforts undertaken by an employee following discharge do not
constitute a mitigating circumstance.[55] Likewise, financial difficulties experienced by a discharged grievant and his family have
been viewed as irrelevant.[56]

By contrast, factors that support a relatively severe penalty
within the framework of the company's penalty system might
include misconduct that was highly dangerous;[57] additional mis-

---

occur, the Company should remove the means by which the rule is to be broken." See
also *Zinsco Elec. Prods., Inc.*, 65 LA 487 (Erbs, 1975) (employer failed to take steps to
prevent fight it knew was impending); *AFG Indus.*, 87 LA 1160 (Clarke, 1986) (employer
at fault in failing to provide proper supervision at company picnic where it furnished
beer); *Greenlee Tool Textron Co.*, 88-1 ARB ¶8102 (Fischbach, 1987) (employer's failure
to provide remedial instruction contributed to grievant's second instance of negligence);
Mead Corp., 89-2 ARB ¶8367 (Haemmel, 1989) (penalty for negligence reduced because
supervisor guilty of gross negligence in failing to train properly).

[51]*Basic Vegetable Prods., Inc.*, 70-1 ARB ¶8020, 3083 (Koven, 1969) (falsification of
time card): "[D]espite the very serious character of the grievant's misconduct, that
conduct did not include the elements of a deliberate and premeditated theft."

[52]*Hooker Chem. Co.*, 74 LA 1032, 1034 (Grant, 1980) (smoking marijuana on job):
"Although the Company states its concern about the possibility of dangerous mistakes
caused by the erroneous mixture of chemicals, the Grievant did not work in a sensitive
area; his job was in the boiler house unloading and shoveling coal."

[53]*Graphic Communications Union*, 89-1 ARB ¶8018 (Koven, 1988) (insubordination)
(some doubt whether grievant fully understood direct order because of difficulty with
English).

[54]*Phillips 66 Co.*, 88 LA 617 (Weisbrod, 1987) (habitual gambling and probable
presence of mental illness viewed as mitigating circumstances); *New Jersey Bell Tel.
Co.*, 89-2 ARB ¶8381 (Nicolau, 1988) (alcoholism a diagnosable and treatable disease;
presence of such a disease and possibility of recovery can be considered mitigating
circumstances). For a review of this general category of mitigating circumstances, see
M. L. Greenbaum, *The "Disciplinatrator," the "Arbichiatrist," and the "Social Psychotractor"—
An Inquiry Into How Arbitrators Deal With a Grievant's Personal Problems and the Extent to
Which They Affect the Award*, 37:4 ARB. J. 51–64 (1982).

[55]*Pittsburg & Midway Coal Mining Co.*, 91 LA 431, 434 (Cohen, 1988): "If Grievant's
actions after this discharge could be used to reverse the Company's decision, the Company would be placed in an impossible position, *i.e.*, whenever employees are discharged
for intoxication, they need only seek some sort of rehabilitation programs to be able to
then proclaim that they are changed persons and should be reinstated." See also *Lick
Fish & Poultry*, 87 LA 1062 (Concepcion, 1986); *Baltimore Tin Plate*, 89-1 ARB ¶8308
(Aronin, 1988); and cases cited in Ch. 5, note 72, where several contrary rulings may
also be found.

[56]*Georgia Kraft Co.*, 84-1 ARB ¶8127 (Yancy, 1984) (falsification of records); *Thomas
Steel Strip Co.*, 87 LA 994 (Feldman, 1986) (testing positive for drugs).

[57]As in *Decar Plastics Corp.*, 44 LA 921, 923 (Greenwald, 1965), in which placing
lighted cigarettes in someone's pocket was considered far more serious than other types
of horseplay for which lesser penalties had been imposed. "All horseplay, ranging from

conduct that compounded the original offense (for example, profanity caused by intoxication);[58] malicious intent;[59] and lack of truthfulness or failure to cooperate with the employer's investigation.[60]

In some instances both mitigation and aggravation are present, and a balancing act is called for. "Just cause is essentially a standard of reasonableness and fairness. It requires that the penalty imposed must fit the seriousness of the offense and must take into consideration the total circumstances, both those in aggravation and those in mitigation."[61]

Finally, there is an area within which management may exercise discretion. As Harry Shulman put it: "[The arbitrator's] power is only to modify penalties which are beyond the range of reasonableness, and are unduly severe. If the penalty is within that range, it may not be modified."[62]

Industrial Due Process. One of the factors to which arbitrators may pay heed is industrial due process. Aside from the preliminary and basic requirement that a progressive discipline system must consist of

> the successive application cumulatively for employee infractions beginning with oral reprimands, written reprimands, suspensions, and finally discharge where really compelled . . . progressive discipline requires still more, namely, industrial due process to the end that the employee also may be more fully informed as to the charge and have an opportunity for a hearing for himself

joking involving a more remote possibility of injury to that involving a high risk of serious injury, need not be uniformly regarded as requiring the same penalty, regardless of the facts of the particular situation."

[58]*White Pine Copper Co.*, 63-2 ARB ¶8548 (Larkin, 1963).

[59]*E.g., Calmar, Inc.*, 51 LA 766 (Turkus, 1968), in which an employee's insubordinate act was deliberately designed to humiliate and embarrass a supervisor in front of other employees.

[60]*Arden Farms Co.*, 45 LA 1124 (Tsukiyama, 1965). See also cases cited in Ch. 3, notes 102–08.

[61]*Fulton Seafood Indus., Inc.*, 74 LA 620, 622 (Volz, 1980). Other cases balancing mitigating and aggravating factors include *Louisville Cooperage Co.*, 70-2 ARB ¶8652 (Volz, 1970) (draining untaxed whiskey out of barrels; discharge set aside); *F. E. Olds & Son*, 64 LA 726 (Jones, 1975) (setting fire to dramatize safety problems; discharge sustained).

[62]*Ford Motor Co.*, Opinion A-2, June 17, 1943. See also *Jackson County Medical Care Facility*, 65 LA 389 (Roumell, 1975) (unbecoming conduct); *Arrow Lock Corp.*, 84 LA 734, 735 (Nemaizer, 1985) ("I do not conceive it to be my role as Arbitrator to grant clemency where the disciplinary penalty assessed was not excessive"); *Ohio State Highway Patrol*, 94 LA 58 (Bittel, 1990) (only if employer's decision "lacks rationality and fairness" can arbitrator reduce penalty).

as to his alleged offense. Counsel or union representation is essential, too.[63]

Notice. In addition to the requirement that progressive discipline must function within the framework of industrial due process, progressive discipline must also operate within the framework of notice.

> **EXAMPLE:** A foreman, suspecting that an employee's poor production might be due to her long fingernails, ordered her to cut them. The employee refused, and was suspended first for three days, then for 10 days. Returning from the second suspension, the employee displayed her freshly clipped nails to the foreman and declared that she was ready to go back to work. Deciding her nails were still too long, the foreman fired the employee.

Progessive discipline, yes—but the discharge was set aside on notice grounds.

> [A]ccording to the believable evidence . . . the orders given the grievant *at no time* specified the length to which the grievant's nails should be cut, in order to satisfy her employer's rquirements. That failure to articulate may have been permissible for suspensions, but it was impermissible for discharge. It is one thing to be insubordinate; it is quite another to seek how not to be, and to be rebuffed.[64]

Where Progressive Discipline Does Not Apply

Certain types of misconduct often are considered not to be subject to the requirements of progressive discipline, either because the misconduct is so serious that the employment relationship cannot survive it or because corrective measures could not be expected to have much effect. Some of the more common exclusions are the following:

"*Malum in se.*" In addition to the standard *malum in se* offenses that call for summary discharge, such as theft[65] ("even though

---

[63]*Giant Eagle Markets, Inc.*, 1975 ARB ¶8145, 3608 (Emerson, 1975) (drinking).

[64]*Honeywell, Inc.*, 80-1 ARB ¶8270 (Belshaw, 1980).

[65]*American Motors Corp.*, 52 LA 709 (Keefe, 1969). The view that progressive discipline is inapplicable to violations involving money was stated in *Niagara Frontier Transit Sys.*, 24 LA 783 (Thompson, 1955) (falsification of time cards): "It seems more appropriate to apply the idea of 'progressive' discipline to loafing, negligence, incompetence, even damage to machines and equipment, etc., than to infractions which more or less deprive the Company of money directly."

the amount of money involved is very small"[66]), arbitrators have recognized the propriety of summary discharge for other serious offenses, among them striking a foreman,[67] gross insubordination,[68] destruction of company property,[69] lending money to a fellow employee at usurious rates,[70] and fighting.[71] The existence of a progressive discipline system does not mean that management has given up the right to discharge summarily for serious offenses.[72] It has also been held that a past failure to discharge for a given offense of this nature cannot "be considered a waiver of the right to discharge."[73]

Alcohol and drug use. In some industries, such as transportation, drinking or drug use on the job is considered to be so serious an offense that it is beyond the reach of corrective discipline. "Where the safety of the public is at issue, arbitrators are exceptionally hesitant about upsetting a decision of management."[74]

---

[66]*United Hosiery Mills Corp.*, 22 LA 573, 576 (Marshall, 1954). Other cases sustaining discharge for dishonesty involving trivial sums include *Tri-City Nursing Center*, 84-1 ARB ¶8289 (Keefe, 1984) (one onion); *Greyhound Food Management*, 89 LA 1138 (Grinstead, 1987) (58-cent can of orange juice); *Timken Co.*, 88-1 ARB ¶8056 (Duda, 1987) (claim of 8.0 hours worked rather than 7.9 hours). However, in *Defense Gen'l Supply Center*, 89-2 ARB ¶8473 (Veglahn, 1989), discharge for attempted theft of three rolls of Scotch tape was reduced to a two-month suspension because there was no established practice of discharging for theft. The arbitrator said that attempted theft was tantamount to theft, but under company rules discipline was stated to be corrective in nature.

[67]*E.g., White Front Stores, Inc.*, 61 LA 536 (Killion, 1973); *Continental Fibre Drum Co.*, 83 LA 1197 (Yaney, 1984).

[68]See *Link-Belt Co.*, 17 LA 224 (Updegraff, 1951) (leaving work without permission); *International Tel. & Tel. Corp.*, 54 LA 1110 (King, 1970) (insubordination; making speech in company cafeteria during lunch); *Fourco Glass Co.*, 84 LA 693 (Cantor, 1985) (defiance of order to return to work); *Rockwell Int'l Corp.*, 88 LA 418 (Scholtz, 1986) ("blatant" insubordination consisting of directing obscenities at two managers and refusal to surrender badge to supervisor or guards).

[69]*R. E. Phelon Co.*, 75 LA 1051 (Irvings, 1980) (unauthorized absence); *Southern Bell Tel. & Tel. Co.*, 25 LA 270 (McCoy, 1955) (strike misconduct).

[70]*Glenn L. Martin Co.*, 27 LA 768 (Jaffee, 1956).

[71]*Harry M. Stevens, Inc.*, 51 LA 258, 260 (Turkus, 1968): "On job physical fighting standing alone is just cause for dismissal. It need not be buttressed by prior misconduct or offensive behavior." Many other cases also stand for this proposition; see F. ELKOURI & E. A. ELKOURI, HOW ARBITRATION WORKS 694 (4th ed. 1985). But mitigating circumstances have often been cited as ground for setting aside the discharge penalty; see, e.g., *Teledyne Monarch Rubber*, 89-1 ARB ¶8295 (Prusa, 1989), where the discharge of the aggressor in a fight that caused incapacitation of the victim for 27 days was reduced to a disciplinary suspension. The grievant's clean 16-year work record and the fact that the attack was an unpremeditated outgrowth of a verbal altercation were cited as mitigating factors.

[72]*Inland Steel Prods. Co.*, 47 LA 966 (Gilden, 1966).

[73]*Gries Reproducer Corp.*, 47 LA 747 (Cahn, 1966).

[74]*Deluxe Saw and Tool Co.*, 70-2 ARB ¶8639 (Hon, 1970) (on-the-job drinking by truck drivers).

More generally, Arbitrator Koven has identified five factors which, singly or in combination, will be held to justify discharge for drinking or intoxication on the job without resort to progressive discipline (or further steps in progressive discipline):

> (1) where the grievant has previously been disciplined for alcohol-related misconduct or been warned that further incidents of drinking or intoxication may lead to discharge; (2) where the grievant has compounded his alcohol-related offense with some additional act of misconduct such as insubordination, profanity, fighting or the like, or where his drinking is tied to excessive absenteeism; (3) where the grievant is a chronic alcoholic who has refused treatment or who has lapsed in his rehabilitation efforts; (4) where the grievant's seniority is very short and/or his disciplinary record is poor overall; (5) where the grievant's job has special hazards, so that intoxication on the job poses particular dangers to persons and property.[75]

The use of illegal drugs in the workplace is similar to drinking on the job in that the result may be impairment and consequent danger to persons and property. But there is an additional factor which is critical in the eyes of many arbitrators—drug use is a criminal activity, whereas alcohol use is not. Making this point, Arbitrator Harry Dworkin has ruled that suspension is not an effective way to deal with employees guilty of selling, using, or providing drugs to fellow employees. His reasoning is as follows:

> A suspension is simply not an adequate corrective action in this situation. Given the potential profit involved in providing drugs, the risk of suspension provides little deterrent to one who might engage in this activity. This is particularly true given the known difficulty of actually proving such involvement. The only effective, and appropriate corrective action is to separate the provider from his "market."[76]

---

[75]*Armstrong Rubber Co.*, 77 LA 775, 778 (1981) (footnotes omitted), cited with approval in *Maintenance Central for Seniors*, 86 LA 288 (Roumell, 1985) (drinking during break).

[76]*Burger Iron Co.*, 92 LA 1101, 1106 (1989). Dworkin also gave this response to a union argument that enlightened employers frequently deal with alcoholism and drug addiction as an illness rather than as a disciplinary problem: "[S]uch commendable endeavors do not serve to deprive management of its contractual rights to discipline for just cause, nor do they grant the Arbitrator authority to modify contractual language, or to add new language that the parties had not deemed appropriate to incorporate in their agreement." See also *San Francisco Police Dep't*, 87 LA 791 (Riker, 1986) (progressive discipline not required in case of cocaine use by police dispatcher, since such use is incompatible with functions as dispatcher).

Sickness. In some contracts, chronic absenteeism due to illness is not subject to progressive discipline.[77] Inherent in misconduct that is responsive to progressive discipline is that the employee can voluntarily improve his conduct; to put it another way, it is misconduct the employee can do something about. Obviously, this is not the case with sickness, which by its very nature is involuntary. Therefore, it is often said, "[p]unishment for illness is not logical procedure."[78]

> *Arbitrator J. Dworkin:* Sickness is not just cause for discipline. But at the same time, no company is required to retain a person in the workforce whose illness disables him or her from working. Such individual is not a candidate for discipline *in the classic sense.* However, it is well understood that one who will not or cannot report to work regularly, even through no fault of his own, may be discharged for non-disciplinary reasons. In such instance, the Company is required to consider factors that are not necessarily appropriate to normal disciplinary cases. A person who is ill is not subject to termination of employment unless recovery from the illness and resumption of duties is not something that is likely to occur in the foreseeable future.[79]

Incompetence. Poor workmanship and negligence are obvious candidates for progressive discipline when the cause is inattention or attitude.[80] But if poor work performance results from genuine incompetence (because the employee lacks either native ability or proper training), progressive discipline cannot reasonably be expected to have any corrective effect.[81] Some other response may be called for—demotion, transfer, training, or

---

[77]*Logan Metal Stampings, Inc.,* 53 LA 185 (Kates, 1969).

[78]*Atlantic Richfield Co.,* 69 LA 484, 491 (Sisk, 1977), with additional citations. In *Mead Paper,* 91 LA 52 (Curry, 1988), progressive discipline requirements were held not to apply to an employee whose absences because of accidents and illness constituted almost a quarter of his 18 years of employment, where the discharge was based on unsuitability for work in the mill and not on chronic absenteeism, and the termination letter stated that the action was nondisciplinary.

[79]*Airco, Inc.,* 84-1 ARB ¶8121, 3557 (1984).

[80]See, e.g., *Home Bldg. Corp.,* 74-2 ARB ¶8652 (Goetz, 1974) (incompetence, inefficiency); *Photo Color, Inc.,* 76-1 ARB ¶8178 (Cohen, 1976) (incompetence and inefficiency); *Eagle Picher Indus., Inc.,* 77-1 ARB ¶8099 (Ipavec, 1977) (negligence, carelessness, defective work); *J. P. Miller Artesian Well Co.,* 78-1 ARB ¶8001 (Doppelt, 1977) (negligence); *Stuck Mold Works, Inc.,* 78-1 ARB ¶8255 (Dyke, 1978) (improper job attitude, neglect of duty).

[81]Such a case was *Kerr-McGee Refining Corp.,* 88-2 ARB ¶8330 (Allen, 1988), where the grievant's test score was less than half that of the next lowest scorer and where the grievant, even after retraining, could not meet the requirements of the job.

even termination if no other work is available, depending on the employee's past record, length of service, and what the contract permits.[82]

Safety. Some kinds of behavior in some industries simply cannot be tolerated or dealt with by means of progressive discipline. A prime example of this principle concerns safety. As Arbitrator Seward put it:

> In dealing with the general run of offenses, the proper function of discipline is to correct the employee's conduct; discharge is justified only where an employee's prior disciplinary record indicates that he is incorrigible. It is universally recognized, however, that there are some offenses which are of so serious a nature that the employer cannot properly be required to run the risk of their repetition. . . . Unimportant as [the grievant's] failure to stop may seem after the event, the fact is that he risked the lives of the passengers who were entrusted to his care. If a train had come while his bus was on the tracks, all of his prior good record as a driver would not have saved a life.[83]

II. Penalty: In Practice

Up to this point the focus has been on the conceptual foundation for penalty systems and the standards on which arbitrators rely in deciding whether progressive discipline should have been applied and, if so, was applied properly. The focus of this section is upon some immediate and everyday practical questions involved in evaluating penalty.

---

[82]*General Tel. of Cal.*, 44 LA 669 (Prasow, 1965). The arbitrator in this case also suggested that where an act of negligence, or a lapse in performance, results not from willful misconduct but from "errors in judgment, where the good faith of the employee is not in question," the appropriate response is not punitive action like suspension, but a warning that will improve the employee's understanding of what is expected.

[83]*Pennsylvania Greyhound Lines, Inc.*, 19 LA 210, 212 (Seward, 1952). In *J. R. Simplot Co.*, 77-1 ARB ¶8272 (Conant, 1977), the arbitrator found that penalties associated with safety rules are intended to protect employees and are not for punitive purposes. Hence, an arbitrator "should not so strictly consider all the due process questions concerning rules and their strict application as one would review these questions in a discipline case." The logical extension of that position is that safety rule violations ought not to be subject to progressive discipline.

Warnings and Suspensions In Progressive Discipline

Warnings as Notice Versus Warnings as Reprimands

> Arbitrator Dean: The purpose of a warning is to bring a halt to the offensive activity and to afford the offending individual an opportunity to reform. If, after sufficient warning, the individual does not improve to the degree desired, he may be deemed incorrigible and dismissed.[84]

The term "warning" is used in two different senses within the context of progressive discipline: as notice and as reprimand. In the sense of notice, a warning (whether oral or written) tells an employee what behavior is expected and what penalties may be imposed for particular acts of misconduct. In the sense of reprimand, a warning constitutes a formal record that an employee has committed a disciplinary offense. In that dual sense, warnings are the cornerstone of progressive discipline.

Because the accepted purpose of industrial discipline is corrective rather than punitive, the purpose of any disciplinary system obviously would be defeated if an employee could be discharged without having been given notice that correction is necessary. The critical role of notice in progressive discipline is most evident in cases where notice is entirely lacking. A good example is management's reaction to an employee who was spotted drinking beer in the locker room. Instead of calling him on the carpet immediately for his violation, his supervisors decided to keep watch on him, and after he was observed drinking several more times he was discharged. Because he had no warning prior to discharge that his job was in jeopardy, the employee had no opportunity to correct his conduct; in fact, the company's conduct had the opposite effect of allowing him to compound his misconduct. Under these circumstances, discharge was without just cause and the employee was reinstated with full back pay.[85]

As a necessary concommitant of this goal of rehabilitation,"[t]he concept of a warning implies an opportunity for correction. This in turn implies opportunity for sober reflection

---

[84]*Hoover Co.*, 82-2 ARB ¶8524, 5345 (1982) (writing lewd remarks about female coworker on men's room wall). The purpose of warnings is also discussed in *Northern Cal. Grocers Ass'n*, 53 LA 85 (Eaton, 1969) (violation of check-cashing rules).

[85]*Industrial Plastics Corp.*, 58 LA 546 (Willingham,, 1972).

and in many cases resolves itself into a question of how much time has elapsed between the warning and the final discharge."[86]

A warning in the sense of reprimand (whether it is called a reprimand, a warning notice, an incident report, or something else) has two closely related functions: From the employer's point of view, a reprimand becomes part of the employee's disciplinary record that management may ultimately use to justify a more severe penalty, including discharge. From the employee's point of view, a reprimand does more than tell him what conduct is acceptable or unacceptable; it places him on notice that he can no longer count on the advantages of a "clean" disciplinary record if he commits another act of misconduct, and that more severe disciplinary action is likely to follow.[87]

While every warning functions as a form of notice, a warning does not necessarily have a disciplinary component. A case in point is the employer that adopted a new rule reducing the time given employees to put away their tools and thereafter suspended several employees who violated the rule. The employer believed that the posting of the rule amounted to the verbal warning which the contract required as the first step in progressive discipline. The arbitrator pointed out, however, that management's action had neither of the characteristics of a disciplinary warning. That is, it was not entered on the record of any of the employees, and it was directed to all employees affected by the rule, irrespective of whether any individual had been guilty of an "abuse" of the rule.

> Such action being in the nature of the promulgation of a rule or in the nature of a general instruction to the employees cannot properly be considered as the type of warning for a 'first offense' which the contract contemplates.[88]

---

[86]*Standard Shade Roller Div.*, 73 LA 86, 90 (Dawson, undated) (refusal to work overtime), also citing *I. Schumann Co.*, 65 LA 674 (Cohen, 1975). For an extreme example of the lack of such opportunity, see *Rockford School Dist.*, 88-2 ARB ¶8367 (Traynor, 1987) (improper behavior toward student), where the grievant was given an oral and a written warning and then discharged, all on the same day, for three unexcused absences. Such a compression of the steps of progressive discipline, the arbitrator held, gave the grievant no chance to improve.

[87]*Armco Steel Corp.*, 52 LA 101 (Duff, 1969) (poor record).

[88]*Ingalls Shipbuilding Corp.*, 39 LA 419, 429 (Hebert, 1962). Similarly, in *San Mateo County Restaurant-Hotel Owners' Ass'n*, 59 LA 997 (Kenaston, 1972) (violation of work rules), the arbitrator found that a supervisor's oral direction that the grievant take the rules home and study them if she could not remember them did not constitute an oral warning in a disciplinary sense.

One arbitrator has made the point that, if a reprimand is to become a part of the employee's record and form the basis for discipline in the event of further misconduct, the employee should have an opportunity to correct the behavior in question and thus clear his or her record. At issue was a written reprimand issued to an employee for disrespectful and disruptive behavior during a training session. The arbitrator found the reprimand justified; but because the employee was not put on notice that his conduct was intolerable until it was too late for him to do anything about it, or told that he could be disciplined if it continued, the arbitrator directed that the reprimand be removed from the employee's record at the end of one year if he did not engage in misconduct during that period.[89]

The Need for Suspensions in Progressive Discipline

One View: Disciplinary Suspension Required Before Discharge. Three reasons are given for this majority position on suspension.

(1) *The notice factor.* As discussed in Chapter 1, a major reason why suspension is considered an indispensable step in progressive discipline is the notion that loss of earnings is a more effective form of notice than a simple warning. In Arbitrator Marshall's words, "[o]ne of the purposes of disciplinary suspensions is to demonstrate that an employer means business. This before-discharge action . . . affords a tangible indication to the employee that the Company will carry through with a warning."[90]

(2) *The rehabilitation factor.* From a retrospective vantage point, suspension has served for many arbitrators as a tangible guarantee that the employer used all means available to rehabilitate the grievant within the accepted range of disciplinary penalties. If the grievant failed to respond, it is not the employer's fault.

> *Arbitrator Jones:* Escalation of unwanted consequences is the crux of progressive discipline. The employee who has nonetheless remained uncorrectable despite those increasingly unwanted experiences is then, in all fairness, subject to discharge either as one who understands and still refuses to cooperate in the joint

---

[89]*Southern Gravure Serv., Inc.*, 89-2 ARB ¶8469 (Sergent, 1989).

[90]*Eastex, Inc.*, 69-2 ARB ¶8459, 4574–75 (1969) (absenteeism). See also *Rochester Tel. Corp.*, 45 LA 538 (Duff, 1965) (obscene language).

enterprise or who simply cannot grasp the essentials necessary to perform the work properly assigned.[91]

Or in the words of Arbitrator Dworkin, "[d]ischarge is warranted only in such cases where corrective measures appear to be futile."[92] To prove that corrective measures short of discharge are futile, all such measures, including suspension, logically need to be tried.[93]

(3) *Punishment should fit the crime.* For those who take the view that "the punishment should fit the crime," a penalty system needs to include not only discharge for very serious misconduct (theft, assault, and the like) and warnings for minor offenses (such as a single lateness), but also a penalty of intermediate severity for offenses that fall somewhere in between (drinking on the job is a frequently encountered example).[94] Suspension is the obvious candidate, with variations in the length of suspension to accommodate offenses of intermediate gravity.[95]

Another View: Suspension Not Always Necessary. Not all arbitrators agree that suspension is a necessary component of progressive discipline. Cases in which discharge has been upheld in the absence of a prior suspension fall into one of these two categories:

(1) *Where the company has established a formal "warnings only" penalty system.* Warnings-only systems of progressive discipline are based on the dual premise that the heart of progressive

---

[91]*Pete Pasquinelli Co.*, 68 LA 1068, 1971 (1977) (leaving work).

[92]*Babcock & Wilcox Co.*, 41 LA 862, 866 (1963) (absenteeism).

[93]Among many other cases that take this line, see, e.g., *Rexall Drug Co.*, 65 LA 1101, 1105 (Cohen, 1975) (garnishment, other violations): "Grievant had previously been suspended for disciplinary reasons. Therefore, following the concepts of progressive discipline, discharge is the only remaining discipline left to the Company." See also *Smith & Wesson-Fiocchi*, 60 LA 366 (Traynor, 1973) (absenteeism and offensive body odor leading to complaints by coworkers); *Colgate-Palmolive Co.*, 64 LA 397 (Allen, 1975) (insubordination); *I. Schumann Co.*, 65 LA 674 (Cohen, 1975) (refusal to work overtime); *Memphis Light, Gas and Water Div.*, 77-1 ARB 8202 (Flannagan, 1977) (unauthorized reconnection of personal utility service). And see "last straw" cases cited in note 112 *infra.*

[94]See, e.g., *Packaging Corp. of America*, 56 LA 856 (Anrod, 1971), where the arbitrator concluded, "It is axiomatic that the penalty must fit the offenses committed by the Grievants," and found that a disciplinary suspension would be an "equitable, fair and just penalty" for drinking that does not lead to intoxication.

[95]See, e.g., *General Elec. Co.*, 74 LA 578 (Schor, 1980), for a three-part system of progressive discipline that divides misconduct into (1) misconduct serious enough to warrant summary discharge; (2) less serious misconduct that justifies a reprimand accompanied by a one-week suspension; and (3) relatively minor offenses that call for no suspension but only written warnings.

discipline is notice and that, to be effective, notice need not be punitive in the sense or depriving the employee of his earnings. Indeed, warnings-only systems have been applied most frequently in the case of absenteeism, for the reason that most (though not all) absenteeism is due to illness, an involuntary condition that is unresponsive to punitive measures.[96]

Logically, a warnings-only system is effective to the extent that it fulfills the critical function of giving notice. That means that the number of steps leading to discharge must be clearly spelled out;[97] that the system must be consistently applied; and that employees must be informed clearly and unequivocally at each step where they stand and, most critically, at what point another infraction will result in discharge. The importance of notice in warnings-only systems has been emphasized by Arbitrator High.

> I appreciate that technically Grievant was on notice of the possibility of discharge upon the accumulation of his fourth offense within 12 months. I find, however, that the lack of a progressive nature in this provision makes it all the more important that the imminence of discharge, in fairness, be underlined to the Grievant before he accumulated the fourth violation.[98]

(2) *Where the employer has been "patience personified."*

---

[96]For cases supporting this rationale, see note 135 *infra*. Cases in which discharge for absenteeism has been upheld, without the necessity of a prior suspension, include *Pacific Tel. and Tel.*, 32 LA 178 (Galenson, 1959); *Cannon Elec. Co.*, 46 LA 481 (Kotin, 1965); *American Brakeblok Div., Abex Corp.*, 52 LA 484 (Wagner, 1969); *Sterling Drug, Inc.*, 70-1 ARB ¶8033 (Berkowitz, 1969); *Koenig Iron Works, Inc.*, 53 LA 594 (Ray, 1969); *Globe-Union , Inc.*, 57 LA 701 (High, 1971); *Doxsee Food Corp.*, 57 LA 1107 (Farinholt, 1971); *Beaunit Fibers*, 71-2 ARB ¶8455 (Amis, 1971); *Avco Corp.*, 64 LA 672 (Marcus, 1975); *Husky Oil Co.*, 65 LA 47 (Richardson, 1975); *Hoover Ball and Bearing Co.*, 66 LA 764 (Herman, 1976); *Pacific Southwest Airlines*, 70 LA 833 (Jones, 1978). The contrary view is taken in *Park Prods. Co.*, 68-1 ARB ¶8330 (Kates, 1968), and *Harsco Corp.*, 70-2 ARB ¶8757 (Klein, 1970), and in a number of cases where the contract expressly mandated suspension as a progressive discipline step, including *Babcock & Wilcox Co.*, *supra* note 92; *Amerace Corp.*, 68-1 ARB ¶8238 (Roberts, 1968); *Eastex, Inc.*, *supra* note 90; *Cleveland Burial Vault Co.*, 69-2 ARB ¶8554 (Kallenbach, 1969); *Niagara Mach. & Tool Works*, 76 LA 160 (Grant, 1981). For an example of an accepted warnings-only system not restricted to absenteeism, see *General Elec. Co.*, *supra* note 95, where the system provided that four reprimands for minor infractions would result in discharge.

[97]*Canton Drop Forging & Mfg. Co.*, 80-2 ARB ¶8450 (Kabaker, 1980) (absenteeism and abuse of washup time).

[98]*Wolf Mach. Co.*, 72 LA 510, 513 (1979) (various rule infractions). See also, e.g., *Philips Petroleum*, 64-3 ARB ¶8907 (Mittenthal, 1964); *Kaiser Aluminum & Chem. Corp.*, 68-2 ARB ¶8606 (Hebert, 1968) (absenteeism); *General Elec. Corp.*, 69 LA 707 (Jedel, 1977) (unauthorized break, other misconduct).

EXAMPLE: During her three years of employment, according to her supervisors, a practical nurse had been unable to get along with many patients, had failed to master routine nursing procedures, had reacted with hostility to instructions and suggestions, and had just not "carried her weight." Counseling and "talkings to" by her superiors had made no impression on her. When the hospital finally discharged her, the union argued that suspension or perhaps transfer to another department should have been tried as a last resort to persuade the nurse to mend her ways.

Some arbitrators might have agreed with the union. But here, looking at the nurse's deplorable record, the arbitrator found not a shred of evidence to suggest that suspension would have done any more to improve her attitude than the intensive counseling the hospital had already given her. Notice, too, was a factor: "[The grievant] could not have been lulled into a false sense of security, in view of the numerous times she was spoken to. She must have known about the various "incidents" testified to, as they were called to her attention and corrected as they occurred. By giving her more than average help, over a longer period of time, her supervisors should be praised—not faulted." Discharge was sustained.[99]

This case exemplifies an argument that is heard with some frequency. The employer says, "Don't blame us for not being hard on this employee. We bent over backward to give him a chance." Essentially what it is saying is, "We're good guys." One might say that when an employer does not give proper notice or does not apply a suspension when it should, there is an implication of bad faith and underhanded dealing. Arbitrator Stouffer has addressed this point, holding that when there is ample evidence that this is not the case, the conclusion should be that the employer simply has been patient and *is* a "good guy."

It appears that all of the Company's prior reprimands were justified; at least no grievances were filed contesting the same. The Company's reluctance to impose progressive disciplinary layoffs on grievant for past misconduct does not indicate negligence on its part. It indicates patience and willingness to help the grievant. The Company should not be criticized for this.[100]

---

[99]*Elizabeth Horton Memorial Hosp.*, 74-2 ARB ¶8588 (Sandler, 1974).

[100]*Pretty Prods., Inc.*, 51 LA 688, 691 (1968). Arbitrator Stouffer took the same position in *American Cyanamid Co.*, 68-2 ARB ¶8674, 5341 (1968) (sleeping on job), where he quoted Arbitrator Kreimer as follows:

There can be no doubt that every one of the Company's prior reprimands was

Number and Length of Suspensions

The conventional wisdom on disciplinary suspensions, as expressed by Arbitrator Duff, is that "the Company should impose layoffs of increasing degree" when an employee fails to respond to reprimands.[101] But exactly how many suspensions? And should a suspension be one day, three days, or three weeks? Arbitrator Jonathan Dworkin has suggested that 30 days is the outside limit for a corrective suspension, and that any longer suspension is punitive.

> A two-month suspension for negligence . . . stands out as arbitrary and punitive. If correction was the goal, it is unreasonable to believe that the second month . . . added any corrective influence . . . . Stated another way, if a 30-day suspension was not going to remedy Grievant's faulty performance, it is clear that the faults were not going to be remedied. In such case, Grievant should have been dismissed.[102]

Arbitrator Justin has proposed that a suspension should be not less than three working days and not more than 10 days, reasoning that the corrective effect of a disciplinary suspension derives from the shame that an employee feels when he has been suspended. Less than three days away from work, Justin suggested, does not provide enough time for the suspension to sink in; furthermore, an employee can "explain away" a day or two off to his family and friends more easily than a longer period of time. On the other hand, more than 10 days off, in Justin's view, becomes more punitive than corrective.[103]

Some arbitrators take the position that if misconduct is proved, selecting the appropriate penalty is exclusively the function of management, and the arbitrator has no authority to modify that penalty. Where the penalty is discharge, a majority of arbitrators do not hesitate to substitute a lesser penalty if in their judgment discharge was unreasonably harsh. Where the

---

thoroughly justified. Certainly the Company's reluctance to inflict progressive disciplinary layoffs to Grievant for his wrong-doings cannot be attributed to weakness. Rather, it indicates patience and strength, a willingness to help Grievant, not to hurt him. For this the Company cannot and should not be criticized."
In agreement, see *Jaeger Mach. Co.*, 55 LA 850 (High, 1970), where the arbitrator declined to penalize the employer for its leniency in withdrawing the grievant's prior suspensions; and *Avco Corp., supra* note 96.
[101]*Armco Steel Corp.*, 52 LA 101, 104 (1969) (poor overall record).
[102]*Red Cross Blood Serv.*, 90 LA 393, 397 (1988).
[103]J. JUSTIN, HOW TO MANAGE WITH A UNION 420–21 (1969).

original penalty was something less than discharge, and the impact on the employee not so drastic, however, those same arbitrators, like leopards changing their spots, often switch to the position that the arbitrator has no business substituting his or her judgment for that of management. As Sanford Kadish has put it,

> it is in reviewing relatively fine differences in punishments that these objections have their greatest force. Is the proper discipline a reprimand or a one-day lay-off? A two-day lay-off or a week? Here there are no substantial standards for the arbitrator to apply beyond protecting against inconsistency with past practice and unfair surprise where the practice is altered, and assuring equal treatment for like cases.[104]

Arbitrator Shulman is often cited in support of the proposition that arbitrators should follow a strict hands-off policy when the appropriate length of suspension is in issue:

> Even when all the circumstances are considered, the exact size of the penalty is still a matter of judgment. . . . If the penalty for a particular violation may reasonably range from one week to one month's lay-off, for example, two different persons might very well choose two different penalties, one a week, the other perhaps two weeks. But the Umpire does not have the power to substitute his judgment for that of the company in all cases and compel the acceptance of the precise measure of discipline which the Umpire would have imposed had he had the initial responsibility for discipline. . . . His power is only to modify penalties which are beyond the range of reasonableness, and are unduly severe.[105]

But one reading of Shulman suggests that he is riding two horses at the same time. With one hand, Shulman "gives" to management, by stating that an arbitrator has no power to substitute his or her judgment for that of management so long as the penalty is within the "range of reasonableness"; but he "takes away" with the other hand, by implicitly retaining the authority to decide what the range of reasonableness is. Shulman thus offers only a conditional answer when the arbitrator (or employer) asks what penalty is appropriate for a given of-

---

[104]S. Kadish, *The Criminal Law and Industrial Discipline Sanctioning Systems: Some Comparative Observations*, LABOR ARBITRATION: PERSPECTIVES AND PROBLEMS 143–44 (Proceedings of the 17th Annual Meeting, National Academy of Arbitrators 1964).

[105]*Ford Motor Co. and UAW*, Opinion A-2 (1943), cited in, among other opinions, *Jackson County Medical Care Facility*, 65 LA 389, 393 (Roumell, 1975) (unbecoming conduct); and *Grand Haven Brass Foundry*, 68 LA 41, 45 (Roumell, 1977).

fense. When, for example, the employer has imposed a five-day suspension, the arbitrator who feels that a three-day or even a one-day suspension would have been long enough can avoid the uncomfortable feeling of appearing to be arbitrary simply by invoking the Shulman view that management's judgment should be respected. The same would apply when the question was how many suspensions should be imposed prior to discharge.

Take a typical set of facts: The grievant was discharged after his third refusal to work Sunday overtime. After the first refusal, he was reprimanded; after the second, he was suspended for three days. The union argued that, at most, another three-day suspension would have been appropriate. But the arbitrator refused to step in. "It is arguable," he observed, "that another disciplinary step short of discharge might have been taken or that another management might have used a different combination of penalties." But the issue was whether there was just cause for the grievant's discharge. He had repeatedly refused to comply with legitimate directives to work on Sunday; there were no extenuating circumstances to justify his refusal; and the penalty was neither arbitrary nor capricious. Under these circumstances, another suspension was no more appropriate a penalty than discharge.[106]

But change the facts somewhat: Say that the grievant had been reprimanded for a first offense of refusing overtime and suspended for 30 days for a second refusal, and that the issue before the arbitrator was whether the 30-day suspension was proper. For at least some arbitrators, the loss of 30 days' wages might well be a penalty outside the "range of reasonableness" for the misconduct in question (or "an abuse of discretion" or "arbitrary and capricious"), and the just cause standard would require the substitution of a shorter suspension. The implication of the Shulman view for management, then, is that the number and length of disciplinary suspensions is a matter of management discretion—but only within limits.

Discharge for Cumulative Misconduct

The "Last Straw" Case

Here is a scenario that arbitrators have experienced many times: Over a period of time, an employee builds a record of

---

[106]*Yale Univ.*, 52 LA 752, 754 (Dunlop, 1969).

unsatisfactory conduct, in which no incident standing alone (although each violates a rule) is of such moment as to warrant discharge.[107] Or perhaps the various prior incidents, or some of them, are more serious but none has inspired the penalty of discharge for one reason or another. Finally, something happens, maybe only a little infraction in itself, and the employer decides that enough is enough and discharges the employee for the most recent offense as well as for the totality of past infractions.

These are what are referred to as "last straw" or "rain on the roof" cases.[108] From one perspective, if "last straw" is defined very generally as the last incident of misconduct that leads to discharge, most discharges would fall into this category. But what is typically meant by last-straw cases is not cases where the last act is very serious in itself.[109] Instead, the term "last straw" is reserved for situations in which the last event or incident is a trifle. An example is the case of an employee who had a tiff with his shop steward. This would not have justified discharge standing alone, but his conduct over the preceding two-month period, in which lesser penalties had been repeatedly given, demonstrated that further efforts at corrective discipline would be futile.[110]

Or an employee engages in all sorts of acts which in themselves are not misconduct but are inappropriate in the workplace. For example, an employee leaves a note with his time card requesting a date with a female payroll clerk; when asked why he is riding a piece of equipment he does not belong on, he responds that he is "freaking out, man"; he leaves his machine during working hours, stands in the doorway gazing outside, and, when asked what he is doing, replies, "I'm looking at the sunset"; and while doing his work, he merrily sings and hoots

---

[107]*National Fireworks Ordinance Corp.*, 20 LA 274 (Roberts, 1953) (uncooperativeness, troublemaking); *Ebinger Baking Co.*, 47 LA 948 (Singer, 1966) (varied misconduct).

[108]For the spectrum of "last straw" cases, see *Rowe Mfg Co.*, 36 LA 639 (Turkus, 1961) (improper attitude, conduct, performance); and *Great Atl. & Pac. Tea Co.*, 41 LA 887 (Cahn, 1963) (overstaying lunch period, time card violations, past record). For "last straw" cases where discharge was not sustained either because misconduct was not sufficiently proved or progressive discipline was not applied, or for other reasons, see *Abbott Linen Supply Co.*, 35 LA 12 (Schmidt, 1960); *Northwestern Bell Tel. Co.*, 37 LA 605 (Davey, 1961); *Ohio Crankshaft Co.*, 48 LA 558 (Teple, 1967).

[109]See, e.g., *Birmingham-News Co.*, 79-1 ARB ¶8039 (Grooms, 1978); and *Neville Chem. Co.*, 74 LA 814 (Parkinson, 1980), among many other cases.

[110]*American Motors Corp.*, 51 LA 945 (Dunne, 1968).

so loudly that the foreman warns him, "You just can't be making loud noises in this department."

This is the so-called "Peck's Bad Boy" case. This employee is not necessarily a "bad apple"—what sets him apart is a "can't get it together" personality and attitude. At some point the employer reaches the end of its patience and gets rid of the employee. And even though the violations with which he is charged may be minor (or not even improper in another setting), discharge is not necessarily an overly stringent penalty. That is so because even petty infractions can build up to a critical point where the employee has become such a liability that the employer cannot reasonably be expected to tolerate his behavior any longer.

> *Arbitrator Koven:* Cause for discharge is not found in his final [act of misconduct], but in the established fact that he is incorrigible. It is upon this logic that the grievant's conduct, though in each instance a picayunish matter, in its totality amounted to a serious matter and a burden which one could not expect the Company infinitely to sustain.[111]

Typical Questions in Last-Straw Cases

Is There a Genuine Last Straw? "[A]n employee cannot be penalized by discharge merely for a past record unless he has committed a present offense";[112] and because an employee was fundamentally blameless in the incident that provoked his discharge (leaving work early without permission), no discipline was called for despite his lengthy history of rule violations and written warnings.[113] "[T]he final act . . . must stand by itself as a proper and justifiable trigger for some discipline. Unless this factor is present, . . . past steps in a progressive discipline program become meaningless."[114]

---

[111]*Ampex Corp.*, 44 LA 412, 416 (Koven, 1965). See also *Electronic Corp. of America*, 3 LA 217 (Kaplan, 1946); *Rochester Tel. Corp.*, 45 LA 538 (Duff, 1965); *Arden Farms Co.*, 45 LA 1124 (Tsukiyama, 1965); *Friden , Inc.*, 52 LA 448 (Koven, 1969); *Pacific Bell*, 87-1 ARB ¶8037 (Killion, 1986).

[112]*Turco Mfg. Co.*, 74 LA 889, 895 (Penfield, 1980) (cumulative misconduct, abuse of union office). See also *Wyandotte Chem. Co.*, 70-2 ARB ¶8830 (Ellman, 1970) (absenteeism); *Whirlpool Corp.*, 65 LA 386 (Gruenberg, 1975) (possession of marijuana); *Alabama Dep't of Mental Health*, 66 LA 279 (Spritzer, 1976) (absenteeism).

[113]*Ogden Food Serv. Corp.*, 75 LA 805 (Kelman, 1980) (leaving plant without permission).

[114]*Overhead Door Co.*, 70 LA 1299, 1303 (Dworkin, 1978) (absenteeism, excused absence).

A garden-variety "last straw" is present when an employee indulges in the last of several refusals to obey a reasonable order. For example, take the "melancholy list of charges" against a 21-year employee who, over a long period, consistently refused or loudly protested her work assignments, constantly complained about being overworked, talked incessantly in a loud voice, refused to stop terrorizing the secretaries whom she supervised, and finally on one fine day could not resist producing the "last straw" that justified her dismissal by refusing to help one of her colleagues.[115]

Do All the "Straws" Have to Be of the Same Type? The answer, of course, is no. Take this situation: A waitress was reprimanded for loafing; next she was discharged for refusing an order but then was reinstated with a reprimand; next she was cautioned about leaving the job without permission; she was then given a reprimand for refusing a work assignment together with a final notice; after which she was cautioned for chronic tardiness. Then came the day when she threatened a customer with a knife because, she claimed, he had spit at her. Result: Enough is enough.[116]

Can the Arbitrator Review Past Incidents, as Well as the Last Straw? As noted in Chapter 5, arbitrators expect the charge for which the employer offers proof to be the charge for which discipline was originally imposed, not something the employer cites for the first time at the arbitration hearing. Thus, "[i]t is well-settled that when an employee is discharged for a particular alleged violation and no mention is made of his past record, the latter should be considered later only in connection with the quantum, or relative severity, of the discipline meted out."[117]

"Last straw" cases by their very nature involve a course of past and cumulative misconduct. Nonetheless, the rock-bottom

---

[115]*National Council of Jewish Women, Inc.*, 57 LA 980 (Scheiber, 1971). But compare cases along the same lines where discharge was overturned: *Magnavox Co.*, 29 LA 305 (Dworkin, 1957); *Metropolitan Transit Auth.*, 39 LA 855 (Fallon, undated); *Revere Copper and Brass, Inc.*, 45 LA 254 (McCoy, 1965); *Olin Mathieson Chem. Corp.*, 49 LA 573 (Belshaw, 1967).

[116]*Prophet Foods Co.*, 55 LA 288 (Howlett, 1970). See also *W-L Molding Co.*, 72 LA 1065 (Howlett, 1979) (assault on vending machine). But compare *Olin Mathieson Chem. Corp.*, *supra* note 115.

[117]*American Airlines, Inc.*, 46 LA 737, 739 (Sembower, 1966). By the same token, said the arbitrator in *Martin-Brower Co.*, 89-1 ARB ¶8221 (Miller, 1988), the employer's failure to notify an employee of an alleged infraction or to reprimand him for it precludes use of that infraction to support disciplinary action for a later infraction.

requirement is still the same as in cases that involve only a single incident.

> Since it is basic that a dischargee should know at the time he files his grievance what he is accused of doing wrong, so that he may make proper remonstrance and prepare his case, the aspect of his prior record should appear in the charge itself in order to be an appropriate consideration in direct connection with whether or not he is "guilty."[118]

Often the shoe is on the other foot. Rather than the employer seeking to display the grievant's employment history before the arbitrator, it may be the grievant who points to his or her past history and argues that some of the earlier absences, for example, should have been excused and, indeed, that the prior warnings were unwarranted. The employer can then be expected to argue that any such offered evidence is inadmissible because the grievant never grieved any of the past warnings. And the arbitrator would at first agree: "[I]n most instances, it would be improper for an arbitrator to expunge the aspects of an employment background which had not been submitted to the grievance procedure with requisite timeliness."[119]

But that might not be all. Some arbitrators would go on to say that because, as a "fact of industrial life," employees do not contest such warnings, some latitude is in order. An arbitrator "may justifiably review prior discipline to determine whether it should be permitted to form a link in the chain leading to suspension or discharge. . . . Evidence which refutes the presumption that former discipline was proper must be such as creates a positive conviction contradicting personnel records."[120]

Does Consideration of the Employee's Whole Record Amount to Double Jeopardy?[121] When an employee is charged with a single act of misconduct, the question of double jeopardy is not likely to arise. But where his problem is a course of conduct and past

---

[118]*American Airlines, Inc., supra* note 117.

[119]*Overhead Door Co., supra* note 114.

[120]*Id.*

[121]Another type of double jeopardy problem, the overlap between criminal penalties and industrial penalties, was discussed in Ch. 5, pp. 290–92. For additional double jeopardy issues, see F. ELKOURI & E. A. ELKOURI, HOW ARBITRATION WORKS 677–79 (4th ed. 1985); and FAIRWEATHER'S PRACTICE AND PROCEDURE IN LABOR ARBITRATION 301–04 (R. J. Schoonhoven, ch. ed., 3d ed. 1991). These issues include the classic situation where two penalties are imposed for the same offense and the difference between double jeopardy and suspension pending investigation of suspected misconduct.

record culminating in a last incident for which he is punished, a claim of double jeopardy is more likely to be asserted.

Take the case of an employee who failed to report for his scheduled shift and was thereupon discharged. His prior bad record of attendance and punctuality was held admissible in arbitration even though some of the evidence put forward was previously presented at the arbitration in which a prior three-day suspension was protested. No double jeopardy was found.

> [T]he very nature of the offense is cumulative and significant as such. If the earlier grievance (i.e. the three day suspension) had been sustained, then that decision would perforce, have knocked out the supporting props and those papers could not be accorded the same respect here that they are if the grievance is overruled, as was the case.[122]

> *Arbitrator Tsukiyama:* Since penalties become progressively harsher with each repeated offense, progressive discipline is necessarily cumulative [cites], necessitating review and consideration of any past record of previous offenses, prior warnings and discipline in determining the propriety of discharge and penalty. Thus, the argument against "resurrection of past offenses and double jeopardy" is inapplicable to a discharge coming at the culmination of management's efforts toward corrective discipline . . . .[123]

When Is Enough Enough?

Aside from the specific issues that last-straw cases tend to raise, such as those discussed above, the perennial and underlying question is at what point can the employer feel reasonably secure in saying "Halt—that is enough!" Obviously, the answer cannot be reduced to a simple formula since each case has its own particular facts and flavor. However, setting up a system in advance (for example, one under which four violations of company rules within a 12-month period will result in discharge) is an effort to define when "enough is enough." Such a system

---

[122]*American Airlines, Inc., supra* note 117, at 741:
The familiar statutes in many states providing for suspension of an automobile driver's license for three rolling traffic law violations within a certain period, is an example [of no double jeopardy]. If the motorist successfully challenges in court any of the first two violations, it is wiped out. Otherwise, it persists and provides a cumulative foundation for the ultimate forfeiture.
[123]*Arden Farms Co.,* 45 LA 1124, 1130 (1965). Omitted citations are *Michigan Seamless Tube Co.,* 24 LA 132 (Ryder, 1955); *Pacific Press Ltd.,* 42 LA 947 (Hebert, 1964).

is itself intended to define when enough is enough—the last step becomes the "last straw" for all employees similarly situated.[124] (The intervening consideration, that is, reconciling the problem of uniformity and consistency with a system of progressive discipline, was discussed above at pp. 393–97).

Even in the absence of a self-executing system of standards, the fact that an employee has been frequently reprimanded and finally suspended because there has been no improvement becomes evidence that the employer has gone as far as can reasonably be expected—thus suggesting the parameters of "enough is enough."

> **EXAMPLE NO. 1:** For four years an employee violated the rules as a way of life. He refused to take orders; interpreted the rules his own way; observed only the rules he liked; was rude to his superiors; and when he was caught eating in the kitchen in violation of the rules became abusive and banged pots and pans. All of this ultimately earned him 11 warning notices and two disciplinary suspensions. Finally came the "last straw." He was ordered to appear at a disciplinary hearing for using the telephone for personal business, and he failed to show up. At this point the employer threw up its hands and fired him.

Despite the attention he had received through counseling, warning, and suspension, this employee by his own actions proved himself to be incorrigible. "This record leads the Arbitrator to conclude that progressive, corrective disciplinary procedures utilized by the Employer proved to be futile only because [the grievant] refused to accept the concept that an employer possesses the right to issue legitimate orders and to expect employee compliance."[125]

---

[124]Having thus loaded the gun, the employer must be careful not to pull the trigger prematurely. In *Master Builders, Inc.*, 92 LA 1021 (Curry, 1989), an employer which had adopted an absenteeism-control plan that provided for discharge only after 13 absences in a 12-month period fired an employee for failing to improve his attendance record after several warnings, charging him with chronic absenteeism. The employee, however, had been absent only eight times, leading the arbitrator to reduce the penalty to a three-day suspension—the penalty specified by the plan itself after eight absences. The arbitrator agreed with the employer's contention that the plan was not its sole weapon against absenteeism, but he found that this employee's pattern of absence did not amount to chronic absenteeism. Rather, he said, the absences were of the type which the attendance program was intended to address.

[125]*St. Mary's Hosp.*, 68 LA 1199, 1202 (Falcone, 1977). See also *Thiokol Chem. Corp.*, 52 LA 1254 (Williams) (pattern of filing groundless charges of wrongful acts, including racial discrimination, conspiracy, defamation of character, and unsafe practices, held ground for discharge).

EXAMPLE NO. 2: Three times an employee failed to wear his hard hat in violation of a rule calling for discharge for the fourth violation. Three times he was disciplined—two warnings and a suspension. When asked if he was going to wear his hard hat in the future, he said he was not—that the rule was stupid and the hat gave him a headache. As a result he was discharged.

This case puts in focus the niggling problem of projecting what a particular employee is likely to do in the future. Will he continue his old ways, or will he finally shape up? The arbitrator, like it or not, is in the business of being a predictor. In this case the arbitrator chose to conclude that the book was not yet closed on this grievant.

> Nothing in the contract permits Company to substitute an employee's attitude, charges of insubordination not having been made, for a step of the discipline procedure. . . . [F]or one to say he'll not obey a rule does not mean that thereafter he'll actually disobey it. "Second thoughts" by the employee . . . cannot be discounted as factors encouraging compliance with the rule.[126]

Compare this case to one in which an employee issued a threat to "throw a fit" and to kill the superintendent. Discharge was held to be justified.[127] The difference is that here the threat was *to do* something bad (*malum in se*), whereas the threat not to wear a safety hat was a threat *not to do* something that was required (only *malum prohibitum*). The threat to kill the superintendent became an act in itself by virtue of its effect upon the person to whom it was directed: it put that person in apprehension. The vow not to wear a hard hat, in contrast, did not put anyone in apprehension—it was simply a "non-act." Thus, where an act has already taken place, a penalty may or may not be applied, but the question of prediction does not arise. It is only non-acts that raise the question of prediction.

Last-Chance Agreements

A special kind of last-straw situation occurs when the employee has been put on notice that one more violation of com-

---

[126]*B. Green & Co.*, 81-1 ARB ¶8259, 4158 (Whyte, 1981). In *Allied Employers, Inc.*, 71-1 ARB ¶8078 (Kleinsorge, 1970), the arbitrator took the contrary position and sustained the discharge of an employee who had refused to comply with the employer's hair-length rule, holding that the rule was reasonable and that it made no sense to put the grievant back to work because he had already stated he would not comply with the rule.

[127]*Georgia Power Co.*, 76 LA 761 (Foster, 1981).

pany rules—perhaps of the same rule he or she previously violated, perhaps of *any* company rule—will be curtains.[128] In other words, the employee has been told in advance that further misconduct will be regarded as the "last straw" and has acknowledged that this will be the case. Such a "last chance" agreement often is the result of a settlement negotiated by the union on behalf of a grievant whose misconduct clearly warranted discharge.

Arbitrators have held that last-chance agreements, as a general rule, are not subject to the usual requirements of just cause. To put it another way, violation of the last-chance agreement provides the "just cause" required for discharge. Arbitrator Jonathan Dworkin has explained: "[J]ust cause is not essential to the formation of a [an agreement]. A company and union could negotiate to eliminate the benefit. . . . A union also can enter into a last-chance bargain relieving an employer of some or all of its just-cause obligations to an employee." He continued:

> When encountering a last-chance settlement, an arbitrator can presume its validity even though it places the subject employee at a distinct disadvantage. It should be inferred that the settlement was negotiated in good faith to grant the employee something s/he could not otherwise achieve—continued employment. The arbitrator should recognize that there was a trade-off for the advantage—relinquishment of certain employment rights. . . . An employer would have no reason to enter into them if they were illusory or unenforceable.[129]

All this said, an employer does not have complete freedom in dealing with the employee working under a last-chance agree-

---

[128]For a discussion of the last-chance agreement as a form of notice, see Ch. 2, p. 64.

[129]*Butler Mfg. Co.*, 93 LA 441, 445 (1989) (insubordination). To similar effect, see *Joy Mfg. Co.*, 86 LA 517, 519–20 (Duff, 1986) (absenteeism): "The Company does not have to grant any Last Chance Agreement, and having granted it, it has no other obligation but to refrain from being arbitrary or capricious in revoking it." See also *Allied Maintenance Corp.*, 87 LA 121, 86-1 ARB ¶8240 (Duda, 1986) (improper checking of baggage); *U. S. Steel Corp.*, 87 LA 973 (Neyland, 1986) (alcohol-related absenteeism); *National Steel Corp.*, 88 LA 457 (Wolff, 1986) (failure by alcoholic to abide by rehabilitation program). But see *Northrop Corp., Aircraft Div.*, 96 LA 149 (Weiss, 1990), where the arbitrator held that an employee was improperly terminated for talking and leaving his post without permission, even though he had signed a last-chance agreement calling for his immediate discharge for any further offense. The current offenses were minor, the arbitrator pointed out, they were unrelated to the misconduct (absenteeism) that occasioned the last-chance agreement, and the employee had worked for the company for 10 years. See also *Monterey Coal Co.*, 96 LA 457 (Feldman, 1990) (last-chance agreement invalid insofar as it provides that any violation of terms will result in discharge without resort to "grievance, claims, arbitration, or lawsuit").

ment. It remains true that there must be *some* violation of company rules, however trivial, to justify discharge. And what looks like a violation to the employer may not be so viewed by the arbitrator. Take the shop steward who, after receiving a "final warning" that any further violation of written or unwritten shop rules would result in suspension or discharge, filed a spurious claim for overtime pay. The employer, viewing the filing as a dishonest act, discharged him. The arbitrator, on the other hand, pointed out that the mere filing of the claim, even if it was faulty and outrageous, was innocuous, especially since the supervisors who would have had to approve the claim were present at the meeting for which he was claiming overtime compensation. In the absence of clear evidence that the parties intended an unacceptable overtime claim to be regarded as an offense triggering discharge under the last-chance agreement, the arbitrator concluded that the discharge could not be allowed to stand.[130]

A further qualification is that extreme extenuating circumstances may be recognized by the arbitrator even if the violation of the last-chance agreement was clear-cut. An example is the case of an employee who was discharged for being absent without notice while working under a last-chance agreement. It turned out that the employee was faced with a serious family emergency—his pregnant wife had become violent and the employee feared for the safety of their two small children. To top it all, his wife had ripped the telephone out of the wall. Returning the employee to work, the arbitrator nevertheless refused to award him back pay on the theory that the employer was not financially responsible for the employee's problems.[131]

Absenteeism and Progressive Discipline

Absenteeism is probably the occasion for progressive discipline more often than any other type of misconduct, but what kind of

---

[130]*San Francisco Newspaper Agency*, 93 LA 322 (Koven, 1989). In *Ohio Dep't of Highway Safety*, 96 LA 71 (1990), Arbitrator Dworkin held that a last-chance agreement which held the grievant's discharge "in abeyance" on condition that she complete a rehabilitation program and refrain from further drug or alcohol abuse was unreasonable on its face and contrary to the just cause standard because it failed to specify an expiration date. But see *University of Mich.*, 96 LA 688, 690 (Sugarman, 1991), where the arbitrator ruled that a last-chance agreement "without a term continues in effect until the parties themselves modify, amend, or change it."

[131]*Chicago Transit Auth.*, 89-1 ARB ¶8129 (Goldstein, 1988).

absentee record it takes to justify the firing of an employee is not of concern here. All that need be said in this connection is that "[a]dmittedly, there is no precise standard for determining what is excessive absenteeism."[132] The focus in this section is the overall relationship of progressive discipline to absenteeism.[133]

> *Arbitrator Eaton:* [T]he general rule is that where a discharge is to be sustained for absenteeism there must be aggravated circumstances, formal notification to the employee of the consequences of further absences, and effort, either of consultation or progressive discipline, or both, to remedy the situation short of discharge. The last of these elements is of particular importance. It must be required that the employer make good faith efforts, over a reasonable period of time, to eliminate the cause of absenteeism before resorting to the "capital punishment" of discharge. This is particularly true in the case of an employee with long and satisfactory service to the company.[134]

What has been previously set forth with respect to progressive discipline as it applies across the board is incorporated here, so to speak, by reference. Absenteeism has already been discussed in reference to reasonable rules (pp. 139–42) and notice (pp. 63, 70).[135] In addition, the following points should be emphasized:

- An employer has the right to expect an employee to be available on a reasonably consistent basis and to take corrective measures if he or she is not.[136]
- "Once guidelines are established and publicized, only in 'extraordinary circumstances' may an employer disregard

---

[132]*Worthington Corp.*, 47 LA 1170 (Livengood, 1966).

[133]*Electric Hose and Rubber Co.*, 47 LA 1104 (Kerrison, 1967).

[134]*Peerless Laundry Co.*, 51 LA 331, 335 (1968).

[135]Absenteeism due to illness is covered in ELKOURI & ELKOURI, *supra* note 121, at 578–80. Absenteeism in general is discussed in J. R. REDEKER, DISCIPLINE POLICIES AND PROCEDURES 55–69 (1983); and by L. STESSIN, EMPLOYEE DISCIPLINE 67–86 (1960). An exhaustive compendium of citations on absenteeism is set forth in *Husky Oil Co.*, 65 LA 47 (Richardson, 1975). Another key case is *Sperry Rand Corp.*, 70-1 ARB ¶8149 (Kesselman, 1969). See also *American Airlines, Inc.*, 47 LA 266 (Dworkin, 1966); *Electric Hose and Rubber Co.*, *supra* note 133; *Park Prods. Co.*, 68-1 ARB ¶8330 (Kates, 1968); *U. S. Pipe and Foundry Co.*, 68-2 ARB ¶8665 (Seinsheimer, 1968); *Rockwell Int'l, Flow Control Div.*, 1975 ARB ¶8036 (Knee, 1975); *Central Tel. Co. of Va.*, 68 LA 957 (Whyte, 1977); *St. Francois County*, 77-2 ARB (Elbert, 1977); *Werner-Continental, Inc.*, 72 LA 1 (LeWinter, 1978); *General Mills, Inc.*, 78-1 ARB ¶8188 (Madden, 1978); *Union Carbide Corp.*, 74 LA 681 (Bowers, 1980).

[136]*Gerstenlager Co.*, 66-1 ARB ¶8331 (Teple, 1966); *U.S. Pipe and Foundry Co.*, *supra* note 135; *Carter-Wallace, Inc.*, 69-1 ARB ¶8372 (Kerrison, 1968); *General Mills, Inc.*, *supra* note 135.

his own guidelines. Otherwise, the guidelines would be meaningless."[137]
- A progressive discipline program will not necessarily be invalidated because it does not provide for suspension but jumps, after a suitable number of warnings, all the way to discharge.[138] Those who take this view argue that absenteeism due to illness cannot be corrected by traditional forms of progressive discipline.[139] Indeed, according to some arbitrators, absenteeism due to sickness is not subject to progressive discipline at all, since it is illogical to punish someone for being ill.[140] Only intermittent absenteeism, not chronic absenteeism, is governed by progressive discipline if so provided for in the contract.[141]
- The employer does not necessarily have free rein to do as it pleases with its progressive discipline system. For example, an employee cannot post an individual employee's work and attendance records for all in the plant to see since by doing so it may "subject the employee to irreparable, speculative, and conjectural harm by his fellow employees or any other observer."[142]

Demotion as a Penalty

Arbitrators disagree as to whether demotion is a legitimate form of penalty.[143] Decisions in particular cases have turned on

---

[137]*Metal Container Corp.*, 81-2 ARB ¶8610, 5652 (Ross, 1981). Illustrating this point is *Master Builders, Inc.*, 92 LA 1021,89-2 ARB ¶8583 (Curry, 1989), where the grievant was discharged after accumulating eight absences during a 12-month period although the absenteeism-control plan provided for discharge only after 13 absences. The employer argued that the grievant was guilty of chronic absenteeism and that it could resort to discharge under its inherent management rights. The arbitrator agreed that unusual circumstances might arise in which the plan would not apply. But in the grievant's case, the absences were of the type intended to be curbed by the plan, and a three-day suspension was the prescribed penalty after eight absences.

[138]*Hoover Ball and Bearing Co.*, 66 LA 764 (Herman, 1976).

[139]*Worthington Corp., supra* note 132.

[140]*Atlantic Richfield Co.*, 69 LA 484 (Sisk, 1977), with additional citations. In *Airco, Inc.*, 84-1 ARB ¶8121, 3557 (Dworkin, 1984), the arbitrator upheld the discharge of an alcoholic who had repeatedly been absent, but he directed that the reason for termination be changed to "failure to carry out his responsibilities" rather than chronic absenteeism. Said the arbitrator: "[I]t was unfair to *discipline* the Employee for absenteeism which was not voluntary, but which was caused by an illness. The taint of discipline on Grievant's record was unwarranted."

[141]*Logan Metal Stampings, Inc.*, 53 LA 185 (Kates, 1969).

[142]*Electra-Gas Appliance Corp.*, 64 LA 1185 (Rinaldo, 1975).

[143]Many cases on both sides of this issue are cited in F. Elkouri & E. A. Elkouri, How Arbitration Works 565–69 (4th ed. 1985). Hill and Sinicropi, in Remedies in

such issues as whether the demotion was temporary or permanent (permanent demotion sometimes having been regarded as unreasonable because it is comparable to an "indeterminate sentence"); whether the contract expressly or impliedly permitted demotion as a penalty;[144] whether the grievant was demoted for inability to perform his or her job duties satisfactorily or for some reason unrelated to job performance;[145] and whether progressive discipline had been applied prior to the demotion. The majority view is that demotion should not be used as a *disciplinary* penalty, but should be reserved for cases in which the employee has demonstrated an inability to perform his or her job.[146]

> *Arbitrator Platt:* But I do not believe that permanent demotion is a proper form of discipline where an employee's capabilities are conceded and his performance is generally satisfactory but where his attitudes of the moment are improper. For improper work attitudes—as experienced by occasional carelessness and failure to obey instructions—can usually be corrected by suspending or laying off the employee for a reasonable but definite period.[147]

ARBITRATION (2d ed. 1991), quote Arbitrator Volz to the effect that, where permitted by the contract, demotion is a more appropriate remedy than discharge for substandard work performance that is due to lack of mental or physical ability rather than to carelessness, indifference, etc., and cite *Sunshine Biscuits, Inc.*, 60 LA 197 (Roberts, 1973), as a case in accord with that position. In *Southwest Petro-Chem, Inc.*, 92 LA 492, 89-2 ARB ¶8323 (Berger, 1988), the arbitrator held that, although demotion may not be used as a form of discipline, an employer could properly allow an employee to return to a lower-rated job where the latter was guilty of a major violation of company rules and could have been terminated.

[144]Arbitrator Thornell, in *City of Omaha*, 86 LA 142, 143 (1985):
As a general rule demotion is not a proper form of discipline, absent a specific contractual provision permitting such. This is because demotion must be related to an employee's ability to perform the work on a continuing basis in terms of his competence and qualifications. Discipline is properly related to infractions of rules or misconduct.

[145]An example of a case where demotion was held to be improper is *U.S. Army Tank-Automotive Command*, 93 LA 767 (Smith, 1989), where an employee demotion solely because he refused to admit fault in entering a non-work-related program into a government computer was held to be improper. Said the arbitrator: "Thus management has put the cart before the horse in requiring the grievant to accept fault and loss of his grievance, usurping the authority delegated to the Arbitrator, as a preliminary to its assessment of penalty."

[146]*Weyerhaeuser Co.*, 51 LA 192, 195 (Whyte,1968): "[A]rbitration authority is generally uniform to the effect that non-disciplinary demotions—that is, because of inability, lack of efficiency or lack of competence—is a management right limited only by the requirement that such action not be arbitrary, capricious or discriminatory." See also *Gilbarco, Inc.*, 87-2 ARB ¶8338 (Flannagan, 1986) (inability to perform).

[147]*Republic Steel Co.*, 25 LA 733, 735 (1955) (careless workmanship). Platt went on to point out that demotion under such circumstances is inconsistent with the concept of progressive discipline, which has as its fundamental purpose the correction of faults

A problem sometimes faced by an employer is that of the employee who returns to work following rehabilitation from alcohol or drug dependency. In many cases the contract, or the terms of the rehabilitation agreement, will specify that the employee is to be returned to his or her former job or to an equivalent job. But what if this is not the case? In such a situation, the arbitrator ruled that it was proper to reinstate the employee to a lower-paying, temporary nonunit job since the employee's seniority was unimpaired and he could bid on unit jobs as they became available.[148]

On occasion, the arbitrator's use of the remedy power may result in the grievant's demotion. This occurs when a discharge is found to have been improper but the employer nevertheless proved to the arbitrator's satisfaction that the grievant was unable to do his or her job acceptably. In one such case the arbitrator directed the employer to reinstate a discharged employee to his former job because of his unblemished 14-year work record prior to his promotion, even though the employer had warned him that he risked discharge if he bid on the higher job.[149]

Seven Pitfalls in Progressive Discipline

1. The Off-the-Record Past Record

Discharge is difficult to support when past incidents of misconduct have not been brought to the employee's attention or made a matter of record. In part, this is a notice problem, as Arbitrator Dworkin clearly noted in the case of a journalist who had been discharged for, among other things, tardiness, excessive use of the telephone, uncooperative attitude, poorly written copy, and grammatical errors:

> Although the evidence does indicate that oral criticisms were voiced on some occasions, these were not made a matter of record, and the grievant was not aware that she was being subjected to

---

and behavior and not the imposition of "an indeterminate sentence" of punishment. See also *Metromedia, Inc.*, 46 LA 161 (Dworkin, 1965) (insubordination; refusal to sign memo concerning new company rule). Cases holding that if demotion is to be used as a disciplinary penalty, the principles of progressive discipline must be applied include *Safeway Stores, Inc.*, 78-2 ARB ¶8557 (Tyler, 1978); *Firestone Tire & Rubber Co.*, 74 LA 565 (Whyte, 1980) (poor work, making false accusations against supervisor).

[148]*E G & G Fla., Inc.*, 93 LA 1141 (Abrams, 1989).

[149]*Rohm and Haas Tex., Inc.*, 92 LA 850 (Allen, 1989).

disciplinary action. . . . An employee should be permitted an opportunity to respond to corrective measures and guidance before a decision is justified that the employment relationship should be terminated.[150]

The employer that fails to put an employee's misconduct formally on record, with appropriate warnings and/or suspensions, also makes itself vulnerable to a later protest by the union that the employee's record was not really so bad. When, for example, a supervisor testified that an employee had been reprimanded for violating a rule against making personal telephone calls but could not cite one concrete violation or reprimand, the arbitrator drew the inevitable inference that any telephone violations the employee might have committed were insignificant and could not be held against her at a later time.[151]

2. Stale Past Record

Discharge may also be set aside, even if progressive discipline has previously been applied, if the grievant's last reprimand or suspension was too far in the past.

> *Arbitrator Ipavec:* There is a further consideration that the foregoing progression of discipline be within certain reasonable time limitations in that it has also been widely accepted that a rehabilitated employee . . . may have any prior discipline for poor performance, ignored; and the employee's slate to be, so to speak, clean.[152]

What is "too far in the past"? Sometimes the contract or a company rule answers that question by providing, for example, that any disciplinary action older than one year will be erased

---

[150]*Times Publishing Co.*, 40 LA 1054, 1059 (1963). See also *Wade Mfg. Co.*, 21 LA 676 (Maggs, 1953) (grievant not advised oral warnings could be held against him in future); *Standard Shade Roller Div.*, 73 LA 86 (Dawson, undated) (statement to grievant that he could be fired for refusing to work overtime given too casually to qualify as a formal warning); *U. S. Steel Corp.*, 68-2 ARB ¶8772 Dybeck, 1968). Additional cases in this line are cited in F. ELKOURI & E. A. ELKOURI, *supra* note 143, at 680.

[151]*San Mateo Restaurant-Hotel Owners Ass'n*, 59 LA 997 (Kenaston, 1972). See also *Patton Sparkle Market*, 75 LA 1092, 1095 (Cohen, 1980) (lack of documented warnings taken to show prior misconduct "did not reach a level of seriousness to warrant the issuance of a written warning"); *Abilene Flour Mills Co.*, 61-1 ARB ¶8049 (Granoff, 1960) (damage to company property); *Licek Potato Chip Co.*, 82-1 ARB ¶8074 (Belcher, 1981) (incompetence, inefficiency); *Martin-Brower Co.*, 89-1 ARB ¶8221 (Miller, 1988) (assault on fellow employee).

[152]*Belmont Hotel*, 74-1 ARB ¶8316, 4189 (1974) (incompetence, inefficiency).

from an employee's record and not be made the basis of a later, more severe penalty.[153] Otherwise, it depends.

> **EXAMPLE:** An employee of some 13 years' seniority maintained an unblemished record for the first 11 years or so. Then, however, she received a written warning for being intoxicated on the job. About 15 months later, when she again showed up for work intoxicated, the employer discharged her, claiming that she had been observed under the influence on at least one other occasion and that she had been prohibited from leaving the premises during her lunch hour for fear that she would return intoxicated.

Was this a past record justifying discharge? It might have been, were it not for two considerations. First, the employee's written warning had been given more than a year prior to her discharge. Second, none of the other drinking violations the employer cited had ever found their way into her personnel file. "Her past record indicates that this is not the first occurrence. At the same time her official work record . . . would indicate that the problem has not been extreme. She has received only one written warning concerning her drinking . . . ." For an employee with long and, until recently, creditable service, that one relatively old warning was not enough to justify discharge; a suspension would have been a more reasonable penalty.[154]

3. No Opportunity for Improvement

> *Arbitrator Dawson:* The concept of a warning implies an opportunity for correction. This in turn implies opportunity for sober reflection and in many cases resolves itself into a question of how much time has elapsed between the warning and the final

---

[153]*E.g.*, *Champion Spark Plug Co.*, 67 LA 254 (Kates, 1976) (firearms violation, tardiness, etc.); *Champion Spark Plug Co.*, 93 LA 1277 (Dobry, 1989) (insubordination).

[154]*Eden Hosp.*, 56 LA 319, 320 (Eaton, 1971). In *Huntington Chair Corp.*, 24 LA 490, 492 (McCoy, 1955), the arbitrator found that management acted unreasonably when it discharged the grievant for leaving work three minutes early, when his work had been completed, adding: "This is particularly true where the last offense prior to this incident had occurred 11 months before. This is not the exercise of corrective discipline." See also *Ideal Cement Co.*, 13 LA 943 (Donaldson, 1950) (loafing); *General Controls Co.*, 34 LA 432 (Roberts, 1960) (poor work record); *Interstate Brands-Four S*, 76 LA 415 (Adler, 1981) (leaving work before completing overtime assignment); and additional cases cited in F. ELKOURI & E. A. ELKOURI, *supra* note 143, at 680. For a contrasting ruling, see *Wells Badger Indus., Inc.*, 67 LA 56 (Jones, 1976) (fact that suspension was year old did not preclude employee's discharge for continued excessive absence, where contract made no provision for removal of suspensions from record).

discharge. . . . It is not permissible to warn and discharge an employee in the same act if not the same breath.[155]

EXAMPLE: An employee was discharged for failing to follow his foreman's direction to clean the filters in the air conditioning system. The union pointed out that the discharge violated the contract, which required at least two warning notices prior to discharge. Conceding the point, management reinstated the employee and substituted two warning letters for the discharge, the first referring to several earlier failures to follow orders and the second, dated the next day, reprimanding the employee for the filter-cleaning episode. A few days after returning to work, the employee was again discharged for failing to carry out his work assignments properly.

The timing of the two warnings gave the arbitrator a problem. "It is axiomatic that the purpose of such warnings is to enable the employee to improve his performance so that he may not incur suspension and/or discharge." The two letters technically may have satisfied the two-warnings requirement; but because the second letter followed the first in quick succession, the employee did not have a second opportunity to improve as the parties intended. So that letter was invalid as a step in progressive discipline, and the employee's discharge was set aside.[156]

A similar situation arose where, for two days running, an employee refused to comply with a new procedure requiring employees to submit to lunch box inspections. The employer determined that he should be given a written warning for the first refusal and a suspension for the second; the employee was told simultaneously of both disciplinary actions and filed a grievance protesting the suspension. Here, too, the employee prevailed on the theory that the employer had not given him an adequate opportunity to comply with the lunch box rule.[157]

---

[155]*Standard Shade Roller Div.*, supra note 150, at 90 (refusal to work overtime).

[156]*Western Lithograph Co.*, 71-1 ¶8276, 3965 (Shearer, 1970).

[157]*Nipak, Inc.*, 76-2 ARB ¶8434 (Ruiz, 1976). See also *A & M Metal Casket Co.*, 70-2 ARB ¶8871 (Altrock, 1970) (improper attitude, loafing); *Safeway Stores, Inc.*, 64 LA 563 (Gould, 1974) (rudeness to customers); *Grain Processing Corp.*, 75 LA 1254 (Stix, 1980) (refusal to pick up gum from floor). The grievant was likewise warned one day and improperly discharged the next in *Standard Shade Roller Div.*, supra note 150. But in *Women's Gen'l Hosp.*, 74 LA 281, 290 (Klein, 1980), the grievant's discharge was sustained, despite the fact that she had been notified only a few days before that she was being suspended for three days for failing to work as scheduled, because in that short interval she "seriously compounded her record of misconduct by acts of insolence, belligerence, gross insubordination and by failing to perform critical work assignments on two consecutive days."

4. Suggestion of "Building a Record"

The issuance of too many warnings in too short a time has been interpreted as evidence that the employer was out to build a case against the grievant. Where, for example, the employer discharged a driver-salesman after it had given him three warnings in three days for minor infractions, the arbitrator drew the conclusion that "the reasons for discharge were pretextual, designed as a subterfuge for some other undisclosed reason."[158] In another case, the evidence convinced the arbitrator that "on those occasions where [the grievant] could not complete all of his work there were specific circumstances not within his control which prevented him from doing so and . . . the Company representatives made careful note of these instances in order to buttress a discharge for an entirely different and unwarranted reason."[159]

Record-building of a different sort was condemned by the arbitrator in another case. Upon discovering that an employee had falsified his employment application by denying that he had ever been convicted of a felony, the employer did nothing right away. Instead, it waited some nine months before discharging him. Though the falsification was material and the conviction would have influenced the hiring decision, the arbitrator nevertheless reinstated the employee, though without back pay. He inferred that the employer waited to see how the employee would work out and only then made the decision to discharge him. This, he concluded, was improper.[160]

5. Discipline Not Imposed Promptly

The corrective purpose of progressive discipline is likely to be frustrated if the employer delays for an unreasonable length of time before imposing a penalty.

Arbitrator Lipson: [C]ommon sense requires a reasonably speedy connection between an offense and the discipline imposed there-

---

[158]*Licek Potato Chip Co.*, *supra* note 151, at 3356.
[159]*Food Giant Markets, Inc.*, 70-2 ARB ¶8477, 4574 (Helbling, 1970) (improper job attitude).
[160]*V. A. Medical Center*, 91 LA 588 (Howell, 1988). Other cases holding that the employer must act reasonably promptly after discovering false statements on an employment application include *Tiffany Metal Prods.*, 56 LA 135 (Roberts, 1971); *Price Bros. Co.*, 62 LA 389 (High, 1974); *Huntington Alloys, Inc.*, 74 LA 176 (Katz, 1980); *Wine Cellar*, 81 LA 158 (Ray, 1983).

after. Otherwise, the memory of the offender and those around him will become dim with regard to the event, and the punishment will inevitably become less logical with the passage of time.[161]

Furthermore, additional misconduct committed by an employee while the employer is waiting to impose discipline may be "thrown out of court," so to speak, if the penalty is later protested in arbitration. The employer's case went up in smoke, for example, when it waited to suspend the grievant for smoking marijuana on his lunch break until several months after an undercover agent first discovered what he was up to. "When an employee embarks on a course of conduct that is potentially harmful to his employer, he is entitled to be advised at an early opportunity that his actions are improper and must stop." The employer was not entitled to discipline the grievant for "repeated instances" of smoking marijuana when the employer had known of his activities but elected to give him enough rope to hang himself.[162]

---

[161]*Inland Tool & Mfg. Co.*, 65 LA 1203, 1207 (1975) (sale of marijuana). *Federal Aviation Admin.*, 87 LA 697, 700 (D'Spain, 1986): "Discipline cannot be postponed for the benefit of the employer . . . . To delay such action for seven (7) months is contrary to recognized labor standards. Discipline should be corrective in nature rather than punitive." In *Astro-Valcour*, 93 LA 91 (Rocha, Jr., 1989), the arbitrator cited a two-day delay in imposing discharge as evidence that the employer did not view the grievant's insubordination as "gross" insubordination. And in *Bureau of Alcohol, Tobacco & Firearms*, 93 LA 393, 89-2 ARB ¶8511 (Kravit, 1989), the arbitrator ruled that the employer should have promptly applied progressive discipline to an employee who submitted an inaccurate report and false travel voucher, not wait 21 months and then discharge him. The delay was unfair to the employee, said the arbitrator, and showed that the efficiency of the agency was not adversely affected by keeping the employee on the job. See also *Weatherhead Co.*, 56 LA 159 (Maxwell, 1971) (absenteeism); *Frontier Airlines, Inc.*, 61 LA 304 (Kahn, 1973) (excessive coffee breaks). In *Pratt & Whitney Aircraft Group*, 91 LA 1014 (Chandler, 1988) (poor performance), on the other hand, the arbitrator found the employer's delay in discharging the grievant not fatal, where it was occasioned by the employer's considerable efforts to rehabilitate the grievant. In *Zenith Elecs. Corp.*, 88-1 ARB ¶8229 (Patterson, 1987), the arbitrator ruled that a seven-month delay in discharging an employee for possession and sale of drugs on company premises did not invalidate the discharge, where the delay was caused by the employer's cooperation with a police investigation and the union was not prejudiced in its ability to defend the employee. *Union Tribune Pub. Co.*, 89-2 ARB ¶8542 (McBrearty, 1989), is to the same effect, except that the employer in that case was seeking to protect the confidentiality of its own investigation. See also *City of St. Paul*, 92 LA 641 (Scoville, 1989) (two-year delay in imposing penalty for accepting gifts from contractor not improper, where delay caused by city's desire to maintain secrecy of investigation of alleged corrupt practices in planning agency).

[162]*Air Force Logistics Command, McClellan Air Force Base*, unpublished opinion (Koven, 1984). To similar effect, see *Lawrence Gen'l Hosp.*, 55 LA 987, 990 (Zack, 1970), where the arbitrator noted that the absence of a warning or other discipline prior to the grievant's discharge "contributed to the build up of the record against her without giving her an opportunity to correct her conduct prior to the imposition of the demotion

6. Increase in Penalty

If management wishes to reserve judgment on the penalty to be imposed on an employee, it should be careful to make clear that whatever action it takes initially is not necessarily final. To impose a relatively light penalty and later to increase it in the absence of additional facts has been held to be a form of double jeopardy.[163]

> **EXAMPLE:** An auto mechanic who got into a fight with a co-worker was given a two-day suspension by his supervisor. The other combatant, given five days off, asked in the mechanic's presence, "Well, is that going to be it? Am I going to get fired?" The supervisor replied, "No, that's it." The next day higher management, having given the matter further thought, decided both employees had to go.

The arbitrator held that the mechanic's discharge was not for just cause for two reasons. Given the circumstances of the fight, he said, the mechanic did not deserve discharge. But beyond that, the fact that he was initially given an unconditional two-day suspension precluded the employer from discharging him later for the same misconduct. The company's rules, the arbitrator noted, permitted but did not require discharge for fighting.[164]

7. "Out of Bounds" Penalty

In addition to being commensurate with the offense, penalties imposed for misconduct should be designed to encourage the employee to mend his or her ways. Penalties that might have other effects—for example, to humiliate the offending employee—have been held by arbitrators to be outside the compass of progressive discipline.

> **EXAMPLE:** When a shop steward showed up for work wearing tennis shoes, which the rules stated could not be worn anywhere

---

penalty." See also *Allstates Air Cargo, Inc.*, 61 LA 640 (Sands, 1973) (excessive coffee breaks).

[163]*Misco Precision Castings*, 40 LA 87 (Dworkin, 1962) (card playing on break time). See also *Durham Hosiery Mills*, 24 LA 356 (Livengood, 1955) (fighting); *Georgia Power Co.*, 76 LA 761 (Foster, 1981) (threat, disruptive behavior); *City of Orlando*, 88 LA 572 (Frost, 1986) (substandard performance); *Marin Honda*, 91 LA 185 (Kanowitz, 1988) (fighting); *Transit Management of Southeast La.*, 95 LA 74 (Allen, 1990) (dishonesty).

[164]*Marin Honda, supra* note 163. See also *Ralston Purina Co.*, 88-1 ARB ¶8039 (Roumell, 1987) (grievant's act, initially treated as unauthorized absence, could not later be treated as insubordination).

within the plant, the guard refused to let him through the gate. The steward protested that he had safety shoes in his locker and had every intention of putting them on before he actually got to his work area. The guard called his chief, who agreed to admit the employee to the plant to get his shoes, but only if he was escorted to his locker by his foreman. The steward complied, but thereafter filed a grievance protesting that the tennis shoes rule was unreasonably applied in his case and that the "penalty" was improper.

The arbitrator found the tennis-shoes rule clear on its face, and the steward would have violated it had he worn tennis shoes anywhere on plant premises. But the penalty was another matter. The employer could have penalized the steward for showing up for work in the wrong shoes; but it was "at variance with the prevailing norms of imposing discipline" to subject him to the embarrassment of having other employees see him enter the plant with a supervisorial escort as a form of punishment.[165]

The case mentioned previously in which an employer tried to control excessive absenteeism by posting the attendance records of employees who missed more than their share of work offers another example of a penalty that falls outside the range available to the employer.[166] The theme of this case, as well as of the tennis shoes case, is that the corrective effect of the penalty chosen by the employer was overshadowed by its punitive character, and for that reason the purposes of progressive discipline would not be served.[167]

III. The Remedy

The Arbitrator's Options

"Penalty" and "remedy" might be regarded as first cousins. "Penalty" is what is applied as a punishment in the first instance

---

[165]*Allegheny Ludlum Steel Corp.*, 66 LA 1306, 1309 (Yagoda, 1976).

[166]*Electra-Gas Appliance Corp.*, 64 LA 1185 (Rinaldo, 1975).

[167]In *Hercules, Inc.*, 78-2 ARB ¶8535, 5489 (Owen, 1978), where the company required the grievant to perform cleanup work without pay as a penalty for being remiss in not making sure the cleanup was performed after his shift, the arbitrator found that "withholding the employee's wages for work performed as a means of discipline was contrary to accepted industry practice and was possibly a violation of the federal wage laws." See also *Dillingham Mfg. Co.*, 91 LA 816 (Nicholas, 1988) (improper to withhold holiday pay because of failure to work pre-holiday overtime, where employee met contractual holiday-pay-eligibility requirements).

by the employer; "remedy" is the subsequent relief provided by the arbitrator when he sustains, overrules, or modifies the penalty. But there is a basic difference in the decision-making process: The arbitrator and the employer have different sets of chips in the pot.

> *Arbitrator LeWinter:* The arbitrator does not live with the parties, he has not actually experienced the problems management may have which might require strong disciplinary measures. He also makes his decision and promptly becomes *functus officio* and leaves the parties behind to adapt to the ramifications of his award.[168]

Standard Remedies

Assuming the arbitrator orders that a discharged employee be reinstated, one of three remedies generally will go along with the reinstatement order.

Full Back Pay. The relief which the union almost always seeks (even when it does not expect to get it) is that the grievant be "made whole" for all wages and other benefits lost as a result of unjust discharge. But reinstatement with full back pay is normally awarded only when it is clearly established that the grievant engaged in no misconduct—which occurs only in a minority of cases.[169]

No Back Pay. Typically no back pay is awarded where the grievant's misconduct was serious but strong mitigating circumstances, discriminatory application of penalty, or procedural violations by the company bar discharge; or where the grievant

---

[168]*Werner-Continental, Inc.*, 72 LA 1, 10 (1978) (absenteeism). For a discussion of the scope of the arbitrator's remedy power, see D. E. Feller, *The Remedy Power in Grievance Arbitration*, 5 Indus. Rel. L.J. 128–55 (1982–83). Feller's position is that the arbitrator's function is the narrow one of providing the remedy intended by the parties, as expressly or impliedly set forth in the contract, and he criticizes the more expansive view taken by some arbitrators that their task is to "do justice." "[T]he institution of grievance arbitration as we know it today has been built upon the assumption that arbitrators are not courts and do not have power of discretion to see that justice and equity are done. They are, and should be, restricted to performing the limited role defined by the parties."

[169]Three studies concerning the disposition of published discharge cases indicate that reinstatement with full back pay is awarded in 32% of discharges analyzed (A. A. Malinowski, *An Empirical Analysis of Discharge Cases*, 36 Arb. J. 34 (Table I) (1981); 23% (K. Jennings & R. Wolters, *Discharge Cases Reconsidered*, 31 Arb. J. 169, 174 (1976); and 29.1% (D. L. Jones, *Ramifications of Back-Pay Awards in Discharge Cases*, Arbitration and Social Change 167 (Proceedings of the 22nd Annual Meeting, National Academy of Arbitrators (1970).

has contributed to his or her own difficulties by, for example, engaging in self-help or refusing to cooperate with a reasonable investigation by management. (The employer often will argue that, should the arbitrator decide to reinstate the grievant, back pay in any amount is out of the question.)

Some Back Pay. A partial back-pay award may result where the grievant engaged in misconduct that was deserving of a disciplinary suspension but not discharge, or where other mitigating circumstances are present. (It is rare that either party argues for "some back pay"; this remedy almost always turns out to be a creature of the arbitrator's making.[170])

Where the penalty in dispute is something less than discharge, the arbitrator ordinarily has the following options: disciplinary suspension—rescind, reduce, convert to a warning; warning—remove from the grievant's record or convert written warning to oral warning.

Unconventional Remedies

To provide three standard forms for remedies is like dividing suits of clothes into only three sizes—small, medium, and large. They fit most situations, but because the varieties of industrial experience and misconduct are infinite, the standard remedies often are not responsive to the problems at hand. As a consequence, the arbitrator may have to look beyond the three standard options for a remedy that will address itself directly to the reasons why the grievant got into difficulty and what can be done about it, if anything. Truly innovative remedies are rare. In order to deal with the in-between "sizes," however, some less standard options have evolved.

Conditional Remedies. The key to conditional reinstatements is that the arbitrator's remedy requires the grievant to make his own remedial efforts as a condition of his return to work. Such reinstatements are seen particularly in drug and alcohol cases, especially where the arbitrator views the alcoholic or drug-using grievant as having a medical as well as a disciplinary problem. The condition may be that the grievant enroll in the employer's employee assistance program or other rehabilitation pro-

---

[170]For further discussion of the circumstances under which no back pay and some back pay are called for, see *Western Die Casting Co.*, 79 LA 391 (Koven, 1982) (strike misconduct; propriety of penalty).

gram;[171] that he or she agree to submit to periodic or random testing;[172] or both.[173] Or it may simply be that the grievant abstain from the use of alcohol and/or drugs.[174] Some arbitrators, on the other hand, have taken the position that, praiseworthy though rehabilitation efforts may be, it is not their place to require the employer to resort to them in the absence of a clear past practice of doing so.[175]

Other conditions imposed by arbitrators have included res-

---

[171]As in *Jim Beam Brands Co.*, 89-2 ARB ¶8575 (Katz, 1989), where the grievant, who was discharged for working while intoxicated, was reinstated on condition that he present proof of participation in the employer's alcohol-abuse program, with continued employment to be dependent on the program leader's judgment. See also *Armstrong Cork Co.*, 56 LA 527 (Wolf, 1971); *Monte Mart–Grand Auto Concession*, 56 LA 738, 71-1 ARB ¶8267 (Jacobs, 1971); *American Synthetic Rubber Corp.*, 73-1 ARB ¶8070 (Kesselman, 1973); *Land O'Lakes Bridgeman Creamery*, 65 LA 803 (Smythe, 1975); *Giant Eagle Markets, Inc.*, 1975 ARB ¶8145 (Emerson, 1975); *Armstrong Rubber Co.*, 77 LA 775 (Koven, 1981); *Arcata Graphics, Buffalo Div.*, 83-1 ARB ¶8127 (Curry, 1983); *Iowa State Penitentiary*, 89 LA 956 (Hill, 1987); *County of Martin, Fairmont, Minn.*, 87-2 ARB ¶8328 (Flagler, 1987).

[172]In *W. R. Grace & Co.*, 93 LA 1210 (Odom, 1989), the arbitrator conditioned reinstatement of an employee who had pled guilty to off-duty, off-premises drug charges upon his remaining drug-free throughout the ensuing five years and submitting to random and scheduled drug tests. In *Bay Area Rapid Transit Dist.*, 92 LA 444 (Koven, 1989), the grievant, reinstated after being discharged for intoxication while on duty, was to be subject to daily drug testing for a substantial period in view of the nature of his misconduct and the hazards posed by any repetition. See also *Eden Hosp.*, 56 LA 319 (Eaton, 1971) (grievant discharged for intoxication must submit to "sobriety test" whenever she might again be suspected of some offense); *Aeroquip Corp.*, 95 LA 31 (Stieber, 1990) (grievant must agree to random testing and summary discharge upon proof of illegal drug use).

[173]In *Capitol Plastics of Ohio, Inc.*, 89-2 ARB ¶8309 (Duda, 1989), an employee who was discharged for being absent while serving a 30-day jail sentence was reinstated on condition that he furnish certificates of alcohol abstinence and drug abstinence; pay $35 toward the cost of a drug test; agree to 12 random drug/alcohol tests during the ensuing two years; and participate in an alcohol rehabilitation program for two years. In *Engelhard Corp.*, 89-1 ARB ¶8033 (Mathews, 1988), a grievant who was improperly discharged for testing positive for cocaine was to be reinstated upon his return from medical leave on condition that he undergo a physical exam. If he passed the physical, he was to be reinstated without back pay; if he tested positive for drugs, he was to be so notified and allowed to seek help at his own expense. In *Southern Cal. Permanente Medical Group*, 92 LA 41 (Richman, 1989), an employee who was found not guilty of charges of selling drugs on company property was reinstated with back pay on condition that he agree to the same rehabilitation and random testing made available to other employees, since he admitted to being a drug user. And in *Southern Cal. Rapid Transit Dist.*, 93 LA 20 (Christopher, 1989), the employer was to restore the grievant to his bus operator position if he tested negative for drugs; if he tested positive, he was to be placed in the employee assistance program.

[174]In *Trans World Airlines*, 89-1 ARB ¶8186 (Eisler, 1988), a flight attendant discharged for showing up drunk was reinstated on condition that she abstain from medication or drugs unless prescribed and abstain from alcohol in any form. Rather than being discharged, the arbitrator said, the attendant should have been given the option of participating in the airline's employee assistance program.

[175]See, e.g., *Stanley Door Sys.*, 89-1 ARB ¶8141 (Doering, 1988); *Sheriff of Broward County, Fla.*, 92 LA 937 (Seidman, 1989); *Burger Iron Co.*, 92 LA 1100 (Dworkin, 1989).

ignation from a second job found to be causing problems on the primary job[176] or withdrawal from outside business activity found to create a conflict of interest;[177] medical testing for employees with emotional or health problems;[178] evidence of ability to meet job requirements in the case of an employee who misrepresented her physical condition;[179] completion of school in the case of an employee whose absenteeism problems were caused by carrying a full school load while working full time;[180] counseling in race and human relations at his own expense in the case of a delivery driver who used a racial epithet on a customer's dock;[181] counseling on "the meaning and implications of sexual harassment" in the case of an employee whom the arbitrator judged to be not beyond rehabilitation and the reach of progressive discipline;[182] weight loss for an individual whose excess poundage prevented him from working safely;[183] and reimbursement of the employer for two thirds of the cost of opening,

---

[176]*E.g.*, *Climate Control*, 89 LA 1062 (Cromwell, 1987), where the grievant was directed to quit her moonlighting job within two weeks.

[177]*E.g..*, *New York Post Corp.*, 62 LA 225 (Friedman, 1973), where a newspaper sports writer was directed to sell his interest in a race horse as a condition of returning to work.

[178]In *Bay Area Rapid Transit Dist.*, 79-1 ARB ¶8015 (Koven, 1978), psychiatric testing was prescribed for a grievant who carried firearms as part of his job to determine whether he was psychologically stable. See also *Island Creek Coal Co.*, 88-2 ARB ¶8530 (Goldman, 1988), where the grievant's misconduct was held to warrant discharge, but the arbitrator found that the company did not pay enough attention to the emotional problems resulting from the breakup of his marriage. Reinstatement was ordered provided the employee submitted to an examination at his own expense by a psychiatrist or other specialist designated by the company; the psychiatrist determined that the grievant was able to be a safe, reliable employee; and the grievant continued in any program of treatment that might be professionally prescribed for him. And see *Brock-Hall Dairy*, 54 LA 448 (Johnson, 1969) (reinstatement of employee discharged for absenteeism caused by back injury conditioned upon producing doctor's clearance to return to work); *Kost Bros., Inc.*, 86 LA 65 (Berquist, 1986) (epileptic to provide physician's statement that he may return to work and periodic similar reports thereafter); *Lever Bros. Co.*, 87 LA 260 (Traynor, 1986) (two years of treatment by psychiatrist for grievant with mental problems, followed by reinstatement if able to work reliably); *The Bucklers, Inc.*, 88-1 ARB ¶8238 (Braufman, 1987) (grievant with AIDS to be examined promptly by specialist and reinstated if found able to perform all job duties; if not, to be continued on involuntary medical or disability leave); *Delta-Macon Brick & Tile Co.*, 92 LA 837 (O'Grady, 1989) (grievant discharged because of off-duty back injury to be examined by medical expert acceptable to both company and union).

[179]*Firestone Tire & Rubber Co.*, 93 LA 381 (Cohen, 1989). The misrepresentation was found not to have been willful. If the grievant proved to be unable to meet the physical requirements of her job, her case was to be handled in accordance with contractual disability provisions.

[180]*Springday Co.*, 70-2 ARB ¶8476 (Bothwell, 1970).

[181]*Rustco Prods. Co.*, 92 LA 1048, 89-2 ARB ¶8351 (Watkins, 1989).

[182]*Hyatt Hotels Palo Alto*, 85 LA 11, 17 (Oestreich, 1985).

[183]*Reynolds Metals Co.*, 71 LA 1099 (Bothwell, 1978).

reinspecting, and resealing cartons in some of which the grievant had inserted religious sermons.[184]

Last-Chance Remedies. Just as employers and unions sometimes
agree upon giving an employee guilty of serious misconduct
"one last chance," so arbitrators may use their remedy power to
direct that a grievant whom the employer has discharged be
reinstated on a last-chance basis. Whatever the source of the last
chance, the grievant is on notice that if he engages in further
misconduct—perhaps of the same kind, perhaps of *any* kind—
he will be discharged without recourse. Generally speaking,
whereas conditional remedies allow the grievant to *return* to
work only if certain requirements are met, last-chance remedies
allow the grievant to *remain* at work only if he engages in no
further misconduct.[185] In the case of reinstatements conditioned
upon the employee's agreeing to submit to periodic drug or
alcohol testing, however, the distinction between the two becomes blurred.[186]

The last-chance remedy is motivated by the arbitrator's
belief that the grievant is not a hopeless case, and that some
factor—a long period of good service, perhaps,[187] or procedural
errors or unfairness on the part of the employer—argues for
giving him or her a reprieve. The thinking that may underlie
the last-chance remedy is exemplified by the case of the grievant,
discharged for being absent without notice too many times,

---

[184]*Eureka Co.*, 93 LA 513 (Wolff, 1989).

[185]In *Safeway Stores, Inc.*, 75 LA 430 (Winograd, 1980), a grievant who was discharged after a series of absences connected with motorcycle accident injuries was
reinstated on condition that for six months after returning to work he had no absence
longer than one day that was related to his prior injury and total absences not exceeding
the bargaining unit average. See also *Intalco Aluminum Corp.*, 68 LA 66 (LaCugna, 1977)
(employee discharged after pleading guilty to unlawful delivery of marijuana reinstated
with stipulation that possession of drug on company property or conviction of drug-
related charge in court would subject him to summary discharge); *Kroger Co.*, 88 LA
463 (Wren, 1986) (nongrievable dismissal upon positive test for any drug); *Cleveland
Elec. Illuminating Co.*, 88 LA 781 (Morgan, 1987) (any tardiness or unexcused absence
during six months after reinstatement ground for termination); *GTE Fla., Inc.*, 92
LA 1090 (Cohen, 1989) (further sexual harassment or similar misconduct cause for
immediate discharge).

[186]See *supra*, notes 171–74.

[187]As in *Mosler, Inc.*, 89-1 ARB ¶8067 (Katz, 1988), where the grievant was discharged for striking a supervisor. His last-chance reinstatement was based on his 28
years of good service as well as the fact that there was some provocation. He was to be
subject to immediate discharge for any similar conduct, or threat thereof, or for any act
of serious insubordination. See also *Air Treads, Inc.*, 86 LA 545 (Allen, 1986) (insubordination; "substantial" seniority); *Weyerhaeuser Co.*, 88 LA 270 (Kapsch, 1987) (absenteeism; 26-year good record).

whom the arbitrator ordered put back to work "by the thinnest of margins" one month after the date of his award. Said the arbitrator:

> He should spend the time until his reinstatement thinking about whether or not he is capable of adhering to the Company's rules on his own, including making the requisite notification when absent. If he decides he cannot act responsibly in the future, he would be doing all involved a favor by seeking employment elsewhere.[188]

Transfer. Transfer has been selected as an appropriate remedy where an employee appears to be salvageable, but personal problems or some other factor makes it predictable that the difficulties will persist if reinstatement to the former job is directed. Say that longstanding personal conflicts between the grievant and her fellow workers might have contributed to her uncooperative attitude. If the arbitrator finds that her misconduct was not so bad as to warrant discharge, or if her discharge is washed out on other grounds, the award might direct her reinstatement to a job in another department to prevent the same personality clashes from erupting again.[189]

Transfer has also been part of the remedy where, for example, the grievant had been subjected to sexual harassment by her former supervisor, and the arbitrator ordered her reinstatement to another store rather than put her back under his supervision.[190] Another possible occasion for transfer is where the nature of the grievant's misconduct disqualifies him for one type of job but not necessarily for others. Thus, where two truck drivers were discharged because their poor driving records led the insurance carrier to exclude them from coverage, the arbitrator reinstated them to nondriving jobs commensurate with

---

[188]*Franke, Inc.*, 88-1 ARB ¶8342 (O'Connell, 1988).

[189]*Times Publishing Co.*, 40 LA 1054 (Dworkin, 1963), is a case of this type. The animosity of other employees was one reason why the grievant was reinstated to another job in *Hawaiian Tel. Co.*, 44 LA 218 (Tsukiyama, 1965) (incompetence); her inability to perform her former job because of aging was another. See also *Social Sec. Admin.*, 84 LA 1100, 1104 (Weinstein, 1985), where an employee found to have used foul language to her supervisor was ordered reinstated to another job in a different work area. If a comparable job was not available, the arbitrator said, she could be offered a lesser job, with termination the alternative to acceptance.

[190]*Osborn & Ulland, Inc.*, 68 LA 1146 (Beck, 1977) (various work rule violations). In *U.S. Dep't of Justice*, 89-1 ARB ¶8069 (Weisbrod, 1988), a victim of sexual harassment who was demoted for complaining was reinstated and transferred to another facility of her choice. The transfer of her husband, preferably to the same facility, was recommended.

their qualifications and seniority.[191] And where a drug company subject to employee screening requirements of the Drug Enforcement Administration improperly discharged an employee for being an "unacceptable security risk" following his guilty pleas to a charge of obtaining money through false pretenses, the arbitrator directed the company and union to negotiate the possibility of relaxing transfer or bidding rules to allow him access to a nonsensitive job.[192]

In still another case, a grievant who had been discharged for committing an indecent act toward a passenger was reinstated to a job that would minimize his contact with the public.[193]

Back Pay Without Reinstatement. Where discharge is found not to have been for just cause, but the employer-employee relationship has deteriorated to the point where it is no longer viable or there is little doubt that the grievant, if returned to work, would just be fired again, reinstatement may make no sense. The arbitrator may then award full or partial back pay but permit the termination to stand.[194]

Back pay without reinstatement may also be the remedy where the employer committed a procedural error that was not, however, viewed by the arbitrator as serious enough to warrant overturning the discharge. For example, the arbitrator ruled that the grievant was denied due process when the company discharged him for assaulting the company president and vice president and did not hold a hearing until two days later. This did not render the discharge improper, but since the contract

---

[191]*Inland Lumber Co.*, 62 LA 1150 (Wilmoth, 1974). In *Transit Auth. of River City*, 95 LA 137 (Dworkin, 1990), a bus driver found to have been discharged improperly even though a breathalyzer test showed a blood alcohol level of 0.05% was ordered reinstated to a different position because the employer could never be confident of the driver's ability to drive safely. The duty to put a disabled employee in a job he can perform, the arbitrator said, arises with respect to an employee disabled by alcoholism as well as to employees suffering from other illnesses.

[192]*Parke Davis*, 86 LA 935 (Keefe, 1985).

[193]*Philadelphia Transp. Co.*, 49 LA 606 (Gershenfeld, undated).

[194]*E.g., Safeway Stores, Inc.*, 64 LA 563 (Gould, 1974), where procedural errors on the employer's part made the grievant's discharge not for just cause, but the arbitrator's conclusion that he was incorrigible precluded his return to work. See also *Sunshine Specialty Co.*, 55 LA 1061 (Levin, 1970) (poor work performance, belligerence toward coworkers); *Bay Area Union Professional Center*, 67 LA 960 (Griffin, 1976) (deterioration of work performance); *Hollytex Carpet Mills, Inc.*, 79-1 ARB ¶8181 (Anderson, 1979) (theft, refusal to cooperate with investigation); *Chromalloy Am. Corp.*, 93 LA 828 (Woolf, 1989) (threats against management).

said no employee would be discharged without a hearing, the employee was entitled to two days' pay.[195]

Special Remedies. Special circumstances may convince the arbitrator that none of the remedies discussed above will set matters right, or that they simply do not address the problems presented by the case at hand. In such situations, arbitrators have shown great ingenuity in fashioning tailor-made remedies. The following are some of these remedies:

Where the employer suspended an employee for misappropriating company funds and then waited two years before discharging her, the arbitrator awarded back pay *or* reinstatement. Because of the employer's unfair delay, he noted, the question of whether the employee's discharge was proper normally would not have been reached—the discharge would have been overturned and the employee reinstated with back pay. But the employee concocted a story to cover her misdeeds and impeded the procedure designed to protect her rights. The arbitrator therefore gave the employer a choice—reinstate the employee without back pay or, if the employer believed her effectiveness had been irreparably damaged, give her back pay from the date of discharge to the date of the arbitration hearing.[196]

Where a grievant had twice been guilty of negligent operation of equipment, the arbitrator found contributory fault on the part of the employer because it had failed to provide remedial instruction after the first incident. His reinstatement order directed management to provide remedial training and reorientation for at least 30 days, followed by close monitoring until the grievant's supervisor was satisfied he could do his job properly without close supervision.[197]

An arbitrator found no contractual basis for *any* penalty in the case of an employee who was discharged for having a can of beer outside the plant but on company property. But the

---

[195]*State Paper & Metal Co.*, 88-1 ARB ¶8112 (Klein, 1987). See also *Trailways Commuter Transit, Inc.*, 92 LA 503, 89-1 ARB ¶8168 (Marcus, 1989) (back pay but no reinstatement for bus driver improperly discharged after completion of probationary period for events during that period, since driving infractions concerned safety); *Lancaster Electro Plating*, 93 LA 207 (Bressler, 1989) (back pay from date of suspension to date of discharge, even though discharge justified, where grievant denied union representation prior to discharge).

[196]*Virgin Islands Water & Power Auth.*, 89 LA 809 (Watkins, 1987).

[197]*Greenlee Tool Textron Co.*, 88-1 ARB ¶8102 (Fischbach, 1987).

employee left work after two hours and spent the rest of the shift at a nearby saloon. The arbitrator said he had the power on equity grounds to impose a two-month disciplinary suspension.[198]

Where a nursing home was found to have improperly discharged an AIDS-infected employee, rather than placing him on medical leave until he could return to work, the arbitrator ordered that he be permitted to reinstate his group insurance coverage; and that the nursing home pay his medical bills for the period he was not covered by group insurance. The arbitrator conceded that, barring a medical breakthrough, the employee probably would never be able to return to work at this health-care facility but should remain in a suspended-employee status indefinitely.[199]

Where a library assistant was wrongly suspended for defying his superiors' orders to desist from helping two women being attacked in the library foyer, the arbitrator awarded back pay and, as an additional remedy, directed the city and the director of library services to apologize to the assistant and to present to him a commendation for assisting others in the presence of staff members on duty at the time of the incident.[200]

Back Pay Awards—A Closer Look

No Back Pay or Some Back Pay?

> *Arbitrator Teele:* [I]t is frequently hard to find the rhyme or reason which justifies the choice between the outright denial of back pay and a reduction in the amount of the penalty. The monetary 'fines' involved are frequently large and sometimes seemingly out of proportion to the alleged offense—particularly if, as in 35 percent of the cases studied here, fault is also found (by the arbitrator) on the company's part.[201]

Say that the arbitrator finds that, although the grievant was guilty of *some* misconduct, the penalty of discharge was clearly

---

[198]*Interbake Foods, Inc.*, 88-2 ARB ¶8478 (Howlett, 1988).

[199]*Nursing Home*, 88 LA 681 (Sedwick, 1987).

[200]*City of Berkeley*, 93 LA 1161 (Riker, 1989). See also *Federal Bureau of Prisons*, 91 LA 277 (Statham, 1988), in which the arbitrator reduced a five-day suspension for directing racial slurs at a coworker to a written reprimand, but ordered the grievant to make a public apology to the coworker and thank him for his restraint in not responding.

[201]"*But No Back Pay Is Awarded* . . . ," 19 ARB. J. 104 (1964).

too harsh to "fit the crime" or for some other reason was not justified. A year or more has passed since the discharge—consumed by filing of the grievance, discussions by the parties, selection of the arbitrator, holding of the hearing, and receipt of transcripts and briefs. Here is where the arbitrator meets his perennial dilemma—what should he do about back pay, if anything? He comes face to face with the standard choices—full back pay, no back pay, or some back pay. How does he decide which one?

A few arbitrators operate on the theory that even though there may have been misconduct, if the discharge was not for just cause the grievant is entitled to full back pay. Because the company's action *ab initio* was improper, they reason that the company must shoulder the financial burden.[202] It can be reasonably objected, however, that the grievant then reports back on the job without any penalty at all to induce him to "mend his ways," and (especially if a long time has passed between discharge and reinstatement) a "windfall" in his pocket.

Other arbitrators will more often than not opt for no back pay on the theory that the grievant, by engaging in misconduct (*any* misconduct), signed on for what happened thereafter, however long the "suspension" that resulted from the time needed to take the case through arbitration.[203] However, critics of this view point out, if the grievant's misconduct was not really serious, the loss of earnings that results from a denial of back pay may be greatly disproportionate to the offense, especially if the time between discharge and suspension is lengthy.

Many arbitrators avoid the extremes of full back pay and no back pay and choose an award that penalizes the grievant *to some degree* for his or her misconduct and penalizes the employer

---

[202]A few collective bargaining agreements make reinstatement with full back pay mandatory if the arbitrator finds that the discharge penalty was improperly imposed for any reason. Where the agreement so provides, the arbitrator has no other remedy option. See, e.g., *City Prods. Corp.*, 67 LA 27 (Goetz, 1976).

[203]See, e.g., *Grant Hosp.*, 88 LA 587 (Wolff, 1986) (theft). Another rationale is seen in *Foote & Davies*, 88 LA 125 (Wahl, 1986), where the arbitrator ruled that a refusal to take a test for intoxication was not an admission of guilt but such refusal was ground for denying back pay because the grievant frustrated the only objective means of determining his condition. Still another possible measure is the grievant's lack of contrition, seen in *Pan Am Support Servs.*, 89-1 ARB ¶8306 (Odom, 1988). Normally, said the arbitrator, the grievant would have merited at most a short suspension for having violated the company's human relations policy by using offensive sexual references in training sessions. But because he failed to recognize that he had done anything wrong, the arbitrator denied back pay altogether.

to some degree for imposing a discharge without just cause. But where to draw the line? Should the grievant get a suspension of one month, three months, three months and two weeks, five months and a day—what? Should the arbitrator just "split the difference"?[204] For the arbitrator simply to "pick a number" is arbitrary, for, as in the case of the well-known Chancellor in Equity, there ordinarily is no standard for guidance other than the length and width of the arbitrator's own foot[205]—that is, his or her own knowledge of what penalty the "reasonable man" in the industrial community would find appropriate under all the circumstances. And whether that "foot" will turn out to be the same size as those of the parties—their reasonable expectancies based on their particular history and practice—is a matter of guesswork.

On the other hand, when the arbitrator tries to avoid being arbitrary by reinstating without back pay (because he or she cannot decide how much back pay is proper without being arbitrary), the result still is arbitrary. That is so because the time the grievant has been off work prior to being reinstated is controlled by such arbitrary factors as the length of time it takes to get an arbitrator, to arrange for a hearing, and finally to receive the arbitrator's award.

Reducing the Options

Reflective of the concern with the arbitrary character of back pay awards is a case in which, by agreement of the parties, one arbitrator imported in modified form the "baseball" (or final offer) procedure commonly used in "interest" arbitration into the "rights" arbitration framework as a means of minimizing

---

[204]The doctrine of "comparative fault" was applied in *Panhandle E. Pipeline Co.*, 88 LA 725, 88-1 ARB ¶8021 (Yarowsky, 1987), to determine that an employee wrongfully discharged for filing for and accepting benefits under both the employer's and his wife's group insurance plans should receive one-half back pay. The employee was guilty of carelessness and inattentiveness, the arbitrator found, not of intent to defraud.

[205] Equity is a roguish thing. For law we have a measure, know what to trust to. Equity is according to the conscience of him that is Chancellor, and as that is larger or narrower, so is Equity. "'Tis all one as if they should make the standard for the measure we call a 'foot' a Chancellor's foot; what an uncertain measure this would be! One Chancellor has a long foot, another a short foot, a third an indifferent foot. 'Tis the same thing in the Chancellor's conscience." It is the same for arbitrators.
P. Seitz, *Substitution of Disciplinary Suspension for Discharge (A Proposed "Guide to the Perplexed" in Arbitration)*, 35 ARB. J. 29–30 (1980), quoting from J. SELDEN, TABLE TALK. EQUITY.

arbitrary "no back pay" and "some back pay" awards. After deciding there was no just cause for discharge, the arbitrator remanded the question of back pay (and therefore also the length of the suspension) to the parties for negotiation. He directed further (also with their prior consent) that if they failed to reach agreement by a specified date, they would submit to him what had been their respective final or "last best" offers. The arbitrator would then make a selection between the two "last best" offers, which would then become his own back pay award.[206]

"The Grievant Shall Be Made Whole"

When an award states that the grievant is to be reinstated with full back pay and other benefits, what is intended is that the grievant be "made whole." But what does "made whole" really mean? Does it mean getting paid for overtime the grievant might have worked? Is the grievant entitled to the job he or she might have been eligible to bid into? What about interest on the back pay award, or attorney's fees?

The standard definition of "made whole" is that the grievant is entitled to whatever he or she would have earned during the period away from work, were it not for the discipline imposed by the employer, plus seniority and fringe benefits for that period.[207] It generally does not mean that the grievant is entitled to interest on the back pay award, unless the parties provided for this in their contract. (The same is true of attorney's

---

[206]*Western Die Casting Co.*, 79 LA 391 (Koven, 1982) (strike misconduct). In his article *Substitution of Disciplinary Suspension for Discharge, supra* note 205, Arbitrator Seitz advocated a slightly different approach. He suggested the back pay issue be remanded to the parties without first obtaining their consent and, if they were unable to settle the matter, that a second hearing or "in chambers" discussion with the arbitrator be held for the presentation of evidence and arguments relevant to the back pay question. See also D. M. Young, *My Use of the Final-Offer Principle*, ARBITRATION 1985 239–46 (Proceedings of the 38th Annual Meeting, National Academy of Arbitrators 1986), in which Arbitrator Young describes a procedure much like the *Western Die Casting* remedy, except that he includes the grievant in the back pay negotiations, and his use of it over an eight-year period. Only once, in 1985, was he required to choose between two final offers (he picked the company offer, a 90-day suspension, over the union's offer of a 60-day suspension); in all other cases the parties reached agreement.

[207]Numerous questions that arise in calculating the exact dollar figures involved in any back pay award, e.g., whether lost earnings should be computed on the basis of calendar quarters, monthly periods, or some other standard; whether lost overtime opportunities should be added in and, if so, how lost overtime should be calculated; and whether allowance should be made for normal absenteeism, are discussed in M. F. HILL, JR., & A. SINICROPI, REMEDIES IN ARBITRATION 190–235 (2d ed. 1991).

fees.) That is because, it is argued, the arbitrator's remedy, as well as the rest of the award, "is only enforceable as long as it draws its essence from the agreement."[208] If the "common sense" remedy that seems to be called for cannot be found somewhere within the four corners of the contract, the arbitrator cannot reach beyond what the parties have signed on to for some other standard of fairness.

Similarly, very few arbitrators have been willing to assess "punitive" damages in discipline cases—that is, monetary penalties against the company over and above what is required to make the injured grievant whole.[209] However, some courts have in principle upheld the arbitrator's right to award punitive damages, in order to deter future contract violations, in cases where such damages were within the scope of the contract.[210]

The notion that the grievant should not profit from his discharge has another consequence. Most back pay awards include a proviso that unemployment benefits and earnings from other jobs during the period between discharge and reinstatement will be deducted from the back pay award.[211] Moreover, the grievant may be considered to have an obligation to take reasonable steps to mitigate damages by, for example, seeking other work and applying for unemployment benefits.[212] The grievant does not, however, have to prove that he or she made

---

[208]P. PRASOW & E. PETERS, ARBITRATION AND COLLECTIVE BARGAINING 256–57 (1970).

[209]See HILL & SINICROPI, supra note 207, at Ch. 19.

[210]See, e.g., Sheet Metal Workers v. Helgesteel Corp., 335 F. Supp. 812, 80 LRRM 2113 (W.D. Wis. 1971); Bakery & Confectionery Workers Int'l Union v. Cotton Baking Co., 514 F.2d 1235, 89 LRRM 2665 (5th Cir. 1975), reh'g denied. 520 F.2d 943; Niagara, Wheatfield, Lewiston & Cambria Cent. School Dist. No. 1 Bd. of Educ. v. Niagara-Wheatfield Teachers Ass'n, 46 N.Y.2d 553, 415 N.Y.S.2d 790, 101 LRRM 2258 (1979); Operating Eng'rs Local 450 v. Mid-Valley, 347 F. Supp. 1104, 81 LRRM 2325 (S.D. Tex. 1972).

[211]For a discussion of the outside-earnings question, see D. E. Feller, Remedies in Arbitration: Old Problems Revisited, ARBITRATION ISSUES FOR THE 1980s 122–24 (Proceedings of the 34th Annual Meeting, National Academy of Arbitrators 1982).

[212]Feller, supra note 211, at 123–24, takes the position that "[t]here is, or should be . . . no requirement that the employee seek other employment and no deduction from back pay because of his failure to do so." For discussion of the obligation to mitigate, see HILL & SINICROPI, supra note 207, at 214–23; F. ELKOURI & E. A. ELKOURI, How ARBITRATION WORKS 408–10 (4th ed. 1985). For an example of a case in which a reinstated employee was denied back pay because he failed to take reasonable steps to mitigate his damages, see Sheraton Westgate Hotel, 88-2 ARB ¶8488 (Klein, 1988). In Flohr Metal Fabricators, Inc., 88-2 ARB ¶8462 (Perone, 1988), the arbitrator ruled that it was up to the grievant to decide how best to get money after being fired; any reasonable attempt, without regard to success, was enough. Thus, the fact that the grievant failed to apply for unemployment compensation was viewed as irrelevant, where he made a conscientious effort to find work at his established trade.

a reasonable effort to find other work; rather, the employer must prove that such an effort was *not* made.[213]

From at least one union's point of view (and probably unions generally), an employee can never be adequately compensated for an unjust discharge, even if he or she is reinstated with full back pay and benefits.

> *Union representative Ben Fischer:* You never make a discharged employee whole by putting him back to work. In this day and age, when workers are developing dignity and status in the community and in their family, and you operate almost in an industrial goldfish bowl, you can't make him whole. He was offended; he was embarrassed; his family was embarrassed. . . .
>
> [W]hat do you do to avoid the stigma? How do you make that whole? What do you do about the guy who loses his car, whose TV is picked up, who has to borrow money and pay interest, who loses his home? . . .
>
> Labor has to face up to the fact that it must extract from management a termination of this "less deductions" baloney. You can't really make the wrongfully penalized employee whole, no matter what you do, so at least give him the few pennies or the few dollars that are involved instead of adding insult to injury.[214]

The Reinstated Employee—A Bad Risk?

Take a grievant who, in management's eyes, was a defiant employee, a sustandard employee, or an employee who engaged in unacceptable conduct such as gross insubordination. The grievant saw it differently, and after a long and costly grievance and arbitration scenario finally was reinstated with back pay. Management believed when it fired him that he was guilty as charged and unacceptable, and it feels the same way now. No wonder it is a galling experience for management to see him back at work, sure he will take up his old ways.

Are management's fears justified? Arthur Malinowski has said no. In a study of the subsequent employment histories of 73 reinstated employees, Malinowski found a difference of opinion as between front office personnel and first-line supervisors. Those in the personnel department reported that

---

[213]*Cleveland Pneumatic Co.*, 88-1 ARB ¶8116 (Sharpe, 1987).

[214]B. Fischer, *Implementation of Arbitration Awards: The Steelworkers View*, ARBITRATION AND THE PUBLIC INTEREST (Proceedings of the 24th Annual Meeting, National Academy of Arbitrators 1971).

few reinstated employees returned to work with a poor attitude—that is, with an air of having "beaten the system." More
commonly, the reinstated employee seemed to have "gotten the
message" and settled down to his job. However, "[f]irst-line
supervisors did not necessarily share the personnel department's assessment of reinstated employees' performance, but
were somewhat dissatisfied with their progress (about 30% for
upper management vs. 40% for the first-line supervisors)."[215]
Malinowski suggested a reason for that difference of opinion.

> Perhaps this difference in attitude between the personnel depart-
> ment and the supervisor exists because immediate supervisors do
> not like to supervise a previously discharged employee, especially
> if the supervisor who fired or recommended firing again becomes
> that employee's supervisor.
>
> If the relationship between supervisor and employee was
> strained before discharge, the arbitrator's order of reinstatement
> would not have improved it. Indeed, from the supervisor's point
> of view, the relationship could have been made worse.[216]

But whatever first-line supervisors would like to believe,the
figures themselves show that most returned employees turn out
to be not such "bad apples" after all.[217] In specific terms, of the
63 employees who accepted reinstatement, only five, or *about 8
percent*, were again discharged by the time of Malinowski's study;
four retired or were laid off; seven quit voluntarily. Forty-seven,
or *about 75 percent*, were still on the job, and their employers
rated their performance generally favorably.[218]

---

[215]A. Malinowski, *An Empirical Analysis of Discharge Cases*, 36 ARB. J. 43 (1981).

[216]*Id.* at 42. Although Malinowski's sample may have been too small to draw a firm
conclusion, his figures suggest that continued resentment on the part of supervisors
may have been an important factor in the five subsequent discharges of reinstated
employees considered in his study; their immediate supervisors were dissatisfied to
some degree with four of the five, while there was no response from the supervisor of
the fifth.

[217]*Id.* Professor Jones's figures show that reinstatement was ordered in approxi-
mately 54% of the cases analyzed. D. L. Jones, *Ramifications of Back-Pay Awards in
Discharge Cases*, ARBITRATION AND SOCIAL CHANGE 167 (Proceedings of the 22nd Annual
Meeting, National Academy of Arbitrators 1970). Jennings and Wolters show the same
reinstatement frequency. K. Jennings and R. Wolters, *Discharge Cases Reconsidered*, 31
ARB. J. 174 (1976).

[218]Malinowski, *supra* note 220, at 36–37, 39–41. Malinowski unfortunately did not
make clear exactly how long the reinstated employees in his survey had been back on
the job when he compiled his figures. The arbitration cases he considered were all
published between September 1977 and October 1978, and his article was published in
March 1981. An earlier study by D. L. Jones and A. M. Ross, *The Arbitration of Discharge
Cases: What Happens After Reinstatement*, CRITICAL ISSUES IN ARBITRATION 21–56 (Pro-

A study by Arbitrator William E. Simkin involving the experience of a single large company over a 12-1/2-year period (1970–1982) revealed a somewhat less successful post-reinstatement history. The cause of discharge usually was absenteeism or tardiness or both, sometimes complicated by poor performance or related reasons. Of 116 employees reinstated in the grievance procedure or through arbitration, 45, or 39 percent, were discharged again and not reinstated, either because the subsequent discharges were upheld in arbitration or because they were not taken to arbitration. Only 9 percent were given excellent or good ratings by management, 20 percent were rated average, 25 percent below average, and 7 percent poor but good enough to avoid being discharged again. As of December 1983, just under half were still with the company.[219]

---

ceedings of the 10th Annual Meeting, National Academy of Arbitrators 1957), yielded basically similar results about employers' assessment of reinstated employees.

[219]W. E. Simkin, *Some Results of Reinstatement by Arbitration*, 41:3 ARB. J. 53–58 (1986).

Appendix

Decision of Arbitrator Carroll R. Daugherty
in
Enterprise Wire Co. and Enterprise Independent Union

March 28, 1966

46 LA 359

Factual Background

On October 8, 1965, the Company communicated to grievant X an employment termination notice, signed by the plant manager and by the assistant plant superintendent and giving as the reasons for X—'s dismissal unsatisfactory work, including absenteeism, plus insubordination or refusal to work as directed.

The aggrieved employee had been hired on April 13, 1965, and had been trained as a wire rod cleaner in the Cleaning Department, second shift. The Company receives coils of wire rod from its suppliers, and said coils vary in diameter and metallurgical composition. Before the coils reach the cleaner employee, they are welded together at the ends in sets of three to form a "pin" and are tagged for identification as to diameter and composition. The cleaner's job is to clean the pins in an acid tank, preserve their identities, and respectively to re-tag them after they have been so pickled and as they are left suspended from a sort of beam called a "yoke." The tag is a rectangular piece of cardboard with spaces to be filled in as to size and other characteristics of the wire rod in the pin and as to the identity of the wire-drawing machine to which the pin is to go. At the top of the tag is a reinforced hole through which a fine, flexible

449

wire is placed by the cleaner, fastened to a strand of rod in the pin, and wound or twisted to prevent detachment.

Failure properly to tag each pin results in production delays, cost increases, and customer dissatisfaction (when orders for wire are not filled according to specifications). Alleged continued failure to tag some of his pins properly—either through allegedly not tagging some pins at all or through allegedly not marking the machine number on some of them—was the immediate cause of X—'s discharge.

Other material facts are set forth below under *Findings and Opinion* in respect to the issue of "just cause."

Contract Provisions

The provisions of the Parties' controlling Agreement cited by the Company read as follows:

ARTICLE IV
Hours of Work and Overtime

Section 10. Absence From Work. Any employee absent from work for any cause is required to report at once to the Superintendent and arrange his next scheduled work shift. Any employee unable to report on his regularly scheduled shift shall notify his foreman or the Superintendent at least two hours prior to the start of the shift. Any employee failing to report as described above will, on the second offence, be given disciplinary layoff of one shift. Repetition of this practice without proper cause will be considered basis for discharge.

ARTICLE VII
Management

The union hereby recognizes that the management of the plant and the direction of the working forces, including, but not limited to the right to direct, plan and control plant operations, to establish and change working schedules, to hire, transfer, suspend, discharge or otherwise discipline employees for cause, to promulgate, administer and enforce plant rules, to relieve employees because of lack of work or for other legitimate reasons, to introduce new or improved methods or facilities and to manage its properties, is vested exclusively in the Company. It is understood that the aforesaid rights of management shall not be exercised in a manner inconsistent with the other provisions of this Agreement.

Any rights not specifically abridged, qualified or limited by this Agreement are reserved exclusively to the Company.

ARTICLE VIII
Discipline

Section 1. Proper Cause. No employee shall be discharged or otherwise disciplined except for proper cause.

Section 2. Discharge or Discipline Grievance. Any case of discharge or other discipline may be taken up through the grievance procedure, but any such grievance must be presented within three working days after the disciplinary action occurs.

Section 3. Notice to Union. The Union shall be notified within one working day of any disciplinary action taken against any employee covered by this Agreement.

The Union contends that the Company's disciplinary action violated the Agreement but cites no provisions thereof alleged to have been breached.

Arbitrator's Findings and Opinion

Article VII, quoted above, affirms the Company's right to discipline for "cause"; and Article VIII, Section 1, requires "proper cause" for discipline, including discharge. No provision in the Agreement defines these terms; that is, no contractual criteria exist for determining from the facts of any disciplinary cases, including this one, whether or not the Company had just cause for its decision. Therefore it is necessary for the Arbitrator to supply and apply his own just cause standards. Same are set forth in detail as an Appendix to this decision. In what follows, the Arbitrator makes findings of fact from the evidence of record in respect to each criterion.

Question No. 1: The record establishes that the Company gives to each employee a copy of a booklet labeled "INTRODUCTION TO ENTERPRISE WIRE CO." Pertinent portions thereof are reproduced just below:

PLANT INFORMATION AND RULES

In order to have our plant operate at maximum efficiency and insure the safety of the individual and plant property, it is necessary for all workers to abide by certain rules and regulations. We believe this will provide for our mutual protection and benefit.

Rules cover the following areas: instructional, standard practice, and disciplinary.

GENERAL INFORMATION AND RULES

ABSENTEEISM. Employees are required to notify or call their foreman or superintendent when, for any reason, they are unable to be present or anticipate a late arrival. (Shop employees are referred to Article IV, Section 10 of the union contract.)

ADMINISTRATION OF DISCIPLINE: The welfare of the company as a whole must be considered first, because it represents the total welfare of the entire group. Rules and regulations are established for the guidance and protection of all employees. Employees should be familiar with the rules and govern themselves accordingly. Failure to do so will result in disciplinary action, including suspension and discharge.

Disciplinary action may be in the form of verbal reprimand or written notice type. Our written notice type is based upon three notices within a twelve month period. The first warning notice is issued as a serious warning when verbal reprimand has failed. The second written notice carries a time off penalty related to the seriousness of the offense. The third notice requires suspension or discharge.

Disciplinary action will be taken in the following instances:

. . .

16. Insubordination, inability or refusal to perform assigned duties.

. . .

18. Unsatisfactory performance of duties assigned to the employee.

From the above, the Arbitrator must find that X— had been put on notice in respect to (1) the necessity of notifying the Company about impending absence or tardiness; (2) the necessity for satisfactory compliance with job requirements and supervisory directions when actually at work; and (3) the possible disciplinary consequences of failing to fulfill said requirements.

In addition to the above finding, which is general in nature, the evidence of record supports the firm conclusion that X— had been put on much more specific notice in respect to absenteeism, absence notification and work performance: (1) On June 16, 1965, X—'s foreman spoke to him about his absences and placed in his personnel file a written memorandum (not a formal warning notice) summarizing said interview. (2) On July 27, 1965, a formal written warning notice was issued to X— (and placed in his file) and a one-day suspension was imposed for his having been absent on two preceding days and for his not having notified the Company thereon. Said notice also promised further discipline for repetition of the offense. (3) On September 13, 1965, X— received a second such notice and one-day suspension for the same offense. He was also then put on a three-month probation. "Further action" was promised for his next "warning for any Reason." (4) During the first week in October, 1965, X—received four oral communications from three management persons—his two immediate foremen (who divided supervision of X—'s shift) and the assistant plant superintendent—in respect to his alleged failure to tag some of his cleaned pins or properly to mark some of the pins he did tag. Neither of the foremen explicitly warned that continued dereliction of tagging duty would lead to discipline; but on the evening before the discharge the assistant superintendent told X— that if he (the assistant superintendent) found the next morning that X—'s pins were not identified, the assistant superintendent would have to discharge him.

From all of the above, the Arbitrator must find that the answer to Question No 1 is clearly and strongly "Yes."

Question No. 2: The record contains no evidence, nor indeed does the Union contend, that the Company's rules and warning against absenteeism, against failure to notify the Company on same, and against tagging laxity were and are not reasonably related to Company efficiency and X—'s work capability. The answer to the second criterion must also be a strong "Yes."

Questions Nos. 3 and 4: On this Question the weight of the evidence of record warrants the following conclusions: (1) As to absenteeism and failure to notify: (a) The offense is of such a nature that, given X—'s records thereon, a prior further investigation into the fact was unnecessary. (b) But there was no explicit testimony about whether or not the Company asked X—to explain or excuse his lapses in this area. (2) As to X—'s alleged tagging failures: (a) This offense was of a different sort. At the hearing there was no controversion of the Company's evidence that on the three mornings preceding the date of X—'s discharge some of the pins that he had cleaned the prior evenings either lacked tags entirely or, if tagged, lacked wire-drawing-machine identification. Then, given the Company-conceded possibility that X— *might* have tagged all his cleaned pins properly those evenings and some one else or some post-shift occurrence *might* have caused the tickets to be removed or lost after

X— went home, the Company would be on firmer ground if it had taken the pains to question material handlers and other employees who conceivably might have been involved in order to remove as much doubt in this area as possible. On the other hand, if some of the tags that X— did attach on those evenings did not bear machine numbers, no further inquiry into this portion of his alleged offense was needed. (c) X—, at the times he was spoken to by management, had ample opportunity to try to justify or explain his tagging deficiencies if same existed. The Company cannot be held to have been seriously remiss in this field of its investigation. The Company is not shown actively to have solicited from X— any justification for his alleged sins of omission; but the Company may not rightly be found *to have denied* him such opportunity. (d) A relatively detached management official, higher than X—'s foremen, made the determining inquiries.

On balance, the Arbitrator holds that the answer to these two Questions is a moderate "Yes."

Question No. 5: Of all the seven questions, the fifth is the crucial one here. This statement is grounded on two facts of record: (1) The evidence on this Question is in direct conflict. At the hearing the Company witnesses testified forthrightly that on the mornings of that October week, after X— had left the preceding nights, some of his cleaned pins lacked tags entirely or, if tagged, lacked machine numbers. They also testified that, although X— at first denied any tagging failures whatever, he later (twice) admitted having tagged only "most" of his pins. On the other hand, X— himself at the hearing just as forthrightly testified that he had tagged all his pins and only two tags lacked machine numbers because some one came to take them immediately to the right machine, thus obviating any need for so identifying them. He also denied ever conceding to the Company that he had tagged only "most" of his pins. (2) No management person checked on X—'s tagging at the ends of his shifts that week. His foreman spot-checked his tagging those evenings and found same entirely satisfactory; but his checking ended one hour before X—'s shifts ended; and no further checking was done until the next mornings. Thus the record is blank on what happened from 10 p.m. until the morning checks.

This Arbitrator has no means for resolving the conflicts in testimony for filling in the blank area in facts. His function here is to determine whether the Company's decision-maker or "judge" (the plant manager) had reasonable, non-arbitrary grounds for accepting the word and conclusions of his managerial subordinates rather than any denials X— may have made.

On this issue the Arbitrator finds as follows: He has no proper basis for ruling that the Company's decision that X— was guilty of the alleged tagging offense was so unreasonable or arbitrary as to have constituted an abuse of managerial discretion. The record contains no probative evidence that either the Company or some fellow employee was trying to "frame" X—. The Company's evidence on the tagging matter must be ruled to have been sufficiently substantial to support its decision.

In respect to the absenteeism question, the Company must be held to have had amply substantial evidence of X—'s failures.

Given all the above, the answer to Question No. 5 must be a fairly strong "Yes."

Question No. 6: The record contains no evidence of probative value that would support a finding of Company discrimination against X— in the action it took. The answer to this Question is "Yes."

Question No. 7: This Question is a two-fold one. In the light of the Notes set forth in the Appendix hereto, as applied to the facts of record here, the answer to Question 7(a) must be "Yes." The Arbitrator has held that the Company properly found X— guilty of violating its reasonable rule on absenteeism and its reasonable shop rules Nos. 16 and 18. Such violations in the context of this case constituted a serious offense. The Company may not be found to have been unreasonable or arbitrary in deciding on discharge rather than on some lesser penalty.

As to Question No. 7(b), the Union makes two contentions: (1) X—'s record on absenteeism has no bearing on his discharge, for he had already been penalized for same. (2) The Company violated the contractual provision that three warning notices for the same offense are necessary before discharge can be imposed.

The Arbitrator is forced to reject both these contentions. As to (1), the reasons will be evident from the Appendix Notes to Question No. 7. As to (2), the following should be noted: (a) There is nothing in the Agreement about the necessity for three warning notices for the same offense before discharge. The Company's own discipline rules (previously quoted) were unilaterally issued and are not a part of the Agreement because not referred to there. (b) Even if same were in the Agreement, (i) they can not be interpreted in the manner contended for, because there is no statement that the three notices have to be for the same sort of offense; and (ii) nothing therein would prevent the Company from discharging an employee for a truly serious first offense.

The Arbitrator finds that the Company's decision was not unreasonably related to X—'s record.

Then the answer to the whole of Question No. 7 must be held to be "Yes."

The arbitrator has found that all seven Questions merit affirmative answers. Accordingly, he must now rule that there is no proper basis for sustaining X—'s grievance.

Award

The grievance is denied.

TESTS APPLICABLE FOR LEARNING WHETHER EMPLOYER HAD JUST AND PROPER CAUSE FOR DISCIPLINING AN EMPLOYEE

Few if any union-management agreements contain a definition of "just cause." Nevertheless, over the years the opinions of arbitrators in innumerable discipline cases have developed a sort of "common law" definition thereof. This definition consists of a set of guide lines or criteria that are to be applied to the facts of any one case, and said criteria are set forth below in the form of questions.

A "no" answer to any one or more of the following questions normally signifies that just and proper cause did not exist. In other words, such "no" means that the employer's disciplinary decision contained one or more elements of arbitrary, capricious, unreasonable, or discriminatory action to such an extent that said decision constituted an abuse of managerial discretion warranting the arbitrator to substitute his judgment for that of the employer.

The answers to the questions in any particular case are to be found in the evidence presented to the arbitrator at the hearing thereon. Frequently, of course, the facts are such that the guide lines cannot be applied with precision. Moreover, occasionally, in some particular case an arbitrator may find one or more "no" answers so weak and the other, "yes" answers so strong that he may properly, without any "political" or spineless intent to "split the difference" between the opposing positions of the parties, find that the correct decision is to "chastize" both the company and the disciplined employee by decreasing but not nullifying the degree of discipline imposed by the company—e.g., by reinstating a discharged employee without back pay.

It should be clearly understood also that the criteria set forth below are to be applied to the employer's conduct in making his disciplinary decision *before* same has been processed through the grievance procedure to arbitration. Any question as to whether the employer has properly fulfilled the contractual requirements of said procedure is entirely separate from the question of whether he fulfilled the "common law" requirements of just cause before the discipline was "grieved."

Sometimes, although very rarely, a union-management agreement contains a provision limiting the scope of the arbitrator's inquiry into the question of just cause. For example, one such provision seen by this arbitrator says that "the only question the arbitrator is to determine shall be whether the employee is or is not guilty of the act or acts resulting in his discharge." Under the latter contractual statement an arbitrator might well have to confine his attention to Question No. 5 below—or at most to Questions Nos. 3, 4, and 5. But absent any such restriction in an agreement, a consideration of the evidence on all seven Questions (and their accompanying Notes) is not only proper but necessary.

The Questions

1. Did the company give to the employee forewarning or foreknowledge of the possible or probable disciplinary consequences of the employee's conduct?

Note 1: Said forewarning or foreknowledge may properly have been given orally by management or in writing through the medium of typed or printed sheets or books of shop rules and of penalties for violation thereof.

Note 2: There must have been actual oral or written communication of the rules and penalties to the employee.

Note 3: A finding of lack of such communication does not in all cases require a "no" answer to Question No. 1. This is because certain offenses such as insubordination, coming to work intoxicated, drinking intoxicating beverages on the job, or theft of the property of the company or of fellow employees are so serious that any employee in the industrial society may properly be expected to know already that such conduct is offensive and heavily punishable.

Note 4: Absent any contractual prohibition or restriction, the company has the right unilaterally to promulgate reasonable rules and give reasonable orders; and same need not have been negotiated with the union.

2. Was the company's rule or managerial order reasonably related to (a) the orderly, efficient, and safe operation of the company's business and (b) the performance that the company might properly expect of the employee?

Note 1: If an employee believes that said rule or order is unreasonable, he must nevertheless obey same (in which case he may file a grievance thereover) unless he sincerely feels that to obey the rule or order would seriously and immediately jeopardize his personal safety and/or integrity. Given a firm finding to the latter effect, the employee may properly be said to have had justification for his disobedience.

3. Did the company, before administering discipline to an employee, make an effort to discover whether the employee did in fact violate or disobey a rule or order of management?

Note 1: This is the employee's "day in court" principle. An employee has the right to know with reasonable precision the offense with which he is being charged and to defend his behavior.

Note 2: The company's investigation must normally be made *before* its disciplinary decision is made. If the company fails to do so, its failure may not normally be excused on the ground that the employee will get his day in court through the grievance procedure after the exaction of discipline. By that time there has usually been too much hardening of positions. In a very real sense the company is obligated to conduct itself like a trial court.

Note 3: There may of course be circumstances under which management must react immediately to the employee's behavior. In such cases the normally proper action is to suspend the employee pending investigation, with the understanding that (a) the final disciplinary decision will be made after the investigation and (b) if the employee is found innocent after the investigation, he will be restored to his job with full pay for time lost.

Note 4: The company's investigation should include an inquiry into possible justification for the employee's alleged rule violation.

4. Was the company's investigation conducted fairly and objectively?

Note 1: At said investigation, the management official may be both "prosecutor" and "judge," but he may not also be a witness against the employee.

Note 2: It is essential for some higher, detached management official to assume and conscientiously perform the judicial role, giving the commonly accepted meaning to that term in his attitude and conduct.

Note 3: In some disputes between an employee and a management person there are not witnesses to an incident other than the two immediate participants. In such cases it is particularly important that the management "judge" question the management participant rigorously and thoroughly, just as an actual third party would.

5. At the investigation did the "judge" obtain substantial evidence or proof that the employee was guilty as charged?

Note 1: It is not required that the evidence be conclusive or "beyond all reasonable doubt." But the evidence must be truly substantial and not flimsy.

Note 2: The management "judge" should actively search out witnesses and evidence, not just passively take what participants or "volunteer" witnesses tell him.

Note 3: When the testimony of opposing witnesses at the arbitration hearing is irreconcilably in conflict, an arbitrator seldom has any means for resolving the contradictions. His task is then to determine whether the management "judge" originally had reasonable grounds for believing the evidence presented to him by his own people.

6. Has the company applied its rules, orders, and penalties evenhandedly and without discrimination to all employees?

Note 1: A "no" answer to this question requires a finding of discrimination and warrants negation or modification of the discipline imposed.

Note 2: If the company has been lax in enforcing its rules and orders and decides henceforth to apply them rigorously, the company may avoid a finding of discrimination by telling all employees beforehand of its intent to enforce hereafter all rules as written.

7. Was the degree of discipline administered by the company in a particular case reasonably related to (a) the seriousness of the employee's proven offense and (b) the record of the employee in his service with the company?

Note 1: A trivial proven offense does not merit harsh discipline unless the employee has properly been found guilty of the same or other offenses a number of times in the past. (There is no rule as to what number of previous offenses constitutes a "good," a "fair," or a "bad" record. Reasonable judgment thereon must be used.)

Note 2: An employee's record of previous offenses may never be used to discover whether he was guilty of the immediate or latest one. The only proper use of his record is to help determine the severity of discipline once he has properly been found guilty of the immediate offense.

Note 3: Given the same proven offense for two or more employees, their respective records provide the only proper basis for "discriminating" among them in the administration of discipline for said offense. Thus, if employee A's record is significantly better than those of employees B, C, and D, the company may properly give a lighter punishment than it gives the others for the same offense; and this does not constitute true discrimination.

Note 4: Suppose that the record of the arbitration hearing establishes firm "Yes" answers to all the first six questions. Suppose further that the proven offense of the accused employee was a serious one, such as drunkenness on the job; but the employee's record had been previously unblemished over a long, continuous period of employment with the company. Should the company be held arbitrary and unreasonable if it decided to discharge such an employee? The answer depends on all the circumstances. But, as one of the country's oldest arbitration agencies, the National Railroad Adjustment Board, has pointed out repeatedly in innumerable decisions on discharge cases, leniency is the prerogative of the employer rather than of the arbitrator, and the latter is not supposed to substitute his judgment in this area for that of the company unless there is compelling evidence that the company abused its discretion. This is the rule, even though an arbitrator, if he had been the original "trial judge," might have imposed a lesser penalty. Actually the arbitrator may be said in an important sense to act as an appellate tribunal whose function is to discover whether the decision of the trial tribunal (the employer) was within the bounds of reasonableness above set forth.—In general, the penalty of dismissal for a really serious first offense does not in itself warrant a finding of company unreasonableness.

Index

Q